Globalisation, Governance Reforms and Development in India

Globalisation, Governance Reforms and Development in India

Edited by

Kameshwar Choudhary

SAGE Publications
Los Angeles ▪ London ▪ New Delhi ▪ Singapore

First published in 2007 by

Sage Publications India Pvt Ltd
B 1/I 1, Mohan Cooperative Industrial Area
Mathura Road, New Delhi 110044
www.sagepub.in

Sage Publications Inc
2455 Teller Road
Thousand Oaks, California 91320

Sage Publications Ltd
1 Oliver's Yard
55 City Road
London EC1Y 1SP

Sage Publications Asia-Pacific Pte Ltd
33 Pekin Street
#02-01 Far East Square
Singapore 048763

Published by Vivek Mehra for Sage Publications India Pvt Ltd, typeset in 9.5/12 pt Stone Serif by Star Compugraphics Private Limited, Delhi and printed at Chaman Enterprises, New Delhi.

Library of Congress Cataloging-in-Publication Data

Globalisation, governance reforms and development in India/editor, Kameshwar Choudhary.
p. cm.
Includes bibliographical references and index.
1. India—Economic conditions—21st century. 2. India—Politics and government—21st century. 3. India—Social conditions—21st century. 4. Globalisation. I. Choudhary, Kameshwar.

HC435.3.G565 330.954—dc22 2007 2007001255

ISBN: 978-0-7619-3583-4 (HB) 978-81-7829-744-6 (India-HB)

The Sage Team: Sugata Ghosh and Koel Mishra

Contents

List of Tables

List of Figures

Preface

India is currently passing through a period of momentous change in different spheres—economic, social, cultural and political. A set of neoliberal reforms has been introduced in the country specifically since the 1991 balance of payments crisis, first, as stabilisation and structural adjustment programmes and later, as 'good governance' reforms. This has promoted greater integration of India with the globalising world. There is a shift in the model of development adopted in the country, i.e., from a centralised planning within a 'Mixed economy' framework for four decades after independence to a private sector/market-centred outward looking model of development particularly since 1991.

In such a scenario, the theme 'globalisation, governance reforms and development' emerges as very important from the angle of both academic understanding and development policy and practice. Globalisation, governance reforms and development are highly contentious issues and have been largely studied separately. A modest attempt is made in this volume to analyse and understand these issues in an integrated manner with theoretico-conceptual clarity focusing on India.

There is a vast literature already available and increasing day by day on globalisation. The issue has been studied from different theoretico-conceptual angles and there is no unanimity in this regard. Similarly, there are several studies on the current reforms introduced in India. But the emphasis is largely on national-level economic reforms. State-level reforms have not received much attention. A large number of studies examine the economic dimensions of reforms, which seem to be rich both theoretically and empirically. However there is a lack of theoretical and empirical depth in the studies on social, cultural and political dimensions of reforms and development in India. This volume tries to fill these existing gaps in a limited way. Accordingly, it is divided into five sections. Section I presents the conceptual spectrum. It has three chapters. Chapter I serves as an introduction to the volume and provides a synoptic overview of the theme. Section II has four chapters which deal with the state-level reforms in India by covering a few select states representing high, medium and low level of introduction of reforms. Social dimensions of globalisation and reforms in India are analysed in seven chapters of Section III, while cultural dimensions are dealt with in three chapters of Section IV. Finally, Section V has three chapters on certain major issues related to the political dimensions of globalisation, reforms and development in India. Given the limitations of space, time and other resources it was not possible to include in the volume, analysis of certain other important issues like business and politics, gender, rising fundamentalism and identity politics in India in the context of globalisation.

The volume is significant in several ways. It is not confined to the analysis of merely a single dimension of globalisation, reforms and development in India which is common in most studies, but tries to present an overview of multiple dimensions—social, cultural, political and state-level reforms. Quite understandably, it has contributors from different disciplines such as sociology, political science, economics and media studies. The Introductory chapter is contributed by the editor of the volume. It delineates the major theoretico-conceptual perspectives on globalisation and makes an attempt to apply these in the analysis of social, cultural and political dimensions of globalisation and reforms in India. It has a wide canvas so as to fully cover the contours of discussions and analyses in different chapters of the volume and thus make it a unified work. The contributors to the volume had the freedom to approach the issue of their concern from the theretico-conceptual perspective of their choice. This volume clearly demonstrates that 'good governance' reform is not confined to the traditional notion of governance but basically is just another conceptualisation (the other being SAP, i.e., structural adjustment programme) of the neoliberal agenda of reforms meant for firmly reorganising 'developing' countries like India along the path of global capitalism. It is shown that reforms have a significant impact in the social, cultural and political domains in the country. Further, it is observed that the introduction of reforms at state level has not led to 'competitive developmentalism' as claimed by neoliberal/neoclassical advocates of market, but to an exacerbation of the existing inequalities, across states in the country, and at the intra-state level, higher economic growth is not necessarily related to human/social development. Obviously, the study emphasises the need for an alternative development model and policies to promote a democratic (substantive), egalitarian and sustainable development in India rather than clutching to the largely 'dependent development' paradigm of globalisation and reforms. This may be applicable to the other Third World countries as well. (Though the second world has collapsed, the term Third World is used here keeping in view its historical significance.)

It needs to be mentioned that the volume is the outcome of a national workshop organised during 14–16 December 2004 at the Institute of Rural Management Anand (IRMA), Gujarat (India) as part of the silver jubilee symposium of the institute. A background paper was prepared on the theme of the workshop, which provided a synoptic view of the theme and also identified specific issues/topics for contribution of papers. This paper was circulated much in advance among the contributors. The intention was to have a thematic unity in the papers to ensure focused discussions in the workshop as well as to have a publication thereafter. All the papers have been suitably revised after the workshop for publication in the volume in which all the contributors cooperated fully despite their busy schedule. I am thankful to them for their valuable contributions to the volume. I am also thankful to the editor of the journal *Economic and Political Weekly*, C. Rammanohar Reddy for kindly permitting me to include the chapter contributed by Surinder S. Jodhka in this volume. In April 1996, the journal had carried a modified version of the paper contributed to the IRMA workshop by Prof. Jodhka in 2004.

Further, I would like to thank the Swedish International Development Agency (SIDA) and Sir Dorabjee Trust for the financial support extended to the institute (IRMA) to hold the silver jubilee symposium of which the workshop on the theme of the volume was also a part. The symposium organising committee of IRMA was quite helpful in the successful conduct of this workshop and for this I am thankful to them. The fellow programme students at IRMA, Ms Maitraiyee Mukerji and T. Kumar assisted me in conducting the workshop. Ms Maitrayee also helped me in preparing the paper on Gujarat. I thank both of them.

On a personal count I feel happy to have the long, warm relationship, both as friend and family with Smita and Haribandhu which gives me support and strength to feel human in a highly unsettling world. Interaction with their children, Tatu and Niki has given me a taste of innocence and playfulness in life. The love and affection of the family was available to me in abundance during and before the period of working on this volume. I would not just say thanks for what I have received from them, but would like to treasure all this close to my heart. Also, I feel grateful to the ever welcoming family of Ballabhji and Geeta Bhabhiji who provided their warmth and jovial conviviality whenever I dropped in, including the period of preparation and finalisation of this volume. I thank Ms Alice Jose for providing me with excellent secretarial assistance at IRMA in preparation of the volume.

Dr Sugata Ghosh, Vice President, Commissioning at Sage Publications, New Delhi, has been very supportive and patient with the finalisation of this volume. I express my sincere thanks to him. Ms Mimi Choudhury, while at Sage, took keen interest in the volume through her professional approach and personal touch. I feel thankful to her as well. I am highly thankful to the first production editor Ms Janaki Srinivasan for her excellent copy editing and cordial approach in handling the volume so efficiently and with utmost rigour. The second production editor, Ms Koel Mishra beautifully gave the final touch to the volume which further improved its quality and for this I am very much thankful to her.

Last but not the least, I own up responsibility for the errors, if any, remaining in the volume despite my best efforts.

Kameshwar Choudhary

Section I
Conceptual Spectrum

1

Globalisation, Governance Reforms and Development: An Introduction

Kameshwar Choudhary

In recent years, globalisation has emerged as a very popular term amongst academics, policy makers, businessmen, development practitioners and in common parlance. But there is no consensus on its meaning and theorisation. Broadly, the term is used to describe the global processes of change taking place in the world over the last two decades. Concerted attempts have been made to introduce certain sets of reforms to promote globalisation. It may be noted at the outset that with the cessation of the Cold War, Western industrialised capitalist governments have identified a cluster of policy prescriptions which, according to them, constitutes a model for good economic and political management. This is usually referred to as 'Washington Consensus' by economists and 'good governance' when approached from the perspective of politics (Archer 1994: 7). It is this model which has been operational in most Third World countries in recent years especially under the fiscal stabilisation and structural adjustment programme (SAP) of the World Bank (WB) and the International Monetary Fund (IMF).

Some scholars refer to two generation of reforms introduced in the third world countries under the aegis of the WB and IMF in the recent decades—the first generation reforms aimed at liberalising the economy (i.e., 'getting prices right') and the second generation reforms meant for redesigning the state and its institutions (i.e., 'getting institutions right'—referring to political and institutional reforms). Moreover, it is added that the second generation reforms complement the first. It is affirmed that 'Promotion of good governance has become an integral part of the emergent global economic order' (K. Singh 2005: 106).

Introduction of a new paradigm of governance reforms, i.e., 'good governance' reforms is advocated particularly by the major multilateral and bilateral development agencies for adoption especially in the third world countries, including India. A close scrutiny demonstrates that this new governance paradigm represents a market/private sector-centred model of development which signifies the current era of globalisation. In fact, it marks a shift in the model of development adopted in India, i.e., from a centralised planning within 'mixed economy' framework for five decades after independence to a private sector/market-centred outward looking model particularly since mid-1991.

An attempt is made in this chapter to provide an overview of what globalisation is and what are its different facets with a focus on the current agenda of 'good governance' (reforms) paradigm of development. The analysis made here is distinct in terms of applying a broad theoretical spectrum on the theme drawn from the diverse interpretations of globalisation in the analysis of its major dimensions. The discussion in the chapter is divided into six parts. First, it delves on the concept and interpretations of globalisation. Second, it analyses the current agenda of 'good governance' and development as advocated by select multilateral and bilateral development agencies, and the agenda adopted by the Government of India in this respect. Analysis of the social, cultural and political dimensions of globalisation and reforms with a focus on India is provided in Parts 3, 4 and 5 respectively. In part 6 some concluding observations are made relating to governance reforms and development in India. Finally, a brief outline about organisation of this volume is given.

Globalisation: Meanings and Perspectives

The term globalisation is said to have appeared in 1962 and has gone from being a jargon to a cliche (Chanda 2002). In 1964, McLuhan (2002) talked about 'the global village' in his celebrated study of media. Over the years the concept of globalisation has been defined differently by scholars and institutions. Steger (2004: 19) has noted the varied description of the term offered by different scholars as 'increasing global interconnectedness', 'the rapid intensification of worldwide social relations', 'the compression of time and space', 'a complex range of processes, driven by a mixture of political and economic influences', and 'the swift and relatively unimpeded flow of capital, people, and ideas across national borders'. Walby defines globalisation as 'a process of increased density and frequency of ... international or global social interactions relative to local or national ones' (Walby 2003, cited in Mazlish 2005). She does accept the notion of 'supraterritoriality' but holds that 'global processes still have a territorial component'.

Broadly, globalisation can be said to refer to the current phase of growing complex linkages, interdependence and integration among countries and people in the world (in the last two decades). Parker (2005: 7) observes that the growing interconnections are rapid and discontinuous, following a jagged upward way. The process is disorganised and incoherent (Veseth cited in ibid). So, the effect of the same global phenomenon can differ. Effect of interconnections can vary at different times for nations, businesses and individuals as witnessed in the case of the 1997 Asian economic crisis.

In fact, the meanings of globalisation available in the vast literature on the subject can be broadly categorised as referring to: (*a*) a process of increasing interdependence and integration, (*b*) the contemporary global capitalism, including a normative or political prescription/ideology, (*c*) a myth, not a reality, and (*d*) an abstract concept.

It is observed that those viewing globalisation as a process also differ in their understanding. For instance, as a process, globalisation is regarded as one-dimensional, two-dimensional, and multi-dimensional in nature. Most commonly globalisation is conceptualised as a one-dimensional process of economic integration/interdependence that has been occurring on a very rapid pace in the present. In this sense, Harris defines it as an economic process, i.e.,

'The increasing internationalisation of the production, distribution and marketing of goods and services' (cited in Streeten 2001: 167). The two-dimensionality of the process covers economic integration facilitated by new technology. As an example, for Thomas Friedman globalisation is 'that loose combination of free trade agreements, the Internet and the integration of financial markets that is erasing borders and uniting the world into a single, lucrative, but brutally competitive market place' (ibid.: 171). Taking it as a multi-dimensional process, Streeten states, 'Globalisation is transforming trade, finance, employment, migration, technology, communications, the environment, social systems, ways of living, cultures, and patterns of governance' (Streeten 2001: 8). Holm and Sorensen (1995, cited in ibid) view it as 'the intensification of economic, political, social and cultural relations across borders'. A World Bank publication defines globalisation as 'the growing integration of economies and societies around the world'. This is 'a complex process that affects many aspects of our lives' (World Bank 2002: ix). UNDP (1999: 7) holds that 'globalisation is a process integrating not just the economy but culture, technology and governance. People everywhere are becoming connected—affected by events in every corner of the world'.

Further, globalisation is viewed, in its essence, as the phase of global capitalism (Kurien 1995). Moreover, it is regarded as a normative prescription/ideology affirming that it is 'the only possible road to the full liberalisation and integration of world markets'. It is seen as 'the inevitable and desirable fate of all humankind' (United Nations 2002: 18). Mahbub ul Haq avers, 'Globalisation is no longer an option, it is a fact. Developing countries have either to learn to manage it far more skilfully, or simply drown in the global cross currents' (MHDC 2002: 1). Wallerstein (2000) holds that the concept of globalisation is primarily a political prescription involving exhortation for the third world to opt for all kinds of shortcuts to integration with the capitalist global economy.

But there are others who greatly differ in the understanding of globalisation. Hirst and Thompson hold that globalisation is a myth, not reality. They assert, 'Globalisation is a myth suitable for a world without illusions, but is also one that robs us of hope' (cited in Streeten 2001: 170). It is held that the label of 'global village' has been uncritically adopted like a slogan. One should remember the fact that over one half of humanity has not made even a phone call and around two billion people in the world are still living below poverty line. In India and in other developing and poorer countries, still the overwhelming majority of people have no access to the new information and communication technologies in any meaningful way. In this sense, global village is in fact not global. Some scholars deny that globalisation is a process with its own logic, and hence inevitable. For example, Ian Clark holds that globalisation has often been a result of state policies, and so it is not irreversible (1997, cited by Hudson 2002: 103). He argues that economic, technological and cultural changes are different things, with different dynamics and time frames, hence it would be wrong to merge them. So, it may be useful first to posit them and then examine the relationship among them. In addition, it is denied that globalisation exists in one or more determinate senses. A recent study by the United Nations (2002: 17), conducted by ECLAC (Economic Commission for Latin America and the Carribbean), specifically highlights the multi-dimensional nature of globalisation. It also notes that the economic dimension of globalisation 'acts concomitantly with non-economic processes, which have their own momentum and therefore are not determined by economic factors' (ibid.).

Lubbers holds that globalisation is 'an abstract concept'. In his opinion, 'It does not refer to a concrete object, but to (an interpretation of) a societal process. Therefore, the concept cannot be defined easily. To understand clearly the meaning of 'globalisation' it is necessary to explain the theory in which one's use of the concept is embedded' (cited in Hudson 2002: 101). Lubbers demands greater 'logical clarity' from writers on globalisation about the theoretical framework deployed and the specific empirical data that would validate their thesis/hypothesis (ibid.: 104).

Further, there are different types of orientations reflected in the interpretations of globalisation. There are cheerleaders, cynics and worried doubters (Birdsall 2003). Martinelli (2003: 96) places the growing literature on globalisation conceptually along three main axes (which ideologically/politically can be broadly put under two broad categories, i.e., advocates and opponents of globalisation). His categorisation is:

(*i*) **Hyperglobalisers vs. sceptics:** Here, the key distinction between the two positions relates to the degree of novelty of globalisation and its impact on nation states.

(*ii*) **Neoliberals vs. neo-Marxists and radicals:** Here, the key points of difference is the balance between positive and negative impact of globalisation and its truly global or Western hegemonic character.

(*iii*) **Homogenisation vs. heterogeneity/hybridisation:** The focus here is on the cultural dimension of globalisation.

In the three-fold axis of categorisation, the first is regarded as the main and the other two as specifications. It is noted that the varied conceptualisations on globalisation differ in terms of the type and number of aspects analysed—causal dynamics, periodisation and trajectory, major actors, (differential) social impact on people, and political implications for state power and world governance. Analyses also differ in terms of the type of countries, social groups, institutions and cultural phenomena under investigation (ibid.).

Broadly speaking, it can be said that hyperglobalisers are the advocates of globalisation with a neoliberal ideology/prescription and focus on its homogenising nature. The sceptics are mainly the neo-Marxists and radicals who focus on the negative aspects of globalisation and also some of them notice the heterogeneity/hybridising cultural side of the process. Neo-Marxists/Marxists highlight the hegemonic character of globalisation. Besides these two main strands, some scholars in recent years have taken a different view and are known as 'transformationalists' (like Baylis and Smith [2005: 20]). This strand stands somewhere in between the other two, i.e., the hyperglobalisers (neoliberals) and sceptics (neo-Marxists/Marxists/radicals). Held et al., (1999) clearly identify three perspectives on globalisation, e.g., hyperglobalist, sceptical, and transformationalist.

Hyperglobalisers draw their basic ideas from the neoliberal gurus like Milton Friedman and F.A. Hayek. Friedman emphasises on individual freedom, both economic and political. He affirms an 'intimate connection' between economic and political freedom. Private enterprise and market, in his view, constitutes the bedrock of freedom and growth. Market operates on the principle of freedom of exchange and benefits all—the consumer, the seller, the employee and the employer. He affirms, 'the market does this impersonally and without centralised authority' (Friedman 1962: 15). Market provides diversity and scope for choice and thus, provides economic freedom, which also enables the individual to assert political freedom. It reduces the range of issues to be decided through political means and thus minimises direct participation of the government in the game. However, he recognises the need of government, but only of a minimal one. For him it is essential as a forum to determine the 'rules of the game', and as an umpire to interpret and enforce the rules.

Hyperglobalisers conceptualise globalisation mainly as an economic phenomenon—a new phase of human history through which business activities have supplanted the power of nation states. It implies that it is the businesses rather than the nation states which have emerged as the primary economic and political units of world society. Ohmae (2002) speaks of the existence of a 'borderless world' in the economic realm today. It is held that people are getting increasingly integrated into the global marketplace. Economies are being increasingly de-nationalised due to the formation of transnational networks of trade, finance and production. This is regarded as 'a novel condition, hardly reversible'. It is affirmed that globalisation is 'inevitable and unavoidable' (Friedman 2005: 47). It is argued, 'The world is being flattened. I didn't start it and you can't stop it, except at a great cost to human development and your own future. But we can manage it, for better or for worse' (ibid.: 469). So, there is a need to adapt to this process. It limits the range of choices for nation states and individuals and compels them to follow neoliberal economic policies to be able to compete in the world market. It is held that the benefits of globalisation outweigh the costs. The neoliberals view globalisation as the triumph of economic liberalism, i.e., the application of economic rationalism to 'nation societies'. It is believed that (*i*) markets provide the most dependable means of setting values on all goods, and (*ii*) economies and markets can deliver better results than states, governments and the law (Hudson 2002: 102).

Further, there is proclaimed, in a philosophical vein, the 'end of history' and the triumph of the Western economic and political liberalism ruling out the possibility of any alternative to it (Fukuyama 1992). It is affirmed that there would no more be deep conflicts or ideological divisions in the world. The 'new world order' interdependence based on economic liberty and democratisation created both wealth and solidarity. The spread of market-oriented policies, democratic polities and individual rights promoted the well-being of all. It not only produced greater economic efficiency and prosperity, but also extended the idea of liberty. Globalisation is good for the poor as, besides growth, it raised their income and reduced the inequality between rich and poor countries (Dollar and Kraay, in Lechner and Boli eds. 2004). There are potential benefits of global integration, though it also had unjust consequences that need to be addressed (Sen, in Lechner and Boli eds. 2004). Globalisation is presented as 'a moral imperative with some amount of economic freedom as basic to prosperity. Markets are seen as a force that propel production, provide means of sustenance outside government and thereby also strengthen democracy (Bhagwati 2004). It is argued that globalisation has a human face (hence, no need to add a human face) and on balance it advances, rather than harms, social agenda like reduction of poverty and child labour, and gender equality. Its economic and social impact is not only beneficial, but also correlated. We hear songs like 'In Praise of Empires'. It is averred that empires are good as they maintain peace and promote prosperity better. Today, United States is an empire and the need is to accept it. The US is pleaded to accept the role of an emperor and push forward economic globalisation further, creating market economies based on economic and civil liberties (Lal 2004). It is affirmed that globalisation 'works', that it is sensible, practicable and desirable. Its alternatives like the planned economies of Soviet design and also other isolationist attempts have been a failure. The policies meant for integration of 'economic activities via markets' have proved to be the best path of increasing the welfare of the largest number of people (Wolf 2004). It is argued that globalisation does not lead to an increase in the exploitation of workers, of inequality and of poverty or pollution of environment as there is competition between countries to attract investment and thus forcing a race to the bottom. Rather, economic growth achieved by the globalising regions, like East and South Asia, have witnessed decline in illiteracy rate, child labour rate and in fertility rate, and improvement in environmental quality. There is, in fact, a 'race to the top' (Geddes nd). For the third world, participation in the ILE (interlinked economy of USA, Europe, and Japan) is considered key to prosperity, where there were no absolute winners or losers (Ohmae 2002).

But even certain noted supporters of globalisation express strong reservations about the way it is operating currently. Soros (2004), a stalwart in global finance, regards the current global capitalist system as 'unsound and unsustainable', in fact, disintegrating due to the increasing distress at the periphery and imminent breakdown in the global financial system/international trade. In his view, 'market fundamentalism' is invading even non-economic spheres of life, and hence the urgent need to 'rethink and reform the global capitalist system'. Despite being a supporter of globalisation, Stiglitz (2004) notices duality in the policy of dominant states. For instance, US preaches privatisation and opening of markets while simultaneously preventing free trading in its markets. He also observes that tax cuts, deregulation in the sense of privatisation and retreat of the state have led to making the wealthy even richer without benefiting the lower income groups. No wonder, he advocates restoring the balance in the relation between the state and the free market. Sachs (2004) is a firm supporter of globalisation. He affirms that 'open markets (including free trade) are necessary for economic growth, but they are hardly sufficient'. Process of global production helps rich countries in terms of low-cost products. Poor countries also benefit with the creation of jobs, experience with advanced technologies and investment. There are several winners in the developing world from globalisation, but many countries are not beneficiaries. In fact, economic crisis is rather intensifying in several poor and remote parts of the world. So, he suggests the need to adopt a serious approach to achieve a balanced globalisation in which everyone participates and benefits as well. In this connection, the most urgent task is to meet the basic needs of the world's poorest people. Only in some cases people's suffering can be tackled through better internal governance. 'The truth is that economic performance is determined not only by governance standards, but by geopolitics, geography, and economic structure'. Greater foreign assistance is needed to alleviate the conditions of poorer countries, besides their economic integration with the global economy and debt cancellation. 'Rather than rich countries giving more lectures about poor governance, real solutions will require that rich countries give sufficient financial assistance to overcome the deeper barriers'. There is a need for partnership between the rich and the poor countries, he asserts.

But sceptics/critics view the neoliberal version of globalisation as a prescription/ideology, not a reality. Sceptics include neo-Marxists/Marxists and radicals. They do not consider globalisation as either beneficial to all or being irreversible. There are two main arguments made here—periods of growing interconnections across borders have also occurred in the past and the future would be much like the past. Sceptics paint a gloomy picture of increasing inequalities and dominance by the stronger economic actors. There is a fear of the world ruled by profit seeking global corporations. Economic interdependence is said to make countries more vulnerable to the destructive consequences of market shifts. The social fabric/ties also get strained as the winners in the global game become detached from losers. The whole process is lopsided. It is repressive, exploitative and harmful to most people in most countries. Globalisation is considered a 'false dawn' (Gray, in Lechner and Boli 2004). There is loss of sovereignty and autonomous power of nation states. Market forces are getting more powerful than the states (Strange 1996). The main concern of governments now is to compete for attracting investments. 'National governments are torn between the need to foster economic competitiveness and that of enhancing social cohesion' (Martinelli 2003).

Sceptics reject the talk of globalisation as 'globaloney'. They do not consider globalisation to be a novel phenomenon. They regard it as another wave of internationalisation, involving interactions among predominantly national economies. They criticise the hyperglobalist thesis of demise of the nation state for not distinguishing among states with different power and influence. The patterns of inequality and hierarchy continue to prevail and most 'third world' countries remain marginalised. The governments continue to play a key role, particularly the powerful Western states, in determining economic relations. States and geopolitics continue to be the main forces shaping world order. Moreover, it is observed that transnational corporations are not truly global, because they have their own home state and regional base. Some sceptics interpret the current phase of internationalisation as the byproduct of the US-initiated multilateral economic order after the Second World War (Gilpin 2000). Callinicos et al. (1994) call it a new phase of Western imperialism with governments operating as agents of monopoly capital. It is opined that the current process of globalisation is 'incomplete and asymmetric'.

At the theoretico-ideological level, the current phase of globalisation is labelled by neo-Marxists/Marxists as neoliberalism. Certain important features of neoliberalism, which Giddens (1999: 8) calls the New Rights, include market fundamentalism, minimal government, welfare state as safety net, autonomous civil society, moral authoritarianism (including strong economic individualism), acceptance of inequality, low ecological consciousness, etc. Neoliberalism is affirmed by Paul Krugman. He has highlighted the doctrinal and normative/prescriptive nature of the views of the advocates of globalisation, for instance, the 'Washington consensus'. He affirms that conclusions with little basis are constantly put forth and provide the doctrinal support for policy (cited in Chomsky 1999: 25). Chomsky mentions two varieties of neoliberal doctrine which characterise modern history. 'The first is the official doctrine imposed on the defenseless. The second is what we might call "really existing free market doctrine": market discipline is good for you, but not for me, except for temporary advantage'

(1991: 34, 39). Giddens (1999: 6) also refers to two strands of neoliberalism, (*i*) the conservative variety (the New Right like Thatcherites) upholding free market and traditional institutions like family, and (*ii*) the liberal variety which favours free market and other freedoms such as sexual freedom.

Further, the contemporary process of worldwide change is treated by Marxists/neo-Marxists as the latest phase of capitalism, and variously characterised as 'global capitalism' (Kurien 1995) 'pancapitalism' (Tehranian, in Lamberton 2002: xv), 'transnational capitalism' (Rivero 2001: 40), 'technocapitalism' (Kellner 2002: 289) and 'multilateral (capitalist) imperialism' (Harshe 2005: 2076). Amin (2003) diagnoses (the current phase of) globalisation as the third phase of imperialism—'collective imperialism of the Triad' (US, Europe and Japan), wherein, comprador bourgeoisie are 'acting as transmission belts for transnational capital that remains a monopoly of the Triad'. Moreover, he differentiates 'active peripheries' from marginal peripheries forming part of the system. The uniqueness of the late 20th century is seriously questioned by Wallerstein (see Lechner and Boli 2004). He opines that capitalism was always global but it is not yet fully globalised. According to him, the core of the world economy is only over 30 of the world's 200 countries.

Market is eulogised by the advocates of globalisation and reforms. But Dev Nathan (2006: 1893) clearly underlines the basic positive and negative features of the market system of equality. According to him, the market system marks an advance over the feudal or casteist systems which prescribe, on socio-cultural lines, who can consume what. But the market treats all buyers as equal at the formal level. It 'does not recognise the individual behind the buyer' (ibid.). It offers equality of access/opportunity to all. But at another level—the substantive level—the market is unconcerned with existential inequalities. It is 'blind to the strengths and weaknesses and the capabilities that the buyer and seller bring to the market'. In the absence of equal capabilities, equal access/opportunity in the markets is likely to lead to highly unequal outcomes at domestic or international (trade) level.

Different arguments are made regarding the limits under capitalism to the spontaneous diffusion of industrial development—natural resource constraints, exhaustion of world's labour reserves, etc. Patnaik (2006), however, highlights a more immediate limit to such spontaneous diffusion, i.e., 'unwillingness of the leading capitalist economy to sustain a growing claim upon its wealth by outsiders'. In view of this, he affirms that 'an authentic development strategy for backward economies cannot take the direction of neoliberalism' (ibid.: 1771). In his edited volume Jomo (2006: 26) recognises that international economic integration might be beneficial in some respect. But on balance, '... the economic and political circumstances of globalisation during the long twentieth century have resulted in outcomes, which have principally benefited the dominant powers in the world economy in the North, often at the expense of the developing Third World or South'. There is noted net economic outflows from the South through various process (changing over time) like trade, finance, investment, human and other resource flows.

The 'transformationalist' view represents another perspective. It differs from the understanding of both the advocates and opponents of globalisation. It is argued here that both the hyperglobalists and sceptics exaggerate their arguments and thus misconstrue the current world order. It claims to take globalisation seriously. It is held that global interconnections and interdependence will forge new links and dilute some existing ones. Relationships among nations and people are getting reconfigured and power relationships restructured. But it is argued that the end point of globalisation is not yet clear.

In this vein, the emergence of a new society i.e., a global society is observed. Several noted sociologists tend to interpret globalisation as a 'process at a new level of social reality'. The term 'global society' is sometimes used to describe this 'new reality'. In the opinion of M. Albrow (1990, cited in Hudson 2002), globalisation refers to all those processes that involve bringing the people of the world into a single society in which 'humanity' emerges for the first time as a 'collective actor'. The latter aspect is connected with the concept of 'globalisation' defined as 'those values that take the real world of five billion people as the object of concern, the whole earth as the physical environment, everyone living as world citizens, consumers and producers, with a common interest in collective action to solve global problems' (ibid.: 101). A United Nations publication (2002: 21) talks about both the economic and non-economic dimensions of globalisation. One of the non-economic dimensions mentioned here includes ethical and cultural aspects which ECLAC terms as the 'globalisation of values' and refers to the gradual spread of shared ethical principles as manifested in declarations on human rights covering two main issues: (*a*) civil and political rights, and (*b*) economic, social and cultural rights. The 'globalisation of values' is increasingly manifested in the aspirations and formation of a 'global civil society' whose capacity for mobilisation and exchange of information has multiplied by the new information and communications technologies.

To Giddens, globalisation is not merely or even primarily, about economic interdependence. It is rather about the 'transformation of time and space' in our lives. Distant events, economic or non-economic, affect us more directly and immediately than ever before. Also decisions taken by individuals are often global in their implications. He states, 'Globalisation, in sum, is a complex range of processes, driven by a mixture of political and economic influences. It is changing everyday life particularly in the developed countries at the same time as it is creating new transnational systems and forces ... taken as a whole, globalisation is transforming the institutions of the societies in which we live' (Giddens 1999: 33).

Further, the global economy is found reshaping the existing division of labour between the centre and periphery countries and between the North and the South in the world. It is replacing the existing relations with 'more complex patterns of hierarchy of inequality', which has winners and losers both among and within countries and with new tacit transnational class affiliations. To Martinelli (2003: 96), globalisation implies deep transformation in the spatial organisation because of relations becoming more stretched and intensively interconnected. Transcontinental and transregional flows and networks of activities and exchanges have been taking place. This generates power relations which has major implications on decision making processes. 'New patterns of hierarchy and inequality of inclusion and exclusion are shaped, that cut across national borders'. Kellner (2002) also seems to take a transformationalist view of globalisation. He does not stress on the aspect of integration. Rather, he focuses on the transformation currently occurring in different spheres of life and the emergence of webs and networks of global relations. He sees globalisation as having both negative and positive consequences and also both homogenising and hybridising impact plus emergence of identity based defences.

In fact, transformationalists seem to take a middle position on globalisation. They view it as a multifaceted process with multiple causes like economic, technological, cultural, and political. This perspective does not stress on global integration. It focuses on the emergence of webs and networks of relations among individuals, groups, communities, states, international organisations and transnational actors. Globalisation is seen as leading to an 'unbundling of relationships between sovereignty, territoriality and state power'. It involves a basic restructuring of the nation state. Moreover, 'globalisation reinforces old patterns of inequalities, but also forms new social hierarchies which penetrate all regions of the world, thus recasting the traditional patterns of inclusion and exclusion. However, significant opportunities for empowerment of individuals, communities and social groups also exist' (Martinelli 2003: 98–99). It is accepted that global corporations have a homogenising impact on lifestyles and consumption patterns. However, increasing hybridisation of cultural traits and the staunch defence of specific identities are also observed. Moreover, it is affirmed, 'Globalisation brings about a variety of adjustment strategies by national policies that require a rather active state—not the neoliberal minimum government, but the 'developmental' or 'catalytic' state' (Martinelli 2003). Nation states are one of the major actors in the emerging 'global governance as a polyarchic mixed-actor system'. As a result of globalisation there is not so much of demise of the sovereign state but a globalisation of politics. There is 'emergence of a conspicuously global politics in which the traditional distinction between domestic and international affairs is no longer valid. Under these conditions "politics everywhere, it would seem, are related to politics everywhere else"' (Baylis and Smith (2005: 20). The need for democratic global governance based on the principles of universal rights and responsibilities is suggested (ibid.).

Thus, it is observed that globalisation is a highly contentious concept. On the one hand, it is viewed as a real process of rapidly increasing integration and interdependence across countries and people in the world. On the other, it is regarded as a normative prescription, a myth. Similarly, there are widely diverging interpretations of globalisation. On the one hand, there are strong advocates professing neoliberal perspective, pushing forward economic/financial integration through private sector/market-led development which, according to them, is most efficient and dependable, yielding more benefits than loss to all, particularly in the long run. On the other hand, the bitter critics/sceptics holding neo-Marxist/Marxist persuasion call it a new phase of Western imperialism/global capitalism which, in their view, would adversely affect particularly the weaker nation states and people. There is also a middle position, i.e., the one adopted by the transformationalists. Their focus is on the emerging new level of social reality (global/single society) that is happening due to increasing transnational/regional flows of networks/exchanges and growing global values. But the process has, in their opinion, both positive and negative implications for different countries and people. What is advocated here to redress the problems is a democratic global governance and a catalytic state. These contrasting conceptualisations and theoretical perspectives need to be kept in view in the analysis of globalisation and reforms focussing on any particular country and people, including India. A synoptic view of the analytical framework that emerges from the foregoing discussion is provided in Figure 1.1.

Figure 1.1: Meanings and Interpretations of Globalisation

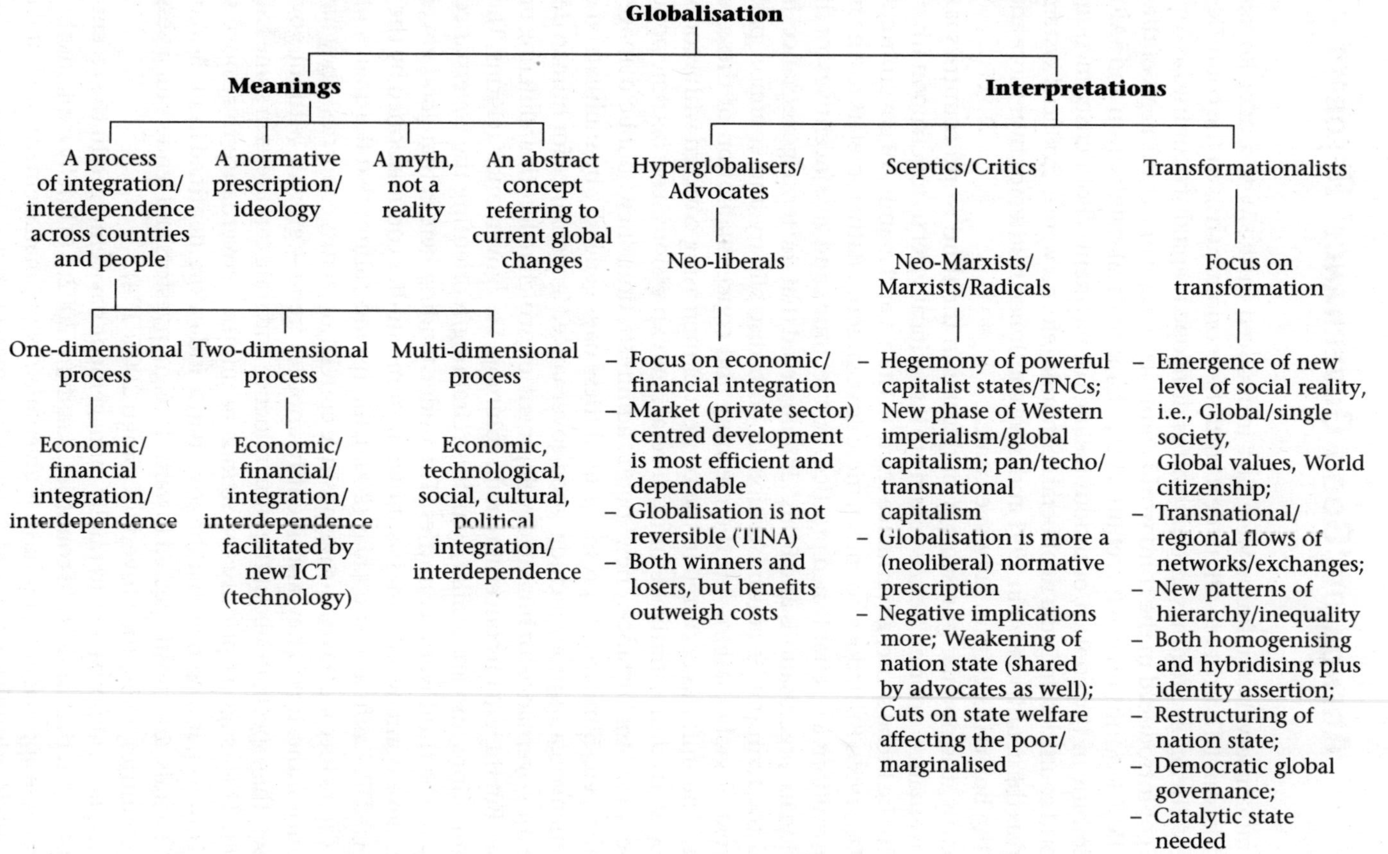

Agenda of 'Good Governance' Reforms

Neoliberal/conservative reforms were first introduced in the West under Ronald Reagan in US and Margaret Thatcher in UK to deal with the economic crisis in the countries concerned. Gradually, the reform regimes spread to other developed capitalist countries as well. Neoliberal reforms got introduced in the third world countries mainly under the aegis of the World Bank and the IMF. Reforms moved forcefully in the shape of fiscal stabilisation and SAP of the Fund-Bank combine in the context of serious balance of payments (BoP) crisis encountered by the third world countries. In India neoliberal economic reforms were introduced systematically due to the crisis the country faced in 1991 and have continued further to cover more and more areas despite the BoP crisis getting fully overcome.

Currently, the popular phraseology of reforms in the third world countries is expressed as 'good governance' reforms. Before coming to it specifically, let us touch upon what governance means. In the literal sense, governance refers to the act and manner of governing. According to the UNDP (1999: 8), it 'does not mean mere government'. Rather it refers to 'the framework of rules, institutions and established practices that set limits and give incentives for the behaviour of individuals, organisations and firms'. It is observed that the term 'governance' has gradually replaced the term public administration in both disciplinary and common parlance in the current era of globalisation. But the meaning and conceptualisation of these terms are not identical. The shift has occurred in the context of increasing concern with economic reforms and associated administrative reforms. Several new expressions have become popular with the adjective 'new', for instance, 'new' public administration, 'new' public management, 'new' governance, etc. Similarly, expressions used these days generally by multilateral and bilateral development organisations include 'good governance,' 'governance for human development,' 'democratic governance for human development' etc which reflect their differing programmatic emphasis. But their main concerns remain common, i.e., 'governance' reforms. Their objectives and assumptions also are similar, which is reframing/reorienting the governance system particularly in the third world countries. The understanding here is that good governance leads to better development outcomes as shown in some studies commissioned by the World Bank and the UNDP. Kaufmann and Kraay (2003), for instance, affirm that the quality of governance and per capita income have a strong positive correlation across countries. They have identified governance indicators. They also identify another trend—'growth without governance'. In such cases, they speculate about the elite influence and state capture as in some Latin American countries. They suggest priority for actions to improve governance to remove state capture (2004). However, it is opined that the governance indicators identified in studies commissioned by multilaterals, are 'mostly geared towards foreign investors and lenders for assessing political risks in countries where they invest' (K. Singh 2005: 134).

Further, newer approaches to public management have emerged in the recent past and are being applied in the third world countries. Salamon (2002: 16) briefly explains the distinctions between these approaches. Emphasis is given mainly on 'management' skills in both the traditional public administration and 'new public management' approaches. Skills required in this connection involve manipulation of a large number of people arranged hierarchically in bureaucratic organisations. However, in the 'new public management' approach, the emphasis is substantially shifted from control (traditional public administration) to performance. Despite that it remains preoccupied with internal agency management and the manager is regarded as the key to success. (Private corporate) business management practices are introduced into the public sector to improve performance. Managers are free to manage, but they are subjected to increased competition and held accountable for results.

In contrast, the 'new governance' approach shifts the focus from management skills and the control of large bureaucratic organisations to enablement skills. Here the required skills are meant to engage partners arranged horizontally in networks and to bring multiple stakeholders together for a common objective in a situation of interdependence (Salamon 2002: 16). The 'new governance' paradigm is said to mark 'perhaps the greatest political revolution of our times' (Dahl and Lindblom, cited by Salamon 2002). It symbolises a new approach to solving public problem for the current era of 'third party government' (This involves sharing of public authority with a host of non-governmental or other governmental actors in a complex collaborative system. There are a wide variety of 'third parties' such as commercial banks, private hospitals, social service agencies that deliver publicly financed services and are closely involved in implementation/management of the public's business). Here there is a major shift in the role of government, from one of doing to one of arranging. The focus is on forging and managing collaboration among different sectors/agencies and enablement rather than hierarchy and control (Salamon 2002: vii).

Moreover, privatisation theories advocate reliance on the private sector to be more effective/efficient than public agencies in delivering public services. It is argued that the protection provided to the civil service/bureaucracy from political pressures, isolates them from the citizens and makes them free to pursue their self-interests. Hence, the remedy for attaining effective government becomes 'privatisation' which involves reducing the size of the public sector, shifting responsibilities to the private sector and providing private sector alternatives (E.S. Savas 1987 and S. Butler 1985, in Salamon 2002).

The intellectual origin of the current 'good governance' approach is traced to the neoliberal theory that treats conservative governments and organised business interests in unison. It is considered a product of two strands of thinking that originally appeared in the form of Thatcherism and Reaganism in the world since the late 1970s. One line of argument relates to efficiency and accountability. It affirms that the state faced a crisis of governability because of its overloaded tasks and demands from civil society which had a state-centric view. Second, the state suffered from legitimacy as it was not able to perform. The first argument is linked with the broader neoliberal thinking that involved re-establishing the notion that the market is an institution that makes use of available resources and skills with proficiency. The interventionist state is blasted for stifling the self regulating propensity of the market. Its welfarism weakened the economy and hence it needed to roll back from many areas.

Further, (pluralist) theories of governance assume that distinct institutions pursue overlapping goals, even if they follow different paths to the same goal. The state is held as 'just one and not necessarily the most important institution of governance'. The role of state is regarded as contextual as well as contingent. Theories of civil society consider the domain of social associations as more important than the state for the citizen. So, what has emerged as the concept and the practices of good governance involves 'the decentring and the pluralisation of the state into a number of levels that stretch horizontally from civil society and market organisations on the one hand, and vertically from the transnational to local self-government institutions on the other' (Chandhoke 2003). This view of governance is argued to be both descriptive (as already existing) and prescriptive (sought to be established). This model emerged as a response to the crisis of the welfare state in the advanced capitalist countries. But now it has been extended to the countries, especially of Asia and Africa through the conditions attached to financial loan/aid, policy prescriptions and new notions of development. This model is 'part of a wider project that was to restructure the economy, the polity, and society in the last two decades of the 20th century' on post-Fordist, postmodern neoliberal lines (ibid.).

Under the new model of governance, a collaboration between state and market interests is advocated. This is currently, enthusiastically promoted by the trinity of WB/IMF/WTO. In connection with the third world, good governance is meant to complement SAP by political reforms to ensure greater accountability, transparency and efficiency in public service along with the protection of civil and human rights and maintaining rule of law through an independent judiciary (Oommen 2004: 146). Governance is conceived as encapsulating government, but going beyond and covering non-governmental agencies as well to meet the needs and aspirations of citizens. So, civil society is made co-responsible with the state for promoting citizen welfare. Thus the relationship between state and civil society is recast from the earlier confrontational orientation into a collaborative mode. It is suggested that 'good governance should be viewed as a conjoined effort of the citizen, the market and civil society. Its aim should be to transcend state-centrism, moderate the rapacity of the market and exorcise extremist orientations from civil society' (ibid.: 147). It is even opined that 'good government' approach marks a break with neoliberalism. It does not consider market as the whole answer and rehabilitates the state which is given central, social and economic responsibilities (Archer 1994: 7). Nevertheless, it remains 'a market-driven competitive model which favours the strong in every area—technical, educational, political, economic, financial' (ibid.: 8).

Currently, in the context of the third world, the concept of 'good governance' has a wider meaning which amounts to replacing the concept of government itself. The new concept is embedded in the paradigm of liberalisation. It involves laying explicit emphasis on the dominance of individual over collective concerns. The state/government is required to reduce its scope and nature and provide more space to the market that operates on the basis of economic efficiency. This condition is observed when market determines allocation of resources for production and consumption. State intervention is viewed as causing distortion in allocative decision-making and thus creating inefficiencies. So, the governance reforms require curtailing state intervention and ensure at the same time a change in the quality of interventions in the desired sectors. In essence, the role of government/public administration is redefined. Its main task in the globalisation/liberalisation framework is to 'facilitate decision-making by the market (Mathur 2003: 51). Kothari (1995) considers the current reforms as 'a response of the ruling circles round the world (both domestic and international) to the challenge being thrown by the masses—the so far ostracised, depressed, and backward social classes that were somehow held at bay through a combination of small crumbs and elitist theory of democracy'. In fact, there are noted two broad concepts of governance. There is one that is people-centred and there is another which takes us away from democracy and possibilities of genuine development including the attainment of the Millenium Development Goals (MDGs). The latter is predominant these days, being promoted by the multilateral/bilateral development financing agencies (Bendana 2004).

Governance Reforms and Multilateral/Bilateral Organisations

Sometimes the concept of 'good governance' is used by multilateral agencies in a limited sense, referring only to institutional reforms and an effective government (IMF 2002: 8). But overall, the concept has a very broad canvas in their agenda. The major multilateral and bilateral development financing agencies' view of good governance is an integral part of their globalisation agenda as set largely by dominant capitalist countries in the world. Decision-making in these agencies is dictated by the rich Western countries, which have a pro-market and anti-state intervention focus (Dasgupta 2005: 33). Neoliberal ideologisation of these agencies has been observed. These institutions are systematically pushing the 'good governance' agenda of reforms particularly in the third world countries. The World Bank and IMF, in particular, are working in tandem to effect institutional restructuring in the third world countries through their loan conditionalities. What they follow is a 'you twist their right arm and we'll twist their left arm' kind of cooperative strategy (Polak, cited in Dasgupta 2005: 36). With the onset of SAP in the 1980s, the Bank made a clear break with its past narrow, project-based lending to influence overall policy direction in the country concerned. In certain cases, the Fund-Bank teams have been involved in the details of the country's budget-making and even in implementing cuts in government expenditures (Dasgupta 2005: 37–39).

In 1989, the World Bank pointedly raised the issue of improving development performance. In its document on sub-Saharan Africa, it was affirmed that due to a 'crisis of governance' the Bank's programmes of adjustment and investment were not proving effective there. So, there came up a push for good governance as 'sound development management' which was defined by the Bank as 'the manner in which power is exercised in the management of a country's economic and social resources for development' (World Bank 1992). But later, the Bank elaborated its view on governance in terms of economic role for the state, a set of policy reforms and other non-economic aspects (Munshi 2004). In its 1992 report *Governance and Development*, the Bank states,

> Governance, in general, has three distinct aspects: (*a*) the form of a *political* regime (parliamentary or presidential, military or civilian, and authoritarian or democratic); (*b*) the processes by which authority is exercised in the management of a country's *economic and social* resources; and (*c*) the capacity of *governments* to design, formulate, and implement policies, and in general, to discharge governmental functions (World Bank 1992, emphasis added).

It can be noted here that the first aspect clearly falls outside the Bank's mandate. The Bank's focus is, therefore, supposed to be on the second and the third aspects. In the opinion of the Bank (1994 report), 'Good governance is epitomised by predictable, open and enlightened policy making (that is *transparent* process); a bureaucracy imbued with a *professional ethos;* an executive arm of government *accountable* for its actions; and a strong *civil society* participating in public affairs; and all behaving under the *rule of law*' (Mander and Asif 2004: 14).

In its 1994 report, the Bank clearly identified four major components of governance reforms. These cover:

(*i*) **Public Sector Management:** This includes civil service reforms (e.g., downsizing, professionalisation), prudent financial management and *state enterprise sector* (i.e., corporatisation, disinvestments/privatisation).

(*ii*) **Accountability of Government:** This implies macrolevel accountability (political, administrative) and also its reinforcement by microlevel *accountability* through decentralisation, participation and competition; decentralisation of government; financial accountability (e.g., improved budgeting, accounting and information systems); and anti-corruption measures.

(*iii*) **Legal Framework for Development:** This includes formulation of clear laws and efficient legal institutions; a set of rules securing *property rights*, governing civil and commercial behaviour and *limiting the power of the state*—all this clearly aimed at private sector development.

(*iv*) **Transparency and Information:** This requires access to information essential for competitive *market economy*; the government to value transparency, i.e., to rely more on market mechanisms for economic management; transparency in privatisation; beneficiary participation in programme design and implementation; freedom of the media; and making public processes more open (e.g., public procurement tenders) (italics added).

So, the Bank agenda of governance reforms covers economic, social, administrative/government and political domains. Its policy statement on governance argues that economic reforms involve a parallel effort at restructuring governmental institutions (Jenkins 1999: 52). The main features of reforms include public sector management (capacity and efficiency), accountability, the legal framework for private sector development, and information and transparency.

The IMF has also paid increasing attention to the issue of 'good governance' in recent years (Abed and Gupta 2002). Its view calls for a transparent and accountable system of government. It is noted that poorly run institutions provide scope for the vested interests to 'capture the state' and promote their interests through preserving monopolies and extracting rent, hindering competition and preventing economic reforms. Moreover, those occupying positions of authority make personal gains through corrupt practices which add taxes on the economy and undermine the rule of law that is essential for the operation of a market economy. So, the Fund has emphasised the need to foster transparency in the management of public funds and in the legal regulatory frameworks, competent and impartial courts of law, trustworthy law enforcement agencies, and better trained and properly paid civil servants and judges. The Fund has made systematic efforts to introduce a market/private sector-centred agenda of development, including the above measures as the third world countries have approached it for tackling their fiscal crisis. Intervention in domestic economy is made to ensure macroeconomic stability and non-inflationary sustainable growth that is central to its mandate. It is reflected in its three core activities, i.e., surveillance of economic policies of member countries, financial support for adjustment programmes, and technical assistance to strengthen economic and financial management. Support is provided for economic policies and structural reforms with a view that there will be reduction in ad hoc decision-making, rent seeking and preferential treatment of individuals and organisations. Technical assistance is offered for strengthening capacities for effective design and implementation of economic policies that include public expenditure management, tax administration, banking systems, foreign exchange, etc. The Fund emphasises on deregulation, liberalisation and privatisation. Its technical assistance is aimed at strengthening the budgetary process and institution building, improve economic governance and reduce rent-seeking behaviour. It has adopted a proactive role along with the Bank, besides other international financial institutions (like the regional development banks), stressing the importance of country ownership of policies for improving governance on the suggested lines. International Financial Institutions (IFIs) have shown increasing interest in the question of good governance which is evident also in several PRSPs (Poverty Reduction Strategy Papers). One such paper concerning Kenya, for instance, states, 'Good governance is fundamental building block of a just and economically prosperous society and therefore, is an essential component of action to reduce poverty' (Singh 2005: 135). The agenda of good governance and structural conditionality has been an important concern also at the G-7 summits. IFIs have been encouraged by G-7 leaders to play an active role in governance reform in the borrowing countries through lending investment and technical assistance activities (ibid.: 136).

Further, it is found that the term 'good governance' was used at the Second United Nations Conference on Least-developed Countries held in 1990. It was concluded at the Conference that 'Good governance is basic to the economic and social progress of all countries'. The UN Secretary-General Kofi Annan opines that, 'Good governance is perhaps the single most important factor in eradicating poverty and promoting development' (UNDP 2002: 51). UNDP (ibid.: 51–2) notes that the focus in debates on good governance is on what makes institutions and rules more effective, including transparency, participation, responsiveness, accountability and the rule of law. Good governance for UNDP is what promotes human development (i.e., 'governance for human development') and democratic governance. It is 'much more than effective institutions and rules'. It is 'partly about having efficient institutions and rules that promote development and ensuring that public services live upto their name'. It is also about protecting human rights, promoting wider people's participation and achieving 'more equitable economic and social outcomes'. It is 'concerned not just with efficient, equitable outcomes but also with fair processes'. It 'must be democratic in substance and in form—by the people and for the people'. The UNDP begun to examine government efficiency and effectiveness to explore good governance-type projects. Its annual Human Development Reports have started linking human development/sustainable human development and human rights with good governance. In fact, it sponsored studies on the efficiency and effectiveness of government provided services in many countries in the late 1980s and 1990s. It examined the public administrative sectors in developing countries. In this connection, it suggested reforms in areas such as civil service (including training), budgeting and finance, organisation and management, government structure, public decision-making and women in development. UNDP takes a broad view of governance like the World Bank. In this context, it refers to the exercise of economic, political and administrative authority's management of a country's affairs at all levels. In its annual report, emphasis is given on the human rights and sustainability dimensions of good governance (LaPorte 2002). Economic and Social Commission for Asia and the Pacific (ESCAP), a UN organisation, regards governance as good only if measures are taken to minimise corruption and there is inclusion of the voices of the most vulnerable sections of society including minorities in decision-making.

According to the Office of the High Commissioner of Human Rights (OHCHR), the real measure of 'good' governance lay in the degree to which it delivers the promise of human rights—civil, cultural, economic, political and social rights. It requires effective guarantee of the right to health, adequate housing, sufficient food, quality education, fair justice and personal security (Mander and Asif 2004: 17). According to the European Union, good governance requires the context of a political and institutional environment that upholds human rights, democratic principles and the rule of law. It defines good governance as 'the transparent and accountable management of human, natural, economic, and financial resources for equitable and sustainable development (ibid.: 15).

Further, it is already noted that the World Bank is not supposed to interfere in the affairs of recipient countries on the basis of political considerations. That is why the Bank appears to define 'good governance' mainly as a technical instrument in terms of maximising development outcome and promoting growth. But a clear political definition of good governance is found in the aid and foreign policies of the Organisation for Economic Cooperation and Development (OECD) countries (Jayal 1997: 407). The discourse of governance has gained solid ground in the development assistance programmes. A clarion call for governance is given by most agencies, including the European Community, the Commonwealth, the OECD and the Organization for African Unity (OAU). Moreover, it is observed that countries like the US, France and Japan have explicitly built political conditionality into their policies of bilateral assistance. OECD also derives from the World Bank's view of governance and links that with participatory development, human rights and democratisation (ibid.: 15).

In the recent decade, bilateral development agencies also began to emphasise 'good governance' in their programmes. For instance, the US Agency for International Development (USAID) focuses on the areas like civil service reform, local government decentralisation and development, public auditing reform, government restructuring and reorganisation, legislative development, legal reform, judicial system reform as well as traditional areas of government streamlining, efficiency and effectiveness. Civil society is regarded as a key player in promoting democratic development. It is affirmed that only an accountable government can deliver development. Accountability would depend upon the existence of 'autonomous centres of social and economic power' that can act as watchdogs over the activities of the state. Civil society comprises both the associations making these 'centres' and the 'enabling environment'.

The aims of fostering, supporting or nurturing civil society through aid are: (*i*) transitions to competitive politics, (*ii*) the consolidation of fledgling democracies, and (*iii*) the establishment of market-oriented economic policies, and subsequently positive development performance (Jenkins 1999: 212).

For the Government of the Netherlands, good governance demands responsible economic and financial management of public and natural resources for the purpose of economic growth, social development and poverty reduction in an equitable and sustainable way. This ensures participatory procedures for public decision-making, transparent and accountable institutions, primacy of law in the management and distribution of resources, effective steps to prevent and combat corruption, support for leadership development and empowerment of men and women (Mander and Asif 2004: 15). Overseas Development Administration or the ODA (renamed, Department for International Development or DFID) of UK emphasises on two facets of good governance. One is competence, i.e., the capacity to formulate policies and strategies, to take timely decisions, e.g., long term and short term issues, and to implement decisions. The second is accountability which among other things requires 'transparency of decision-making and relationships' (Jenkins 1999: 52).

Moreover, there is observed in the international aid agencies emphasis on promoting decentralisation and local self-governance by involving local bodies and NGOs in the developmental projects with a view to reduce poverty and expedite economic growth. In this context, developmental tasks are being assigned to these bodies without properly evaluating their performance, capacity to deliver and sustainability. The accountability of NGOs is highly problematic as they intend to be answerable to donors rather than people. Unequal power structures exist at local level and in such situations it would be erroneous to presume that these institutions can function in an impartial manner. Further, the programmes for promoting popular participation are also found to be highly constricted. Participation is largely viewed as a technical issue and is meant to ensure efficient implementation of policies without much say in the decision-making processes. A survey of participation in the PRSPs in many countries revealed very low level of participation in projects even by NGOs (what to talk of common people) who expressed disenchantment with the process. (K. Singh 2005: 148–49).

So, on the whole, the agenda of good governance propounded by the multilateral and bilateral financial/development agencies is quite broad. In the new agenda is embedded an explicit/implicit view of a liberal democratic state with a pluralist polity that guarantees human rights and separation of powers. These political requirements 'subsist within economic structures that are essentially capitalist'. The 'democratic capitalist political regime, presided over by a minimal state ... is also part of the wider governance of the new World Order' (Leftwich 1992, cited in Jayal 1997: 408). So, 'it is no surprise that the governance agenda should express, and be perfectly consistent with, neoliberal principles of politics and economics' (ibid.). It is affirmed that 'good governance' agenda is deeply embedded in the Washington Consensus (K. Singh 2005: 137). Promotion of good governance has become an integral part of the emergent global economic order (ibid.: 139). The Washington Consensus is reinforced through the governance agenda. The first generation reforms of the Consensus focused on economic reforms in the third world (getting the prices right). The second relates to governance agenda which involves redesigning of the state and its institutions (getting institutions right) to promote smooth development of market economy (ibid.: 138). Market does not operate in vacuum. Globalisation requires uniformity of institutions across states. Diverse forms of institutions are considered as obstacles in the development of market economy. So, legal and institutional reforms are oriented towards securing property rights, enforcing contracts and expansion of the private sector. 'IFIs and the WTO are insisting on harmonised national political, institutional and legal processes in order to ensure smooth operations of transactional capital' (ibid.: 138). The private sector dominated market model of good governance agenda under globalisation is clearly evident in what Paul O'Neill, former Treasury Secretary of the US stated:

> Good governance means enforcing laws and contracts fairly, respecting human rights and property rights, and fighting corruption. Encouraging economic freedom means removing barriers to trade with neighbors and the world, opening the economy to foreign and domestic investment and competition, and divesting government from business operations. Economic freedom also means recognizing that it is the private sector that creates prosperity, not central planning or bureaucracies (ibid.: 130).

Good Governance Agenda of the Government of India

In recent decades, it is observed that multilateral institutions as well as several bilateral development agencies have come forward with the 'good governance' package and are forcing/helping introduce it in the third world countries. In case of India, increasing directive/assistance is provided to the government by these agencies to introduce the package of reforms through loan conditionalities, policy advice, projects (also with NGOs in different areas in different parts of the country) and training of personnel.

The Government of India has paid special attention to governance reforms. The reforms in economic governance started in the country under fiscal stabilisation and SAP over a decade ago with the World Bank/IMF loan conditionalities to improve the balance of payments and fiscal discipline, and the reorganisation of economy, polity and society, as in several other third world countries. The measures for administrative reforms also followed. The country could overcome the BoP problems, but has continued apace on its own with governance reforms in a comprehensive manner. The agenda of reforms has been clearly stated in the recent official documents and reports of the government.

The Tenth Five Year Plan (2002–07) of the government has a full chapter (Chapter 6, vol. II of the plan) on 'Governance and Implementation'. It categorically states that governance issue is at the forefront of the development agenda and says, 'good governance' is one of most crucial factors for development. Here, the notion of governance is broad and comprehensive, and not confined to just the administrative sphere. This is similar to the agenda of governance reforms of the major multilateral and bilateral agencies. The Tenth Plan states,

> *Governance* relates to the management of all such processes that, in any society, define the environment which permits and enables individuals to raise their capability levels, provide opportunities to realise their potential and enlarge the set of available choices.

These processes, *covering the political, social and economic aspects of life* impact every level of human enterprise, be it the individual, the household, the village, the region or the national level.... It *covers the state, civil society and the market,* each of which is critical for sustaining *human development* ([emphasis added] GOI 2002a).

In this schema, the state is regarded as responsible for 'creating a conducive political, legal and economic environment' for building individual capabilities and encouraging private initiative. The market is expected to create opportunities for people. And the role of civil society is to facilitate the mobilisation of public opinion and people's participation in economic, social and political activities (ibid.: 177). This is meant for sustaining an 'efficient and productive social order'. Moreover, *National Human Development Report* (NHDR), 2001, brought out by the Government of India has a full chapter (Chapter 7) on 'Governance for Human Development'. It notes that the issue of governance has emerged at the forefront of the agenda of 'sustainable human development' which implies 'A development that, while being sustainable in terms of resources over generations and across space, recognises the legitimate claim of each person in a society to be an active and a productive participant in the development process' (GOI 2002b: 114). While presenting a recent score card of India's governance, NHDR includes economic, political and civil governance.

NHDR recognises quality of governance as one of the primary factors in the most remarkable development successes of human history. Good governance is regarded as helpful in achieving human well-being and sustained development. Moreover, 'it is equally important to recognise that poor governance could well erode the individual capabilities, as well as institutional and community capacities to meet even the basic needs of sustenance for large segments of the population' (ibid.: 115). NHDR notes with appreciation that there is currently adaptation in governance practices. This is seen as reflected in the changing role and scope of the state, the market and the civil society vis-à-vis each other. There is acceptance of market liberalism and globalisation. The state is yielding to the market and the civil society in several areas where it is said to have 'a direct but distortionary and inefficient presence', as in production of goods and services that are also produced in the private sector. Even in its role as a 'development catalyst', the state is considered inferior as 'perhaps the civil society presently has better institutional capacity'. On the whole, 'It means extension of the market and the civil society domain at the expense of the State in some areas. It also implies an increase in the area of their respective overlaps' (ibid.: 123). This is shown in Figure 1.2.

The governance issues and strategies identified in the Tenth Plan (chapter 6) include: people's participation, decentralisation, right to information, civil society involvement, civil service reforms (rightsizing, transparency, accountability, professionalism), procedural reforms (single window clearance, investor assistance cell), judicial reforms (speedy delivery of justice), using information technology, empowerment of the marginalised, etc. These issues largely relate to administrative reforms (including judicial) and partial political reforms (decentralisation plus people's/civil society participation). But at the core are the reforms in economic governance in terms of increasing privatisation/disinvestments/corporatisation, liberalisation/deregulation, and social sector reforms (growing entry of private sector and NGOs) as evident from other sections of the plan document and the actual policy changes in the recent years.

Figure 1.2: Changing Face of Governance

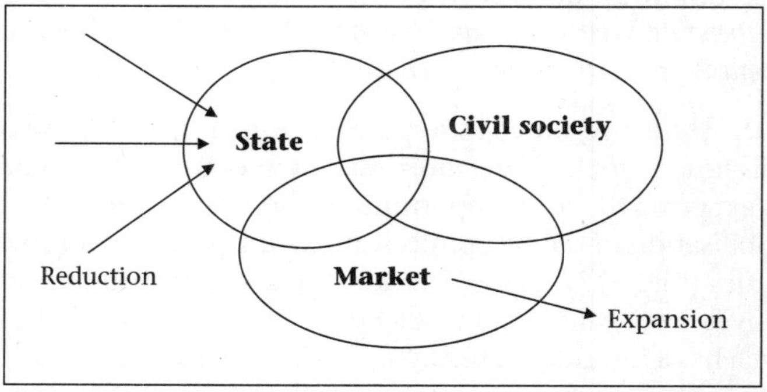

Source: GOI (2002b).

The first report to the people issued by the Manmohan Singh-led UPA (United Progressive Alliance) lists out NCMP's (National Common Minimum Programme) six principles of governance which includes ensuring sustained economic growth of 7–8 per cent per year, and unleashing the creative energies of entrepreneurs, businessmen, scientists, engineers and all other professionals, besides vague generalities about people's welfare and well-being (PMO 2005a). The policy thrust areas for each ministry/department of the Central government is identified. In case of almost all ministries/departments one item is common, viz, institutional reform in terms of decentralisation, simplification, transparency, accountability and e-governance (ibid.: 2005b).

In fact, the Asian Development Bank (ADB) (2004) expresses its appreciation for the reforms in India. It appreciates the focus on high growth, reforms and private sector development. It regards India's focus on good governance in the Tenth Plan as an attempt in 'a new kind of planning' that marks continuing decline in the role of the state in production and creation of a better environment for private enterprises. 'The strategies of the Government, and ADB thus fit together well'. Moreover, ADB emphasises that linking its assistance to reforms in India would remain important. The Bank's involvement at the state-level also is to continue. For the period 2003–06, the ADB proposed 33 loans for India with a total of $7.5 billion (ADB 2004).

Further, the major thrust in the reforms agenda is on the 'rolling back of the state', and its retreat from redistributive commitments that are viewed by hyperglobalisers as morally unacceptable. A staunch advocate of reforms Arun Shourie (2004: 21, 255) affirms the need to transform the nature of the Indian state into an enabling state by disentangling the government, 'whose job is to enable others to do what they can best', 'not to tinker with this procedure or that institution, but to just jettison the function, to hack away the limb wherever this is possible.... A leaner machine, like a leaner body will then be easier to improve'. Bimal Jalan (2005) who was Governor of RBI (1997–2003), emphasises that India is facing a crisis of governance. So, there continues to be the need to launch a bold programme of reforms in the role of the state and the governance structure. 'A priority for the future is to reduce the political role of the government in the economy'. Given a comfortable BoP position, India 'must adopt an aggressive open economy policy'. There is a change in the global environment in India's favour. 'As never before, India's destiny is now truly in our hands' (Jalan 2005: 20, 36, 152, 202).

So, the good governance project according to Jayal (1997) emerges as 'a project for the elimination of politics, for its banishment from the nation state'. It negates the generation of a governance agenda as a product of democratic politics. This poses a serious question on the real nature of the concerns for audit/accountability in the agenda. Here, even the notion of participation is highly constricted. It is mainly viewed as a means (not end), a component of project design to achieve better project effectiveness (less cost and time) and sustainability. It does not provide space for democratic discussion about the model of development, decision about development priorities, and non-acceptability of particular development intervention. In this sense, the agenda of good governance is concerned with marginalising politics. In this paradigm 'the citizen is transformed into a subject: a passive recipient of rights, enjoyer of governance, beneficiary of development'. In the third world context viewing governance as a technical facilitator of development and delinking it from democracy and welfare, emerge as 'a highly impoverished notion' (ibid.).

Thus, the new governance package, popularly known as 'good governance', is advocated by the major multilateral and bilateral development/financing agencies. They share the view that better quality of governance would promote development, which, in their opinion, is not happening in the third world. So, there is an urgent need to introduce governance reforms. Here, good governance is not confined only to traditional civil service/public administration reforms. The agenda of reforms is very comprehensive in nature. It covers economic, social, administrative and political reforms. The agenda primarily propounds a model of development that places the private sector/market in the centre and treats other sectors (viz. state and Civil Society Organization [CSO]/NGO/third sector) as agencies to promote private sector growth. It is basically a private sector/market-centred model of development, though it provides for partnership/collaboration between state, market and third sector/civil society/NGOs. This model of development/reforms has been largely accepted by the Government of India. In the sphere of economic governance, reforms involve pro-actively promoting private sector development, reorganisation of public sector on market lines (through privatisation, disinvestment) and re-orienting social/welfare sector on market lines. In the domain of public administration, there is emphasis on civil service reform for enhancing efficiency, effectiveness, transparency and accountability of government, curtailing corruption and also maintenance of rule of law, including judicial reforms. In the political realm, the state is required to adopt a partnership approach (with private sector and NGOs/CSOs) through collaboration with plurality of actors/agencies, and promote decentralisation and devolution of government and people's participation. This is supposed to provide stability to the government and ensure achievement of development goals in terms of human development, human rights, equity and empowerment of the marginalised and sustainable development. The crisis of governance thesis emerges as a rationalisation of the prevailing system and has become the 'central call of the forces of liberalisation and globalisation in the era of reforms' (Mohanty 2004: 109).

Figure 1.3: New Governance Package of Reforms under Globalisation (Good Governance Paradigm)

Major dimensions

Economic governance reforms (Management of country's economic and social resources)

Public sector management
- State enterprise reform, Corporatisation of state enterprises, Disinvestment/Privatisation

Private sector development
- Enabling legal framework, Clear laws—set of rules securing property rights, civil and commercial behaviour, and limiting power of the state, Removal of market unfriendly policies/control
- Procedural reforms, Single window clearance, Investor assistance cell
- Information and transparency, Access to information for competitive market economy, Relying more on market mechanisms for economic management, Transparency in privatisation, Open public processes (tendering, etc.)

Social sector reforms
(areas of health, education, poverty reduction, etc.)
- Involvement of private sector and NGOs/CSOs

Administrative reforms (Government capacity to discharge its functions)

Civil service reform
- Government streaming, Efficiency and Effectiveness Downsizing/rightsizing, Professionalism (competence of civil servants), Improving quality of public service provisions

Accountability of Government
(both macro and micro levels)
- Financial accountability, Improving budgeting, public accounting and information system
- Anti-corruption measures (impact on business environment and service delivery)

Transparency/ Accountability
Right to information, E-governance(use of IT), Citizen's charter
- Freedom of media

Rule of law
Effectiveness of judiciary, Enforceability of contracts, Crime control, Judicial system reform (legal reform), Measures for speedy delivery of justice

Political governance reforms (Government restructuring and reorganisation)

Legislative development
Promoting democratisation i.e. Multi-party competitive politics, Fair elections

Political/government stability, and (low/no) use of violent means

Partnership approach/ Pluralism
Role of multiple actors in development—State, private sector, NGO/CSO/CBO

Decentralisation of government
Promoting local government, devolution of powers

People's/Beneficiary participation
in programme design and implementation

Achievement of development goals:
Human development (indicators relate to education, health, income),
Human rights—Exercise of civil liberties and political rights (reducing crime, including against SC/ST),
Equity (reducing inequality—income gap); ***Empowerment*** of the marginalised (SC/ST/women/minorities),
Sustainability (tackling environmental degradation, promoting improvement)

The whole package of 'good governance' represents nothing but the neoliberal agenda of globalisation. Globalisation is facilitated by the good governance reforms. So, it would, in fact be apt to view globalisation and good governance reforms conjointly. The volume edited by Leo Panitch et al. (2006) rightly suggests us to view neoliberal globalisation in its totality, 'not as a mere series of "reforms" ... but as a radical programme to reshape the entire economic, political, legal and ideological landscape of capitalism' (Zuege et al., in Panitch, et al. 2006: 1).

A synoptic view of the comprehensive package of governance reforms is provided in Figure 1.3.

Social Dimension

There are two main concerns in the studies dealing with the social dimension of globalisation and reforms. These include: (*a*) social base/driving social forces in terms of social classes and castes, and (*b*) socio-economic impact in terms of poverty, income inequality, unemplcyment, etc. This is analysed at different levels, i.e., global, regional, national and state/local. Sceptics seem to dominate over the hyperglobalisers in the studies dealing with these aspects in the case of India. And there is a dearth of studies on the country from a tranformationalist perspective. This would be evident from the discussion below.

Social Base—Gainers and Losers

Both foreign and Indian scholars have delved on the social dimension of globalisation. Some scholars have examined globalisation from broad theoretical perspectives while others have focused their attention on the specific social aspects of globalisation. At the macro-level, Wallerstein (2004) insists on treating the modern world system as capitalist which originated in the 16th century and has grown further passing through different phases. The system formed a hierarchy of states and at its 'core' existed strong states that supported the dominant classes who continue to exploit labour, resources and trade opportunities, most notably in the 'peripheral' countries. The countries located in the 'semiperiphery' reduced polarisation between the two and helped keep the system relatively stable. This historical view of capitalism is complemented by Sklair (2004) who emphasises on the role of transnational corporations (TNCs) and transnational classes in the contemporary capitalist global system. According to him, the driving forces and dominant institutions of globalisation include the transnational corporation, transnational capitalist class and the culture-ideology of consumerism in the economic, political and cultural domains respectively. He notes the rapid growth in recent time of a transnational class which consists of TNC executives, globalising bureaucracy and politicians (who occupy positions in international multilateral/regional structures of governance and lend services to nation states), globalising professionals, merchants and media. He affirms that a global consumerist ideology promotes the exploitative structure commanded by TNCs and helps the dominant transnational class becoming ever stronger.

Pedersen (2000: 266) identifies two main theoretical perspectives in the debate on (policy) reforms in developing countries with a focus on national level. First, there is a debate on the relationship between state and social structures and actors and its significance for explaining reforms/social change. Second, there is a focus on the nature of developing societies and their insertion into the world economy. This relates to the reforms package of the Bank-Fund duo. But the moot issue is about the driving force for reforms, whether it is internal (state elites or social classes) or external/foreign hand (Bank-Fund-WTO trinity) or may be a combination of both, but with dominance of one or the other factor. Pedersen is in favour of adopting a state-society oriented approach, not merely statist or otherwise, for properly understanding the nature and dynamics of reforms. He observes, 'The state is "embedded" in and reflects the configuration of articulated interests in its own society, and while substantial reform measures may be initiated autonomously by state officials, they will only take effect when supported by strong and organised social interests' (ibid.: 278). Moreover, reforms might get started under the pressure of foreign agencies, but 'the actual implementation and the long term effect of polices depend much more on the nature of the society in question and, in particular, on the nature and strengths of the various social forces within it' (ibid.).

Coming to India, Patnaik et al. (2004) analyse the 'shift from a dirigiste to a neoliberal economic strategy' that has occurred in India since 1991. As regards the external push, they refer to certain basic changes that the world capitalism has undergone with the 'emergence of a new form of international finance capital which sees the global promotion of neoliberalism as serving its interests'. This explains the domestic social (class) support base for reforms in India. There are beneficiaries of reforms which include the Indian capitalist class, upper class/caste, urban middle classes, the non-resident Indians (NRIs) (new diaspora), agricultural capitalists (initial support), and (top) elements within the bureaucracy/professional classes/the intelligentsia (Patnaik 1994). These sections of society are hence the supporters of reforms. The interests of the domestic supporters of reforms well coincided with the Fund-Bank schema of reforms to serve basically the interests of MNCs and globalised finance (Patnaik et al. 2004: 95). Kothari (1995: 1593) also finds a convergence between the external and domestic interests that are involved in pushing forward the reforms agenda. No wonder the reforms have broadly had a smooth sailing in India even after the 1991 crisis, as external forces could find 'junior partners' in the domestic turf. Here, the attempt is to integrate the upper and the middle classes with the simple aim of retaining and enhancing the privileges and perquisites of these classes (ibid.: 1595). Currently, a pro-business model of development is followed in the country which rests on a 'fairly narrow ruling alliance of the political and the economic elite' (Kohli 2006: 1368).

The Bombay Club representing the old group of big industrialists was initially reluctant to support economic reforms because of the fears of takeover or peripheralisation by MNCs. But their stance gradually changed with increasing success both within and outside. Some Indian brands have gained global repute. For instance, Asian Paints has entered markets of developing countries. Moser Baer is a major global player in optical media and compact disc, and Ranbaxy and Dr. Reddy's Laboratories in generics (TOI 2006a). Besides, certain Indian companies are acquiring firms abroad, like TATA acquiring a giant UK firm Corus and Ranbaxy a Romanian firm Terapia. 'Today the times have changed so much as to make those [earlier] protestations seem absurd' (ibid.).

In the Forbes 2000 list of Corporate Titans, 33 Indian companies found place. This consists of both private and public sector Indian firms, the ratio being 49 per cent and 51 per cent respectively. These largely operate in the areas of banking, oil and gas, IT and software. The major firms in the public sector include ONGC, SBI Group, Steel Authority of India; and in the private sector, Reliance Industries, ICICI Bank, TCS, Tata Iron & Steel Company Ltd., Infosys Technologies, Bharti Televentures, Wipro, etc. (TOI 2006b).

In fact, a major segment of the Indian big business is currently worried and uneasy with the slow pace of reforms, but at the same time, supports a cautious approach to globalisation. It expresses its uneasiness with the current Congress-led UPA government at the centre. For instance, Mr Rahul Bajaj (2006), Chairman of Bajaj Auto, finds the government reverting to its 1970s mindset of government control and redistributing poverty by wasting public money. He clearly supports economic reforms over social ones, efficiency over equity. In his view, 'economic reform needs support and encouragement. Because, in the final analysis, it facilitates social reform'. Moreover he favours globalisation, but with caution. He states, 'I believe that on the whole globalisation presents an opportunity for India. However, mindless globalisation is not in our interest. The situation of our agriculture, industry and services sectors, and within these of the sub-sectors varies tremendously and we have to modulate our engagement sectorally.... What we need are reforms that facilitate economic and human development based on a good understanding of what is required, not some World Bank or IMF prescription'.

There is emergence of a new kind of transnational capitalist class in India with the recent growth of the IT industry (Upadhya 2004). This class consists of NRI tech entrepreneurs and venture capitalists, the founders and top executives of large and medium-sized Indian IT companies, top managers of MNC software centres in India and entrepreneurs of the new breed of high-end start-ups. Most IT entrepreneurs have middle class origin, who build on their cultural capital of higher education (e.g., engineering) and social capital through professional careers. This class is distinct in terms of having close global integration and relative autonomy from the 'old' Indian economy dominated by the public sector and a nationalist capitalist class. Particularly, the growth of cross-border IT companies marks a shift to a new type of transnational corporate structure in the software industry wherein ownership and control generally lies outside India (mainly with NRIs in the US) but actual work or production of value occurs within the country. These companies are US based multinationals with wholly owned subsidiaries operating in India, while other major inputs, other than capital, are Indian. IT industry seems, both in physical and financial terms, to be 'more an extension of the global information economy than an integral part of the Indian economy'. Given the structure and linkages of the IT industry, the IT business class is one of the most vociferous votaries of liberalisation and globalisation and has significant influence on public policy in India.

The Indian diaspora is a strong advocate of globalisation and associated reforms. It comprises NRIs, OCIs (overseas citizen of India) and PIOs (persons of Indian origin)—about 20 million in number. Their recognition, appreciation and influence in the country is on the rise. A study by investment banker J.P. Morgan says that India is the largest recipient of remittances by overseas workers, estimated at $21 billion. This study reaffirms the RBI figures showing that remittances were double the amount of net foreign institutional investor inflows and one-fourth of the merchandise export earnings of the country. It is reported that the stock of deposits by NRIs comes to about $32 billion or 23 per cent of foreign exchange reserves. (It may be noted that portfolio and real estate investments are mainly concentrated in the IT area). Dhawan (2006) notes, 'It is no wonder that the government is keen to recognise and pander to the interests of the growing diaspora'. There is an 'opening up' of Indian citizenship through the introduction of extra-territoriality with the enactment of the Citizenship Amendment Act, 2003 and the Citizenship Amendment Act, 2005 (Roy 2006). The earlier provision of termination of Indian citizenship on the assumption of the citizenship of a foreign country does not hold anymore. In addition to NRIs, the Indian diaspora now has the 'overseas citizen' of India which is based on the association between Indian citizenship and ethnic Indian-ness—their Indian origin, cultural heritage and emotional attachment to India. Besides their emotional ties, other considerations have been important in this connection. While speaking on this issue in 2003 in the Rajya Sabha Manmohan Singh, as the then leader of the opposition, referred to overseas Indians as 'a great national reservoir', whose 'knowledge, wealth, experience and expertise' could be tapped to benefit the country. Now, overseas Indians have been granted dual citizenship of sorts, though not in a full fledged sense. They are not provided with an Indian passport, but an overseas citizen card. Two such cards were given to overseas Indians at the fourth Pravasi Bharatiya Divas held at Hyderabad in January 2006. This card provides overseas Indian a greater flexibility in entry and registration with local police authorities. They can also apply for a new kind of visa called 'U' visa which is a multipurpose, multiple entry lifelong visa. They are placed at the same level as NRIs in economic, financial and educational matters, but not in acquisition of agricultural or plantation properties. In fact such stance towards the diaspora is being adopted by several countries which are getting significantly integrated in a 'hierarchical' world economy. These countries are trying to reach out to their diaspora in several ways including provision for investment in the country of origin (Roy 2006: 1422). Visvanathan (2005) calls Indian diaspora 'the happy Trojan Horse of globalisation'. He finds the diaspora projected as representing the new 'idea of India' of the present as successful, professional, competent and globally recognisable'. 'They are the new consumers of culture who gradually become the new producers'. They symbolise India's citizenship at Stanford, Oxford or Silicon Valley and partially reconstruct India abroad as in *The Argumentative Indian* of Amartya Sen and *The Fortune at the Bottom of the Pyramid* of C.K. Prahalad.

Deshpande (1997) highlights the emergence of the new middle class as 'a key actor' today on the national stage in India which is 'playing a role of unprecedented importance in the public life of the nation'. It has an 'important role in promoting the paradigm shift' from state-led planned nationalist development to market-oriented structural adjustment and globalisation in the country. There is change in self-understanding and social position of this class. It has acquired the position of 'an indispensable member of the ruling bloc, the dominant segments of which are agrarian capitalists and industrial and financial bourgeoisie'. Deshpande finds upper middle class (managerial professional) segment acquiring the maximum benefits of globalisation. This segment consolidated its position on the basis of the (previous) developmental state. It is today interpellated by globalisation and is now ready to kick the developmental state away as the ladder it no more requires. It has 'graduated to thinking of itself as a "portrait" of the nation'. The middle class no more claims merely to represent the people, but rather thinks that 'it is itself the nation' (Deshpande 1997: 310). Palshikar (2004: 153) finds an alliance between the bourgeoisie and the middle classes. The size of the middle class has increased and it has acquired a central position in the current situation. India's ruling classes require a hegemonic project in the context of globalisation. 'The middle class can now develop the hegemonic project on behalf of the capitalist class. In exchange, the core of the middle class will gain entrance to the ruling coalition'. Lele indicates the trends of global integration through both formal and informal channels. The NRIs, for instance, send remittances for quick and shady windfall returns and for building temples/mosques. They also participate in the culture of predatory capitalism (Lele, in Vora and Palshikar eds. 2004).

Further, it is observed that increasing stronghold of transnational agribusiness in modern agriculture is leading to continuous rise in production costs and lower net income for farmers (Jomo 2006: 10). Moreover, there are huge subsidies support from the Western governments for agricultural export. This causes lowering of farm-gate prices for the produce in the third world countries. Surplus producing farmers are said to be the beneficiaries, and hence supporters of economic liberalisation in India (Panini 1997). They see the advantages of deregulation, as in the case of Sharad Joshi of Shetkari Sangathan in Maharashtra. But another segment of rich farmers (large and medium) have expressed apprehension about issues like cut in agricultural subsidies and entry of agribusiness MNCs, and so oppose globalisation as visible in Karnataka, western Uttar Pradesh, Gujarat, etc. Increase in input costs and decline in prices of primary agricultural commodities in the international market affect even the surplus producing farmers in a negative way. The farmers are split broadly into two segments, one for and the other against globalisation (Omvedt 1993).

The impact of globalisation is regarded as being largely negative in India on the weaker and marginalised sections of society, e.g., small and marginal farmers and agricultural labourers. Globalisation tends to turn agriculture more capital-intensive. There is spread of corporate controlled agriculture—control by global agribusiness and bio-technology corporations. It is geared to grow food and non-food commercial crops for the market, especially for exports. Capital-intensive export-driven agriculture has severely affected the poorer peasantry, which is reflected in frequent cases of suicides as in Andhra Pradesh and Punjab (Arvind 2002). Minimum food security has emerged as a serious problem for both the poor peasantry and agricultural labourers.

A recent issue of the journal *Economic and Political Weekly* (April 12, 2006) focuses on the current agrarian crisis and suicide by farmers in several states in India (Jodhka 2006, Mishra 2006, Mohankumar and Sharma 2006, Rao and Suri 2006, Sridhar 2006, Suri 2006). In the case of Maharashtra, there is noted withdrawal of the state from agriculture as reflected in declining public investment, poor government agriculture extension services and the diminishing role of formal credit institutions. As a result the farmer depends on the input dealer for advice and informal sources of credit with higher interest rate. Input costs have increased due to shift to commercial crops. Change in cropping pattern has adversely affected the livelihoods of the people. Returns are generally low or negative. Moreover, in the event of crop failure or low output price, farmers' indebtedness is compounded forcing them to commit suicide. In case of

Kerala, there is noted a close link between the neoliberal policy regime and the agrarian crisis and farmers' distress. The worst affected are the smaller farmers due to their higher vulnerability to crop failure and a fall in prices of the produce like coffee and pepper. In Andhra Pradesh it is indicated that the process of economic liberalisation began particularly since 1990s and increasingly imposed a new kind of stress on the peasantry due to the state withdrawal and a greater play of market forces. There is a paradox here, most of the political representatives come from agricultural background but farmers' interests still get marginalised. This is explained by the increasing differentiation/fragmentation of farming classes and lack of organised farmers' movement in the country. K.C. Suri wonders, 'Are we any more a nation? What kind of citizens are these farmers? What happened to the solemn resolve to constitute India into a socialist democratic republic and to secure for its citizens justice, liberty, equality and fraternity?' He warns, 'If nothing positive happens in Indian agriculture in the coming years and if farmers continue to be squeezed by the global and domestic markets as well as the rentier classes, they will have to either abandon agriculture or rebel against governments; or else the spate of suicides continues to haunt the country' (Suri 2006: 1529).

An adverse impact of globalisation on labour and their unions in the country is noticed. SAP generally leads to a freeze in public sector employment. In the organised private sector also employment rarely increases due to the low level of private investment and high capital intensity. So, most of the unemployed people enter the low productivity and low paying informal sector. Moreover, the organised sector takes advantage of the surplus labour condition. It gets into contract labour, casualisation and putting out systems. Thus, they save on establishment costs and are able to offload surplus workers when demand decreases (Dasgupta 2005: 247). No wonder, most studies on SAP with its attendant policy of sacking workers and reduction of wages, find rise in poverty, unemployment, decline in wages and in access to health and education as a result of government slashing social spending and subsidies (ibid.: 250). In India, in recent years, a hardening of attitude towards labour by the government, including the judiciary, is observed. There is increase in casualisation of labour force, and contract labour is on the rise. There is decline in the employment in the organised sector. Moreover, the number of knowledge professionals in the growing Indian IT sector is very small (Debroy and Kaushik 2005: 131–34, 239, 240, 294, 316). Advocates of globalisation demand reforms in labour laws and the introduction of an exit policy with the right of the employer to hire and fire to maximise profit. But there is a lot of opposition to this, though not much effective, in India. A large number of industries have closed down, leading to increased unemployment and poverty. There are attacks on the wage rates of workers/employees, which has been static in real terms. Both the government and the private sectors have introduced schemes like the Voluntary Retirement Scheme (VRS) to throw out employees. It is common to find these days the government arbitrarily stopping payment of bonus, freezing Dearness Allowance, refusing payment of wages/salary for months and harassing of employees to leave (Arvind 2002: 213). Traditional industrial working class is getting badly hit due to processes of tertiarisation, feminisation, casualisation and precarisation.

Recently, the Supreme Court of India has shown a favourable stance for a flexible labour law regime in the country. It has ruled that in case of governments closing down departments for financial constraints and administrative streamlining there will be no obligation to provide reemployment to those who lose their jobs due to such closures or restructuring. The court has also ruled in favour of strict action against employees found guilty of sleeping on the job, and abusing and assaulting their seniors. The unanimous verdict passed in case of a petition filed by the Karnataka government, by a five judge constitution bench headed by the apex court Chief Justice, dashed the hopes of lakhs of daily wagers ruling out regularisation of service even if they worked for years. The verdict clearly states, 'There is no right of regular employment for those who have been given employment on a daily basis' (Mahapatra 2006).

But giving a faint glimpse of the 'human face', the National Commission for Enterprises in the Unorganised Sector, set up by the UPA government, has proposed a national minimum social security scheme for the unorganised sector which employs 93 per cent of the workforce (about 360 million people) in the country. The scheme covers healthcare costs, life insurance, provident fund and pensions. It is to be funded by the centre and the state governments plus nominal contributions from workers themselves. The implementation of the proposed scheme would include Panchayati Raj Institutions (PRIs), NGOs and trade unions. If implemented, the scheme would imply widening of the social base of the welfare state in the country (TOI 2006d).

It is asserted that the new economic policy reforms in India have serious negative implications for the SCs and STs. Reforms have 'nothing to offer them except marginalisation and displacement' (Jogdand 2000: 10). Increasingly privatisation deprives them of jobs. Growing privatisation and commercialisation in education affects their social mobility. 'As a result of the receding social security and PDS, displacement of the traditional labour in the agrarian economy and privatisation of jobs, the Dalits will encounter a major threat to their survival. The Dalits will get crushed between the increasing price structure and growing unemployment and underemployment' (ibid.: 11).

Instances of shifting landownership from small tribal peasants to private companies, including transnational corporations, due to liberalisation and privatisation are noticed. This is leading to displacement of landless tribals. Moreover, there is a threat of their cultural invasion (Pathy 2000). As the majority of tribals are dependent upon agriculture, further penetration of market economy would increase their marginalisation (Chalam 2000). The new economic policy is meant for intensive utilisation of agricultural land through free market mechanism/capitalist farming. Despite government regulation, the tribals are found leasing out land to bigger cultivators or for plantation crops, horticulture and also grass cultivation. Agriculture is increasingly becoming a losing proposition. Wage-employment is emerging as more remunerative for them. The apprehension is that the tribal primitive agriculture (now non-viable) would get replaced by big farms, ranches, plantation estates, farm houses and holiday resorts. Their forest would become private/corporate estates and the tribals would be expected at the most to serve as labourers. Harnessing water resources of tribal areas for power and irrigation projects and extraction of mineral resources would lead to massive displacement of the tribal people. Moreover, the water resources would be polluted and thus, pose problems of even drinking water scarcity for them. They will then be hard hit (Sharma 1995).

Mohanty (2004: 109) observes that there was, by 1980s, a change in the social basis of power in the country from a landlord-capitalist-middle class combination to a capitalist-rich peasant-regional bourgeoisie-middle class combination. This trend further crystallised in the 1990s with globalisation and liberalisation that linked the Indian bourgeoisie and the rich peasants with the world capitalist system and the Indian middle class with global information technology. Power, however, remained confined to the privileged sections of society. The Dalits and adivasis continued to stay outside. Their elites remained dependent agents of the privileged castes and leaders. Swamy (1994) finds the model of dependent industrialisation shaped by globalisation as the force that created in India a class of industrialists unabashedly subservient to foreign capital. It also created a middle class obsessed with Western culture and intensely consumeristic in orientation. 'This compradorisation of the upper layers of the society is an important cause of the structural crisis' (Swamy 1994). The latest scenario in India presents a picture of diminishing employment, narrowing of markets and increase in foreign debt. 'It presents development impasse', for the common people.

On the whole, there are two types of exclusion under globalisation in the contemporary societies, in both the developed capitalist countries and others including India. The top social class reflects voluntary exclusion in the form of detaching itself from the social mainstream. There is a withdrawal from public institutions on the part of the more affluent social groups which is evident from their pulling out from public education and public health system and living in 'fortress'/'gated' communities. This symbolises the 'revolt of the elites'. Another type of exclusion is of those at the bottom. This is forced exclusion in a way, signifying their exclusion from the mainstream of opportunities society has to offer (Giddens 1999).

Panini (1995) focuses his attention on the early years of economic liberalisation, which signified adoption of a new strategy of development. He finds a new social logic that generated 'pragmatic consensus' on economic reforms in India. Private enterprise and business have gained remarkable social legitimacy. But 'it is not yet clear that economic reforms are irreversible. There is an increasing trend of social inequalities, deterioration in the conditions of women and rising ethnic conflicts and communalism. However, the social logic of liberalisation, in his opinion, is such that it 'may counter the ... tendencies of disharmony and disintegration'. The prevailing condition, in fact, is unstable and uncertain. There may occur a swing from one extreme (harmony) to another (disharmony). 'Economic liberalisation may create prosperity but in the process may increase ethnic strife and conflict' (ibid.: 60).

Poverty, Inequality and Unemployment

Neoliberals affirm that globalisation-friendly policies (greater economic integration) have led in recent years to a reduction of poverty and also claim globalisation to be the causal factor in this connection. It is asserted that absolute poverty declined at the world level from 1237 million in 1990 to 1100 million in 2000. According to the World Bank the number of people living in absolute poverty reduced from 1.4 billion in 1980 to 1.2 billion in 1998. But critics do not accept these figures because of serious measurement faults in the estimates and underestimation. For instance, the income of $1 a day used here to determine poverty is based on purchasing power parity (PPP) exchange rate (not US $) which is adjusted and hence the cost of living tends to be lower in poorer countries than richer ones. The basket of goods forming PPP is not considered appropriate for measuring poverty correctly. The estimates are based on two different comparative indices which create distortions (Kiely 2005). Moreover, poverty reduction is said to be mainly due its decline in the most populous countries viz China and

India which, in fact, are not as open (e.g., in terms of trade openness, capital control, etc.) as many other third world countries. There is an increase in the level of poverty in several regions such as Sub-Saharan Africa, Latin America and the Carribean. It is largely the moderate liberalisers that show a better record of poverty reduction, not those countries having highly open or an extremely closed economy.

As regards inequality trends, average income gap between the 20 richest countries and 31 least developed countries (LDCs) is found to have increased from 11: 1 in 1960 to 19: 1 in 1999 (based on 1985 PPP dollars and population weighted). But the gap increased less in case of those LDCs that diversified into manufacturing and services but more in case of those still most dependent on (non-oil) primary commodities (Kiely 2005: 900). Income inequalities also exacerbated within countries. For instance, in the US 60 per cent of income gains during 1980–90 went to the top 1 per cent of the population, but real income of the poorest 25 per cent of the population remained static for the last 30 years. In UK the gap between the highest and lowest-paid workers is found to be greater now than it was for the last 30 years. Moreover, the real income of the poorest 10 per cent of the working population showed a decline (Giddens 1999: 106–7). Wage inequality was thus, on the rise between mid-1980s and mid-1990s in some industrialised countries.

There is also an increase in the open unemployment in the world in the recent decade. International Labour Organisation (ILO) gives the total unemployment figure as approximately 188 million (in 2003). There is a variation across regions and countries regarding unemployment trends. Industrialised countries reflect a mixed trend. There is increase in unemployment in Japan, but decline in the US and UK. However, there is an increase in the rate of unemployment within the third world since 1990 as in Latin America and Carribean, and South-East Asia. The developing regions on the other hand generally showed increasing share of self-employment which is linked with stagnation or slow growth in modern sector employment and hence an increase in labour absorption in the informal economy. (Giddens 1999).

Further, Pulin Nayak (2006) notes certain encouraging trends in the Indian economy in the recent years—in terms of growth rate of GDP reaching about 8 per cent, saving rate rising to about 29 per cent of the GDP in 2004–05 (compared with 23.5 per cent in 2001–02), gross domestic investment rate for the first time crossing 30 per cent mark in 2004–05, reduction in revenue deficit, and direct taxes reaching 5 per cent of the GDP for the first time (stuck at around 2.5 per cent for decades prior to the 1990s). But he also observes serious negative trends. India is faced with a wide gap in inter-sectoral growth rates (about 9 per cent in industry and services but only 2.3 per cent in agriculture in 2005–06). This implies accentuation of income inequalities in the economy at large (60 per cent of the population dependent on agriculture which has a low growth rate). There is a professional industrial class flaunting a luxurious life, which is in clear contrast with periodic reports of suicide deaths of farmers due to inability to repay relatively small debts. The recent 60th round of National Sample Survey Organisation (NSSO) data reveals increase in unemployment rate both in rural and urban areas among males as well as females. Unemployment for rural males increased from 5.6 per cent in 1993–94 to 9 per cent in 2004. In case of urban males the rise in the same period was from 6.7 per cent to 8.1 per cent. The unemployment rate for women also went up. Increase in unemployment has direct impact on the incidence of poverty in the country. Kohli (2006: 1368) observes that higher economic growth rate in India in the recent decade is accompanied by increasing inequalities,

Figure 1.4: Social Dimension of Globalisation and Reforms in India

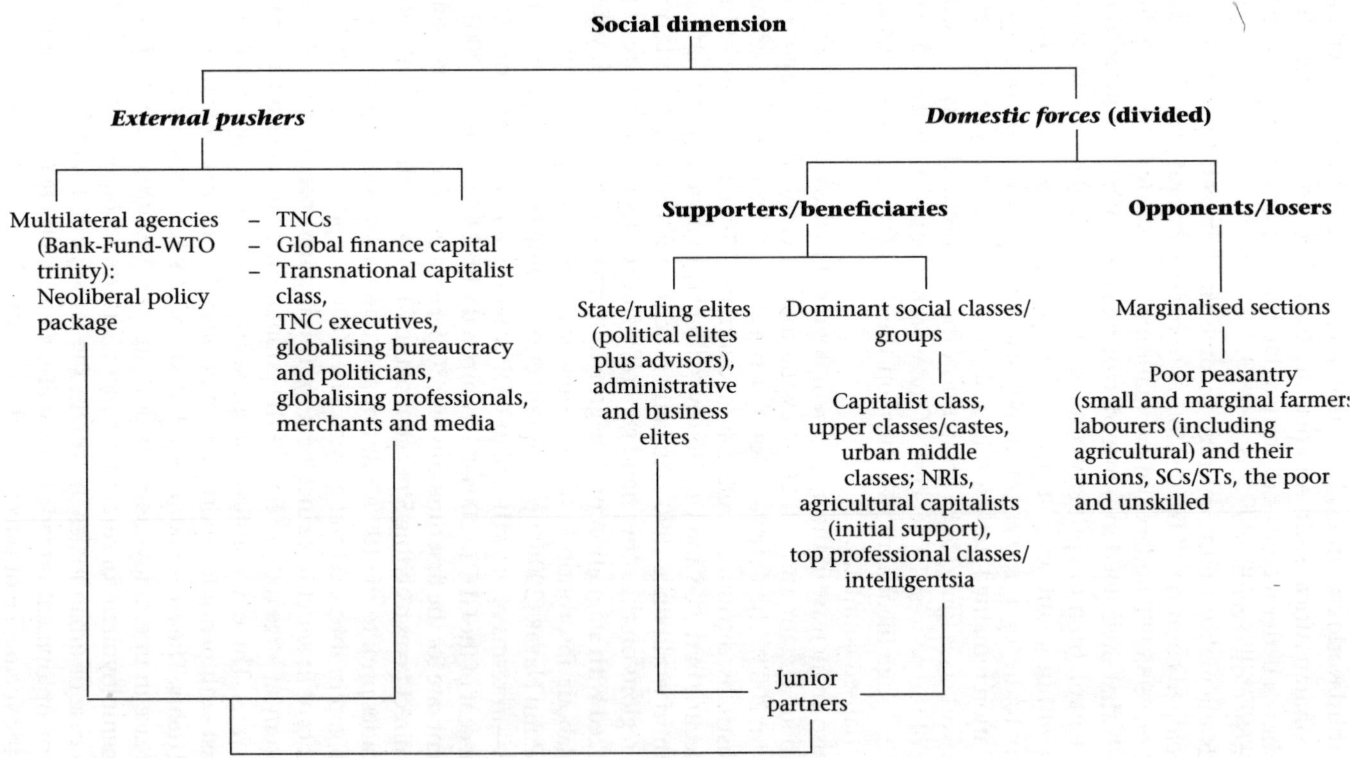

growing capital intensity of the economy, increasing concentration of ownership of private industry and nearly stagnant growth in employment, particularly, in manufacturing industries. Nayak (ibid.) states,

> The latest Economic Survey talks of demographic dividend, referring to a large and younger labour force in coming years. But there is an India where significant sections of the youth in remote villages and tribal belts have only a bleak landscape before them, and no gainful employment. And this comes along with a steady and unprecedented growth in aspirations. This combination can hardly be salutary for stable and equitable economic development.

Thus, as regards the social dimension of globalisation and reforms in India, it is evident that there are external pushers as well as internal supporters/junior partners. The former includes multilateral and bilateral development/financing agencies, TNCs, global finance capital and the emerging transnational capitalist class. At the domestic front, globalising reforms are steered by the state/ruling elites (political, administrative and business elites and advisors) and supported by the beneficiary social classes/groups like capitalist class, upper classes/castes, urban upper middle class, top professional classes/intelligentsia, NRIs and agricultural capitalists (initial years). There is, however, ambiguity regarding decline in poverty but inequality has increased. There is increasing informalisation of labour and weakening of their unions. Reforms have created losers who are opposed to it. This includes the marginalised sections of society, e.g., the poor peasantry, landless labourers, industrial/service sector labourers, the lower middle classes, SCs and STs. The apprehension is that they would get further marginalised.

But the actual situation may not be as simple. Are their no winners at all from the lower classes and castes, even a small section as a result of the reforms? Are there no losers at all from the upper classes and castes? Increasing socio-economic polarisation may accentuate conflict and ultimately lead, maybe to the end of reforms. But increase in internal differentiation within classes and castes would fragment the resistance against reforms and allow its forward march, even though haltingly as is happening after the severe thrashing of the reforms-oriented regimes during elections in the country. There is a need to closely and critically examine the role of different classes/castes/strata of society in the reforms process and the impact of reforms on them. A synoptic view of the social dimension of globalisation and reforms is provided in Figure 1.4.

Cultural Dimension

In a broad sense culture refers to the values, beliefs and lifestyles of people. Fast changes are observed at this level as a result of increasing globalisation and reforms in the third world countries in recent decades. There are widely divergent views on the cultural dimension of globalisation and reforms. Theoretical frameworks are not clearly stated in most studies in this area. However, three major paradigms of cultural change under globalisation seem to emerge. The paradigm of cultural 'homogenisation' reflects basically the neoliberal hyperglobalist view which would imply harmonious acceptance of the homogenising cultural changes. But cultural homogenisation is also viewed from neo-Marxist perspective which discerns 'cultural imperialism' in the current cultural changes. Then there are the heterogeneity and hybridisation paradigms. Increasing cultural heterogeneity is said to provide more cultural choices to people and individuals and might be said to imply a neoliberal persuasion in the cultural domain. Hybridisation paradigm can be said to be embedded in the transformationalist perspective. The paradigm of cultural 'clash' provides a culturalist interpretation of the current cultural changes.

General Scenario

In fact, Pieterse (1996) identifies three clashing notions of cultural change in the era of globalisation, which include cultural homogenisation, clash, and heterogeneity/hybridisation paradigms. The homogenisation paradigm focuses on the current phenomenon of increasing global interdependence and interconnectedness leading to growing cultural standardisation, uniformisation, convergence and compression into a single global culture (such as an European or a US culture). This is manifest in the increasing homogeneity of world values like rationalisation, market competition, commodification and democratic/human rights. The prominent popular American/Western cultural symbols such as Coca-Cola, blue jeans, rock music and McDonald's Golden Arches are getting spread all over. So, homogenisation of consumption patterns and lifestyles is reflected in increasing McDonalisation, CocaColisation and Disneyfication of the world.

Berger (2002) observes an emerging global culture which, in origin and content, is mostly of Western and American provenance. Emerging global culture is penetrating the rest of the world through diffusion at both elite and popular levels. He talks about two types of elite vehicles of diffusion. First is the 'Davos culture' which signifies an international culture of business and political leaders, Davos being the locale of the annual World Economic Summit. Those participating at the Summit are socialised in its culture and carry the cultural baggage from there for diffusion in their countries and regions. This culture also includes the culture of 'Yuppie internationale' (a global network of ambitious young people in business and professions spread across countries) who speak, dress and think alike. Another elite vehicle of diffusion is represented by the 'faculty club culture' signifying globalisation of the Western intelligentsia. It consists of a variety of carriers such as academic networks, foundations, NGOs and some governmental and intergovernmental agencies. They create markets throughout the world for their products which include ideas and behaviour invented by Western (largely American) intellectuals, e.g., ideologies of human rights, feminism, environmentalism, multiculturalism and associated politics and lifestyles. In this the success of those from other cultures depends on their adaptation to this intellectual culture. Moreover, diffusion at the level of popular culture is reflected in the consumption of items of cultural import like TV programmes, internet, jeans, shoes, hamburgers, Disney cartoons, rock music, T-shirt with inscriptions, etc.

According to Tomlinson (1991), such cultural merging represents a form of neo-imperialism that will destroy cultural variety. In this sense cultural globalisation poses a threat to nation states. The main concern is that the existing cultural variation at national, regional and local levels would get reduced and subsumed by global culture. There is a growing influence of global media through television, internet, etc. in the shaping of the culture of the new generation all over. The role of institutions like family and nation in shaping the values, attitude and behavioural pattern is declining fast. Programming of the global media is largely dominated by the US. It is feared that European/US culture will erode and displace other cultures. This cultural homogenisation/imperialism has attracted varied responses from other cultures, ranging from one extreme to another, i.e., complete acceptance to complete rejection. The culture of the yuppie internationale, for instance, reflects passive acceptance of cultural Westernisation/ Americanisation.

But another view emphasises militant rejection of cultural imperialism in the present times. It could be referred to as the cultural clash/identity assertion paradigm. It presents a bleak picture of cultural globalisation because of its negative impact. It is noted that the market-centred globalisation is making deep inroads into local, national and regional cultures that is seen as a threat to their survival. The result is the increasing assertion of cultural identities to defend against the onslaught of globalisation. Barber opines that the American-inspired homogenising popular culture of the McWorld overwhelms other cultures that lose the capacity to govern themselves and hence evokes a defense of indigenous national or religious traditions around the world, giving rise to a variety of movements he labels as 'Jihad' (Lechner and Boli 2004). The negatives are reflected in the rising trend of cultural violence, armed reactions to cultural imperialism and increasing dominance of a consumer and self-oriented society leading to erosion of spiritual and community-oriented values worldwide. There are different types of violent responses to cultural clash such as terrorism, vigilantism, and extremism (Parker 2005: 218). There are also less totalistic forms of rejection of cultural onslaughts as typically practised by certain governments. In China, for instance, the government is engaged in balancing global economic participation with resistance against global culture (Berger 2002).

Huntington (1997) talks of clash of civilisations. He considers culture as a dominant source of potential clash among eight major civilisations in the world today, which include Western, Islamic, Confucian, Japanese, Hindu, Slavic-orthodox, Latin American, and African. Cultural conflicts, he avers, would happen due to unresolvable differences based on important social principles like equality, individuality and human rights. Mobilisations of cultural groups in the clash would occur at the level of a single nation or as multiple nations (such as Western civilisation). The ultimate clash would be between the West vs. the Rest because of their basic differences in value frameworks. Moreover, he does not consider the defence of distinct cultural values as being merely reactive. Rather, the world is now divided into several civilisations with often irreconcilable worldviews and hence the clash. Maybe this could ultimately lead to the reduction of the Western influence.

The heterogeneity and hybridisation paradigms are different from the others. Heterogeneity signifies mixing of culture across borders. Increasing heterogeneity might imply expansion in cultural options/choices for people. Hybridisation, on the other hand, emphasises on the process of translocal cultural mixing. It can be regarded as a specific type of cultural heterogeneity. It signifies cultural borrowing and is known by aliases like syncretisation, creolisation, metissage, *mestizaje*, cross-over, etc. It involves deliberate efforts to synthesise foreign and native cultural traits. It represents postmodern sensibility which involves 'cut "n" mix' transgression. It privileges border crossing. It subverts nationalism, racialism and identity politics (modernity embodies an ethos of order and clear demarcation of boundaries). The culture of the new diaspora is its excellent example.

Glocalisation is another frequently used term, which signifies a particular kind of cultural heterogeneity. It is explained as insiderisation or internal globalisation. Roland Robertson (1995) views glocalisation as the way in which the global and the local intertwine. In this interaction, the global (element) can be the same across countries, but its relation to the local may vary significantly in different settings (Mazlish 2005). Also, the term 'localisation' is used to denote acceptance of global culture with significant local modifications (Berger 2002). There is observed the phenomenon of 'world products' adapting to local cultures and markets, for instance, McDonald adapting to local tastes in different parts of the world. In Asian countries housewives and children are found relaxing in McDonald's and the management has to adapt to its economic consequences. This is called 'looking in both directions' (Ohmae 1992: 93). The phenomenon of 'revitalisation' of indigenous cultural forms is also noticed as in the opening of fast food outlets for traditional foods in several countries like India and Japan (Berger 2002).

Cosmopolitanism, which also indicates heterogeneity in some sense, is considered an important attribute of globalisation. It refers to the 'stance of openness toward divergent cultural experiences' (Hannerz 1990, cited in Roudometof 2005: 114). In Beck's view, 'cosmopolitanisation means internal globalisation, globalisation from within the national societies' (Beck 2002, cited in ibid.: 116). It implies pluralisation of social borders and 'life-world' of individuals living within the same state. 'People from within the same state can inhabit markedly different life-worlds and be closer to or farther from people who live outside the borders of the state they live in' (Roudometof 2005). Glocalisation leads to cosmopolitanism of both the thick type (rooted or situational) and thin type (transcending the boundaries of one's culture or locale). Roudometof (2005: 128–29) conceptualises cosmopolitan and local as forming a continuum, not as polar opposites, because people are likely to adopt highly complex attitudes towards these two. Individuals might adopt different positions within this continuum. Also they might or might not be consistent in their preferences in different spheres. Some, for instance, may support local culture but oppose economic protectionism at the same time.

It is observed that increasingly closer social bonds across borders are intensified by the virtual filaments of the internet and by the messages and images bouncing off the satellites. An e-mail correspondent far away becomes as close a neighbour (virtual) as the one next door with whom face-to-face interactions take place. 'We must recognise that our interests and identities have become more and more a matter of larger levels than the traditional local.' A globalisation of existing cultures seems to be occurring. There is also emerging a global culture of sorts. But this does not mean cultural uniformisation. 'As we move further into a global epoch, fostered by science and technology, we can expect moves toward more diversity of cultural behaviours—the local—and asymptotic approximations of a global culture' (Mazlish 2005).

Berger (2002) talks of 'alternative globalisations' which denotes the process of emissions to the West, i.e., impacting the impacter. This refers to cultural movements with a global outreach originating outside the Western world. There is noted rise of a 'new age culture' which signifies cultural influence of Asia on the West. This culture is unorganised and diffused and has influenced millions of people in Europe and the US. This also involves change in beliefs (e.g., belief in *karma*, reincarnation and mystical connection with almighty) and behaviour (like adopting meditation and yoga) and use of alternative medical traditions. This is conceptualised as

'Easternisation' by Colin Campbell. This is of both religious and secular types. From India, for example, the Hare Krishna movement and Sai Baba movement have originated, the latter having more than 2000 centres in 137 countries. Berger also talks of 'subglobalisations' which refers to movements with a regional rather than global reach. There is presently occurring, for instance, 'Europeanisation' of certain former socialist countries as a result of increasing German influence. There is diffusion of Japanese popular culture in Taiwan. Mexican and Venezuelan media is penetrating other Latin American countries. Here it may be added that alternative globalisations are operating in smaller spaces (compared with Americanisation) and add to global cultural heterogeneity.

Further, it is opined that the emergence of a global culture of Euro-US combination might not necessarily lead to the death of other cultures. It is quite common for people to live within the same nation and follow different cultural rules of family, religion, ethnic group and nation. So it is technically possible for people to live comfortably in a global (business) culture and a differing national culture (Parker 2005: 219). But the global culture is developing rapidly, and hence for many people the process of transition to a new culture may be painful (ibid.).

Cultural heterogeneity would mean multiplication of cultural differences and increased cultural option. It is observed that compression of time and space brings us closer to one world (homogenisation). But it also exposes us at the same time to the large variety and diversity of the world. This causes tension which may operate as opportunities and also exact costs at the cultural level. Opportunities could open up in terms of mustering ability to confront and modify stereotypes, identify with new affinity groups, improve knowledge and understanding, and gain familiarity with new options, but the costs also seem to be heavy in terms of erosion of culture, identity and hence clash (Parker 2005: 219). Breidenbach and Zukrigl (1999) hold that 'cultural globalisation is a highly dialectic (sic) process, in which globalisation and localisation, homogenisation and fragmentation, centralisation and decentralisation, conflict and creolisation are not excluding opposites, but inseparable sides of the same coin'.

Griffin (2004: 262) takes note of the argument that globalisation has strong homogenising influences that weaken and destroy existing cultures, and move towards a world culture under US hegemony. 'The American way of life, or more likely a pale imitation of it, will become the world's way of life'. However, he thinks that the emergence of a single 'world culture' is highly unlikely. 'Instead, globalisation and the associated cultural interpenetration are more likely to lead to new permutations, new combinations, new options, and new cultures' (ibid.: 254). With the increasing pace of globalisation, in his opinion, the idea of 'global citizenship' would gain support. But it would not pose a threat to the existing loyalties and identities—local, national, regional. It would neither supersede existing loyalties nor represent the creation of a global culture. But 'It would be a step towards recognition of the fact that globalisation affects us all and we should all have a voice in determining how the effects are managed' (ibid.: 262).

Cultural Scenario in India

There are different interpretations of current cultural changes under globalisation in India. According to Ahmad (2004), a 'massive reorganisation of culture' has taken place in the recent decade with the emergence of a worldwide capitalist civilisation. National, regional and local level cultures are being reorganised as variants of a singular civilisation, i.e., the capitalist civilisation. This leads to civilisational homogeneity at the deepest level in the form of commodification. But at the surface level of reality, i.e., in the phenomenal form of the commodity, differences/variety/diversities are maintained and even manufactured. This gives the 'illusion of freedom and choice' reflecting the essence of the market. Commodification of culture increases. Freedom in the market is exercised by those having money. Moreover, 'The aesthetic pleasure and the purity of the use values of a work of art necessarily diminishes, or at least gets transformed, when it gets caught in circuits of exchange, market pricing, advertising, and so on' (Ahmad 2004: 105). Even ethnicity (for example in fashion design) is incorporated as a commodity in the global/national market. Local culture gets more and more dominated by the market and the autonomous spheres increasingly contracts. Even some well-intentioned NGOs working for 'empowerment' of poor peasants and tribals mobilise them to produce ethnic items for elite consumption at national and/or international level. The power of the market is able to subsume such projects in quasi-cultural sphere of petty production for its expansion and to 'use perfectly well-intentioned people as its moral agents and cultural representatives ... those projects of empowerment which work within the market economy often turn out to be the other face of globalisation' (ibid.: 106).

Coming to the Indian context, Ahmad notes the differential impact of the culture of globalisation which destroys certain ways of life and sustains others. A particular type of culture globalisation supports ideologically and strengthens materially through varied means, such as, the electronic means (means of telecommunication and digitisation), concentrations of investible capital, etc. So, Ahmad is opposed to the cultural intervention of globalised capital in India, not in a nationalistic jingoistic sense but in a much more fundamental way. Indian culture, he avers, is not static. He notices a cultural struggle in India involving domestic contenders on the issue of radical democratic social change which is oriented towards the future shape of India. But this is being fatally undermined by the culture of globalisation which is pre-empting the possibility of resolution of cultural struggle at the domestic level. Ahmad stands for defending the cultures of the victims of globalisation, not that of its beneficiaries. What 'one wants to defend, in the teeth of globalisation, (is) the right to make one's nation, hence one's own national culture, according to the needs and requirements of our own people' (ibid.: 108). But Ahmad considers the demagogic jingoistic protests against the 'so-called western invasion', e.g., by the *Shiv Sainiks* and the *Swadeshi Jagran Manch*, as an exercise in 'deflecting attention from the real problems of anti-imperialistic nationalism'. This is evident from their intimate proximity with parties and governments strongly committed to liberalisation, Privatisation and Globalisation (LPG) agenda of reforms (ibid.: 115–16).

Panikkar (2002) views globalisation in the cultural arena as an attempt to establish cultural imperialism, imposition of the culture of capitalism to be more specific. He identifies two aspects of cultural invasion—homogenisation and construction/commodification. He holds that globalisation involves building capitalist hegemony by creating favourable ideological climate. New cultural infrastructure is being developed by global/corporate forces. This marginalises indigenous culture/commonsense (heterogeneous and plural in nature) and cultural practices, projects them as anachronistic and replaces them with the 'universal' (singular) character of cultural commonsense of the advanced capital. Corporate giants run/dominate the global culture industry (television, fast foods, clothes, etc.), exploiting the third world market through different products—pizza to pornography. This can be viewed as a cultural project of neoliberal persuasion. Mohan (1999) also deliberates upon the issue of cultural invasion under globalisation. The (current) project of Western modernity, in his view, is seeking to standardise cultural patterns, perceptions, expectations and responses in the third world. The basic philosophy here is that of consumer capitalism.

Panikkar observes that in the dissemination of the dominant global (corporate dominated) culture, there is collaboration of the Indian bourgeoisie and the (upper) middle classes. There is no free cultural interaction. There are 'new constructions' of the traditional indigenous cultural forms/styles/items in artificial spaces (e.g., studios). This reflects decontexualisation and dehistoricisation of the indigenous cultures. Indigenous popular culture is turned into commodities for the global media and generates huge profits to the corporates and their junior partners/collaborators. The process leads to cultural fossilisation of the third world, which has the political implications of undermining resistance both to global domination and also internal domination. Moreover, the emerging cultural crisis is leading to search for roots, identity and therefore to fundamentalism. He holds that there is convergence of interests and collusion between communal and global forces, which may destroy the very foundations of the republic, for instance, in India.

But Appadurai (1997) is strongly predisposed to the view that globalisation is not the story of homogenisation. In his view, globalisation is a deeply historical, uneven and even 'localising' process. 'Globalisation does not necessarily or even frequently imply homogenisation or Americanisation'. The geneology of cultural forms, in a theoretical vein he says, is 'about their circulation across regions, the history of these forms is about their ongoing domestication into local practice' (ibid.: 17). In case of India he talks about how history and geneology inflect one another and how global forms take local forms. Another important phenomenon he is concerned with, is that of the diaspora which is part of the cultural dynamic of urban life in most countries of the world. In this connection, the joint force of electronic mediation and mass migration 'coconstitute new sense of the global as modern and the modern as global' (ibid.: 10). The diasporic phenomenon of today, he observes as explicitly transnational—even post-national.

Appadurai finds the nation state in 'terminal crisis' today. There is emergence of a 'post-national imaginary' (ibid.: 21) as reflected in the increasing diasporic public spheres—transnational discourses/movements and multiculturalist debates powered by mass media, refugees, students, labourers and activists/organisations working on issues like environment, women, human rights and even transnational separatist fundamentalist movements. Thus, the diverse public spheres of the diaspora seem to form the 'crucibles of a post-national political order'. This emerging order is very much uncertain and challenging. 'This unsettling possibility could be the most exciting dividend of living in modernity at large' (ibid.: 23).

Bhargava (2004) also is not in favour of treating globalisation as Americanisation, or even Westernisation. He recognises that there is a certain degree of cultural uniformity 'but there is also a lot of cultural heterogeneity'. Ideas and models move from one place/country/community to another. In the process they are transformed and in some ways indigenised. This does not result into homogenisation in the sense of complete uniformisation. However, it produces 'something new' some forms of hybridity' (Bhargava 2004: 305). Globalisation has, in fact, much to do with the emergence of a 'sub-culture' that is found largely among the elites of different countries and also at a pretty superficial level. But this is a reality. Another associated process is that of deterritorialisation particularly typical of the diaspora (ibid.: 306).

Singh (2002) recognises that globalisation is bound to put pressures on the Indian culture. He envisages some degree of acceleration towards homogenising of cultural forms and activities (lifestyle, dress, food etc.) in the country. However, he asserts that 'the social structure and cultural system in India are intrinsically based on pluralism and diversity'. The Indian society (both caste and tribe) is segmented in communities which enjoy 'enormous cultural autonomy'. 'This provides enormous cultural resilience to communities in India to filter the effects of globalisation through refractory and prismatic adaptations' (Singh 2002: 64). Moreover there is an enhanced sense of self-consciousness and awareness of identity. Those elements of globalisation that encroach upon or do not promote the core cultural values of society are resented. So, globalisation has both facets—homogenisation and (cultural) identity enhancement. In case of the Indian diaspora, he finds the trends of cultural fusion. Also in India, at the level of popular culture (of music, dance, dramatics, cinema etc.), the new trend is one of fusion of traditional Indian forms/styles and Western/global forms/styles. This emergent popular (fusion) culture, he regards as posing 'a threat to the indigenous local, regional or ethnic identity of cultural traditions in so far as it abstracts culture from people's rhythm of life and its natural expressiveness or vitality and converts its new packaging into a commodity' (ibid.: 103). In this process, the traditional identity deeply embedded in community life (caste, class, tribe, principles of hierarchy and reciprocity) are 'metamorphosed into a faceless "audience"'. This, he thinks, is not entirely due to globalisation, but rather 'germane in the very paradigm of modernisation which we along with the rest of humanity wilfully celebrate' (ibid.). As regards modernisation, Gupta (2000) talks about the process of westoxication in India.

Pathak (2006) notes the early stirrings of the emergence of a fluid/hybrid global culture due to continued overlapping of cultures today with widespread tourism, migration and rising diasporic communities along with economic globalisation. Moreover, despite diffusion of a packaged global culture from the dominant global metropolises, there is, in his view, 'a possibility of a localised appropriation of global culture'. There is observed a process of localisation and contextualisation of global products (like film, music, eatables—Coke popularised in local/Hindi idiom as *Thanda Matlab Coca-Cola*). So, local cannot be treated as finished and dead because global is influenced by local in the latter's domain. 'Instead of a thoroughly homogenized culture, a creative/complex interplay of the global and the local is possibly taking place' (Pathak 2006: 87). Pathak does not view globalisation as just Americanisation or cultural imperialism, but sees diverse possibilities in its ability to generate a cross-cultural conversation and an open/fluid/inclusive culture. However, he expresses anxiety about and opposition to the prevailing asymmetrical and hegemonic globalisation which is reflected in the increasing 'helplessness of developing countries to have any control on the ongoing flow of media-inducted/market-oriented cultural commodities and symbols'. He advocates symmetrical globalisation which would involve developing a new global culture based on the ideals of harmony, reciprocity and aesthetic calmness—replacement of the current one by 'a more humane, egalitarian and symmetrical one'. It would mean exorcising exclusivist identity and experiencing 'a collective bond with the larger humankind'. Moreover, it would involve resistance to excessive consumerism, technologisation and depthlessness. It would also require an alternative mode of living affirming that 'there is a world beyond global capitalism and its seductive consumerism' (ibid.: 109). This, in fact, would be a 'quest for something more broader, more inclusive and more universal' without getting culturally uprooted. This search would require an 'authentic cross-cultural conversation' by adopting 'dialogue as a mode of cultural practice'. Such a dialogue would essentially demand 'reciprocity, the willingness to learn from others, and at the same time the courage to stand up and resist all sorts of hegemony and domination'. It would be an experience of the 'fusion of horizons' and an 'unifying experience' without supplanting native cultural rootedness and identity. Becoming global here would not mean death of national identity. 'In such a world differences prevail, but differences are not limiting, hierarchical and exclusivist. Instead, a complex/dialectical interplay of unity and differences enriches the world' (ibid.: 158–59).

Media and Culture

It is observed that the media sector particularly is undergoing rapid transformation. New technology-driven mass media is playing an important role in promoting cultural globalisation and associated reforms in recent time. The prominent ones include both the electronic and the print media. The discussion here concerns television, newspapers and Information and Communication technology (ICT) which deals with news, entertainment and information. There are highly contrasting perspectives on the issue of media and culture today as in case of globalisation and culture in general as indicated already.

One view is that the mass media forms the driving force of cultural homogenisation/Americanisation/Westernisation and of hegemony/domination over the third world (MacBride and Roach 2004). The global media is controlled mainly by Euro-American companies that have spread their tentacles all over. They impose their powerful images and advertisement on people who succumb to their messages that are meant to enhance profits of the capitalists. The main trends in recent years have been larger cross-border flow of media outputs, the growth of media TNCs and increasing spread and intensification of commercialisation. There is increasing control and monopolisation of the sector by a handful of transnational corporations, which treat media as any other business, based solely on the principle of profit maximisation. Moreover, the rapid integration of global telecommunication systems has strengthened the symbolic and psychological means of control of the neo-colonial powers in pushing mainly the American culture with the ideologies of consumption, instant gratification, self-absorption and global capitalism. There is increasing commercialisation of the media which focus on sex and violence-based entertainment. Pressure is exerted by media TNCs to open up the third world's domestic media sector (both electronic and print) for foreign participation. The government of India has, for instance, made policy changes to allow entry of TNCs in the electronic media (TV) (Mukherjee 2003). The opening up of the print media seems to be next in line, though, at present, there is stiff resistance to it.

Today internet/website cuts across all boundaries. Life in the cyberworld is quite vibrant with Online groups (yahoo groups, msn groups) and Internet (social networks) communities like Friendster, Orkut, OkStupid, etc. Besides, the webworld is used for advertising and sales for profit. This has a political dimension that involves web-based mobilisations and movements of varied types, including those at global level. The cyberspace is viewed as having the innovative potential of electronic public space for democracy, particularly when applied to a deliberative transnationalism. Internet is considered inherently democratic and dialogical. However, according to critics, transnational democracy lacks an egalitarian public sphere for mass participation in a shared political culture. There is no unified public sphere based in a common culture or identity (Crossley and Roberts 2004).

People's exposure to media is increasing all over. Uniformisation is increasing as more and more people now, particularly the new generation, watch the same television programmes and films, listen to the same music and read the same books. The media is generally said to shape the way most of us live our lives—affecting the way we think, act and dream. But a close view reveals that the media is experienced differently across the world (Steven 2005). In countries like US there is 'super-saturation' of media where it is said to have profoundly altered the American psyche. On the other side, half the population of the world has never made even a single phone call, illiteracy is rampant and there is rigid state control of news and entertainment. Though in the poorer and remoter parts media saturation may be less but 'the influence can still be considerable'. According to Steven, the distinctiveness of the media today is that they have emerged as 'entities unto themselves' as they are no longer simply devices or neutral carriers of ideas. They are now 'the source of these ideas and meanings'. They constitute 'a central element of power' and represent 'powerful forces of capitalism in most societies—in economic terms they are hugely wealthy and wield political as well as cultural and ideological power' (ibid.: 17).

Ahmad (2004) notes the high intensity of invasion of the household by the global electronic media, particularly television. This is changing 'not only thought processes but also the lived value systems, consumption patterns, and even the very nature of such human desires as love and sexuality'. Watching TV operates as 'a study circle for acquisition of certain sorts of ideology and cultural taste'. Electronically mediated culture has a wider reach covering even the poor families, particularly in urban areas, who participate as passive, fantasising consumers. The globalised electronic cultural form seeks to transform both elite and mass cultures in one go. There is increasing integration of the institutions of mass culture and popular entertainment in India into the dominant American media—politically, aesthetically and in an expressive form. But this culture of globalisation, Ahmad opines, cannot be simply treated as an external imposition. It also occurs 'spontaneously, as it were, from the life process of the affluent classes within India' (Ahmad 2004: 115). The print media, i.e., several newspapers in India also show a distinct shift in becoming increasingly advertisement-driven (as a 'semi-pornographic broadsheet' in case of the *Times of India*, for example) and which uses bits of news to fill up the spaces between advertisements and specialises in trivia. Moreover, on the other hand, there is also admirable reportage of the great technological wonders of American weapons in war games deployed in the 'automated battlefield' as in Iraq. In fact, there is 'strong intersection of commerce and entertainment which passes for culture'. On a broader plane, 'the main thing about culture is that it exists in all aspects of life and is simply inseparable from zones of the economic, political, military and so on' (ibid.: 14).

The growing critical approach focuses on the increasing monopolisation and commercialisation of media which, in political terms, is regarded as having highly depoliticising effects and thus considered to pose a serious threat to public sphere and democratic order based on citizen participation in public life and agenda setting. Herman and McChesney (1998: 9) observe that 'The commercial model ... being privately owned and relying on advertiser support, tends to erode the public sphere and to create a "culture of entertainment" that is incompatible with a democratic order. Media outputs are commodified and are designed to serve market ends, not citizenship needs.' The media is getting integrated into the capital accumulation process. Even media professionalism is rarely found to be neutral and 'tends to reflect the interests not only of media owners and advertisers, but of business and powerful social forces as well'. There is spread of advertising and commercial values into new areas like education, politics, public media, and sport (McChesney 2001: 5–6). The ideas propagated by the dominant economic institutions/agencies and the academic circle is picked up by the information media, particularly the business section of national and international newspapers, economic dailies/weeklies, popular magazines, and news and commentary shows on TV and radio. The media comments on policy keeping in view its own interests and also helps decide among competing policy directions responding on behalf of public opinion. There is a link between commodification and the advertising revenues that underwrite the apparent neutrality of 'all the news that's fit to print or fit to surround advertisements'. It is affirmed that 'the entire discursive process from ideological conceptualisation to policy implementation is structured by class, gender and ethnic power relations (Peet et al. 2003). In her analysis of the world of advertisements in the print media in India, Chaudhuri (1999: 255) finds 'privileging of the self-seeking individual, the inalienable right of the individual to pleasure, to choice [as] the essence of the new economic order'. The ideology of globalisation pushes outside its frame of reference, the grime and filth created in this process. Hence, the global media industry has serious implications for a free and independent media, and also for society, economy, culture and politics. It may lead to even wiping out the domestic media industry particularly in the third world countries like India.

But the advocates of globalisation in the media sector have a different understanding. They do not accept the cultural imperialism thesis. It is recognised that cultural homogenisation is growing in some respects. But local transformation and interpretations of imported media products reflected cultural diversification (see Tomlinson, in Lechner and Boli eds. 2004). For instance, there is 'indigenisation' of many TV formats and genres coming from the West as reflected in their local equivalents and adaptations. There is a growing variety of media content and the growth of new regional centres of media production. So, it is questioned whether the 'peripheral visions' of the media in the less developed world could be considered the products of imperial Western design (Sinclair et al., in ibid. 2004). Moreover, it is held that the audience/viewer now has access to better quality services/programmes with wider choice and thus they benefit. Global media has exerted competitive pressure on the state controlled broadcasting

Figure 1.5: Cultural Dimension of Globalisation and Reforms

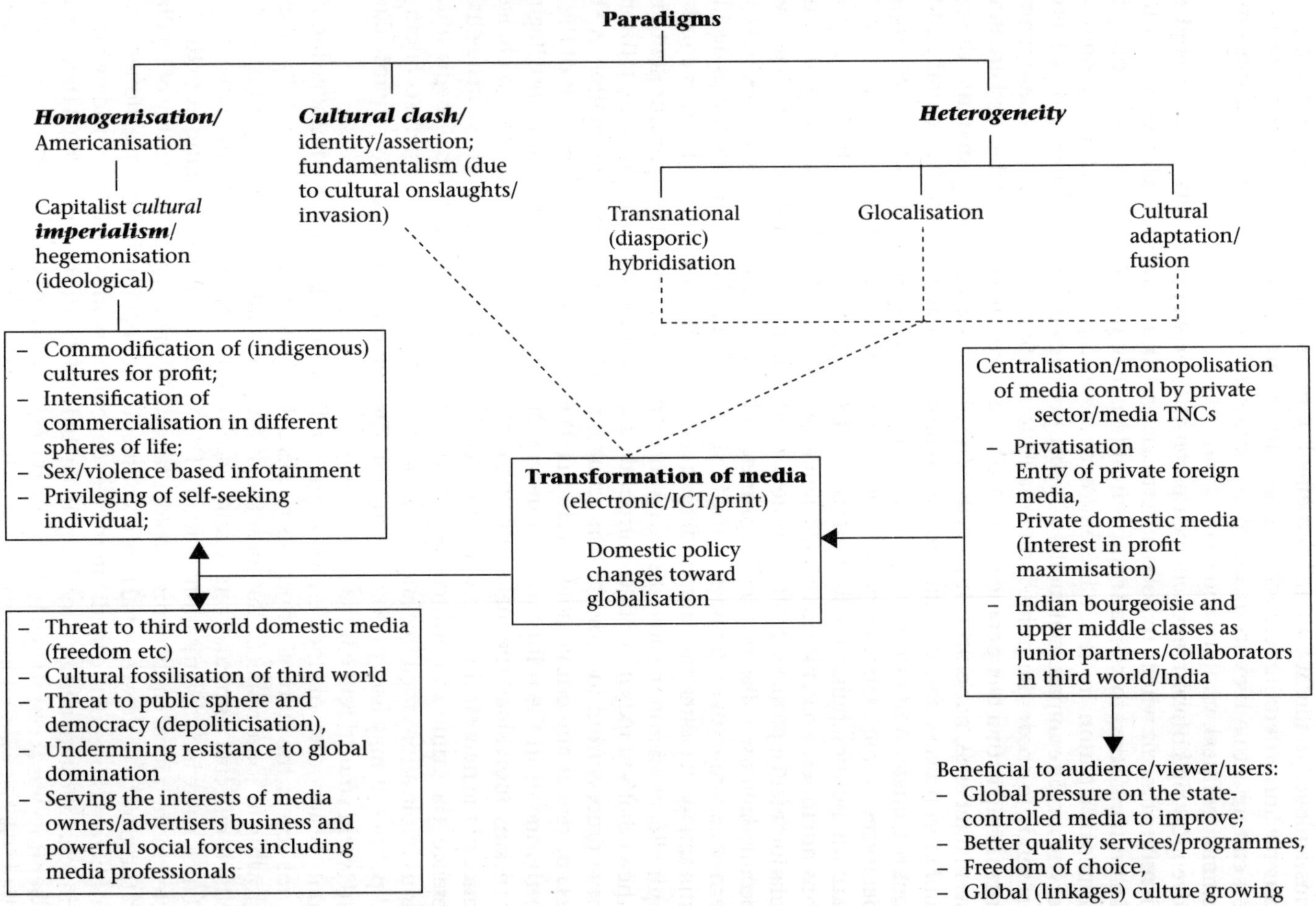

systems and thus energised them to improve services. There is rapid dissemination of the popular culture all over. There is also greater connectedness and linkage among people, and so there is emergence of some form of global culture. Moreover, fundamental Western values are also spreading fast across borders.

Steven (2005: 22) observes numerous patterns of exchange and flow in the media world. He identifies three different types of international relationships in this domain: a diffusion of dominant media (largely of the US provenance), encounters and cross-pollination. The dominant media, according to him, has the power to shape political agendas and the cultural landscape. The media companies exhibit significant economic and symbolic roles. These 'cultural industries' have shown immense growth and concentration of power. Yet they are not omnipotent. There are observed many contradictions and conflicts within the companies and also between companies and states. This provides the scope for initiatives to build the democratic media. Steven comments, ...'despite common media experiences and a shrinking world simple notions of globalisation and cultural imperialism will not suffice. Some elements of technology, science and economics are leading to universal (global) standards and practices, yet politics and culture remain stubbornly local, fractured and diverse' (ibid.: 36).

Thus, there seem to emerge broadly two levels of analysis on the cultural dimensions of globalisation and reforms. In one set of writings, the focus is on 'what' aspect, i.e., what changes are occurring in the cultural sphere in the era of globalisation. This relates to identifying the patterns of changes like homogenisation/imperialism, heterogeneity/hybridity and identity assertion/clash. The media, both electronic and print, is found to play an important role in this process, as important changes have been introduced in policies regulating the media. Another set of writings delve deeper and try to find out 'why' such changes are happening in the cultural sphere, including the media. It finds links between the external and internal forces and brings out the negative implications of the changes particularly for the third world countries and the marginalised people. But there are also those emphasising the benefits to the countries and people as a result of growing cultural globalisation. On the whole it does not seem easy to generalise. However, a synoptic view of the cultural dimension of globalisation and reforms is given in Figure 1.5.

Political Dimension

The major issues that have emerged in the discussions on political globalisation and reforms include those concerning the nation state, welfare state, democracy, decentralisation, rise of global civil society and movements against globalisation, etc. A close scrutiny of the studies on India in this matter, as elaborated below, would reflect the application, explicit or implicit, of mainly two perspectives, i.e., hyperglobalist/neoliberal and sceptical/radical/neo-Marxist. Only rarely is noticed the application of the transformationalist perspective which deals with issues like democratic global governance and cosmopolitanism. The analysis in the studies as regards political dimensions of globalisation and reforms is generally related to two/three levels, i.e., global, national/local.

General View

Different interpretations are offered on the current political scenario at the global/international and national levels. Neorealists attempt to present classical realism in a theoretically more rigorous way. Most of them do not think that globalisation has changed the game of international politics in any significant manner. They hold that currently the world is competitive and uncertain. The structure of the international system is such that power politics continues to be the dominant policy framework. States are still the major actors in international politics. 'Politics is still international' rather than global or transnational. However, they accept that forces of globalisation pose a challenge to state sovereignty and autonomy in certain areas, though states have not lost their authority and control. It is feared that push and pull of globalisation could cause loss of key industries and resources threatening national security. There is concern with the uneven nature of economic globalisation. It is held that increasing inequality and conflict in the international system might create instability in strategic regions, pose new security challenges, and hence the need to ensure security which would include military preparedness to protect one's national interests (Baylis and Smith 2005).

Neoliberalism does not accept the more utopian or cosmopolitan versions of liberalism. Its dominant philosophy of statecraft privileges markets and Western democratic institutions as the chosen means to promote growth and improve lives. It advocates a careful use of power to promote peace through trade, investment and commerce. (Western governments are promoting free trade and democracy weaved into their foreign policy programmes.) Business and markets are given priority over human rights, environment, and social justice. In fact there are two types of neoliberals. Free market neoliberals who are dominant, regard globalisation as a positive force which would economically benefit all states. Hence, states should not oppose globalisation or try to control it with unwanted political interventions. Neoliberal institutionalists regard institutions as the mediator and the means to gain cooperation in the international system. They regard institutions as essential to govern a competitive and anarchic international system. This may involve multilateralism and cooperation to secure national interests. Cooperation enables states to achieve absolute gains. They support (limited) state intervention to promote capitalism with a human face or a market which is sensitive to the needs and interests of all the people. This would involve creation of new institutions and reform of the old ones with a view to control uneven flow of capital, protect the rights of citizens and ensure environmental sustainability. This neoliberal institutionalism emphasises on international cooperation, institutions and regimes essential for developing rules and norms to deal with the challenges of globalisation and achieve developmental goals.

It is opined that despite certain differences between them, the neorealist and neoliberal debate does not represent completely opposed perspectives. They have large areas of agreement. They are concerned with similar issues and assumptions about international politics. Both consider the current international system as anarchic, address status quo issues and are concerned with ways to keep the system going. These theories do not pose questions about the dominant belief system or the distribution of power and linkages with problems of poverty and violence. But neorealists hold that anarchy imposes more constraints on foreign policy. They criticise neoliberals for minimising the importance of survival as the objective of each state. Neoliberals on the other hand, object to the neorealists minimising the importance of international interdependence, globalisation and the regimes built to manage these interactions. They believe that all parties/states would be able to maximise the total amount of gains and focus more on economic welfare or international political economy issues and other non-military issues like international environmental concerns and human rights. Neorealists, on the contrary, focus on relative gains and hold that the fundamental objective of states in a cooperative relationship is to prevent other states from gaining more. They hold that prevailing anarchy demands of state focus on relative power, security and survival in a competitive international system. In a way the two are concerned with different worlds of international politics. (Baylis and Smith 2005).

The classical 'realist' view is that independent states pursue their interests, but get constrained by the power of others. In the current global context, this notion is considered very simplistic. Neoliberal institutionalism finds globalisation producing a more complex system of interdependent states in which transnational rules and organisations have gained more influence. New organisations critically influence world politics. States are still a major force pursuing their interests. However, there is no clear hierarchy of states. World society consists of many centres of power. There exists 'complex interdependence' (see Keohane and Nye 2004). However, global power structure is not symmetrical in nature. It is undergirded by the powerful interest of dominant classes and states. The military power of the states is still crucial and state security outranks other issues (Keohane and Nye 1998, cited in Olesen 2005: 434).

In fact, globalisation is not just a neoliberal economic project, but is said to be a political project as well (Sampat 2003: 104). The former is about promoting free movement of goods and capital. But this free movement is hindered by diversity of legal, administrative and political systems across countries. A smooth operation of global market economy requires uniformity in legal and institutional terms. So, the political project of globalisation aims at globalising/uniformising national political and legal processes. Interventions are made by the developed capitalist countries, particularly the US, at unilateral, bilateral and especially multilateral (IMF/WB) level to achieve such uniformity. It is stated, 'Promotion of democracy has, therefore, become an integral part of the emergent global economic order' (ibid.).

It is observed that the neoliberal agenda of governance reforms is sweeping the world in the recent times. There is presently a trend of 'globalisation' of national policies and policy-making mechanisms (Khor 2001: 10). National policies relating to different spheres of life, which were until lately under the domain of states and their people, are being increasingly influenced by international agencies and processes or by big private corporations. Even in the developed countries the large corporations have acquired large part of decision-making at the cost of the power of the state or political and social leaders. Western national governments have to compete with each other in terms of tax concessions, deregulation and wage restraint to retain or attract investments from MNCs. 'In fact, ... we are in an era where the old-fashioned autonomy of the nation state is being eroded by the multinational corporation *everywhere*, both in the First World and in the Third World, but at different speeds' (Bhaduri and Nayyar 1996: 70). The nation state in the developing countries is at a double disadvantage because they have to compete not only with the developed countries but also among themselves in enticing the MNCs (ibid.). They have to lower domestic wages and social welfare and offer tax holidays in this fierce competitive bid. Globalisation seems to signify 'new dictatorship of international finance' (Stiglitz 2002). When the third world countries facing financial crisis approach the IMF, they are 'forced to give up part of their sovereignty to let capricious capital markets, including the speculators whose only concerns are short term ... discipline them, telling what they should do and should not do'. Growing global civil society also puts pressure on the nation-state curtailing its autonomy on an increasing number of issues.

Further, there has been a shift from government-speak to governance-speak. But the imperative for this shift is very different in the North and the South. In the North, the policies of deregulation and cutbacks in social spending were made by the state due to a fiscal crisis. It forced them to introduce new strategies of public management to change the inefficient and huge welfare state bureaucracies, even if it involved reorganising the state itself along the lines of the private sector. Here, privatisation and liberalisation did not mean reduction in the role of the state, but rather a shift in the means of intervention from decommodifying bureaucracies to marketising ones. 'Reinventing government', for example, meant the replacement of bureaucracies which directly produce public services by those which closely monitor and supervise contracted-out and privatised services, according to complex financial criteria and performance indicators (Cerny 2000: 129). There is a tendency of truncation of the state's role as the regulator of economic activity and a provider of social services, but not as the 'orchestrator of social consensus' (Hirst 2000, cited in Jayal and Pai 2001: 14).

In the South, governance discourse entered in a different context. It was pushed in by the Bretton Woods institutions. Besides the MNCs, the global institutions like the World Bank, IMF, WTO and UN bodies have emerged as major makers of an increasingly wide range of policies that were previously under the national governments. It is noted that the 'unholy trinity' of the Bank, Fund and WTO have imposed a virtually synonymous set of neoliberal policies on countries all over as loan conditions, debt relief, etc. (Peet 2003). What has practically emerged is 'a single global institution governing the world economy', whose three parts specialise in stabilisation (IMF), structural adjustment (WB) and trade liberalisation (WTO). Their joint action has 'increasingly enabled private sector actors, primarily MNCs, to enjoy unprecedented freedoms in the processes of deepening and broadening the globalisation of the international economy' (Rowden 2001, cited in Peet 2003: 200). As a result of their deepening debt crisis and fiscal deficit in recent times, most of the third world countries had/have to approach these multilateral bodies for assistance. These countries have been helped out on the condition of introducing the popularly known package of fiscal stabilisation and SAP which has impacted their sovereignty in terms of decision-making relating to social, economic, administrative and even cultural life. The new development model being advocated and implemented by these multilateral institutions is that of liberalisation, privatisation and globalisation (LPG). In this process, a new paradigm of governance and development has emerged which has serious implications particularly for the developing countries—their nation state and the people. Both the multilateral and international development institutions/agencies have played an important role in this connection. Moreover, it is noted that 'in recent years, the UN has lost a lot of its policy and operational influence in economic matters, and correspondingly the powers and authority of the World Bank, IMF and GATT/WTO have expanded' (Khor 2001: 12).

IMF (2002) advocates greater global economic integration as the way to tackle the problems of increasing income gaps and poverty. It avers, 'No country, least of all the poorest, can afford to remain isolated from the world economy. Every country should seek to reduce poverty. The international community should endeavour—by strengthening the international financial system, through trade, and through aid—to help the poorest countries integrate into the world economy, grow more rapidly, and reduce poverty. That is the way to ensure that all people in all countries have access to the benefits of globalisation' (IMF 2002: 2). The World Bank (2000) also focuses on economic globalisation in the areas of international trade, FDI, and capital market flows. It generally favours greater openness to trade and FDI because of their higher benefits in terms of economic development and poverty reduction compared to potential costs and risks. But recently it has tried to adopt a cautious stance about liberalisation of other financial or capital market flows whose volatility sometimes causes boom-and-bust cycles and crises with high economic costs. Both the Bank and IMF recognise that globalisation brings both opportunities and risks. While reaping the benefits of opportunities there is a need, the Bank (2000) holds, to face the 'challenge of mitigating the risks for the poor, vulnerable and marginalized, and of increasing equity and inclusion'.

Currie (1996) observes an extension of the policy concerns of many Western development agencies and aid donors in the recent decade. Democracy and good governmental practice is recognised by these agencies as essential prerequisites for development. The multilateral agencies like the World Bank and IMF showed a largely similar trend. In the recent decade, it was noted that the World Bank, particularly, has broadened the domain of its conditionality and policy advice. Greater attention is given to the process of governance within a borrower country. Moreover, its concern with 'sound economics' is reflected in practice as neoliberal economic policy which pushes the state back from the operations of the market. 'Good governance in the political and administration sphere is seen as essential to make laissez-faire economic policies work, and vice versa' (Currie 1996: 787).

As per the provisions, the World Bank is neither supposed to interfere in the political affairs of any member country, nor to base its lending decisions on the basis of any political considerations. But there is a clear shift in the Bank policy in practice, since the late 1980s. Its agenda is overlain with an additional concern, i.e., policy formation and administration in the borrower country. The belief is that corrupt and unaccountable authoritarian governments do not possess the required governmental and administrative infrastructure to introduce the neoliberal development package suggested by the international financial institutions. So, the shift in policy is justified for promoting pluralistic democracy, social justice, and administrative accountability and efficiency. 'The Bank deems governance of borrowing countries to be of direct relevance to its work' (World Bank 1994, cited in Currie 1996: 788). The Bank performs a dual role to effect good governance in the third world—that of 'supervision' and 'facilitator'. It is charged with acting as rule enforcer or disciplinarian and thus supervising the operation of 'good governance' in a borrower country. In addition, it has to play an enabling role to establish the favourable conditions for this to happen (ibid.: 789). It is observed that the Bank uses the CPIA Country Policy and Institutional Assessment rating system in case of the third world countries. The rating involves assessment of the economic, social and political performance of the borrowing government to the extent of compliance with its own definition of 'good' policies and institutions. The system represents a new and powerful kind of conditionality that interferes in a country's domestic affairs. It is used to reward those countries that conform to donor and creditor policy preferences. As a result donors and creditors are able to 'dominate the policy-making of low-income countries more than ever before ... no matter what a country's own development strategy on Poverty Reduction Strategy Paper (PRSP) says, a country is likely to adhere to CPIA-derived policy prescriptions if it expects to retain external support'. But the same rating system is not applied to developed countries. Hence, the IMF and World Bank reveal a 'shocking double standard' that makes a mockery of national sovereignty for most of the countries in the world (Social Watch 2004).

Under the loan conditionalities, central banks and financial regulators have been given greater autonomy in the formulation of economic policies in some countries and fiscal responsibility laws have been enacted to restrain the scope of fiscal policies. Therefore, technocrats have gained more weight. So, it is observed, 'Delinking of economic decision-making from the political processes through such technocratic forms of governance is thoroughly undemocratic as it subverts democratic accountability and popular participation in policy-making' (Singh 2005: 146).

There are highly contrasting interpretations regarding the shape that the nation state is taking in the current globalising world. Neoliberals see rapid erosion of the nation state and predict its ultimate demise as a result of globalisation. Globalisation exposes states to the global market place. 'When a country's political, economic, and developmental activities become globalised, the national government may cease to be dominant' (Shun'ichi 2003, cited in Mazlish 2005). Sceptics/neo-Marxists and radicals also agree that the nation state is gradually eroding but do not accept the possibility of its demise. Rather, they see reframing of the nation state in general and welfare policy in particular along market lines which could be disadvantageous to the marginalised sections of the society. Transformationalists hold that the very nature of the state is changing with gradual erosion of the very foundation of its sovereignty and autonomy. But it is not going to die. It is undergoing a process of transformation because of its being reconstituted (Martinelli 2002). There is 'internationalisation' of the state as it has to share with other states and international institutions the political responsibilities to manage the new global economy (Zuege et al. 2006). Giddens (1999) talks of the three-way movement of globalisation affecting the position and powers of states all over the world. Globalisation 'pulls away' from the nation state some powers of management of the national economy. It 'pushes down' the nation state by creating new demands and also new possibilities for regenerating local identities. It also 'squeezes sideways' by creating sometimes new economic and cultural regions which cross-cut the borders of the nation state.

The shape of welfare is affected by globalisation. In a broad sense, welfare state refers to the transfer of resources by the state. Its basic rationale is to prevent the exploitation of weaker members in an unequal society. The traditional notion of welfare was characterised by 'charitable mentalities' as in the relief of poverty. But the modern welfare state adopts a notion of citizenship based entitlement. There is a shift in the welfare logic with the recent dominance of neoliberalism which blames welfare state for creating dependency and obstructing development and also for inefficient delivery. Neoliberals consider the welfare state as destructive of growth and hence propose its dismantling. They advocate a smaller but stronger state with less scope (no direct participation in economic/productive activities) but more strength/capacity/effectiveness in ensuring the play of market forces.

In the US, neoliberal/conservative welfare reforms signify an attack on the New Deal/Great Society ideas of collective responsibility. ('New Deal' refers to the set of policies adopted by the Roosevelt administration for the US economic recovery and collective well-being after the Great Depression of 1929). Here, emphasis is given on 'personal responsibility'. Welfare state is blasted for encouraging degrading forms of 'dependency'. A barrage of rhetorical attack has helped discredit welfare and 'liberalism' (Piven and Ehrenreich 2005) and also paved the way for the agenda of 'upward income redistribution that was always the goal of the right's campaign'. There is another dimension to it. Individual churches receive public money through the (Republican) administration's 'faith-based' social service initiatives. This helps them expand their social services and membership. In return they extend political support to Republicans, who are hostile towards welfare or at least vote against those who favour abortion and gay rights. Thus, there is a vicious cycle in operation: 'declining public services push people toward the churches, which in turn promote a political agenda involving still further decreases in public services. As this process continues, the outcome ... is that an increasingly free market economy combines with a compensating form of religiosity that reflects an intellectually, artistically and sexually repressive culture' (ibid.: 87).

Critics of the neoliberal position see this as a retreat of the state and consequent deterioration of the life of the disadvantaged people. But some scholars consider this retreat as merely a neoliberal rhetoric. Hartman (2005: 58), for instance, holds, 'Contrary to their claims that welfare provisions must be dismantled for the health of the nation, neoliberal rationalities have in fact pursued a strategy of reshaping but not abolishing welfare regimes, which ... form an integral component of a neoliberal governmentality'. No doubt, welfare is becoming leaner and meaner for some. But the welfare state has not diminished. Different forms of welfare have emerged which are coupled with new modes of administration and a changed theoretical rationale which marks a shift from 'entitlement to obligation' (Harris 2001, cited in ibid.: 63). Debate on the issue of welfare has shifted from the earlier focus on citizenship rights to now around the notion of contract and mutual obligation. There is increasing devolution of provisioning and administration of welfare to the community, NGO and quasi-markets. This is in line with the neoliberal strategy of dispersal of sites of government and would not imply the abolition of welfare. Welfare assistance is extended to help individuals to 'align their individual desires with those of the government and to acquire the requisite virtues in order to become self-governing, enterprising individuals'. This does not imply dismantling welfare. Despite acerbic rhetoric neoliberal regimes in the advanced capitalist countries continue with a comprehensive arrangement for the transfer of resources by the state. According to Hartman, neoliberals know the functionality of welfare to capitalism, but they use anti-welfare rhetoric as a purposeful device. 'This combination of discourse and practice has secured some approximation to the ideal conditions for capitalism to flourish, rather than creating the self-paralysing tendencies earlier theorists attributed to the inherent contradiction between market forces and decommodification via welfare' (Hartman 2005: 64). Welfare state sustains neoliberalism by underwriting the flexible labour market and managing populations and thus keeps the society intact. 'At first glance they may seem antagonistic, but if this analysis is correct neoliberal and welfare rationalities are bedfellows nevertheless' (ibid.: 70). Giddens suggests reform of the welfare state. He finds such reforms already underway in several developed capitalist countries in the shift in state policy from welfare to 'workfare'. But critics demonstrate that neoliberal hostility to welfare state is more a matter of rhetoric at ideological level, but in practice there is no retreat of the state from welfare as shown by the expenditure pattern on welfare which has been quite stable in 1990s (Giddens 1999: 113–14, Kiely 2005).

Further, neoliberals hold that globalisation and democracy are compatible and complementary phenomena (Singh 2005). It is argued that political liberalisation, in terms of replacement of authoritarian regimes by democratic regimes based on multiparty system and periodic elections, is occurring rapidly along with economic globalisation in the recent decade. Moreover, political liberalisation is advocated as a part of governance reforms package in the third world countries.

Also, in recent years there has been direct intervention by dominant powers for regime change in some third world countries. Certain states in the third world are labelled as 'failed states' and outside intervention is justified in such cases for preventing threat to the stability of the world system. Fukuyama (2004) expresses serious concern about the problem of weak or failed states (incompetent or non-existent government) particularly in the third world, also former socialist countries after the end of the Cold War. He argues that state weakness/collapse impeded economic growth and created humanitarian and human rights disasters in countries like Somalia, Cambodia, Kosovo etc. Weak governance in such regions was ill-equipped to face up to the 'radical Islamic terrorism'. So, state-building (creating new institutions and strengthening capabilities of the old ones) is on the top of the global agenda as a major condition for ensuring security in the world. In his view, it is not enough for the developed countries to construct state institutions only within their borders, but in other more 'disorganised and dangerous countries' as well. This is justified on the grounds of promoting democracy, self-government and human rights. This is not a matter of worry because such efforts 'to rule other people are merely transitional rather than imperial in ambition' (Fukuyama 2004: 164).

However, sceptics strongly differ and oppose imposition of the (Western/US brand) democracy from outside and support nurturing of democracy from within. Neoliberals are faulted for privileging Schumpetarian procedural democracy which view 'democracy as a set of rules and procedures devoid of specific content related to distributive justice or fairness in society, ignoring the ethical and normative content of idea of democracy' (Boron in Panitch and Leys 2005: 28). They equate democracy with political democracy valourising the right of franchise, elections, and civil and political rights, and ignore basic economic and social rights (Singh 2005). The current global crusade for democracy is found to be more for setting up polyarchy rather than genuine democracy. Such regimes are variously described as low-intensity democracy, pseudo democracy, illiberal democracy, restricted democracy, mechanical democracy, etc. Periodic elections are held for gaining democratic legitimacy, but democratic norms and institutions are violated in a systematic manner by using money and muscle power, rigging polls, patronage-based political support, rule by a coterie of leaders in parties, lack of inner party democracy, etc. Democracy exists largely in form, rather than content. However, it operates as a safety valve to deflect popular aspirations and maintain an unjust and undemocratic society. Such polyarchic regimes are conducive for legitimising the domination of powerful ruling elites and providing political stability desired by transnational capital for its smooth operation across borders. 'Under the dictates of transnational capital, political democracy cohabits with unequal distribution of income and wealth' (ibid.).

Further, in the context of globalisation there is reorganisation of institutional jurisdictions which involves creating space for the private sector, NGOs/CSOs, on one hand, and reorienting the state on market lines, on the other. Adoption of neoliberal reforms makes it incumbent upon the state to push policy towards deregulation, privatisation, selective state withdrawal, expenditure cuts and finally integration with the global economy. The state curtails its traditional regulatory powers and turns into a 'facilitator' of the private sector. The existing legislative/legal framework is radically changed for this purpose. There is a growth of new institutions for market governance. The new regulatory agencies operate along the lines of neoliberal agenda. There is introduction of market mechanism in the state sector itself as reflected in measures like policy of outsourcing and contracting out of services, rightsizing of workforce, hiring management consultants for policy advice, introduction/raising of user charges, reduction of subsidies to transfer costs to users of social services, sharing of government responsibilities with NGOs, etc. 'The displacement of political processes which provide space for public debate on policy issues is the real effect' (Arora 2002: 50).

There is weakening of democratic influence on economic policy-making. Sovereignty of nation state is undermined by financial globalisation concerning macro-economic policies. There is strengthening of the technocratic form of economic governance which is independent of democratic control and accountability (Singh 2005). The way policy-making is done by the state these days, conceals the fact that 'economic and social policy has to now be made on capital's terms'. What is done can often be unpalatable to the voters. Hence, 'these policies are increasingly made in secret and their likely effects concealed'. The state has not become only more and more responsive to capital, 'but more and more closely integrated with it'. The problem here is that risks involved and costs of this is borne by the common public. 'In effect the corporate agenda is installed in the state' (Leys in Panitch and Leys 2005). In fact, globalisation and associated reforms are generating democratic deficit at all levels—national, local and global.

The Indian Scene

In case of India, it is observed that certain economic reform measures were initiated by the Central government in the 1980s. However, a systematic and comprehensive agenda of reforms unfolded with the BoP crisis of 1991. The reforms package first came as conditionalities attached by the IMF and World Bank as part of the financial loans provided to the country to overcome the immediate crisis. In addition, other major multilateral and bilateral agencies such as ADB (Asian Development Bank), USAID (United States Agency for International Development), DFID (Department for International Development, UK) and NOVIB (Netherlands Organisation for International Cooperation) that operate in India, made governance reforms an important part of their agenda. Reforms started systematically at the central level (Mukherji 2002) and have later moved on to the state level as well (GOI 2003). It is observed that 'a wave of reforms have been sweeping India at the state level' since the second half of 1990s (Howes et al. 2003). However, the pace and depth of reforms seem to vary particularly at the state level. In introducing reforms, some states have moved faster like Andhra Pradesh (Mooij 2003, Rao 1998) and Gujarat (Dholakia 2000, 2003); some are very slow like Bihar (Kumar nd), and some may be in the middle like Kerala (Nayar 2004). It is held that in some states the reforms are introduced in a remarkably centralised manner with the dynamism of the chief minister and a small group of advisers (as under Chandrababu Naidu in Andhra Pradesh), but in a slower and more collegial way relying heavily on consensus rather than command (like in Karnataka) (Beschel Jr. 2003). However, the package of reforms is similar both at the central and state levels. The State-specific factors (like the general environment, political dynamics and the nature of ruling regime) could be responsible for unevenness in reforms.

It is opined that as a result of reforms, the state (national level) is weakened and altered from within. Multilateral and bilateral organisations (like WB, ADB, DFID, NOVIB) enter into direct relationship with the provincial/state governments in India and thereby shape their policy developments and socio-economic activities. External funds granted to state governments have substantially increased, though not in equal measure to all states. There is more effective penetration of top-down agenda of external aid agencies at this level and increased competition between state governments to obtain external assistance that generates more pressure to implement the reforms agenda (D. Arora 2002). Also, greater autonomy of state governments is facilitated by the emergence of coalition governments at the central level though this kind of formation has not yet been fully accepted by dominant political parties (B. Arora 2002). The experiences of reforms are not all that pleasing. For instance, the World Bank package of reforms in Andhra Pradesh has made it a highly indebted state and also contributed to the overthrow of the proactive (regarding reforms) regime there in the assembly elections.

India's federal system shows a unique dynamics of reforms. It is noted that impetus for reform derives from a relatively small circle of advisors around the finance minister and the prime minister at the centre. But the state governments are forced to respond in their own way as per their needs and the stance of the ruling regime. The responses of the ruling regimes and the interest groups differ from state to state. Also the impact of reforms in different states vary. Reforms are generally introduced in the form of successive micro-reforms in different states at different times and in different situations. 'This combination means that the political impact of economic reform is refracted through the prism of federal India, resulting in a slower pace than many proponents of reform would prefer'. An important advantage here is that it helps to 'blunt the edge of opposition'. A united political opposition is dissipated in such a fragmented environment (Jenkins 1995: 42). Union Finance Minister P. Chidambaram recently emphasised the need for having 12 per cent growth in manufacturing to boost industrial expansion and achieve 10 per cent growth rate of the economy. Action in this regard has come in the form of the Central government proposing five manufacturing investment regions (MIRs) on the lines of Special Economic Zones (SEZs). To prevent political controversies in this regard, the Central government has taken advantage of the federal structure and provided that states should frame laws relating to MIRs (TOI 2006e).

Further, deregulation of industrial licensing at the central level has made state governments the key point of contact for entrepreneurs. The fluidity of India's democratic system (e.g., frequent regime change) and the nature of policy change creates a general expectation that new situation brings opportunities. The importance of state governments have increased due to 'their role as ... inaugurators of new political alliances and as accommodating initiators in the process of incremental reforms' (Neale 1988, cited in Jenkins 1995: 44). Now, the individual entrepreneur is free to decide and the state governments have to compete with each other to attract investment, both foreign and domestic. The states have to create an investor-friendly environment for this purpose. Inter state competition weakens the reform-related dissidence among state-level politicians (ibid.). The components (interest groups—winners and losers) of coalitions under reforms are easily interchangeable. But it is not as simple in the Indian case. Political support bases are not easily substituted. There have been mediation of conflicts between contending economic interests at different levels, both central and state.

Under the loan conditionalities attached to the fiscal stabilisation and SAP, the WB and IMF facilitated through the Indian government the rollback of the state sector and changed regulatory framework, which includes delicensing, privatisation and removal of restrictions on monopolies, trade and foreign participation in the country. The underlying thrust is to promote the operation of market forces in different sectors. In the supervisory capacity, these agencies have applied pressure on the government to remedy drawbacks in accountability and transparency. Thus, they have played a consultative/facilitating and supervisory role in overseeing the implementation of the reforms programme.

However, it is noted that direct external pressure has been used 'only selectively' on the government to improve its political and economic governance. A more overt 'disciplinary' role has been played in other sectors like environment and resettlement policy (e.g., Sardar Sarovar Project) by the World Bank, and in trade, finance (Super 301) and intellectual property (Special 301) by the US government and the WTO. In fact, 'the governance agenda is applied in a partial and ad hoc manner' in India (Currie 1996: 802). Moreover, in the case of India, it is held that the arguments for reforms were articulated in 1970s in the writings of economists like Bhagwati and in several Government committee reports (i.e., the Dagli Committee report). 'If anything, the IMF and the World Bank simply recycled these arguments, using slightly different jargons' (Debroy and Mukherji 2004). This is strongly disputed by Byres (1998). A systematic departure in development strategy by the Government of India began only in 1991 (Kurien, cited in Byres 1998). But the reform process is said to reflect a continuum as it started in the eighties and got expedited as a result of the BoP crisis in 1991.

For the advocates of globalisation, the current phase of reforms heralds a 'second independence' in India (Das 2001: xi). On the contrary, there is an erosion of the sovereignty, authority and legitimacy of the Indian state, or its retreat from the economic and social spheres (Kothari 1995: 1595). There is reorientation or shrinking of state's autonomous jurisdictions that has changed its real nature and capacities. The goals of the state have been redefined to serve the interests of powerful external and domestic economic interests. There is a 'virtual hijacking of policy space' by the non-state players. There is devaluation of democracy. Political process has been reduced to a legitimation function. Formal political institutions like legislatures are engaged in formalising the policy decisions taken elsewhere, usually in corporate circles that lack any accountability to the people. 'There is a clear subordination of public policy to the global and international power dynamics'. This curtails the space for the domestically defined and democratically shaped politics. This is done though 'in close league with some vested interests at home' (D. Arora 2002: 47). It is argued that reforms have been introduced in India 'by stealth' (Jenkins 1999). This is so when reforms are viewed from the perspective of democracy and policy participation. It is observed that the power of the government and of the employers has been further consolidated at the cost of weaker sections of people (such as labour, including trade unions) in policy making. Globalisation has significant adverse impact on welfare as it exposes common citizens to greater economic risk and increased insecurity. 'This is particularly true of poor countries such as India, which do not have adequate social security arrangements' (Sikdar 2004: 6). Besides, in India there is also a vitriolic rhetoric against the welfare state. Attempts are made to involve NGOs and allow entry of even the private sector in the social development sector. But the total government expenditure (centre and state combined) does not reflect any significant cut in the social sector. In the period of reforms, i.e., 1990–91 to 2004–05, the total expenditure on social services (education, health, etc.) remained largely stable at around 20 per cent of the total government expenditure (Sezhiyan 2005: 113).

Noted Western/US media and other agencies—*Time* and *The Economist*, Goldman Sachs and CIA (US intelligence agency), have given appreciative coverage of the recent growth in India and predicted India's rise as an economic superpower in the near future, by 2050. An avid votary of reforms, Aiyar (2006) feels gratified by the West's new discovery of India, though he is quite sceptical about the prediction getting validated. He observes, '... much of this (prediction) is unwarranted hype. India has a thin veneer of world-class people. But beneath this lies a cesspool of injustice, corruption, poverty and callousness. The impressive outer layer is thickening, but much too slowly'. India being labelled as a future superpower completely ignores the country's super heavy burden of backwardness in social development areas. For instance, according to a UNICEF report, India has the largest number of malnourished children in the world. One out of every three malnourished children in the world is Indian. To be more specific, out of the world's 146 million malnourished children, 57 million are in India which is 47 per cent of under-five in the country. The corresponding figures for Bangladesh and Ethiopia is about 47 per cent each, but only 8 per cent in a comparable country like China (TOI 2006c).

Kohli (2006) expresses deep concern about the quality of democracy due to the adoption of the current pro-business model of development in India. He hints at the country increasingly getting stuck with a 'two track democracy' in which common citizens are required only at the time of periodic elections and then forget politics and allow the 'rational' elite smoothly run a pro-business show. Shiv Viswanathan (2005) notices emergence of a 'new behavioural consensus' across party lines since the 1991 reforms in India. Democracy is viewed tactically and as a discrete set of indicators rather than as a value frame and a way of life. '... [C]onsumer defines the new contours of citizenship. Ideas of justice and equality lose out to those of mobility and opportunity. The politics of livelihood yields to the civics of lifestyle'. Political movements are losing out and pressure groups gaining strength. Radical politics is getting replaced by 'NGOisation' of life. The media is 'enzymatically central' in building this new consensus. It selectively picks up issues, frames and defines them. It 'homogenises issues and those who formulate them'. 'Left, Right and liberal begin to look affably alike in the democracy of media bytes'. The new consensus privileges mobility over equality, professionalism over ideology, pragmatism over value embeddedness, consumption above subsistence. The media has played an important role in its creation and legitimation.

Further, decentralisation and devolution of power is an important plank of the reforms agenda in India. This is proposed for promoting local level people's participation and empowerment. But the recent experiences show that there is little by way of actual empowerment happening on ground. Local social conflicts and asymmetrical power relations have largely rocked the boat. Moreover, the guiding logic here is that of capital and narrow economic efficiency in terms of improving service delivery. There is an interest in promoting market institutions by strengthening certain civil society institutions in the local context. NGOs are roped in to build state capacity, e.g., by holding training programmes for local Panchayats. This is expected to promote efficiency and responsiveness to help the growth of market institutions (D. Arora 2002). So, there is a move towards building state-NGO/CSO partnership to contribute to improve local level governance and efficiency (ibid.). In fact, NGOisation of social issues is increasing. The state is required to abandon social issues. But there is also a need to take care of the limits of markets that is inherently discriminatory against the poor. Hence, the general tendency is to leave social issues increasingly with the voluntary sector. Donor agencies and the state pour in huge funds to this sector. At the same time these funds are used to determine the political agenda of NGOs/CSOs. 'These become instrumental in coopting these and redefining their very approaches to issues, often in line with the concern for market-orientation as well as policy objectives of global significance' (ibid.: 62). There is donor-directed partnership at work, aimed at coopting the NGO/CSO sector as a part of the system. There is an attempt to 'coopt or divide' the civil society initiatives/movements by influencing the perspectives and approaches to development through funded programmes. Those not falling in line have to face state repression. Moreover, democracy is conceptualised in purely procedural terms. Politics as self-realisation—as human awareness and rights, is put at a discount when different agencies (NGOs etc.) involved in administration or management hijack political initiatives and the common people are constituted as consumers of services. In fact, in the new governance paradigm, 'civil society has lost the potential for democracy because it has been depoliticised' (Chandhoke 2003).

Measures have been taken in the area of administrative reforms, which include downsizing. New information technology is used, particularly through computers initiated as a tool to tackle the problem of inefficiency, corruption and lack of responsiveness of the state sector. Computerised information and facilitation counters are being set up. The Right to Information

Bill has been enacted. Citizen's Charters have been brought out by several government ministries/departments/organisations stating the details of citizen's entitlement to public services. However, these remain largely symbolic gestures, without much substance at the ground level (D. Arora 2002: 57). Secrecy obstructs access to information despite technological innovations. Citizens' charters remain non-justiciable. Moreover, citizen's rights, especially collective rights have been curtailed. Public and private interest/domain have been redefined. Consequently, rights of citizens have been redefined as those of consumers. Consumer rights are expanding. But the poorer non-consuming public is folded out of the framework of rights. The new value is to protect consumers rather than citizens. 'The privileging of consumer over citizen ... has serious implications for the democratic principles of equal rights of citizenship' (ibid.: 56).

Another concern of reforms under globalisation is to make the system more transparent, accountable and thus root out inefficiencies and corruption from economic, political and bureaucratic administration. However, studies relating to India reveal a completely different picture. Regular exposes of massive scams, diversion of funds from public sources into private hands, flight of capital and endemic corruption are reported. Though corruption is an old problem, it appears to have increased in recent years. There is growing corruption in the private sector as reflected in huge tax evasion, manipulation of loans, loan defaults, excessive pricing, etc. Besides, black money is increasing and corruption at the highest levels has gone up. There are instances of voluntary disclosure schemes initiated by the government to declare black money, which benefits mainly the richest 10 per cent of the population (Kabra and Upadhyay 1999). One opinion is that the system is corrupt. But, according to another argument, people are corrupt. There is a 'hopeless' strategy with inadequate anti-corruption measures where political leaders are not concerned with curbing corruption (Quah 2003). Currently reforms are supposedly meant to curtail it. But they, on the contrary, seem to have generated new forms of corruption which are 'aimed at evasion of policy, to secure the withdrawal of State, to obtain its silence on conflict-oriented issues to let them be settled in favour of the dominant forces' (D. Arora 1995).

Kohli (1990) delves into the issue of feasibility and pace of reforms in a democratic set-up. He notices a growing crisis of governance in India. The roots of this, in his view, are more political than socio-economic, i.e., they are located mainly in political structure—highly ineffectual national government and weak political parties, besides overpoliticisation of the marginalised. Referring to the Rajiv Gandhi regime, he opines that 'it is indeed difficult for a democratic regime to undertake a major shift in development strategy' (Kohli 1989). He notes that some economic reforms were introduced in the 1980s. And reforms have some social support base also. But it also evokes opposition (as clearly reflected in the recent elections). So, there are 'fairly sharp limits on how far and how fast a liberalisation programme can be implemented in a democracy' (ibid. 1989: 324). In India, like social settings, cultures of efficiency are not well grounded. So, the measures for enhancing efficiency and competitiveness do not create wide political support. The necessity to forge broad coalitions forces fragile democratic governments to adopt policy directions away from promoting the best and efficient competitive economy. (So, these issues of 'political rationality' and 'economic rationality', Kohli feels, have to be integrated in the analysis and policy advice offered to the governments in the third world) (ibid.: 325).

But commenting on the reforms in India in the early 1990s, Robert Jenkins (1995: 46) affirms that there is a 'potential for promoting policy change in a liberal democracy'. 'A democratic political system need not be an impediment to reform ... [though] there is no belief that democratic political system are better at implementing liberal economic reforms (Jenkins 1999: 43). Liberal democracy reflects resilience. In India, liberal democracy has provided a system for negotiating bargains and sharing spoils that is conducive to incremental change. Incentives are there for both political elites and leaders of interests to take risks on the basis of their assessment. Three basic features of India's political system are said to facilitate sustainability of adjustment over decades—political mechanisms, skills, and incentives. It is demonstrated from the experiences of the last decade that a democratic system is capable of dismantling its state-controlled economy without fatally undermining either reforms or democracy itself. [However, the difficulty in replicating India's case needs to be recognised, as its strength may lie in its unique features which evolved over the last half-a-century.] So, Jenkins looks closer than Kohli in understanding the prevailing Indian scenario.

Responses to Globalisation

There are varied responses to globalisation and reforms in India, as in several other countries of the world. Established political parties are largely supportive—ranging from ardent advocacy to reluctant and qualified support. Large numbers of professional developmental NGOs are knowingly or unknowingly engaged in implementing the agenda of globalisation. But there are also organisations and mobilisations strongly opposed to it—ranging from extreme left and Gandhian to those with extreme right ideological persuasions. In fact, mobilisations against globalisation have been taking place at different levels—global, national and local. There are alternative conceptualisations of globalisation as well as of good governance. There is advocacy of symmetrical globalisation. Also, there is advocated the need for broadening the agenda of good governance to the international level and in all sectors in terms of introducing transparency, accountability and democratic global governance (Singh 2005: 156). From a people's perspective governance is considered 'good only if it benefits the social groups that are most impoverished and socially vulnerable' (Mander and Asif 2004: 17). It is affirmed,

> For the vast majority of people, good governance also means a better quality of life; an equitable distribution of wealth, income and natural resources; dismantling of highly concentrated structures of property ownership; full employment; access to housing, health and education; restraining privileges of elites; the right to choose alternatives; cultural development and so on and so forth. A good governance system is the one under which all public policy affairs are managed through broad consensus in a transparent, accountable, participatory and equitable manner. Such an ideal system of good governance remains a far cry in the developed world, leave alone the poor and the developing world (Singh 2005: 158).

It is quite aptly pointed out that the focus of governance reforms of the international financial/developmental agencies is exclusively on the domestic institutions in the third world countries.

They are not much concerned with introducing 'good governance' at their own organisational level. Moreover, the technocratic approach of the reforms agenda ignores the role of external factors being responsible for the bad plight of the third world countries (such as protectionism especially in agriculture, declining commodity prices, external debt and volatile capital flows). So, the reforms agenda is very much questionable.

Omvedt (2005) refers to the major strands of thinking on 'alternative' globalisation, i.e., the market economy/neoliberalism/LPG. Alternative globalisation for eco-romantics means 'an alternative to the market and the state', i.e., a socialist society based on subsistence production which she considers an impossibility. Second, there is the alternative represented by the traditional left which advocates development of the forces of production and of human capacities along the left lines. (Currently this happens to be only a discredited model.) Then there is an alliance between the eco-romantics and the traditional left. This, according to her, is 'opportunistic on both sides' because eco-romantics are theoretically opposed to not only the market but also statism which the left symbolises. A true alternative, to Omvedt, would be a replacement of the present capitalism as well as to the current left and eco-romantics/ecological challenge. This would have 'a role for both the state and the market' and for 'sunrise industries' such as information technology and alternative energy sources. She advocates 'a true equalitarian, classless, casteless, non-patriarchal [ecologically] sustainable society' which can be constructed by 'using the seeds formed within the womb of the current society'. This would involve supersession of the existing capitalist society. This process, she notes, has already begun with the rise of 'new forces of production' as reflected on the social front, in the corporate leaders talking of social justice, philanthropy and corporate responsibility, and on, the material/environmental front, in production of electrically-powered cars, windmills, etc. Also, there are worker-owned companies, various types of home-based production and services, and not-for-profit enterprises. Finally, it is the responsibility, according to her, of the revolutionaries to develop them, direct them, link them up to reach a stage of conflict with the existing relations of production and thus begin an era of revolutionary change (2005: 4885).

Omvedt identifies two main tendencies among anti-globalisation activists working particularly in the Scheduled Tribe belt in India. This involves resistance to market incorporation and extraction by (*i*) returning to subsistence production, traditional cultivation methods, etc., and (*ii*) gaining local (community) control over the forest and its resources. She considers the first effort as a 'romantic impossibility' in the current stage. The second one, according to her, is the most progressive and important demands of today. Local control would 'mean that resources will be extracted more sustainably, that local people will get a share of the profits and raise their standard of living .... And this will primarily mean getting a better deal from world capital'. 'Simply put, it is impossible and even undesirable to withdraw from the global economy and social system', she affirms. So, this approach does not involve resistance to the world market and extraction, and can be seen as representing adaptation with assertion.

Further Gupta (2005) suggests an 'alternative paradigm' which takes a broad view of development. It is not confined to just improving health and education related indicators but includes the making of an active citizenry—the one with assertive self-confidence rather than reflecting clientelist dependence. The new paradigm, he suggests, aims at meeting the 'felt aspirations' of the poor (the kind of hopes and ambitions they have for the future) rather than confining to meeting just felt needs (immediate and pressing) such as under the poverty amelioration programmes. It would require building social capacities (structural capacity of the economy) of different categories of people (like farmers, fisherfolk, workers, intellectuals, etc.) to complement individual capabilities to enable 'achieving the life one values'.

Gupta expects that 'globalisation can show us the way' towards such an alternative paradigm of development as it draws us away from the 'nation state rhetorics'. To him, globalisation marks an ideological shift from the protection of producers to meeting the needs, desires and aspirations of users. But the challenge before globalisation, in his view, is to 'create enough purchasing power at lower levels so that aspirations can be met'. He advocates 'globalisation with equity' aimed at 'creating wealth, or at least open avenues whereby classes locked in poverty and that are aid-dependent can become self-generating producers of wealth' (Gupta 2005: 133). And this needs to be done quickly as people are quite demanding in democracy and would like to fulfil their aspirations in their own lifetime. The state has to play 'a major role' in this as the market on its own would not be able to ensure alternative development. In developing countries, the state has to extend a helping hand. Gupta concurs with Stiglitz regarding the role of the state in 'creating, shaping and guiding markets, including promotion of new technology'. Moreover, the state has to provide for building infrastructure and social security measures (ibid.: 140). There is also a need for sequencing globalisation-related reforms (in individual countries) in such a manner that 'a greater number of people benefit from an open economic system, not just the elite or those who have been privileged by the accidents of birth' (ibid.: 142). Income and employment generation would be a must 'to give substance to citizens and to their aspirations as consumers of services and of opportunities'. Provisions for health and education are essential but these may not be of real substance if opportunities for employment and income generation are not adequately created and thus give a real substance and meaning to development.

For overcoming India's current problems Dreze and Sen (1998) emphasise the need to 'go well beyond liberalisation'. They advocate a widely shared 'participatory economic expansion'. They affirm, 'there has to be growth for it to be participatory' (Dreze and Sen1998: 198). They hold that the roots of failure on the growth front included the continuation of overregulated economic governance that has blighted the prospects of economic expansion all over India for many decades (ibid.). They support expansion of social opportunities open to people and in this the use of market can be 'an important yet quite incomplete part'. 'In so far as these opportunities are compromised directly or indirectly—by counterproductive regulations and controls, by restrictions on economic activities, by the stifling of competition and its efficiency-generating advantages, and so on, the removal of these hindrances must be seen as extremely important' (ibid.: 203). The broader challenge is the creation and use of social opportunities which would require much more than 'freeing' of markets. 'What needs curing is not just "too little market" or "too much market". The expansion of markets is among the instruments that can help to promote human capabilities, and given the imperative need for rapid elimination of endemic deprivation in India, it would be irresponsible to ignore that opportunity. But much more is involved in freeing the Indian economy from the cage in which it has been confined, and many of the relevant tasks call for more—not less—government activity and public action' (ibid.).

A radical restructuring of the contemporary globalisation process is considered necessary to achieve genuine democracy at all levels. It is affirmed that democratic values like human dignity, freedom, equity and justice cannot gain strength in a polity obsessed with neoliberal orthodoxy (K. Singh 2005: 128). Hyperglobalisers suggest strengthening of the current pattern of global governance; polished neoliberals wish to add a 'human face' to globalisation. But sceptics advocate restructuring of the contemporary globalisation process to promote democratic, equitable and sustainable development. Transformationists suggest the need for global democratic governance, cosmopolitan democracy and a catalytic state.

Finally, it emerges that both external and internal forces/factors are responsible for the introduction of a comprehensive package of market-based neoliberal reforms in India (economic, social, administrative and political). The fiscal crisis (BoP) faced by India in 1991 provided an opportunity to the American/Western dominated multilateral institutions to push the reforms agenda in the country under the fiscal stabilisation and SAP programmes. The Western bilateral development agencies also gave a push to the reforms programmes through their projects in different spheres in many parts of the country. Elite circles of advisors, including the top bureaucracy, particularly around the prime minister and the finance minister have played a very important role in the introduction and steering of the reforms programme in the country. On the whole, the business elites backed the reforms. At the state level also efforts have been made to introduce similar reforms at the centre level. Federal structure, coalition governments at the centre and the motivations of individual chief ministers along with his/her elite circles of advisors/bureaucrats/ministers/business people have influenced the pace and depth of reforms in different states. Multilateral and bilateral development/financing agencies have directly or indirectly penetrated and are influencing all levels of governance in the country—national, state and local levels through their new policy thrusts, programmes and projects. In India, the overall impact of all this has been the erosion of sovereignty and autonomy of nation state, *reframing* of the state (shift from statist to partnership approach), retreat of the state from directly undertaking welfare functions, weakening of the state's welfare functions, devaluation of democracy, new forms of corruption, and (huge) benefits to the powerful external and internal interests/classes. There are varied responses to globalisation. A large number of political parties and professional development organisations work closely with the forces of globalisation. There are also many organisations which are mildly to highly opposed to globalisation and reforms in the country. The last parliamentary elections broadly showed that the higher the rate and depth of reforms introduced by the governments, both at the centre and state levels, the lower the electoral support by the people plus higher the degree of loss of political power by the ruling regimes. Yet, the process of reforms continued along the same lines as before, though a little slowly, with a thin topping/rhetoric of 'human face'. A synoptic view of the political dimension of globalisation and governance reforms is provided in Figure 1.6.

Figure 1.6: Political Dimension of Reforms in India

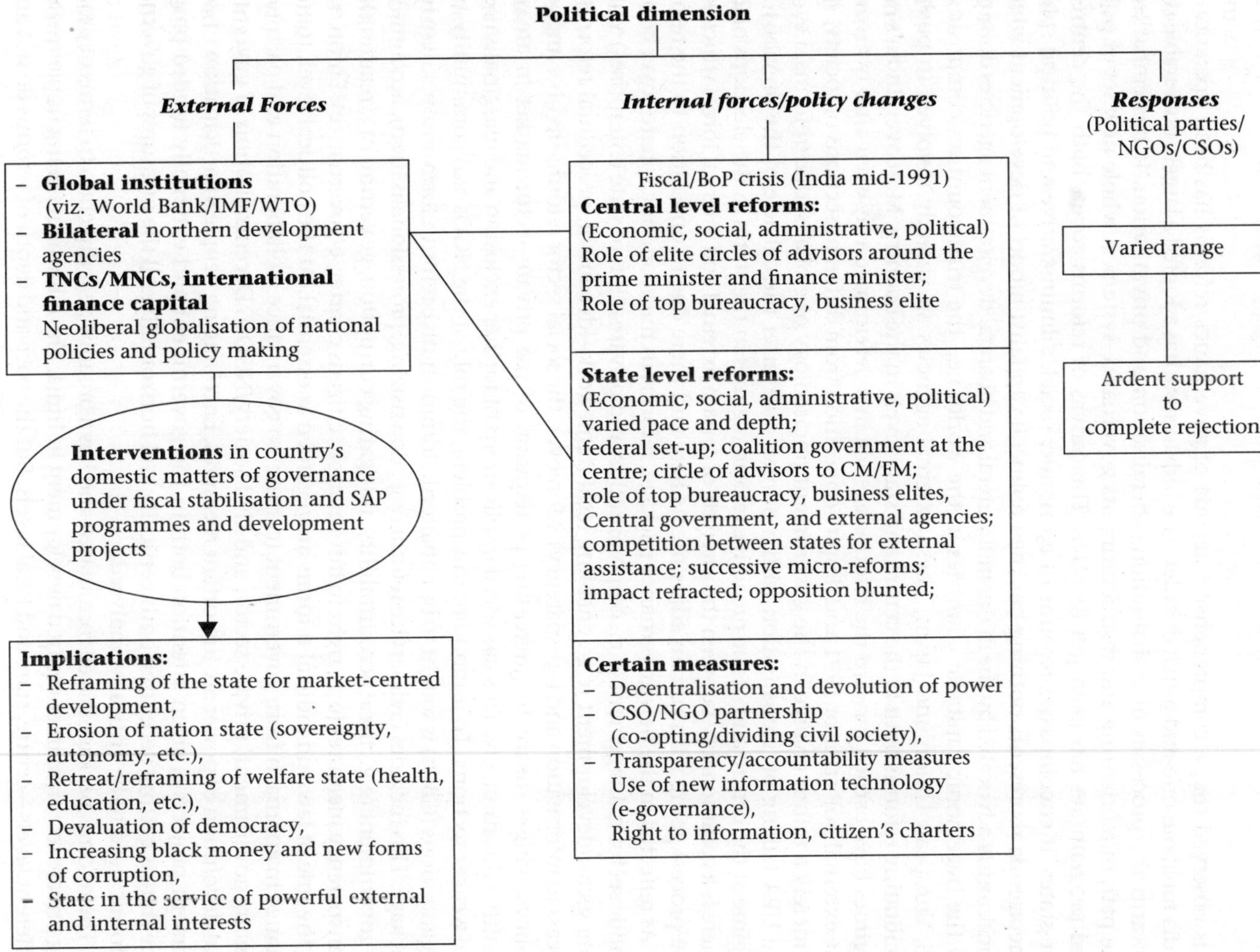

Concluding Observations

It is observed that a comprehensive agenda of governance reforms has been operational in India for about one-and-a-half decades. The Indian state has adopted a largely favourable stance towards the processes of globalisation, liberalisation and privatisation. It has embarked on the path of reörienting and restructuring its governance system. A whole new set of policies and programmes has been put in place. The canvas of reforms covers both the centre and the states. It encompasses reforms in economic, social, administrative and political spheres. The agenda represents nothing but the neoliberal capitalist model of development which is vociferously advocated by the major multilateral and bilateral development agencies dominated by the hegemonic capitalist countries in the world, i.e., the triad countries comprising the US, European Union and Japan. These external agencies are directly involved in pushing/facilitating reforms both at the centre and state levels in the country. Moreover, India's ruling regimes have carried forward the reforms agenda in a determined way even after overcoming the external BoP crisis of 1991 and despite opposition from different sections of society. There is merely a minor change in the government phraseology of globalisation/reforms, i.e., with the UPA talking of 'globalisation with a human face' after the debacle of the previous NDA regime at the centre and of the proactive reform regimes in the states in the elections of 2004. There is a commonality between the interests of certain external and internal forces which keeps the process going with certain adjustments here and there due to opposition to the reforms.

As reflected in the new governance package, reforms in the economic sphere cover both the public sector management (e.g., corporatisation and privatisation of state enterprises) and private sector development (e.g., enabling legal framework—decontrol, procedural reforms and access to information and transparency). Moreover, the social sector reforms involve important policy changes meant for increasing penetration of the private sector/market in areas like health, education, etc. This has social implications of further exclusion and marginalisation of the weaker sections. To respond to this problem, the role of the NGOs and community-based organisations (CBOs) is sought to be enhanced. Administrative reforms form another item in the package. This includes civil service reform (e.g., downsizing, professionalisation), accountability of government (e.g., fiscal accountability, mitigating corruption, government streaming), and transparency measures (e.g., right to information, citizens charter, e-governance). Enforcement of the rule of law and judicial reforms are regarded as essential. At the political level, there is a change in approach from government (centric) to governance (collaboration and partnership among government, private sector, and civil society/NGOs). Decentralisation of government and devolution of power are important measures. Encouraging people's participation in development projects is given attention both in the government and externally funded projects. The state is getting decentred both vertically and horizontally. All the measures of governance reforms need to be critically analysed.

The reforms package is well formulated and has a broadly clear direction in terms of promoting private sector/market-centred development in India. The reforms are being implemented at different levels—centre, state and local levels. But the pace and depth of reforms do not appear to be the same at all levels and across different spheres—economic, social, cultural, political and also across different sectors. Though the agenda is the same, there seem to be contrasting experiences in this connection across states. The dynamics of reforms varies across different spaces. The implications of reforms have some commonalities and also certain variations across states as regards development reflected in terms of human development, human rights, equity and empowerment. To have a broad snapshot of reforms at the state level, this volume covers select states representing high, medium and low categories in terms of introduction of reforms and development. More studies are required in this area.

In fact, there are several studies which deliberate upon the issue of globalisation and reforms in India. But the focus has generally been on the economic dimension. So, this aspect is not much emphasised in the present volume. Not much systematic attention seems to have been paid to closely understand the agenda of governance reforms in a systematic manner covering other important spheres of life—social, cultural, political and administrative. So, certain major issues concerning these spheres are analysed in detail in the volume.

The process of globalisation and reforms relates differently to the major sections of society in India. It has a strong social base in the privileged castes and classes in India, including the Indian diaspora, who are the driving forces backing it and are also the main beneficiaries. Their nexus with the forces of global capitalism is becoming increasingly stronger, though they remain a junior partner in the formation. On the other side, the overwhelming majority of the marginalised people are adversely affected and are losers in this process. So, there are both winners and losers. There are certain classes/castes/social strata and their spokespersons and representatives in government, (higher) bureaucracy, academia and media who are supportive of the reform package, there are also losers and their spokespersons and others who are opposed to it but are largely on the margins.

The media is playing a very important role in popularising and promoting the LPG package in which is embedded the culture of commodification, consumerism, money making, hedonism and infotainment characteristic of the American/Western society. This type of homogenisation seems to be the dominant trend. This has serious socio-political implications. Moreover, the instances of increasing cultural heterogeneity and glocalisation/adaptation are also rising. Also there is a trend of increasing identity assertion and conflict in the country. The situation is quite complex and difficult to generalise with certainty.

As regards the political domain, undermining of the sovereignty and autonomy of the nation-state is being undermined as a result of increased influence of external forces—particularly multilaterals and international finance. The state is on the retreat in the economic domain in terms of direct involvement in productive business activities. Its role is being reframed mainly as facilitator of the private sector/market-centered development. The welfarist stance of the state is under attack, more so at the rhetorical level which is in line with the policies in the advanced capitalist countries. Its approach to welfare is changing from being state-centric to being collaborative in nature. It may be mentioned here that the 'overloaded' welfare state in the West may like to change its strategy to be more efficient and effective. But load-shedding by the 'underloaded' welfarist state in the third world countries like India would have strong adverse consequences for the marginalised sections of society. The very nature of democracy is adversely affected by reforms as the consumer is gradually becoming more important than the citizen. It can be added that the prevailing system of governance in India lacks transparency, public accountability, efficiency/effectiveness, responsiveness and people's participation. The scourge of corruption is not decreasing, but rather devouring the whole body politic in newer forms. These problems need to be tackled seriously and sincerely which may require substantive changes that have to be different from the LPG.

The overall pattern of changes in India in the era of globalisation would be quite aptly described as 'dependent development' as formulated by Cardoso (1982). On the whole the privileged classes have benefited and developed quite a lot as a result of governance reforms on the lines of globalisation, further consolidating their status and influence in the country. The reforms have been possible due to their domestic alliance among the privileged classes and their collaboration, as a junior partner, with the global/'metropolitan' forces. The condition of a large section of marginalised people has either stagnated or further deteriorated.

Most studies on the social, culture and political dimensions of globalisation and reforms in India are reflective general commentaries. So, there is an urgent need to have comprehensive empirical studies to find out the dominant national trends and also regional, state/local specificities relating to globalisation, governance reforms and development in the country. In this connection, it must be understood that neoliberal globalisation is not merely an economic project, but also, directly or indirectly, a social, cultural and political project meant for reorganising the society at the global level. A theoretical sensitivity in the studies would facilitate better understanding of the theme, which would also help formulating an appropriate response to the challenges posed by globalisation, both at the political and people/civil society levels, with a view to promoting equitable, participatory, largely autonomous and sustainable development *in practice*. A modest attempt is made along these lines in this volume. But there is a need to do much more on a larger scale.

Organisation of the Volume

From the foregoing discussion, it is clear that globalisation is a multi-dimensional phenomenon. It has covered under its wings the third world countries with the introduction of a set of reforms signifying a shift in the development paradigm. Scholars belonging to different disciplines have tried to grapple with specific dimensions of globalisation from their particular disciplinary perspective. Hence, it is essential to have a joint attempt to analyse and understand some of its major dimensions in an integrated manner. Keeping this in view, contributors to the volume include sociologists, political scientists, economists and media experts. On the whole, a modest attempt is made in the volume to have a broad understanding of certain major issues/aspects of state-level reforms and the social, cultural and political dimensions of globalisation and governance reforms in India. Contributors to the volume had all the freedom to analyse different issues from their own conceptual angle as no specific theoretico-conceptual framework was prescribed to them. They had to relate their analysis of the issue concerned to the broad framework of the study delineated in the Introduction of the volume, which they have tried to do in their own ways.

There is a vast literature already available and increasing day by day on globalisation. The issue is studied from different theoretico-conceptual angles and there is no unanimity in the resultant observations. Similarly, there are several studies on the current reforms introduced in India. But the emphasis is mainly on national-level economic reforms. State-level reforms have not received much attention. There is a lack of both theoretical and empirical depth in the studies on social, cultural and political dimensions of reforms and development in India. The volume tries to fill these existing gaps in a limited way.

Keeping in view this backdrop, the volume is divided into five sections with specific thematic focus. Section I presents the conceptual spectrum on globalisation and associated reforms. It has three chapters. Chapter 1 serves as an introduction to the volume. It is contributed by the editor and provides a synoptic overview of the theme, i.e., globalisation, governance reforms and development with a focus on India. In Chapter 2, Dolly Arora delves into the vital question of reorganisation of institutional space in the time of globalisation. In Chapter 3, Niraja G. Jayal deals with the burning issue of democratic deficit in the current era of globalisation. Section II has four chapters dealing with state-level reforms in India which covers a few select states representing high, medium and low level of introduction of reforms. Discussions in this include the experiences of reforms in Gujarat (Chapter 4) by the editor, in Andhra Pradesh (Chapter 5) by G. Krishna Reddy, in Kerala (Chapter 6) by K. Ramachandran Nair and in Bihar (Chapter 7) by Shaibal Gupta. Social dimensions of globalisation and reforms in India are analysed in seven chapters of Section III. Here K.L. Sharma analyses the general issue of continuities and changes in caste and class (including middle class) under globalisation in Chapter 8. In Chapter 9, Surinder S. Jodhka discusses the conditions of farmers in contemporary Punjab. Sharit K. Bhowmik portrays the situation of labour (excluding rural labour) in Chapter 10. The issue of exclusion and assertion of Dalits is covered by Vivek Kumar in Chapter 11. Prakash Louis analyses the plight of the scheduled tribes in Chapter 12. In Chapter 13, Manoranjan Mohanty focuses on the poor. The issue of the Indian diaspora is dealt with by R.K. Jain in Chapter 14. Cultural dimension of globalisation and reforms in India are covered in three chapters of Section IV. The focus here is on the role of mass media in the cultural domain. In Chapter 15, J.S. Yadav broadly discusses mass media but focuses on the print media viz. newspapers. Biswajit Das delves into the debates on Indian television and culture in Chapter 16. In Chapter 17, Santosh Panda deals with the ICT and culture. Finally, Section V has three chapters on major issues related to the political dimensions of globalisation and reforms. Vidhu Verma deliberates upon the question of globalisation and the state in India in Chapter 18. Mohan Rao discusses in Chapter 19 the health scenario which reflects the changes in the shape of welfare state in India. In Chapter 20, Anand Kumar briefly discusses the political and civil society responses to globalisation and reforms in India against the backdrop of the project of modernity and nation-building. However, given the limitations of space, time and other resources it was not possible to include in the volume, analysis of certain other major issues like business and politics, gender, rising fundamentalism and identity politics in India in the context of globalisation.

The volume is significant in several ways. It is not confined to the analysis of just one dimension but tries to present an overall view of multiple dimensions—social, cultural, political, state-level reforms of globalisation, reforms and development in India. Quite understandably, it has contributors from different disciplines. The introductory chapter delineates the major theoretic-conceptual perspectives on globalisation and attempts to apply these in the analysis of social, cultural and political dimensions of globalisation and reforms in India. The volume clearly demonstrates that 'good governance' reforms are not confined to the traditional notion of governance but are basically another conceptualisation (the other being SAP, i.e., structural adjustment programme) of the neoliberal agenda of reforms meant for firmly reorganising the 'developing' countries like India along the path of global capitalism. It is shown that reforms have a significant impact in the social, cultural and political domains in India. At the inter-state level what is actually happening in the country as a result of reforms is not 'competitive developmentalism', as claimed by advocates of the market, but exacerbation of the existing inequalities and at the intra-state level higher economic growth is not necessarily related to human/social development. Obviously, the study emphasises the need for an alternative development model and policies to promote a democratic (substantive), egalitarian and sustainable development in India rather than clutching to the largely 'dependent development' paradigm of globalisation and reforms. This could be applicable to the other third world countries as well.

References

Abed, George T. and Sanjeev Gupta (eds) (2002). *Governance, Corruption & Economic Performance*. Washington DC: International Monetary Fund.

Ahmad, Aijaz (2004). *On Communalism and Globalisation: Offensive of the Far Right*. New Delhi: Three Essays Collective.

Aiyar, Swaminathan S. Anklesaria (2006). "West's Discovery of India", *The Times of India* (Ahmedabad edn), 25 June.

Amin, Samir (2003). *Obsolescent Capitalism—Contemporary Politics and Global Disorder*. London and New York: Zed Books.

Appadurai, Arjun (1997). *Modernity At Large—Cultural Dimensions of Globalisation*. Minneapolis: University of Minnesota Press.

Archer, Robert (1994). 'Markets and Good Government', in Andrew Clayton (ed.), *Governance, Democracy and Conditionality—What Role for NGOs*? Oxford: INTRAC Publication.

Arora, Balveer (2002). 'Negotiating Differences: Federal Coalitions and National Cohesion', in F.R. Frankel, Z. Hasan, R. Bhargava and B. Arora (eds). *Transforming India: Social and Political Dynamics of Democracy*. New Delhi: Oxford University Press.

Arora, Dolly (1995). 'On the Tragedy of Public Domain: Corruption, Victimisation and the New Policy Regime', *Indian Journal of Public Administration*, 42(1).

——— (2002). 'Reorganisation of Institutional Space: State, Market and Public Domain', *Man & Development*, 24(4), December.

Arvind (2002). *Globalisation: An Attack on India's Sovereignty*. New Delhi: New Vistas Publications.

Asian Development Bank (ADB) (2003). *India—Country Strategy and Program 2003–2006*. Available at http://www.adb.org/Documents/CSPs/IND/2003/default.asp, accessed on 30 July 2004.

Bajaj, Rahul (2006). 'Reforms Take a Back Seat', *The Times of India* (Ahmedabad edn), 20 January.

Baylis, John and Steve Smith (2005). *The Globalization of World Politics*. New Delhi: Oxford University Press, first Indian edition.

Bendana, Alejandro (2004). 'Good Governance and the MDGs: Contradictory or Complementary?'. Available at http://www.globalpolicy.org/socecon/2004/1012goodgovernance. htm, accessed on 26 May 2005.

Berger, Peter L. (2002). 'Introduction—The Cultural Dynamics of Globalization', in Peter L. Berger and Samuel P. Huntington (eds), *Many Globalizations: Cultural Diversity in the Contemporary World*. London and New York: Oxford University Press.

Beschel Jr., Robert P. (2003). 'Civil Service Reform in India: Perspectives from the World Bank's Work in Three States', in Stephen Howes, A. Lahiri and Nicholas Stern (eds), *State-Level Reforms in India—Towards More Effective Government*. New Delhi: Macmillan India Ltd.

Bhaduri, Amit and Deepak Nayyar (1996). *The Intelligent Person's Guide to Liberalization*. New Delhi: Penguin Books India (P) Ltd.

Bhagwati, Jagdish (2004). *In Defense of Globalisation*. New Delhi: Oxford University Press.

Bhardwaj, Prem R. (2003). 'Globalisation: Politics of US Hegemony and Democratic Processes in Developing Countries', *Man and Development*, 25(4), December.

Bhargava, Rajeev (2004). 'Globalisation and Culture', in Achin Vanaik (ed.), *Globalisation And South Asia—Multidimensional Perspectives*. New Delhi: Manohar Publishers.

Birdsall, Nancy (2003). 'Cheerleaders, Cynics and Worried Doubters'. http://www.globalagendamagazine.com/2003/nancybirdsall.asp, accessed on 24 May 2005.

Boron, Atilio A. (2005). 'The Truth About Capitalist Democracy', in Leo Panitch and Colin Leys (eds), *Telling The Truth: Socialist Register 2006*. New Delhi: Leftword Books. (First pubn by The Merlin Press, 2005).

Breidenbach, Joana and Ina Zukrigl (1999). 'The Dynamics of Cultural Globalization—The Myths of Cultural Globalization'. Available at http://www.inst.at/studies/collab/breidenb.htm, accessed on 10 August 2005.

Byres, Terence J. (ed.) (1998). *The State, Development Planning and Liberalisation in India*. Delhi: Oxford University Press.

Callinicos, Alex (ed.) (1994). *Marxism and the New Imperialism*. London: Bookmarks.

Cardoso, Fernando H. (1982). 'Dependency and Development in Latin America', in H. Alavi and T. Shanin (eds), *Sociology of Developing Societies*, London: The Macmillan Press Ltd.

Chanda, Nayan (2002). 'Coming Together—Globalization Means Reconnecting the Human Community'. Available at http://yaleglobal.yale.edu/about/essay.jsp, accessed on 2 June 2005.

Chandhoke, Neera (2003). 'Governance and the Pluralisation of the State: Implications for Democratic Citizenship', *Economic and Political Weekly*, 38(28), 12 July.

Chaudhuri, Maitrayee (1999). 'The World of Advertisements and Globalisation—A Look at the Print Media', in Raj Mohini Sethi (ed.), *Globalisation, Culture and Women's Development*. Jaipur and New Delhi: Rawat Publishers.

Chomsky, Noam (1999). *Profit over People—Neoliberalism and Global Order*. Delhi: Madhyam Books (by arrangement with Seven Stories Press, New York).

Crossley, Nick and J.M. Roberts (eds) (2004). *After Habermas—New Perspectives on the Public Sphere*. Oxford: Blackwell Publishing/Sociological Review.

Currie, Bob (1996). 'Governance, Democracy and Economic Adjustment in India: Conceptual and Empirical Problems', *Third World Quarterly*, 17(4).

Dasgupta, Biplab (2005). *Globalisation: India's Adjustment Experience*. New Delhi: Sage Publications.

Das, Gurcharan (2001). *India Unbound: From Independence to the Global Information Age*. New York: Alfred A. Knoff.

Debroy, Bibek and Rahul Mukherji (eds) (2004). *India—The Political Economy of Reforms*. New Delhi: Bookwell.

Debroy, Bibek and P.D. Kaushik (eds) (2005). *Reforming the Labour Market*. New Delhi: Academic Foundation.

Deshpande, Satish (1997). 'From Development to Adjustment: Economic Ideologies, the Middle Class and 50 years of Independence', *Review of Development and Change*, 2(2), July–December.

Dhawan, Himanshi (2006), 'NRI Remittances Twice the Amount of FII Inflow', *The Times of India* (Ahmedabad edn), 14 June.

Dholakia, Ravindra H. (2000). 'Liberalisation in Gujarat', *Economic and Political Weekly*, 35(35–36): 3121–25, 26 August–2 September.

——— (2003). 'The Role of the State Government in Promoting Private Sector Growth: The Case of Gujarat', in Stephen Howes et al. (eds), *State-Level Reforms in India—Towards More Effective Government*. New Delhi: Macmillan India Ltd.

Dreze, Jean and Amartya Sen (1998). *India—Economic Development and Social Opportunity*. Delhi: Oxford University Press.

Friedman, Milton (1962). *Capitalism And Freedom*. Chicago: The University of Chicago Press.

Friedman, Thomas (2005). *The World Is Flat—A Brief History of the Globalised World in the Twenty-first Century*. London: Allen Lane—Penguin Books Ltd.

Fukuyama, Francis (1992). *The End of History and the Last Man*. London: Penguin Books.

——— (2004). *State Building: Governance and World Order in the Twenty-First Century*. London: Profile Books.

Geddes, Pete (nd). 'Globalisation—A Race to the Top'. Available at http://www. aworldconnected.org/article.php?id, accessed on 24 May 2005.

Giddens, Anthony (1999). *The Third Way*. Cambridge, UK: Polity Press.

Gilpin, R. (2000). *The Challenge of Global Capitalisation: The World Economy in the Twenty-First Century*. Princeton: Princeton University Press.

Government of India (GOI) (2002a). *Tenth Five Year Plan, 2002–2007*, vol. II. New Delhi: Planning Commission.

——— (2002b). *National Human Development Report (2001)*. New Delhi: Oxford University Press.

——— (2003). *Successful Governance Initiatives and Best Practices—Experiences from Indian States*. New Delhi: Academic Foundation.

Griffin, Keith (2004). 'Globalisation and Culture', in S. Cullenberg and P.K. Pattanaik (eds), *Globalisation, Culture, And the Limits of the Market: Essays in Economics and Philosophy*. New Delhi: Oxford University Press.

Gupta, Dipankar (2000). *Mistaken Modernity: India Between Worlds*. New Delhi: HarperCollins Publishers India.

——— (2005). *Learning To Forget: The Anti-Memoirs of Modernity*. New Delhi: Oxford University Press.

Harshe, Rajen (2005). 'Changing Profile of Imperialism in Global Political Order/Disorder', *Economic and Political Weekly*, 40(20): 2071–76, 14 May.

Hartman, Yvonne (2005). 'In Bed with the Enemy: Some Ideas on the Connections between Neoliberalism and the Welfare State', *Current Sociology*, 53(1): 57–73.

Held, David, Anthony McGrew, David Goldblatt and Jonathan Perraton (1999). *Global Transformations*. Stanford, CA: Stanford University Press.

Herman, E.S. and R.W. McChesney (1998). *The Global Media—The New Missionaries of Corporate Capitalism*. Delhi: Madhyam Books.

Howes, Stephen, A.K. Lahiri and N. Stern (eds) (2003). *State-Level Reforms in India—Towards More Effective Government*. New Delhi: Macmillan India Ltd.

Hudson, Wayne (2002). 'What Is Globalisation?', in Donald Lamberton (ed.), *Managing the Global—Globalisation, Employment and Quality of Life*. London and New York: I.B. Tauris Publishers.

Huntington, S.P. (1997). *The Clash of Civilisations And the Remaking of World Order*. New Delhi: Penguin Books India (P) Ltd.

International Monetary Fund (IMF) (2002). 'Globalisation: Threat or Opportunity'. Available at http://www.imf.org/external/np/exr/ib/2000/04/200.htm, accessed on 7 January 2006.

Jalan, Bimal (2005). *The Future of India—Politics, Economics and Governance*. New Delhi: Viking/Penguin Books India Pvt. Ltd.

Jayal, Niraja G. (1997). 'The Governance Agenda: Making Democratic Development Dispensable', *Economic and Political Weekly*, 32(8): 407–12, 22 February.

Jayal, N.G. and Sudha Pai (2001). *Democratic Governance in India—Challenges of Poverty, Development and Identity*. New Delhi: Sage Publications.

Jenkins, Robert S. (1995). 'Liberal Democracy and the Political Management of Structural Adjustment in India: Conceptual Tensions in the Good Government Agenda', *IDS Bulletin*, 26(2).

Jenkins, Rob (1999). *Democratic Politics and Economic Reform in India*. Cambridge: Cambridge University Press.

Jodhka, Surinder S. (2006). 'Beyond "Crises": Rethinking Contemporary Punjab Agriculture', *Economic and Political Weekly*, 41(16): 1530–37, 22 April.

Jogdand, P.G. (ed.) (2000). *New Economic Policy & Dalits*. Jaipur and New Delhi: Rawat Publications.

Jomo, K.S. (ed.) (2006). *Globalisation Under Hegemony: The Changing World Economy*. New Delhi: Oxford University Press.

Kabra, K.N. and V. Upadhyay (1999). *Alternative Economic Survey 1997–98*. New Delhi: Rainbow Publishers.

Kaufmann, Daniel and Aart Kraay (2003). 'Governance and Growth—Causality Which Way?'. Available at http://www.worldbank.org/wbi/governance/pdf/growthgov-synth.pdf, accessed on 12 December 2003.

——— (2004). 'Growth without Governance', World Bank Policy Research Working Paper. Available at www-wds.worldbank.org/servlet, accessed on 5 July 2005.

Kellner, Douglas (2002). 'Theorizing Globalization', *Sociological Theory*, 20(3), November.

Khor, Martin (2001). *Rethinking Globalisation—Critical Issues and Policy Choices*. London and New York: Zed Books.

Kohli, Atul (1989). 'Politics of Economic Liberalisation in India', *World Development*, 17(3).

——— (1990). *Democracy and Discontent: India's Growing Crisis of Governability*. Cambridge: Cambridge University Press.

——— (2006). 'Politics of Economic Growth in India, 1980–2005', *Economic and Political Weekly*, 41(14): 1361–70, 8 April.

Kothari, Rajni (1995). 'Under Globalisation: Will Nation State Hold?', *Economic and Political Weekly*, 30(26): 1593–1603, 1 July.

Kumar, Ajay (nd). 'Poverty In Bihar: A Crisis of Governance'. Available at http://www.bihartimes.com/poverty/ajay_kumar.html, accessed on 19 November 2003.

Kurien, C.T. (1995). *Global Capitalism and the Indian Economy*. New Delhi: Orient Longman Ltd.

Lal, Deepak (2004). *In Praise of Empires—Globalization and the World Order*. New York: Palgrave Macmillan.

Lamberton, Donald (ed.) (2002). *Managing The Global—Globalisation, Employment and Quality of Life*. London and New York: I.B. Tauris Publishers.

LaPorte, Robert (2002). 'Governance—A Global Perspective' (paper presented at South Asia Regional Conference, Kathmandu (Nepal), 20 February. Available at http://www.fulbrightnepal.org. np/word%20 files/hhhcon, accessed on 31 December 2002.

Leys, Colin (2005). 'The Cynical State', in Leo Panitch and Colin Leys (eds), *Telling the Truth: Socialist Register 2006*. New Delhi: Leftword Books.

Lechner, Frank J. and John Boli (eds) (2004). *The Globalization Reader*. Malden, USA and Oxford, UK: Blackwell Publishing Ltd, second edn.

Mahapatra, Dhananjay (2006). 'A Daily-Wager Can't Lay Claim to Job: SC', *The Times of India* (Ahmedabad edn), 12 April.

Mahbub ul Haq Human Development Centre (MHDC) (2002). *Human Development In South Asia 2001*. Oxford: Oxford University Press. (This report was prepared by a research team of the centre and Director of the team was Sarfraz Quereshi).

Mander, Harsh and Mohammed Asif (2004). *Good Governance—Resource Book*. Bangalore: Books for Change.

Martinelli, Alberto (2003). 'Global Order or Divided World', *Current Sociology*, 51(2), March.

Mathur, Kuldeep (2003). 'Good Governance and Pursuit of Transparency in Administration—The Indian Efforts', in P. Sahni and U. Meduri (eds), *Governance for Development: Issues and Strategies*. New Delhi: Prentice—Hall of India Pvt Ltd.

Mazlish, Bruce (2005). 'The Global and the Local', *Current Sociology*, 53(1): 93–111.

McChesney, Robert W. (2001). 'The Political Economy of Global Communication', in R.W. McChesney, E.M. Wood and J.B. Foster (eds), *Capitalism and the Information Age: The Political Economy of the Global Communication Revolution*. Kharagpur: Cornerstone Publications.

McLuhan, Marshall (2002). *Understanding Media—The Extensions of Man*. London and New York: Routledge.

Mishra, Srijit (2006). 'Farmers' Suicides in Maharastra', *Economic and Political Weekly*, 41(16): 1538–45, 22 April.

Mohan kumar, S. and R.K. Sharma (2006). 'Analysis of Farmer Suicides in Kerala', *Economic and Political Weekly*, 41(16): 1553–58, 22 April.

Mohan, Kamlesh (1999). 'Implications of Globalisation and Cultural Invasion for India', in Raj Mohini Sethi (ed.), *Globalization, Culture and Women's Development*. Jaipur and New Delhi: Rawat Publishers.

Mohanty, Manoranjan (2004). 'Theorizing Indian Democracy', in R. Vora and S. Palshikar (eds), *Indian Democracy: Meaning and Practices*. New Delhi: Sage Publications.

Mooij, Jos (2001). 'Economic Reforms and Political Interpretations', Working Paper No. 41, Hyderabad: Centre for Economic and Social Studies.

——— (2003). 'Smart Governance? Politics in the Policy Process in Andhra Pradesh, India', Working Paper 228, London: Overseas Development Institute, October.

Mukherjee, Arpita (2003). *Audio-visual Policies and International Trade—The Case of India*, HWWA Report 227, Hamburg: Hamburg Institute of International Economics.

Mukherji, Rahul (2002). 'Administrative Reforms in India', Agenda for Improving Governance-8, New Delhi: Rajiv Gandhi Institute for Contemporary Studies, October.

Munshi, Surendra (2004). 'Concern for Good Governance in Comparative Perspective', in Surendra Munshi and B.P. Abraham (eds), *Good Governance, Democratic Societies And Globalisation*. New Delhi: Sage Publications.

Nathan, Dev (2006). 'Rules for Fair Trade', *Economic and Political Weekly*, 41(19): 1893–94.
Nayak, Pulin B. (2006). 'In the Shadow of Growth', *The Times of India* (Ahmedabad edn), 7 April.
Nayar, K.R. (2004). 'Kerala—Confusing New Approach to Public Services', *Economic and Political Weekly* 39(21), 22 May.
Ohmae, Kenichi (1995). *The End of the Nation State*. London: Harper Collins.
——— (2002). *The Borderless World—Power and Strategy in the Global Marketplace*. London: Profile Books Ltd. (Mckinsey & Co. 1990).
Olesen, Thomas (2005). 'Transnational Publics: New Spaces of Social Movement Activism and the Problem of Global Long-Sightedness', *Current Sociology*, 53(3): 419–40.
Omvedt, Gail (1993). 'Farmers Movement—Fighting for Liberalisation', *Economic and Political Weekly*, 28(50): 2708–10, 11 December.
——— (2005). 'Capitalism and Globalisation—Dalits and Adivasis', *Economic and Political Weekly*, 40 (47): 4881–85, 19 November.
Oommen, T.K. (2004). *Nation, Civil Society and Social Movements*. New Delhi: Sage Publications.
Palshikar, Suhas (2004). 'Whose Democracy Are We Talking About? Hegemony and Democracy in India', in R. Vora and S. Palshikar (eds) *Indian Democracy: Meaning and Practices*. New Delhi: Sage Publications.
Panini, M.N. (1995). 'The Social Logic of Liberalisation', *Sociological Bulletin*, 44(1).
Panitch, Leo (2000). 'The New Imperial State', *New Left Review* (Second series), No. 2, March–April.
Panitch, Leo and Colin Leys (eds) (2005). *Telling The Truth: Socialist Register 2006*. New Delhi: Leftword Books.
Panikkar, K.N. (2002). *An Agenda for Cultural Action and Other Essays*. New Delhi: Three Essays Press.
Parker, Barbara (2005). *Introduction to Globalisation & Business*, New Delhi: Response Books.
Pathak, Avijit (2006). *Modernity, Globalisation and Identity: Towards A Reflective Quest*. Delhi: Aakar Books.
Pathy, Jaganath (2000). 'The End of Millennium: Liberalisation and Accentuation of the Tribal Problematique', in P.G. Jogdand (ed.), *New Economic Policy & Dalits*. Jaipur and New Delhi: Rawat Publications.
Patnaik, Prabhat (1994). 'Notes on the Political Economy of Structural Adjustment', *Social Scientist*, 22 (9–12), September–December.
——— (2006). 'Diffusion of Development', *Economic and Political Weekly*, 41(18): 1766–72.
Patnaik, Prabhat, C.P. Chandrasekhar and Jayati Ghosh (2004). 'The Political Economy of the Economic Reform Strategy—The Role of the Indian Capitalist Class', in Manoranjan Mohanty (ed.), *Class, Caste, Gender*. New Delhi: Sage Publications.
Pedersen, Jorgen D. (2000). 'Explaining Economic Liberalisation in India—State and Society Perspectives', *World Development*, 28(2).
Peet, Richard (2003). *Unholy Trinity—The IMF, World Bank and WTO*. Kuala Lumpur, SIRD and London: Zed Books.
Pieterse, Jan N. (1996). 'Globalisation and Culture: Three Paradigms', *Economic and Political Weekly*, 31(23), 8 June.
Piven, Frances F. and Barbara Ehrenreich (2005). 'The Truth About Welfare Reform', in Leo Panitch and Colin Leys (eds), *Telling The Truth: Socialist Register 2006*. New Delhi: Leftword Books.
Prime Minister's Office (PMO) (2005a). 'Government of the United Progressive Alliance: Report To The People I', May 2004–February 2005. Available at http://www.pmindia.nic.in/report, accessed on 20 May 2005.

Prime Minister's Office (PMO) (2005b). 'Policy Thrust Areas for Ministries/Departments'. Available at http://www.pmindia.nic.in, accessed on 5 May 2005.

Quah, Jon S.T. (2003). 'Combating Corruption in India: Some Lessons from Asian Experiences', in Stephen Howes et al. (eds). *State-Level Reforms in India—Towards More Effective Government*. New Delhi: Macmillan India Ltd.

Rao, P. Narsimha and K.C. Suri (2006). 'Dimensions of Agrarian Distress in Andhra Pradesh', *Economic and Political Weekly*, 41(16): 1546–52, 22 April.

Rao, R.S. (1998). 'World Bank and Economy of Andhra Pradesh', *Economic and Political Weekly*, 30(25): 1499–1502, 20 June.

Rivero, Oswaldo de (2001). *The Myth of Development—The Non-Viable Economies of the 21st Century*. London and New York: Zed Books & other publishers.

Robertson, Roland (1995). 'Glocalisation: Time-space and homogeneity-heterogeneity', in Mike Featherstone et al. (eds), *Global Modernities*. London: Sage Publications.

Roudometof, Victor (2005). 'Transnationalism, Cosmopolitanism and Glocalization', *Current Sociology*, 53(1): 113–35.

Roy, Anupama (2006). 'Overseas Indian Citizen', *Economic and Political Weekly*, 41(15): 1421–24, 15 April.

Sachs, Jeffrey D. (nd). 'The Diseases of Globalisation'. Available at http://www.project-syndicate.org/commentary/sachs67/English, accessed on 23 July 2005.

Sezhiyan, Era (2005). 'Budget for Whom?', *Frontline*, 22(17), 26 August.

Salamon, Lester M. (ed.) (2002). *The Tools of Government—A Guide to the New Governance*. Oxford: Oxford University Press.

Sampat, Preeti (2003). *Economic Globalisation Today*. Bangalore: Books for Change.

Sharma, B.D. (1995). *Globalisation and the Tribal Encounter*. New Delhi: Har-Anand Publications.

Shourie, Arun (2004). *Governance and the Sclerosis That Has Set In*. New Delhi: Rupa & Co.

Sikdar, Soumyen (2004). *Contemporary Issues in Globalization—An Introduction to Theory and Practice in India*. New Delhi: Oxford University Press.

Singh, Kavaljit (2005).*Questioning Globalisation*. Delhi: Madhyam Books.

Singh, Yogendra (2002). *Culture Change in India—Identity & Globalisation*. Jaipur and New Delhi: Rawat Publications.

Sklair, Leslie (2004). 'Sociology of the Global System', in F.J. Lechner and J. Boli (eds), *The Globalization Reader*. Malden, USA and Oxford, UK: Blackwell Publishing Ltd.

Social Watch (2004). *Annual Report*. Published by The Third World Institute, Jackson, Montevideo, Uruguay. Available at http://www.socialwatch.org/en/InformeImpreso/pdfs/judgeandjury2004_english.pdf, accessed on 29 August 2004.

Soros, George (2004). *The Crisis of Global Capitalism*. New Delhi: Viva Books Pvt. Ltd.

Sridhar, V. (2006). 'Why do Farmers Commit Suicide? The Case of Andhra Pradesh', *Economic and Political Weekly*, 41(16): 1559–65, 22 April.

Steger, Manfred B. (2004). *Globalisation—The New Market Ideology*. Jaipur and New Delhi: Rawat Publications.

Steven, Peter (2005). *Global Media*. Jaipur: Rawat Publications.

Stiglitz, Joseph (2002). *Globalization and Its Discontents*. London: Penguin Books.

——— (2003). *The Roaring Nineties*. New York: W.W. Norton & Company.

Strange, S. (1996). *The Retreat of the State—The Diffusion of Power in the World Economy*. Cambridge/New York: Cambridge University Press.

Streeten, Paul (2001). *Globalisation—Threat or Opportunity*. H. Forlag, Copenhagen: Copenhagen Business School Press.

Suri, K.C. (2006). 'Political Economy of Agrarian Distress', *Economic and Political Weekly*, 41(16): 1523–29, 22 April.

Swamy, Dalip S. (1994). *The Political Economy of Industrialisation: From Self-reliance to Globalisation*. New Delhi: Sage Publications.

Tehranian, Majid (2002). 'Preface', in Donald Lamberton (ed.), *Managing the Global—Globalisation, Employment and Quality of Life*. London and New York: I.B. Taurin Publishers.

Times of India (*TOI*) (2006a). 'Right Formula: Ranbaxy, Mittal Lead Indian MNC Charge' (editorial), (Ahmedabad edn), 31 March.

——— (2006b). 'PSUs Dominate List of Forbes 2000', (Ahmedabad edn), 4 January.

——— (2006c). 'Hidden Hunger—Unicef Reports India has Highest Number of Malnourished Children' (editorial), (Ahmedabad edn), 5 May.

——— (2006d). 'Leg-up for Labour—Social Security Proposed for Unorganised Sector' (editorial) (Ahmedabad edn), 22 May.

——— (2006e). 'Something Special—After SEZs, Govt plans Manufacturing Investment Regions' (editorial), (Ahmedabad edn), 20 June.

Tomlinson, John (1991). *Cultural Imperialism*. Baltimore: John Hopkins University Press.

United Nations Development Programme (UNDP) (1999). *Human Development Report 1999*. New Delhi: Oxford University Press.

——— (2002). *Human Development Report 2002*. New Delhi: Oxford University Press.

United Nations (ECLAC) (2002). *Globalisation and Development*. Brasilia (Brazil): Economic Commission for Latin America and the Caribbean.

Upadhya, Carol (2004). 'A New Transnational Capitalist Class? Capital Flows, Business Networks and Entrepreneurs in the Indian Software Industry', *Economic and Political Weekly*, 39(48), 27 November.

Visvanathan, Shiv (2005). 'The New Consensus In India', *The Times of India*, (Ahmedabad edn), 5 October.

Wallerstein, Immanuel (2004). 'The Rise and Future Demise of the World Capitalist System', in F.J. Lechner and J. Boli (eds). *The Globalization Reader*. Malden, USA and Oxford, UK: Blackwell Publishing Ltd.

Wolf, Martin (2004). *Why Globalization Works*. New Haven: Yale University Press.

——— (2000). 'What is Globalisation' (prepared in April 2000 by the PREM Economic Policy Group and Development Economics Group). Available at http://www1.worldbank.org/economicpolicy/globalization/ag01.htm, accessed on 7 January 2006.

World Bank (1992). *Governance and Development*. Washington.

——— (1994). *Governance—The World Bank Experience*. Washington, D.C.

——— (2002). *Globalisation, Growth and Poverty—Building an Inclusive World Economy*. A World Bank Policy Research Report. New York: Co-publication of the World Bank, Washington and Oxford University Press.

Zuege, Alan, M. Konings, C. Leys, and L. Panitch (2006). 'The Globalisation Decade: An Introduction', in Leo Panitch, Colin Leys, Alan Zuege and Martijn Konings (eds), *The Globalisation Decade: A Critical Reader*, New Delhi: Aakar Books (first pubn by the Merlin Press, London, 2005).

2

Globalisation and Reorganisation of Institutional Space: Meaning for Democracy and People's Rights

Dolly Arora

Introduction

Globalisation is the key word in the political and economic analysis of contemporary developments. There are, however, multiple discourses on globalisation, which emerge from multiple vantage points and lead to a wide variety of interpretations, explanations and prescriptions. While there is little agreement on the extent, nature and effects of globalisation, one also finds that even its meaning is strongly contested by scholars and practitioners alike. The only point which is common across the wide range of perspectives and analysis pertaining to globalisation has been the admission of a major transformation in the relationship of time and space in defining social, economic and political processes (Harvey 1989; Giddens 1990; Held et al. 1999). This has given rise to an increased speed of interactions across the globe, evident in the growing bearing, which actions in one context have over those in other contexts.

This chapter, first, seeks to put forth five points of contention/propositions regarding globalisation. Second, it discusses the process of institutional reorganisation brought forth by the globalisation project. Third, it delves on the implications of globalisation for citizenship and democracy. Finally, some concluding observations are made.

Globalisation

Globalisation as an On-going Project

Globalisation is not an event that has just taken place, but a project, which is still on. Its nature, form, content, meanings and motives are continually recast as several competing or cooperating sub-projects are executed through multiple agencies in varied locations. These include multilateral agencies, state actors, corporate players as well as civil society institutions executing their respective plans, policies, strategies and every day decisions. It is not surprising that efforts to measure the extent and implications of globalisation lend different results when measured in terms of the new possibilities of global integration as compared to the actual integration, which has taken place. In that sense, one finds that technology and global policy initiatives, especially with respect to liberalisation, deregulation and free flow of goods have enhanced these possibilities immensely and one can say that an increasingly large range of activities related to economic, social and political life across the world are exposed to global influences (Held et al. 1999). However, when measured in terms of actual integration, there is a considerable difference across regions, activities and socio-economic groups. Besides, the character or influence of national and regional policy and the context of socio-economic and technological development are still the defining factors in shaping its reality—in the latter framework, globalisation is in fact considered to be a mere myth (Hirst and Thompson 1996). The explanations as well as the understanding of the impact of globalisation would essentially depend upon the approach to the issue of defining globalisation itself.

While it may be useful to measure globalisation in terms of the changing meaning of time and space for the actions and experiences of human beings and economic, social and political entities, it is important to realise that contextual variations—related to techno-economic structures as well as policy discourses and political institutions and processes do not permit the altered meaning of time and space to be uniform for all. Not all aspects of change in social, economic and political life can, therefore, be understood in terms of globalisation though its influence is quite significant in some dimensions and in relation to some people. Historical compulsions of space and time do leave many trapped in different patterns of evolution, which defy all signs of globalisation and which may not be altered through other intervening processes. Such contexts should also be understood to delineate the real nature and patterns of globalisation processes across the globe.

Economic Globalisation as the Dominant Project

The most powerful of the ongoing projects on globalisation, which has dominated the world so far takes shape under the influence of multilateral agencies like World Bank, IMF and WTO, and the transnational corporations working in close alliance with the political elites of the more powerful of the nation states. World Bank defines globalisation as freedom/ability of individuals and firms to initiate voluntary economic transactions with residents of other countries and measures it in terms of the share of world trade, capital movement, movement of people and spread of knowledge/technology related to production/management techniques (World Bank 2000). The IMF, while focusing on economic globalisation, describes it as 'a historical process, the result of human innovation and technological process', and underlines the need for increasing integration of economies around the world, particularly through trade and financial flows (IMF Staff 2002). Globalisation is advocated by these institutions as a win-win game from which everyone can benefit provided that the 'right kind' of policy environment is created.[1] WTO too seeks to redefine the framework of rules to shape the world order in the context of globalisation through multiple rounds of negotiations, wherein similar forces that dominate the World Bank and IMF exercise direct or indirect influence (Arora 2002a). This project to further economic globalisation, it emerges, has the interest of capital as its primary concern and makes use of both structural and discursive spaces to further it. It is noteworthy that the globalisation processes along these lines have gained strength from and contributed further to the growing concentration of economic power in the world. According to the *Human Development Report*, 2000, the wealth of the world's 200 billionaires exceeds the combined income of 582 million people in all least developed countries (UNDP 2000). The economic power of many transnational corporations in fact far exceeds that of the national economies of several states. The 2004 Report of United Nations Conference on Trade and Development (UNCTAD) reflects on the growing role of FDI and TNC activity in the global economy. The degree of transnationalisation is increasing for both TNCs and the countries in which they operate.[2] It is noteworthy that International production is carried out by over 900,000 foreign affiliates of 61,000 TNCs worldwide. These affiliates account for an estimated one-tenth of world GDP and one-third of world exports and their shares are increasing. It is noteworthy that less than 0.2 per cent of the total number of TNCs, i.e., the top 100 of them account for 14 per cent of the sales of foreign affiliates world-wide, 12 per cent of their assets and 13 per cent of their employment in 2002, compared with 27 per cent, 21 per cent and 21 per cent respectively in 1990 (UNCTAD 2004). Conditions for an increase in the transnationalisation of economic activity are sought to be accomplished through multilateral agencies as well as the state policy processes. In fact, multilateralism has emerged as a powerful tool for furthering the globalisation of capital. Worldwide there were 244 changes in laws and regulations affecting FDI, 220 of them in the direction of increased liberalisation. Bilateral investment treaties, bilateral free trade agreements and regional free trade agreements have been on the rise (UNCTAD 2004). Significantly, even the UN has provided an increasing legitimacy and space to corporations through the UN Global Compact and enabled them to actively shape global policies.[3]

As mentioned earlier, this project of economic globalisation has involved a complex range of processes. On-going technological developments, especially those related to information technology, growing complexity of economic structures and processes, and increasing concentration of economic power, have both induced and facilitated its evolution towards present manifestations. The keenness of concerned interests to execute this project with minimum resistance created imperatives for a major reorganisation and rearticulation of institutional space, whereby the direction and content of globalisation processes could appear inevitable, unidirectional and lacking a design even when in effect these were influenced in subtle ways through policy recommendations and conditionalities or advice on grounds such as promoting good governance, furthering growth and stabilisation of economies, addressing poverty or even simply promoting globalisation, which was to take care of all other needs or concerns.

Globalisation Processes are Exclusionary and Marginalising

Globalisation does not have an inherent integrationist thrust, nor does it create a framework for an inclusive pattern of development. Many aspects of the process of globalisation have created direct as well as indirect victims, who may not sustain themselves long enough to assess its claims of long-term benefits (Khor 2001). There are some beneficiaries in all countries, which seek to embrace its logic, but the victims far outnumber them everywhere (Mittelman 2000). This has been particularly true of economic globalisation which has led to large scale unemployment and overburdening of retained employees even at the cost of safety and security in many countries, only to serve the interests of big capital and its owners who manage to lobby and obtain policies favourable to themselves. The IMF brief issued on April 12 2000 and altered in January 2002 admits that poverty and inequality across the world have increased and that periodic crisis are an inevitable consequence of globalisation (IMF 2002). A similar admission has been made by the World Bank also (World Bank 2000a). However, globalisation continues to be seen by them as crucial for growth and pro-poor policies in well-targeted social expenditures considered capable of reducing poverty. The UN advocates millennium development goals but considers globalisation as a key goal that needs to be pursued. In effect, the *race to the bottom* has itself put pressure on the poor nations to compromise on social security, labour rights, environmental and health safety issues. These countries compete for capital in the face of globalisation pressures while the hard-won rights of people are readily sacrificed. At the same time, the opportunities for employment in the industrialised countries are adversely affected as jobs shift to the more competitive labour markets in the South. The presumed dispensability of a large section of world population in both rich and poor countries, while goals of globalisation are pursued, turns it into a project for exclusion and marginalisation rather than integration and inclusion as claimed by its proponents (Arora 1998; 2000b; 2002c).

Alternative Globalisation Projects are Significant Too

The ongoing processes of globalisation do not present a one-dimensional road that rips off all possibilities of alternative projects. A growing number of people feel that if only 'globalisation from below' substituted 'globalisation from above', the benefits to common people would be tremendous. These perspectives seek to make use of possibilities to alter the very nature of globalisation which has actually unfolded. The use of information technology to create global networks of civil society groups is seen as capable of moving in this direction. It is argued that 'globalisation from above' must meet an assertive and effective 'globalisation from below', strengthening global solidarity through networking and new communicative and organisational modes of linking local, national, regional and global level strategies for reform. Labour, social movements and state are seen as the countervailing forces if they can retreat from the narrow location of traditional nationalism (Falk 1999). Need for unifying strategies by resistance and emancipatory movements to confront global capitalisation is underlined. New forms of universalism must flow from 'bottom' upward, i.e., from people to their organisations, not the other way around and they should not take the form of homogenising imperialism, according to this perspective (Gills 2000).

At the same time, there is a growing movement for localisation to foster and build sustainable local communities to help rebuild local economies everywhere on a permanent and inclusive basis. It involves a better thy neighbour supportive internationalism where flow of ideas, technologies, information, culture, money and goods has, as its end goals, the protection and rebuilding of local economies worldwide. Its emphasis is not on competition for the cheapest but cooperation for the best (Hines 2000). On the other hand, there are supporters of the democratic globalisation movement, who aspire for an institutional system of global democracy, which would expand democracy to a system of global governance, bypassing national states and corporate oligopolies to give world citizens a say in global activities (Held 1995; Archibugi et al. 1998). Advocacy of alternative governance mechanisms and democratisation of existing institutions at the international level, including the World Bank, IMF and UN system, is considered important in this framework. Still others look towards states to evolve appropriate policy responses for putting the changing global marketplace in order (Boyer and Drache 1996).

Alternatives to Globalisation are a Survival Strategy for Many

That globalisation is an all encompassing phenomenon, which cannot be escaped and which leaves no alternatives is far from the evidence which is available. Alternatives to globalisation-led development are not only possible; these appear to be the only promise for millions whose life experiences defy the integration claims of its discourse. There is an increasing realisation among people everywhere that exclusion and victimisation processes leave little hope for them except to turn to locally-centred and locally-driven patterns of assuring collective fulfillment and humane existence. It is this striving towards alternatives to globalisation which is gaining ground in numerous local contexts and which is likely to pose a major challenge to those eager to move further towards the present pattern of globalisation.

Globalisation Project: Institutional Reorganisation

Since globalisation is neither inevitable or invincible, nor does it take uniform manifestations, supporters of various globalisation projects have attempted to make use of discursive as well as structural instruments to move towards their specific agendas. In the process they confront each other, as also those various aspects of structural reality, which pose a challenge to their design. What emerges is not a simple straightforward economic globalisation project that may have a bearing for other social, cultural, political dimensions of life or vice versa but a constant struggle to move in accordance with their respective visions of globalisation or even anti-globalisation. As mentioned earlier, the dominant globalisation project of our times seeks not only to privilege the global over the local, but also the interests of capital over people's needs. The imperatives of this model of globalisation have given rise to a concern for reorganisation of institutional space in order to smoothen its journey towards a neoliberal pattern of reforms and alter, to the extent necessary and possible, the very framework of governance in favour of the interests of capital. This is also aimed at weakening the possibilities of effective challenge and resistance to globalisation processes at the multiple points of its operation. Since competing projects which make use of increasing integration possibilities have been on, competing exercises towards reorganisation of institutional space have also been evident, though these have yet to acquire as much hold over the actual developments as the former. This section seeks to discuss the nature of the dominant globalisation project and the pattern of reorganisation of institutional space, which has been under way to facilitate its execution with particular reference to the Third World countries.

Discursive space has undoubtedly been created for the reorganisation of institutional arrangements to influence the exercise of power in desired directions by presenting globalisation as a technology-driven process, which has already arrived and is likely to displace the economies and societies unless they adjust their institutional framework appropriately and become integrated with the global economy. This has been the primary thrust of the Washington Consensus,[4] evident in the analysis and policy prescriptions emanating from organisations like the WB, the IMF, the WTO and, to a considerable extent, even the UN. Most First World countries felt such a need as they began to apprehend capital *flight* following new technological possibilities unless such changes were introduced. In case of most Third World countries as well as the erstwhile socialist economies, however, it was the pressure of aid conditionalities offered through the structural adjustment and reforms programme which they embraced following their indebtedness that speeded up the processes of redefining institutional relations and roles.

As institutional jurisdictions are redefined, power spaces are effectively reconstituted and rights and obligations assigned new meanings with far-reaching implications for the respective claims of different interest configurations. There has been a significant shift in the articulation of the position and role of state, civil society and market institutions in relation to each other as well as internally, while a significant increase in the role of institutions located outside the jurisdictions of state sovereignty has also become evident. It is important to look into the nature and likely effects of these developments for the very organisation of social, political and economic life, as also, the value-shifts which mark it.

Four significant shifts are noteworthy in the emerging scenario of institutional relations. These are evident in the privileging of (*a*) supra-state/global governance institutions on an increasing range of policy issues; (*b*) private sector operations and market institutions; (*c*) the subnational and local state itself; and (*d*) the civil society institutions, particularly, non-governmental organisations. Developments in these respects both reinforced and contradicted each other. While some aspects of these have been widely shared by many countries, others acquired their precise meaning in the specific space-time contexts. These have had serious implications for the state of public domain and citizens' rights. It is relevant, therefore, to examine the nature of these developments, how these have altered the organisation of institutional power and the meaning of public domain, and their bearing on the state of people and their capacity to shape governance and public domain.[5]

Supra-state/Global Governance Institutions

In most Third World countries, following the adoption of SAP-driven globalisation agenda, the power of state to shape the economy and society has been either considerably fractured or redefined. There is also a growing pressure to engage in the search for global governance mechanisms/solutions to deal with specific policy concerns such as environmental problems, social development, global crime, etc. through international/intergovernmental fora. The ability of states to address the growing complexity of problems is challenged as much as their capacity to make rational policy choices by themselves. At the same time, however, the state is expected to take active interest in creating conditions through intervention for the growth of markets. Strengthening public agencies, legal systems, financial institutions, and education and health systems are considered significant for the success of market economies. Improving state capacity for creating conditions for the growth of markets by laying down clear property rights and supportive conditions for their implementation is considered necessary (World Bank 1997). State capacity is also considered crucial for binding economies and markets of specific regions to the complex framework of trade negotiations at the level of WTO and for ensuring debt repayments—the total external debt of low-income countries is more than $520 billion and they pay $100 million in debt service everyday.[6]

States, therefore, are expected to remain significant but their role is required to change with the expectations of the aid-providing multilateral agencies and the interests which dominate them. They are expected to follow the prescriptions offered on 'good governance', which is defined essentially in terms of the conditions which are conducive to the promotion of economic globalisation. Policy and programme consultancies by agencies like WB, UNDP and some donor agencies have grown manifold on grounds of their commitment to promote good governance, though, often, these prescriptions are found to lack sensitivity to the political and social contexts of specific nations. Other influential mechanisms for collective shaping of policy environment and economic management have been the regional alliances like NAFTA, G7, ASEAN, OECD, etc. and organisations like the Bank for International settlements (BIS), the International Organisation of Securities Commission, etc. Non-state agencies like the International Securities Market Association and the International Accounting Standards Committee have developed their own rules to govern their respective spheres, often creating pressure on states to harmonise the legal frameworks.

Private Sector and Market Institutions

Reorganisation of institutional jurisdictions, which is under way, is intended to create space for private enterprises on the one hand and reorient the state towards market institutions on the other. The boundary between public and private sector is dwindling in some significant respects as a consequence. It is noteworthy that commitment to neoliberal reforms supposedly implies a commitment to market orientation of the economy, and incorporates a presumed obligation of the state to push policy towards deregulation, privatisation, selective state withdrawal and expenditure cuts, and ultimately integration with the global economy. States are expected to concentrate on core competencies and leave the rest to the private sector. While the economy is expected to be liberated from political directions and interferences, the state is refrained from taking up a competing or restrictive role vis-à-vis private enterprise (World Bank 1996). States have also sought to off-load judicial responsibilities to informal mechanisms like Alternative Dispute Resolution mechanisms so that capital does not feel inhibited by the delays in delivery of justice which characterised the formal judicial institutions (Arora 1999). Public interest is conveniently redefined in terms of the growth of private sector, with special affinity towards the big and foreign capital.

A close look at the pattern of state functioning in the process of carrying out globalisation-driven reforms in most Third World countries clearly suggests that the primary interest of their proponents involves procuring more space for the dominant market players by using state apparatus itself to selectively orient the economy in the direction of their interests. Its legitimate hold over policy domain makes it relevant for altering the very framework of market operations as well as the precise direction in which markets would operate. Budgets continue to be an extremely powerful instrument through which the state still provides numerous kinds of direct or indirect support to the growth and profitability of market economies. While there is a dismantling of the existing regulatory regime, new institutions for market governance and new regulatory agencies have also been created—their terms of existence and operation have indeed been along the lines of neoliberal agenda. Space for genuine politics and democratic interventions, however, is significantly contained through other economic and political instruments wherever it clashes with the power of the big private enterprise. The politics of 'small' is no longer considered to be either 'rational' or in 'public interest'. To integrate with the global is offered as the new mantra for development in this discourse.

To the extent state continues to be of interest, and is expected to support the growth of markets, introduction of market mechanism in state sector itself is considered desirable. Several states have resorted to the policy of outsourcing and contracting out of services, in many cases without any serious analysis of the long-term costs involved. The introduction or raising of user charges and reduction of subsidies in order to transfer costs of service to the consumer are other trends evident in the public sector. Many public services, including those in the sphere of health, education and public distribution system have seen a change of orientation and objectives. The emphasis on cost recovery is justified in terms of prospects of improved service quality. Users are expected to value efficiency far more than the lower cost of its provision.

Advocacy of Sub-national and Local Institutions

State power has been challenged and altered from within also, by state and local governments. Multilateral organisations have increasingly established a direct relationship with state/provincial governments and have shaped policy developments and politico-economic activities at their level where much of the effective decision-making and implementation powers are vested. Especially since the shift in the strategy towards reforms advocacy, which became evident in the World Bank's Country Economic Memorandum of 1996, interest in sub-national governments as vehicles to carry out reforms and promote a climate for globalisation has increased.

Direct loan negotiations with sub-national governments are preferred where possible, offering them assistance to execute reforms. This has increased internal competition among the sub-national governments to rush towards recommended directions. Decentralisation is also expected to ensure effective service delivery. The dominant logic guiding this, however, remains the logic of capital and narrow economic efficiency. This is expected to help the growth of market institutions.

Despite international and national political discourse overplaying their interest in the value of the 'local' and underlining the significance of 'empowerment', there is, however, very little by way of actual empowerment happening on the ground. The need for creating local institutions is admitted but there is a note of caution, which informs action. World Development Report 1997, expressed the apprehension that local power may pose problems for macroeconomic stability and also come in the way of the 'reforms' process. It is not surprising that structures created to pursue the objectives are either too dependent or too superficial to make any substantive effect. While much decision-making power is passing out of control of even the Central government, to expect any real empowerment from the setting up of local institutions is to disregard the complexity of the situation.

Strengthening of Civil Society Institutions

Civil society is becoming an arena of interest to multilateral agencies not only because of its perceived potential to encourage democratic processes and good governance practices, but more importantly, to further the ends of development in the context of globalisation and state withdrawal. Social capital has moved to the centre-stage in the Social Fund Programmes of the World Bank. Defined in terms of public goods networks, culture, local knowledges, etc., social capital is seen to foster reciprocity, facilitate information flows for mutual benefit and trust and, therefore, success of development programmes. State is advised to help build social capital as well as to make use of the existing stocks.

Non-governmental organisations are provided enormous funds to promote the goals of development. Their existence is considered crucial to improve governance which is no longer seen as the task of the state alone. States are expected to engage them in taking over many welfare responsibilities and developmental functions, which the former may withdraw from. Increased participation of stakeholders in the arenas where market forces are not likely to take much interest has been considered desirable. Partnership between state and civil society organisations is also encouraged and expected to contribute towards efficiency. Many development programmes of the state are also required to be executed by the voluntary sector. In many cases, there is an attempt to provide state funding too. Increasingly, however, external funding of NGOs is on the rise. Many of them have their own agenda and interest to look after, though, others may be able to advocate public interest in an effective manner.

There are other elements of civil society which derive strength from their struggle among the people and which do not submit to the basic framework of neoliberal reforms. Many of them are actively struggling against globalisation. Little interest is shown towards strengthening these or supporting their position. Their perspectives and viewpoints remain unattended to or are even condemned for their failure to appreciate the value of growth-oriented reforms which have been initiated under the structural adjustment programme. These include strong people's movements enveloping concerns like environment, women, civil rights, right to information, human rights, Dalits, tribals etc. It is also noteworthy in this context that even as there has been an increasing interest in creating new institutions to enhance the possibilities of citizen participation, for instance by supporting the growth of the NGO sector, space available to traditional organisations like trade unions has been significantly contained. There is clearly a lack of interest in responding to people's struggles, but a need to adopt symbolic gestures of support to enlist sensitivity towards them despite a growing disinterest in taking up their genuine cause. At the global level too, organisations of business interests like the World Economic Forum, International Chambers of Commerce, etc., have assumed a significant role in the shaping of public policy. While an alternative World Social Forum has also come to be organised, its capacity to shape policy is far from being of comparable magnitude.

Implications for Citizenship and Democracy

The preceding discussion brings home the point that the reorganisation of institutional framework for power has been aimed at redefining the position and role of state, civil society and market institutions in relation to each other as well as internally. It has also created space for an active role of institutions located outside the jurisdictions of state sovereignty. In a large measure, it reflects that influence. It is important to mention that not only the actual alterations in institutional relations but also the discourse, which accompanied these steps, is significant in as much as it reflects the imperatives and directions which these alterations are aimed at.

Although there is little ground to doubt that much of what is emerging from the reorganisation is in line with the imperatives of globalisation which shape the discourse of multilateral agencies, it is important to reiterate that globalisation continues to be a project that is being continually recast and there are multiple agencies, competing or cooperating, which are engaged in shaping it. Even the impact of their respective plans, strategies, actions and inactions are not always in accordance with their expectations. Yet, so far the most powerful actors in the context of the Third World countries have been the multilateral agencies and transnational corporations, which have been actively engaged in and often dominating the policy discourse and processes in these agencies.

States, Democracy and Policy Autonomy

The most important institution to be adversely affected in terms of power by the imperatives of globalisation has undoubtedly been the state. States have faced a loss of power to the suprastate institutions, to civil society institutions, to market institutions and to the local institutions within. Some of this loss has been self-imposed, especially in the industrialised part of the world. This is because of a realisation of its need on the part of states themselves, either on account of the growing power of capital to move in and out at great speed or because of the challenges posed by technological developments, which defy territorial jurisdictions. In the Third world countries, however, this has considerably been accepted under pressure of aid conditionalities.

It is not without reason that while the rising power of global capital has been read by some to carry enough threats to the very existence of nation states and as emergence of a de-territorialised borderless world, other analysts have found the state well in its place, although, with somewhat altered roles and responsibilities. Confronted with the increasing structural power of capital concentrated in a small number of TNCs, states have felt the pressure to compete with other states to attract capital and offer favourable terms for its operation. They have given up significant rights to interfere and protect the welfare needs of their workers in particular and citizens in general, only to avert the possibilities of capital flight. Globalisation processes have, therefore, not contributed to the disappearance of the state but the emergence of 'competition state', eager to appease capital at the cost of other domestic constituencies (Cerny 1997). States have adjusted in accordance with the expectations of global capital and multilateral agencies.

The quest for enhancing the state's institutional capacity to ensure the implementation of policy in line with the needs of capital as well as the recommendations of multilateral agencies and other global governance mechanisms has generated contradictory imperatives. For state capacity is at once weakened on account of lack of policy autonomy or sovereign rights of states to opt for a different set of policies which this implies. This has resulted in a near closure of the public's right to debate on the policies of the state, implying a devaluation of the political process, and a virtual denial of scope for public accountability. A clear subordination of the state to the imperatives of global and international power dynamics has accompanied a significant containment of space available to the domestically defined and democratically shaped politics at the instance of politics controlled from outside in alliance with some vested interests at home. State power has thus been redefined in ways which strengthen its alliance with capital while weakening its relationship with people, as it increases its subordination to inter-governmental as well as extra-governmental institutions.

Redefinition of Social Concerns

The reorientation of public sector to incorporate market mechanism in its activities, however, has not meant a simple step towards improved institutional performance. It has, in effect, implied a transformation of goals, which no longer reflect any commitment to a broader socio-political perspective, as would cover the values of equity and social justice. These goals have been displaced by a narrow perspective, which gives priority to organisational efficiency and profitability. This kind of substitution is likely to dilute the very objectives of having these tasks in the public sector.

Institutional reorganisation in favour of market institutions has delegitimated the relevance of social concerns in defining economic activities. On the contrary, there is a growing inclination towards marketisation of social issues too. Social concerns are not expected to interfere with the economic processes of state or market but market principles are supposed to become the defining rule of social issues. Under this logic, many social problems are likely to be dismissed as individual problems requiring individual solutions. Unemployment, for instance, becomes a problem of acquiring skills; insecurity in jobs, a matter of skill upgradation; health and education, matters of consciousness raising; thereby delinking the structural content of problems from anything but market opportunities.

Markets are increasingly expected to solve social problems too. The fact, however, remains that they do so only at the cost of redefining the issues themselves. Privatisation of social sectors, or even other essential services, is likely to alter the very essence of service and not simply imply a change in the source of provisioning. The marketisation of social sectors like health and education, for instance, are likely to not only redefine rights in terms of purchasing power but also service in terms of commercial interest. The very content of education or health will be affected adversely as a consequence of both these problems. These aspects of reorganisation are not assessed in the light of wider social needs and prevailing socio-economic contexts. This will have wider implications for the very legitimacy of state institutions which fail to respond to social needs and expectations.

Decentralisation and devolution of power to sub-national and local governments can go a long way towards strengthening the capacity of systems to address social concerns. However, in the absence of real policy jurisdictions and resources for their implementation, these remain only symbolic and ineffective initiatives for improving the possibilities of responsive and accountable governance. There is a difficulty with the approach towards conceptualisation of the local too. Local social conflicts and power relations are overlooked and the 'local' is perceived as a homogenous entity, quite isolated from the broader political and economic context. The forces of change and resistance in the local context are not comprehended in their complexity as they relate to each other and affect the developments in the local as well as wider political economy context.

Civil society institutions can certainly prove to be effective mechanisms of citizen empowerment as well as regulators of state and market players. However, for this to happen, it is important to ensure both this autonomy and participative content. The accent on civil society institutions in the globalisation and reforms discourse does not, however, provide any significant support to those elements in society which derive strength from their struggle among people. Mere reduction of civil society to NGOs, with little or no regard for movements for people's rights which may pose a challenge to all manner of top-down reforms cannot be seen very positively. The latter are either bypassed or sought to be co-opted, or else they are also faced with a repressive state. It is not possible to overlook their significance, for despite such adverse conditions of operation, they remain in struggle and strive to institute alternative patterns of reforms which may be able to take care of people's real needs and concerns rather than simply ensure the survival and growth of market institutions, in complete disregard to their elitist character and anti-people bias.

Changing Terms of Political Discourse: Privileging Consumers Over Citizens

The reorganisation of institutional space which has been under way indicates and further instigates a weakening of the borderline between the national and global, public and private, citizen and consumer. There is much more ambiguity in the defining features of these. One finds issues changing places and affecting the very nature and role of the state as well as its relationship to market institutions, private sector, local institutions, and civil society and the citizens. The ultimate defining variable emerges to be the imperatives of globalisation.

In significant respects, neoliberal reforms have implied giving away the rights vested in the domain of citizenship to dominant market forces. These have virtually contained the public space available for negotiating the 'political' itself. States have arbitrarily disowned responsibility towards meeting the basic needs of citizens. Efforts towards legitimation of these changes, of course, continue to be made through careful exercises aimed at displacing the discourse of basic rights and instituting the discourse of efficiency and profitability, often used interchangeably. State responsibility is no longer the issue for discussion. Scope for the growth of private is the primary concern. There is thus, a complete change in the terms of political discourse at the instance of the globalisation logic.

The empowerment discourse is central to the exercises meant to redraw the line between public and private. The public cannot be confined within the control of state. Citizens have a right over it and, therefore, there is an accent on participation of the concerned public in policy making and implementation processes. They also have a right to directly take care of their affairs in many contexts. These exercises are apparently aimed at broadening the rights of the public by taking them away from the state. Yet, in effect, these are contributing to a growing hiatus between the wider public and the small elite, which, as individuals or as a group, can afford the possible efforts involved in realising the rights made available to them as constituents of the public.

Despite the fact that empowerment discourse has been extensively used to redraw the line between the tasks appropriate for public and private sector institutions or state and civil society institutions respectively, the real imperatives for such reorganisation come from the concerns for creating room for globalisation of economy. Citizenship rights have been the real casualty of such processes meant to serve the ends of globalisation, and its attendant doctrine of strengthening market institutions and non-governmental sectors to the extent they support the objectives of the dominant globalisation project. This has happened on account of growing concentration of economic power, widening disparities in societies and a virtual abandonment of state commitment on questions of equity and welfare. This has also been accomplished through a systematic displacement of the citizen and the institution of the consumer in the rights discourse. Consumer rights are expected to expand beyond the confines of state and touch the horizon of global citizenship. Global markets, global standards, global range and global reach are expected to liberate the citizen-consumer from the limits of state boundaries.

Increasing the range of consumer choices is the primary meaning of rights in the globalisation discourse. Protection of consumer rights may be an important addition to the rights of citizens. However, in as much as these are meant to substitute the rights of citizens, there is a problem involved.

The privileging of 'consumer' over the 'citizen' in matter of rights has far-reaching implications for principles of democracy. While equal rights of all citizens give way to the rights of those who can afford the privilege of becoming consumers, the former are doubly victimised—once for their inability to become consumers, and a second time, for their failure to enjoy rights because of being non-consumers. The concerns of the non-consuming public are thereby dismissed in the name of consumer rights. This is really problematic. For, in effect, denial of right to consume, for instance, by increasing user charges to offer more efficient service, may itself be a serious infringement and cannot be handled through the framework of consumer rights. These exercises at redefining the framework of rights pose a serious challenge to the democratic principles and the rights of people. These are likely to have a bearing on the possibilities of rights struggles, which may be necessitated on account of the negative fall-outs of globalisation processes in course of time. Survival, sustainability, equity, democracy and social justice stand to lose out to consumer rights in case of a conflict in this discourse.

Concluding Remarks

If concerns of capital for global expansion have provided imperatives for seeking a redefinition of the nature, role and relationship between state, market and civil society institutions, and if this raises questions about the prospects of democratic institutions and processes in the coming days, this is not without reasons. The shrinking of public domain, the creation of global networks and agencies for providing mechanisms for global governance, the selective freezing of state jurisdictions, the hijacking of policy processes by institutions and agencies which lack accountability to the people, the dismissal of people's aspirations as irrelevant for making policy choices and rejection of pro-people policies as populist, the privileging of consumer over citizen and dismissal of social issues as individual problems—all these are part of the same striving to create spaces for the global expansion of capital. This globalisation project does not further global integration on equal terms but within the framework of hierarchical, inegalitarian and undemocratic structures, protecting and reproducing power asymmetries across the globe, between and within nation states.

It is such developments which raise questions about the need to challenge and resist such endeavours towards globalisation. There have no doubt been serious problems with existing institutions and their performance when evaluated from the perspective of people. There has definitely been a need to rethink the manner in which power spaces were organised and institutional relations evolved over the years of capitalist expansion, with or without state support and a formal commitment to rights. The processes which created alienation in societies, made democratic aspirations difficult to take shape, and turned struggle for rights extremely hard, certainly call for a reorganisation of institutional relations. But, institutional reorganisation under the imperatives of global capital has only worsened the existing scenario. It amounts to an increasing closure of public domain, denial of democratic spaces and delegitimation of people's rights. Any concern for people's rights and democratic principles necessitates striving towards alternatives wherein people can experience a collective existence and put an end to exploitative social and economic relations. The struggles are unlikely to be easy, especially on account of the powerful presence of visions of globalisation as an integration mechanism, which many people have embraced. Yet, for those who cannot be of much use in carrying forward the aspirations and dreams of global power elites and who do not accept their victimisation as destiny, collective struggles offer the only site for redefining the possibilities. Whether these can be launched on a global scale or remain confined to the local contexts, they remain significant channels of hope in this rapidly globalising, yet not integrating world.

Notes

1. It is noteworthy that these institutions are dominated by the developed nations. At the IMF and World Bank, the prime mechanism of control being the size of the countries' capital subscriptions, 48 per cent of the voting power lies with the G-8 countries alone. In the IMF, US alone is entitled to 17 per cent of the votes and on that ground, a veto power on the decisions it dislikes. These countries operate in close alliance with the corporate interests in their respective countries. Suggestions for reforming these institutions have come from both critics and supporters of globalisation (Stiglitz 2002; Nayyar 2002).
2. In its annual World Investment Report, UNCTAD in collaboration with Erasmus University (Rotterdam) compiles key data on TNCs. The Report focuses on the largest TNCs from developed, developing and Central and Eastern European countries, analyzing recent trends in their internationalisation strategies. The UNCTAD/ERASMUS database includes data about these companies' foreign assets, total assets, foreign sales, total sales, and foreign and total employment. Based on the key variables, a Transnationality Index (TNI) is calculated.
3. The only condition for corporates to join Global Compact is to agree to follow 10 principles of human rights, labour rights, environment and anti-corruption principles, regardless of their actual performance on these counts. This, however, provides them an easy forum to shape the framework of global governance and the pattern of globalisation to be aimed at.
4. An overview of the way in which Washington Consensus evolved and later the discourse on the need to go beyond its framework is provided by Williamson (2000).
5. For a discussion on how these developments have taken shape in the Indian context, see Arora (2002b).
6. A very strong campaign for seeking debt relief for the poor countries has been going on for some years now. Jubilee 2000 is one of the chief campaigners on the issue. Although, some initiatives have been taken at the international level to provide relief to the highly indebted poor countries, debt recovery continues to remain an important concern with lending institutions and governments (Jubilee Debt Campaign).

References

Archibugi, Daniele, David Held and Martin Kohler (eds) (1998). *Re-imagining Political Community: Studies in Cosmopolitan Democracy*. Stanford: Stanford University Press.

Arora, Dolly (1998). 'Reforms and Reality: Emerging Contradictions', in Alternative Survey Group, *Seven Years of Structural Adjustment 1991–98*. New Delhi: Lokayan, Rainbow and Azadi Bachao.

——— (1999). 'Judicial Reforms and Market Institutions: The Emerging Scenario', *Indian Journal of Public Administration*, July–September.

——— (2000a). 'Public Management Reforms', *Administrative Change*, 28(1), January.

——— (2000b). 'The Privatisation of Governance', in Alternative Survey Group, *Alternative Economic Survey—Two Years of Market Fundamentalism*. New Delhi: Lokayan and Rainbow.

——— (2002a). 'WTO Regime, State Processes and People's Rights', in Surjit Singh, D.N. Reddy and Dolly Arora (eds), *Political Economy of WTO Regime: Some Aspects of Globalisation and Governance*. New Delhi: Rainbow.

——— (2002b). 'Reorganisation of Institutional Space: States, Market and Public Domain', *Man and Development*, 24(4), December.

——— (2002c). 'Globalisation, Governance and Rights Struggles', *Mainstream*, 40(19), 27 April.

Boyer, Robert and Daniel Drache (eds) (1996). *States Against Markets—The Limits of Globalization*. London: Routledge, Kegan Paul.

Cerny, Philip G. (1997). 'Paradoxes of the Competition State: The Dynamics of Political Globalisation', *Government and Opposition*, 32(2), Spring.

Falk, Richard (1999). *Predatory Globalization*. Cambridge, UK: Polity Press.

Giddens, Anthony (1990). *The Consequences of Modernity*. Stanford: Stanford University Press.

Gills, Barry K. (ed.) (2000). *Globalization and the Politics of Resistance*. Houndmills: Macmillan Press.

Harvey, David (1989). *The Condition of Postmodernity*. Oxford, UK: Blackwell.

Held, David (1995). *Democracy and the Global Order: From the Modern State to Cosmopolitan Governance*. Cambridge: Polity Press.

Held, David, A. McGrew, D. Goldblatt and J. Perraton (1999). *Global Transformations—Politics, Economics and Culture*. Cambridge: Polity Press.

Hines, Colin (2000). *Localisation: A Global Manifesto*. London: Earthscan.

Hirst, Paul Q. and Grahame Thompson (1996). *Globalization in Question: The International Economy and the Possibilities of Governance*. Cambridge: Blackwell.

IMF Staff (2002). 'Globalization: Threat or Opportunity?'. (First posted in April 2000, corrected in January 2002). Available at www.imf.org/external/np/exr/ib/2000/041200.htm, accessed on 7 January 2006.

Jubilee Debt Campaign: Facts and Figures, www.jubileedebtcampaign.org.uk.

Khor, Martin (2001). *Rethinking Globalization: Critical Issues and Policy Choices*. London: Zed Books.

Mittelman, James H. (2000). *The Globalization Syndrome: Transformation and Resistance*. New Jersey: Princeton University Press.

Nayyar, Deepak (2002). *Governing Globalisation: Issues and Institutions*. New Delhi: Oxford University Press.

Stiglitz, Joseph E. (2002). *Globalization and its Discontents*. London: Penguin Books.

United Nations Development Programme (UNDP) (2000). *Human Development Report*. New Delhi: Oxford University Press.

United Nations Conference on Trade and Development (UNCTAD) (2004). *World Investment Report 2004: The Shift Towards Services. New Delhi:* Academic Foundation.

Williamson, John (2000). 'What Should the World Bank Think about the Washington Consensus', *The World Bank Research Observer,* 15(2), August.

World Bank (1996). *World Development Report 1996: From Plan to Market.* New York: Oxford University Press.

——— (1997). *World Development Report 1997: The State in a Changing World.* Washington D.C.: World Bank.

——— (2000). 'What is Globalization'. Available at www1.world bank.org/economicpolicy/globalization/ag01.html, accessed 7 January 2006.

——— (2000a). 'Poverty in an Age of Globalization'. Available at www1.worldbank.org/economicpolicy/globalization/documents/provertyglobalization.pdf, accessed on 7 January 2006.

3

A Democratic Deficit: Citizenship and Governance in the Era of Globalisation

Niraja Gopal Jayal

Introduction

As with all concepts that acquire sudden currency, the meaning of governance in contemporary political discourse varies with the interlocutor in whose speech it occurs. I would like to frame my remarks on the discourses of governance by invoking the argument familiar to political theorists that there is a relationship of mutual constitution between concepts and the political reality they seek to describe.[1] The claim here is that language informs and is informed by the practice of politics, and that linguistic disagreements are also about social and political reality. A shared understanding of political practices would suggest some agreement among political actors on the use of political concepts. To quote Quentin Skinner, such an agreement would encompass three dimensions: agreement about when it is appropriate to apply these concepts; the range of things in the empirical world to which these concepts refer; and the range of attitudes which these concepts express (Skinner 1989).

One more dimension needs to be added to these: the temporal. Meanings of political concepts are notoriously changeable as they evolve over time. Democracy is a classic example: a concept that, until the middle of the 19th century, was marked by opprobrium, and viewed as dangerous and unstable. Theorists from C.B. Macpherson in the 1970s to John Keane in the present have pointed to the multiple appropriations of democracy by all manner of regimes, including the rulers of Nazi Germany, the Soviet Union and many others whose title to it is by all reckonings highly dubious. By the end of the twentieth century, however, democracy had acquired an unparalleled sheen of virtue, becoming 'a global entitlement' (Franck 2000: 46). Something similar is happening to governance today, at least in the Indian context. I would like to suggest that, rather like the idea of democracy over the last century or two, the concept of governance is still in the process of evolution and this is taking place partly in the discursive realm and partly in the realm of political practice [see, e.g., the engagement of political theorists with this question, in Jon Pierre (2000) and Paul Hirst (2000a, 2000b)].

In India, for instance, governance as a buzz-concept has been variously appropriated and deployed by political actors. In the domain of politics, its meaning may be viewed as contested, making it a subject of negotiation in the democratic process. In academic discourse, by contrast, the concept of governance is not generally viewed as contested. It is seen as a consensual concept that carries the taint of genetic sin—in this case, its perceived origin in the prescription of the doctors of the Bretton Woods institutions—and repudiated for that reason. Here, it is the presumed *absence* of contestation and the *lack* of multiple meanings that become the basis of its rejection. Thus, arguments of the following form become possible:

- Chandrababu Naidu claims to be implementing governance reforms.
- I reject Naidu's policies.
- Ergo, I reject 'governance'.

But, it may be asked, does the interlocutor here, thereby reject the idea of governance, or simply Naidu's conception of governance? If, further, the interlocutor believes that Bihar or Uttar Pradesh or Gujarat could be better governed than they presently are, then clearly, we have some disagreement here about what Skinner describes as the range of things in the empirical world to which these concepts refer and the range of attitudes which these concepts express. The ultimate trivialisation of the idea of governance could be said to have occurred with its entry into mainstream political discourse in the Assembly elections of December 2003 when the governance argument raced ahead of 'anti-incumbency' to become *the* explanation for the election result. The Congress had claimed that good governance in terms of BSP (*bijli, sadak, pani*) had won it the Delhi election and the BJP had claimed that the absence of these public goods in the other states coupled with its credible promise of providing them, had helped it to come to power. Because its campaign platform had been overtly developmental, focussing on the failures of incumbent Congress governments to provide development; because development was encapsulated in the holy trinity of electricity, roads and water; and because the only state election the BJP lost at this time was in Delhi where the Congress government was seen to have actually delivered on these fronts—governance became, for both the major parties, a shorthand term for *bijli, sadak* and *pani*. To emphasise this rather banal image of governance which translates into electricity, roads and water is not to belittle the importance of these public goods, which is unarguable. It is only to observe that in popular political discourse, at least in the English language media and in the pronouncements of both the major political parties, the idea of governance had been so trivialised as to be drained of all content other than the provision of electricity, roads and water. However, even in this form, it did not appear as a particularly sincere commitment to public goods provision but was more an electoral strategy of coining a slogan that could respond to what was perceived as the pulse of the people. The primary concern was not to secure responsiveness of governance, but rather to discover the rhetoric that would fetch the votes. In the electoral discourse of the recent past, this is the only discernible connection between the ideas of democracy and governance.

It is precisely this connection that I wish to explore further in this chapter: the connection between governance, on the one hand, and democracy and citizenship, on the other, both framed by the context of globalisation. There are arguably two schools of thought on the relationship between democracy and governance. Their points of departure are different, and the difference is of consequence. The point of departure of the first is governance and that of the second is democracy. For the first, favoured by a variety of donor agencies and multilateral institutions, governance subsumes democracy, and democracy is but one component of governance. Many, if not all of us would have strong disagreement with a notion of democracy that is as anaemic and skeletal as the one favoured by institutions like the World Bank, for whom the regular holding of free and fair elections is a sufficient condition of democracy.

The second school of thought is one that we recognise in some fragments of our own democratic experience. This school adopts a slightly more, though by no means adequately robust conception of democracy which has little patience with the nitty-gritty of governance. This is also an impoverished conception of democracy which believes that representation in legislative assemblies and parliaments is an end in itself, and the purpose of participation is rather cynically restricted to the process by which political elites can be consecrated in power. Such democratic practices often engage in a cynical manipulation of the electorate, instead of expressing a genuine commitment to enhance the deliberative competence of citizens.

Thus, on the one hand, we have an essentially managerial view of governance which accommodates—more or less as a concession to the liberal democracies in which it originates—a certain modicum of democracy, in the form of electorally-conferred legitimacy. On the other hand, we have what we might call the rather instrumentalist, even vehicular, view of democracy, in which the people are literally taken for a ride, their legitimate aspirations for a better quality of life and better governance are ridiculed, and the commitment to social equality reduced to the self-aggrandisement of the political class. Both these views have some—albeit more or less concealed—affinity with the Schumpeterian model of democracy. Both these views, I would submit, are more or less insulting and diminishing to the citizen in a democracy.

Should we then give up the ghost? Can the twain—democracy and governance—ever meet on their own terms? Is there a theoretical framework that can bind them closer, in such a way that we end up neither with a technocratic view of governance that entails an anaemic and emaciated notion of democracy, nor with the view of vehicular democracy built upon complete disregard for the rights and welfare of all citizens? I would like to argue that to engage with the project of governance is at least partly to simultaneously engage in a restoration of democracy, i.e., to restore to democracy some of its own basic foundational principles that have been lost for a long time. The emphasis on representation in democratic practice has led to a neglect of another dimension central to democratic theory: accountability. The justification of democracy is not limited to securing representation in the political process, but based upon the assumption that democracy is a form of government in which people's opinions and interests are represented on an ongoing basis, with the democratically elected government acting in fulfilment of people's will as expressed in their mandate. Accountability in governance is, thus, a central component of the principle of democracy. Democracy is only partially realised at the time of electing a government. It is more fully realised as it gives expression to the will of the people on an ongoing basis. It is another matter that the institutions of democracy make it difficult for the people to exercise control over government on a daily basis: this task is performed by the Opposition in a parliamentary system, by free press and, in the last resort, at the time of re-election. Today, issues of accountability, transparency, and governmental responsiveness—which constitute governance concerns—can contribute to the refashioning of the idea of democracy to endow it with more substance than its common Schumpeterian meaning.

Such an exercise is necessarily premised upon a separation of the purposes of democracy and governance. One is deeply informed with a normative vision of the good society and citizenship; the other is more concerned with the mechanisms, rules, norms and policies which give effect to this normative vision. They have somewhat different jurisdictions and a completely different normative status. The important task is not to make democracy the handmaiden of governance, but rather to make governance the handmaiden of democracy. The former is objectionable because democracy has an undeniable intrinsic value that is widely cherished and defended. It is a noble and a worthy end, but the democratic project is never complete or finished. On the other hand, to make governance the handmaiden of democracy is to suggest that the normative vision of democracy must inform, inspire and lead the project of governance. However, there is no call to belittle the importance of governance just because the concept does not possess any independent normative or ethical content of its own. Indeed, this is precisely why the term governance is frequently qualified by terms such as 'democratic' or the very dodgy prefix 'good'.

The normative implications of governance are necessarily contested and political. Different societies, and indeed social theorists, will have different interpretations of what constitutes the acceptable core of 'good' governance. In descriptive terms, however, the contemporary usage of the term captures elements of institutional change that have become part of the reality of the world economy and society today. It warns us that governance is more than simply what governments do. It asks, and encourages many answers to, the question of how power in society is exercised in both form and practice (Doornbos 2001: 96). It refuses to prejudge the locus of actual decision-making, admitting the possibility that this could lie with the state, but equally with the norms and informal rules of local institutions, or even institutions of global governance.

What then does the task of democratising governance entail? Contemporary scholarship on governance recognises that—whether we like it or not—power is no longer concentrated in the state, but that it is dispersed both laterally as well as vertically. The former is signified by the recognition of at least three broad *domains* of governance: the state, the market and civil society (encompassing both social movements and the non-governmental sector). The latter is signified by the displacement of the 'national' level of governance and a parallel process of proliferation in the *levels* of governance, from the local, through the regional/sub-national and the national, to the global. In each of these domains and at each of these levels, there are important, indeed vital, concerns about democracy.

Several interlocutors of the new governance discourse have suggested that despite the dispersal of power upwards, downwards and outwards, the state remains central to the practices of politics and democracy, and should remain central therefore to ways of thinking about them. They argue that these displacements of power have generally, at least in the Western world, occurred with the consent of states, if not as a consequence of consciously exercised policy choices by them. As such, states are adapting and transforming themselves rather than, as is commonly assumed, being rendered weak or invisible. Indeed, in some contexts, it is argued, states are actually strengthened.[2] By no means, then, are states obsolete or threatened with extinction.

This chapter suggests that, if states are undergoing processes of transformation—ranging from absolute retreat to adaptation and modification—it is only reasonable to suppose that democracy is also being transformed, and so correspondingly are the practices of citizenship. More specifically, it argues that while some elements of new governance could encourage the project of citizenship, others tend to undermine it. Clearly, the proliferation of the sites of governance, of agencies and actors other than the state, as also their partnerships with it, can neither be refuted nor simply wished away. The 'how' and 'on whose behalf' questions must nevertheless be asked of governance. Hence, we must evaluate the discrete institutional components of new governance, and their inter-relationships with each other, in the light of some overarching normative principle. That principle, this chapter suggests, is that of democratic citizenship.

What, it asks, are the consequences of these multiple displacements on the practice of democratic citizenship? It reflects on possible ways of disaggregating and studying the impact of the new structures and processes of governance for the way in which citizenship has been conceptualised in 20th century political thinking. If the state is no longer the exclusive locus of citizenship and identity, what is? If power is more dispersed than it was, does that make it more or less accountable? How is this picture of redistributed power different from the traditional, pluralist one, and how different are its consequences for citizenship?

In the pluralist picture, the state was explicitly the arbiter and the referee, standing above and beyond society, seen as an agglomeration of individuals organised into pressure and interest groups. Further, the pluralist account of power attached normative value to both the disconnectedness of state from society and to the deconcentration of power. In contemporary discourses on governance, on the other hand, the state is seen as embedded in society, though in varying degrees, its role as an agency of 'steering' and co-ordination is emphasised, as opposed to its role as arbiter and referee. There is, moreover, no special moral merit attached to the deconcentration of power, which is here presented more as description than prescription.

Multiple Domains of Governance: The Locus of Citizenship

The contemporary political imagination has tended to conceptualise the lateral dispersal of power in the rather flat and clichéd terms of state, market and civil society. What are the possible implications for democratic citizenship, of power moving outwards from the state to markets and civil societies? Has the role of the state really changed in the new governance and what does this imply for conventional state-centered conceptions of citizenship?

Today there is a considerable body of scholarship that agrees to the fact that proliferation of agencies and levels of governance does not necessarily imply that the state has diminished or is likely to diminish in importance. At least three reasons are adduced for this. First, to the extent that a dispersal of power takes place, it is a result of the conscious exercise of a policy choice by the state. By legislating and guaranteeing such dispersal, states ensure the effective distribution of power at the levels most appropriate to its exercise. Even where policy networks are assuming greater importance, the choice of groups to be consulted by official agencies remains very much the preserve of the state. It is, therefore, very likely that groups with broadly compatible visions and perspectives would be invited for consultation rather than oppositional groups with alternative agendas. In this, among other senses, states retain their primacy.

Second, states—certainly in the North—are spending more, rather than less, on a variety of public services, such as state shrinkage in some areas is more than compensated for by state expansion in others. Even where public spending has been cut, the payrolls, budgets and regulatory scope of states have not been reduced. Apart from the new surveillance and military technologies available, states are more energetically pursuing environmental and consumer protection, and trying to provide a framework of regulation for an effective global market (Scholte 2000: 134). A survey of social policy in OECD countries reported that the share of national resources devoted to social spending has continued to inch upwards in OECD nations, despite the pressures of economic restructuring (Kymlicka 1999: 114).

Finally, the nation state remains arguably the most important locus of identity for most people, and even supra-national regional bodies have not managed to attract the loyalty of citizens in quite the same way. It is hard to envision markets or institutions of global governance replacing the state in this dimension. As such, nation states cannot but remain so long as the world is organised around territorially constituted populations, conferring legitimacy on (hopefully) democratically elected national governments. As representatives of these populations, states remain the constituent units of the world order. Citizens have also remained, as Michael Mann put it, 'true zoo animals, dependent on and emotionally attached to their national cages' (Mann 1993: 117).

It is often presumed that states are necessarily on the road to retreat in the face of globalisation. Peter Evans has powerfully questioned this assumption by pointing to, on the one hand, evidence from East Asia showing that intense state involvement actually helps to achieve successful participation of developing economies in global markets and, on the other, the fact that even transnational economic actors would like to limit the state only in so far as it places constraints on their activities, but otherwise look up to the state to protect their returns. 'In this optic,' says Evans, 'the persistence of the state's institutional centrality looks more likely than eclipse' (Evans 1997: 20).

Despite the continuing centrality of the state in the ways outlined above, there are other ways in which the project of citizenship is threatened. To the extent that public services and welfare functions are 'franchised' out to private firms and non-governmental organisations, they are placed beyond the reach of the citizen. Indeed, the citizen is re-invented as a *consumer* of market-produced goods or as a *user* of the civic services provided by public institutions. As the category of the citizen is thus recast in relation to different spheres, the space for citizenship ineluctably shrinks.

The corporation is probably the most compelling example of the lack of accountability. The new catechism of 'corporate governance' was first spelt out in the Cadbury Committee Report (1992).

Of the Indian attempts in the same direction, the SEBI (Securities Exchange Board of India) Code of Corporate Governance, drafted by a committee headed by Kumaramangalam Birla Committee, is the best known. Corporate governance generally translates as shareholders' interests, intended to reassert the control of the shareholders vis-à-vis that of management. In this perspective, however, while shareholders count, organised labour still does not. The stakeholder's conception of corporate accountability is more likely to ensure that the interests of the latter are represented through a more democratic and representative form of governance than either management or shareholder control.

The definition of stakeholders varies widely in different situations. Apart from shareholders, it generally includes employees and trade unions, and sometimes also the local community in terms of local schools, local amenities and charities. Others extend this list to include new and emerging stakeholders such as the natural environment and future generations. However, the dominant emphasis remains on maximising shareholder value while all others who can claim to be considered stakeholders without actually contributing to the success of the company have to be 'managed'. The board of a company is expected to balance conflicting claims, 'to steer a middle course, one that protects and enhances shareholders' wealth while satisfactorily "managing" the real stakeholders' aspirations in a manner not prejudicial to shareholders' interests' (Balasubramanian 2004: 71).

In the Indian context, a study of corporate governance in the large private sector companies in India, highlighted 'the ineffectiveness of boards, the lack of transparency surrounding transactions within business groups, the divergence of Indian accounting practices from international standards, and the changing role of, and controversy surrounding, institutional shareholders ... a more active approach to corporate governance on the part of institutional investors requires larger changes in the nature of the FIs' (Foreign Investors) ownership and control by government, greater autonomy for institutional managers, and the active development of a market for corporate control' (Banaji and Mody 2001: 1).

Even this study, perhaps because it is based on interviews with 170 representatives of business interests, interprets the Indian evidence within the parameters of British and American discourses on corporate governance and does not raise the question of economic democracy within the firm, or of workers' participation and voice.

Should we then turn to civil society to restore the accountability and responsiveness that we find woefully missing in the state and the market alike? As Evans writes,

> The revitalization of 'civil society' was portrayed, at least by conservatives, as a solution to the social and political side of public well-being, one that could make the state obsolete, just as global markets made the state economically obsolete.... Just as neoclassical political economy negated the state's role in the development of a more productive and efficient society, the growing charisma of civil society (and other more parochial and exclusionary forms of community) negated the state's ability to speak to nonmarket needs (Evans 1997: 21).

However, the amorphous character of civil society and the diverse nature of the actors that populate it, make this a question that does not admit of an easy or unambiguous answer. Social movements, for instance, are more likely to be more representative of popular aspirations than non-governmental organisations engaged in development work. The latter often typify the 'donor' approach to civil society, which can be deeply conservative. In this perspective, civil society is a check against arbitrary government, the preserver of a civic culture that binds and the ultimate defender of individual freedom. While it is concerned with the defence of negative liberty, it is (in this version, at least) much less concerned with the social and economic inequalities that beset societies, making the meaningful exercise of their rights of citizenship difficult.

While the relationship between civil society and the state has engaged the attention of many scholars, that between civil society and the market has not. Similarly, while donor discourses highlight tensions between the state and civil society, the relationship between civil society and the market is implicitly viewed as harmonious and complementary (Howell and Pearce 2001). In fact, in the discourse of multilateral economic institutions, civil society (and its ungainly cousin, social capital) is often projected as that which would compensate for the shortcomings of the state and the market by making development possible in ways that the latter have failed to do. This is the underlying theme of the Third Way which sees civil society as an equilibrating mechanism, a supplement and an alternative to state and market.

Among the many incarnations of civil society is its description as the 'non-profit' sector. To the extent that civil society is content with its non-profit role, it fails in its function of political vigilantism and legitimises the state; if it fails to question social and economic inequalities, it legitimises the functioning of the market which generates many of these inequalities. Of course, it may be argued that this is only one version of the civil society argument. But, it must be remembered that when civil society is conceptualised as the 'third sector', this is generally the role it is assigned.

The more radical possibilities of civil society are best exemplified by social movements like the environmental or feminist movements, which have emancipatory political programmes. The relationship between these and the state is largely conflictual and mutually hostile. It is, therefore, quite different from the collaborative relationship which frequently exists between NGOs and the state. NGOs as 'public service contractors' provide efficient mechanisms of public service delivery, in ways that social movements—such as the Narmada Bachao Andolan or the MKSS (Mazdoor Kisan Shakti Sangathan) movement for the Right to Information—do not. An altogether different model is, of course, that of partnership between the state and local communities, for instance, in the management of forests and national parks, through Joint Forest Management or Joint Protected Area Management Programmes. Though many of the familiar social constraints such as caste and patriarchy impact the effectiveness of such programmes, they remain more accessible to citizens than NGOs which replicate state structures and bureaucracies with more efficient, though not necessarily more accountable, ones.

One area where civil society and market may be encountered at the point of their intersection is arguably the media. Dreze and Sen have famously argued the importance of a free press and adversarial politics for public action (including but not exclusively popular action). Clearly, the importance of a free and responsible media for the effective performance of citizen roles is indisputable insofar as it makes possible the transmission of information, the ventilation of a variety of opinions, and the exercise of freedom of thought and speech. While state-controlled media have their limitations in this respect, it is worth asking, to what extent a corporatised media—possibly even controlled by transnational corporations—fulfils this objective? Is it equal to the task of facilitating the exercise of citizenship?

Multi-Level Governance: The Fragmentation of Citizenship?

Global Governance

The emergence of the transnational, the subnational and the local as significant levels of governance suggests different implications for the practices of citizenship. Even the mechanisms of transnational governance that are associated with globalisation carry contradictory tendencies in this respect. Some of these are enabling, while others are manifestly not. Ecological citizenship in a global commons, for instance, is a good example of the enabling character of globalisation. There is a widespread recognition today that environmental problems—from acid rain to ozone depletion and global warming—are not restricted to national boundaries and that their causes and consequences routinely and recklessly transgress such borders. The 'environmental community of fate' that emerges from this recognition of the global commons and its degradation is arguably far larger than the citizenries of many nation states (Goldblatt 1997: 80). Similarly, many feminists believe that, like the worldwide environmental movement, the internationalisation of the women's movement has expanded political spaces for the articulation of women's exclusion and so helped address the 'democratic deficit' (Dickenson 1997: 97).

What are the implications of these developments for citizenship? On the one hand, the recognition of an environmental community of fate has accelerated transnational environmental activism aimed at creating sensitised citizens on planet earth. On the other hand, given the scientific and technical nature of the knowledge involved, all citizens are not sufficiently empowered to contribute to these debates or express informed preferences on these issues. It is, further, but a natural outcome of the admission that some of these environmental problems cannot be handled within the territorially defined limits of the sovereign nation state, and that states should submit to a whole set of international treaties, protocols and conventions on environmental issues. The globalisation of the problem mandates the globalisation of solutions, and so gives rise to anxieties about the undermining of the autonomy of the nation state. Of course, while states are often bound by international treaties to act in certain ways to combat environmental problems, it is possible for them to effectively avoid these obligations through lack of action, with the international institutions created to enforce them rarely possessing the moral or political clout to do so.

In 1991, in the course of international negotiations on biodiversity, the Group of 77 countries asked for the inclusion of biotechnology with biodiversity. This demand sought to link Northern access to the genetic resources of the South with Southern access to biotechnology research in the North, and even to a share of the benefits arising from the commercial exploitation of genetic resources (Rajan 1997: 206ff). This proposal had thus far been strenuously resisted by USA and the business community in America had also lobbied strongly against it. At the seventh and final round of negotiations at Nairobi, just a month before the UN Conference on Environment and Development (the Earth Summit) was held at Rio de Janeiro in June 1992, a document was drawn up which remained contentious even on the eve of the summit. Though it embodied substantial concessions for which the US had driven a hard bargain—in not, for example, providing the South with the guarantees it had sought for the transfer of biotechnology or on the question of intellectual property rights. The US refused to sign the Biodiversity Convention at Rio. It is significant that the reason cited by President Bush for this rejection was that the convention 'threatens to retard biotechnology and undermine the protection of ideas' (McConnell 1997: 51). More recently, the US stand on the Kyoto Protocol has confirmed the suspicion that it is committed to resisting any environmental initiative that limits its freedom of action or involves the sacrifice of corporate interests.

Indeed, business interests influence environmental policy not merely through individual governments, but also through international agencies (which seek funding from, and collaboration with, them in this area), raising significant questions about democracy and accountability. Apart from environmental issues, even the creditworthiness of states is determined by essentially private international credit rating agencies like Moody's.

Of a positively disabling character, as far as citizenship is concerned, are three other identifiable forms of direct or indirect global governance. These are the activities of the World Trade Organization; the peregrinations of transnational capital; and the handouts of bilateral and multilateral donors of aid and development assistance to the Third World, which have often, in the past, arrived with a price tag labelled 'good governance' that claims virtue by its endorsement to formal democracy. None of these however contain any possibility of accountability to citizens, least of all in the developing world. From the vantage-point of citizenship, therefore, these institutions and agencies of global governance are singularly unaccountable.

From an institutional point of view, the troika of multilateral economic institutions that form the cornerstone of the world economic system are the World Bank, the International Monetary Fund (IMF) and the World Trade Organization (WTO). Unlike agencies of the United Nations, such as the International Labour Organization or the United Nations Conference on Trade and Development (UNCTAD), which ultimately depend upon persuasion and moral pressure, these organisations have indisputably greater power in legislating for the international economy. Through their governance of the financial and production structures of the world, these 'econocrats' exercise an enormous influence over the daily lives of much of the world's population.

Who do these public institutions of global governance represent? The G7 countries, along with the remaining countries of the European Union (EU), represent 14 per cent of the world's population, but control 56 per cent of the votes in the IMF Executive Board. Since the voting power of a country is proportionate to its share of IMF capital, the United States alone has 17.4 per cent of the voting power, which makes it the only country to have unilateral veto power. Though decisions are taken by consensus, and not by majority vote, the very existence of this veto power renders disagreements and divisions unnecessary (Thomas 2000: 17ff). Indeed, it has been observed that the US Treasury plays a central role in the formulation of World Bank and IMF policies and has attempted to suppress public debate and criticism of the policies made by these bodies (Stiglitz 2002: 245–46).

Quite apart from the democracy-undermining effect of political conditionalities, the quota-based voting system in all the Bretton Woods Institutions (BWIs) implies that it is the interests of the richer, capital-exporting countries that dominate. The IMF's retreat from Keynesian social democracy in favour of financial conservatism; the politically motivated nature of loan decisions, often to further American political and foreign policy interests; and the exclusion of borrowing countries from the decision-making processes have been attributed to the flawed governance structures of the BWIs (You 2002: 218–19). This is only exacerbated by the lack of accountability and transparency in the functioning of these institutions and the complete absence of public scrutiny of their operations and decisions. As Joseph Stiglitz has argued, the IMF typically—and mostly under conditions of secrecy—interacts with the finance ministry of a country, which more often than not reflects the elite financial community of the country, rather than the people as a whole. His case for a re-examination of the governance structures of the IMF is justified by the real risk that what so often happens within national governments—that power is used not to advance the general interest but to further special interests—will happen at the international level. One might argue that the problems at the international level are even more severe, for the electoral process provides at least a partial check on the abuse of these powers within countries. The international financial institutions and the IMF in particular are sufficiently far removed from systems of direct electoral accountability and there is no effective check on abuses of this kind (Stiglitz 2002: 244).

The WTO also suffers from the same problems of accountability, transparency and inadequate representation. The apparently democratic principle of one-country, one-vote is in practice not so democratic, because decisions are not arrived at through a vote but through consensus, and the legacy of the 'green room' practices of its institutional predecessor, the GATT, endures. Though developing countries are in a majority in the WTO and their citizens therefore form a majority of global citizens, they are not in a position to determine its agenda or participate meaningfully in its decision-making processes. The WTO has been a particular target of criticism because, through instruments like the TRIPS and TRIMS, it is perceived to reflect the interests of the North and its transnational corporations. Developing countries provide markets but do not receive any corresponding benefits in terms of, say, access to technology; similarly, they permit the mobility of foreign capital, but receive no corresponding benefits in terms of the mobility of their labour.

The extent to which the troika of multilateral economic institutions has engaged (or not) with social movements also varies. Of the three, the World Bank has had the most extensive contact with global social movements and non-governmental organisations, especially with environmental and women's groups, whose concerns have, therefore, found some spaces within its structures and programmes. More monolithic, and less tolerant of dissent, the IMF and WTO have been more reluctant and slower to engage in such initiatives. To the extent that the WTO has been involved with global social movements, it has done so instrumentally to gain the support of important states and to placate the environmental and labour movements in advanced industrial countries. It has, in fact, been argued that the varying levels of success encountered by the women's, environmental or labour movements depends upon the degree to which such a movement can pressurise key states. Thus, the environmental movement has met with some success in the World Bank and the WTO, but pressure on the US has been decisive in both these cases. By contrast, the women's movement has had some of its concerns incorporated in the Bank, but since they have less influence in the American political system, they have made little impact upon the IMF and the WTO (O'Brien et al. 2000: 218–25).

Describing international organisations as 'bureaucratic bargaining systems', Robert Dahl has argued that if citizens find it difficult enough to exert control over the foreign policy of their own nations, the obstacles to their influencing international organisations would be far greater. By extension, just as citizens routinely delegate their powers of decision-making to political elites, they might delegate control in international organisations to international political elites, taking the principle of delegation 'well beyond any acceptable threshold of democracy' (Dahl 1999: 32).

As the power of decision-making in key areas is transferred to remote levels that are completely unaccountable, it becomes clear that global governance is completely delinked from its putative global citizenry. The institutions of global governance neither reflect the interests of the latter, nor are they structured so as to allow their participation. The processes and the outcomes are thus equally weighted in favour of the developed nations.

Sub-National Governance

The trend towards supraterritoriality that has accompanied processes of globalisation everywhere, has also in several countries witnessed a growth in regional or substate arrangements of governance, which have acquired a certain autonomy from the national state. In India, too, the processes of economic reform and liberalisation have seen a dramatic shift from a nominally federal but effectively centralised state structure to one that has become considerably more federal—at least in economic terms than was possibly envisaged when the constitution was written. Lloyd and Susanne Rudolph have argued that economic liberalisation was necessary, but by no means the sufficient, condition for the emergence of what they call the 'federal market economy'. As public investment declined, consequent upon the centre's mounting debts and fiscal deficit, its financial leverage was also reduced. The sufficient condition for transformation, however, was provided by the simultaneous political change from one-party dominance to 'a regionalised multiparty coalition government system' (Rudolph and Rudolph 2001: 1548).

The enhanced autonomy of states may, as the Rudolphs argue, have simultaneously placed them under greater constraint in terms of fiscal discipline. However, states have substantially emancipated themselves from the centre in competing with each other for foreign direct investment. In the pre-reform days, regional disparities were, more often than not, created and fostered by the centre; today, it is the direct linkages with transnational capital that encourage these, and potentially also encourage a certain hardening of regional identities. Among the important questions of the future, that of how autonomous the states of the federation can and should be, is certainly one. As individual states embark on their own developmental journeys, whose responsibility will the resultant disparities be? Within the formal legal structure of single citizenship that obtains, is it right that the citizens of some states should be less fortunate in their access to public goods and services than those of other, more prosperous ones?

Local Governance

The local is arguably the most hospitable site of citizenship. It enables the most direct citizenship participation, and even acts as 'a school of political capacity', to simultaneously invoke J.S. Mill's phrase and Aristotle's sentiments. Despite the cynicism of some and the carping criticism of others, the relative success of the new Panchayati Raj Institutions (PRIs) in India is undeniable. Even where caste, class and patriarchy have exerted a stranglehold on the functioning of these institutions, sometimes even preventing elected functionaries such as Dalit women from assuming office, the institutional framework has provided a site and a space for struggle which, with the assistance of the judiciary, has eventually yielded encouraging results. Of course, critical gaps remain, of which the lack of awareness of and, therefore, minimal participation in, the Gram Sabha is the most significant. From an institutional point of view, of course, the most severe constraint has been an inadequate devolution of functions and powers, and the finances to perform these. Here again, the variations between states are a result of differences in the manner of translating the intent of the constitutional amendment while drafting conformity acts. Thus, while the West Bengal, Karnataka and Maharashtra legislations explicitly design these as institutions of self-government, Haryana's conformity act interprets panchayats as administrative mechanisms. With all these limitations—both institutional and social—the panchayat institutions still provide a potentially empowering space for citizen action.

If the local appears to be the most hospitable site of democratic citizenship, should this suggest that complexity and participation are incompatible? What are the ways in which citizenship concerns can be realised at every level of multi-layered governance, from the global to the local? How may the project of inclusion be furthered at each level?

However promising the local may be, there are important caveats to the issues outlined above. The first and most important of these relates to the virtual disappearance of the national as the level of governance that mediates the global and the local. Its role in this respect is crucial not merely in functional terms, but also in the sense that if local political institutions constitute the most proximate level of accountable governance, national political institutions are the last bastion of accountable power for the citizen. How effective or otherwise even local institutions are likely to be is contingent upon the extent of devolution—of powers, functions and resources—which is generally determined by the national state. The extent to which the state resists or capitulates to intrusions on its sovereignty or to foreign capital is likewise centrally determined.

A second caveat relates to the nature of society. While the debate on state-society relations that so preoccupied political scientists from the mid-1980s through the 1990s is now all but concluded, to the satisfaction of all, with a consensus on a state-*in*-society perspective, the importance of the two most important forms of social stratification—class and caste as well as of patriarchy cannot be underestimated. These are by all reckoning severe constraints that militate against the individualist universalism suggested by liberal democratic ideas and institutions. It is difficult to interpret the consequences of the multiplication of levels of governance for a society so riddled with heritable forms of inequality. Is it, for instance, arguable that the multiplication of levels of governance produces another kind of fragmentation of identity, which is secular instead of cultural or ascriptive. Could this have a secularising impact on identity in the long run? This is a tempting argument, tempered however by Benjamin Barber's argument of the parallel courses of tribalism and globalism.

The multiplication in the domains and levels of governance discussed above essentially posit an alternative distribution of power. Does, however, the exercise of power become more transparent, simply because it is more widely dispersed? The claim that the lateral and vertical dispersal of power encapsulates an essentially democratising impulse is also contestable. The lateral dispersal of power may well lead to fragmentation and even proliferation, but that does not logically imply democratisation. It also does not spell out or suggest any relationship between the domains so created, on the one hand, and the vertical multiplication of levels, on the other.

The assumption that deconcentrating power is inherently democratising was, in fact, the fallacy of the pluralist theories of yore. Even if concentration and dispersal are opposing tendencies, the one does not presume less transparency and accountability, any more than the other presumes their opposite. The location of power is an important indicator of the nature of its exercise, but by no means the only determinant of this. We arguably still need to closely examine the constraints and conditions—social, economic, and political—under which it is exercised, as also other forms of power which intersect with it. A reframing of the problem of democratic citizenship is clearly warranted.

What are the possibilities for such a reframing? If, as Habermas has said, citizenship is not conceptually tied to national identity, what can take its place? Some suggest the strengthening of transnational citizenship and cosmopolitan democracy (Held 1999), while others posit 'multiple citizenship'—ranging from municipal citizenship to world citizenship of a cosmopolitan democracy—as an alternative (Heater 1999). Postmodern perspectives endorse the idea of multiple citizenship on the grounds that citizenship can have an emancipatory potential only when its links with the state and market are severed. Opposed to these arguments is a point of view that suggests that globalisation has not in fact undermined the sense of national collectivity or historical solidarity among the members of nation states. This argument goes further to suggest possibilities of democratic renewal in the opportunities offered by globalisation, which makes for less political apathy, encourages public debate and opens up political processes to new, hitherto excluded groups (Kymlicka 1999: 118–19). On this account, creating a transnational citizenship could have a deleterious effect on citizenship at the domestic level, the proper home of the citizen. Clearly, the negotiation of citizenship within the reconfigured structures and processes of governance will require not only struggles to prise open spaces, but also renewed reflection about the sources and practices of social power.

Notes

1. Cf. Ball, Farr and Hanson (1989).
2. Pierre and Peters (2000) argue that since power is not a zero-sum game, governance processes in today's world actually add to the strength of the state by increasing the points of contact between the state and society. Jan-Aart Scholte (2000: 134–5) claims that state shrinkage in some areas has been more than compensated by its expansion in others and that the spread of supra-territoriality has tended to create a *different* kind of state, rather than contracting or eliminating it. Philip G. Cerny (2000: 133) likewise claims that the nation state is not dead, it is simply assuming a role different from that of the welfare state of industrialised societies. Ronen Palan (2000: 139) describes this simply as recasting of political authority and a reinvention of the state.

References

Balasubramanian, N. (2004). 'Economic Reforms, Corporate Boards, and Governance', in Darryl Reed and Sanjoy Mukherjee (eds), *Corporate Governance, Economic Reforms, and Development: The Indian Experience*. Delhi: Oxford University Press.

Ball, Terence, James Farr and Russell L. Hanson (eds) (1989). *Political Innovation and Conceptual Change*. Cambridge: Cambridge University Press.

Banaji, Jairus and Gautam Mody (2001). 'Corporate Governance and the Indian Private Sector', *QEH Working Paper Series QEHWPS73*, Oxford.

Cerny, Philip G. (2000). 'Restructuring the Political Arena: Globalization and the Paradoxes of the Competition State', in Randall D. Germain (ed.), *Globalization and its Critics: Perspectives from Political Economy*. London: Macmillan.

Dahl, Robert A. (1999). 'Can International Organizations be Democratic? A skeptic's View', in Ian Shapiro and C. Hacker-Cordon (eds), *Democracy's Edges*. Cambridge: Cambridge University Press.

Dickenson, Donna (1997). 'Counting Women In: Globalization, Democratisation and the Women's Movement', in Anthony McGrew (ed.), *The Transformation of Democracy? Globalization and Territorial Democracy*. Cambridge: Polity Press, in association with The Open University.

Doornbos, Martin (2001). '"Good Governance": The Rise and Decline of a Policy Metaphor?', *Journal of Development Studies*, 37(6), August.

Evans, Peter (1997). 'The Eclipse of the State? Reflections on Stateness in an Era of Globalization'. Mimeo.

Franck, Thomas M. (2000). 'The Emerging Right to Democratic Governance', *The American Journal of International Law*, 86(1): 46–91, January 1992.

Goldblatt, David (1997). 'Liberal Democracy and the Globalization of Environmental Risks', in Anthony McGrew (ed.), *The Transformation of Democracy? Globalization and Territorial Democracy*. Cambridge: Polity Press, in association with The Open University.

Heater, Derek (1999). *What is Citizenship?* Cambridge: Polity Press.

Held, David (1999). 'The Transformation of Political Community: Rethinking Democracy in the Context of Globalization', in Ian Shapiro and C. Hacker-Cordon (eds), *Democracy's Edges*. Cambridge: Cambridge University Press.

Hirst, Paul (2000a). 'Globalization, the Nation State and Political Theory', in Noel O'Sullivan (ed.), *Political Theory in Transition*. London: Routledge.

——— (2000b). 'Democracy and Governance', in Jon Pierre (ed.), *Debating Governance: Authority, Steering and Democracy*. Oxford: Oxford University Press.

Howell, Jude and Jenny Pearce (2001). *Civil Society and Development: A Critical Exploration*. Boulder: Lynne Reinner Publishers.
Kymlicka, Will (1999). 'Citizenship in an Era of Globalization: Commentary on Held', in Ian Shapiro and C. Hacker-Cordon (eds), *Democracy's Edges*. Cambridge: Cambridge University Press.
Mann, Michael (1993). 'Nation States in Europe and Other Continents: Diversifying, Developing, Not Dying', *Daedalus*, 122(3).
McConnell, Fiona (1997). 'The Convention on Biological Diversity', in Felix Dodds (ed.), *The Way Forward: Beyond Agenda 21*. London: Earthscan.
O'Brien, Robert, Anne Marie Goetz, Jan Aart Scholte and Marc Williams (2000). *Contesting Global Governance: Multilateral Economic Institutions and Global Social Movements*. Cambridge: Cambridge University Press.
Palan, Ronen (2000). 'Recasting Political Authority: Globalization and the State', in Randall D. Germain (ed.), *Globalization and its Critics: Perspectives from Political Economy*. London: Macmillan.
Pierre, J. (ed.) (2000). *Debating Governance: Authority, Steering and Democracy*. Oxford: Oxford University Press.
Pierre, J. and B.G. Peters (2000). *Governance, Politics and the State*. London: Macmillan.
Rudolph, L.I. and S.H. Rudolph, (2001). 'The Iconisation of Chandrababu: Sharing Sovereignty in India's Federal Market Economy', *Economic and Political Weekly*, 36(18): 1541–52, 5 May.
Rajan, Mukund Govind (1997). *Global Environmental Politics: India and the North-South Politics of Global Environmental Issues*. Delhi: Oxford University Press.
Scholte, Jan Aart (2000). *Globalization: A Critical Introduction*. London: Macmillan.
Skinner, Quentin (1989). 'The State', in T. Ball, J. Farr and R. L. Hanson (eds), *Political Innovation and Conceptual Change*. Cambridge: Cambridge University Press.
Stiglitz, Joseph E. (2002). 'Globalization and the Logic of International Collective Action: Re-examining the Bretton Woods Institutions', in Deepak Nayyar (ed.), *Governing Globalization: Issues and Institutions*. Delhi: Oxford University Press.
Thomas, Caroline (2000). *Global Governance, Development and Human Security: The Challenge of Poverty and Inequality*. London: Pluto Press.
You, Jong-Il (2002). 'The Bretton Woods Institutions: Evolution, Reform, and Change', in Deepak Nayyar (ed.), *Governing Globalization: Issues and Institutions*. Delhi: Oxford University Press.

Section II
State-Level Reforms and Development

4

Governance Reforms and Development in Gujarat

Kameshwar Choudhary

Governance reform has emerged as a big buzzword in the domain of development in the recent decades, particularly in the context of the third world countries. There is no clear unanimity on the concept of governance among the different sets of actors such as donor agencies, governments, academics, activists and civil society organisations. However, one could observe two types of orientations on this issue, that is, the dominant and the marginal ones. The currently dominant paradigm of governance, popularly known as 'good governance' is advocated by the multilateral and bilateral international agencies backed by dominant capitalist countries led by US, dominant ruling elites and establishment intellectuals in the third world countries, and associated civil society organisations/NGOs operating at different levels (local, national, regional, global). They are the votary of reforms promoting liberalisation, privatisation and globalisation (LPG). But another set of people and organisations are critical, and some even completely opposed to the 'good governance' agenda of LPG type reforms. The external forces pushing for the current neoliberal agenda of reforms are the multilateral and bilateral development agencies, that is, the World Bank, the Asian Development Bank (ADB), IMF, USAID (bilateral development agency of the US), DFID (bilateral development agency of UK), etc. The introduction of this agenda in the third world countries has spread from the national to provincial to local levels. Governments in these countries are working in collaboration with the external agencies to transform their policies and programmes in a very systematic manner. Though the pace of governance reforms may vary, the agenda is common across and within borders in the third world countries. Reforms have serious impact in different spheres—economic, social, political, and administrative—in the third world countries.

This chapter is divided into four parts. First, it provides a brief overview of the agenda of governance reforms and highlights the context of state-level reforms in India. Second, it deals with the reforms agenda of the ADB in India, particularly in Gujarat. Third, it focuses on the package of reforms introduced in Gujarat, especially in collaboration with the ADB. It covers reforms in the areas of economic and human development. Finally, certain broad concluding remarks are made.

Agenda of Governance Reforms

The introductory chapter of the volume provides a synoptic view of the package of governance reforms advocated by the multilateral/bilateral institutions that is under implementation in India. The package of reforms is very wide in scope covering economic, social, administrative and political domains. These reforms mark a shift in the development paradigm from the state-centred to market-led model of economic development in India (RoyChowdhary 1995: 19). It symbolises a departure from the 'socialistic' to the neoliberal private sector-centred development. Several reasons are cited which necessitated the shift. It is argued that the 'socialistic' state in India has failed to deliver development. The 'Hindu rate of growth' has always been low. The state was 'overloaded' with direct interventionist/production activities and welfarist baggage. The service delivery by the bureaucratic state was very inefficient and corrupt. Corruption also hampered the endeavours of private entrepreneurs due to heavy control and regulation ('*license-permit raj*', 'inspector *raj*') by the state. Anti-poverty measures remained badly targeted and hence do not have the desired impact. The administrative system lacked accountability. The inward-looking economy and administration symbolised a rigid state system lacking scope for economic growth and marked improvement in the quality of life of the people (Krueger 2002). Hence, to remedy the situation, a retreat and reframing of the state and introduction of the market-led model of development has been advocated in India.

A favourable opportunity arose for the advocates of reforms, both within as well as outside, in 1991 when India faced a serious balance of payment (BoP) crisis and had to approach the IMF and World Bank for assistance. The assistance was provided but with strict conditionalities as a part of the stabilisation and the structural adjustment programmes (SAP) which ushered in the era of systematic overhaul and transformation of the system along neoliberal lines in the country. Reforms were first introduced at the Central level by the Union Government.

It was soon realised by the external agencies and the pro-reform domestic elites that Indian economy/society cannot be significantly restructured unless the reforms are introduced at the state (provincial) level as well. Indian Constitution recognises the states as the second level unit which has exclusive domains of operations in several economic, social and administrative matters. Moreover, the LPG package and recent emergence of coalition governments at the Centre with the support of regional parties has enabled the states to have more room and influence in the polity (Joshi and Little 1996). It is observed that most states faced serious fiscal crisis and that provided the opportunity to the external agencies, the Union government and the state-level ruling elites (political, administrative and business elites) to introduce reforms at the state-level mainly from mid-1990s. The state governments followed the Union government in introducing the same set of governance reforms. The state-level fiscal crisis is considered particularly important as a causal factor behind reforms at this level. In the context of the crisis, 'bureaucrats' were able to approach their political masters with the harsh reality that reforms were inevitable. This required additional finance and therefore states began approaching the Government of India as well as multilateral funding agencies for 'cash for reforms' (Howes et al. 2003: 5–6). External assistance is dovetailed with Government of India's own state-related incentives and measures for promoting reforms (ibid.: 21). The top echelons of bureaucracy have been quite supportive of reforms (RoyChowdhary 1995). A combination of all these external and domestic forces has led to a 'paradigm shift' that is underway in India in terms of the perspective of state governments of their own developmental role (ibid.: 20). The shift is indicated in Table 4.1.

It is observed that since the second half of the 1990s a wave of reforms has been sweeping the states in India. Prior to the 1990s there was relative uniformity of policies across states. The main role of the state government was to implement policies of the Central government. But the situation is quite different now. Certain states have taken the lead in introducing reforms and are far ahead, some lag far behind, and some others are in the middle. As a result, there has emerged diversity, in place of past uniformity, in India's economic policies at the state-level.

Table 4.1: Shift in Development Paradigm with Reforms at the State-level

Government responsibility	*Old paradigm: Role of government as*	*New paradigm: Role of government as*	*Examples of the shift*
(i) Economic management and growth	Central planner	Facilitator and regulator of market economy	• Privatisation and closure of public enterprises • Establishment of power sector regulators • Business deregulation
(ii) Provision of employment opportunities	Provision of employment through public sector hiring	Facilitator of employment opportunities	• Emphasis on physical and social infrastructure • Freeze of public sector hiring on non-critical areas
(iii) Financial management	Cash-flow manager	Fiscal manager	• Development of medium-term fiscal frameworks • Passage of fiscal responsibility legislation • Fiscal adjustment through tax and expenditure reforms • States making borrowing decisions on the basis of affordability rather than availability
(iv) Policy role	Implementer of Central policies	Policy maker in many areas as well as implementer	Variation in policies now seen across states
(v) Service provision	Broadening scope of services	Improving quality and access of existing services, as well as expanding their scope	Greater attention to education quality, rather than exclusive focus on increasing the number of schools

Source: Stephen Howes (2003: 20), in Stephen Howes et al. (eds), *State-level Reforms in India*.

One view is that reforms have brought in a healthy process of competitive developmentalism driving out competitive populism (Howes et al. 2003: 4). Neoclassical/neoliberal growth theory suggests decrease in regional inequalities and increasing convergence as a result of growth. But ironically there was rapid absolute divergence growing across the states in the 1990s and afterwards which coincides with the economic liberalisation programme (Aiyar 2001). The poor states have become further marginalised. Now the reformers, both internal and external, advocate that the poorest states stand most in need of reforms to promote growth (Howes et al. 2003: 21).

But the question is whether the poorer people in the leading reformist states have benefited from reforms? What is the nature of reforms in different sectors within a state and who are the winners and losers in the process? What reforms have been introduced in the economic and human development domains in particular and what are the results thereof? What is the role of external agencies in the process? To examine all this, we will focus in this chapter on the state of Gujarat which is regarded as a leading state in introducing reforms. Certain comparisons will be made with three other states that can be said to fall in the upper, middle and lower categories in terms of introduction of reforms. These include Andhra Pradesh (AP) in the upper category, Kerala in the middle and Bihar in the lower category. But in terms of overall ranking in 2004 (based on eight parametres), *India Today* placed Kerala, Gujarat, AP and Bihar at position 2, 7, 11, and 20 respectively (Saran 2004: 20–31). Further, it may be noted that reforms started when Gujarat was ruled by a national level right-wing political party BJP and AP and Bihar by regionally based political parties—TDP and RJD respectively (now AP is under the Congress rule and Bihar under a non-RJD coalition)—and Kerala by a left party coalition. Thus, the states covered here represent a cross-section of states in the country in terms of overall development, governance reform and ruling political party.

Asian Development Bank in India

ADB (set up in 1966) is a multilateral development finance institution covering Asia and the Pacific. It is owned by 63 members, from both within and outside the region. Its largest shareholders include USA (15.8 per cent), Japan (15.8 per cent), China (6.5 per cent), India (6.4 per cent), etc. It provides development assistance to the member countries in different forms both to governments and private enterprises. Assistance includes loans to public and private sectors for projects which promote socio-economic development, technical assistance for preparing projects, giving advice on operations and supporting regional activities. It also manages and administers funds for grants from bilateral donors, offers guarantees for and equity investments in private sector projects and holds policy dialogue with governments. Moreover to increase the impact of its projects, it also arranges co-financing from official and commercial sources. [The operations of ADB are financed by issuing bonds, recycling repayments and receiving contributions from members. Around 70 per cent of lending comes from its ordinary capital resources (OCR)—from borrowing through private placements and capital markets, paid-in shareholder capital and accumulated reserves. It also provides concessional loans from the Asian Development Fund (ADF) to the least developed countries. Its Technical Assistance Special Fund was US $1.0 billion at the end of 2003. Funding for technical assistance also comes from the Japan Special Fund (JSF) and other sources] (ADB 2004).

ADB extends assistance in varied sectors of development such as governance, finance, energy (electricity), industry, transport and communication, and social sectors like education and health. In the mid-1990s, the Bank shifted its macro-level strategy to a more focused state-level approach in its operations in India in the form of project financing, technical assistance and policy dialogue. In 2000, it decided to increase its state-level assistance to 50 per cent of its total lending in the coming years in India (ADB 2004).

The vision of ADB is dedicated to reducing poverty in Asia and the Pacific. In 1999, ADB's Board of Directors announced the Poverty Reduction Strategy which aims at combating poverty through the three following pillars:

(*i*) **Pro-poor, Sustainable Economic Growth:** To generate employment and incomes, and promote policies that encourage labour intensive growth;

(*ii*) **Inclusive Social Development:** To promote the development of human capital that is the primary asset of the poor, improve access to basic social services, and strengthen the social participation of the poor (including women and other groups vulnerable because of age, illness, disability, shocks from natural disasters, economic crises, or civil conflict); and

(*iii*) **Good Governance:** To facilitate participatory pro-poor policies and sound macro-economic management, ensure the transparent use of public funds, *encourage private sector growth*, promote effective delivery of public services and help establish the rule of law. (ADB 2004, emphasis added).

Good governance agenda of the ADB involves leveraging development impact through programmes of fiscal consolidation, sector reforms, state-level reforms and core governance interventions. The fiscal consolidation programme includes improvement in public sector management and tax administration. Other major areas of its interventions include private sector development, infrastructure development, and agriculture and rural development. ADB leverages with the multilateral and bilateral development institutions to enhance its impact through proper coordination, complementarity and avoiding duplication or operations at cross-purposes. This includes institutions like the World Bank, USAID (USA), DFID (UK), CIDA (Canada), NORAD (Norway), DANIDA (Denmark), AusAID (Australia), European Union, UNDP, etc.

ADB's Country Portfolio Review 2002 provides the details of sectoral distribution of loans extended to India as of 31 December 2002. The approved 66 loans to India were worth $ 11,481.2 million, and the ongoing 27 loans were $ 5,173.6 million only. The sectoral loans in terms of amount was highest for energy sector (34 per cent), followed by transport and communications (30 per cent) and social infrastructure (12 per cent) (see Figure 4.1, Table 4.2). Further, ADB's annual lending to India is expected to increase two times the existing level in the next three years and thus reach over 2 billion annually. Finance Minister P. Chidambaram recently announced that the bank's

Figure 4.1: Sectoral Distribution of ADB Loans to India as of (31 December 2002) (Number and Amount)

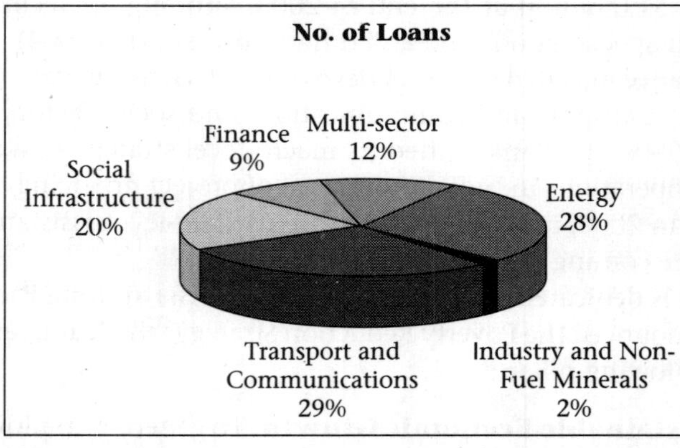

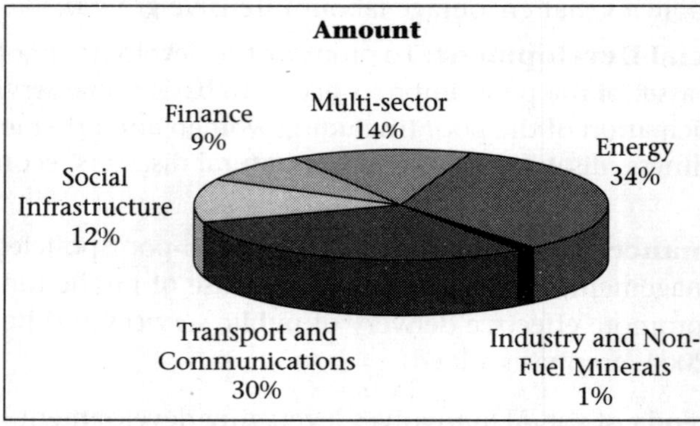

Source: Asian Development Bank (2003), *India—Country Portfolio Review 2002* (Joint Report of the Asian Development Bank and the Government of India), p. 3.

Table 4.2: Sectoral Distribution of ADB Loans to India (as of 31 December 2002)

	Approved		Ongoing	
Sector	*No.*	*Original loan Amount ($ million)*	*No.*	*Original loan Amount ($ million)*
Energy	19	3,842.0	7	1,375.0
Industry and Non-Fuel Minerals	1	150.0	0	0.0
Transport and Communications	19	3,419.2	8	1,688.6
Social Infrastructure	13	1,400.0	7	960.0
Finance	6	1,020.0	0	0.0
Multi-sector	8	1,650.0	5	1,150.0
Total	66	11,481.2	27	5,173.6

Source: Asian Development Bank (2003), *India: Country Portfolio Review 2002,* (Joint Report of the Asian Development Bank and the Government of India), p. 2.

lending to India would be $2.25 billion, $2.45 billion and $2.65 billion respectively in 2006, 2007 and 2008, which in total comes to 7.35 billion in the three year period (TOI 2006h). The loan is meant for both the Central government projects and for projects in several states.

ADB-led Reforms in Gujarat

The state of Gujarat was carved out of Maharashtra in 1960. It is situated in the western part of India. There are around 50 million people in the state. It is ranked third in terms of urbanisation, with about 38 per cent of the population living in the urban areas. The population of SCs, STs and Muslims in the state is 7 per cent, 15 per cent and 8.7 per cent respectively. The long coastline of the state measures 1600 km. A significant section of NRIs consists of Gujaratis. It is one of the more developed states in India.

ADB is the major international agency promoting governance reforms in different sectors in Gujarat. ADB's Country Operation Strategy study noted that the states in India lagged behind in fiscal adjustments and structural reforms. So, to address the next phase of reforms there was, it emphasised, a need to shift from the national to state level and support them for broadening and deepening of the macroeconomic and structural reform process. It required measures for corrections of the state's macro dynamics and thus prepare them to receive sectoral and project specific assistance. The bank considered the case of five states in India and finally selected Gujarat for its interventions. There were clearly favourable factors for Gujarat. The Gujarat State Finance Commission (set up in 1992) had already formulated a clear agenda for restructuring the state's public sector units, which included measures like closing down and disinvestment of units. Moreover, the bank found a strong political will in the state. 'There was broad consensus across all political parties to carry forward the reform process' (ADB 2000). Gujarat faced daunting structural problems. Its fiscal position was precarious because of stagnation in tax revenues and rising current expenditures. State-run enterprises were becoming increasingly inefficient. There were huge gaps in infrastructure which hindered industrial and economic growth. Hence, it was thought that if Gujarat succeeded, which had a better chance due to its favourable stance, it could serve as a 'role model' for other states (ibid.).

ADB extended loans to the state for development of a number of projects, offered technical project assistance, and held policy dialogue with the state government. The list of select approved loans and technical assistance provided to Gujarat by ADB (as of 31 December 2002) is given in Table 4.3(a) and (b). The bank assistance programme covers:

(*i*) Public Sector Resource Management Programme(PSRMP)
(*ii*) Reform of Public Finance
(*iii*) Restructuring of State-owned enterprises
(*iv*) Infrastructure development—particularly power/electricity sector, roads, etc.
(*v*) Private sector development

ADB provided a loan of $250 million to Gujarat under the Gujarat Public Sector Resource Management Programme (PSRMP), effective from December 1996. The programme focused on three aspects—

(*i*) Public finance reforms for improving the management of public resource.

(*ii*) Public sector reforms which involved closing down unviable units and privatisation and restructuring of others.

(*iii*) Creation of an enabling environment for private sector participation in critical infrastructure sectors by strengthening the policy, regulatory, legal and institutional framework.

Table 4.3(a): ADB's List of Select Approved Loans for Gujarat (by Sector) (as of 31 December 2002)

Sector/ Sl. no.	*Project name*	*Amount ($ million)*	*Approved date*
Energy			
1.	Gujarat Power Sector Development—Program Loan	150.000	13 Dec 2000
2.	Gujarat Power Sector Development—Project Loan	200.000	13 Dec 2000
Multisector			
3.	Gujarat Public Sector Resource Management Program	250.000	18 Dec 1996
4.	Gujarat Earthquake Rehabilitation and Reconstruction	500.000	26 Mar 2001
Transport and Communications			
5.	Surat-Manor Tollway	180.000	27 Jul 2000

Source: Asian Development Bank (2003), *India—Country Portfolio Review 2002* (Joint Report of the Asian Development Bank and the Government of India), pp. 14–16.

Table 4.3(b): ADB's List of Select Approved Technical Assistances (TAs) for Gujarat (by Sector) (as of 31 December 2002)

Sector/ Sl. no.	*Project name*	*Amount ($ million)*	*Approved date*
Energy			
1.	Preparation of a Power System Master Plan for the State of Gujarat	0.600	17 Dec 1996
2.	Development of a Framework for Electricity Tariffs in Gujarat	0.300	17 Dec 1996
3.	Review of Electricity Legislation and Regulations in Gujarat	0.235	17 Dec 1996
4.	Financial Management Support to Kheda and Rajkot Distribution Centers of Gujarat Electricity Board	0.580	17 Dec 1996
5.	Reorganization Plan for Gujarat Electricity Board	0.600	13 Dec 2000
6.	Support for Gujarat Electricity Regulatory Commission	0.450	13 Dec 2000
Finance			
7.	Capacity Enhancement of Gujarat Industrial Investment Corporation	0.500	30 May 1996
8.	Institutional Strengthening of the Gujarat Infrastructure Development Board	0.850	18 Dec 1996

(*Table 4.3(b) continued*)

(*Table 4.3(b) continued*)

Sector/ Sl. no.	Project name	Amount ($ million)	Approved date
Multisector			
9.	Capacity Building for Earthquake Rehabilitation and Reconstruction of Housing	1.300	26 Mar 2001
Transport and Communications			
10.	Vadodara-Bombay Expressway	0.600	15 Jun 1990
11.	Vadodara-Bombay Expressway (Supplementary)	0.250	19 Mar 1991
12.	Vadodara-Bombay Expressway TA Project Environmental Impact Assessment	0.090	10 Sep 1993
Others			
13.	Restructuring Program for State-Owned Enterprises in Gujarat	0.600	02 Apr 1996
14.	Gujarat's Reform of Public Finances	0.600	23 Oct 1996

Source: Asian Development Bank (2003), *India: Country Portfolio Review 2002*, (Joint Report of the Asian Development Bank and the Government of India), pp. 17–22.

This loan was to be released in three tranches ($100 million, $50 million and $100 million). The first transfer was released soon. But the other tranches were to be obtained upon systematic compliance with the agreed upon conditions. For getting the second tranche the state was to undertake tax reforms, initiate the first phase divestment of state public sector units and announce the road and power sector policies. In addition, the bank provided technical assistance grants totalling $1.9 million. This was meant to build capacities for implementation of fiscal reforms and privatisation of state's public sector units, to enhance capacities of the Gujarat Industrial Investment Corporation, for infrastructure development, and to develop the roles and functions of Gujarat Infrastructure Development Board (GIDB) (ADB 2000).

Reforms Introduced in Gujarat

Indian democracy is a union of states, with substantial extent of federal features. After Independence, different Indian states followed distinct trajectory of economic and social development within the broad national framework of Five Year Plans under which the state operated as the most important agency of development. The process of economic reforms was initiated and pursued haltingly on a low key by the Central government in the 1980s. Further, in the immediate context of the BoP crisis in 1991, the Central government embarked in a systematic way on the path of private sector-centered reforms popularly known as LPG, and in this the IMF and World Bank have played a key role by making loans conditional upon introduction of the reforms package as these agencies had already done in case of various other countries in the third world. It is observed, 'The process of shift in ideology from state intervention to market orientation, which was initiated and speeded up since 1991 in India, implies the restoration of the functioning of market forces in all markets by removing or reducing quantity restrictions on supply, removing price controls and other distortions and reducing unjustified or unnecessary market interventions by the government' (R. Dholakia 2003: 303). The LPG agenda provided to the states ample scope to introduce governance reforms to move towards private-sector led growth. However, the pace of reforms differs from state to state depending upon the state specific correlation of forces.

Economic Reforms

There are several lobbies in the state of Gujarat which influence policies and programmes of the government in the state (Mahadevia 2005: 301–02). The industrial lobby has exercised considerable influence from the very beginning of the formation of the state. Rich farmers who arose with the green revolution form another lobby. They largely belong to the canal-irrigated regions of Kheda, Bharuch and Surat districts and the cash crop producing areas of Mehsana and Saurashtra districts. Industrialists engaged in production of groundnut oil constitute a third important lobby (groundnut is an important cash crop grown in the Saurashtra region). A fourth important lobby of those involved in real estate (land) emerged in the 1990s and continue to gain support from the government in the reform period.

On the official website, the Government of Gujarat claims itself to be the 'business state' of India (GOG 2006). It has introduced a series of reforms in recent years relating to the public sector enterprises, private sector development, human development sector and administration in general. Gujarat has come out with a slew of visions and new set of policies such as Infrastructure Vision 2010, Agro Vision 2010 and Human Development Vision 2010. Since its creation in 1961, Gujarat has given emphasis on industrialisation. However, the state got a new opportunity to speed up industrialisation with the launch of economic reforms by the Central government in 1991. Three industrial policies were announced by the state government in the 1990s. These include the State Industrial Policy 1990–95 (already operational when the Central government declared the New Industrial Policy in 1991), the New Industrial and Incentive Policy 1995–2000 (with the title 'The Best Now Becomes Even Better'), and then a policy statement known as 'Gujarat 2000 AD and beyond'. The goal of the state was to become a 'tiger economy' like Southeast Asia and East Asia (Mahadevia 2005: 296).

Economic reforms cover Public Sector Enterprises (PSE), fiscal reform and private sector development. Reforms of PSE relate to disinvestment, restructuring and closure. The Gujarat government had initiated measures towards privatisation even when the country's economic environment was highly protective and government control was comprehensive (Wadhwani 2006). As of 24 January 2002, out of a total of about 54 State Public Enterprises in Gujarat, 24 were identified and the process of reform was initiated. Six were closed and three privatised (see Table 4.4). Though a little change/slowing down in the approach of the Central government was observed with respect to privatisation of PSEs, the Government of Gujarat identified 12 more PSEs for disinvestment in 2004 (see Table 4.5) which set the share prices of these companies rise very significantly. In April 2006, the Government of Gujarat accepted the expert group advice to give up control over Gujarat Alkalies and Chemicals Ltd (GACL) by disinvesting its stake in the company, which has a market capitalisation of Rs 1,532 crore (Shah 2006i). The state has stuck to moving in a determined way on the reforms front while some other

Table 4.4: Disinvestment in States

State	*Approximate number of SLPEs*	*SLPEs identified for disinvestment/winding up/restructuring*	*No. of SLPEs in which process initiated*	*No. of SLPEs privatised*	*No. of SLPEs closed down*
Gujarat	**50**	**24**	**24**	**3**	**6**
Andhra Pradesh	128	87	79	13	38
Kerala	111	55	40	–	10
Bihar	54	6	6	–	–
Orissa	72	33	10	9	11
Arunachal Pradesh	7	–	–	–	–
Assam	42	–	–	–	–
Delhi	15	–	1	1*	–
Haryana	45	8	6	1	4
Himachal Pradesh	21	15	8	3	2
Jammu & Kashmir	20	7	2	–	–
Karnataka	85	39	20	2	12
Madhya Pradesh	26	14	14	1	–
Maharashtra	66	11	4	–	–
Manipur	14	10	–	–	–
Mizoram	5	–	–	–	–
Punjab	53	11	11	1	6
Rajasthan	28	10	6	1	1
Sikkim	12	–	–	–	–
Tamil Nadu	59	29	29	–	7
Uttar Pradesh	41	25	25	1	14
West Bengal	82	15	15	–	–
Total	1036	399	300	36	111

Source: Government of India (2006), Department of Disinvestment, Ministry of Finance.
Notes: SLPE—State Level Public Enterprises; * Delhi Vidyut Board.

Table 4.5: PSUs Identified for Disinvestment in Gujarat, 2004

Sl. no.	*Public sector undertaking*	*Listed company*
1.	Gujarat State Finance Corporation (GSFC-Finance)	Yes
2.	Gujarat State Fertiliser and Chemicals (GSFC-Fertiliser)	Yes
3.	Gujarat Narmada Valley Fertilisers Company (GNFC)	Yes
4.	Gujarat Alkalies and Chemicals Limited (GACL)	Yes
5.	Gujarat Mineral Development Corporation (GMDC)	Yes
6.	Gujarat Industries Power Company Limited (GIPCL)	Yes
7.	Gujarat Industrial Development Corporation (GIDC)	No
8.	Gujarat Industrial Investment Corporation (GIIC)	No
9.	Gujarat Power Corporation (GPC)	No
10.	Gujarat State Petroleum Corporation (GSPC)	No
11.	Gujarat Agro-Industries Corporation (GAIC)	No
12.	Gujarat State Warehouse Corporation (GSWC)	No

Source: *Times of India* (Ahmedabad edn), 'Gujarat Takes First Step to Disinvestment', 24 September 2004.

states seem to be holding on in this connection. It is found that till January 2002, 18,000 employees were affected under PSRP in Gujarat and 17,702 employees relieved at the cost of Rs 324.53 crore. Moreover, in 1999 under the VRS package 3,040 employees were relieved at the cost of Rs 96 crore.

The state of Gujarat has taken numerous measures in a systematic manner to promote private sector-led growth particularly with the onset of the LPG regime since 1991. Since its inception in 1961, the state had deliberately adopted industrialisation as the path of development, and initiated certain measures in late 1980s, which fed into the reforms steps undertaken after 1991.

The Gujarat government adopted different instruments, like certain other states, for promoting private sector development. The instruments used by the government include the following:

(*a*) providing tax and cost-related incentives;
(*b*) provision of infrastructure and input supplies;
(*c*) granting various approvals and clearances, especially to the small scale, cottage and the tiny sector units (since these sectors, unlike the big and medium ones, are under effective control of the state government); and
(*d*) restoring market forces in the land market in the state (R. Dholakia 2003: 304).

Industrial policy adopted by the state government in the 1990s provides a clear idea of the tax and cost-related incentives offered to the private sector. For encouraging the private enterprises, the main instrument used by the government, in the early phase of reforms, included reduction, exemption and deferment of sales tax payments by the new business and industry. This led to substantial reduction in the sales tax revenue collected by the state. On this score, there are estimates showing loss of revenue to the government to the tune of Rs 2.10 billion per annum during 1991–95, increasing to Rs 13.43 billion in 1998–99 and Rs 41.2 billion during 2000–01 (R. Dholakia 2003: 305).

Other states, besides Gujarat, also entered into a competition to offer tax-related concessions to attract private enterprises, and in the process lost the score which caused fiscal problem for them. The Central government intervened and a consensus was reached by states to introduce sales tax reforms which included stopping all exemptions from January 2000, uniform floor rates, etc. Gujarat government implemented these measures. At the same time it reviewed its industrial policy to ensure incentives to the private sector. As a result, tax concessions were substituted by subsidies to the private sector. Gujarat Industrial and Agro-Industrial Policies 2000 made ample provision for such subsidies offered in different forms.

So, a change in the strategy of the state government is observed, i.e., the replacement of the hidden subsidy in the form of tax benefits by the explicit subsidies. But there is

> 'no change in the basic philosophy, theory, or approach of the government of Gujarat for attracting private sector activities in the state. Under both the policies, the government believes in first allowing directly productive activity and leaving the infrastructure development to the felt need, or shortages, or political pressures, rather than first creating the social overhead capital and waiting for its utilisation' (R. Dholakia 2003: 307).

Besides changes in strategy, this approach reflects that 'the government never becomes irrelevant and inconsequential. Under both these policies, discretion is retained with the bureaucrats and politicians' (ibid.). There continues to exist the illegal but private market for favours and discretion which involves the politicians, bureaucrats and the potential beneficiaries of the subsidies (ibid.).

The New Industrial and Incentive Policy 1995–2000 ('The Best Now Becomes Even Better') offered tax concessions for industries to set up their own infrastructure like residential colonies, roads, water transportation facilities, etc. This largely benefited the large industries. There are also other measures taken by the state government with regard to tax concessions. In 1997, the turnover tax was abolished. In May 2001, octroi was abolished from 143 towns and 14,000 villages (but not from the major municipal corporation areas in the state). Though fiscal crisis forced the government to reduce certain earlier tax exemptions, the 2000 policy provided assistance to private entrepreneurs in several ways, thus playing the role of enabler of private sector-led development in the state. Further, to accelerate growth a number of incentives are provided to the private sector development under the Industrial and Agro-industrial Policies 2000. The government has offered support for new units and also for expansions and diversifications. Incentives offered to the private sector as per 2000 Policies include (R. Dholakia 2003: 306)

(*i*) **Interest subsidy:** It is for new units in small scale industries (SSI) and service sector industries, and offered at the rate of 5 per cent per annum up to a cumulative maximum of Rs 2.5 million and Rs 0.5 million respectively. For expansion and diversification of existing units, the interest subsidy is at the rate of 3 per cent per annum upto a cumulative maximum of Rs 1.5 million.

(*ii*) **Research and development (R&D) subsidy:** Financial assistance is offered up to Rs 50 million per industrial cluster for establishing common facilities covering quality improvement, technology upgrade, market promotion and technical skills. Similarly, a subsidy at the rate of 50 per cent of expenses up to Rs 0.5 million is offered for filing patents on research by industries or R&D institutions.

(*iii*) **Quality improvement assistance:** Industrial units obtaining quality certification from approved institutions/research laboratories are offered a subsidy at the rate of 50 per cent of expenditure up to a maximum of Rs 0.2 million

(*iv*) **Backward area development:** Industrial units coming up in the identified backward Taluka are offered additional incentives at the rate of 25 per cent under all schemes.

(*v*) **Capital subsidy:** For self-financed new SSI units, there is a subsidy at the rate of 10 per cent of fixed capital investment (up to Rs 1 million); for employment park with employment in excess of 2,500, a subsidy at the rate of 10 per cent of capital investment (up to a maximum of Rs 20 million); for hi-tech park, a subsidy at the rate of 50 per cent of capital investment (up to a maximum of Rs 25 million); and a subsidy of up to Rs 5 million for trade centres with more than 500 square metres of constructed area.

(*vi*) **Environmental protection assistance:** An interest subsidy is offered for industrial units that undertake environment protection measures.

(*vii*) **Land provision:** Priority accorded to the allocation of required land to industrial units with the 'Deemed NA' concept is made more effective. Land is proposed to be offered at affordable prices to industrial units.

(*viii*) **Airfreight subsidy:** For agro-industries and food industries, a subsidy (a maximum of Rs 1 million per exporter) and a subsidy for market development abroad (a maximum of Rs 50, 000 per exporter) are offered.

(*ix*) **Project report preparation assistance:** A subsidy is offered at the rate of 50 per cent of the cost of project proposal preparation for agro-industries.

It is stated that most of the subsidies offered by the government benefit the Small Scale Industries (SSIs), which cover those with investment in plant and machinery up to Rs 10 million. A 1999–2000 survey showed that only 3 per cent of 0.25 million SSIs have made investment (plant and machinery) exceeding Rs 2.5 million. So, the main objective of providing subsidies seems to be for protecting the SSIs, which generate employment opportunities for the people outside agriculture (R. Dholakia 2003).

The state government has taken several steps to improve supplies of certain critical inputs (like coal and water) to promote the private sector growth. Measures relating to water supply concern the construction of dams, better water conservation practices and hike in user charges to reflect the scarcity value of the resources. Importing better quality coal is an option to increase efficiency and reduce costs. It is observed that the state achieved high annual growth rates of value added during the 1990s in the registered (12.7 per cent) and unregistered (7.1 per cent) manufacturing sectors. In the early 1990s, an impressive growth was observed in the number of new SSI units registered in the state but a decline in later years. For the promotion of small and cottage industries, the district industries centre (DIC) has been made more effective by delegation of power by the government with regard to registration for several developmental and subsidy purposes. Periodic meeting of the District Industrial Executive Committee is held to discuss and resolve problems of industrialists. An important measure is the provision of a citizen's charter for all DICs, which gives details of procedural requirements and time limits for various clearances and approvals required. Strict monitoring is done regularly through a computerised process.

Large scale units have grown faster in comparison with the SSI units in the state. The favourable SSI policy does not seem to have led the investors to split enterprises into fragmented smaller units. State governments have only a limited role in case of larger units as these lie mainly in the domain of the Central government. But in Gujarat, the DICs and the office of the industries commissioner provide assistance to such units in what they need. DICs undertake follow-up and monitoring of the progress in these cases. In 1997, the state government granted permission for conversion of agricultural land to non-agricultural (NA) uses without much hiccups up to the limit of 10 hectares. For curtailing delays, the process was simplified for getting the NA permission for land from the collectorate. This measure helped the large-scale industries and helped up industrialisation.

LPG is reflected in the fast growth of Special Economic Zones (SEZs) in the country with the policy changes at the central level (Exim Policy) and supportive role of state governments. Exim Policy 2000 was introduced by the Central government to provide an internationally competitive and hassle-free environment for export of goods and services. SEZs are treated as foreign territories for trade operations. They are offered huge incentives in terms of tax exemptions, labour flexibility and provision of infrastructural facilities to operate as foreign exchange earners (Rai 2005). The Gujarat Industrial Policy 2000 pushes for further industrial diversification to enters into new sectors such as IT and other knowledge-based industries. Moreover, it aims at stimulating industrial clusters through, for instance, promoting the establishment of private sector, employment-intensive industrial parks like biotech parks, IT parks, trade centers, etc. An important concern is promotion of exports from the state. For this purpose, the policy specifies the procedures and incentives for setting up SEZs which are offered several tax exemptions. There is, for example, complete exemption on the payment of stamp duty and registration fees on the transfer of land for industrial purpose in the SEZ area. Transactions within the SEZ are exempted from all state taxes like sales tax, VAT, luxury tax, etc. The environmental and labour laws compliance processes have been streamlined. Thus, a SEZ is 'treated as an independent foreign authority' for all practical purposes (Mahadevia 2005: 304). In 2005, Gujarat had seven approved SEZs. Kandla SEZ is the first one (earlier an Export Processing Zone, converted as SEZ in March 2000) in the state, Positra is a public-private venture and Surat is the first private sector SEZ in the country. In case of Kandla SEZ, a sum of Rs 2003 million was invested on infrastructure development of the zone by the Central government. Private entrepreneurs have invested Rs 762 million which includes Rs 29 million by NRIs and Rs 9 million by foreign companies (Rai 2005: 18). With the Central government approval (in June 2006) of eight fresh proposals to set up SEZs, the total number of SEZs in the state has gone up to 17. The latest eight proposals include three SEZs to be developed by the state-run Gujarat State Indsutrial Development Corporation (GIDC) concerning apparel park (one in Ahmedabad and another at Surat) and electronics (at Gandhinagar). Two will be developed by private developers—a multi-product one in Jamnagar by Essar and a pharma SEZ by Cadila near Dhandukha in Ahmedabad district. Three have been given 'in principle' approval (Adanis—multi-product, Essar—Engineering, Welspun—textile). (Shah 2006k).

Two SEZs are fully functional in the state, as indicated already. Three sector-specific SEZs are expected to be functional by the end of 2007, which includes the apparel parks at Surat and Ahmedabad and the gems and jewellery park at Surat. Six are in the pipeline and another six are under consideration by the state government. This covers two big multipurpose SEZs, spread over 10,000 hectares each, being developed by Adani group at Mundra and by Reliance at Jamnagar. It is proposed that Zydus-Cadilla will set up a pharma SEZ at Changodar, GIDC will develop an electronics SEZ at Gandhinagar and an IT SEZ will be built by a private party near Ahmedabad (TOI 2006c). In March 2006, 150 SEZs were approved at the first meeting of the Board of Approval (BoA) of the Union Commerce Ministry. Of these, nine are from Gujarat. According to the opinion of the state officials, the state would get a lion's share of almost 40 per cent of the expected total investment of Rs 1,00,000 crore over the next three years. This would be because of the sheer magnitude of some of the SEZs coming up in the state (Shah 2006f).

Further, reversal of the land reform policy of the pre-reform period has been observed in Gujarat. The Bombay Tenancy and Agricultural Lands Act 1948 was there to prevent absentee landlordism. But it was amended in March 1995 to permit the purchase of agricultural lands anywhere in the state. This was to benefit those willing to acquire large landholdings for capital-intensive farming and the urban real estate developers. The Tenancy Act 1948 provided protection to the tenant farmers who got land as a result of redistribution of land under this Act. Such *navi sharat* land belonging to tenants was not allowed to be sold. But in 1993, this Act was amended and the sale/purchase of *navi sharat* land was permitted. Under the Bombay Land Revenue Code 1979, it was necessary to obtain No Objection Certificate (NOC) from the government authority for conversion of agricultural land to non-agricultural use. But in 1996, the government exempted, by an ordinance, purchase of land up to 10 hectares for industrial use from NOC requirement and such a purchase needs only to be notified by the district collectorate. The Urban Land Ceiling and Regulation (ULCR) Act 1976 fixed a ceiling on land ownership by individuals in urban areas. This was repealed in 1999. This has facilitated free transaction of land in urban areas and is expected to release the excess land locked up with many industrial units for sale and development purposes like housing and construction. In October 2001, the government also amended the Rent Control Act to deal with the problem of vacant premises and boost building construction in urban areas. Thus, the new land policies adopted during the reform period catered to the demands of the industrial lobby and further their interests (Mahadevia 2005: 306). With the annual budget 2006–07, the state government reduced stamp duty on registration of immovable properties from the existing 8.4 per cent to 6 per cent, which met the long-standing demand of the construction industry. This budget also proposed full exemption from electricity duty and luxury tax for five years and also from stamp duty on the purchase of land for those who develop 'good hotels at strategic places' as part of the 'Tourism Year' celebration. (TOI 2006e).

Furthermore, the Gujarat Infrastructure Agenda 2010 provides a blueprint for privatisation of infrastructure in the state. The document follows the Government of India report titled 'India Infrastructure Report'. It offers a new development framework of the state. It marks a shift in perspective which indicates moving away from regional planning to project-based planning with cluster development in specific locations. Issues of regional inequalities and distribution of benefits are sidelined. The document provides a framework for the involvement of the private sector in the construction and operation of infrastructure projects. The state government took several measures in the latter part of the 1990s in connection with extending infrastructural support and input supplies to the productive enterprises. This mainly covers areas like electricity, ports and roads. Policy changes have been made to permit private sector participation in the power, ports and road subsectors. For this the government has formulated Build-Own-Operate-Transfer (BOOT) policy. There is also the BOOT law, i.e., the Gujarat Infrastructure Development Act 1999 which provides a legal framework for private participation in financing, construction, maintenance and operation of infrastructure projects in the areas of power, ports, dams, and also health facilities, water supply and education (Mahadevia 2005: 202–03). Measures also involve introduction of guidelines for transparent competitive bidding, restructuring of government agencies dealing with infrastructure to have commercial orientation and effective partnership for public and private sector development. In March 2006 the state government passed an amendment to the Gujarat Infrastructure Development Act 1999, which permits project developers to profitably invest in the state without entering into competitive bidding under specific conditions (TOI 2006f). While introducing the amendment, the Minister of State Industries expressed the hope that the memoranda of understanding for infrastructure projects could now be implemented quickly and the state would be able to attract an investment of Rs 3.40 lakh crore by 2020.

As per the recommendations of the Gujarat State Finance Commission 1994 report, power sector reforms started in 1995–96. The participation of the private sector was permitted in the power sector. The government policy statements relate to CPP (captive power policy) for own use and IPP (independent power projects) for private power supplier to the power grid with guarantees against demand risks and losses. IPP attracted private parties and thus led to the creation of additional power generation capacity, sometimes leading to marginal oversupply of power in the state. But the power purchased from the private parties cost relatively higher which led to deterioration of the financial conditions of the Gujarat Electricity Board (GEB). So in 2000, the government formed the Gujarat Electricity Regulatory Commission (GERC), an independent regulatory body to monitor the functioning of both the GEB and the IPPs, and to decide on the pricing and investment in the power sector. Steps were taken to make obligatory installation of meters by the consumers. The GERC made tariff revisions in 2001, with the agricultural rates raised five times and the industrial rates by 4 to 15 per cent. But there has been opposition to the introduction of this measure, particularly by the farmers' lobby agitations due to the steep hike. Other concerns of the government included cutting the cost of raw materials (such as coal used for power generation) and downsizing the staff strength of GEB (R. Dholakia 2003). Unbundling/trifurcation of the GEB into production, transmission and distribution units has been completed. Privatisation is to gain more strength. Private sector participation in power generation is already operational. Private sector entry in distribution of power is actively under government consideration and may not be far off. In 2006, the government of Gujarat boasted of being a power surplus state. But later it turned into a power deficit state. The power shortage is reported to be of the order of 15,000 MW—the maximum demand being 8,957 MW as against the supply of 7,567 MW. This has led to load-shedding mostly affecting the farm sector which gets only about 8 hours of power supply a day. The deficit is said to be caused by rising demand related to 'rapid' economic growth. No wonder, the Minister of State for Energy, Saurabh Patel, recently held a pre-bid conference with about 40 prospective investors to enter into power purchase agreements with the state-run Gujarat Energy Development Corporation Ltd (GEDCL). The participants at the conference included private investors like Reliance Power, Tata Power, Birla Power, Jindal Power, Larson & Toubro, etc. (TOI 2006i).

The Gujarat government was the first in the country to work in conjunction with the private sector in developing port facilities, estates and roads. The Gujarat Infrastructure Development Act is meant to facilitate setting up of infrastructure projects with the help of private sector investment. The government is actively promoting private participation in sectors like ports and roads. In this connection it has adopted the policy of BOOT. The Pipavav port (Saurashtra) and the Mundra port in Kachchh are the first greenfield ports in the country developed on a BOOT basis. At the Pipavav Port, the government has introduced the concepts of private port and private companies owning their jetties. In the new port projects, the government is promoting private ports as well as joint ventures. The Gujarat Maritime Board is undergoing bifurcation and unbundling. There are projects of the private sector under BOT schemes in road construction. There are policy proposals to have private participation in the storage of specialised cargo at the air cargo complex in Ahmedabad and other such complexes. Around 400 infrastructure projects have been proposed to be implemented by 2010 with the participation of the private sector. The Gujarat Industrial Development Corporation (GIDC) has started transferring (on long-term lease) the operation and management of the industrial estates and sheds built by the government to the private sector, that is, associations. (In the annual state budget of 2006–07, land allotted in the GIDC estates on lease for 99 years is allowed to be converted to free hold (TOI 2006e)]. Moreover, since 1998–99, the representatives of the private sector from the Gujarat Chamber of Commerce and Industries (GCCI) are being inducted in to the board of the state government bodies concerned with the infrastructure and related matters, that is, the Gujarat Electricity Board, the Gujarat Infrastructure Development Board, the Gujarat Pollution Control Board, etc. (R. Dholakia 2003).

In 2000, the Government of Gujarat prepared its 'Agrovision 2010'. The preparation of this vision document was not done by the government, but entrusted to be done jointly by A.F. Ferguson & Co. (an Indian private consultancy firm) and Rabo India Finance Pvt. Ltd., a subsidiary of Rabo Bank of the Netherlands. The vision set in the document aims at linking up farmers of the state with international markets. In this, major emphasis is given to technological means like biotechnology and information technology for raising agricultural productivity (Mahadevia 2005: 305).

Reforms also include measures for reduction of fiscal deficit in the state. The state government took measures for its rightsizing. In 1991, due to financial crisis it imposed a 20 per cent ban on recruitments in government departments. Fiscal measures also involve tax reforms and expenditure reforms. It is noted that the sales tax structure required simplification and rationalisation to increase transparency and efficiency, and eventually introduction of VAT as in other states. Most states in the country have accepted VAT as a result of the efforts of the Central government, but Gujarat took time to decide and finally joined the rest from April 1 2006. The reform programme includes rationalisation of the role of structure of stamp duty, entertainment tax and motor vehicle tax. In the expenditure reform, an important element in the state is the introduction of the Core Investment Programme at aggregate and sectoral levels (Shelat 1997: 106).

As regards performance, Gujarat is said to have emerged as a 'role model for the entire nation' (Wadhwani 2006). It is claimed that year 2005 belonged to Gujarat, which showed the highest economic growth rate in the country. The state received the national award for Investment Environment and Economic Freedom. In its report of 2005, Department of Industrial Policy and Promotion (DIPP) of the Government of India put Gujarat at number one in attracting investment. A study by Debroy and Bhandari (2005) (of the Rajiv Gandhi Institute for Contemporary Studies, New Delhi) placed the state at the top in 2004 and second in 2005 on the economic freedom index. The state government regularly organises Annual Global Investors Summit with the slogan of 'Vibrant Gujarat' which generally coincides with the Uttarayan festival held in January in the state. The last Vibrant Gujarat Investors' Summit was held in January 2007.

The proactive approach of the state government towards industry has led to a huge increase in industrial investments. During 1991–2002, the state got about 6,000 industrial entrepreneur's memorandum and a total investment of Rs 1,662,720 million. Hence, annual investment has come up to about Rs 1,511.6 million. This is around 16 per cent of the annual investment occurring in India (CMIE 2003, cited in Mahadevia 2005: 296). So, Gujarat emerged as second only to Maharashtra in attracting investments in the reform period. It needs to be noted that these are mainly national investment, not FDI. (See also Table 4.6 for more details on investment in large and medium industries).

Table 4.6: Industrial Investment Sanctioned in Large and Medium Industries in Gujarat (1983–2002)

Particulars	*1983–90*	*1991–96*	*1997–2002*	*1991–2002*
Total number of projects	886	4,423	2,529	6,952
Number of projects per year	110.75	732.00	422.00	632.00
Total Investment (in Rs million)	2,138.6	17,011.69	7,893.83	24,905.52
Investment per year (in Rs million)	267.22	2,835.28	1,315.640	1,336.866
Total Employment (in number)	1,41,637	8,43,673	1,95,399	10,39,072
Employment per project (in number)	17,704	1,40,612	32,567	94,461
Investment per project (in Rs million)	2.414	3.846	3.121	3.582
Employment per project	159.86	190.74	77.26	149.46

Source: Hirway and Mahadevia (2003), drawn from Mahadevia (2005: 296).

Quoting Chief Minister Narendra Modi, the Gujarat Information Bureau, Gandhinagar reported a significant growth in terms of projects commissioned and actual investment made in the state worth Rs 14,856 crore which is claimed to be 84.35 per cent of the investments in the country during the period from March to October 2005. But this abnormally high percentage is found to be actually a result of the proactive approach of the Gujarat government to quickly provide investment figures to the DIPP of the Central government. In fact, this figure is in sharp contrast to the figures of the Centre for Monitoring Indian Economy (CMIE) (December 2005). According to CMIE, a total of Rs 8,49,503 crore projects were being implemented in the country. In this, Gujarat's share is Rs 73,497 crore, i.e., 8.65 per cent (not 84.35 per cent as claimed), and Maharashtra is at the top with Rs 99,160 crore, i.e., 11.6 per cent. Gujarat comes only next to Maharashtra rather than topping the list. 'Creating a hype is one thing, but realities lie elsewhere' (Shah 2006c).

Dholakia (2003: 317) observes that Gujarat's secondary sector and modern service sector have certainly benefited from the national policy on liberalisation. Moreover, the state government has adopted consistent policies and further measures to liberalise the state economy and facilitate private sector development. As a result, impetus to accelerated growth is witnessed in the industrial sector of the state.

It is observed from Table 4.7 that the growth rate of the economy of Gujarat in terms of per capita SDP was very high in the post-reform period (7.62 per cent per annum during 1993–94 to 1997–98) than in the pre-reform period (only 2.5 per cent per annum during 1983–84 to 1993–94). Its growth rate (per capita SDP) in the post-reform period is about three times higher than states like

Table 4.7: Annual Rate of Growth of Per Capita SDP (1993–94 to 1997–98)

Sl. no.	*State*	*1983–84 to 1993–94 (per cent per annum)*	*1993–94 to 1997–98* (per cent per annum)*
1.	Gujarat	2.50	7.62
2.	Andhra Pradesh	3.49	2.40
3.	Kerala	4.11	3.79
4.	Bihar	0.78	2.14
5.	All 14 States**	3.16	3.87

Source: Drawn from M.S. Ahluwalia (2000: 1640, Table 5).

Notes: * Growth rates in this table have been calculated as compound growth rates between the two end years and not as log-linear trends. This is partly because of the limited number of observations in the second period and partly also because these growth rates are being used to explain changes in poverty between the two end years of the first period which makes the calculation of growth rates based on end years more appropriate.

** Other states include Rajasthan, Uttar Pradesh, Orissa, Madhya Pradesh, Tamil Nadu, Karnataka, West Bengal, Haryana, Maharashtra and Punjab.

AP and Bihar. In this connection, only Gujarat shows improving performance unlike AP, Kerala and Bihar. Increased liberalisation occurring in Gujarat is clearly reflected in the Economic Freedom Index for the states in India, prepared recently by Debroy and Bhandari (2005). The composite economic freedom index for the states placed Gujarat on rank 1 in 2004 and rank 2 in 2005 (Tamil Nadu replaced Gujarat to occupy the top rank in 2005). (The economic freedom index for Indian states is similar to the Economic Freedom of the World index. However, in measuring economic freedom, the world index covers five major areas whereas this state-level index includes only three, that is, (*i*) size of the government-expenditures, taxes and enterprises (small government size implies more economic freedom), (*ii*) legal structure and security of property rights, and (*iii*) regulation of credit, labour and business (lower degree of regulation is considered indicative of more economic freedom). This economic freedom index is very much in line with the agenda of governance reforms in the LPG map.) Reforms have raised the pace of industrialisation and urbanisation in the state due to the higher growth in secondary and tertiary sectors. But the agriculture sector has lagged behind, even pulling down the overall SDP growth rates in recent decades in the state.

In terms of per capita income, Gujarat occupied third position amongst 15 major states in India in 1970–71 (after Punjab and Haryana), but slided to fourth position in 1980–81, 1990–91 and 2000–01 (after Punjab, Maharashtra and Haryana) (Hirway and Mahadevia 2004: 306, Table 53). In 2000–01 per capita income in the state was Rs 12,975, compared with Rs 3,859 in Bihar and Rs 15,390 in Punjab (at 1993–94 prices).

In case of Gujarat low overall SDP growth rate has been noted in the last two decades, 4.96 in 1980–81 to 1990–91 and 5.98 during 1993–94 to 2000–01 (Mahadevia 2005: 294), compared with India as a whole. Revenue deficit in the state shot up from Rs 592 crore in 1996–97 to Rs 3,546 crore in 1999–2000, to Rs 3,546 crore in 1999–00 and Rs 6,732 crore in 2001–02. This shows over eleven-fold increase in revenue deficit in the six year period. Further, fiscal deficit of the state increased from Rs 2,359 crore in 1996–97 to Rs 6,705 in 1999–00 and Rs 6,511 in 2001–02, reflecting about three-fold increase during the period (see Hirway and Mahadevia 2004: 69, Table 3.10).

In fact Gujarat does not show an encouraging trend regarding its fiscal and revenue situation. Its revenue deficit declined in the early 1990s (2.51 per cent of NSDP in 1990–91 to 0.34 per cent in 1995–96), but reached a higher level (2.75 per cent of NSDP) in 1999–2000. Similarly, Gujarat's fiscal deficit significantly declined in early 1990s (6.42 per cent of NSDP in 1990–91 to 2.71 per cent in 1995–96), but shot up again to 6.01 per cent of NSDP in 1999–2000. Its fiscal deficit trend is similar to Kerala, though AP and Bihar have deteriorated in this regard over the years (see Table 4.8). Further, the debt servicing burden of the state is quite high in the post-reform period (around 13 per cent of the total expenditure) compared to the 1980s (4 per cent to 6 per cent of total expenditure) and early 1990s (around 9 per cent). This has happened despite cut imposed by the state on the subsidy particularly in the late 1990s (see Table 4.9). The burden of public debt has increased in the post-reform period in the state. The

Table 4.8: Fiscal Imbalances in Select States (% of NSDP)

		Revenue deficit			Fiscal deficit		
Sl. no.	*State*	*1990–91*	*1995–96*	*1999–2000*	*1990–91*	*1995–96*	*1999–2000*
i)	Gujarat	2.51	0.34	2.75	6.42	2.71	6.01
ii)	Andhra Pradesh	0.46	1.03	2.34	2.79	3.36	5.16
iii)	Kerala	2.67	1.15	3.88	5.06	3.71	5.49
iv)	Bihar	2.17	2.81	5.45	6.11	4.09	9.37
	All states	0.93	0.73	2.94	3.30	2.60	4.75

Source: M. Govinda Rao (2002: 3269).
Notes: All states is sum of 25 states.
For states, major states and special states it is ratio to NSDP new series. For all states it is ratio to GDP new series.

Table 4.9: Selected Expenditures in Gujarat's Budgets

	% of total expenditure	
Year	*Debt service*	*Subsidies*
1980–81	4.57	4.20
1985–86	6.67	4.20
1990–91	9.26	6.40
1995–96	12.28	15.26
1997–98 (R)	12.66	9.68
1997–98 (B)	13.27	N.A.

Sources: Directorate of Economics and Statistics, *Budget in Brief*, Annual Publication, Government of Gujarat, Gandhinagar; *Economic and Purpose Classification of Budgets of Gujarat State* (Annual). (Drawn from: Archana R. Dholakia [1999: 273]).
Notes: R — Revised, B — Budgeted.

ratio of public debt to GSDP increased from 0.20 in 1996–97 to 0.38 in 2001–02 (Hirway and Mahadevia 2004: 69, Table 3.10). According to an RBI publication on state finances, the Gujarat government's total debt increased from Rs 8,075 crore in 1991, to 12,998 crore in 1995, Rs 41,003 crore in 2001, 73,669 crore in 2005, and was likely to reach a whopping Rs 81,491.5 crore in 2006. As percentage of GSDP it comes to 20.5 per cent in 1991 to 26.5 per cent in 1995, 37.8 per cent in 2001, 46.6 per cent in 2005 and 45.7 per cent in 2006. The publication observes that in 2006 the debts of only three state governments (UP, Maharashtra and West Bengal) would reach a higher figure than that of Gujarat. No wonder, the Comptroller and Auditor General's report sounded an alarm about the unsustainability of such debt burden and emergence of a debt trap situation. Gujarat government passed a fiscal responsibilities legislation in 2005. However, it is said to be ironical that in the same year the debt-GSDP ratio rose very high-reaching 46.6 per cent (Shah 2006e).

Further, Gujarat reflects a high degree of regional inequalities which might get further exacerbated due to the ongoing reforms. The Golden corridor is the area connecting Mumbai and Ahmedabad. It is known as the 'core' or the heartland of economic growth in the state. It is inhabited by the prosperous, the well-to-do, the industrial, the developed and the educated Gujaratis. The core is encircled by a vast 'periphery' comprising the regions of Saurashtra, Kachchh, the northern districts and the eastern belt. The periphery is poor, agricultural, non-industrial and less educated. As a result of successive droughts in the 1980s, the inequalities between the core and the periphery is said to have only increased (Mahadevia 2005: 297). In the period of recent reforms, increasing investments have occurred largely in the coastal belt of the periphery (Saurashtra and Kachchh) in the state. There are rising investments in Kachchh also due to special tax concessions offered to entrepreneurs after the recent earthquake there. The share of Saurashtra and Kachchh in the industrial investment has increased from merely 2 per cent in 1983–90 to 42 per cent in 1997–2002. But the new industries in north Gujarat represent islands of modern production in an impoverished hinterland. They are located in the coastal region and involved in exporting products or importing raw materials. The general backwardness of the local people in terms of literacy and skill would not provide them much opportunities to benefit. Moreover, big industries cause alienation of land from the farmers and diversion of water resources to industries which would only increase the vulnerability of the local population (Mahadevia 2005: 300). At the Planning Commission meet in New Delhi with the state Chief Minister Narendra Modi in April 2006, concern was expressed over continued backwardness of various regions in Gujarat. 'In Gujarat, one can find poverty-stricken regions with lowest literacy rates and health indicators, even though the state has progressed well in industry and commerce sector'. This was in sharp contrast with several states particularly Punjab and Haryana, which do not reflect the type of extreme backwardness with some of the poorest indicators existing side-by-side with extreme prosperity (TOI 2006g).

Further, wide sectoral inequality is noticed between agriculture and industry in the state. Table 4.10 clearly reflects that the secondary and manufacturing sectors maintained high growth rates in the 1980s and also in the reform period, but agriculture registered negative growth rates. In recent years, a skewed growth is observed in Gujarat of the gross state domestic product (GSDP)—the main indicator of a state's economic growth. Recent government figures reveal

Table 4.10: Sectoral Growth Rates (CARG) in Gujarat (1980–81 Prices) (%)

Item	*1960–61 to 1970–71*	*1970–71 to 1979–80*	*1980–81 to 1989–90*	*1990–91 to 1999–2000*
Primary sector	2.91	4.15	–0.44	1.95
Agriculture	2.27	4.22	–0.59	–0.18
Secondary sector	3.62	5.64	6.51	7.25
Manufacturing	3.04	5.55	7.33	7.33
Tertiary sector	3.51	5.86	7.10	7.39
Overall SDP	3.32	4.95	5.02	5.53
Per capita income	–	–	3.14	3.94
Trade	–	–	6.08	10.34
Banking & insurance	–	–	12.11	12.94

Source: Hirway and Mahadevia (2003); (Drawn from Mahadevia (2005: 295, Table 10.2), in Jos Mooij (ed.).
Note: Compound Annual Rate of Growth.

two disturbing economic trends—sharp fluctuation in the farm economy/primary sector, and the failure of the manufacturing sector to catch up with the national average. In case of the primary sector the fluctuation in growth was minus 11.1 per cent in 2002–03, then increased by 50.3 per cent in 2003–04, again declined by minus 8.9 per cent in 2004–05, and then jumped to 20.8 per cent in 2005–06. The secondary sector, with manufacturing as the backbone, did not grow fast enough in the state. It grew by a huge 17 per cent in 2002–03, but only by 7.6 per cent in 2003–04, 9.3 per cent in 2004–05 and 8.7 per cent in 2005–06. As for manufacturing, the country's GDP has been growing at 9.2 per cent which is a little higher than that of Gujarat. (But the overall growth of the country's GDP was lower than that of Gujarat.) The high fluctuation in the overall GSDP of the state is reflected in its growth by 7.5 per cent in 2002–03, 15.1 per cent in 2003–04, 5.2 per cent in 2004–05 and 11 per cent in 2005–06. The tertiary sector showed a steady growth between 8 to 9 per cent in the last four years in the state. A senior economic advisor to the state government observed, 'Gujarat is not able to sustain a steady growth mainly due to wide fluctuation in agricultural growth' (cited by Shah 2006h).

At the same time, the magnitude of workers employed in the primary sector remained high. 'A large discrepancy between the proportion of the population employed in a particular sector, on the one hand, and the contribution of that sector to overall growth and income, on the other' (Mahadevia 2005: 298) is observed.

Reforms in Human Development Sphere

The Government of Gujarat entrusted Tata Consultancy Services, a private firm to prepare 'Social Sector Vision 2010'. The document covers several social sectors such as education, health, social welfare, housing, water supply and sanitation, environment, employment and training. It notes the inability of the state and Central governments to provide the needed allocation for social sector development and hence, recommends private sector participation. The report is faulted on the grounds of a lack of conceptual understanding, disregard for existing studies and evaluations, and ignoring consultations (Mahadevia 2005: 305).

There are shifts occurring in social sectors in the state in recent years. Private investment is growing and would grow further in the human development sector, e.g., education and health. It is expected that secondary and tertiary education would be gradually privatised by eliminating controls over fees. The government seems to have paid more attention to primary education. This includes increasing school rooms and appointment of *Vidya Sahayaks* (46,000 already) but on a small monthly honorarium of Rs 1,000 only, which would curtail the state's spending of about $20 million. The state government has already enacted laws to set up a private university. And they have already set up few such universities like the Nirma University at Ahmedabad. Private commercial professional/technical institutions are increasing.

It is observed that the annual rate of increase in literacy in Gujarat was much higher in 1980s than in 1990s (see Table 4.11). Moreover, it is disconcerting to note that the increase in literacy rate of SCs in Gujarat was very high, i.e., by 21.3 per cent (point) during the decade 1981–91 (39.8 per cent in 1981 and 61.1 per cent in 1991), but their literacy rate declined by 3.8 per cent (i.e., 57.3 per cent) in 1999–00 (Hirway and Mahadevia 2004: 151, Table 6.3). In early 2000s there was observed almost no increase in the number of teachers in higher education, though there was a little increase in case of secondary/higher secondary level, and a little more increase at primary level (particularly due to appointment of *Vidya Sahayaks* at a very low honorarium) (see Table 4.12). It is noticed that the Gujarat government is reducing its responsibility towards education, except at the primary level. The rate of retention at school level (completing Vth standard) was found to be 100 per cent for Kerala, 50 per cent for AP, 52 per cent for Gujarat and 28 per cent for Bihar (Hirway 2000: 3117, Table 4.19). Hence, Gujarat shows an average performance in this regard. In fact, in the 1990s Gujarat moved down in ranking regarding overall literacy and also female literacy among the 15 major states in the country (Hirway and Mahadevia 2004: 175). The performance of the state in human development slowed down significantly in the 1990s (ibid.: 228).

Removal of illiteracy does not seem to be an important concern for the Gujarat government in the recent years. The 2001 Census data showed that number of illiterates were 387 out of 1,000 persons in rural areas and 181 out of 1,000 persons in urban areas in the state. The latest National Sample Survey data (2006) reveal that the number of illiterates has only marginally improved by about 1 per cent in last five years, the figures being 374 illiterates per 1,000 persons in rural and 171 per 1000 in urban areas. It is noted that more than 10 out of 25 states continue scoring better than Gujarat. The state has fared worse in female literacy. Even rural Orissa is found to perform better in this respect (Shah 2006a). One reason for this dismal performance of the state, according to a senior state official is that the state failed to use virtually any central grant under the literacy programme (like the Continuing Education [CE] project under NLM) for half-a-decade because accounts for even payment to motivators (*preraks*) appointed to spread literacy was not submitted. After first bearing all expenses, the submission of accounts by the state to the centre is essential to obtain 75 per cent of expenditure as central grant. There are 15,000 *preraks* in the state to educate illiterates or neo-literates, but only 500

Table 4.11: Total Literacy Rate (%)

Sl. no.	State	1981	1991	1997	Annual increase 1981–91	Annual increase 1991–97
i)	Gujarat	43.40	61.29	68.00	1.79	1.12
ii)	Andhra Pradesh	29.84	44.09	54.00	1.43	1.65
iii)	Kerala	70.42	89.81	93.00	1.94	0.53
iv)	Bihar	26.20	38.48	49.00	1.23	1.75
	All India	36.23	52.21	62.00	1.60	1.63

Source: Drawn from: M.S. Ahluwalia (2000: 1646, Table 9).
Notes: (a) 1981, 1991 data related to literacy rates are based on Census.
(b) 1997 data of literacy rates are based on NSSO Survey.

Table 4.12: Number of Teachers in Primary, Secondary and Higher Education in Gujarat (2000–03)

Sl. no.	Item	2000–01	2001–02	2002–03
i)	Primary	1,95,919	2,07,787	2,17,898
ii)	Secondary/Higher Secondary	64,076	65,253	68,816
iii)	Higher Education	11,041	11,197	11,197

Sources: Directorate of Primary Education, Gandhinagar; Commissionerate of Schools, Gandhinagar; Commissionerate of Higher Education, Gandhinagar; (Drawn from: Government of Gujarat [2004], *Socio-Economic Review, Gujarat State 2003–04*, Table 12.1).
Note: Figures of Primary Education for the year 2002–03 are estimated.

are active. 'The rest have either lost interest or have not got any stipend (Rs 700 per month) for long or have withdrawn from CE as they feel none cares for them,' as told by a state secretariat source. Another state official associated with adult education attributes the socio-economic conditions of those who are illiterate as a factor hindering the literacy drive. Gujarat's literacy performance is so dismal despite the well-orchestrated literacy drives for last three years, these drives include taking out *Kanya Kelavni Raths* for the literacy of girl child and *Sarva Shiksha Abhiyan* for adult literacy (Shah 2006b).

There are more and more elite schools being set up or expanded mainly in the major cities of the state, like Ahmedabad and Vadodara. These schools provide world class facilities with a view to offer best quality education. They present themselves as international schools, with state-of-the-art infrastructure and a special emphasis on meeting the requirements of NRI children, besides the locally affluent classes. Now in Vadodara, there is (starting June 2006) Billabong High School (of Kangaroo Kids Education Ltd.) managed by Aditya Education Trust, covering play school, nursery, KG and class I to V. It is an international school with both ICSE and IGCSE curriculum, air condition facilities (including hostels) and latest infrastructure like semi-olympic size swimming pool, tennis court, football and cricket ground, a multi-media centre, gymnastics and yoga centre, a music and drama room, jazz ballet, skating rink and such overall 15 extra curricular activities. Its view of holistic education includes curricular plus sports and performing art programmes besides regular field trips and educational tours. Hostels would have Internet connectivity to enable children to keep in touch with their parents abroad. The student-teacher ratio is maintained as 1: 8 at pre-primary level and 1: 12 at primary level with two teachers per class. The aim of the school is to allow children to be thinkers, innovators and problem solvers. American School of Baroda classrooms have modern equipments such as overhead projector, audio-visual facilities, air condition and close-circuit camera to monitor the activities of students in the class. Ambe Vidyalaya aims at developing 'future citizens ready to join hands with their counterparts all around the world'. Delhi Public School with its presence in 13 countries, has a branch in Vadodara and strives to maintain world class standards. Navrachna International School (nursery to class XII) has a campus coming up on the outskirts of the city with an ambience of greens and woods to complement its international curriculum, where 'every aspect of teaching and learning is supported by modern technology'. Facilities at the school are 'planned to achieve holistic development of the students to successfully operate in a global environment without detaching oneself from the roots'. Chairperson of Navrachna Education Society, Tejal Amin states, 'keeping with the needs of globalisation, it's time to bring in international education with an Indian ethos and we at Navrachna International are geared towards creating a cultural identity for the children, especially needed in case of NRIs' (TOI 2006a). Such an international school (viz, Shree Narayan Vidyalaya, popularly called SNV International school) is operational even at a smaller town like Nadiad in Kheda district in the state which advertised in a national daily stating its Vision 2020 as ' We plan to prepare students to take on challenges of year 2020, when our nursery students will enter in the university' (TOI 2006b).

On the other hand, a general negative trend in terms of increasing teacher-pupil ratio over time was observed in Gujarat: the ratio showing marginal increase at primary level, substantial increase at middle and higher secondary level and the highest increase (i.e., most adverse) at university/higher education level (see Table 4.13). A slight improvement in the ratio in 2000–01 over 1998–99 in case of primary education seems to be due to the introduction of the scheme called Vidhya Sahayaks, who are not full-fledged teachers like those in the formal system of primary education.

Table 4.13: Teacher-pupil Ratio in Gujarat

Year	*Primary*	*Middle and Higher Secondary*	*University/Higher*
1980–81	39.29	26.72	23.81
1985–86	40.23	26.95	27.64
1990–91	41.61	28.50	35.44
1995–96	41.65	30.00	38.54
1998–99	44.01	31.32	39.08
2000–01	41.78	–	–
Increase in 1990–91 over 1980–81	2.32	1.78	11.63
Increase in 1998–99 over 1990–91	2.40	2.82	3.64

Source: Drawn from: Hirway and Mahadevia (2004: 64, Table 6.19).

Further, there is a remarkable increase in social sector expenditure of the centre as percentage of aggregate expenditure and GDP in the reform period. But states have shown decline in social sector spending. The increase at the centre level has occurred at the cost of lower allocations made from the central plan outlay to the states (Joshi 2006: 365).

In the annual budget of Gujarat there is a noticed decline in the per cent share of social services on both revenue account and capital account during the post-reform period in the state. In case of economic services, there is slight increase on revenue account but sharp decline on capital account in the late 1990s. Social services show sharp decline on capital account and a little less decline on revenue account in the late 1990s in the state. The details are provided in Table 4.14.

Table 4.14: Percentage Share of Social and Economic Services in Annual Budget in Gujarat (1980–81 to 2001–02)

	Social Services		*Economic Services*	
Year	*Revenue account*	*Capital account*	*Revenue account*	*Capital account*
1980–81	39.83	6.46	33.17	51.50
1985–86	43.81	9.62	31.07	41.66
1990–91	39.36	4.84	31.19	60.43
1995–96	36.68	7.68	31.48	57.62
2001–02	33.99	1.99	34.38	2.09

Source: Drawn from: Hirway and Mahadevia (2004: 68, Table 3.8).

As percentage of expenditure on social services in the state, revenue expenditure on education was 48.14 per cent in 1986–87, increased and hovered between 54 per cent to 59.90 per cent during 1990–91 to 1999–2000 and then declined to 42.19 per cent in 2001–02. The capital expenditure on education was 1.70 per cent in 1986–87, increased gradually to 11.51 per cent in 1995–96, hovered between 2.76 per cent to 6.19 per cent during 1996–97 to 1999–2000 and then declined to mere 0.63 per cent in 2001–02 (Hirway and Mahadevia 2004: 64, Table 3.2). So, there is a clear decline in expenditure on education, particularly capital expenditure after 1999–2000, though increase as well as fluctuations during the 1990s have been broadly noticed. Further, within the education sector, there was very marginal change in the expenditure pattern across major sub-sectors in the 1990s. Expenditure on elementary education was 52.40 per cent in 1990–91, and marginally increased to 53.86 per cent in 2001–02 with some minor fluctuations in between. Secondary education showed a marginal decline in expenditure from 35.20 per cent in 1990–91 to 33.42 per cent in 2001–02. Similarly, university and higher education reflected a minor decline in expenditure from 10.50 per cent in 1990–91 to 9.89 per cent in 2001–02 with some fluctuations in between. Expenditure on technical education was 2.80 per cent in 1990–91, hovered around 3.5 per cent till 2000–01, but declined again to 2.80 per cent in 2001–02. Expenditure on adult education declined from 0.80 in 1990–91 to a mere 0.03 per cent in 2001–02 (ibid.: Table 3.2).

As percentage of total budget of Gujarat, expenditure on education was 16.03 per cent in 1990–91, declined and gradually increased (slightly) to 17.45 per cent in 1995–96, then gradually declined to 11.83 per cent in 2000–01, and sharply reduced to 4.95 per cent in 2001–02. As percentage of SDP, the expenditure on education in the state was 3.77 per cent in 1990–91, slightly increased to 3.82 per cent in 1995–96, then marginally declined and increased to 4.00 per cent in 2000–01, and significantly reduced to 3.11 per cent in 2001–02 (for figures, see, Hirway and Mahadevia 2004: 161, Table 6.15). So, as percentage of total budget, significant reduction in expenditure on education is evident mainly since 2000–01 in the state. Further, taking a comparative view, it is observed that share of education in the total budget (revenue account) of AP was 25.7 per cent in 1980–81, started declining since 1990–91 and came down to around 21 per cent during 1995–96 and 1997–98. In Kerala there was more reduction: the share of education was 35.5 per cent in 1980–81, declined to 30.4 per cent in 1990–91 and 27.4 per cent in 1997–98. In Gujarat the share of education was 23.6 per cent in 1980–81, increased to 28.3 per cent in 1985–86, then declined sharply to 24.3 per cent in 1990–91, and remained at over 23 per cent in 1995–96 and 1997–98. So, in general there was not much change in the share of education in the total budget expenditure in Gujarat. In contrast with these states, the share of education in Bihar increased from 26.5 per cent in 1980–81 to 28.8 per cent in 1997–98 (see ibid.: 163, Table 6.17).

To reduce expenditure, the Government of Gujarat imposed in 1991 a substantial ban on recruitment in different departments. This has affected the social sectors in particular quite adversely. The quality of public higher education has deteriorated because a large number of vacant faculty positions are not filled up in the universities, instead some teachers are employed on a daily basis with very heavy workload that badly affects the quality of education. In this regard, recently a government official observed that the continuous ban on recruitment in important sectors like health and education has led to chaotic conditions and if the ban is not lifted, the situation would deteriorate further.

Educational scenario at the national level is also a cause for concern particularly because the new trends have serious negative implications for the marginalised sections. Seema Joshi's (2006) analysis shows that India's expenditure on education in the reforms period of 1990s remained around 3.5 per cent of GDP. It reached 4.1 per cent only in 1999–2001, which was equal to the level of expenditure in the pre-reform year 1989–90 (ibid.: 362, Table 8). In the budgets (centre plus state), an overall decline in allocations to secondary education, university education, adult education and also in technical education is observed. Only elementary education reflects a rising allocation trends (ibid., Table 9). Though literacy rate in the country reached 65 per cent in 2001, there are 296 million illiterates in the age group of 7 years and more. About 48 per cent children could not reach grade 5 in 1995–99, compared with 38 per cent during 1990–95, which is a worrying trend. So, on the whole, education and skill formation continued to remain low. This is contrary to needs as globalisation requires better education and a skilled labour to compete and derive benefits.

In the health sector growing involvement of private donors and institutions to supplement the infrastructure of government hospitals in Gujarat has been proposed. Also, private doctors would be allowed to use the facilities in government hospitals and dispensaries, thus reducing their costs and fees (Shelat 1997: 109–10). Extremely expensive and highly specialised private hospitals like Apollo hospital are expanding in major cities in the state such as Ahmedabad and Vadodara which cater to the well-to-do people including NRIs and foreigners, especially from Africa. In fact, Gujarat is emerging as a favourite destination of medical tourism. Multi-speciality hospitals are fast increasing. They are equipped with modern infrastructure facilities and offer cost-effective treatment, relative to the Western standard, to the affluent people, including the NRIs and foreigners. The state government is formulating a medical tourism policy to further develop this sector (Wadhwani 2006).

Medical tourism is high on the agenda of both the government and private sector in the state, especially for the NRIs. Through newspaper advertisements Navrang Hospital of Vadodara allures patients/clients with its swanky look (building) and offers of treatment using the most advanced technological gadgets. It claims to offer 'international amenities, national charges'. Bankers Heart Institute, Vadodara is advertised as a super speciality cardiac hospital 'redefining cardiac care through innovative technologies and dedicated human touch'. Hospitality industry in the city—hotels like Surya Palace, Express Hotel, Taj Residency—take special care of NRI patients coming for treatment, in terms of accommodation and food to support medical tourism. General Manager of a Vadodara hotel said, 'We take care of the diet control to be exercised by the patients and also arrange for those who wish to go on site-seeing in and around Baroda. We provide guidance by giving references of doctors and also shopping places if desired'. The staff of another hotel stated, 'Our menu satisfies European standards'. Hotels also have tie-ups with hospitals and provide customised lunch and dinner delivery at the hospital (TOI 2006a).

Gujarat shows a much higher density of health facilities in comparison with India as a whole with regards to, for instance, hospital, dispensaries, beds, doctors and nurses. The number of hospitals and dispensaries per lakh population in the state is found to be more than three times that in the country (Acharya and Ranson 2005). But the nature of health care in the state is quite distinct. It is 'largely privately financed, individually purchased by out-of-pocket expenditure, privately produced, unregulated, and geared more towards curative instead of preventive care' (ibid.). Table 4.15 makes the difference very clear regarding the importance of private health care provision, especially inpatient. In case of outpatient care, the share of private sector in the state is 65 per cent in rural areas and 80 per cent in urban areas (Mahadevia 2002, cited in ibid). So, the dependence of people on private facilities is very high in both rural and urban areas of the state.

The condition of government hospitals is not improving in the state. Primary health centres (PHCs) run by the government are neither increasing nor improving. The expenditure on social services in the state government budgets has declined in recent years as noted earlier.

Table 4.15: Presence of Private Sector in Health Care—Gujarat and India (%)

Sl. no.	*Particulars*	*Gujarat*	*India*
i)	Hospitals in private sector	85	68
ii)	Inpatient beds in private sector	58	37
iii)	Hospitalisations among rural males in private sector	67.8	38
iv)	Hospitalisations among urban males in private sector	72.8	39.9

Source: Sundar 1995; (drawn from Acharya and Ranson 2005: 4144).

As percentage of expenditure on social services, the revenue expenditure on health (including health, family welfare, social welfare and nutrition) in the state was 30.66 per cent in 1986–87, declined to 25.49 per cent in 1990–91, further declined to 21.82 per cent in 1995–96, but increased to 26.38 per cent in 1999–2000 and further to 44.97 in 2001–02. The capital expenditure on health was 3.94 per cent in 1986–87, declined to 2.78 in 1990–91, further declined to 2.62 per cent in 1995–96, gradually increased to 7.6 per cent in 1998–99, then again started declining and reached as low as merely 1.60 per cent in 2001–02 (see Hirway and Mahadevia 2004: 64, Table 3.2). Within the health sector, expenditure on medical and public health in the state increased in the early 1990s but started declining in the later years. For instance, expenditure on public health in 1990–91 was 11.60 per cent, increased to 15.51 per cent in 1996–97, and gradually declined to 9.34 per cent (of the total expenditure on health) in 2001–02. Expenditure on family welfare hovered around 12 per cent during 1990–91 to 1999–2000, but declined to 8.76 per cent in 2001–02 (ibid.: 65, Table 3.4). Further, there is a move by the state government to hand over service delivery in the health sector at the local level to NGOs. This withdrawal would in a way absolve the government from direct delivery of services and then NGOs can be the blamed for drawbacks. In contrast, even in the advanced countries, the state role has been extremely critical in assuring that health care is available universally and more or less equitably (Acharya and Ranson 2005).

The adverse sex ratio in Gujarat is getting worse in recent years. The number of girls per 1,000 boys was 928 in 1991, 878 in 2001, 848 in 2003 and 824 in 2004. Forty-three talukas have been identified for having the least number of girl children. Certain districts are more affected by this problem like Mehsana, Rajkot, Patan, and Ahmedabad. There are several worst hit places like Unjha with 742 girls, Visnagar with 766, Vijapur with 777 and Mehsana with 779 girls per 1000 boys in the 0–6 age group (Sharma 2006c). Certain communities are affected more, like Patels, Chaudharys and Prajapatis. Patels are a well-off community and a dominant caste in Gujarat, but the most affected in terms of adverse sex ratio. In Morbi in Rajkot district, the Patel community reported an alarming 40 per cent less girls compared to boys in the 0–10 age group. Jayaram Patel, president of the Saurashtra Patidar Sangathan (a community organisation of Patels), stated the problem to be very serious as the Patel community in the region is facing an average 30–40 per cent deficit of girls.

The major reason of this problem is the high infant mortality rate (IMR) among girls compared to boys in the state. Urban areas are generally considered more progressive and modern. But IMR is found to be higher for girls in urban areas than in rural areas of the state. Though mortality in urban areas is lower than in rural areas, female mortality is 18 points higher than male mortality in urban areas (Shah 2006j). Modern high-tech medical equipments have reinforced regressive cultural beliefs in the superiority/preference for male child over girl child. Several gynaecologists and radiologists having clinics with facilities for sonography reveal the sex of the unborn child (foetus) through sex determination tests. This is done in a clandestine way by using pictures of deities like Lord Krishna and Goddesses like Ambaji and Laxmiji, and also using standard greetings like 'Jai Matajji' and 'Jai Shri Krishna' to symbolically tell the sex of the foetus (Sharma 2006e). This helps willing couples to terminate the female foetuses leading to the declining sex ratio.

But the highly skewed sex ratio has turned out to be a big business for some people in the state. Tribals in the state do not suffer from skewed sex ratio. In some areas of Netrang, Valia, Dediapada, Sakbara, Rajpipla and Jhagadia, certain tribal communities sell off their daughters in marriage through brokers (locally known as Vachetias) to the daughter-deficit communities like Patels and Thakurs. Generally, the price ranges between Rs 30,000 to Rs 90,000. Tribal girls are also supplied at a very low rate of even Rs 500 to a few thousands depending on the degree of desperation of the girl's family. The broker/agent makes a huge profit in the deal. He could, for instance, charge Rs 70,000 from a Patel and pay only Rs 20,000 to the tribal family for the daughter given in marriage. A committed broker is reported to make Rs 1.5 lakh to Rs 2 lakh every month (John and Rupera 2006). In such marriages, some cases of the brides disappearing from the groom's place after staying for a few days under the pretext of going to her parent's home has been reported (Sharma 2006d).

In addition, instances of 'rent-a-wife' and even wife swap are noted. There are 'reports of husbands agreeing to their wives staying with higher caste men who are not able to find a match in their community for a monthly rental charge!' In Netrang taluka there was the case of Atta Prajapati permitting his wife Laxmi to live with a Patel in Mehsana for a monthly rental of Rs 8000 (John and Rupera 2006). Also bride shortage has forced bachelors to buy sex. In places like Unjha there is a growing number of forced bachelors veering towards sex workers, thus increasing prostitution in the region. A project officer with the organisation Yoganjali, stated, 'many young people, frustrated with not being able to get married, are buying sex for Rs 50–100. There is also an increased male-sex-with-male activity' (see Sharma 2006b).

No wonder, these distressing problems related to the declining sex ratio has prompted the state government to launch the *Beti Bachao Andolan* (save the daughter campaign) in the state. Certain community organisations like the Patidar Samaj have held awareness camps and Patel couples are encouraged to take a vow at their weddings not to get sex-determination tests done (Sharma 2006a). Such initiatives may be expected to bear fruits in the long run, but the problem currently is very distressing.

But health does not seem to be a high priority area for the government of Gujarat as in many other states. More than half the expenditure on health in the state is borne by households rather than the government in terms of per capita expenditure. As of 1993, Gujarat falls in the lower category compared with other select states as regards health expenditure as percentage of SDP, which was only 2.8 per cent for Gujarat and 4.6 per cent for a backward state like Bihar (see Table 4.16). It is worth noting that Gujarat has one of the fastest growing NSDP. But this has not led to higher government spending on health. In 1990–91, Gujarat was ranked fourth from the bottom out of 25 states, in terms of the proportion of NSDP spent on health. Health expenditure as a proportion of NSDP declined in the state in the last decade from 2.16 per cent to 1.56 per cent. The NSS 52nd round data shows that per capita public health expenditure was Rs 54 in Gujarat, i.e., lower than national average of Rs 70 (Mahadevia 2002, cited in Acharya and Ranson 2005). Further, for the year 1995–96, a World Bank publication (2001) shows that Gujarat's per capita public spending on health is quite low compared to Kerala, though it is higher than AP and Bihar (see Table 4.17).

Table 4.16: Per Capita Health Expenditure and State Domestic Product, 1993

(Rs)

State	*Households (HHs)*	*Government*	*Total*	*% of HHs in total*	*Health expenditure as % of SDP*	*SDP per capita*
i) Gujarat	173	83	256	0.68	2.8	9,103
ii) Andhra Pradesh	244	75	319	0.76	4.6	6,930
iii) Kerala	266	99	365	0.73	5.6	6,547
iv) Bihar	103	51	154	0.67	4.6	3,365
v) All India	201	79	280	0.72	3.8	7,358

Source: Drawn from: Kasturi Sen (ed.), (2003: 233).

Table 4.17: State-level Per Capita Public Spending on Health (Rs)

State	*1995–96*
i) Gujarat	99
ii) Andhra Pradesh	85
iii) Kerala	132
iv) Bihar	57

Source: World Bank (2001). *India: Raising the Sights—Better Health Systems for India's Poor*. (Drawn from: R. Misra, R. Chatterjee and S. Rao [2003: 31]).

It can be mentioned that lower public expenditure on health or increase in health care expenditure adversely affects the poor households in multiple ways. One, they are compelled to spend more money and resources on medical care. Two, they are not able to earn during the period of illness. In addition, rural people (especially the poor) have to bear a relatively higher burden of indirect costs associated with illness like expenses on transport, food/stay, tips given to gain access to any person or facility, opportunity cost of lost wages of the accompanying person, etc. Rising cost of health care forces them to borrow money generally from informal sources at high interest rate which leads them into increasing indebtedness. The problem is compounded as the poor do not have access to any safety nets such as health insurance (Acharya and Ranson 2005).

Further, it is worth noting that the number of Government owned family welfare clinics/centres in Gujarat increased substantially during 1980s, i.e., the pre-reform period (4,971 in 1980–81 to 7,152 in 1990–91), but there was no such increase in the 1990s, i.e., the reform period; rather it stagnated during late 1990s (7,294 only during 1995–96 to 1999–2000 (see Table 4.18). In 1994–96, IMR was found to be 15 for Kerala, 66 for AP, 63 for Gujarat (quite high compared to Kerala) and 71 for Bihar (Hirway 2000: 3118, Table 21). The decline in IMR (by place of residence) in the 1990s was found to be substantially higher in Bihar than in Gujarat and AP More specifically, decline (by point) in IMR during the period 1991–93 to 2001 was by 9 points in Bihar (71 to 62), 4 points in Gujarat (64 to 60), 3 points in AP (69 to 66), and 4 points in Kerala (15 to 11) which could be a standard for backward states and the developing countries in general (for figures, see Hirway and Mahadevia 2004: 59, Table 2.33).

Table 4.18: Number of Family Welfare Clinics/Centres in Gujarat State (2000)

Year/District	Total	Rural	Urban	Government owned	Other bodies
1980–81	5,058	4,951	107	4,971	87
1990–91	7,240	7,132	108	7,152	88
1995–96	7,381	7,274	107	7,294	87
1999–2000	7,279	7,274	105	7,294	85

Source: Drawn from: Government of Gujarat (*2000*: 126, Table 8.11), *Statistical Abstract of Gujarat State 2000.*

Decline in IMR in Gujarat was by 29 points during 1971–81 (i.e., from 145 in 1971 to 116 in 1981), 47 points during 1981–91 (i.e., from 116 in 1981 to 69 in 1991) and merely 9 points during the reform period 1991–2001 (i.e., from 69 in 1991 to 60 in 2001 (ibid.: 120, Table 5.2). Yogendra Mathur (2005) who works with the UNICEF, observed that IMR (which is a sensitive measure of social development) in Gujarat is similar to a backward state like Bihar (IMR: Kerala 14, Gujarat and Bihar 62 each, Orissa 95). Life expectancy at birth (1996–2000) was found to be slightly lower in Gujarat than the all-India average (see Acharya and Ranson 2005: 4144, Table 1).

A World Bank team visited various cities and towns in Gujarat, held meetings with the Minister for Urban Development and concerned state officials. In June 2005, the Bank agreed in principle to provide a loan of Rs 750 crore ($150 m) for the government's urban reforms project. The loan was provided with international market rate of interest. Moreover, it is linked with reforms like introducing area-based property tax, double entry account system, reduction of stamp duty to 5 per cent, abolition of the Bombay Rent Control Act whose amended version still weighs against house owners, sustainable user charges for water and sewerage facilities and a guarantee not to revert to the already repealed urban land ceiling law provisions (*Indian Express* 2005). Recent indications are that the state would privatise and outsource civic services such as water supply, solid waste management, road construction, etc. This is one of the main tasks assigned for a detailed study by the government to a high-level committee headed by former bureaucrat Vithal Cowlagi who opined that outsourcing should be absorbed in a big way in government services.

The approach to poverty reduction under the reforms programme is predominantly growth-centric. It is held by reformers, including ADB, that to make a major dent in reducing poverty, it is very essential to be on a fast growth track. The bottlenecks hindering financial growth and infrastructure have to be removed to speed up economic development. A direct targeting on core poverty groups like the slum dwellers and poor people living in backward areas and uneducated women so that they are not bypassed has been suggested. In this connection, the role of NGOs is considered important, besides urban development programmes like slum upgradation. This marks a shift in approach in terms of poverty reduction.

In line with this in recent years the Gujarat government has given heavy emphasis on growth-oriented approach. Alongside it is observed that the decline in the percentage of BPL families is quite high during the reform period in Gujarat (13.5 per cent over 1993–94 to 1999–2000) compared to other select states. But this is reported to be due to certain errors (overvaluation) in poverty figures in the past. Here, even an element of politics of poverty figures could be involved implying that the higher the level of below poverty line (BPL) families a state shows, the higher will be the allocation of food stock from the centre for poverty alleviation programmes. It is noted that BPL list is a 'politically sensitive' issue in Gujarat. The powers to identify BPL families in a village is vested with the *talati-cum-gram sevak*. This lowest rung rural official worked under local political pressure which led to constant updating/raising the numbers which reached 33 lakh families in the late 1990s. A Central team identified the errors in poverty/BPL figures in Gujarat and corrected them which apparently show high rate of poverty reduction in the state. On the directive of the Planning Commission, a complete survey of all the 67 lakh rural families was conducted in the state and only 11.4 lakh families were found to fall under BPL category as against 23.29 lakh on the current list. The revised list is with the state government for approval (Shah 2006g).

According to the Planning Commission, the percentage (of total population) of poor people in Gujarat was 33.27 in 1983, 23.92 in 1993–94 and 12.78 in 1999–2000. So, there was a slightly higher degree of decline (11.14 per cent) in poverty during 1993–94 to 1999–2000 than the decline (9.35 per cent) during 1983 to 1993–94. Datt, Kozel and Ravallion estimated decline in poverty in the state from 33.7 per cent in 1993–94 to 19.9 per cent in 1999–2000, that is, by 13.8 per cent. According to Sundaram and Tendulkar, the decline in poverty (HCR on MRP) was from 26.38 per cent in 1993–94 to 18.12 per cent in 1999–2000, i.e., only by 8.26 per cent (for estimates by Datt et al. and Sundaram and Tendulkar, see Hirway and Mahadevia 2004: 51–52, Tables 2.26, 2.27). According to Hirway and Mahadevia experts' view is that the finding of the Planning Commission is overestimated. They put poverty level in Gujarat at about 17 to 19 per cent on the basis of alternative estimates (ibid.: 50).

According to the recent statistics released by the National Sample Survey, the average daily wage paid to the unskilled casual worker in Gujarat is one of the lowest in India, both in rural and urban areas. The average wage in the state is lower than the national average of Rs 51 and Rs 69 for rural and urban areas respectively. People in Gujarat get much lower than the minimum wage they are supposed to, that is, Rs 53 in rural areas and Rs 89 in the urban areas. In Gujarat's rural areas it is Rs 45, compared to Rs 51 in Jharkhand, Rs 77 in Punjab, Rs 112 in Kerala and Rs 123 in Delhi. It is, in fact, lower than the 15 major states. On the other head, in Gujarat's urban areas, the average daily wage is Rs 57, compared to Rs 61 in Andhra Pradesh, Rs 63 in Bihar (also Jharkhand), Rs 76 in Punjab, Rs 100 in Delhi and Rs 127 in Kerala. The states reporting lower urban wages than Gujarat include Chhatisgarh, Uttaranchal, Madhya Pradesh and Orissa. So, Gujarat is bracketed with some of the most backward states in terms of wage rates. There is also male-female divide in this. Whereas the average wage (unskilled) for urban male is Rs 68, it is Rs 49 for rural male. The respective wages for females are Rs 39 and Rs 36. Also, there exists high level of regional disparity in wages—quite low in dry areas and the eastern tribal belt, and high in fertile areas of Saurashtra and Central Gujarat (Shah 2006d). There is high degree of rural-urban disparity in Gujarat in certain other terms. The NSS data shows that in urban Gujarat 93.2 per cent people live in pucca houses, but this figure is only 59.3 per cent in case of rural people (TOI 2006d).

There is also a paradox on the employment front. General (neoliberal) economic argument is that increase in investment would create more job opportunities. But that is not true of the state in the reform period. There is sizeable increase in investment in the state. But there is decline in creation of jobs in the organised sector. The number of persons employed in the organised sector in the state was 17.17 lakh in 1995, which declined to 16.22 lakh in 2005. In case of PSUs, the employed persons declined from 9.60 lakh in 1996 to 8.19 lakh in 2004 (i.e., a decline of 1.41 lakh). The state's recent development programme (DP) explains this decline due to the nature of investments being capital intensive in industrial sectors such as chemical, petrochemical, refining, etc. In case of public sector, it is said to be caused by the closure of sick textile mills especially in Ahmedabad (Shah 2006).

A study covering the period 1999 to 2005 shows that about 40 per cent workforce in Vadodara district have been either retrenched or given voluntary retirement and thus a large number of people are unemployed. It is stated that about 10,000 employees are sitting idle at home with the Voluntary Retirement Scheme (VRS) offered by their companies. Several small and big industries have closed down in Vadodara in the last five years. A 2001 survey by the Ministry of Labour found nearly 592 factories closed down in the city. This is said to be, besides other reasons, due to the dumping of cheaper foreign products into the local market (Rao 2006).

There is a significant decline in employment opportunity in Gujarat in the reforms period of the 1990s (4.54 per cent) compared with 1980s (19.09 per cent). Public sector employment declined sharply and a little increase in the private sector employment could not absorb the impact of the job decline in the public sector (see Table 4.19). It is observed that the creation of employment is insufficient in the state. Highly capital intensive large and medium industries came up in the state during the reform period. In 1980–81, investment of Rs 48,000 created one direct job, which increased to Rs 408,000 in 1992–93 at current prices and Rs 157,000 at constant prices. Hirway and Mahadevia estimate that the average investment per project in large and medium industries has increased from Rs 240 million in the pre-reform period to Rs 360 million

Table 4.19: Employment (in '000) in Public and Private Sectors in Gujarat

		Number of persons employed as on 30 June						
Sl. no.	*Category*	*1980*	*1990*	*Change in '90 over '80 (%)*	*2000*	*Change in 2000 over '90 (%)*	*2001*	*2002*
1.	Public Sector	737	940	21.60	934	(–) 0.64	872	844
	Central Government	127	140	9.29	138	(–) 1.45	123	133
	State Government	187	217	13.82	210	(–) 3.33	199	193
	Quasi-Government	189	293	35.49	298	1.68	283	266
	Local Bodies	234	290	19.31	288	(–) 0.69	267	252
2.	Private Sector	573	679	15.61	762	10.89	740	723
	Total of 1 and 2	1,310	1,619	19.09	1,696	4.54	1,612	1,567

Source: Directorate of Employment and Training, Gujarat state, Gandhinagar. (Drawn from: Government of Gujarat [2004], *Socio-Economic Review: Gujarat State 2003–04*, Table 16.1).

in the reform period, but the average employment per project has declined from 160 in the pre-reform period to 149 after the reforms (Mahadevia 2005: 299). Increasing unemployment has led only to increase in poverty. However, as per the estimates of the state government, the absolute number of registered (with Employment Exchanges) unemployed in the state increased by 486,093 during 1980–90 and by 110,770 during 1990–2000; i.e., increase was less in the post-reform period compared with the pre-reform period; i.e., the rate of increase in registered unemployment was less in the latter period. The absolute number of registered educated unemployed kept increasing, though at a lower rate in the 1990s. But there was reported decline in the absolute number of registered uneducated unemployed in the 1990s; the number of registered uneducated unemployed in 1980, 1990 and 2000 was 200,635, 363,826 and 212,234 respectively (Hirway and Mahadevia 2004: 43, Table 2.23). There are varied estimates of decline in poverty level in Gujarat as indicated earlier.

In comparative terms, it is observed that unemployment rate (based on current daily status [CDS]) has slowly declined in Gujarat, i.e., from 5.79 per cent in 1987–88 to 5.73 per cent in 1993–94 and 4.63 per cent in 1999–2000. But unemployment rate has increased in case of Bihar, i.e., from 4.04 per cent in 1987–88 to 6.25 per cent in 1993–94 and 7.35 per cent in 1999–2000. AP also has witnessed slight increase in unemployment rate with certain fluctuations, that is, from 7.35 per cent in 1987–88 to 6.67 per cent in 1993–94 and 7.94 per cent in 1999–2000. A similar fluctuating trend is found in Kerala, the rate being 21.19 per cent in 1987–88 to 15.50 per cent in 1993–94 and 20.77 per cent in 1999–2000 (Hirway and Mahadevia 2004: 317, Table 76). It can be noted that only Kerala has unemployment rate in double digits whereas other three states have it in single digit.

Further, it is observed that in Gujarat the proportion of both male and female self-employed workers in both rural and urban areas has increased in the late 1990s in comparison with the late 1980s and in this the female proportion has increased much more than males in their respective categories, both in rural and in urban areas. The proportion of both males and females in regular employment declined in the 1990s, much more in case of females than in males, both in rural and urban areas while that of the casually employed declined in rural areas, more in case of females in rural areas. However, the proportion of casually employed males and females increased in urban areas, more so in case of males. (see Table 4.20).

There is a growing inequality in the state as regards the social indicators. Among the 15 major states, Gujarat was placed 4th in per capita income throughout the 1990s, but its human development index (HDI) rank was 6th. It was 6th on the education index and 9th on health index in 2001. As regards gender development measure (GDM), it ranked 4th in 1991, but slided down to 6th in 2001. On gender equality index (GEI), it stood in the 8th position in 1991 as well as in 2001 (Mahadevia 2005: 301). It is held that the relatively low HDI and human development measure (HDM) ranks in the state are related to the poor achievements in education among the state's tribal population and the decline in performance in the dry regions of the state (ibid.: 301).

Further, though industrial employment of contract labour was a long-term tendency in the Valsad industrial region with the Contract Labour Act (1970) in Gujarat, from the late 1980s there has been increased use of contract workers, which comprises both migrant workers and

Table 4.20: Employment Status of Workers, Gujarat (%)

Year	Self-employed		Regular employed		Casually employed	
	Male	*Female*	*Male*	*Female*	*Male*	*Female*
Rural						
1987–88	46.2	40.2	12.8	4.5	41.0	55.3
1993–94	46.9	55.4	9.9	1.5	43.2	43.1
1999–2000	50.4	59.8	9.7	1.8	39.9	38.5
Urban						
1987–88	38.1	35.2	45.2	36.4	16.7	28.4
1993–94	37.3	42.6	44.9	24.1	17.8	33.3
1999–2000	40.5	43.8	35.6	24.7	23.9	31.5

Source: National Sample Survey Organisation. (Drawn from: Hirway and Mahadevia [2004: 39, Table 2.21]).

local workers, more of the former. Contract workers are hired and paid by labour contractors and not by the company. It is preferred by owners and managers because it offers them flexibility and saves money. They are exploited more (in terms of wages, security of job, etc.) than the temporary workers who could hope to become permanent, the privilege not being open at all to the former. 'The increase in casual labour in the local industrial workforce has been a major change over the last 30 years. At present, more than 60 per cent of local industrial workers are either temperwali (temporary) or contract workers' (Streefkerk 2002: 142). In his study of the industrial complex of Atul-Atic in the Valsad region, Streefkerk (ibid.: 136) found that the Central government policy of liberalisation brought Atul-Atic to face foreign competitors, forcing automation of parts of production process which led to hundreds of workers becoming redundant and hence pensioned off.

Furthermore, there are huge social disparities within the agricultural sector in Gujarat. Farmers in the 'core' area of the state have opted for diversification of their economic interests. They are also relatively better connected with political circles. Rich farmers belonging to the middle caste, namely, Patels (Patidar caste) have been able to raise their social and economic status. But there are a large number of small and marginal farmers in the state who belong to other middle castes popularly known as OBCs (Other Backward Castes). The recent agriculture census found that small and marginal farmers have about 55 per cent of the operational holdings which comes to merely 2.13 per cent of the total cultivated area (Mahadevia 2005: 299). The current pattern of development shows growing marginalisation of the workforce. It is estimated that the share of marginal workers in the total workforce of the state increased from 13.33 per cent in 1981 to 15.20 per cent in 1991 and to 19.96 per cent in 2001. The proportion of main workers in the workforce reduced form 34.1 per cent in 1991 to 33.60 per cent in 2001 (ibid.: 300).

Globalisation and liberalisation entail increasing commercialisation in the agricultural sector. In fact, there are several studies showing the uneven impact of the commercialisation process on different social groups with some groups acquiring greater access to and control over resources than others who are further marginalised. In fact, 'rural differentiation is exacerbated as divisions between, for example, the landed and the landless become more pronounced and entrenched' (Kothari 2002: 115). In her study of Sera village in South Gujarat in late 1980s and early 1990s, Kothari found that the dominant landholding caste of Patidars benefited quite a lot both economically and socially through the adoption of sugarcane cultivation. They preferred to employ predominantly migrant workers (in place of local Halpati landless labourers), who could work on a seasonal basis, without involving any long-term obligations. The inflow of seasonal migrant labour reduced the bargaining power of the local Halpati labour, and there were more overt expressions of class hostility between landowning Patidars and the landless Halpatis. Local workers formed work gangs to protect their interests. But their tactics was undermined by alternative labour supplies and new technologies. 'In this sort of unequal conflict, which depends on responses to volatile changes and contingencies, the worker is in a danger of becoming further marginalised by virtue of the farmer's greater access to knowledge, resources and networks, and his ability to move beyond the local terrain for information and class allegiance' (ibid.: 129).

Increasing privatisation in the state would adversely affect the people benefiting from the policy of reservation. This includes people belonging to SC, ST and OBC categories. Private enterprises do not follow the policy of reservation. Privatisation of state-owned enterprises would curtail the existing job opportunities for the reserved categories. Growing private sector enterprises create jobs which may not necessarily benefit the reserved categories and, thus, exacerbate social inequalities. For instance, increasing growth of private educational institutions at all levels, particularly higher/professional education, would not benefit the reserved categories, particularly the poorer ones. Likewise, increasing commodification of health sector facilities would also make access more and more difficult for the poor.

There is lack of adequate sensitivity on the part of administration to respond to the needs of the SCs. Vice-chairman of the National Commission for Scheduled Castes, Fakirbhai Vaghela, holds that civil servants often refuse to perform the work they are supposed to do for uplifting the conditions of the SCs, particularly in Gujarat. This is because the administration is 'manned by upper caste officials with vested interests in perpetuating the existing system'. In his meeting with the top police brass of Gujarat, including police commissioners, superintendents of police and other police officials, it was revealed that 'the entire law and order machinery is hopelessly ignorant about the rights of SC people'. The top cops reflected ignorance particularly about two Central Acts—Protection of Civil Rights Act 1955, and SCs and STs (Prevention of Atrocities) Act 1989. He states, 'I was pained by their Himalayan ignorance about the social, economic and legal aspects of these two Acts and their traditional mindset and antipathy towards the downtrodden SCs' (TOI 2006b).

Tribals continue to be the most deprived and backward community in Gujarat, in terms of both economic and human development as reflected in their lower income, low literacy rate and poor health facilities. There was in early 1990s, violence in the Dangs district by the state machinery against them in course of their struggle essentially meant to regain their rights over land which they have been cultivating since centuries. The struggle resulted in the state government giving land titles to those who were cultivating forest land before 1980. But the government notification required those claiming rights over land to produce some written evidence of their continued cultivation. Due to lack of such written evidence, the notification remained largely a right on paper only. The problem continues to remain unresolved with continued persistence of two sets of conflicting views: one, the tribals have the right to cultivate their land which is based on ancient customs and tradition, and two, the forest officials hold full right under the law to determine the use of reserved forest in the tribal areas. There are 'degrading consequences of this conflict for the tribal population of the Dangs, who continue to live in a state of fear and terror' (Joshi 2002).

There was the problem of land alienation and tribal assertion in Bharuch district in the 1990s. The main demands of the Vasavas (tribals) there relate to reclaiming the land they had been cultivating from outsiders (non-tribals). Besides non-tribals, 'the state has dispossessed them of their resources and denied them justice, rights and equality, while .... [ironically] the same system speaks of empowerment through sustainable development'. This method of negotiation with the forces of oppression and disempowerment is reflected currently through identity politics. They have formed their organisation and demand autonomy to have some say in the affairs of their development. 'The various slogans for autonomy are expressions of this cry that grows out of the marginalisation of Adivasis from the mainstream economy and polity, especially in the light of the continuing rift between Adivasis and non-Adivasis in the socio-cultural, economic and political spheres' (Pinto 2002).

Tribals also have been a major victim of environmental degradation and involuntary displacement inherent in the mainstream development paradigm, which infringe their fundamental rights, including the right to life and livelihood. Randeria (2002) refers to Breman's studies which demonstrated the growing polarisation between the beneficiaries and victims of Gujarat's rapid economic transformation, the trend towards further marginalisation of the labouring poor and the complicity of the state in these developments. For instance, the displaced people could not be protected adequately despite the long-drawn battle by the Narmada Bachao Andolan (NBA) and even the eviction of the World Bank from the Narmada Valley project (Randeria 2002).

Concluding Remarks

Globalisation related reforms introduced by the Central government since 1991 broadened the scope for different states in the country to promote private sector development and growth according to their own priorities and strategies. Reforms are manifested in Gujarat in the form of transnational/regional (ADB)/national flows of capital, power and discourse, and they help in understanding the specificities of local transformations and power relations. Introduction of the reforms signifies entry and increasing influence of supra-national agencies at the state (provincial) level and the 'changing contours of governance within and beyond the nation state' involving the complex interaction among regional/international organisations, and national and state government. Despite decentering and restructuring occurring due to the contemporary dynamics of global capitalism, the state continues to remain an important actor which mediates the processes of economic globalisation in Gujarat as in several other states in India (Randeria 2002: 266–67).

Mahadevia (2005: 307–08) identifies certain important features of the recent reforms policies adopted by the Government of Gujarat. One, academicians and government departments have been replaced by private sector consultants in the preparation of important vision and policy documents. The process of awarding contracts for this purpose is not transparent. No open discussion is held on the documents, neither are the documents shared with the public. 'In a way, this is reforms by stealth'. Two, the current development vision is largely limited to enhancing economic growth rates by raising investments in all the three sectors. The main thrust is 'to promote the privatisation process and reduce the role of the government to being a facilitator'. Of all the sectoral policies 'social sector development has been taken least seriously'.

Hirway (2000) notes mixed results of the development path chosen and reforms introduced in Gujarat. Economic growth has accelerated in the state but performance on other fronts is not satisfactory. The state stands in the forefront of economic development in the country. It has acquired and maintained fourth rank in per capita NSDP. It has attracted a high level of industrial investment (especially in large and medium industry), and demonstrated the highest growth in per capita NSDP in the reform period. The economy of the state has become highly diversified. But this process might not be sustainable because the primary sector, particularly agriculture, has lagged far behind which distorts the agriculture-industry linkages. There is severe degradation of environment which also would constrain sustainability of economic growth. Moreover, there exists an unsatisfactory scenario in several important areas of social and human development. In the reform period there is fall in the rate of decline in poverty and deceleration in the rate of progress in human development. There are serious problems of concern particularly with respect to female literacy, enrolment and retention of children in schools, infant mortality rate, etc. There are problems of significant backlog of employment, besides the poor quality of new employments.

Further, it may also be noted that the convergence thesis advocated by neo-classical/neoliberals does not hold good. Kohli (2006) clearly notes the neo-classical/neoliberal strand of market logic which holds that capital would move to capital-scarce areas where it might get higher returns and, thus, lead to some convergence across regions following liberalisation. But his analysis demonstrates that the rates of economic growth across Indian states started diverging more with liberalisation in the 1990s than in the 1980s. Growth showed deceleration by more than a point in 1990s in poor states like Bihar, Orissa, Rajasthan and UP (Punjab was an exception where decline occurred mainly due to decline in the agricultural growth rate). The main reasons indicated here are the decline in public investments and failure of private investment to fill the gap. In contrast, economic growth rate accelerated in certain other states such as Gujarat, West Bengal and Kerala—Gujarat being a rich state but the other two not as rich (rather closer to the national average regarding per capita income). Industrial growth in post-reform period in better-off states either increased (as in Gujarat and Tamil Nadu) or remained similar to that in 1980s (as in Maharashtra, Karnataka and Punjab). Besides initial conditions of the states, the role of varying state governments, Kohli holds, has played an important part. States which have adopted a clear pro-business approach have attracted more investments. Private investors have continued to favour better-off states over the backward states. So, recent reforms proved to be advantageous to some states and disadvantageous to others. '... [S]tates that have effectively created a pro-business alliance for growth seem to be experiencing the most rapid economic growth'. The underlining fact, according to Kohli, is that 'the pattern of economic reforms in India is not following the free market logic of capital moving to capital scarce areas. The logic evident instead is more akin to a Mathew effect, namely, to him who hath shall be given' (2006: 1367).

Subramanyam and Rao (2000) have analysed data on per capita net state domestic product of 17 major states of India for the periods 1965–85 (the green revolution period) and 1985–1996 (the liberalisation period). They found no evidence of convergence of per capita income across states in either period. What they found is that the tendencies of divergence were mild and not statistically significant in the green revolution period but quite strong in the liberalisation period. In fact, the green revolution period showed a modest growth rate of 1.35 per cent per annum, but the performance of poor states was good during this period. In contrast, the liberalisation period experienced a higher growth rate of 3.37 per cent per annum, but the growth rate of most of the poor states was lower than the average. This stands contrary to the claim of convergence. They affirm that 'the path is highly divergent since mid-eighties and the divergence has increased sharply after the foreign exchange crisis and consequent structural adjustment measures since 1991' (ibid.: 19).

Based on the preceding discussions, it could be affirmed that:

(*i*) The agenda of current governance reforms in Gujarat, as at the Centre, marks a shift from the state-led to a market/private-sector-led model of development. This shift is pushed and facilitated in a systematic manner in Gujarat by the ADB in collaboration with the Central government and the state-level ruling elites. The package of reforms introduced in Gujarat is quite comprehensive. But the emphasis of reforms is more on the economic side and not as much in the human development sector.

(*ii*) The overall growth in the state is higher than the national average. But the state is not able to sustain a steady growth as reflected in wide fluctuations in the recent years. Moreover, growth in manufacturing in the state is lower than the national average. There is skewed growth both in inter-sectoral and inter-regional terms in the state.

(*iii*) Human development sector in the state has suffered as a result of reforms happening in the shape of retreat and reframing of the state, and increasing privatisation and commercialisation. Overall, there is widening of gaps between the better-off and poorer sections of society in terms of access and use particularly in education and health. This trend would continue to grow only with deepening of reforms. Public spending on higher education is stagnant or on the decline which will hinder global competitiveness in several areas for Gujarat in particular.

(*iv*) In standard economic/neoliberal thinking, increase in investments is expected to create more employment opportunities. There has been increase in investments in Gujarat during the reform period. But overall there is decline in employment in the organised sector in the state. Employment in the public sector has sharply decreased, which has not been compensated by a small increase in employment in the formal private sector. Quality of employment has deteriorated with increasing informalisation/casualisation of labour which could only indicate increasing marginalisation of the working people.

(*v*) The major benefits of reforms have gone to the private entrepreneurs as a result of economic growth. Despite increase in the growth rate in the reform period in Gujarat, the fiscal conditions of the state has not really improved. This has happened because of the tax sops and subsidy given to private investment which has benefited the business classes. But the poorer sections have not benefited. Socio-economic inequalities are on the rise. This would further deepen as a result of increasing privatisation and commercialisation particularly in the areas of health and education.

(*vi*) The conditions of the overwhelming mass of backward sections of society such as SCs, STs and OBCs would only worsen with reforms, though a small fraction of elites belonging to these groups might benefit like the elites in general.

(*vi*) Interstate divergence in economic growth has increased during the reform period in spite of increase in the overall growth rate in the country. There does not seem to be a healthy growth of 'competitive developmentalism' between states in the country. This goes against the neo-classical/neoliberal position which is advocated in studies like Howes et al. (2003). Reforms unleashed a process of interstate competition which has serious fiscal consequences. It is noted, 'The prudence of ensuring sufficient revenue generation to be able to afford various sops to attract industry into the state is often sacrificed, with disastrous fiscal consequences in several states' (R. Dholakia 2003: 304).

All these problems, according to Hirway (2000: 3120), are 'the consequences of the path and dynamics of development chosen by the state'. And, 'Solution lies in correcting the path of development of the state,' she affirms (ibid.). Broadening of the base of development through employment intensive and environment friendly development path would lead to rapid reduction of poverty and faster human development. She observes, 'It is important that the state shifts towards this path. It is high time that the political leadership in the state realised that attracting industrial investments to the state at any cost will not serve the long-term interests of the state' (ibid.).

Current government thinking on development can be inferred from the view of a senior Economic Advisor to the state government who recently held that the agricultural sector contributes only a little to world trade. 'Therefore, Gujarat must focus on industry, mainly supported by the service sector, for its sustainable growth in the future' (cited in Shah 2006h). The state's 'development programme' underscores the need to reverse the trend of declining employment. For this it proposes 'an appropriate policy intervention by the government as a facilitator in terms of promoting knowledge-based industries, like IT industries, service sector which have very high employment potential' (Shah 2006). But the knowledge-based industries would largely benefit only a small section of the large army of educated ones. Educated unemployment would not end. The problem of uneducated unemployment would continue to remain a daunting problem afflicting mainly the poorer sections of the society. Sustainable growth in the government parlance is mainly confined to sustaining a high rate of economic growth. So, environmental sustainability remains marginalised.

The case of Gujarat testifies to the fact that increase in economic growth does not necessarily lead to improvement in human development as affirmed in the human development perspective advocated by Amartya Sen and other such scholars. Adoption of an employment intensive path of development, which is emphasised by Hirway, is not an important concern of the current agenda of 'good governance' reforms. Privileging employment would involve transforming this agenda which would imply a different notion of governance reforms and globalisation—making the agenda good from the perspective of the marginalised people. An employment-intensive path may reduce poverty. But the problem of inequality would continue to prevail and there could be strengthening and perpetuation of systemic status quo. The human development approach also does not confront the problem of rising inequalities and systemic status quo. The need of the hour is to look beyond the reformist approaches and come out with an alternative agenda of development which would tackle the multiple and multi-level problems created by the current LPG model of reforms and help move towards achieving an equitable/egalitarian (socially), democratic (substantive, not mere procedural) and sustainable (both economically and environmentally) development in Gujarat in particular and the country in general.

References

Acharya, Akash and M.K. Ranson (2005). 'Health Care Financing for the Poor: Community based Health Insurance Schemes in Gujarat', *Economic and Political Weekly*, 40(38): 4141–50, 17 September.

Ahluwalia, Isher Judge and I.M.D. Little (1998). *India's Economic Reforms and Development—Essays for Manmohan Singh*. New Delhi: Oxford University Press.

Ahluwalia, Montek S. (2000). 'Performance of States in Post-Reforms Period', *Economic and Political Weekly*, 35(19): 1637–48.

Aiyer, Shekhar (2001). 'Growth Theory and Convergence Across Indian States: A Panel Study, in Tim Callen, Patricia Reynolds and Christopher Towe (eds), *India at the Crossroads: Sustaining Growth and Reducing Poverty*. Washington: IMF.

Asian Development Bank (2000). 'News from India: Pioneering State Initiatives'. Available at http://www.adb.india.org/newsrel3.htm.

——— (2003). *India—Country Portfolio Review 2002* (Joint Report of the Asian Development Bank and the Government of India. Available at http://www.adb.org/Documents/CPRMs/IND/2002/default.asp, accessed on 7 December 2004.

——— (2004). *India: Country Strategy and Program Update 2005–07*, September. Available at http://www.adb.org/Documents/CSPs/IND/2004/CSP-IND-2004.pdf, accessed on 10 December 2004.

Debroy, Bibek and Laveesh Bhandari (2005). *Economic Freedom for States of India 2005*. New Delhi: Rajiv Gandhi Institute for Contemporary Studies (in Cooperation with Friedrich Naumann Stiftung, New Delhi).

Dholakia, Archana R. (1999), 'Role of the Centre in Fiscal Balance of States—The Case of Gujarat', *Journal of Political Economy*, 11(2), June.

Dholakia, Ravindra H. (2003). 'The Role of the State Government in Promoting Private Sector Growth: The Case of Gujarat', in Stephen Howe, Ashok K. Lahiri and Nicholas Stern (eds), *State-level Reforms in India*, pp. 302–19. Delhi: Macmillan India Ltd.

GoG (Government of Gujarat) (2000). *Statistical Abstract of Gujarat State 2000*. Gandhinagar: Directorate of Economics and Statistics.
——— (2004). *Socio-Economic Review, Gujarat State 2003–04*, (Table 12.1). Gandhinagar: Directorate of Economics and Statistics. Available at http://www.gujaratindia.com/Useful-Info/Socio%20Economic%20Review/SER-03-04/SERT12-1.htm, accessed 9 December 2004.
——— (2006). 'Welcome to "Gujarat: Business State of India"'. Available at www.gujaratindia.com, accessed 18 January 2006.
Government of India (2006). 'Disinvestment in States', Department of Disinvestment, Ministry of Finance. Available at http://www.disinvest.nic.in/disistates4.htm, accessed 28 March 2006.
Hirway, Indira (2000). 'Dynamics of Development in Gujarat: Some Issues', *Economic and Political Weekly*, 35(35 and 36): 3106–20, 26 August–2 September.
Hirway, Indira and Darshini Mahadevia (2004), *Gujarat Human Development Report 2004*. Ahmedabad: Mahatma Gandhi Labour Institute.
Howes, Stephen, A.K. Lahiri and Nicholas Stern (2003). *State State-level Reforms in India: Towards More Effective Government*. Delhi: Macmillan India Ltd.
Indian Express (2005). 'WB to Assist Urban Reforms Project', Express News Service, 6 June (daily newspaper, Ahmedabad edn).
John, Paul and Prashant Rupera (2006). 'Rent a Wife for Rs 8.000!: Skewed Sex Ratio is Great for Business', *The Times of India* (Ahmedabad edn), 19 June.
Joshi, Satyakam (2002). 'Development, Deprivation and Discontent: A Case of Dangs Tribals', in Ghanshyam Shah (ed.). *Development and Deprivation in Gujarat*. New Delhi: Sage Publications.
Joshi, Seema (2006). 'Impact of Economic Reforms on Social Sector Expenditure in India', *Economic and Political Weekly*, 41(4): 358–65.
Joshi, Vijay and I.M.D. Little (1996). *India's Economic Reforms 1991–2000*. New Delhi: Oxford University Press.
Kohli, Atul (2006), 'Politics of Economic Growth in India, 1980–2005', *Economic and Political Weekly*, 41(14): 1361–70.
Kothari, Uma (2002). 'Landless Labour and Agrarian Change in South Gujarat: The Experiences of Halpati Women', in Ghanshyam Shah (ed.), *Development and Deprivation in Gujarat*. New Delhi: Sage Publications.
Krueger, Anne O (2002). *Economic Policy Reforms and the Indian Economy*. New Delhi: Oxford University Press.
Mahadevia, Darshini (2005). 'From Stealth to Aggression: Economic Reforms and Communal Politics in Gujarat', in Jos Mooij (ed.), *The Politics of Economic Reforms in India*. New Delhi: Sage Publications.
Mathur, Yogendra (2005). 'Challenges for Development Sector', Paper Presented at National Seminar on Development Management, Department of Home Science, Vadodara: M.S. University of Baroda, 4–5 October.
Misra, Rajiv, Rachel Chatterjee and Sujatha Rao (2003). *India Health Report*. New Delhi: Oxford University Press.
Pinto, Stany (2002). 'Land Alienation and Adivasi Assertion in Bharuch District', in Ghanshyam Shah (ed.), *Development and Deprivation in Gujarat*. New Delhi: Sage Publications.
Rai, Shishir Kumar (2005). 'Special Economic Zones: Case Studies and Lessons Learnt', *Spatio-Economic Development Record*, 12(5): 15–22, September–October.
Randeria, Shalini (2002). 'Globalising Gujarat: Environmental Action in the Legal Arena', in Ghanshyam Shah (ed.). *Development and Deprivation in Gujarat*. New Delhi: Sage Publications.
Rao, M. Govinda (2002). 'State Finances in India: Issues and Challenges', *Economic and Political Weekly*, 37(31): 3261–71, 3 August.

Rao, Sudhakar (2006). 'Unemployment on a High Due to Closure of Industries', *The Times of India* (Ahmedabad edn), 21 June.

RoyChowdhury, Supriya (1995). 'Bureaucracies and Management of Economic Reforms', *Vikalpa*, 20(3): 19–26, July–September.

Saran, Rohit (2004). 'India's Best and Worst States', *India Today*, 29(32): 20–31, 16 August.

Sharma, Radha (2006a). 'Girls Gasp for Breath in Garvi Gujarat', *The Times of India* (Ahmedabad edn), 14 June.

——— (2006b). 'Bride Drought Forces rich Unjha to Buy Sex', *The Times of India* (Ahmedabad edn), 15 June.

——— (2006c). 'Communities Get Desperate to Save their Girls', *The Times of India* (Ahmedabad edn), 16 June.

——— (2006d). 'Bride "Sale" Takes Bachelors for a Ride', *The Times of India* (Ahmedabad edn), 17 June.

——— (2006e). 'Gods Scurry for Cover in These Clinics', *The Times of India* (Ahmedabad edn), 18 June.

Sen, Kasturi (ed.) (2003). *Restructuring Health Services—Changing Contexts and Comparative Perspectives*. London: Zed Books.

Shah, Rajiv (2006a). 'Mere 1 per cent Literacy Growth in Gujarat', *The Times of India* (Ahmedabad edn), 4 January.

——— (2006b). 'State May Dropout of Centre's Literacy Drive', *The Times of India* (Ahmedabad edn), 7 January.

——— (2006c). 'Disconnect between Actual Investments and Official Figures', *The Times of India* (Ahmedabad edn), 9 January.

——— (2006d). 'Govt Claims on Poverty Reduction Fall Flat', *The Times of India* (Ahmedabad edn), 30 January.

——— (2006e). 'Gujarat Heads for Debt Trap as Burden Increases', *The Times of India* (Ahmedabad edn), 1 February.

——— (2006f). '9 SEZs to Draw Rs 40K cr in Three Years', *The Times of India* (Ahmedabad edn), 19 March.

——— (2006g). 'Gujarat's BPL List to be Slashed by Half', *The Times of India* (Ahmedabad edn), 9 April.

——— (2006h). 'States's Vibrant Economy Could be a Skewed One', *The Times of India* (Ahmedabad edn), 22 April.

——— (2006i). 'Govt to Divest Stake, Give Up Control in GACL', *The Times of India* (Ahmedabad edn), 29 April.

——— (2006j). 'More Infant Girls Die in Gujarat's Cities', *The Times of India* (Ahmedabad edn), 10 May.

——— (2006k). '5 SEZs Get Nod to Start Work in State', *The Times of India* (Ahmedabad edn), 13 June.

——— (2006). 'Investments in state fail to create jobs', *The Times of India* (Ahmedabad edn), 17 June.

Shelat, S.K. (1997). 'Gujarat Public Sector Resource Management', in Asian Development Bank, *Governance—Promoting Sound Development Management*, (A record of the proceedings of a seminar in Fukuoka, Japan, 10 May 1997 during the 30th Annual Meeting of the Board of Governors) Manila: ADB. Available at http:www.adb.org, accessed 2 December 2004.

Streefkerk, Hein (2002). 'Casualisation of the Workforce: Thirty Years of Industrial Labour in South Gujarat', in Ghanshyam Shah (ed.) *Development and Deprivation in Gujarat*. New Delhi: Sage Publications.

Subrahmanyam, S. and N. Rajagopala Rao (2000). 'Liberalisation and Income Convergence across Indian States', Working Paper no. 36, Centre for Economic and Social Studies, Hyderabad, January.

(TOI) *Times of India* (2004). 'Gujarat Takes First Step to Divestment', 24 September, (Ahmedabad edn).

(TOI) *Times of India* (2005). 'Education Beyond Classrooms', NRI Times Supplement, 6 December, (Ahmedabad edn).
——— (2006a). Special Supplement on Elite schools in Vadodara city in Gujarat, 6 January, (Ahmedabad edn).
——— (2006b). 'Vision 2020: ENV International School', Advertisement for admission, 21 January, (Ahmedabad edn).
——— (2006c). 'Gujarat Upbeat Over New SEZ Policy', 11 February, (Ahmedabad edn).
——— (2006d). 'Progress in Urban Gujarat High, Rural Areas Shockingly Low', 15 February, (Ahmedabad edn).
——— (2006e). 'Budget Highlights', 25 February, (Ahmedabad edn).
——— (2006f). 'Infrastructure development Act amended', 29 March, (Ahmedabad edn).
——— (2006g). 'Planning Commission Concerned Over Backwardness in Gujarat', 6 April, (Ahmedabad edn).
——— (2006h). 'ADB to Lend $7 b to India in Next 3 years', 25 April, (Ahmedabad edn).
——— (2006i). 'Now Gujarat is a Power Deficit State!', 7 May, (Ahmedabad edn).
Wadhwani, Mallika (2006). 'Gujarat Inc!', in Annual Gujarat Review: December 2005–January 2006, *The Indian Express/The Financial Express.*

5

Governance Reforms and Development in Andhra Pradesh: Viewing through Rural Prism

G. Krishna Reddy

Introduction

The economics of globalisation purportedly accepts the primacy of politics for its own survival. Thus, the politics of economic reforms in any Third World region, aided and induced by the international donor community, is characterised. The governance agenda that has come to shape the economic reforms within the Third World countries holds profound implications for the regimes that be[1] and the citizen-state relationship.

This chapter seeks to explain the interplay of politics and economy by tracing it to governance reforms introduced in the state of Andhra Pradesh (AP) following a massive AP Economic Restructuring Programme (APERP) in the mid-1990s funded by the World Bank. While focusing on rural governance, this paper explores the dynamics of economic reforms in the state.

The analysis in the present study is broadly at two levels. First, effort is made to explain what role international and domestic factors played in shaping the political and economic environment in the state since the mid-1990s. It also argues that the changed political and economic environment initiated a new set of governance principles that had a profound impact on the state-citizen relations. Second, while focusing on rural governance in the state, the study seeks to show that new principles of governance such as self-help, stakeholder participation, etc., have made a complete departure from the earlier frameworks and caused marginalisation of the Panchayat Raj Institutions (PRIs). It is also argued that the changed governance norms have paved way for potential tension over the question of resources in the rural setting.

The Background of Reforms

The economic reforms initiated during the mid-1990s by Chandrababu Naidu was marked by the internal dynamics of politics and economy in the state and the intervention of globalisation driven by the international donor community/International Financing Institutions (IFIs) such as the World Bank (WB), International Monetary Fund (IMF), Department for International Development (DFID), British Government's bilateral department agency, which have a strong presence in the state now.

It is widely acknowledged at the international and national level that AP is in the forefront in the country in pushing the reforms agenda with a lightening speed inspite of many stumbling blocks (Manor 2002; Mooij 2003). The process of economic reforms has much to do with Naidu's style of functioning. What is important here is the way the persona of Naidu played a crucial role in shaping the reforms. Seldom personalties became so important in political and economic processes (Balagopal 1999; G.K. Reddy 2002a; Lalitha and Kumar 2005). The present study finds an important link between Naidu's personality traits and political imports thereof, and WB's choice of AP as the first state in the country to have entered into negotiations on aid directly with state governments. Therefore, a brief account of the emergence of Naidu as a leader deserves a place.

The Telugu Desam Party (TDP) founded in 1982 by the charismatic leader, N.T. Rama Rao, popularly known as NTR, came into power in 1983, defeating the Congress Party which was in power undefeated ever since the state was formed in 1956. NTR, became a household name in the state because of his association with Telugu Cinema. The TDP under him was centralised with one leader at the top and the social base was located in a coalition of classes/castes, i.e., Kamma, an upper shudra peasant caste and other backward castes (G.R. Reddy 1989). But it must be noted that the kammas have been emerging as a dynamic entrepreneurial class since the late 1980s (Upadhya 1988), whose role in initiating economic reforms in the state in the 1990s is dealt with in the later part of our discussion.

After losing to the Congress in the 1989 assembly election, the TDP came back to power in December 1994 with a thumping majority. The victory was significant, for it was considered to be the first ever expression of the resistance to economic reforms introduced in the country by the Union Government in 1991. By this time, the impact of the reforms in AP was quite pronounced (Pai 1996). The reforms started appearing on the electoral agendas and in the campaigns fairly frequently from then onwards in the state as well as national elections.[2]

Naidu came into power in September 1995, following a major split in the TDP. Some termed it as a 'Palace Coup' (Manor 2002), and Naidu, the son-in-law of N.T. Rama Rao (founder of the TDP and the then Chief Minister of the state) as the brain behind the 'coup'.[3] Soon after Naidu came into power, he was faced with a dilemma of whether to continue with populist measures of NTR—subsidised rice supply and prohibition of liquor or to make a complete departure from NTR's regime of populism. Naidu opted for the latter.

The economic reforms introduced by the Union Government in 1991 had two kinds of impact on the social classes in AP. In the first place, it adversely affected the poorer sections, which was reflected in the starvation deaths among handloom weavers in Prakasam district due to the shortage of yarn following its massive export as part of economic reforms to earn foreign exchange. Besides, the escalation of subsidised rice from Rs 2 per kg to Rs 3.5 per kg and reduced quota from 25 kg per family to 16 kg by the Congress government in the early phase of reforms troubled the poor who were already facing the problem of steep hike in the prices of essential commodities. NTR had earlier reduced the price of rice from Rs 3.5 to Rs 2 and reinstated the quota at 25 kg per family, immediately after the 1994 Assembly elections. It is to be noted that soon after Naidu assumed power, the price of the subsidised rice was hiked from Rs 2 to 3.5 and later to Rs 6.5 and the quota reduced from 25 kg to 20 kg per family. The third effect of economic reforms on the poor was rather an indirect one but profoundly influenced the course of politics in the state. The anti-arrack movement in the state in 1993 picked up momentum with the economic reforms adversely impacting the lower income groups. The reforms multiplied the strains of arrack consumption on family incomes particularly in the case of women, Dalit landless agricultural labour, who were the main forces that joined the movement. It is well known that the issue of arrack dominated the 1994 elections in the state more than any other.

The debate on subsidised rice and ban on liquor had such a profound impact on the governments during the early phase of economic reforms that the 1994 elections in the state was considered a referendum on economic reforms by both the Congress and the TDP. Thus, it set a clear tone of anti-reformism in the state. And when Naidu came to power, he was carrying this bogey of anti-reform atmosphere.

The Dynamics of Reform Process

Naidu's decision to hike the price of subsidised rise and partial lifting of ban on liquor gave a clear signal for ensuing reforms. However, it must be noted that these reforms which were a departure from the earlier regime impinged on three factors: First, the emerging entrepreneurial class was looking for new avenues in the context of globalisation and liberalisation; the second, imperatives of regime building around Naidu's persona; and third, the fiscal crisis that the state government experienced during this period.

First, the newly emerged entrepreneurial class started perceiving a plethora of avenues opened up by the economic reforms in the state. Its interests were hitherto curbed by license-permit raj. What is largely unique to Andhra Pradesh in the emergence of this class was that its capital base was essentially agrarian surplus. Nowhere in India was the urban industrial capital so well-grounded in capital accumulation from the agricultural front. Thanks to the early advent of green revolution into the fertile and canal irrigated coastal region of AP, a powerful capitalist agrarian class emerged by the 1980s itself which became the mainstay of the social base of TDP. Surplus agriculture prompted this class to convert agrarian capital into agro-based industry, cinema industry and other forms of urban capital (Upadhya 1988; Baru 2000). 'It is not accident that the Telugu Desham Party is dominated by Kammas and its chief functionaries, as well as key leaders, remain Kamma businessmen' (Baru 2000: 219).

Second, though Naidu could wrest power from NTR with the help of legislators, he lacked the image that the latter carried among the rank and file of the party and the masses. What he desperately needed was to build and consolidate his position as the leader. Since his assumption as Chief Minister, Naidu carefully moulded his image by working on the following:

(1) Media management; (2) Depending on a few select bureaucrats combined with a corporate style of functioning (Balagopal 1999; Lalitha and Shashi 2005); and (3) Making use of internationally aided projects for his image and party cadre building (Nayak et al. 2002; Mooij 2003). Naidu's personalistic style was considered more appropriate to push the economic reforms and concomitant governance reforms rapidly. Naidu's centralised style of functioning made the administration appear more composed. Such administrative style was taken to be more appropriate to the times otherwise wrought with the political instability caused by the coalition politics at the national level. Naidu's functioning, characterised as authoritarian within a democratic setup, suited the international donor community's governance agenda well. It focused more on effective management and speedy implementation of projects than on democratic procedures.

The other factor was the fiscal crisis that the state had undergone during the 1990's. 'The basic feature of state finance in the last decade or more is that it has not generated revenues to cover its revenue expenditures, leave alone generating surpluses for capital formation. In fact it has been borrowing to meet its revenue expenses. In AP, revenue surplus was financing expenditure from 1974–75 to 1982–83. Thereafter the capital surplus, i.e., borrowing has been financing the revenue deficit' (M.T. Reddy et al. 2001). Table 5.1 shows the increase in revenue deficit since 1986–87 to 1997–98.

As public debt started increasing, the loan interest payments has disturbed the fiscal balance beyond controllable limits for the state government. Tables 5.2 and 5.3 show the consistent increase in the public debt and the interest repayments. Such fiscal crisis led Naidu's government to go for economic reforms.

The story of economic reforms in the state can be seen in two phases—pre- and post-1999 periods, as the reforms picked momentum at a faster pace after 1999. The pre-1999 phase can

Table 5.1: Revenue Deficits of Andhra Pradesh

Year	*Revenue receipts*	*Revenue expenditure*	*Deficit*
1986–87	2910.88	3099.33	–188.45
1987–88	3353.65	3316.5	37.15
1988–89	3797.31	3764.01	33.3
1989–90	4181.58	4419.81	–238.23
1990–91	5024.9	5182.5	–157.6
1991–92	5935.82	6105.39	–169.57
1992–93	6689.17	6812.98	123.81
1993–94	7814.28	7581.97	–232.21
1994–95	8204.73	8932.46	–727.73
1995–96	9197	9964	–767
1996–97	10498	11386	–888
1997–98	13080	13783	–703

Source: GoAP (1996) *State Finances—The Factual Position, Finance and Planning Department,* and GoAP (2001) *Strategy Paper on Fiscal problems,* Finance Dept. (As cited in M. Thimma Reddy, K.S. Gopal, Raghav Narsalay and Minar Pimple, *Economic Restructuring in Andhra Pradesh,* a report prepared for Centre for Environmental Concerns, Hyderabad & Focus on the Global South India Programme, Mumbai, 2001).

Table 5.2: Public Debt of Andhra Pradesh

(figures in Rs crore)

Year	Loans outstanding as at the end of March					% increase	Average rate of market interest
	Central loans	Market loans	PF	Others	Total		
1986	2538	644	246	694	4122	17.4	4.63
1987	2809	722	299	965	1845	17.54	6.1
1988	3069	933	404	1085	5491	13.33	5.7
1989	3372	1135	523	1193	6223	13.33	5.99
1990	3774	1357	594	1292	7017	12.76	6.71
1991	4368	1596	690	1414	8068	14.98	7.31
1992	5056	1935	819	1563	9373	16.18	7.41
1993	5852	2272	957	1886	10967	17.01	7.56
1994	7094	2609	1109	2085	12897	17.6	7.89
1995	8342	3047	1334	2401	15124	17.6	8.25
1996	9526	3528	1534	2784	17372	14.58	8.7
1997	–	–	–	–	19970	14.96	11.8
CGR (%)	9.64	8	6.5	1.05	11.2	–	–

Source: M. Thimma Reddy, K.S. Gopal, Raghav Narsalay and Minar Pimple, *Economic Restructuring in Andhra Pradesh*, a report prepared for Centre for Environmental Concerns, Hyderabad & Focus on the Global South India Programme, Mumbai, 2001.

Table 5.3: Trends and Major Components of Fiscal Deficit in Andhra Pradesh

(figures in brackets are % of fiscal deficit)

Year	Fiscal deficit	Loan repayments	Interest	Total repayment
1989–90	791.59	256.45 (26.39)	270.94 (48.47)	727.39 (74.87)
1990–91	967.07	217.87 (22.53)	586.52 (60.96)	807.39 (83.49)
1991–92	1125.31	394.45 (35.05)	694.99 (61.76)	1089.44 (69.24)
1992–93	1569	256.73 (16.36)	826.92 (52.88)	1086.65 (69.24)
1993–94	1833.19	329.41 (17.97)	1024.98 (55.91)	1354.39 (73.88)
1994–95	2348.52	746.68 (31.79)	1256.38 (53.50)	2003.06 (85.29)
1995–96	2445	682 (27.89)	1527 (62.45)	2209 (90.35)
1996–97	2763	1208 (43.72)	1839 (66.56)	3047 (110.28)
1997–98	2428	860 (35.42)	2153 (88.67)	3153 (129.11)

Source: M. Thimma Reddy, K.S. Gopal, Raghav Narsalay and Minar Pimple, *Economic Restructuring in Andhra Pradesh*, a report prepared for Centre for Environmental Concerns, Hyderabad & Focus on the Global South India Programme, Mumbai, 2001.

be termed as the 'preparing ground' for reforms. It was a phase of negotiations in both economic and political terms. Naidu's government was preparing itself to enter into negotiations with the World Bank to tide over its fiscal crisis and to put the state on the path of economic reforms. 'The government issued white papers on the state's finances and encouraged extensive and wide ranging debates in all conceivable forms on the need to restore the state's fiscal health' (Prasad 2003: 292). It has also taken some measures to improve the financial position, but more to convince the World Bank that the government has resolved to go for the international donors' way in shaping the economy. These measures included: 1) hike in power tariff (this fetched Rs 9.63 billion), 2) a reduction in rice subsidy (Rs 6.5 billion), 3) an increase in water rates (Rs 1.35 billion), 4) the introduction of turn over tax on trade (Rs 1.2 billion), 5) an increase in the profession tax (Rs 600 million), 6) a bus fare revision (Rs 510 million), 7) an entry tax on motor vehicles (Rs 500 million), 8) luxury tax on tobacco (Rs 250 million), and 9) the rationalisation of the sales tax (Rs 450 million) (ibid.). It also included a highly controversial lifting of ban on liquor in 1997, which is claimed to have fetched Rs 950 crores to coffers. It is interesting to note that the lifting of ban on liquor was preceded by a media campaign and publicity on the benefits that accrue to the state exchequer if the ban is lifted. The debate on this issue was in a typical neoliberal mould—that the financial benefits of the cash-strapped government took a primacy over the strains on the income and health of the poorer sections through the consumption of cheap liquor, which indeed flooded the market following the lift of ban[4], that is, development at the cost of well-being of the poor.

The other major reform that was taken up during this period was *Janmabhoomi* which was meant to encourage people's participation in the development on the principle of self-help. Interestingly, *Janmabhoomi* was dampened after 1999 when reforms were taken up vigorously (Manor 2002).

One can elaborate on this phase of negotiations in Naidu's own words: 'The art of politics is to make such decisions palatable, so that they are not rejected outright by citizens who are the voters. First people should be *convinced* that such steps are necessary' (Naidu 2000: 10, emphasis added). Thus, the new governance agenda makes people mere followers of policies and who only need to be convinced of the rationality of the decisions of rulers, not as active participants who initiate and take part in the decision-making.

It is instructive to note that the World Bank report, 'Agenda for AP Economic Reforms' prepared in 1996 and made public in 1997 (World Bank 1997) and the white paper of the government of AP on the status of finances in the state prepared in 1996 (GoAP 1996) have identical explanations about the reasons for the crisis and solutions to overcome, though both claim to have prepared the documents separately.[5] This exercise provided the grounds for regime shift with pro-liberalisation strategies. The reasons for fiscal crisis were shown to be: the state expenditure on subsidies of various kinds, overstaffing of bureaucracy, non-performance of public sector, etc. The solutions suggested were to activate the market by promoting private investments particularly in the infrastructural and service sector and prune public expenditure by withdrawing subsidies and disinvesting public sector corporations. Privatisation, thus, has come out as a concomitant of liberalisation solutions and the World Bank's conditions. This subsequently paved the way for the World Bank's 'Andhra Pradesh Economic Restructuring Programme' (APERP) with a grant of Rs 2200 crores in 1998. It has several components such as restructuring public sector units, development of irrigation, rural road maintenance, reforms in power sectors and privatising higher education, etc.

The APERP, covering the period 1999–2004, consisted of six components apart from fiscal reforms. The programme visualised spending of Rs 3300 crores on these six components which were: District Primary Education (20.3 per cent), Primary Health (8.5 per cent), Integrated

Child Development (12.4 per cent), Rural Road Upgrading and Maintenance (21.6 per cent), Irrigation Rehabilitation and Maintenance (12.3 per cent) and Public Enterprise Reform (3.2 per cent). The agenda of fiscal reforms cut across all these components. While the World Bank was to meet the project expenditure to the tune of Rs 2200 crore, remaining funds were to be made available by the AP State Government (M.T. Reddy et al. 2001). Subsequently many of the changes in these sectors were effected, despite of major resistance from people. The state has witnessed large scale agitations against hike in the power tariff, the attempts to privatise public sector units such as Allwyn, R.T.C, Singareni coalmines, etc. The restructuring of power sector figured as a major issue in the 1999 assembly elections and 2001 local elections (G.K. Reddy 2002a).

The APERP of The World Bank initiated a comprehensive economic reforms programme in the state. The World Bank's Project Appraisal Document on APERP clearly established a link between the macro level reforms and sectoral level reforms. By the former, it meant cutting down welfare measures such as subsidised rice, and downsizing government expenditure such as salaries and reduction of employment in the government and state level public sector enterprises. It has recommended zero-budgeting for strengthening management of the governments' expenditure. To improve tax mobilisation, the World Bank has suggested expanding the tax base such as sales tax, professional tax, etc. (World Bank 1998).

In sectoral reforms, it focused on physical infrastructure such as power, roads, irrigation and ports, and social infrastructure such as education and health. The reforms at the sectoral level were meant are clearly to open the door for private investment. The World Bank insisted that without these comprehensive reforms at macro and sectoral level, the state would fail to perform (World Bank 1998).

As a major step towards sectoral reforms, the state government entered into an agreement with the World Bank to restructure the power sector. This agreement yielded US$ 210 million in 1999 (World Bank 1999). The project appraisal document stated that APERP and power sector restructuring programme in the state are closely linked as the power sector reforms would ease public expenditure. The power sector reforms in the state have brought in changes in tune with the recommendations made by the World Bank, i.e., power tariff, investment of private capital in power generation projects and setting up of independent Regulatory Authority. Besides, Andhra Pradesh State Electricity Board (APSEB) has been divided into two wings, i.e.. Andhra Pradesh Power Transmission Company (APTRANSCO) and Andhra Pradesh Power Generation Company (APGENCO).

What clearly emerges out of the APERP of the World Bank is that it has provided for a policy framework for economic, fiscal and governance reforms as part of this package of aid by the World Bank and other donor agencies. Following the APERP, AP government embarked on the governance reforms in the state. Importantly, two documents on governance reforms released by AP government need mention here: Swarandhra Pradesh Vision 2020, released in 1999, prepared by American consultancy, McKinsey, and AP Government Strategy Paper on governance and public management brought out in 2002. The former is about growth and development, but also links them with good governance. It looks at governance in terms of effectiveness, that is, how well the institutions help creating congenial atmosphere for growth and development. The document in a nutshell maps out a relation between governance and the market and defines governance in terms of its efficiency to be an enabler of growth which is akin to what the World Bank has been arguing for (World Bank 2001). The vision document proclaims certain objectives of governance, what it terms as SMART—Simple, Moral, Accountable, Responsive and Transparent.

Following the vision document, the strategy paper on governance and public management (GoAP 2002) identified a plethora of areas for administrative reforms which can be broadly grouped under three categories. First includes e-governance (see box for specific measures taken under e-governance). Second covers measures taken up essentially to speed up file movement and for transparency, and the third is concerned with the setting up of new institutions essentially to make policy suggestions, train and mould the attitudes of public officials and employees. This component, in some sense, wields enormous clout with the top administration

E-Governance

- Among the most significant measure is the CARD project (Computerized Administration in Registration Department), which has cut down the time for registration of land sales from a week to less than an hour. The project has been implemented in 214 sub-registrar offices across the state.
- A pilot project, TWINS/e-Seva (Twin Cities Integrated Network Services), has integrated 19 services pertaining to six departments for delivery on a one-stop mode. The services range from utility bill/tax payments and issuing of certificates to provision of information and facilitation. The government had planned to introduce these services throughout the state by entering into a joint venture with a consortium of Singapore companies. It proposed a major innovation in the concept of 'anytime, anywhere government services' or 'non-stop 24-hour government'. However, the idea had to be abandoned when employees, who feared retrenchment, threatened agitation on the eve of general elections. However, now the government is going ahead with the project on its own.
- Under the FAST project (Fully Automated System for Transport), services such as the issue of learner's permits, driving licences, and the registration of vehicles have been computerised on a pilot basis. Eventually, all 37 regional transport offices in the state are to be networked.
- On November 1, 1999, the Andhra Pradesh State Wide Area Network (APSWAN) was made operational. It provides connectivity between the state secretariat and each of the 23 district collectorates in data, voice and video communication. Saving on travel, time and related expenses, officials and ministers now interact through video conferencing.
- A comprehensive database covering the entire population of the state, taking each household as a unit, has been captured on another project—the MPHS (Multi-Purpose Household Survey). The data includes the date of birth, religion, landholding status, type of shelter, occupation and annual income of each citizen. A data warehouse, using a supercomputer, has been set up in the secretariat. Also, the entire geographical and infrastructure data in the state has been captured under GIS (Geographic Information System).
- Besides the above, the SKIMS project (Secretariat Knowledge and Information Management System) was launched in the year 2000, covering the entire secretariat. This was aimed at facilitating and

(Contd.)

(Contd.)

extending the concept of a paperless office among all the heads of government departments and in the districts.

- A comprehensive IT Training Action Plan has been approved by the cabinet sub-committee of the board of governors of the HRD Institute. One of the highlights is to prepare a bank of chief information officers. For this number, of senior officers have been identified for undergoing a special IT package for four months. This is to sensitise them to hardware, software, and other special problems related to implementation of IT in government departments. The Indian Institute of Management, Ahmedabad, and Satyam Computers have been involved in preparing and conducting a comprehensive course with practical orientation. The government has been investing more than Rs 250, 000 to train each functionary.
- Video Conferece Facility for better monitoring and close coordination with district administration.
- AP Portal—It is proposed to develop comprehensive and web-enabled services that would act as an electronic gateway into government and portfolio of services. The portal internet technologies are to deliver an array of services from the GoAP.
- AP NET—GoAP proposes to set up a Satcom network using KU-band transponder of INSAT-3B, for Distance Education, Telemedicine, HRD and E-Governance.
- Treasury computerisation—Better quality service to the clients and internal efficiency in terms of quick and quality accounts.

Source: *Government of Andhra Pradesh Strategy Paper on Governance and Public Management* 2002; P V.R.K. Prasad (2003) 'Governance Reforms in Andhra Pradesh', in Stephen Howes, Ashok K. Lahiri and Nicholas Stern, *State Level Reforms in India: Towards More Effective Government*, New Delhi, Macmillan India Ltd.

in the state—Centre for Good Governance which was established with the aid of DFID (Department for International Development) to make policy suggestions. Similarly, Adam Smith Institute, a London based research and consultancy organisation, has been instituted at the State Secretariat on the advice of the World Bank. Another institute, Marri Channa Reddy Institute of Human Resource Development is to train different officials and employees. The coming up of these institutions has shifted the locus of policy studies from the traditional research institutes to donor-aided institutes (Mooij 2003). The third area that immensely changed most of the sectors was legal framework. Most significant changes in several sectors have been affected through the executive orders, which are referred to as GOs (Government Orders). On very few occassions legislation was resorted to.

Thus, the above two documents on governance and the concomitant changes that are taking shape in various sectors of state administration make things clear. A scholar aptly calls them as four articles of faith: One, there should be no interference in the functioning between bureaucrats and legislators; two, governing for result, with an emphasis on delivery and performance; third, e-governance for speedy file movement and transparency; and fourth, the necessity to increase the participation of stakeholders in development efforts (Mooij 2003). It must be acknowledged that the governance reforms in the state gradually emerged from the process of economic reforms and politics of international aid. Thus, it has been shaped by the imperatives of this process.

It is important to specify the compulsions that a government undergoes, when it enters into agreement with IFIs for financial aid. The World Bank and other Bretton Woods institutions have their own ways of controlling the governments to which they provide aid. The liberalisation in India and AP is marked by IMF aiding the country to overcome balance of payments crisis and forcing it to go for Structural Adjustment Programme (SAP), and later World Bank aiding sectoral development in AP and other parts of the country. It makes a useful exercise, when we analyse the evolution of governance among the international donor community. Donors always viewed governance issues from the point of view of *aid effectiveness* (institutions that render the aid effective in their development programmes) in the recipient countries.

The emergence of the notion of good governance at the global level has a fairly long history. The successive failures of 'economic reform based aid' (on 'pure' economic considerations) in many recipient countries during the 1980s made the international donor community to turn towards 'governance based aid', which means granting aid is contingent upon putting in place suitable political institutions expected to perform for the success of economic reforms (Aubut 2004; Currie 1996). It also shifted the focus from poverty and backwardness as the factors for providing development aid to suitable governance. Aubut argues that the discourse on governance at the international level experienced several mutations owing to the economic and political interests of the donor countries. In the process, more redistributive issues got sidelined. Her exhaustive study on the relationship between aid and governance demonstrates that the debate on governance among the donor community initially was confined to making suggestions on 'good policies' and later it went further in making 'efficient institutions' (good governance) as a conditionality for aid to programmes in the recipient countries. The latest condition is the 'selectivity' principle which means choosing only those countries which already have good governance institutions in place, not 'good governance to be built'. Interestingly, none of these supposedly good governance principles were observed by donors themselves. Aubut (2004) observes that in most of the cases, political factors play an important role in choosing the recipient countries.

In the case of Andhra Pradesh, Naidu's persona and his quick way of pushing the reforms and complete control over management played a crucial role (rather than benevolent reasons) in prompting the World Bank to give aid to the state (M.T. Reddy et al. 2001; Melkote and Kodandram 2005). It is significant to state that the Bank made compromises in order to bail out the Government in the face of growing disenchantment on policies such as hike in power tariff, rising water user charges during the late 1990s which have already become politically sensitive issues having a bearing on the election results. Keeping the TDP's prospects in the 1999 General and Assembly Elections in view, 'the timetable for the reforms in the power sector is structured in such a manner that most politically explosive issues, those regarding 'rationalising' tariffs (on power) for agricultural users, are to be made in the year 2000, well after the elections. Similarly, in the matter of food subsidies, the World Bank has indicated that it is willing to be patient. A substantial increase in water user charges is also slated for a date after the year 2000' (*Frontline* 1999). The principle of 'selectivity' does seem to have been watered down by the Bank in this case. Since the *Vision 2020* (GoAP 1999) of AP government has been prepared on the lines of 'governance' evolved at the global level, it has irretrievably committed itself to the reform process induced by the World Bank's agenda.

Reforms in Rural Governance

Ever since independence, the problem with local governance in India has been one of scepticism of policy makers, bureaucrats and the power elite about the abilities of the genuinely autonomous local institutions. It is important to understand this because the attitudes of national and state leadership always reflected in the policy orientations in shaping the local government institutions. Their ambiguity appears to have emerged out of the mixed conditions prevailing on the eve of independence: widespread illiteracy and caste-ridden feudal structures in rural India, which made them sceptical of the efficacy of the local institutions. Besides the policy makers never allowed them to function to their fullest potential. While this was true in the pre-reforms period, the present rural governance scenario further worsened the situation with its paradigmatic shift from a state-centric system to market orientation.

The present scenario of local governance in AP presents a complex situation with swift changes and multiple agencies working in different directions. One can broadly place them under four major categories: (*i*) PRIs acting under the Andhra Pradesh Panchayatraj Act (APPRA), 1994; (*ii*) Parallel Bodies (PB) which function parallel to the PRIs; (*iii*) Society for Elimination of Rural Poverty (SERP), which runs a poverty reduction programme called *Velugu*—it is a government run non-governmental organisation (one can term it as GNGO) with its structure running from the Chief Minister to the local level mostly headed by senior bureaucrats at different levels; and (*iv*) the recent Village Secretariat and, above all these, the *Janmabhoomi* (land of birth) that worked as an operative framework and channelised the work of these new bodies at the local level.

The *Janmabhoomi* programme, initiated by the TDP government with the objective of involving people in the development programmes ironically operated through a highly centralised nodal mechanism at the top with the involvement of self-help groups, and stakeholders (read 'interested groups') at the bottom. *Janmabhoomi* was so closely identified with Naidu himself that any party that came into power had to face the problem of identity if it continued (G.K. Reddy 2002a; Mooij 2003). The present Congress Government in the state abolished *Janmabhoomi* initiated by the earlier TDP government and introduced it with a different name *Rajiv Pallecs baata* (loosely, 'Road leading to village') and presently it is termed as *Prajapadham* (people's path).

Janmabhoomi and *Prajapadham* are similar at their core as both revolve around the rhetoric of people's participation in development processes. Yet they part ways in one interesting sense. The *Janmabhoomi* was conducted usually in people's gatherings such as *gram sabhas* or special *Janmabhoomi* meetings where people would raise the problems before a group of local officials and politicians generally belonged to the TDP, the then ruling party. The nodal agency at the district level consisting of officials—the district collector and downwards took stock of the problems raised in the programme. The *Janmabhoomi* used to take place periodically twice in a year. In the case of *Prajapadham,* people's representatives along with local officials visit the people door-to-door instead of holding any gatherings. The nodal agency that was set up under *Janmabhoomi* now stands abolished. The *Prajapadham* takes plan once in a year, during summer seasons. Now the present Chief Minister, Y.S. Rajashekar Reddy does visit the villages periodically himself but not with the bureaucratic entourage as it used to be with Naidu. What matters here is that the practice of 'involving people' appears to have caught up with all the regimes. It indicates how deeply it conditions the governance framework of the regime in the state. *Janmabhoomi* as a character of regime politics is discussed by the author elsewhere (G.K. Reddy 2002a).

There are about 7 to 10 stakeholder committees in every village which function almost parallel to the panchayats. The parallel bodies include—Village Education Committee (VEC), *Vana Samrakshana Samithi* (VSS), Water Users Associations (WUA), *Janmabhoomi* Habitation Committee, Mothers Committee, Health Committee, Watershed Committees, Committee for youth to review Chief Minister's Empowerment Programme for Youth (CMEY), and Self-Help Groups (SHGs) like Development of Women and Child in Rural Areas (DWCRA). Among these only two, i.e., VEC and WUA are statutory bodies and the rest are created by government orders. They perform the functions, most of which might as well be performed by the committees of Gram Panchayats (GP), as all these functions fall within the purview of the PRIs (Jayalaxmi 2001). Official nomenclature of these bodies as Community Based Organisations (CBOs) could be seen as an attempt to forge community links between the stakeholders of a particular body on the basis of a person's stake. It would be rather appropriate to call them membership organisations as the criterion to join a body is an individual member's interests (Roy 2002).[6] The PBs such as Water Users Associations (WUA), *Vana Samrakshana Samithi* (VSS), Village Education Committee (VEC), Watershed Committee, DWCRA groups, etc., operated in association with the *Janmabhoomi* programmes, though each of them have their own activities. The binding principle between *Janmabhoomi* or the present *Prajapadham* and Membership Organisations is self-help.

The Parallel Bodies seek to perform the same functions as the PRIs with a different orientation. They envisage a certain kind of collaboration with civil society organisations which is underscored by the notion of self-help. It actually posits the citizen as independent of the social conditions and thereby it calls upon the individual to act on his/her own in managing the resources. Its implication would be serious for those sections not having access to resources as Membership Organisations are concerned with only those who possess resources. Second, these User Groups facilitate the state's new approach to development which could be broadly seen as part of liberalisation. The pro-market reforms regime in Andhra Pradesh has vigorously adopted several strategies to carry out the reforms. The economic reforms adopted by the Government entailed new patterns of relationship between the state and the citizen. Unlike the earlier statist regime, the state in the new scenario cannot hold the responsibility to harness and redistribute the resources as this role has been passed on to the market.

Given the representative character of the PRIs, they cannot fit into the new ambience of liberalisation (Naidu 2000). The PRIs as elected bodies take into account the general interest of people, unlike the stakeholder approach of the newly established bodies which address only those sections that already possess resources, i.e., stakes. This distinction between those people who possess resources and those who do not is important because it characterises the very nature of the present rural governance. The parallel bodies with specific treatment of beneficiaries on the basis of their specific stakes assume more prominence in managing the resources than the PRIs in the new institutional setting.

Another point to be noted is that claims to resources have been traditionally associated with caste structures and sanctions. Conflict resolution mechanisms in the case of resource use were predominantly attributed to the caste hierarchies. The decline of the political significance of the PRIs owing to the gradual ascendance of lower castes and the breakdown in the traditional patron-client relations is instructive in understanding the changing patterns of resource management. One senior political leader puts it aptly that the PRIs have become more important to those sections without resources and they take part seriously in the local elections, and the more advanced sections are shifting their interest to controlling PBs because it would be tangibly helpful for them in accessing resources.[7]

The notion of self-help essentially hinges on the atomising of the citizen. It flows from rational choice theory where it is believed that every individual is capable and has a choice of one's own. All actions of individuals are thus capable of being rational. In a similar way, all the Parallel Bodies address the resources at the local level. The PBs often invoke self-help through two related ways—'stake holders' and 'user groups'. Here it is necessary to clarify these terms as they govern the patterns of use of resources. The PBs presuppose that there are sets of people who have stakes in a particular resource and all those who have common stakes must form into a user group. It tends to ignore the multiple uses of a resource and in the process it prioritises one use of that particular resource over the other uses.

For instance, the WUA was formed through a statute, the AP Farmers' Management Systems Act 1997. It gave total control over all water bodies and canals within the village jurisdiction to the WUA. The Act clearly held the farmers' rights over water for irrigation higher than all the other uses of water such as washing, fishing and drinking which have been traditionally recognised as common. Such prioritisation of use of one resource over others through legal frameworks entailed fragmentation between different user communities, and lead to serious conflicts. In this context, the traditional conflict resolution mechanisms get discredited and one user community gets privilege over the others. For instance, in the case of WUA, the farmers are privileged over the washermen and fishermen communities, and over the people dependent on water only for drinking purpose. The conflict clearly arose out of the new management of water, which is increasingly getting scarce. On many occasions the farmers with newly claimed rights objected to other uses of water such as fishing, washing and drinking water for sheep and buffaloes, resulting in minor skirmishes.[8]

The immediate fallout of the formation of the WUA is reduction of the PRIs to a non-entity in managing water resources. The WUA has the right to maintain and distribute, though they do not have wherewithal to harness water. The rich farmers with considerable size of land with water sources dominate and control these associations.[9] More importantly resource is power and water has been historically linked to land. In the new environment, it reproduces fresh centres of power in the village that becomes extremely contentious.

The presence of the WUAs is quite uneven in the state. They are active only in canal-irrigated districts of coastal Andhra—west and east Godavari districts, Krishna and Guntur. They are relatively inactive in Telangana and Rayalaseema where canal irrigation facilities are scanty. In spite of this, one can perceive WUA's monopoly over whatever water sources available as a potential source of conflict. Sheep Breeders Cooperative Society makes its claims over water as one of the essential demands: 'The chairmen of the WUA are exercising monopoly on village tanks and ponds. Fodder trees like babul and grasses in the tanks and ponds are being auctioned. Though there are GOs to allow free grazing for sheep and goat, the WUAs are auctioning the resources for money. We are not allowed to use the water'.[10]

In the case of Village Education Committees (VECs), the task of primary education has been virtually taken away from the jurisdiction of Gram Panchayats much against the GO No. 120, (31 March 1999) that devolves primary and secondary education to the PRIs. A study conducted by PRIA (Hyderabad), an NGO, observes that the School Education Committee formed under Andhra Pradesh School Education (Community Participation) Act, 1998 invests the responsibilities and the resources with VECs rather than with Gram Panchayats in contradiction with its own GO (Vaddiraju et al. 2001). In the perception of many functionaries and elected representatives, the PRIs have virtually no role in primary education after VECs came into being.[11] Under VECs, the parents come together and form a Parents Committee which is supposed to regulate the functioning of schools. However, the VECs are not concerned with those who do not enter into school education as they deal with only the stakeholders in education.

A study done by *Yakshi,* a Hyderabad based NGO, on the implications of international financing agencies aided projects in Andhra Pradesh observes: 'SAP (Structural Adjustment Programme) based policies in the education sector leads to downsizing the government employees (except teachers) and activities in favour of private provision. In the allocation of public funds, education is not on the priority list. Government expenditure on education has fallen from 3.5 per cent of GSDP to 2.9 per cent during 1986–95. The World Bank has argued for increasing fees for government institutions of higher education, expansion of private unaided schools in rural areas, expansion of multi-grade teaching especially designed materials, and private participation in elementary education.'[12] When this is seen in consonance with the stakeholder approach adopted in management of rural education, it surely opens the gate for the entry of private interests.

What is in fact happening is that the private-public distinction is collapsing as the patterns of use of resource undergo change. Individual usage of resources is increasingly perceived as common. As the relationship between man and the resource is mediated through legal and market mechanisms, the individual is perceived more as a user rather than as a citizen. The resources become increasingly commodifiable things.

Thus, the present legal frameworks not only view the resources as commodities but also legitimise the market logic in accessing them (G.K. Reddy 2002b). As a consequence of this the citizen is perceived as a consumer of resources and the user must pay for it. The question of rights of the citizen over common resources takes a back seat. The resultant conflicts over the access to resources create tensions among different communities. The new framework creates conducive grounds for market expansion and the conflicts are kept outside the purview of political resolution. Perhaps, this is what undermines PRIs in the present scenario.

Coming to the third type of intervention in the local governance in Andhra Pradesh, it appears that the government, so far talking about the collaboration between the government and civil society agencies, is directly entering into that civil society space, by launching the non-governmental organisation in the form of SERP by itself. The idea of *Velugu* originated from its precursor, South Asia Poverty Alleviation Programme (SAPAP), which was launched in Andhra Pradesh in the early 1990s with the help of funds from the UNDP, covering six districts in the state, two each from three regions, viz., Telangana, Rayalaseema and coastal Andhra. When SAPAP was launched, it was purely non-governmental, run by an autonomous structure. Later it took the form of SERP at the behest of the World Bank.[13] The Bank's project appraisal document (World Bank, 2000) dealing with poverty elimination programmes in rural areas of Andhra Pradesh, specifically recommends in its 'institutional arrangements' for establishment of SERP to carry forward the programmes. SERP is an organisation headed by the Chief Minister as the ex-officio chairman and other senior bureaucrats heading different wings at different levels. SERP received Rs 600 crores for its programme, *Velugu,* in the first phase, covering six districts—Adilabad and Mehaboobnagar in Telangana, Anantapur and Chittor in Rayalaseema and Sri Kakulam and Vijayanagaram in the coastal region. At the district level, it is called District Poverty Initiative Programme (DPIP). *Velugu* creates a structure of its own which operates under the SERP. The structure of the SERP is built by the SHGs at the village level to the Mandal, District and the State level.

The *Velugu* programme was initiated as part of the World Bank's strategy to tackle poverty that emerges out of economic reforms in the developing societies. It is intended to provide a cushioning effect for the adverse results of the economic reforms, on one hand, and create conditions for the markets, on the other. Under *Velugu,* different programmes such as Community Investment Fund, Rice Credit Line, Capability Building and so on have been chalked out (SERP, nd). It has been found that these programmes, even as they address the problem of poverty, prepare people for the market. For instance, the Community Investment Fund provides different forms of credit to different communities to access the market. At the ground level most of these programmes have failed to produce any sustained support to the needy communities. However, these programmes create market ethos.

The fact of the matter is that *Velugu* and the SERP have virtually occupied the space of the NGOs and also established a parallel administrative set-up. However, on both counts, the SERP has emerged as an important agency supplanting the NGOs, on the one hand, and the bureaucracy, on the other. Now that the *Velugu* progamme has been extended to all the 22 districts of the state with funding from the World Bank to the tune of Rs 2200 crores, it has assumed more prominence. *Velgu* has been renamed as *Indira Krantti Padham* by the present Congress government.

The fourth and the latest intervention from the state government is the introduction of the Village Secretariat. Here the Revenue and the Panchayat Raj wings are sought to be merged from the village level.[14] The post of Village Secretary, who is supposed to work under the Sarpanch, has been created, who in the new system is burdened with about sixty-four functions to perform (Ravinder 2006). The lower rung employees of the state administration, mostly from the Revenue and the Panchayat wings, are posted as Village Secretaries. Consequently there are reports that they are not aware of the complex realities of the village system as they are not exposed to the system at the village level. The state appears to be in a hurry to build the wherewithal for the changes that have been introduced under the economic reforms. The main motto of the new structure appears to be strengthening of the tax base and legitimising the user charges system at the village level (G.K. Reddy 2005).

While the state is interested in intervening in the local communities on the basis of the new economic rationale that seeks to affect the tax structure at the village level, one crucial link between the resource base and tax mobilisation is missing. Having withdrawn from the responsibility of mobilising the resources, the state intended to make efforts to improve the tax position at the village level. This is a contradiction in itself because the tax base cannot be expanded without developing the resource base with the larger sections having access to them.

Concluding Remarks

There is a general impression, but quite prevalent among scholars that governance reforms in the third world is by and large a result of the designs of the international donor community, which perpetrate the interests of the global finance agencies. While this being substantially true, the view fails to capture more complex dynamics in the process. The question is one of method rather than of substance, as it takes intervention of global factors in the recipient countries as an unnegotiated and superimposed process. It cannot take into account the role that the ruling and subaltern classes in the domestic front play in negotiating with global processes.

The study rather prefers to consider the process of reforms as product of negotiation between regimes in the recipient countries and global actors. It also finds that it is through these negotiations (implies a political process) that the political/economic interests of the regime in the countries that receive aid and global forces get converged. This paper was an attempt to show that the nature and form of the Naidu regime is a crucial factor that attracted the attention of the global donor community. The fact that this state was chosen beyond the principle of 'selectivity' by the Bank is notable. The World Bank has, for the first time, gone in for direct negotiations with a provincial government, breaking the practice of dealing with the national governments. 'AP is the first state not just at the country level but the whole of Asia and only one of the three instances in the world where the World Bank has embarked on a regional/sub-national level SAP' (M.T. Reddy et al. 2001).

It has set the trend that subsequently facilitated the Bank to deal with several other states in India in a similar fashion. It not only cleared the way for speedy negotiations, but also has implications for the federal politics in the country. Dealing with the World Bank and other donors for aid is now one of the important concerns of every state government in the country. As the union government still has to stand for the counter guarantees for foreign aid, the matter of external aid has become an important dimension of financial relations between the center and states. More importantly, it has facilitated the Bank's strategy to influence the formulation and implementation of policies and programmes at the sub-national level.

Naidu's persuation for foreign aid is a result of both fiscal crisis and regime compulsions such as establishing his own persona and managing the opposition to reform process in the state. Thus, it was mutual gain for the donors and the regime. However, the foreign aid has decisively come to shape the policy framework as well as implementation of programmes.

The APERP has prepared the blueprint for the fiscal and sectoral reforms. It also linked up economic reforms with political reforms as it views governance reforms as a crucial factor in the success of economic reforms. It is interesting to note that the Project Appraisal Document (PAD) of the APERP contains the letter of Naidu, the then Chief Minister, assuring the Bank's President, about the reforms to be taken up. And the letter also cites some of the measures already taken up in that direction (World Bank 1998, Letter appeared as Annexure 13). Vision 2020 and the Government's Strategy Paper followed the sanction of the loan under the APERP on governance reforms, which gave a concrete shape to governance reforms.

The Government of Andhra Pradesh's tryst with administrative reforms is linked with global financing agencies like the World Bank and DFID. Most of the programmes initiated under governance reforms are actually aided by these lending agencies. The reforms essentially bring out three characteristics of administration as good governance—efficient management of the market reforms; enhancing the pace of file movement; and transparency and accountability. However, this framework of governance prioritises the interests of a section of people who need a smooth flow of permissions and licenses in the market. In the process, it conveniently takes away the more basic responsibilities towards meeting the problems of the marginal sections from the ambit of governance.

The governance agenda of the Bank is to ensure privatisation and involvement of civil society institutions in all its programmes to make the governments accountable and responsible. It insists on collaboration/partnership of state and society. However, the irony of the situation is that in unequally structured power relations in a society like ours it becomes effectively the collaboration between dominant private interests in the society and the state.

Consequently the accountability of the state in taking decisions is shifted nowhere. Neither the diffused private interests nor the state is held responsible (Joseph 2001). On the contrary, the domination of private interests even in matters of governance come to be legitimised in the name of civil society participation. This is the implication that one can draw out of the notions of minimal state, which is not merely confined to market relations but pervades the whole of state-society relations.

It is important to understand the changing environment with regard to village communities and the state where the relationship between the citizen and the state is being redefined. In the present scheme, the citizen can exist only as a user/consumer of resources, while losing his/her legitimate space in the civil society as the market comes to be treated conterminously with the civil society. The disadvantaged sections would further get marginalised in the new environment of the arrangement of resources.

Thus, in the present institutional framework, the resources are not only regarded as commodities but also accessed through the market logic. The constitutionally recognised rights of citizens to access resources are seriously undermined as the citizens rights now hinge on their ability to pay for the use of the resource. In the context of prevailing social and economic in equalities, the shift in policy orientation renders the question of right of the citizen over common resources meaningless. The resultant conflicts over the access to resources create tensions among different communities.

Two interrelated things emerge out of the present study: First, the declining significance of the PRIs is embedded in the logic of emerging framework of rural governance which is necessarily institutionalised by the economic reforms in the state. It is clear that the representative character of the PRIs is found unsuitable to the management of rural resources in the scheme of things charted by the present regime. The talk of convergence between the PRIs and the parallel bodies held by some quarters in the government and among some NGOs (Bandhyopadhyay 2002) is untenable because the two institutional forms address rural governance in two contrasting ways. Second, the emerging patterns of resources are being legalised and mediated through new institutional forms. In the process of prioritising efficiency of resource management being made central to the rural governance, issues of democracy and social equity often become casualty. It is so because the question of access to resources does not figure in the present framework of governance. Besides, this study finds that the emerging use pattern of resources through SHGs carry potential sites of new conflicts between the communities relying on the traditional and the others who hold these new patterns of resource usage.

Notes

(I greatly acknowledge Dr Limbadri's help in shaping the ideas particularly on the section of rural governance reforms in this paper).

1. The governance reforms that have been introduced across different countries in the third world have profoundly shaped the institutions and political regimes in these countries. The present study on the dynamics of governance reforms in Andhra Pradesh bears insights on similar phenomena happening elsewhere.
2. Elections as an index to understand the politics of economic reforms is dealt with at length by Suri (2005).
3. The event had been publicised as 'August Crisis' in the media. Naidu mobilised 177 MLAs on his side by keeping them captive for about two days in a hotel. It was surprising that when a democratically elected government was manipulated and dethroned, the media maintained conspicuous silence. However, the event marked the beginning of a new era in the state. Naidu, an ambitious leader, though morally incorrect, wanted to potray himself as politically correct.
4. *Eenadu,* a leading Telugu newspaper which spearheaded the anti-arrack movement in 1993, turned back and tacitly supported lifting the ban on liquor in 1997. The rest of the regional media also tacitly sought to support the decision. Media too foresaw economic rationality in lifting the ban and shaped the public opinion in its favour and succeeded in blunting the opposition to it. It is a fine case of the media management skills of Naidu.
5. When both these documents—the World Bank report, Agenda for AP Economic Reforms', and Andhra Pradesh White Paper on Status of Financial Position of the State, gave identical analyses, the media and the intelligentsia came down heavily pointing at the credentials of independent analysis of the AP government. The White Paper was understood to be prepared and released at the behest of the World Bank. It also received criticism against the way the World Bank delayed so much in making its report public so that it appeared after ten months of its submission to the government (*The Hindu,* 27 October 1997).
6. Since the study finds the usage of the word 'Community Based Organisations' inappropriate, it used 'Membership organisations', 'Parallel Bodies' and 'User Groups' interchangeably depending upon the context.
7. Interview with a senior politician of the Telugu Desam Party, 23 February 2002, Hyderabad.
8. Interviews with Primary School teachers in Prakasham District, Ongole, 9 February 2003.
9. Interviews with Mandal Parishad Presidents from Chittore and Nellore Districts, Kalahasthi, 21 December 2002.

10. Position Paper of Andhra Pradesh Sheep and Goat Rearers Association and Andhra Pradesh Sheep Breeders Cooperative Society, presented at the workshop on 'Grazing Issues in the State of Andhra Pradesh', organised by Andhra Pradesh Grazing Fodder Forum, Hyderabad,17 June 2002.
11. PRIA and Partners, *Primary Education and Panchayati Raj Institutions*, New Delhi, 2002.
12. Report on the implications of the World Bank and other allied international agencies funded programmes in Andhra Pradesh, prepared by *Yakshi*, Hyderabad, 2002.
13. An interview with K. Raju, the then commissioner of Rural Development, Government of Andhra Pradesh, formerly CEO of SERP, Hyderabad, 6 December 2004.
14. D. Ravinder, 'Pannupotu, Kendralu Kaagala Grama Sachivaalayalu' (Village Secretariats as tax imposing centres), *Vaartha* (a Telugu daily), 19 January 2002.

References

Aubut, Julie (2004). 'The Good Governance Agenda: Who Wins and Who loses—Some Empirical Evidence for 2001', Working Paper No. 04–48, Development Studies Institute, London: London School of Economics and Political Science.

Balagopal, K. (1999). 'The Man and the Times', *Economic and Political Weekly*, 34(26): 1654–58, 26 June.

Bandhyopadhyay, D. and B.N. Yugandhar (2002). 'Convergence of Programmes by Empowering SHGs and PRIs', *Economic and Political Weekly*, 37(26): 255–61, 29 June–5 July.

Baru, Sanjaya (2000). 'Economic Policy and the Development of Capitalism in India: The Role of Regional Capitalists and Political Parties', pp. 207–30, in Francine R. Frankel et al. (eds), *Transforming India: Social and Political Dynamics of Democracy*. New Delhi: Oxford University Press.

Currie, Bob (1996). 'Governance, Democracy and Economic Adjustment in India: Concept and Empirical Problem', *Third World Quarterly*, 17(4): 787–807.

Frontline (1999). 'A World Bank Agenda for A.P.', 16(12): 89–96, 18 June.

Government of Andhra Pradesh (GoAP) (1996). *White Paper on the State of Finances in Andhra Pradesh*. Hyderabad: Finance and Planning Division, June.

——— (1999). *Vision 2020*. January, Hyderabad.

——— (2002). *Strategy Paper on Governance and Public Management*. Hyderabad: GAD.

Jayalaxmi, K. (2001). 'Panchayat Raj Institution in Andhra Pradesh: Issues and Interventions', Paper presented at South Zone Conference on Panchayat Raj Institutions, Organised by Karl Kübel Institute of Development Education, Thiruvananthapuram, 28–29 December.

Joseph, Sarah (2001). 'Democratic Good Governance: New Agenda for Change', *Economic and Political Weekly*, 36(12): 1011–14, 24 March.

Lalitha, K. and Shashi Kumar (2005). 'Globalisation and the State: Understanding Social Reform in the State of Andhra Pradesh', Paper presented at the First National Conference of the Globalisation and Indian State Research Programme, Organised by The National Foundation for India, New Delhi, 11–12 November.

Manor, James (2002). 'Democratic Decentralisation in Two Indian States: Past and Present', *Indian Journal of Political Science*, 63(1) 51–71, March.

Melkote, Rama and M. Kodandram (2005). 'Contextualising Food Security: Global and Local Articulations and the Declining Role of the State', Paper presented at the First National Conference of the Globalisation and Indian State Research Programme, Organised by The National Foundation for India, New Delhi, 11–12 November.

Mooij, Jos (2003). 'Smart Governance? Politics in the Policy Process in Andhra Pradesh, India', Working Paper no. 228, London: Overseas Development Institute.

Naidu, Chandrababu (with Sevanthi Ninan) (2000). *Plain Speaking*, New Delhi: Viking.

Nayak, Radhika, N.C. Saxena and John Farrington (2002). 'Reaching the Poor: The Influence of the Policy and Administrative Processes on the Implementation of Government Poverty Schemes in India'. Working Paper No. 175, London: Overseas Development Institute.

Pai, Sudha (1996). 'Andhra Pradesh: Elections and Fiscal Reforms', *Economic and Political Weekly*, 31(2–3): 142–48, 13–20 January.

Prasad, P.V.R.K. (2003). 'Governance Reforms in Andhra Pradesh', in Stephen Howes, Ashok K. Lahiri and Nicholas Stern (eds), *State Level Reforms in India: Towards More Effective Government*. New Delhi: Macmillan India Ltd.

Ravinder, D. (2006). 'Dynamics of Administrative Reforms in Panchayatraj System: A Study of Village secreteriat in Andra Pradesh', *The India Journal of Political Science*, 67(1): 109–118, January–March.

Reddy, G. Krishna (2002a). 'New Populism and Liberalisation: Regime Shift Under Chandrababu Naidu in A.P.', *Economic and Political Weekly*, 37(9): 871–83, 2 March.

——— (2002b). *Citizen Participation in Local Governance in South Asia: An Experience from South India*, Logo Link Project Report, IDS, University of Sussex, submitted to PRIA, New Delhi, (available at www.pria.org).

——— (2005). 'Resource Management And Rural Governance: Panchayatraj in Andra Pradesh', pp. 268–285, in A. Majeed (ed.), *Federal India: A Design for Good Governance*, (Center for Federal Studies Jamia Hamdard University) New Delhi: Manak Publications.

Reddy, G. Ram (1989). 'The Politics of Acommodation: Caste, Class and Domination in Andhra Pradesh', in Francine Frankel and M.S.A. Rao (eds), *Dominance and State Power in India: Decline of a Social Order in India*. Delhi: Oxford University Press.

Reddy, M. Thimma, K.S. Gopal, Raghav Narsalay and Minar Pimple (2001). *Economic Restructuring in Andhra Pradesh: An Analytical Introduction to The Andhra Pradesh Economic Restructuring Project*. Mumbai: Centre for Environmental Concerns, Hyderabad and Focus on The Global South India Programme.

Roy, Indrajit (2002). 'Community, Organisation and Reception', *Economic and Political Weekly*, 37(35): 3591–95, 31 August.

SERP. (nd). *Velugu*. Available at www.Velugu.org/what_velugu/what_velugu.html, accessed on 24 November 2005.

Suri, K.C. (2005). 'The Dilemma of Democracy: Economic Reforms and Electoral Politics in Andhra Pradesh', pp. 130–68, in Jos Mooij (ed.), *The Politics of Economic Reforms in India*. New Delhi: Sage Publications.

Upadhya, Carrol (1988). 'The Farmer-Capitalists of Coastal Andhra Pradesh', *Economic and Political Weekly*, 23(27): 1376–82, July 2 and 23(28): 1433–42, 9 July.

Vaddiraju, Anil, C. Venkatesham and K. Saritha (2001). 'A Study on Primary (Formal) Education and Panchayats: Devolution in Primary Education: A.P. Report', PRIA, Hyderabad, November.

World Bank (2001). *World Development Report 2002: Building Institutions for Markets*. Washington DC: World Bank.

——— (2000). *Project Appraisal Document on the Andhra Pradesh District Poverty Initiative Programme*, Report no. 20089–IN, March.

——— (1999). *Project Appraisal Document on Andhra Pradesh Power Restructuring Project*, Report no. 18849-IN, January.

——— (1998). *Project Appraisal Document on Andhra Pradesh Economic Restructuring Project*, Report no. 17710-IN, May.

——— (1997). *Andhra Pradesh: Agenda for Economic Reforms*, Report No. 15901, India, January.

6

Governance Reforms and Development in Kerala in the Context of Globalisation

K. Ramachandran Nair

Introduction

The ongoing debate on globalisation, and economic and governance reforms with a thrust on efficiency, transparency and accountability is both intellectually enriching and refreshingly fascinating. The challenge facing all societies is to create a workable system of governance that promotes, supports and sustains overall human development. People, particularly the poor and the marginalised, are advised to follow either the neoliberal or the radical agenda. Though both are mutually contradictory, they invariably declare that 'there is no alternative' (TINA) other than the one suggested.

The neoliberal agenda suggested for the poor countries of the world having some elemental democratic traditions, consists of a blue print for macroeconomic reforms to strengthen domestic economic fundamentals and is followed by a standardised regimen of governance reform designed and propagated by international financial institutions. However, for countries lacking even a modicum of democratic tradition, this agenda has an 'add-on' in the form of 'political reform' consisting of 'reinventing of democracy' and 'reforming of political system' by pushing the state to the back seat, making 'politics' unnecessary and bringing civil society institutions to the centre stage of governance. 'Governance reform' seems to have thus become an integral part of the anti-state discourse. In this context, the world has witnessed an all-out and well-orchestrated effort by the so-called 'well-meaning' intellectuals, 'think tanks' and global funding agencies backing the neoliberal agenda to counter the propagandist onslaught of the radical agenda.

The radical agenda is founded on Marxist-Leninist ideology and its vision is of a socialist state replacing an imperialist capitalist regime through class mobilisation and class war. However, experiments in Soviet Union and East European socialist countries cast serious doubts on this agenda. This led to a serious ideological debate among the Marxists-Leninists. As an outcome of this, the 'radical agenda' seems to have started shedding some of its primary and fundamental positions by sometimes posing itself as 'reformist social democratic agenda'. The promoters of this reformist view now prefer to work with the existing democratic, political and economic fabric, and reform capitalism in an attempt to make it more equitable through the creation and maintenance of a pro-poor welfare state. In contrast to 'economic fundamentals', they give stress to 'people's fundamentals'.

In India, at the national level and at the level of the states, the relevance of the neoliberal agenda, the radical agenda and the reformist social democratic agenda is now being actively debated. At the national level, the left parties, with faith in and commitment to their respective brands of Marxism-Leninism, have agreed to give political support to the ruling Congress-led United Progressive Alliance (UPA) which is aggressively implementing the 'neoliberal agenda' and its standard policy mix. However, in Kerala the mainstream left political parties are currently engaged in giving a 'local' and 'context specific' interpretation to the radical agenda on the plea that the situation prevailing in this state is not comparable to the all-India one. This gets reflected in their approach to globalisation, economic reform and the new paradigm of 'governance reform' in contrast to the position taken by them at the national level.

This chapter is broadly divided into five major parts. First, it shows that capitalism is a versatile creature having the capacity to get transformed into new forms and acquire new structures to ensure its survival. The international institutions that support it are now propagating globalisation through the refined idea of reforms of governance, democracy and politics. Second, it gives an overview of the development experience of Kerala and what has gone wrong with it since achieving a fairly high level of human development. Third, it looks at state's own reform initiatives and makes a critical study of decentralised governance and civil society initiatives including the people's plan campaign and their inherent strength, weakness and constraints. Fourth, it examines state level reforms driven by external pressure from the Central government as well as the Asian Development Bank (ADB). Finally, the chapter concludes that Kerala urgently needs to correct past mistakes and reinvent good governance that has a local flavour, instead of adopting the standard regimen of governance reform proposed by the promoters of globalisation. It is argued that any success of governance reforms in the contextual situation of Kerala would ultimately depend on basic reforms in the state's 'politics and democracy', particularly in the way they are practised.

Capitalist Globalism and Good Governance

Already a fairly exhaustive literature review on the meaning and perspectives of globalisation, its social, economic, political and cultural dimensions, and challenges of the agenda of 'good governance' has been provided (Choudhary 2004; Shylendra 2004). Therefore, this chapter does not venture to traverse the same path once again. In this section we argue that one cannot ignore the close interconnection between capitalism, colonialism, imperialism, global capitalism and globalisation.

Capitalism in no time became the dominant political, social and economic system until Marxism and Socialism appeared as a vigorous, hostile and competing alternative. The development of industrial capitalism and finance capitalism had serious human costs. Founded on the competitive search for profit, capitalism devised new instruments like colonialism and imperialism to facilitate exploitation of the weak by the strong. The parasitic character of these instruments got reflected in an asymmetrical relationship of interdependence between materially advanced and backward societies. According to Lenin, the essence of imperialism is the division of the world into 'oppressor' and 'oppressed' countries, former being the imperialist power, the latter including the colonial and semi-colonial periphery (Lenin 1967). This seems to be the 'core-periphery' model that underlies the modern theory of underdevelopment, dependency and imperialism, both Marxist and non-Marxist.

The structural and organic inconsistencies and internal contradictions in capitalism threatened recurrent crises and its near total collapse in the 1930s. Marx believed that capitalism could not perpetuate itself indefinitely, the nature of its dissolutions depend on the laws which govern its development and upon specific historical circumstances (Giddens 1971). But contrary to Marx's prophecy, capitalism demonstrated that it was versatile with remarkable resilience and ability to survive and quickly adapt to any situation, at least for the time being. While some countries devoted to capitalism attempted to refine it without compromising on fundamentals, others preferred state-led development with a secondary role assigned to private enterprise, capital and market. The consequent debate on 'state versus market' and 'state and market' highlighted the argument that while 'market failure' could be corrected by timely action, 'state failure' was colossal with tragic consequences (Choudhary 2004). These included unprecedented growth of the state (Leviathan) and state power, concentration of power in the ruling class and bureaucracy, governance breakdown, unsound management of the economy, sheer lack of transparency and accountability, collapse of government performance in delivery of basic services to citizens, and neglect and exclusion of private sector and civil society from political, social and economic decision-making.

Global capitalism then found that the time is ripe for it to reappear as a sensible alternative to state-led development and socialism (Drucker 1997). Sensing people's suspicions about colonialism, imperialism and their 'neo versions', the promoters of global capitalism formulated the neoliberal agenda and the 'anti-state' discourse with attractive offerings like liberalisation, privatisation and globalisation (Amin 1997). People were told that this new paradigm of globalisation has nothing to do with their 'traditional perception of capitalism'. Soon the term 'globalisation' became the buzzword in the lexicon of bureaucrats, consultants and policy analysts. It also acquired legitimacy and an aura of 'sacred', 'goodness' and 'desirable' (Diwan 2000). It created a 'new global order with new markets, tools, actors, and rules/codes/obligations' (UNDP 1999). But the sceptics expect it to accentuate inequalities, create greater dislocation in the common man's life and accelerate the pauperisation of the poor. The polarisation between left and right and between neoliberal and radical discourses on the central issue that market must be allowed to make social, political and economic decisions soon became strong.

In the recent debates on globalisation, the focus has shifted to 'good governance', 'governance reform', 'political reform', 'reinventing of democracy', 'redefining core functions of government', 'transparency and accountability', 'inclusion of civil society institutions in governance'—all meant to achieve 'high quality sustainable human development' (World Bank 1991a, 1992, 1994).

Some argued that the crisis of the state is also a crisis of development (Pieterse 2001). But crisis is an intrinsic part of development and is socially constructed depending on the way people think and talk about social realities. The emergence of a 'fragmented polity' and 'conflictive politics' in party-dominated democracies has made the problem more complex. 'People's power' often failed to set right the misdeeds of the 'Prince' (state/government) and of the 'Merchant' (economic power). We agree that the success of any agenda of governance reform would depend greatly on the working harmony among the multiple actors in a society. If they pull in different directions, even the new paradigm of good governance would surely fail. This is demonstrated by what is happening in Kerala today.

The promoters of governance reform often accuse nation states of critical breakdown in governance and have advocated a standard regimen of refined instruments of governance initiatives (CAGC 1999; Fremond and Capaul 2002; OECD 1999a, 1999b; Pradhan 2003; Wolfensohn 1999). However, this is thrust on countries irrespective of the differing profiles of their history, society, culture, ethics, politics, economy, level and experience of development, citizens' aspirations and their outlook on themselves and others therein. There seems to be some truth in the saying that India had been globalising for the past 150 years, but to some body else's design.

The World Bank has made concrete efforts in developing operationally relevant indicators of governance and government performance to assess 'good and clean government' (World Bank 2000, 2001, 2004a, 2004b; Kaufman et al. 2003). 'Voice and accountability', 'political stability', 'absence of violence', 'government effectiveness', 'regulatory quality', 'rule of law', 'control of corruption', 'high citizen participation', and 'non-disruption of essential public services' (like power and water) are a few indicators constructed for 199 countries. The countries were then classified under good, fair and poor governance, and the values of the composite index ranged from as high as 75 (Switzerland) to a low of 20 (Liberia), with India getting an index of 40, the putting her under the poor governance class (Huther and Shah 2003). However, many have questioned the methodology used for this exercise and its sheer lack of 'local flavour'. One danger of depending on these indicators is its underlying ideology. An Asian Development Bank (ADB) document reveals that the programme to modernise public sector management and improve performance of governments is a part of the transition to a market economy.

Along with these, countries are directed to look to the West for ideas on 'reform of politics and democracy'. They are asked not to rely on 'native prescriptions' on this subject. The tragedy is that even India does not look into such prescriptions provided by our own leaders like Jai Prakash Narain who gave a clear blue print for the reconstruction of the Indian polity (Narain 1959). He had stated: 'political institutions become sound if they draw sustenance from the Indian soil, society and people, their lives'. He argued for a scheme of social engineering to create a 'communitarian democracy' suited to Indian ethos. A strong case has been made for 're-inventing good democracy and correct politics' with a local flavour as a viable alternative to the neoliberal paradigm (Yadav 2001). Whatever paradigm we choose, we must see that *elites* in the society no longer become the decisive factor. If it happens, 'democracy dies and politics fail to deliver'.

The promoters of the new paradigm of globalisation and governance reform assign an important role to civil society institutions (CSIs) and NGOs endowed with social capital (Knack and Keefer 1997; Narayan 1999; Putnam 1993). The CSIs with their face-to-face networks, communitarian feeling, mutual trust and reciprocity are expected to support a high degree of civility, civic group participation and reduce incentives for opportunistic and unethical behaviour by citizens in pursuing their self-interest (Grootaert et al. 2003). They are, thus, said to be capable of reforming the state, market, democracy and politics to a great extent. One criticism of CSIs and social capital is that they deliberately release the state from considerable civic and social obligation, thereby strengthening the anti-state discourse. Though the CSIs may theoretically help the poor and weak, and act as a symbol of people's voice, the great divide existing in India between the social conditions, capabilities, life chances and power of the majority poor and majority rich may erode one's faith in them. In this context, what is needed is a real people's movement spearheading sensitively designed participatory institutions and intervention programmes built on healthy cross-cutting ties among citizens. We also need 'correct politics', building strong 'bonds and bridges' among citizens to replace party-dominated conflictive politics. Kerala's experience throws considerable light on this theme.

Kerala—The Background

Kerala, often described as 'God's own country', the Land of Mahabali, Kathakali and Ayurveda is now fast getting transformed into what Swami Vivekananda had described as the land of lunatics. This is reflected by the increasing evidence of breakdown of good governance and high rate of suicides, crime, high morbidity and life style diseases, liquor tragedies, gender violence, child abuse, family break-ups and divorces, corruption, stagnant economy coupled with high profile consumerism, feeling of helplessness among youth, caste conflicts and unethical practices in political activities. Kerala became notorious for its fragmented polity and conflictive politics caused by the proliferation of political parties, groups and alliances, caste, religious, class and mass organisations, and 'people's movements'. It had the first democratically elected communist government and was also the first to experiment with the innovative multi-party coalition government. Since the 1960s' the state witnessed the convergence of parties into two political fronts, the Left Democratic Front (LDF) led by CPI (Marxists) and the United Democratic Front (UDF) led by the Congress, resulting in 'conflictive politics'. Since roughly 40 per cent each of voters support the two fronts, each of them has alternatively come to power with the support of minor parties that exercise considerable clout in deciding who should rule the state and what policies the state should follow (Pillai 1999). Inner party cliques, factions and groups also cause regular turbulence in state politics. With decentralisation and elections to the local bodies, this turbulence has damaged the vision of decentralised governance, leaving little time to the rulers to think about good governance and development.

'Kerala's development' has always been an interesting area of study and debate among policy makers. Even with her low level per capita income, Kerala's achievements in the field of health and education had been remarkable (in 1989). The National Human Development Report, 2001, constructed a composite index based on three critical dimensions of well-being such as 'longevity' (the ability to live a long and healthy life), 'education' (the ability to read, write and acquire knowledge) and 'command over resources' (the ability to enjoy a decent standard of living and have a socially meaningful life). As per the data available therein, Kerala has the highest ranking among the states. But unfortunately, with respect to unemployment rate, old age dependency rate and suicide rates too Kerala was on the top (GOK 2002a). The sustainability of high level of human development and quality of life made possible till now through popular struggles, social reform movements, pro-poor state intervention/public action is now under serious threat. Many even fear an imminent reversal of the achievements (Oommen 2004; Ramachandran 1996). Already some initiatives have been taken to check it and one such effort is in economic and governance reform discussed at a later stage.

The social history of Kerala is inextricably intertwined with its political history (Gopalan 1952; Menon 1997; Nair 2002). The social renaissance that took place in the state in the 19th and early 20th centuries was at once a cause and the consequence of political awakening and they supplemented each other. The governments, too, were sensitive to the aspirations of people, creating an environment of official support to pro-people socio-economic change. The political parties and mass organisations of workers, peasants, agricultural labour, students, teachers, government servants, women, backward classes and Dalits led popular struggles demanding development based on equity and justice, an indication of a marked progressive social outlook and a conscious assertion of one's legitimate rights and collective strength. It revealed the close interconnection between the state, politics and development, impacting on every attempt at economic and governance reforms in Kerala in recent times. However, the focus of 'so-called popular struggles' is fast shifting from 'public interest' to 'sectional interest', thereby undermining the quality of governance and loss of faith in the state as a pro-people institution.

Following the state reorganisation and formation of Kerala, the first general election brought the communist government led by E.M.S. Namboodiripad to power. His ministry began to lay the foundations of 'good governance'. Some policies of this government sparked off violent protests from the Anti-Communist Front (ACF) led by opposition parties, landlords, private school and college managements, communal organisations, church leaders, employers, estate owners and upper class elites who feared some kind of Stalinist dictatorial rule coming from the communists. Kerala polity soon reached a boiling point, forcing the Central government to dismiss the EMS ministry on 31 July 1959. Soon the Left movement in the state got divided between CPI and CPI (Marxists) in 1964. The period thereafter witnessed unholy, unprincipled and unimaginable alliances among political parties and new splinter groups, tarnishing even the debate on 'good governance and development'. In the 1990s, when attempts were made to introduce initiatives of economic and governance reforms, some of them under external pressure, the political scenario became turbulent. Many started suspecting the dangerous anti-people implications of some of these initiatives, leading to open confrontation between the LDF and UDF groups.

Though the governments in the state tried to remove the basic hurdles in the way of improving investment, efficiency, production and productivity, some critics believe that conflictive politics in the state has neutralised them. This is reflected in the performance of the economy. The state is now facing an acute crisis in the spheres of employment and material production with very little growth of per capita Net State Domestic Product (NSDP) in Kerala since 1970. Production sectors have been witnessing stagnation. While the share of the primary sector and secondary sector has been declining, that of the tertiary/service sector has been expanding substantially. Kerala is, thus, undergoing a big transformation from a 'production economy' in to a 'service/consumer economy'. This has created an illusion of 'Kerala shining', thanks largely due to the massive inflow of foreign remittances of roughly about Rs 3000 billion from the emigrant Keralites during the last four decades. This helped to save the state from utter ruins. However, these remittances have not made any remarkable impact on the productive sectors of the economy (Nair and Pillai 1994; Pushpangadan 2003; Zachariah et al. 1999; Zachariah et al. 2002). Policy makers were wondering how they could utilise the remittance money to revitalise the sinews of growth.

The state is now confronting the serious problem of 'returnees' (return migrants) and their re-absorption in the domestic labour market, which is already burdened with an unemployment rate of 21 per cent and the serious fallouts of a fast changing demographic profile. Kerala's total fertility rate has reached 'below replacement rate', two decades ahead of the all India target of 2001, due to the role played by the State in areas of education and health, universal immunisation, family planning and to some extent radical land reforms (Irudayarajan and Zachariah 1997). The high share of the 60+ and 75+ age groups (due to high life expectancy), rapid decline of school age population (due to falling birth rate) and the consequent changes in the pattern of demand are causing much anxiety to policy makers. The demand for geriatric care and palliative clinics is rising. The 'Kerala Model', which was once described as a 'cheap miracle model' of development is now being questioned seriously.

From early times, farmers in Kerala responded to market signals in deciding their land use pattern. But the exposure to global markets in recent times only contributed to the vulnerability of agriculture, particularly cash crops in the state. From mid-1970s, rice/paddy farmers were caught in the dilemma of diverse perspectives for and against it (Narayanan 2003). It was argued that fragmented politics hampering productive activities needed to be transformed into truly democratic and responsible politics providing a mediating role in the state. Realising the ineffectiveness of the state in helping them, the farmers have started mobilisation to build collective strength.

Industrial backwardness in Kerala is reported to be the result of a long historical process involving commercialisation of agriculture, the colonial capital focusing on export-oriented plantations and agro-processing industries, the indigenous capitalist class focusing on land market, banking and finance sectors, and a nascent bourgeoisie promoting an enclave pattern of development (CDS 1996). Kerala's peculiar topography, resource endowments, poor infrastructure, high density of population, shortage of land and high land prices, and people's high awareness of environmental issues have stood in the way of conventional industrialisation. The export-oriented traditional industries are declining on account of both domestic and global factors.

Structural changes and inter-industry linkages are lacking. The mortality and morbidity rates in small industries are high. Productive capital per capita in the factory sector has been consistently lower in Kerala than in other states. Although it has a large educated and skilled labour force, industry is not well developed. Entrepreneurship is not lacking in making investments in fancy 'bubble sectors' of the economy that offer quick returns and it follows the market signals generated by a distorted distribution of purchasing power in the community. Public investment in industry is shrinking and most of the state level public enterprises (SLPEs) are in bad shape (GOK 2002a, 2003b). Unfair labour practices and incorrect perceptions of investors have made Kerala a poor investment destination. The Global Investors Meet (GIM) held in December 2002 attempted to change it but now stands virtually aborted due to massive popular protests alleging that the proposed projects would not help in sustaining human development already achieved by the state.

Kerala has demonstrated that public action could be constructively used to fight poverty and deprivation through timely interventions in providing food security, universal health care and education, productive employment and adjustment entitlements. Universal statutory rationing was introduced in Kerala in October 1965. Today the state's food security system covers a wide spectrum of beneficiaries from pre-school children to old and disabled poor (Kannan 2000). The state also does market intervention to check undue increase in open market prices. But this is being threatened by the World Bank prescription of a reduced role to the Food Corporation of India (World Bank 1991b). Kerala has made a number of initiatives in the social sector and the extent of coverage looks baffling (Kannan 2002). Currently, Kerala spends 3 per cent of its budget on social security and protection to 3.5 million beneficiaries. The resulting social safety net takes care of all those who are unable to work and earn a decent livelihood and those who are pushed to the periphery of development. Some argue that finding money for sustaining it is not possible given the depressing economic and fiscal scenario facing the state.

Kerala is threatened by fundamental fiscal disabilities caused by its own pattern of development, the impact of the neoliberal policies of the Central government and adverse treatment given to the state by the Finance Commissions in the past. Till the late 1980s, Kerala's fiscal scenario was fairly bright with some control over fiscal and revenue deficits. But after mid-1990s, the situation changed with a substantial jump in revenue expenditure, poor revenue mobilisation, reckless spending by government, rising share of salary, and pension and interest payments, leaving very little for development. The resulting revenue gap forced Kerala to resort to further market borrowing and liabilities (George 1999; Gulati and Narayana 1994; Nair 1997; RBI 1997). The Finance Commissions did not take into account Kerala's unique achievements in human development and expenditure needs for sustaining them in future. The recent report by the 12th Finance Commission contains a plan to restructure public finances, restoring budgetary balance and achieving macroeconomic stability and debt reduction along with equitable growth. It is feared that in this process, the Centre may put pressure on states to implement neoliberal reform policies.

The present situation of a low to no-growth economy in Kerala is neither desirable nor politically sound. Fortunately, both the LDF and the UDF seem to be convinced that Kerala's development has reached a crisis point and if hard decisions are not made, the state's economy would fall into total underdevelopment. However, the analysis of the situation and the remedies proposed by the LDF and the UDF are at variance due to differing ideological perceptions. According to the LDF, the most important task before the state should be revitalising the productive sectors of the economy through decentralised governance, while continuing strong public action as in the past. But the UDF believes that the state cannot continue with public action as in the past due to fiscal constraints and under the circumstances, Kerala must inevitably depend on private capital and enterprise for reviving the economy and help unleash its productive powers. This obviously falls in line with the policy of economic reforms being pursued by the Central government. Given the above scenario, urgent initiatives in economic and governance reforms became imperative.

A close look at the history of such reforms at the state level suggests two broad streams of initiatives. The first was the set of initiatives in reforms with 'local roots and flavour' that got reflected in administrative reforms and decentralised governance taken by the state on its own and supplemented by civil society institutions (CSIs) that promoted people's participation at the grassroot level. The second was those initiatives driven by pressure from the Central government and external agencies like the ADB and inspired by the neoliberal agenda. Chronologically, these two streams often overlapped each other. In this section we discuss the first set of initiatives.

State Initiated Reforms

Administrative Reform Initiatives

It was the first communist government led by E.M.S. Namboodiripad that first laid the foundation for creating 'good governance' based on a state level reform agenda. The reforms in the field of 'agrarian relations' (ban evictions, impose ceiling on land holdings, redistribution of surplus land to the landless), 'education sector' (restructuring universities, guarantee of job security to teachers in private institutions, preparation and printing of textbooks by government, bringing primary schools under government control), and 'industrial relations' (promote bipartism and tripartism, guarantee fair wages and minimum wages, promote collective bargaining, ensure minimum bonus based on the principle of deferred wages) were the corner stone of this government's policy. Besides, the ministry had plans to strengthen the public distribution system by statutory rationing to ensure food security to the entire population in the state. Another step was to promote workers' cooperatives in traditional industries and employments.

Kerala has had three Administrative Reforms Committees (ARCs) since 1956 (GOK 1957 1965 1997a). E.M.S. Namboodiripad, the then chief minister, headed the first ARC. At the political level there was strong conviction to make the administration people oriented.

The ARC (1957) wanted the panchayats to function as agents of government, particularly the bold idea of running schools and hospitals in their area. The Secretariat work was to be confined to framing of policies, rules and procedures, financial control and general direction resulting in some downsizing after decentralisation. The ARC wanted the abolition of Directorates of Panchayats and Municipalities. But they continue even now. Funds to the panchayats were to be allocated based on a formula linked to their level of development needs as well as capacity to raise their own revenue. The efficiency of the departments was to be judged not by their expenditure but by their output in relation to inputs. Both the ARCs (1957 and 1965) had a unity in their vision on reforms.

The ARC (1997) was constituted in the background of the organic linking of decentralisation to people's plan campaign (PPC) taking place in the state at that time. The government was facing severe fiscal stress. Quality of service delivery had reached a bottom with a decline in the work discipline and service ethos of public servants, calling for immediate basic reforms. According to the ARC (1997), the degeneration of governance in the state also got reflected in the culture of rights and demands and rude behaviour by service providers, departmentalism exacerbated by coalition politics and emergence of vertical hierarchies impervious to suggestion for coordination and convergence. The civil service was also constrained by extra constitutional checks and control on its authority and freedom by elected people's representatives and personal staff of ministers. The general idea got circulated that nothing will and can change in Kerala whether it is good for the people or not. By late-1990s decentralisation had created new domains of governance, radically altering existing ones. The ARC felt that as a lot of development functions and a sizable staff were being sent to lower levels to perform new roles in a different domain, there would be a natural downsizing of state bureaucracy. However, this never happened.

The ARC (1997) had a grand vision of 'people-centred governance' based on vibrant local self-government institutions (LSGIs). It submitted 15 reports covering wide ranging subjects, which included citizen's charter, transparency and right to information, financial reforms, personnel reforms, interface between government and public sector, service delivery and general governance reforms. The reports came out of the state's own past experience in governance and the depth and coverage of issues were much more than those contained in the ADB sponsored modernising government programme (MGP). The ARC believed that to cure the ills of democracy, more democracy is the only way. The reason for the breakdown of good governance is the breakdown of democracy. In other words, in the fragmented polity and conflictive politics prevailing in Kerala now, for governance reforms to succeed, one should first reform the way politics and democracy are practised. To concretise this, the ARC suggested initiatives in setting up citizen's juries, public hearings, deliberative opinion polls, public scrutiny of quality of services and issue forums to enhance the quality of public judgement. These were expected to strengthen the democratic system of consultation and participation. Unfortunately, both the LDF and the UDF that were in power seem to have totally neglected these recommendations.

Decentralised Governance

In the planning process since independence, priorities were decided by the centre and the states were asked to comply. People at the grassroot level did not figure in this exercise. They merely looked up to the government to do things for them. It was a kind of patron-client relation. The situation changed with the advent of the 73rd and 74th amendments to the Constitution. In this section, we discuss decentralised governance and in the following section, the role played by civil society initiatives and people's plan campaign.

Though a true Marxist, EMS had always been a champion of decentralised governance. His government initiated the Kerala Panchayat Bill, 1958, and the Kerala District Council Bill, 1959, but could not pass them before it was dismissed in 1959. The governments that came since then went in for decentralisation, but they deviated from the earlier spirit and direction as local bodies were virtually made subordinate agencies under the control of the LSG department of the state government. When EMS became chief minister again in 1967, he tried to resurrect the original Bills but his ministry also fell. When another government led by Left parties came to power in 1987, it passed the District Administration Act and established District Councils with wide powers and responsibilities. It was again the credit of another LDF government in infusing new life and energy into LSGIs with the devolution of 40 per cent of plan funds to enable them to perform better in the field of decentralised governance. However, as a result of conflictive politics, the successive governments seem to have defeated these initiatives.

Today, there are Gram Panchayats (991), Block Panchayats (152), District Panchayats (14), Urban Municipalities (53) and Corporations (5) in Kerala and elections have been regularly conducted to form LSGIs. These elections were fought with as much fanfare as those to the state legislature. The issues focused in the elections were not only local, but national and global including globalisation and neoliberal policies. Conflictive politics soon spread even to the domain of local ward and gram panchayat.

The Sen Committee on Decentralisation of Powers (1997) followed a rigorous methodology in identifying the critical issues concerning decentralisation. It took every effort to strike a balance between the ideals of decentralisation and the requirements of day-to-day governance (GOK 1997b). It wanted to see the citizen at the centre stage and said that it is his voice that has to be listened to and it is his choice that has to be accepted and it is his interest that has to be preserved. It assigned definite functions to people's institutions like gram sabhas and ward committees. Beneficiary committees and social audit groups were to be created as special purpose vehicles for people's participation. Right to information and citizens charter were to be a prominent feature of laws governing LSGIs. Provision in the law has to be made for empowering 'excluded groups'. The Committee redefined the powers and functions, with responsibilities to LSGIs to make them free from interference and executive control from above. Decisions of LSGIs were not to be overruled. Appellate functions with respect to statutory matters were to be removed from the purview of state government and entrusted with a quasi-judicial authority. LSGIs also were to be given total control over their staff and their utilisation. The Committee hoped that with the implementation of its recommendations, Kerala would become a model for decentralised administrative system not only for India but also for the developing world.

The Sen Committee wanted to effect an early shift from welfare to development orientation in governance and this could be made possible only by achieving role clarity and assigning mandatory functions to various tiers of government. This was to be supplemented by a new work culture built on promoting harmony among policy makers, officials and people's representatives. But the most crucial step would be the creation of 'new politics' marked by cooperation in matters of local level development. Kerala was one of the first states to appoint a State Finance Commission (SFC). The second SFC submitted its report in January 2001. Its two major recommendations were streamlining of government grants and creation of a maintenance fund for asset renewal. Now Kerala has also appointed the third SFC.

Decentralised governance in Kerala completed the 'Campaign Phase' and has now entered the 'Institutionalisation Phase'. An assessment report by the IRMA directed its focus on needs, concerns and opportunities thrown up by the decentralisation process (GOK 2002b). The Report said that the methodology for participatory planning was in place, but could be improved by focusing on local data base, rational criteria for prioritisation of needs, long range planning, avoidance of sub-optimal investments, promotion of local development, improvement of quality of services and inclusion of marginalised groups.

There is a general feeling that the government was trying to impose decentralisation from above stifling grassroot initiatives. More than the people, it was the political parties that pressed for decentralisation as it would give them more space for their activities. There is continued reluctance at the top to transfer powers, responsibilities and funds to LSGIs. They question the ability of LSGIs to handle their powers and functions properly. Mere decentralisation has not helped to transform the decadent culture of administrative bureaucracy. Organisational and parliamentary wings of political parties did not want to confront the state bureaucrats and their powerful associations. Conspiracy and open non-cooperation of working class organisations, and service providers also, did their maximum to discourage local level initiatives.

Basic changes in the Kerala Service Rules (KSR), Kerala Financial Code, Treasury Code, and Office and Budget Manuals are yet to take place in Kerala. Similarly, very little change has been brought in to the administrative and organisational structure of Line Departments which have to interface regularly with LSGIs. However, a World Bank Study on Fiscal Decentralisation to Rural Governments gives credit to the Kerala experience (GOK 2003a). According to it, Kerala has devolved more discretion to LSGIs. It has been adopting a 'big bang' approach towards them by transferring functions and resources at one go. There is a built-in mechanism for bottom-up planning and use of funds. Gram panchayats have control over 68 per cent of the expenditure. Therefore, expenditure assignments are much clearer. Functions have been broken up into activities to avoid overlapping. Though administrative autonomy is not complete, there is some amount of freedom in the exercise of limited control over employees. Level of gram panchayat spending is significantly higher in Kerala—1.4 per cent of SDP and 8 per cent of state expenditure. Local revenue mobilisation has increased even with larger transfers. Kerala is the only state in the country where full recognition has been given to the principle that the primary accountability of LSGIs is downward to the local community. The Kerala experience would suggest that a more refined democracy and constructive politics could further improve the quality of decentralised governance in the state.

During the Ninth Plan, the state government transferred Rs 41.30 billion to LSGIs. Sector-wise allocation shows that only 27.29 per cent of the expenditure went to production sectors with agriculture getting just 15.39 per cent. The focus of Kerala's Tenth Plan was on expanding participatory planning, micro enterprises, innovative social service projects, preparation of water-shed development plans, sustainable vegetable cultivation, water supply projects, community-based environment hygiene and localised energy production through micro hydel projects. The Swiss government supported a few initiatives like e-governance in local governments on a mission mode, the formulation of a new accounting, budget and audit system and public works manuals, action research to strengthen gram sabhas, citizens charter and asset register and management for promoting decentralised governance and participatory development under a project called 'Capacity Development for Decentralisation in Kerala' (CAPDEK).

Civil Society Initiatives—KSSP and PPC

The world has witnessed a proliferation of voluntary organisations particularly after the neo-liberal agenda emerged and started the drive for spreading globalisation. Some treat this entire lot as agents of global capitalism and imperialism including the CIA of the USA and most of the critics belong to Left parties and Marxist scholars. In the process they even attack those social/peoples' movements, which launch effective defence and attack on neoliberal agenda and globalisation. Generally peoples' movements have no political ideology and their politics is aimed at pro-poor social change. They generally raise the slogan 'There Are Many Alternatives' (TAMA) in the place of the TINA of neoliberals. The Narmada Bachao Andolan (NBA), All India Peoples Science Network and Kerala Sasthra Sahithya Parishad (KSSP) are some such movements.

The KSSP is a civil society institution actively involved in promoting decentralisation and development in its own distinct way. It is not a political party. 'Power' is outside its agenda. But it is interested in impacting on the power structure. Its vision is reflected in its objectives:

- Democracy of the people, by the people and for the people demand citizens to take more responsibilities than to vote in elections and to engage in protests and supplication.
- Enlarge the realms and levels of people's participation by strengthening their understanding of participatory democracy to ensure higher levels of equity.
- Create and strengthen citizens' organisations/civil society institutions (CSIs) for resistance to globalisation, wastage and inequity.
- Develop actually functioning self-reliant local economies to achieve sustainable and equitable development.

Formed in 1959 by a group of 40 idealistic scientists and writers for spreading scientific awareness in society, the KSSP's work indicates three broad phases: 'democratisation', 'adversarial activism', and 'collaborative mainstreaming'. The KSSP programmes covered a wide range of subjects such as literacy, education, healthcare, environment and energy, taking science to people (KSSP 2003). Three instances of KSSP's contribution need to be mentioned here.

- In the domain of education, it opposed unrestricted privatisation, establishment of self-financing institutions and closure of 'uneconomic' schools, while launching positive initiatives in improving quality of school curriculum, textbooks and teaching methods, improving school infrastructure and quality of education for children through people's and parents' participation. It is at the KSSP's initiative that voluntary contributions from people were collected to meet the expenses of the Ashok Mitra Commission on Education (1999).
- In the domain of health care, KSSP's work was laudable in promoting a popular health movement, health charter, people's alternative, health surveys, health parliament and also campaigns for changes in patent law. New movements like Health Action for People are collaborating with the KSSP.
- In the domain of environment protection, following the Stockholm Conference, the KSSP initiated at the grassroot level as well as the level of the state, campaigns against industrial and water pollution, the bad impact of human interventions in Kuttanad (the rice bowl of Kerala), forests, rivers and bio-reserves, unregulated river sand and coastal mineral sand mining, silting in dams, soil erosion in high ranges and forest fire. The campaign against Silent Valley hydel power project was outstanding as it forced the Central government to declare the area a protected National Park in 1984. Though it expressed serious concern on the ecological fragility of the state and advocated thermal power as an alternative to hydel power, a perspective plan for power development based on environment friendly mini hydel projects, solar lamps and cooker, smokeless chulas and energy saving CFL lamps, the KSSP was attacked for its 'anti-development' stand.

But the KSSP's association with agencies like the Integrated Rural Technology Centre (IRTC) at Mundur, Palakkad and with the state's Centre for Earth Science Studies (CESS), State Land Use Board (SLUB), and Planning Board along with the Centre for Development Studies helped it to provide valuable inputs and collaboration to the exercise of Panchayat Resource Mapping (PRM) and the process of operationalising decentralised governance by evolving and putting into action elemental models of people's participation and the Panchayat Level Development Planning (PLDP) experiment (Menon et al. 2002). In 1988, the KSSP initiated the GALASA programme (Group Approach to Locally Adapted and Sustainable Agriculture) with active participation of farm workers in Thrissur district. In the Kerala Development Congress (1988) organised by State Planning Board, KSSP activists and those who had faith in decentralised governance discussed the experience of People's Plan Campaign (PPC) in the context of the changing global scenario, national development, development perspectives of the state and political economy in general. 'Good governance', 'self governance', 'participatory development', 'politics of development', and 'cultural change and development' were some of the subjects discussed in the seminar.

The KSSP went back to grass root gram panchayats to evolve refined models of 'people's intervention', but these enabling experiments did not get support with a change of government from LDF to UDF (Isaac and Franke 2000; Krishnan 1998). However, the KSSP with its commitment to participatory decentralised governance decided to go alone with an action programme at Kalliasseri panchayat in Malabar. The Kalliasseri model demonstrated the potential for active people's participation, cutting across the fabric of Kerala's 'fragmented polity' and 'conflictive politics'. The experiment with structures like 'neighbourhood groups' (NHGs) or 'ayalkkoottams' (in Malayalam) was novel. The focus was on the use of local level resources and expertise for integrated implementation packages for productivity enhancement, employment generation and improvement in quality of social infrastructure in education and health sectors. The KSSP, thus, demonstrated a design for an 'alternative development paradigm' with a local flavour and people's participation through a democratic process. The vision of the KSSP was to help develop functioning, self-reliant local economies and enable them to resist the bad effects of globalisation. The PLDP project, mentioned earlier, was a process of transformation attempted in five panchayats through decentralised planning and development and was coterminous to PPC. But they soon alienated the left political parties, particularly the CPI (M), though some of its top leaders like E.M.S. Namboodiripad were the initial inspiration behind the experiment. One allegation was that the PLDP project received foreign funds and was led by activists of CSIs and NGOs and this may, in the long run, help to establish the primacy of neoliberal agenda on the people of the state.

Meanwhile, the book '*Naalam Lokam*' (in Malayalam meaning *Fourth World*), by M.P. Parameswaran, nuclear scientist, a member of CPI (M) and a front line activist of the KSSP initiated a public debate on an alternative path to socialism and development (Parameswaran 2004). He examined the relevance of orthodox Marxist-Leninist position in the Indian context and drew inspiration from Gandhian writings. He argued that the transition from capitalism to socialism need not always be through 'class struggle', but can be through people's participation in decentralised democracy and governance. Allegations followed against Thomas Isaac, now a CPI (M) MLA, B. Iqbal, a reputed neurosurgeon and former University Vice Chancellor and a few others who were associated with KSSP and PPC. The PPC also alienated the state bureaucracy and employees' organisations. Service providing departments like Electricity Board, Water Authority, PWD, leviathan structures, also created hurdles to scuttle the PPC.

The PLDP team always tried to work in close collaboration with the panchayats and functioned as a 'collaborator of the state'. The NHGs were the backbone of the PLDP but soon local hardcore politicians hijacked them and kept people away from participating in their meetings. Under these circumstances, sincere local activists and civil society groups formed Panchayat Development Societies (PDSs) and they went out to form NHGs independently following the 'top to bottom' process once again instead of building up from below. An evaluation done by the original designers of the programme reported that citizens preferred just to vote and elect a government and the spirit of participatory democracy has not reached them. The report lamented: 'whatever roots that began to sprout burnt out. But the potential for re-rooting exists' (Menon et al. 2002).

The Kudumbashree programme and the Mararikkulam experiment are two other initiatives whose success is closely watched by people concerned with participatory development. The former started in 1991 as a partnership among four major actors: the centre, state, LSGIs and the National Bank for Agriculture and Rural Development (NABARD). The objective of the programme is to eliminate poverty and is exclusively focused on women from below poverty line (BPL) families. The core activity is women empowerment through micro finance, micro enterprise and convergent community action through community development societies (CDS), a federation of NHGs and the area development societies (ADS). Some studies have reported and commended the rich stock of 'social capital' in Kerala contributing to the level and quality of development (John and Chathukulam 2002; Chathukulam 2002). However, though it has plenty of 'social capital', what it lacks is constructive 'bonds and bridges' to enable people to jointly create a meaningful and sustainable livelihood for all.

The Mararikulam experiment has been examined from an international perspective (Franke 2002). According to Franke, a close observer of Kerala's PPC, the Mararikulam experiment consists of an integrated set of projects to make substantial reductions in poverty in eight villages and two towns of the Aryad and Kanjikkuzhy development blocks in the central coastal region of Kerala. It was a Kerala variant of the Grameen Bank model aimed at job creation through micro credit. The project set up several micro enterprises to produce goods using locally available raw materials for sale in local markets with a view to insulate the local economy from the onslaught of outside forces including globalisation. The experiment was a logical continuation and extension of PPC. We quote Franke (2002):

> While decentralisation has been a key procedure in the PPC, it is strengthening democracy that makes the campaign so significant internationally.... Democracy functioning at the local levels combined with high degrees of participation, mutual trust among individual, compromise, and work together—these elements of PPC effectively extend into the Mararikulam experiment. They are the key to its success or failure.

Reforms under Pressure

Reforms along the National Agenda

It was indeed difficult for any state government to totally disassociate from the economic reforms being implemented by the Centre. Chelliah (2003) has ably listed the reforms to which the states need to give top priority in the coming days. They include reduction of subsidies to power consumers along with restructuring state electricity boards; improvement in the quality of roads; removal of hindrances to the free movement of goods; closing down or sale of loss making public enterprises; reform of tax structure; partial introduction of Value Added Tax (VAT); improvement of tax administration; adopting a planned approach to expenditure growth and achieving zero deficit in revenue account; higher outlays on primary and secondary education; health and family planning along with significant improvement in the standards of services. We shall show below how state level reforms in Kerala till now have progressed and the organic link between economic and governance reforms in it.

A major step in state level reforms was the enactment of the Kerala Fiscal Responsibility Act and the Kerala Ceiling on Government Guarantee Act, both intended to restrain the government from misdirected expenditure and financial profligacy. The practice of seeking a vote-on-account, instead of passing the full budget, which is an exception, has now become a rule. This incorrect practice could be rectified if the budget preparation process is begun sufficiently early so as to pass the budget by 31 March. A beginning has been made to bring out urgently needed corrections in fiscal practices in the state. The state is gradually restoring the budget cycle back to its original time schedule. Recently, following directions from the Centre, Kerala has substituted a large amount of high cost public debt by low cost ones. Kerala has accepted the design of state level VAT as prepared by the Empowered Committee for replacing the sales tax under strong protests from the trading community.

In spite of all these, the spirit of fiscal populism continues to haunt the state government as reflected in the decision to extend the deadline for reaching zero revenue deficit by two years. Fiscal reform in Kerala has virtually taken a back seat halting the reform process. Issues like power sector restructuring, reform of state level public enterprises (SLPEs), public debt restructuring, accentuation of fiscal stress, credible expenditure rationalisation, steady deceleration in capital expenditures and asset maintenance, making forward estimates of fiscal parameters, revenue collection reforms and reform in tax administration are yet to be addressed seriously, though they were in the reform agenda for some years. The revitalisation of productive sectors through universal people's participation in local level development in the context of decentralisation and political and economic empowerment of people at the grass root level with lesser dependence on the state bureaucracy constitute another complementary step that needs to be considered with high priority in the emerging scenario.

Power sector restructuring is an important component in the reform agenda of the Central government. Under pressure from the Centre, Kerala formulated a Power Policy in 1996 and later signed an MOU with the Central government in August 2001 to implement power sector reforms. The state electricity board has been a 'great killer of enterprises', not because of higher power tariff, but because of its poor quality of service and employee arrogance. It had been facing financial distress for some time, but with the help of the state, major crises were averted. Since the government was also in greater distress, power sector reform became inevitable. Now the Kerala State Electricity Board (KSEB) has been functionally disaggregated and made accountable with respect to each of their principal functions of generation, transmission and distribution. The Board has been restructured into profit centres with well-defined roles and responsibilities. Meters have been installed at the interfaces of the profit centres and profit centre-wise energy accounting has been put into force. Grid code to ensure smooth operation of the system is also in place. The restructuring of the distribution sector became all the more important as this sector deals directly with the customers. In the ongoing power sector reform process, power tariff revision by a tariff regulatory authority, human resources development, customer service, safety and environmental aspects are also given focus. The Board and the state government are regularly confronting protests from customers, power workers' unions and political parties against alleged 'anti-people' power sector reforms.

Kerala stands apart in its sensitivity to changes in the national and international trade environment. Following the onset of trade liberalisation in farm products under WTO, Kerala's agricultural products have experienced a price crash of unprecedented proportion. The state appointed a commission on WTO concerns in agriculture in July 2001 under the chairmanship of M. S. Swaminathan (GOK January 2003c). According to its report, at the Government of India level there is a need to review the tariff code and EXIM policies, particularly with reference to oil seeds and edible oils, besides sponsoring a Special Food for Wage and Employment Stabilisation programme for plantation crops sector. At the state level, some urgent steps should be taken to build a Sustainable Trade Security System for its farm products. These steps would include, among other things, a productivity, quality and value addition movement in all agricultural crops, appropriate 'Aquarian reforms' to safeguard the livelihoods of fisher communities, prevention of abuse of the provision for concessional imports for re-exports, promotion of organic farming, establishment of a herbal bio-valley and herbal sanctuaries, and promotion of legal literacy among tribal and rural families in the conservation and enhancement of biodiversity. Following this, the state has set up a WTO cell, but further actions on the lines of the Swaminathan report are yet to be initiated with any seriousness. Here again, the action on the much needed state level reforms in agriculture is yet to take off.

The New Industrial Policy, Report of the Enterprise Reform Committee (to speed up closure and privatisation of SLPEs), sale of state-owned assets and heritage buildings, decision on mineral sand mining, and commercialisation of education, healthcare and infrastructure sectors are some of the new initiatives in the state level reforms. The UDF government argues that it does not have the fiscal strength to undertake public investment and so must go in for private and foreign capital. The post-GIM perspective is that it would be better to assign the task of social and economic development to private capital. But the protestors believe that private capital would always be driven by private profit and exploitation and demand freedom from any kind of social control.

Kerala has the largest number of SLPEs, 111 out of 1071 in the country. They have a capital investment of Rs 164.29 billion and out of this, Public Utilities account for Rs 110.73 billion. The SLPEs have raised Rs 25.16 billion as loan from the government, besides Rs 90 billion with government guarantee. The annual implicit subsidy to them exceeds Rs 5 billion. There is no reliable data on annual as well as total accumulated loss of these SLPEs. But they are plagued by poor standards of corporate governance. The diffused nature of ownership, lack of synchronisation of critical state sponsored interventions for improving their performance, conflicting objectives advocated by trade unions, inadequate incentives for competent personnel, delayed decision-making, redundancy of manpower and blind faith in the goodness of public sector have stood in the way of restructuring and reforming them. There is some truth in the saying that there is hardly any difference between SLPEs and the government, when it comes to their functioning. Both suffer from poor systems for ensuring accountability. They are often not able to balance the social as well as commercial objectives. However, in recent years some steps were taken to close unviable units and initiate most essential restructuring to attract private participation in potentially viable units. But it did not gather momentum due to political and trade union protests and the absence of specialised institutional mechanisms. The absence of a comprehensive reform strategy, shortage of resources and lack of political will have made the problem more difficult.

The government set up the Enterprise Reforms Committee (ERC) in 2001 with the Public Sector Restructuring and Internal Audit Board (RIAB) as its secretariat for initiating a comprehensive SLPEs reform programme. In March 2002, the government approved the approach paper on SLPE reforms produced by the Committee (2002b). It has recommended the government's active participation only in areas with strategic importance and high social relevance. The reform strategy stressed its implementation with a 'human face'. The ERC also recommended a Social Safety Net Programme that consists of a financial compensation package and a welfare and economic sustainability package for retired employees. A study on SLPEs supported by the Dutch Government has estimated a budget of Rs 13 billion for implementing the SLPE reform programme and the state is waiting for the funds. Though the ERC submitted its recommendations on 27 SLPEs and the government took decisions on 12 of them, very little action has been taken on the restructuring of these units. Conflictive politics is a major reason behind this since they are 'hard and risky decisions' for the ruling political front.

The main focus of economic reforms in Kerala during recent years has been on the promotion of investments. Many innovative pro-investor, pro-enterprise policy measures have been initiated to cover industry, biotechnology, information technology and labour sectors, besides promotion of special economic zones. The government claims that these policy measures have set the background for the transformation of the state as an emerging industrial destination. The industrial policy aims to accelerate the industrial growth in the state by attracting a steady stream of investment into core sectors like infrastructure by creating a congenial climate by eliminating all restrictive labour practices, ensuring cordial industrial relations and establishment of a new work culture, with productivity orientation and productivity-linked wages. Industrial zones, parks and estates are to be created. The other initiatives are nurturing entrepreneurial talent; re-engineering government's delivery mechanism to make them responsive, result oriented and transparent; energy conservation; environmental protection; ensuring cost effectiveness and accountability by restructuring public enterprises; and providing a social safety net to those adversely affected by industrial restructuring. The government is also planning to provide investment subsidies, a special package of incentives, exemption from electricity duty and enhanced power tariff, and single window clearance. An Investment Promotion Board (IPB) has been set up as a fast track mechanism for clearing of projects. It performs the functions of an empowered committee of the government. As early as 2000, the Central government has introduced the concept of special economic zones (SEZs). Kerala has adopted this and is planning to set up a number of them in the state.

The state held dialogues with trade unions, but a consensus on 'investor-friendly labour market reforms' has not yet been reached. Trade unions feel that mere amendments to labour laws curbing democratically legitimate trade union activity cannot be a solution. There has been no open debate on the Report of the Enterprise Reform Committee and its recommendations on the outright sale and closure of SLPEs in the name of restructuring public sector. The trade unions have fears on the possible outcomes of labour market reforms with their focus on creating 'labour market flexibility'. A few instances are cited. The Kerala Loading and Unloading (Regulation of Wages and Restriction of Unlawful Practices) Act, 2002, aims at eliminating residual negative perceptions about labour in Kerala by making certain 'retrograde practices' in the loading and unloading sector, cognisable offences. 'Claiming wages above notified ceiling' is also made a punishable offence. Routine inspections by labour law inspectors have been eliminated in key sectors like IT. Establishments can give 'self certification' declarations to labour departments. Sunrise industries like IT have been exempted from restrictions on daily and weekly hours of work, spread-over, opening and closing hours, closing of shops and granting of weekly holidays, employment of women and persons below 17 years during night to facilitate uninterrupted working. New initiatives are steps to discourage stoppage of work and other impediments to productivity. The declaration of services as public utilities has been extended to cover export oriented units, transport other than railways, IT, agricultural products processing, fertiliser and a few others. In these sectors wildcat strikes are made illegal and punishable.

Will these reforms do good for labour, raise the level of real wages, continue to secure social protection and stabilise the traditional industries, but weaken the workers' capacity to fight/resist unjust treatment by the aggressive onslaught of private capital? However, in spite of labour protest, the UDF government has also initiated further steps like promise of prime land, infrastructure, concessional tax rates, speedy clearance of permits and licences and 'all that is required by the investor' to make investment in the state. The LDF has already announced its opposition to these measures assuring the working class that when it comes back to power these measures would be nullified.

A separate IT policy has also been announced comprising a three pronged strategy aimed at: creating an appropriate pro-business, legal, regulatory and commercial framework to facilitate rapid growth of IT industry in the state; establishing Kerala as a global centre for excellence in human resources through the creation of a large pool of diverse, multi-skilled technically competent manpower; establishing an internationally competitive business infrastructure and environment for the IT industry in the state. It has been decided to promote Kerala as a destination for IT business opportunities including IT enabled services.

The above issues currently threaten political stability. A few concrete instances of the dangers, how they lead to wastage of creative energies of people, how they keep Kerala society and politics always in great turbulence, leaving very little time to devote to development are briefly indicated here. Recently, the Kerala government announced its intention to implement a massive project called, 'High Speed Access Controlled Express Highway' as a Joint Venture on Build Operate Transfer (BOT) mode, costing Rs 120 billion by 2012 benefiting just less than 1 per cent of state's population. The Expression of Interest on this project had been presented in the GIM meeting held in 2003 but initially there were no takers for it. The Government is expected to contribute Rs 6.90 billion as its share in equity capital. The details of the project were put on the website of Roads and Bridges Corporation, but it was the KSSP that brought them to the attention of the public in Kerala. The project was even alleged to be a 'part of neo-liberal agenda'. Soon the sensitive issue was publicly debated leading to anti-express highway movements and demonstrations pushing the government on the defensive. The efforts made by the PWD Minister and other supporters of the project did not seem to have impressed the public. The KSSP as usual, was criticised for its 'anti-development' posture. When the issue became very hot, the government withdrew the details of the project from the website and declared that the project will be initiated only after detailed survey and convincing the public about it. It is now reported that the government has entrusted the survey study to Wilbur Smith Associates, a global consultancy based in USA. How much money is going to be spent on this is not made clear.

Similar are the issues relating to unregulated drawing of ground water by the Coca Cola and Pepsi companies from Plachimada and Kanjikkode in Palakkad and several protest movements on the issue are in full swing. The Plachimada struggle attracted world wide attention when the reports of the BBC and the New Delhi-based Centre for Science and Environment confirmed that the Coca Cola sold by the company contained more than the admissible level of harmful chemicals. Soon, Medha Patkar and Vandana Shiva, environmental activists, and several global NGOs arrived in Plachimada to extend their solidarity and support to the agitation initiated by adivasis led by Mayilamma, an ordinary housewife and mother. After long legal battles the Court has now ruled that the company has the same right as the people to draw water and share natural resources. The present UDF government has expressed support to this view.

The Adivasi agitation for asserting the right over forest land in Muthanga (Bijoy and Raman 2003), promotion of self-financing educational institutions after sidelining state run institutions, extremely liberal liquor policy and issue of bar licences, unregulated river sand mining and coastal mineral sand mining and the new hydel project at Pathrakkadavu that lies within the protected and highly fragile bio-diversity region of Silent Valley are a few other vital issues that are being hotly debated in Kerala today. In all these, the governance system lacked transparency in policy formulation and implementation. No government in Kerala, whether led by the left or right, can fool the well-informed people of this state and impose its dictates on them. The people really need some mechanisms or institutions to deliberate upon issues and participate in public hearings to air their views and fears and get them mitigated by the government in a satisfactory manner as envisaged in the reform documents. It is surprising that in the protest movements mentioned above, even the mainstream Left political parties have kept a low profile. As usual, in Kerala politics, the ruling UDF accused the LDF that the latter initiated these projects and proposals and the UDF government is simply implementing them. This is also the stand taken on the controversial ADB sponsored MGP initiative, a set of reforms adopted in Kerala under external compulsions discussed later.

At the time of writing this, Kerala polity is witnessing turbulence caused by the understanding reached on the forthcoming agreement to be signed between the state government and the Dubai Internet City (DIC) to set up the Kochi Smart City project. The LDF led by the opposition leader as well as the people-sensitive media and social activists have come out openly against the project and the conditions agreed to by the government. When the transparency of the government was questioned, it came out with the details of the understanding reached by it (*Hindu*, 28 and 30 June 2005) It shows that DIC, the promoters, has submitted a wish list and the government virtually accepted to fulfil them. The wish list includes: (i) the Infopark built with the exchequer's money in the site shall be handed over to DIC against a payment of just Rs 1097 million and a 7 per cent stake in the Smart City without the government getting representation on the board of directors; (ii) no new IT parks shall be promoted in the central region of Kerala with government participation/support, making the DIC the sole dealer of IT infrastructure for the district; (iii) the DIC seeks for itself all incentives meant for its business partners under the IT policy of the state and also channel the same through it; (iv) exemption be granted from pollution control regulations, and from income tax on business profits; (v) exemption for Smart City, its tenants, employees and residents from all kinds of state taxes and local body taxes, (vi) Smart City to be made a separate local administration unit outside the purview of any local body, (vii) the residents there to be provided with an exclusive passenger check-in counter in the Smart City itself to have hassle-free boarding at the Cochin International airport and (viii) no future changes in law or any new law or regulations will be formulated, which will adversely affect the Smart City, its benefits or its operation. However, the government has given an apologetic reply that some demands are not legally feasible, but they will extend all assistance in fulfilling their wish. Now the UDF government has been put on the defensive on this issue, while it continues its attack on the protestors for their 'anti-development postures'.

ADB Driven Reforms—Case of MGP

In spite of having several reports on administrative and governance reforms from Kerala's own official expert committees, having a better understanding of the specifics of the Kerala situation, one would wonder why the state government went in for the ADB sponsored Modernising Government Programme (MGP) in 2002. The government went for this in keeping with the decision of the National Development Council. It declared 2003 as the year of development and 2004 as the year of implementation of reform initiatives in governance. But people's fears about the nature and implications of MGP have not been properly addressed by the government, leaving scope for popular struggles against it by various sections of Kerala's fragmented polity and society. The Tenth Plan document of the Government of India gives an exhaustive agenda for improving governance that looks like an Indian adaptation of the blue prints given by the World Bank, UNDP, ADB and other similar agencies. Just like the structural adjustment programme (SAP), this agenda of governance reform also has to be treated as a standard regimen prescribed for developing countries that face fiscal stress and slow economic growth irrespective of the historical, social, political and economic context.

The negotiations with the ADB started while Kerala was under LDF rule and in the midst of implementing its PPC. The spirit of PPC was in open conflict with that of ADB on several areas. Due to massive popular campaigns, the ADB has come to be widely known in Kerala as the Asian extension counter of the World Bank since it is alleged to follow the latter's style of functioning and applies the same concepts, tools and policies. ADB's faith in neoliberal, pro-capital, pro-market and anti-state philosophy is also well entrenched in the minds of people through media campaigns. Past history of ADB activities gives a clear evidence of its thrust on fiscal compression and consolidation, efficiency in resource use, privatisation, disinvestments, cost-recovery pricing of public services, improving governance, strengthening of LSGIs through citizens' groups and civil societies, and withdrawal of state from non-core functions. Since the government is yet to become transparent on the MGP, fears continue to circulate, hindering progress towards even urgently required reforms in governance.

The Kerala government entered into two agreements with the centre to address its fiscal crisis and undertake structural reforms. As per this, the ADB and the Dutch government will provide technical and financial assistance to Kerala amounting to $300 million ($200 million loan and $100 million as grant) at a rate of interest based on London Inter Bank Offer Rate (LIBOR) besides a 'Commitment Charge' of 0.75 per cent and a 'Front-End-Fee' of 1 per cent. In the course of negotiations and preparation of documents and agreements, the ADB tactically highlighted themes such as *help build on the social gains achieved in the past, create an enabling environment for pro-poor growth, efficient service delivery, poverty reduction, strengthening of state and local governments, build institutional and human resource capacity*, and *right to information* to allay people's fears about the promotion of anti-state discourse by it. But, it seems that people in the state are not fully convinced about the altruism of the ADB. They feel that it is using a semantic trick to make people first accept 'fiscal reform' and 'governance reform' and get them ready for 'structural reform'. The ADB on its part has stated that theirs is a comprehensive multi-layer reform agenda that includes reform of the power sector and state enterprises. In providing information, the ADB seems to be more transparent than the state government. Its assessment of Kerala's macroeconomic context is fairly realistic but their faith in the TINA approach ignores possibilities of people's alternative to ensure good governance.

The executing agency for the MGP consists of a Steering Committee and a Cabinet Sub-Committee. The former, using methodology and tools of modern management systems, have already prepared a number of Schematic Outlines and Initiatives and Detailed Implementation Plans (DIPs) covering a wide range of departments and activity areas. In the Order issued on 4 October 2002, the government said: the MGP has been drawn up as a part of the strategy of government to overhaul and improve its services to the people. The thrust in MGP is to facilitate public servants and elected officials to serve the citizens of Kerala more effectively, efficiently and equitably with greater accountability. The government claims that this transformation will facilitate the achievement of the human development and poverty reduction targets envisaged in the Tenth Plan.

The MGP strategy document conceptualises a development approach for Kerala around five important pillars, which are: *ensuring assured level of basic public services to the poor and marginalised, building an enabling environment for growth, fiscal sustainability (both state and local governments), enhancing effectiveness and efficiency of core government functions,* and *building on decentralisation for efficient, effective and accessible local self governments*. In each of these areas, the task teams have prepared a total of 26 sub-themes and 100 Strategic Implementation Initiatives (SIPs). They are essentially a set of selected key results in each of the five themes listed above. They also contain performance indicators with target dates as well as the monitoring mechanism for each of them. A few cases are given below for illustrative purpose.

Under the Minimum Needs Programme (MNP) aiming at ensuring assured level of basic public services to the poor, the focus is on seven sub-themes and 28 initiatives. The sub themes are: towards an entitlement based approach to poverty reduction, standardising health services, selected initiatives in education, community level interventions in health, integrated policy for sanitation and water resources, community management in water and sanitation sectors, and innovations for environmental hygiene. The development of an entitlement index, public monitoring of poverty levels, setting minimum standards for costing in government health institutions, community led quality monitoring in schools and hospitals, greater autonomy to government hospitals, unified water resource policy, cost estimation and determination of user charges for public services and propagation of holistic waste management systems through incentive mechanisms are a few initiatives under this SIP. A pilot 'service delivery project' is now being implemented in 2605 institutions that will directly benefit ordinary citizens, especially the poor. A citizen's charter has also been released. A close look at them would suggest that with the exception of a few, like imposing user charges for public services, most of them were the same kind of initiatives undertaken by the KSSP and under PPC earlier, but with the difference that they came not from the government but from the people themselves who were mobilised to realise their capabilities.

Under the pillar of Core Government Functions there are four sub-themes and 17 SIPs covering key result areas like integrated planning, policy formulation and implementation, result based performance oriented public service, policy framework for service delivery, modernised human resource management, rationalising and restructuring the government machinery to make it more efficient, effective and economical, revised system for procurement to make it more transparent and providing value for money, and information management. A monitoring mechanism is to be set up to assess the current status of assets and to conduct independent review of planning process and outcomes as well as performance against standards. Social audits and placing functional reviews/reports in the public domain are also to be provided. A close look at these would suggest that they were also the kind recommended by the earlier ARC reports.

But in spite of all the publicity work and huge quantity of printed materials and entries in official websites, training workshops, seminars and official public campaigns, people continue to have suspicions about the MGP especially when the government fails to give satisfactory answers to specific charges raised against it. The deadlines fixed for completing the SIPs have also not been met. This has invited criticism from the visiting ADB teams. Media has reported unauthorised visits by ADB consultants to government offices scrutinising files, collecting data and initiating discussion with officials. This has provoked organisations of staff including a few department heads, as these exercises did not have prior government clearance.

Let us now look into the specific fears and charges articulated against the MGP (Nair 2004; Raman 2003):

- The ADB employs the services of international consultancy agencies and the enormous cost incurred are adjusted from the loan. Consultancy contracts are given on global tender and Kerala has no right in deciding who should be selected. Many of the consultants are ignorant of the ground realities of Kerala and they hire the services of 'locals', having faith in anti-state discourse, to assist them.

- The new MGP steering committee creates a new power hierarchy and new power centres that override the established democratic process and the state planning board, and promises a 'paradigm shift in the way Government transacts its business'. The bottom line is that the state cabinet does not even have the right to remove from office, the ADB selected bureaucrats in charge of MGP.
- The ADB itself has identified certain risk factors within and outside the MGP. 'Weakness in design', 'poor implementation', 'inadequate resources' and 'weak capacity' are the risk factors within, while the 'weak political commitment of the government', 'challenges of coalition governments', 'lack of commitment of civil service', 'inadequate legislation', and 'unresponsiveness to government directives' are risk factors outside the MGP. Besides, there are a number of uncontrollable factors like 'political opposition' and 'public action against reforms'. The fear is that these factors may force the ADB to use strategies unacceptable to Kerala to overcome the risk factors.
- The ADB has indicated that both central and state governments will maintain separate accounts and provide certified copies to the ADB in accordance with ADB's mandatory guidelines of Programme Performance Management System (PPMS). The ADB will have the right to audit the use of the loan proceeds and verify the accuracy of government's certification. Both central and state governments will maintain separate accounts and records and they will be audited annually in accordance with 'standards acceptable' to the ADB and provide certified copies to the ADB. It seems that the sovereign power in the state will be surrendering many of its rights to ADB, including the right to audit by officers of the department of Local Fund Audit and Accountant General, The legislature committees, too, will have no right to scrutinise the accounts which constitute part of the state budget.
- Further, all future contracts or agreements or even negotiations with other financial agencies/donors would have to be discussed with the ADB, which reserves the right to insist on cross-conditionality. This amounts to a loss of freedom for state government and a clear encroachment on its sovereignty.
- As part of restructuring of SLPEs, the state is to assure a 'minimum annual net attrition rate of one per cent', approve a 'voluntary retirement scheme (VRS)' and 'employee separation scheme (ESS)' to all categories of workers, and implement the recommendations of the Enterprise Reform Committee (ERC). This amounts to virtually accepting the agenda of 'alternative systems of management including privatisation, disinvestments, merger, management contracts and leasing'. The state government has surprisingly failed to secure even a 'withdrawal clause' in the ADB agreement.
- The ADB wants all public utilities to run on 'market principles with cost recovery' and efficiency in delivery. The attempt in this direction has been already initiated as reflected in the hike in fees and user charges in sectors like education, health, electricity and water supply. Some schools are notified 'uneconomic' and marked out for closure. There is a fear

that the public distribution system (PDS), Kerala's pride and which ought to have been replicated in the rest of the country, may stand curtailed. Though the government has stated that the MGP would be implemented with a 'human face', hardly 4 per cent of the adjustment cost was earmarked for poverty alleviation programmes. The ADB is also alleged to render redundant, the poverty survey done by the state, which puts the 'below poverty line (BPL)' population at a shocking 37 per cent. The task of redrawing the poverty line in Kerala seems to have been entrusted with the ADB.

- Another fear is that, in future, all new infrastructure investment would have to be under the BOT mode. It would mean a contraction of public expenditure on vital social sectors.
- In the implementation of the MGP, several exercises like Capacity Building Workshops, Action Plans and Stakeholder Analysis are being undertaken, attended by 'select band of officials and non-officials' (comprador sympathisers), besides ADB officials and consultants who would be visiting Kerala frequently.
- The centre has permitted the ADB and also the World Bank to raise funds from India's own funds market. The money thus raised may get re-lent again to us. (*Hindu*, 24 September 2002)
- Kerala gets the ADB loan through the centre. But it is foolish to believe the state's argument that the ultimate liability of repayment is not on Kerala. People fear that given the ADB loan, there will be less transfer of central funds to the state in future. This has to be read in the background of the terms of reference of the 12th Finance Commission that imply a threat that, in future, devolution may be linked to the implementation of economic reforms, including fiscal reforms based on fiscal compression.
- Under the emerging circumstances, it is argued, that the most politically desirable option is to prefer internal resources to external resources. A strong plea has been made to the state to mobilise tax arrears of about Rs 30.70 billion, which is more than the ADB Loan of $300 million or Rs 13.50 billion at the exchange rate of Rs 45 per dollar.
- In MGP, ADB shifts focus from 'project lending' to 'programme lending'. Frank Paulman, ADB Chief of Public Resources, has said: 'the loan would not be given for Projects, but only for Programmes'.
- People of Kerala have serious reservation on the entire approach of the ADB, which believes that the source of 'good governance' is 'economic' rather than 'political'. By redefining 'Core Functions' of government, the ADB is proposing a withdrawal of the state from many of the areas in which it used to be a major player in the political, social and economic history of Kerala.

We quote a recent critic of the MGP:

> 'If the Kerala government were to adhere to ADB-driven governance, it would culminate in social de-investment, commodification of critical sectors such as education and health and thereby a reversion of whatever remains of the Kerala model of social development: what Karl Polanyi would have called 'disembedding' from social bonds

and civic engagements, vulnerable social sections being the hardest hit. In addition to social de-spending and the mounting of social debt, the ADB loan is likely to strike at the very roots of democracy in the State.' (Raman 2003).

Today Kerala is witnessing strong popular resistance/protest movements against many of the anti-people components in the state level reforms agenda and the use of external pressure used to push it through under the cover of mitigating fiscal stress, poverty, unemployment and poor quality of governance. But unfortunately due to the fragmented polity and conflictive politics, which are the hallmark of Kerala society, these are not held under a common platform or banner. Besides the mainstream left parties and their ranks and people-centred civil society institutions and activists, very recently, radical groups like the CPI(ML) Red Flag also have come to the fighting frontline. Political mobilisation to bring all those people who are opposed to the neoliberal agenda and anti-people reforms is gaining strength in Kerala and much of the reason for this is the failure of the government to take people into confidence about the usefulness and legitimacy of what they are doing. This can come only when the rulers and the ruled collaborate in 'reforming democracy' and reforming politics' in the state at the earliest.

Conclusion

In contrast to other states, Kerala has achieved a fairly high level of human development on account of mass mobilisation, social reform movements, popular struggles and pro-people state/public action. But unfortunately, in the course of it there emerged a complex fragmented polity with anti-development and anti-people conflictive politics indulged in by mainstream political parties. The reinforcement of world/global capitalism through the new, much attractive paradigm of globalisation and governance reform founded on neoliberal agenda crated a support base for the anti-state discourse. The 'terminal crisis' of nation states with its attendant governance breakdown in every sphere of society has forced many among the upper and middle classes to believe in the TINA slogan.

However, in Kerala, due to high political literacy, high density of mass organisations, people-sensitive and people-oriented media and civil society formations like the KSSP at the grass root level with their dynamic activism, greater awareness has been created among people about the anti-people character of the anti-state discourse. They, therefore, are now involved in the search for a real people's alternative founded on decentralised participatory governance and development, reformed democracy and politics. Those who spearheaded the People's Plan Campaign have said: whatever roots that began to sprout, burnt out. But the potential for re-rooting exists. Experience of Kerala indicates that one has to urgently fight absurd and inimical government policies, arrogant and corrupt service providers and transform the prevailing convenience politics to people-centred politics through active democratic participation in governance. Good governance and people-centred development in today's contextual situation would ultimately depend on correct choice of reforms in state politics and democracy, particularly the way they are practised.

References

Amin, Samir (1997). *Capitalism in the Age of Globalisation: The Management of Contemporary Society*. London: Zed Books.

Bijoy, C.R. and K. Ravi Raman (2003). 'Muthanga—The Real Story—Adivasi Movement to Recover Land', *Economic and Political Weekly*, 38(20):1975–82, 17 May.

Chathukulam, Jose (2002). 'Survival through Social Capital Formations: The Case of Women's Self-Help Groups', *Proceedings of International Workshop on Research for Poverty Alleviation*, 16–18 September, Kerala Research Programme on Local Level Development (KRPLLD), Trivandrum: Centre for Development Studies.

Chelliah, R.J. (2003). 'Reducing Poverty through State-level Reforms', in Stephen Howes, Ashok Lahiri and Nicholas Stern (eds), *State Level Reforms in India: Towards More Effective Government*. New Delhi: Macmillan India Ltd.

Choudhary, Kameshwar (2004). 'Globalisation, Governance Reforms and Development in India', Draft Background Paper for the Silver Jubilee Workshop, 14–16 December, Anand: Institute of Rural Management Anand.

Centre for Development Studies (1996). *Workshop on Industrialisation in Kerala*, Trivandrum, August.

CAGC (Commonwealth Association for Corporate Governance) (1999). *Principles for Corporate Governance in the Commonwealth – Towards Global Competitiveness and Economic Accountability*, November. Available at www.cbc.to; accessed 5 October 2004.

Diwan, Ramesh (2000). *Globalisation: Myth Vs Reality*. Available at www.indolinkanalysis, accessed 30 August 2004).

Drucker, Peter (1997). 'The Global Economy and the Nation State', *Foreign Affairs*, 76(5).

During, A.B. (1989). *Poverty and Environment: Reversing the Downward Spiral*. London: World Watch Institute.

Franke, Richard (2002). 'The Mararikulam Experiment: An International Perspective', Seminar on Decentralisation and Sustainable Development and Social Security, organised by Joint Committee of Panchayats of Aryad and Kanjikkuzhy Blocks (Kerala) and the ILO, May.

Fremond, Oliver and Marta Capaul (2002). 'The State of Corporate Governance: Experience from Country Assessment', Working Paper No. 2858, World Bank, July. Available at www.worldbank.org, accessed 5 October 2004.

George, K.K. (1999). *Limits to Kerala Model of Development—An Analysis of Fiscal Crisis and its Implications*. Trivandrum: Centre for Development Studies.

Giddens, Anthony (1971). *Capitalism and Modern Social Theory*. Cambridge: Cambridge University Press.

Gopalan, A.K. (1952). *Kerala's Past and Present*. London: Lawrence and Wishart.

GOK (Government of Kerala) (1957,1965,1997a). *Report(s) of the Administrative Reforms Committees*, Trivandrum: Government of Kerala.

——— (1997b). *Report of the Sen Committee on Decentralisation of Powers*. Trivadrum: Government of Kerala.

——— (2002a). *Economic Review*. Trivandrum: Government of Kerala.

——— (2002b). *Approach Paper for State level Public Enterprises Reforms in Kerala*. Trivandrum: Government of Kerala.

——— (2003a). *Economic Review*. Trivandrum: Government of Kerala.

——— (2003b). *A Review of Public Enterprises in Kerala 2001–02*. Trivandrum: Government of Kerala, February.

GOK (Government of Kerala) (2003c). *Report of the Commission on WTO Concerns in Agriculture: Building a Sustainable Agricultural Trade Security System for Kerala* (chaired by M.S. Swaminathan). Trivandrum: Government of Kerala, January.

Grootaert, Christian, Deepa Narayan, Veronica Nyham Jones and Michael Woolcock (2003). 'Integrated Questionnaire for the Measurement of Social Capital', World Bank Poverty Net Library. Available at www.worldbank.org, accessed 5 October 2004.

Gulati, I.S. and D. Narayana (1994). 'Financial Constraints to Kerala's Economic Development', in *International Congress on Kerala Studies—Abstracts*, Vol. 2, Trivandrum: A.K.G. Centre for Research Studies.

Huther, Jeff and Anwar Shah (2003). *Applying a Simple Measure of Good Governance to the Debate on Fiscal Decentralisation*. Washington DC: World Bank. Available at www.worldbank.org, accessed 5 October 2004.

Irudayarajan, S. and K.C. Zachariah (1997). 'Long Term Implications of Low Fertility in Kerala', Working Paper No. 282, Trivandrum: Centre for Development Studies, October.

Isaac, Thomas, T.M. and Richard Franke (2000). *Local Democracy and Development: People's Campaign for Decentralised Planning in Kerala*. New Delhi: LeftWord Books.

John, M.S. and Jose Chathukulam (2002). 'Building Social Capital Through State Initiative: Participatory Planning in Kerala', *Economic and Political Weekly*, 37(20): 1939–48, 18 May.

Kannan, K.P. (2000). 'Food Security in a Regional Perspective—A View from Food Deficit Kerala', Working Paper No. 304, Trivandrum: Centre for Development Studies, July.

——— (2002). 'The Welfare Model of Social Security for Informal Sector Workers: The Kerala Experience', Working Paper No. 332, Trivandrum: Centre for Development Studies, April.

Kaufman, Daniel, Aart Kraay and Massimo Mastrussi (2003). 'Governance Research Indicators Project: Governance Matters III, Indicators for 1996–2002', 10–13 May, World Bank. Available at www.worldbank.org/wbi/governance, accessed 5 October 2004.

KSSP (Kerala Sasthra Sahithya Parishad) (2003). *Parishad Pinnitta Nalpathu Varshangal*. Kottayam Kochi, KSSP. [Other important KSSP publications include: *Wealth of Kerala* (1976), *Electricity and Kerala Development* (1975), *Pinnitta Moonnu Dasakangal* (1993), *Energy* (1994), *The Silent Valley Hydroelectric Project and Ecological Aspects of Silent Valley* (1997), and their Journal, *Sasthragathi*, Kozhikode and Trivandrum: KSSP].

Knack, Stephen and Philip Keefer (1997). 'Does Social Capital have an Economic Pay off – A Cross Country Investigation', World Bank Poverty Net Library. Available at www.worldbank.org, accessed 13 August 2004.

Krishnan, T.N. (1998). 'The Route to Social Development in Kerala, Social Development in Kerala, Social Intermediation and Public Action', in Santhosh Mehrotra and Jolly Richards (eds), *Development with Human Face*. Oxford: Clarendon Press.

Lenin, V.I. (1967). 'Imperialism—the Highest Stage of Capitalism', in *Selected Works*, volume 1. Moscow: Progress Publishers.

Menon, R.V.G., M.P. Parameswaran and V.R. Raghunandanan (2002). 'PLDP: Problems and Prospects of People's Participation in a Party Dominated Society', in Proceedings of the International Workshop on Research for Poverty Alleviation, Mimeo, 16–18 September, Trivandrum, Centre for Development Studies (Kerala Research Programme on Local-level Development).

Menon, Sreedhara A. (1997). *Kerala and Freedom Struggle*. Kottayam: D.C. Books.

Nair, P.R.G., and P. Mohanan Pillai (1994). *Impact of External Transfers in the Regional Economy of Kerala*. Trivandrum: Centre for Development Studies, August.

Nair, Ramachandran, K. (2002). 'The History of Trade Union Movement in Kerala', Mimeo, Trivandrum, Kerala Institute of Labour and Employment.

Nair, Ramachandran, K. (2004). 'Discussion Note on MGP', Mimeo, Trivandrum: Kerala Sasthra Sahithya Parishad.
Nair, R.P. (1977). 'A study of the Financial Performance of the Kerala State: Part I Emerging Trends in Revenue and Expenditure of Kerala', Mimeo, Trivandrum, Centre for Taxation Studies.
Narain, J.P. (1959). *A Plan for the Reconstruction of the Indian Polity*, written for Akhil Bharat Sarva Seva Sangh, Kashi. Available at website 506, accessed 30 August 2004.
Narayan, Deepa (1999). 'Bonds and Bridges: Social Capital and Poverty', Poverty Group, PREM, Washington D.C., World Bank, July.
Narayanan, N.C. (2003). *Against the Grain: The Political Ecology of Land Use in a Kerala Region*. The Hague: Institute of Social Studies, Shaker Publishing.
OECD. (1999a). *Report by the Business Sector Advisory Group on Corporate Governance—Experience from Country Assessments*. Washington D.C.: World Bank, April.
——— (1999b). *Civil Service Reform: A Review of World Bank Assistance Report, No.19599*, Washington D.C.: World Bank, June.
Oommen, M.A. (2004). *Rethinking Development: Kerala's Development Experience,* Vol. 2. New Delhi: Concept Publishing Company (for Institute of Social Sciences).
Parameswaran, M.P. (2004). *Nalam Lokam: Swapnavum Yadharthyangalum*. Kottayam: D.C.Books
Pieterse, J.N. (2001). *Development Theory*. Delhi: Vistar Publishers.
Pillai, Raman K. (1999). 'Coalition Politics: The Kerala Experience', in Oommen, M.A. (ed.), *Rethinking Development—Kerala's Development Experience,* New Delhi: Concept Publishing Company.
Pradhan, Sanjay (2003). 'Reforming government: International Experience', in Howes et al. (eds), *State Level Reforms in India—Towards More Effective Government*. New Delhi: Macmillan Ltd.
Pushpangadan, K. (2003). 'Remittances, Consumption and Economic Growth, 1980–2000', Working Paper No. 343, Trivandrum: Centre for Development Studies, March.
Putnam, Robert (1993). *Making Democracy Work: Civic Traditions in Modern Italy*. Princeton: Princeton University Press.
Ramachandran, V.K. (1996). 'On Kerala's Development Achievements', in Jean Dreze and Amartya Sen (eds), *India's Development: Selected Regional Perspectives,* New Delhi: Oxford University Press.
Raman, Ravi (2003) 'ADB in Kerala: Playing God in God's Own Country', Working Paper No. 357, Trivandrum: Centre for Development Studies, March.
RBI (Reserve Bank of India) (1997). 'Finances of the State Governments', *Reserve Bank of India Bulletin*, Mumbai, February.
Shylendra, H.S. (2004). 'The Emerging Governance Paradigm and Its Implications for Poverty Alleviation and Equity', Silver Jubilee Workshop, IRMA, Anand, December.
The Hindu (newspaper) (2002). Chennai, 24 September.
——— (2005). Chennai, 28 and 30 June.
UNDP (United Nations Development Programme) (1999). *World Development Report*, Delhi: Oxford University Press.
Wolfensohn, J.D. (1999). 'A Proposal for a Comprehensive Development Framework'. Available at www.worldbank.org/cdf/cdf.text/htm, accessed 2 July 2004.
World Bank (1991a). *The Reform of Public Sector Management—Lessons of Experience*, World Bank Policy Research Series No. 18. Washington DC: World Bank.
——— (1991b). *India: Country Memorandum, Vol. II, Agriculture—Challenges and Opportunities*. Washington DC.: World Bank.
——— (1992). *Governance and Development*. Washington DC: World Bank.
——— (1994). *Governance—the World Bank Experience*. Washington DC: World Bank.

World Bank (2000). *Towards Operationally Relevant Indicators of Governance,* PREMnote, No. 49, December. Available at www.worldbank.org, accessed 4 October 2004.

——— (2001). *Governance: A Participatory, Action Oriented Programme—Programme Brief Document.* Washington: World Bank Institute, October. Available at www.worldbank.org, accessed 4 October 2004.

———(2004a). *Public Sector Governance Reform Cycle: Available Diagnostic Tools,* PREMnotes, No. 88, July. Available at www.worldbank.org, accessed 4 October 2004 (several related documents given under this).

———(2004b). *Reforming Public Institutions and Strengthening Governance: A World Bank Strategy.* Available at www.worldbank.org/public sector/strategy.htm, accessed 4 October 2004.

Yadav, Y. (2001). 'Let's Find an Alternative', *The Indian Express,* 19 June.

Zachariah, K.C., K.P. Kannan and S. Irudayarajan (eds). 2002. *Kerala's Gulf Connections,* Trivandrum: CDS (Studies on International Labour Migration from Kerala State in India).

Zachariah, K.C., E.T. Mathew and S. Irudayarajan (1999). 'Impact of Migration on Kerala's Economy and Society', Working Paper No. 297, Trivandrum: Centre for Development Studies, July.

7

Social Base of Reform Attempts in Bihar

Shaibal Gupta

The Background

In the sultry afternoon of June 20 2004, almost one and a half years before the advent of Nitish Kumar as the Chief Minister of Bihar, Laloo Prasad Yadav, then recently appointed railway minister of the Union Government, flagged off a refrigerated wagon of vegetables to Delhi, the capital of India. The 17 tonne capacity van was half empty in its maiden foray to Delhi. Another wagon was kept ready for linking the Patna market with Kolkata, the metropolitan centre of the east. Laloo Prasad enthusiastically announced that the wagons would commute twice a week initially and its frequency will be increased subsequently (HT 2004, June 21). A half empty wagon in its maiden journey was understandable; but the response to the efforts of Laloo Prasad at both the ends was contrary to the expectations. In Patna, there was no enthusiasm at the farmers' end to send vegetables to Delhi; in Delhi the wholesale traders also did not show any interest inspite of the vegetables from Bihar being of superior quality. When the planned departure schedules could not be maintained in the absence of the supply of vegetables, the state machinery was activated to support the initiative. The officers-in-charge of the police stations within the vegetable growing region around Patna were drafted to influence the traders to send vegetables regularly to Delhi (*Hindustan* 2004a). After all, if the market forces do not operate, the state has to intervene to enthuse it. In the hope of managing the response, the dates of departure of the refrigerated wagon were rescheduled several times. But that was not successful and ultimately the entire project had to be abandoned.

Is charisma in itself sufficient to activate the market forces? For Laloo Prasad, the maverick leader from the most backward state of Bihar, being catapulted to the Union cabinet was indeed a moment of reckoning. After years of living with the reputation of being a non-performer on the development front, and perhaps to stave off the electoral doom in the 2005 assembly elections, he possibly wanted to do something dramatic for the state by attempting this economic integration of the state with the national market. This would have entailed a reversal of trend in exporting goods from the provincial to the national market rather the other way around. In doing this, he inadvertently followed a copybook roadmap of an 'economic reformer' graduating from a social reformer. If the initiative had succeeded, Laloo Prasad would have been on the threshold of creating history. After having liberated the socially deprived from the caste hierarchy, he would have scripted the liberation of the small size provincial market by integrating it with the much larger national market and then, perhaps, international market. As a national political figure, personally, he was transcending himself from social concern to the market concern, which is the ultimate measure of economic dynamism in the increasingly market-centric economy. In this respect, history for a change was on his side. Immediately after independence, the policy of equalisation in the freight rates of the railway, in the matter of coal, iron ore/steel and cement, the most important mineral inputs for industrial development, had devastated the untruncated Bihar. It not only deprived Bihar from being the destination for investment because of its locational advantage vis-à-vis mineral resources, but also subsidised the capitalist industrial transformation of India at Bihar's expense. Laloo Prasad was poised to reverse the trend. Unlike in the case of mineral resources, the freight equalisation would now have worked in favour of agriculture in Bihar, a landlocked state. Even though there was no freight equalisation per se, the vast channels of railway network and its subsidised freight would have favoured the vegetable producers of the state. Unlike Shree Krishna Sinha, the first Chief Minister of Bihar, who could not protect the mineral interest of the state and promote regional capitalism, Laloo Prasad would have ensured the growth of local agrarian capitalism by linking it with the national market. With Laloo Prasad as a de facto head of Bihar, the state would not have suffered from the disadvantages of a limited market or absence of a level playing field. However, this was not to be. Contrary to expectations, Laloo Prasad's optimism for reverse market integration proved to be a damp squib. Why could this highly potent initiative not take shape deserves a close look? Was this only a publicity stunt in view of the then impending assembly elections? Or was its failure related to the structural problems of the economy? Is the debate about centre and periphery still relevant? Or was there no market for the vegetables in Delhi and exports from Bihar would have created a market glut? Or, even if there was a market in Delhi, was there possibly no surplus of vegetables in Bihar to resurge agrarian capitalism in the state? Or, could the failure be attributed simply to lack of forward and backward linkages, a necessary precondition for the market economy? To buttress this point, it was reported that the arrival time of the refrigerated wagon in Delhi was not properly scheduled for its onward connection with the local wholesale market which started at midnight. Is the support for state edifice, in this case the railways, sufficient enough for the market economy to succeed? Can state institutions succeed in promoting the market economy where they have to go beyond the administered prices? Can the pace of the economic forces be increased by the entrepreneurial momentum generated overnight by the state administrative fiat?

Ironically, Patna and its hinterland, during the last one century were not unconnected to the national market. This geographical enclave has developed over the century as a 'vegetable bowl' of the state. This was primarily because of the elevation of Patna in 1912 to a state capital of the newly formed state of Bihar (separated from Bengal Presidency) from a district town, leading to the establishment of military cantonment in its periphery and installation of the railway line connecting Kolkata and eastern Uttar Pradesh. All these created a huge market for vegetables and milk products. This also created opportunity for entrepreneurs from the backward social clan of Yadav, Koeri or Kurmi agro-capitalist. In this context, the refrigerated wagon for vegetables introduced by Laloo Prasad should have further enthused the backward caste entrepreneurs in exploring new frontiers of the market. Apart from the established agro-entrepreneurs, this should have generated interest among those marginal producers who were still outside the market network and cash nexus. However, this did not happen in Bihar when, in contrast, even without any state initiative or support, thousands of refrigerated vans enter with fish from Andhra Pradesh which has, in turn, triggered many other food-based entrepreneurship in Andhra Pradesh. Then why, the question is, did Bihari entrepreneurs behave differently in the case of the Patna-Delhi linkage? Was it because the established Bihari agrocapitalists from the backward castes, by not supplying adequate vegetable to the refrigerated wagon, wanted Laloo Prasad's efforts to fail as he did not belong to their caste? Moreso when truckloads of vegetables were being sent to Ranchi in Jharkhand from Bihar itself (*Dainik Hindustan* 2004b, June 24), with backward and forward linkages operating so smoothly. It was rumoured that Nitish Kumar (Gupta 1995), Laloo Prasad's predecessor in the railway ministry, who had actually initiated the plan of the vegetable export through the refrigerated wagon would have succeeded in this effort because he was the organic leader of this class. He was, like Charan Singh (Byres 1988), careful that the terms of trade between the industry and agriculture was in favour of the latter. Besides, with his administrative ability, he would have ensured backward and forward linkages with the market before initiating the venture. With the rise of Nitish Kumar as the Chief Minister of Bihar, will he succeed where Laloo Prasad had failed? Can Laloo Prasad's failure be attributed to his lack of ability to go into the details of market linkages or is it due to something else? Was it possible that backward linkages would have put certain social categories on the forefront of the market economy? After all, Laloo Prasad had earlier not only effected a paradigm shift between the upper and the backward castes but also brought about a change between them. On the same line, he perhaps planned to use Indian Railways to promote market democratisation in the way 'Mandal Commission' was used for social democratisation?

This chapter, however, is not an attempt to identify the technical or the anthropological aspects of the futile attempt of the vegetable foray, but an exercise in chartering the stunted economic reform attempts in Bihar and the failure of the state to be became a market economy and promote market forces. The first question that begs an answer here is, who is Laloo Prasad in sociological terms or whom does he represent? Was his emergence an indication of a new social group in the political firmament of India? Is his utter failure in creating a market for vegetable trade, at the pinnacle of his political power, indicative of the limitations of his vision or his social class? Can this class be defined in economic terms? Can Bihar be explained by economic or cultural reductionism or does it need a combination of both? To contextualise these questions, it is important to understand the developments that were peculiar to Bihar which ushered Laloo Prasad and Nitish Kumar to power in the 1990s, even though after the latter's exit, the former had an almost unbridled rule for one and half decades. Why did Bihar drift to different political and economic directions? Was the non-ushering of reform, inbuilt in the body polity of the state? Even though Laloo and Nitish originally belonged to the same social philosophy and political ideology, will the new political dispensation under the leadership of NDA in Bihar follow a different reform roadmap?

SOCIAL DETERMINANTS OF BACKWARDNESS

Bihar defies all economic logic to explain its stagnation. The critical factor in this context is not the near collapse of the state, the economic failure or the social conflict that has been endemic for several decades, but the absence of an economic incentive structure, either individual or societal, that could have made the economy and the society move. The neo-classical economics and rational choice theory assume that each individual is a rationally self-interested utility maximising agent. In this context, each individual when supported in pursuing private profits and a collection of individual good, in turn, contributes to public or societal good. The society oscillates around the individual; and the notion of individual action (i.e., private profit seeking) in the neo-classical backdrop yields a fairly complete formula for government economic policies. This formula, then, provides a basis for assessing the quality of governance for the management and nurturing of economy for affecting long-term changes. In the context of Bihar, it is the absence of such an incentive (profit) structure, either individual or societal, that is proving to be detrimental to development, if not a complete waterloo for the government policies. In this respect, for understanding the society in Bihar, the 'increasing return' view may be less relevant than the new institutional view (North 1990) wherein history matters because it shapes institutions. For, if the 'increasing returns' were everything, then one time inflow of aid or other windfall would set the economy on the way to prosperity, which did not happen in the case of Bihar. We have several instances where budgeted outlay remained unspent (World Bank 2004: 36).

State and the Market Dynamics

To what extent states should intervene in markets to promote growth is an old and perennial debate in development studies. One view promoted that 'market imperfections', an impediment for growth, necessitated state intervention. With the advent of globalisation and dismantling of the socialist system, the focus shifted to the 'state imperfections'. This view got further legitimacy with the mandate of the 'Washington consensus' in the 1980s which entailed 'getting prices right, openness and minimal state intervention' (Kohli et al. 2004). However, this policy had its limitation as the issue of 'market imperfections' arises only when there is existence of a substantial market. In both the cases of banishing 'market imperfections' or 'macroeconomic stabililisation', therefore, there is a need for an effective state intervention. With the ushering of reform and the increased role of market, the Central government in India has already abdicated its role. It is now for the state government to provide an enabling atmosphere to attract domestic and international investments. This in turn would entail dismantling some institutions of the state as well as strengthening others. Operationally, it would mean doing away with the flab of the state to make it more market friendly and, at the same time, strengthen organs of the state to entice both national and global investment. Strengthening the organ of the state will depend on the relative size of the tax revenue of the respective states and the pattern of investment in key areas such as industry, energy, roads and urban development. One of the striking features of Indian states prior to the 1990's is the relative uniformity of development policies across the provinces.[1] But with the ushering of the reform and the decline in the role of the Central government, liberalisation entailed that 'the Central government is no longer able to direct investment through licensing; the enabling environment provided by a State has become a major determinant of investment flows' (Howes et al. 2003: 4) But these policy attempts are possible where market, a euphemism for capitalism, has reached a certain threshold level. In India, it is still not spatially uniform. On one end, there is unevenness in the capitalist transformation and on the other, there is duality in the economy. This duality in the economy, in the last few decades, has meant that the 'so called "middle class" (the top five per cent of the income scale) has become rich beyond its wildest dreams. It has literally transplanted itself to the first world without even applying for a visa' (Dreze 2004). Besides, in an underdeveloped country like India with its vast geographical expanse, the state intervention is needed not only for equity and social welfare, but also for developing the productive forces uniformly and creating market across the country. This will bring economic stability which, in turn, assiduously releases the forces of private investment. Table 7.1 indicates the proportionate share of the respective states in the national market, which ultimately indicates its real economic strength. This, however, is not necessarily confined to its geographical territory; exports to other states count as much. The proportionate share of the CST (Central Sales Taxes) indicates

Table 7.1: Share in Size of Domestic Market

	Size of Markets (2003–04)		Population (2001)		Percentage Share of Revenue from CST	States Own Tax Revenue (2001–02)	
States	Value (Rs '000 crore)	Percentage	Number (crore)	Percentage	(2000–02)	(Rs '000 crore)	Percentage
Bihar	106.3	4.8	8.3	8.1	0.6	2.4	2.0
Jharkhand	36.4	1.7	2.7	2.6	1.9	2.0	1.7
West Bengal	178.0	8.1	8.0	7.8	2.6	6.5	5.5
Delhi	74.3	3.4	1.4	1.4		4.9	4.2
Uttar Pradesh	297.8	13.6	16.6	16.2	3.7	10.3	8.7
Uttaranchal	20.9	0.9	0.8	0.8	0.2	0.9	0.8
Madhya Pradesh	99.5	4.5	6.0	5.8	4.7	4.7	4.0
Chhattisgarh	28.3	1.3	2.0	1.9	1.6	1.9	1.6
Rajasthan	135.9	6.2	5.6	5.5	1.3	5.7	4.8
Punjab	68.8	3.1	2.4	2.3	4.2	4.8	4.1
Haryana	60.1	2.7	2.1	2.0	6.9	4.9	4.2
Maharashtra	224.7	10.3	9.7	9.4	15.1	21.2	17.8
Gujarat	128.5	5.9	5.1	5.0	8.6	9.2	7.8
Goa	5.9	0.3	0.1	0.1	0.2	0.6	0.5
Andhra Pradesh	149.9	6.9	7.6	7.4	5.7	12.6	10.7
Karnataka	126.9	5.8	5.3	5.2	5.9	9.8	8.3
Tamil Nadu	159.5	7.3	6.2	6.0	10.3	12.2	10.3
India	2186.0	100.0	102.7	100.0	100.0	118.0	100.0

Source: *The Market Skyline of India—District Profile 2004*, Indicus Analytics, New Delhi.

the share of the export market for the respective states[2] and the distribution here is even more skewed than the same for domestic market. From the classification of Indians vis-à-vis their share of population and share of market, indicating their potential for growth, one can easily understand that Bihar is a seriously disadvantaged state (Table 7.2). The phenomenon of unequal market sizes, however, does not stop at the state-level. Even within a given state, the size of the markets across the districts are also unequally distributed, as indicated by Table 7.3 for the districts in Bihar.

Obviously, the states with stronger industrial base have a much higher command over the market. Second, the condition of the state finances also deters or facilitates the regional effort for attracting industrial investment. This would entail strengthening the department of energy, industry, roads and possibly urban affairs. This 'in turn' will depend on the resource base of the respective states. Some states like Maharastra not only have a larger market share of the country, but its internal resource base is also substantial (Table 7.2). The states with larger resource base, like Maharastra, Tamil Nadu, Karnataka and Andhra Pradesh, have invested substantially in the departments related to investment destination. As compared to them, the capacity of the state government in Bihar to undertake development-related work has become so limited that it now has to depend on outside agencies even when resources are made available (Tables 7.4(a), 7.4(b) and 7.4(c)) The recent example of NHPC, a Central government undertaking, being entrusted with the responsibility of building roads in rural Bihar also is an indication towards its limited capacity for development initiative.[3] Apart from the resource base of the respective governments, those of the respective municipal corporations of Bombay, Pune, Chennai, Bangalore, Hyderabad, Kolkata also play an indirect role in creating the metropolitan and urban ambience, which ultimately attracts investments. In fact, they are important centres and play a crucial role in forging national and global market connectivity. The knowledge base and urbanity of these centres are much higher; they can build bridges with their counterpart at the global level. They are almost like a city-state in the Indian context. In the market economy, lack of urban centres and urbanity in a state like Bihar is a bane for both investment and consequently development. In the absence of a powerful presence of the municipal corporations, Bihar's urban enclave is not able to compete with other metropolitan centres in India in attracting investment. This limitation could have been dealt with, possibly with the

Table 7.2: Share of Markets in Selected States of India

Share of revenue from CST (denoting export)	*Much less than share of population*	*Close to share of population*	*Much above share of population*
Much less than share of population	Bihar, Jharkhand, Madhya Pradesh	West Bengal, Uttar Pradesh, Rajasthan, Uttaranchal	
Close to share of population	Chhattisgarh	Andhra Pradesh, Karnataka	Goa
Much above share of population		Gujarat, Tamil Nadu	Delhi, Punjab, Haryana, Maharashtra

Source: The Market Skyline of India—District Profile 2004, Indicus Analytics, New Delhi.

Table 7.3: Size of Markets in the Districts of Bihar

Districts	Size of market(2003–04) Value (Rs '000 crore)	Size of market(2003–04) Percentage	Population 2001 Number (crore)	Population 2001 Percentage	Percentage of Population (India)	Percentage of National Market size
Patna	7.6	7.15	0.47	5.67	0.46	0.35
Nalanda	2.5	2.35	0.24	2.86	0.23	0.11
Rohtas	2.6	2.45	0.25	2.95	0.24	0.12
Kaimur	1.9	1.79	0.13	1.54	0.12	0.09
Bhojpur	3.0	2.82	0.22	2.69	0.22	0.14
Buxar	1.2	1.13	0.14	1.69	0.14	0.05
Gaya	4.7	4.42	0.35	4.17	0.34	0.22
Jehanabad	1.8	1.69	0.15	1.82	0.15	0.08
Nawada	2.7	2.54	0.18	2.18	0.18	0.12
Aurangabad	2.9	2.73	0.20	2.41	0.19	0.13
Saran	4.6	4.33	0.33	3.92	0.32	0.21
Siwan	4.8	4.52	0.27	3.25	0.26	0.22
Goplaganj	3.5	3.29	0.22	2.59	0.21	0.16
Darbhanga	1.8	1.69	0.33	3.95	0.32	0.08
Madhubani	4.1	3.86	0.36	4.30	0.35	0.19
Samastipur	3.0	2.82	0.34	4.11	0.33	0.14
Saharsa	1.8	1.69	0.15	1.81	0.15	0.08
Supaul	2.3	2.16	0.17	2.10	0.17	0.11
Madhepura	1.5	1.41	0.15	1.83	0.15	0.07
Purnia	2.7	2.54	0.25	3.06	0.25	0.12
Araria	3.0	2.82	0.21	2.55	0.21	0.14
Kishanganj	1.8	1.69	0.13	1.55	0.13	0.08
Katihar	3.1	2.92	0.24	2.88	0.23	0.14
Bhagalpur	3.9	3.67	0.24	2.93	0.24	0.18
Banka	2.8	2.63	0.17	2.04	0.16	0.13
Muzaffarpur	4.7	4.42	0.37	4.51	0.36	0.22
Sitamarhi	2.4	2.26	0.27	3.22	0.26	0.11
Sheohar	0.5	0.47	0.05	0.61	0.05	0.02
East Champaran	5.1	4.80	0.39	4.73	0.38	0.23
West Champaran	4.3	4.05	0.30	3.66	0.30	0.20
Vaishali	3.5	3.29	0.27	3.27	0.26	0.16
Munger	1.3	1.22	0.11	1.36	0.11	0.06
Lakhisarai	0.9	0.85	0.08	0.96	0.08	0.04
Shekhpura	0.6	0.56	0.05	0.63	0.05	0.03
Jamui	1.7	1.60	0.14	1.69	0.14	0.08
Khagaria	1.7	1.60	0.13	1.54	0.12	0.08
Begusarai	1.8	1.69	0.23	2.82	0.23	0.08
All Districts	106.3	100	8.3	100	8.1	4.86
All India	2186.0		102.7		100	100

Source: *The Market Skyline of India—District Profile 2004*, Indicus Analytics, New Delhi.

7.4 (a): States' Own Revenue and Expenditure Pattern 2001–02

	Expenditure						Total dev. expenditure	
States	*Total expenditure*	*Urban dev.*	*Energy*	*Industry + mineral*	*Road and bridge*	*Science and technology*	*Amount (Rs crore)*	*As percentage of total expenditure*
Bihar	14869.29	58.61	NA	45.96	282.04	NA	7312.16	49.18
Jharkhand	7933.75	54.82	33	114.29	329.74	NA	5007.94	63.12
West Bengal	28078.79	989.01	101.85	410.06	714.83	1.42	13108.76	46.69
Delhi	8630.72	500.87	966.72	32.91	295.53	9.22	4086.19	47.34
Uttar Pradesh	38103.75	115.84	1091.36	33.17	749.86	6.99	18113.65	47.54
Uttranchal	3297.76	16.75	21.56	10.28	181.08	1.8	2032.36	61.63
Madhya Pradesh	17319.68	104.65	2209.79	60.94	474.74	2.11	10395.24	60.02
Chattisgarh	5623.89	60.14	82.43	38.14	215.21	0.02	3520.61	62.60
Rajasthan	18994.72	474.54	651.7	52.82	341.42	3.2	10544.34	55.51
Punjab	15692.05	67.52	575.85	23.58	283.29	4.11	5938.73	37.85
Haryana	10728.47	43.75	829.54	24.82	683.92	3.45	6556.05	61.11
Maharastra	42479.58	270.3	1006.28	146.33	653.53	0.84	22922.25	53.96
Gujarat	25650.77	226.09	3502.66	376.43	368.26	3.31	17225.28	67.15
Goa	2352.49	17.02	410.55	17.7	67.33	0.33	1198.38	50.94
Andhra Pradesh	31074.36	345.12	2328.45	212.91	1232.95	5.24	18179.73	58.50
Karnataka	21937.61	98.35	2353.58	351.19	622.04	8.31	13880.72	63.27
Tamil Nadu	24818.18	188.32	134.63	153.98	520.23	5.95	13546.72	54.58
India	377311.62	3988.4	17966.35	3009.53	10019.43	94.36	204515.55	54.20

Source: RBI (2004)—*Handbook of Statistics on State Government Finances*, Mumbai.

Table 7.4(b): Expenditure as Percentage of Total Development Expenditure

States	*Road and bridge*	*Energy*	*Industry + mineral*	*Urban dev*	*Science and technology*
Bihar	3.86	NA	0.63	0.80	NA
Jharkhand	6.58	0.66	2.28	1.09	NA
West Bengal	5.45	0.78	3.13	7.54	0.01
Delhi	7.23	23.66	0.81	12.26	0.23
Uttar Pradesh	4.14	6.03	0.18	0.64	0.04
Uttranchal	8.91	1.06	0.51	0.82	0.09
Madhya Pradesh	4.57	21.26	0.59	1.01	0.02
Chattisgarh	6.11	2.34	1.08	1.71	NA

(Table 7.5(b) continued)

(Table 7.4(b) continued)

States	*Road and bridge*	*Energy*	*Industry + mineral*	*Urban dev*	*Science and technology*
Rajasthan	3.24	6.18	0.50	4.50	0.03
Punjab	4.77	9.70	0.40	1.14	0.07
Haryana	10.43	12.65	0.38	0.67	0.05
Maharastra	2.85	4.39	0.64	1.18	NA
Gujarat	2.14	20.33	2.19	1.31	0.02
Goa	5.62	34.26	1.48	1.42	0.03
Andhra Pradesh	6.78	12.81	1.17	1.90	0.03
Karnataka	4.48	16.96	2.53	0.71	0.06
Tamil Nadu	3.84	0.99	1.14	1.39	0.04
India	4.90	8.78	1.47	1.95	0.05

Source: RBI (2004)—*Handbook of Statistics on State Government Finances*, Mumbai.

Table 7.4(c): Expenditure as Percentage of Total Expenditure

States	*Urban dev.*	*Energy*	*Industry + miniral*	*Road and bridge*	*Science and technology*
Bihar	0.39	NA	0.31	1.90	NA
Jharkhand	0.69	0.42	1.44	4.16	NA
West Bengal	3.52	0.36	1.46	2.55	0.01
Delhi	5.80	11.20	0.38	3.42	0.11
Uttar Pradesh	0.30	2.86	0.09	1.97	0.02
Uttranchal	0.51	0.65	0.31	5.49	0.05
Madhya Pradesh	0.60	12.76	0.35	2.74	0.01
Chattisgarh	1.07	1.47	0.68	3.83	NA
Rajasthan	2.50	3.43	0.28	1.80	0.02
Punjab	0.43	3.67	0.15	1.81	0.03
Haryana	0.41	7.73	0.23	6.37	0.03
Maharastra	0.64	2.37	0.34	1.54	NA
Gujarat	0.88	13.66	1.47	1.44	0.01
Goa	0.72	17.45	0.75	2.86	0.01
Andhra Pradesh	1.11	7.49	0.69	3.97	0.02
Karnataka	0.45	10.73	1.60	2.84	0.04
Tamil Nadu	0.76	0.54	0.62	2.10	0.02
India	1.06	4.76	0.80	2.66	0.03

Source: RBI (2004)—*Handbook of Statistics on State Government Finances*, Mumbai.

higher outlay in the urban sectors, but that has not happened. Further, the investment pattern that has accentuated the duality in India has worked unfavourably for backward states like Bihar and much more favourably for the states with substantial market share and industrial base like Maharastra, Delhi, Punjab, Haryana, Tamil Nadu, Gujarat and Karnataka that have furthered the capitalist growth in India. In this respect, the substantial share of the market of Bengal can be attributed to its dramatic agricultural transformation in the last couple of years in spite of its decline in industrial and trading base over the years.[4] In the Hindi heartland, in no state other than Rajasthan, the proportion of market has outstripped the proportion of its population. Possibly the market strength of even Rajasthan has more to do with its contiguity with Delhi, rather than with the development of the productive forces within the state.[5]

ATTEMPTS OF REFORM IN BIHAR

Fiscal Reform

In contrast to the general impression, Bihar's track record in revenue deficit is not bad as compared to other states. Serious fiscal reform was attempted after the division of the state in 2000 when Bihar lost 96 per cent of the mineral and 78 per cent of the forest resources of the state, and much of economic infrastructure, major industries and technical/training institutions. The state's GSDP, thus, got reduced from Rs 69,764 crores in 1999–2000 to Rs 50,774 crores in 2001–02. The state's own revenue receipt also declined from Rs 4,251 crores in 1999–2000 to Rs 2,606 crores in 2001–02. The 'non-plan revenue expenditure declined from Rs 12,820 crores in 1999–2000 to Rs 10,291.70 crores in 2001–02. This asymmetry in the reduction in revenue receipts and non-plan revenue expenditure has imposed an unbearable burden on the finances of the State' (MOU 2004: 4). The fiscal reform acquired urgency because of the substantial loss of revenue and delay in the division of liabilities. The loss of Rs 1429 crores as tax revenues and Rs 874 crores as non-tax revenue led to an increase in the gross fiscal deficit of the state from Rs 1,348.02 crores (2.51 per cent of GSDP) in 1996–97 to Rs 5,996.05 (8.59 per cent of GSDP) in the year 1999–2000. Apart from the division of the state which took place only in 2000, another cause for the deteriorating fiscal situation of the state has been the fast increase in expenditure in the revenue account during preceding years. The substantial increase in salary, pensions and interest payments led to an increasing proportion of borrowed funds for meeting current expenditures. The rise in revenue expenditure and decline in tax-GSDP ratio along with the fall in non-tax revenue further aggravated the problem. Further, the rise in the size of the debt increased the debt servicing liability of the state and the interest payments as a proportion to GSDP increased from 3.61 per cent in 1996–97 to 5.18 per cent in 2001–02.

The Government of Bihar had signed a Memorandum of Understanding (MOU) with the Government of India on Medium Term Fiscal Reform Programme (MTFRP) on 3 September 2004, 'under which States are required to achieve a single monitorable target of reduction of five percentage points every year, in the ratio of revenue deficit to revenue receipts. The States that subscribe to the programme and achieve the targets envisaged therein are eligible to receive a grant from the incentive fund' (MOU 2004: 6). Though the MOU with the Central government has been signed after the coming to power of the UPA government at the Centre, the deficit management has been going on for a long time. Table 7.5 indicates that the role of the Government of Bihar has been exemplary in matters of reduction of deficit between 2000–01 to 2003–04. Except in the last financial year (2003–04), deficit reduction has always been higher than the planned reduction of five per cent. The deficit was reduced by widening the tax base and revising the tax rates at one end, and 'the revenue expenditure has been compressed through ban on appointment of ad hoc, daily, work-charge and muster-roll workers,' (ibid.: 8) at the other. In 2002–03, tax revenue increased by 19 per cent, recovering lost ground from the first year following bifurcation. During different tenures of Jagannath Mishra as the Chief Minister,[6] thousands of schools and colleges were taken over by the state government. All the lower and upper primary schools which were functioning under the municipality, corporation or the district board, were taken over by the government. After the division of the state, the number of core government employees in Bihãr was nearly 4.51 lakhs. This huge number, even after division, was because of the high number of field posts created in the north and central part of the undivided state. This was due to the fact that the politics of the undivided state was controlled from these parts and creating posts was a major incentive for the political functionaries. In spite of the Mungeri Lall Commission Report and Mandal Commission, the social base of the employees and that of the ruling elite are different. Thus, it was not inconvenient politically to prune the employment flab of the state without drawing much adverse electoral reaction. With the same rigour, about 18 state level public sector enterprises were dismantled[7]. Here too, the non-convergence of social base worked more than the economic logic of reform. However, this helped in pruning the deficit significantly and the deficit is being further managed by keeping the sanctioned post (positions in government organisations for which there are sanctioned resources) vacant. Other than pruning the expenditure, there has not been many authentic attempts at reform of the state finances in Bihar. Tables 7.4(a), 7.4(b) and 7.4(c) indicate further that the expenditure of the state in the departments related to the investment destination has not increased. The outlay on road or industry that is crucial to get investments from outside is extremely meagre. The amount of investment needed to rejuvenate the economy of Bihar is massive.[8] In spite of commitment by the UPA government, the Central government has not given anything yet to Bihar as a separate financial package (CMP 2004). The only alternative left is either domestic mobilisation of resources or investment from outside. Most of the states where economic development has made a breakthrough have a substantial market size as well as an electoral constituency to politically support any reform agenda. Wherever there was a mismatch between the two: market size and reform attempts, there has been electoral destabilisation. In the last two years, several states with their ruling parties known for 'good governance' and 'development' were voted out in the state elections and the succeeding government embraced the earlier policy of reform without any hesitation, notwithstanding instances of extreme 'populism'. However, in Bihar, in contrast, the electoral destabilisation in the assembly was possibly more due to absence of reform rather than due to its presence.

Tax Reforms

One of the first and significant steps in the direction of tax reform by the present Nitish Kumar Government, within one month in office, was slashing of entertainment tax by half. Tax holiday was also announced for revamping the cinema halls and setting up multiplexes in the state. Previously, the Rabri Devi Government, especially after the division of the state, introduced reform, revision and rationalisation in the realm of tax structure. This improved the public finance base of the state. There were several other reforms in the realm of taxation, viz. revision of sales tax, revision and rationalisation of entry tax rates, amendments in the Electricity Duty Act and Rules, provision of advance deduction of tax from the bill of contractors, Brick Kiln dealers to pay tax on compounding basis, abolition of sales tax related incentives to the new industrial units. Bihar was one of the first states to implement VAT. There was not only computerisation of sales tax offices, but also joint check posts of commercial taxes and transport department were established. The tax reform also included revision of stamp duties levi-able under the Indian Stamp Act 1899, amendment to recover loss of revenue on account of registration of property outside the state, amendment in the Indian Partnership Act 1932 to increase the fee payable for registration of partnerships, collection of stamp duty through use of tax meters, etc. The Apartment Act was enacted after prolonged deliberations, which was aimed at substantially increasing the state revenue. A new policy was finalised for the settlement of excise on country liquor and rationalisation of excise duty. The charges for testing vehicular emission for pollution levels at the government and private checking centres and computerisation of the Transport Department on Build Operate Transfer (B.O.T.) basis were also introduced. While the earlier government had revised the road tax rates for all types of vehicles, the present Nitish government is further rationalising the tax structure, e.g., increase in the tax on vehicles temporarily entering the state, increase in the rate of tax payable by dealers and manufacturers of vehicles, introduction of high powered team to check plying of illegal vehicles operating without valid papers, rationalisation of collection of drafts from outside the state, computerised check posts to check vehicles running without proper papers on a B.O.T. basis, revision of land ownership fees and process fees under the Bihar Tenancy Act 1885, higher rate of revenue for commercial use of land, etc. In fact, Bihar has embraced a plethora of reforms with respect to taxation structure that the new regime may probably like to alter so as to give imprint to its philosophical interests (MOU 2004: 10).

Non-Tax Reforms

The strategy of revenue generation was not only limited to taxes, but there was substantial intervention in the non-tax arena as well. The transfer of the management of canal and irrigation system to Water Users Association was primarily aimed at enhancing generation of revenue. Apart from that, there was also an increase in the user charges for technical education, veterinary and hospital services. While revision of higher court fee might forestall litigation, substantial revision of power tariff might act as a dampner for industrial resurgence. However, all possible non–tax efforts were explored to enhance the public finance base of the state (MOU 2004: 12).

Expenditure Reforms

The basic objective of the expenditure reforms strategy of the previous Government in Bihar was to prioritise expenditure in areas like elementary, primary and secondary education, health care, irrigation, power and roads, and to reduce non–productive expenditures. The downsizing of departments was to be done by redeploying the unproductive workforce in more productive sectors. Each department's structure and size was to be reviewed keeping in mind the essential functions it performs. Circulars relating to economy in the use of telephone, vehicles, LTC and contingency expenditure were to be enforced. There was complete ban on ad-hoc appointments, daily wage workers, work-charged staff and muster roll staff. Additional requirements of teachers beyond the present sanctioned posts was to be met by creation of additional posts, which would be filled either by regular teachers or by Panchayat Shiksha Mitras. This has had a salutary effect in keeping the deficit under check. One of the first protest demonstrations, since the takeover of Nitish Kumar, was organised by the Shiksha Mitras for enhancement of salary and regularisation of services. The class position of the present ruling elite will get revealed by the pattern of populist measures and the possible fate of economic reform attempts in Bihar (MOU 2004: 12).

Financial Management Reforms

Lately, some financial management reform has been underway. In this direction, providing a realistic resource framework within which individual departments, specially in education, health, roads, irrigation, power and social security, could plan their sectoral programmes became imperative. After the unveiling of the 'fodder scam', computerisation of treasuries was accorded high priority. Further computerisation of GPF offices, strengthening of data and statistical cell in the finance and planning departments were underway. The technological thrust in the financial management also received further boost in the present dispensation (MOU 2004: 14).

Power Sector Reforms

The Government of Bihar had signed an MOU with the Government of India for power reforms. In pursuance thereof, a State Electricity Regulatory Commission has been established. The implementation of the objectives of APDRP is an important measure in the power sector reform. This strategy will entail reduction of aggregate transmission, distribution and commercial losses of SEBs to around 15 per cent from current levels of 45–55 per cent. The scheme's total outlay, to begin with, has been divided equally between its two components viz. investments and incentives. Over a period of time, the share of investment component will be reduced and the share of the reform-linked incentive component will be raised. To give boost to power sector reform, Nitish Kumar got the National Thermal Power Corporation (NTPC) and Bihar State Electricity Board (BSEB) to sign an MOU for the revival of Kanti and Barauni thermal power stations (Saxena 2005: 3).

Restructuring of PSUs

The state government, after detailed review of the PSUs and their performance, decided to liquidate six of them in the first instance and has filed liquidation petitions in the Court to this effect. Further, on the recommendation of the high-powered committee, the government has also decided to liquidate twelve more PSUs. The state government has also decided to give a one-time relief package to all the permanent and regular employees of these 18 public sector enterprises to be liquidated. Incidentally, there were 88,572 employees in 49 sick PSUs, who were totally dependent on the government for their salaries. These organisations were not generating surplus. There is a severe pressure on the present government to revive the sick and liquidated PSUs which may warrant a thorough review (Saxena 2005: 3).

Budgetary Reforms

There is a substantial change in the way the budget was being presented in the previous government. Separate schedules were attached to the state budget each giving the total expenditure on salaries and allowances on pensions and terminal benefit outflows, and on scheme-wise and sector-wise schedule of direct subsidies. Apart from these, year-wise and department-wise schedules of outstanding guarantees were also attached. The details thus provided, revealed that on account of the reform measures initiated by the state government, the fiscal performance of the state had shown improvement. There had been a marked decline in the revenue deficits of the state, details of which may be obtained in Table 7.5. The state's own revenue also showed a marked increase and reached the same level as at the time when Bihar was undivided. Increase in revenue alongwith compression of expenditure brought about a sharp decline in the revenue deficits as a percentage of total revenue receipts from 34 per cent in 1999–2000 to 13.42 per cent in 2001–02 (Accountant General [A.G.] Figure) making the state eligible for the grant from the Incentive Fund. This example throws light on the state's appreciable performance in medium term fiscal reform designed by the Central government (MOU 2004: 14).

Medium Term Reforms Facility

In pursuance of the recommendations of the 11th Finance Commission, an Incentive Fund meant for the states resorting to fiscal reforms has been set up at the Centre. The release from the Incentive Fund will be based on a single monitorable fiscal objective. Accordingly, each

Table 7.5: Progress under Medium Term Fiscal Reform Programme by Bihar

Year	*Revenue deficit as percentage of revenue receipts target (MTFRP)*	*Revenue deficit as percentage of revenue receipts achieved*
1999–00 (Act)	34.74	34.74
2000–01 (Act)	29.74	20.84
2001–02 (Act)	24.74	13.42
2002–03 (Act)	19.74	11.73
2003–04 (Pre Act)	14.74	11.45
2004–05 (B.E.)	9.74	0.04

Source: MOU 2004.
Note: B.E.—Budget Estimates.

state would need to achieve a minimum improvement of 5 per cent in the revenue deficit/surplus as a proportion of their revenue receipts each year till 2004–05. In order to make the scheme more attractive for the states, the Finance Ministry decided to increase the amount in the kitty from 10,600 crores to about 18,600 crores by adding 4,000 crores of grant funds and 4,000 crores of SLR loans. Bihar has not only improved its tax collections, but also reduced its revenue deficit by an average of 5 per cent a year (see Table 7.5). However, it did not get any assistance under this head in the last two years, but in the current year it may get the arrears too. In all, the size of transfer to Bihar from the Reforms Incentive Fund may be around Rs 400 to Rs 500 crores during the current year (Saxena 2005: 3).

Development Reforms Facility

Under Rashtriya Shram Vikas Yojana an amount of Rs 2500 crore was provided in the Annual Budget 2002–03 towards development reforms facility, but the Government of India did not release any amount during that year. In the year 2003–04, out of three components of the scheme, there was one 'Special Plan for Bihar' for which Rs 500 crore was provided in the Annual Plan of 2003–04. The Planning Commission is thinking of locating central agencies to implement these schemes in sectors like power, rural connectivity and irrigation. The state government has agreed to give full support to this initiative and to the central agencies identified by the Planning Commission with their concurrence. The implementation of projects so identified will be supervised and monitored by the concerned central ministry, which will also be responsible for ensuring the observance of due diligence (adherence to commensurate rules and regulations) with regard to technical and administrative requirements by the Government of Bihar and the implementing agency. The concerned central ministry will also recommend the release of funds to the Planning Commission after assessing the requirements based on the progress of project(s). The Planning Commission will be responsible for the quarterly review of progress of the projects and provide the required funds. Thus, it appears that agencies outside the state government are likely to be used for improvement of infrastructure. 'The perception of Government of India officers who are involved in these projects is that the capability of Bihar's administration is limited, and that they may not be able to deliver the results in time'. Hopefully, hand-holding by the Government of India and implementation by the central undertakings will build up the internal capacity also. The flip side of this aspect is that it might result in greater demoralisation of the state government machinery. With the change in the government in Bihar, the earlier strategy may have to be reoriented. (Saxena 2005: 34).

Externally Assisted Programmes

Bihar is one of the few states where presence of externally assisted projects is practically absent. World Bank made several forays earlier, but it did not get converted into tangible association. With the advent of the present regime, country manager of the World Bank visited Patna and met the Chief Minister and senior officials. It is expected that the external assistance can play a significant role in the development process of backward states like Bihar. The acceleration in the growth rate proposed for the Eleventh Plan cannot take place without tapping the opportunities offered by international investment. However, for Bihar, the state's share in overall externally aided projects of all Indian states in the last three years 1999–02 is only 0.8 per cent and is much low when compared to the share of other backward states such as UP (10.8 per cent) and Orissa (4.8 per cent). It is expected that the present government will be able to attract more funds for the state. (Saxena 2005: 23).

Civil Service Reform

Civil service is a mammoth organisation in Bihar. In the absence of substantial industrialisation or growth of corporate sector, strategy to get absorbed in the civil services has been the principal goal of the elite in Bihar. The edifice of civil service has become more of a threat than an opportunity for the development of Bihar. However, the Fitment Committee Report of 1999 and Fitment Appellate Committee Report of 2000 which resembles a Pay Review Committee, outlined certain steps which could be considered as a civil service reform. Bihar being part of the Zamindari (intermediary) system of land settlement, the revenue records were less developed than in the states with the *ryotwari* system (direct link between the tenant and the state) in southern and western India. There are 38 districts and nine divisions in Bihar and the districts are divided into anchals, that are coterminous with development blocks. The district magistrate (DM) holds the ultimate authority in the district due to which the system of supervision through the Divisional Commissioner and the Board of Revenue is getting undermined. The reforms sweeping other states in administration and economic management seem to have bypassed Bihar. The information on personnel is fragmented across departments. Neither posts have been sanctioned over a period of time nor need-based analysis of staff has been attempted in recent times with reference to functions or schemes or workload or technological improvement. For the first time, the budget of 2003–04 presented information on salary and pension expenditure, broken down into Plan and Non-Plan, departments and major budget heads. The total expenditure on salary and dearness allowance in that financial year was estimated to be Rs 6023 crores, the bulk of which was in Non-Plan, with the balance being predominantly divided between state Plan and centrally sponsored schemes. Wage expenditure represented 41.5 per cent of revenue expenditure or about 180 per cent of own tax revenue in 2003–04. The total number of government employees in undivided Bihar increased steadily from 1961 to 1981. The number nearly doubled during the nine years period from 1972 to 1981, primarily on account of the doubling of intake in Grade 3 and the dramatic increase in the number of teachers in Grade 2 and 3 after the government took over a large number of grant-in-aid schools in the late 1970s. The number also increased due to many illegal appointments, as each project was seen as an opportunity to employ people. Figures of employees obtained from departments and the Treasury vary significantly. The grade–wise figures of sanctioned and working manpower strength for Bihar after bifurcation have been provided in Table 7.6.

Table 7.6: Grade-wise Manpower Strength in Bihar

	2002–03			2003–04		
Grade	*Sanctioned*	*Working*	*% sanctioned*	*Sanctioned*	*Working*	*% sanctioned*
1	4989	3855	77.27	4831	3571	73.92
2	22673	16530	72.91	22815	15737	68.98
3	427888	347529	81.22	425616	339234	79.70
4	117396	94223	80.26	116232	92602	79.67
Total	572950	462137	80.66	569504	451344	79.25

As observed by the Fitment Appellate Committee, the subsistence of the governmental machinery has become its own justification, although the people consider the machinery to be of no use to them. More than 90 per cent of the expenditure in health and education departments is on salaries and pensions. A serious citizens' debate appears to be necessary on whether Bihar can afford the present size of bureaucracy or if government employees should have the same scales as those in Central government with similar promotion benefits, if the resource position results in untimely payment of salaries and delayed promotions. Ironically, in comparison with other states, Bihar is not overstaffed in absolute terms. This appears to be true as government employees on a scale of hundred is 5.6 in Bihar and Karnataka, 7.6 in Andhra Pradesh, 14.6 in Orissa, 11.9 in Rajasthan and 5.4 in UP. The salary expenditure as a percentage of SDP is, however, very high in Bihar at 11.2 as compared to 5.5 in Andhra Pradesh and 4.6 in Karnataka. The percentage would go up if the responsibility for salary expenditure to grant-in-aid institutions is included. The business of government is divided among 48 departments (though the Budget has provided demands for 52 departmental entities including High Court, Legislature, BPSC and the Governor's Secretariat). In terms of manpower strength, secondary and primary education departments account for the largest number followed by home and health departments. The proportion of Grade 3 (or 'C' grade) employees works out to 75 per cent of the total. Delegation of powers to departmental officers are governed by the Rules of Executive Business under Article 166 (3) of the Constitution which, instead of facilitating, obstructs government functioning. Despite the bifurcation of the state, the number of departments have not been reduced. (Sundaram 2003: 3)

Centralisation

Bihar government under the previous regime was highly centralised. All major departments from home to finance were under the Chief Minister, without even a Minister of State to support. Nearly 50 per cent of the budgetary expenditure of the state was routed through the office of the Chief Minister. The personalised system of politics, in the absence of proper cabinet system, tended to resist institutionalisation of the decision-making process. There was a strong resistance to delegation of authority and as a result ministers tended to confine their interest into transfers and establishment matters. The government had taken away a number of powers for recruitment, transfers, purchase and tender and gave it to district officers or heads of departments. Instead of seeking to institute systems to prevent abuse of discretionary powers by individual ministers and to strengthen audit and supervision, the government appeared to have found comfort in reduced risk-taking and collective decision-making over use of public funds or scheme approval. The committee system within the government was poorly managed as the Development Commissioner alone was heading over 100 committees on diverse subjects. The Cabinet Sub-Committee on Economic Affairs, which was set up to deal with major interdepartmental matters was swamped by routine agenda which inhibited its functioning. The system on the whole, did not allow for smooth flow of information on implementation and about local problems that alone should have guided the policy-making process (Sundaram 2003: 12).

Decentralisation

Decentralisation and panchayat election were thrust on Bihar. There was a near show of hostility by the state government in the authentic implementation of decentralisation. Panchayati Raj System did not seem to have been strongly embraced by the then government. The Central government and the Constitution Review Commission had to adversely comment on Bihar's record in the implementation of the 73rd and 74th Constitutional Amendments for democratic decentralisation. However, elections were held to Panchayati Raj Institutions (PRI) in the year 2000 after 23 years. Thanks to the interventions of the High Court and the pressure exerted by the Central government by depriving the state funds from the central ministry for rural development for many years since no elected local bodies existed. After the institution of Panchayati Raj, the High Court has been urging the government through Public Interest Litigation petitions to transfer all the subjects in the 11th Schedule to the PRIs along with commensurate funds and staff but to no avail. It is expected that the new regime in Bihar will restore authenticity to the long awaited democratic decentralisation. (Sundaram 2003: 16)

Further, there are 130 urban agglomerations and 130 towns in Bihar including the major cities (Patna and Gaya). As in the case of PRIs, the process of transfer of subjects listed in the 12th Schedule of the Constitution has not been completed and a number of important areas like water supply and town planning are still handled by functional agencies and city development authorities. Patna blazed a new trail in matters of scientific assessment of property taxes resulting in buoyant revenues for which it received recognition from the UN. Ironically, the measure was not introduced in Patna itself. It is expected that with the Urban Renewal Programme of the Government of India and with the change of regime in the state, urban decentralisation will be introduced seriously.

E-governance

Bihar is late starter in e-governance. There have been isolated departmental initiatives or a few pilot projects but no comprehensive framework for e-governance was developed. It is surprising to note that the use of e-mail for communication across the departments and within the government is limited to littleness because there is an immensely low level of availability of computers because of budgetary constraints. One of the first announcements of the present regime about the large scale initiative to have e-governance, teleconferencing and other modern methods of communication, appears encouraging (Sundaram 2003: 21).

Judicial Reforms

Apart from issues relating to the High Court and the subordinate courts, government litigation is closely linked with administrative reforms on two counts. One is the question of procedural reforms relating to management of litigation, effective monitoring of cases, proper legal defense, appointment of good pleaders and the provision of support and advice to the HODs and Secretaries of the state government. The second issue relates to the need towards addressing systemic causes for recurring petitions to the court for executive inaction, insensitivity to citizen grievances, civil service complaints or payment of admitted dues (committed payment liability of the government). The failure to constitute the administrative tribunal under the Central Administrative Tribunal Act 1985 has meant that the High Court is directly entertaining many service-related cases which include matters of recruitment, regularisation, promotion, transfers, payment of salaries, retirement benefits and punishments in the case of government departments and agencies controlled by them. The highest number of cases relating to all service matters are to do with non-payment of salaries to the employees and non-payment of provident funds and other retirement benefits. The court has also been motivated by the need to ensure the implementation of constitutional provisions relating to the empowerment of elected local bodies. It has assumed the mantle of executive authority in Patna for the shifting of stray cattle, reducing traffic congestion, control of autorickshaws, removal of encroachments, implementation of development plan and the regulated movement of trucks. The third issue is the need to review all the laws and regulations in a comprehensive manner to repeal outdated laws, unify and harmonise laws and regulations and reduce the scope for arbitrary exercise of discretionary provisions. (Sundaram 2003: 23)

Reforms in the Social Sector

Bihar had experienced large scale reform in social sector, mainly mediated through primary education and health. Primary education in Bihar was supported by the World Bank, whereas UNICEF supported the District Primary Education Project (DPEP). The Bihar Education Project (BEP) supported by UNICEF was one of the first large scale donor-supported education programmes in India introduced in the early 1990s in seven districts of the undivided state. In addition to training the teachers, this project developed community groups of Village Education Committees (VECs) to support education at the school level. The BEP was incorporated into the DPEP when it became effective in March 1998. The objectives of the DPEP are to expand access, increase student retention and learning, and improve state and district capacity to manage primary education. The project currently operates in 20 districts of Bihar. Improving service delivery in education and health in Bihar, above all, requires a comprehensive vision for reform which is fully supported by politicians and bureaucrats.

The themes highlighted in the context of the education sector in Bihar, like appropriate financing, administrative reform, strengthening local government and developing public-private partnerships, are also relevant for the health sector. At the same time, the present scenario in the health sector creates challenges specific to this sector alone. It is also useful to look at the models that can be emulated in Bihar—innovative experiments within the state, as well as those undertaken by other states with comparable social and economic indicators. The analysis of health subsidies suggests that better targeting of resources to the poor and disadvantaged will require directing resources in those areas where the poor are likely to derive significant benefit. These include: (i) preventive programmes like immunisation (the proportion of fully immunised children has actually declined to about 10 per cent in recent years); and (ii) primary and community health care facilities. Given that the bulk of current subsidies in Bihar goes to hospital services, it appears that this will only be possible by shifting resource allocation from hospitals to the PHCs. Innovative experiments within Bihar provide useful models for replication on a larger scale, for instance, the experience of Janani—a non-profit society involved in social marketing of birth control through a franchising system. Janani networks a large number of Rural Medical Providers (RMPs) and a smaller number of doctors in a two-tiered franchise structure. The franchisees receive training, advertisement of their clinics and discounted medical supplies in return for a membership fee and a commitment to high quality care and pricing norms. While Janani's commercial principles are sustainable, they do limit the franchisee's ability to reach the poorest of the poor. Subsidising the poor through instruments such as coupons, vouchers or credit, could be explored as possible options. This could be a significant opportunity for public-private partnership, whereby public subsidies are channeled through an existing franchise network (World Bank 2004: 68–74).

Social Context of Reform and Agenda for Change

Techno-Managerial Strategy

It is also necessary to understand the techno-managerial strategy of reform in Bihar. This in turn will help outline the social context of reform and the concomitant agenda for change, in the context of the new regime under Nitish Kumar in Bihar. What was the social base during the time of Laloo Prasad? How can it be different now? In which way will reform in the context of Bihar get accelerated or retarded? Despite the magnitude of problems with the administration in Bihar, it is possible to devise an immediate agenda for change that can bring about perceptible improvement in policy-making, project implementation, service delivery and accountable administration. The question is one of being able to initiate a series of politically acceptable short-term measures to improve decision-making within the secretariat and increase the effectiveness of implementation. The agenda will require sustained support from the central ministries and the Planning Commission as well as flexibility in the use of funds and delivery mechanisms. Some of the key tasks which need immediate attention will be:

(a) procedures involving multiple stages for sanction of new and continuing schemes (barring continuing projects) costing over Rs 25 lakhs and accessing central and state allocations, and improving the effectiveness of public spending for poverty reduction and infrastructure, (b) requirement of approvals from other departments such as information department for printing, personnel and finance department for various matters like scheme approvals, continuation of posts, contingent expenditure, time-bound promotions, etc., (c) dealing with problems of vacancies at operational levels and the secretariat which affect policy making and implementation of schemes and dealing with the urgent issues of recruitment and promotion, after setting up a computerised database, (d) liberating the senior officers for getting attention to policy analysis and evaluation as well as monitoring performance by reducing the time spent on establishment matters, court cases, purchase committees and provision of adequate support for technology inputs, (e) delegation of power for pension, GPF and other routine matters to middle level officers by amendment of rules, (f) two way flow of information to operational levels and strengthening the capacity of District Magistrates (DMs) and Panchayat Raj Institutions (PRIs) at district level, (g) documentation and dissemination of good practices within and outside Bihar, (h) tackling risk aversion and low motivation of officers, (i) addressing issues of citizen interface at various levels and departments of administration and piloting innovations in e-governance and citizen services, (j) demarcating genuinely unproductive expenditure, uneconomic activities (for example, unviable schools), redundant activities (over-staffing or excess regulation), low priority activities and unaffordable policies, (k) focusing on ways to reduce the state's involvement in peripheral, loss-making public undertakings and functions so as to direct its limited financial and administrative resources on core tasks, (l) support efforts to contain the wage bill and anticipate future pension liabilities based on a computerised and dynamic database, (m) articulate the human resource management function and address issues relating to services, internal communication, recruitment, performance management, incentives and sanctions, and training, (n) integrate efforts to converge efforts for poverty reduction and improve service delivery in critical areas such as education, health, power, and rural development and mainstream into the reform agenda advocated by the Central government and the Planning Commission, and (o) initiate efforts to strengthen accountability through greater transparency and public participation in government decision-making, especially at the local levels. The final area will explore the prospects for growth in agriculture and agro-processing, which constitute the state's primary hope for development and the major source of employment for its citizens (Sundaram 2003: 27).

Social Trigger

While the techno-managerial strategy will work out the nuts and bolts of the reform agenda, the innocence of social context often leads to grotesque political consequences. Before contextulising the reform agenda, one needs to comprehend the social base of unbridled rule of Laloo, and his unceremonious ouster. While many of the state based governments (or ruling elite) were ousted on the ground of vigorous reform, Laloo's ouster is attributed to the absence of reform and development agenda. Is development or reform possible in an underdeveloped regime, in the increasing market-centric economy?

In any discussion on reform in the context of Bihar, away from the techno-managerial strategy, it is essential to understand the broad contour of the society in the state. Contrary to general impression, there has been reform attempts in Bihar, specially that which entailed dismantling of the state. Because the class and the social base of the state and the ruling elite were different and dismantling the state suited the then ruling elite, will the current ruling elite resurrect the past and put a stop to dismantling? In any case, anything that happens in a society or economy is attributed to one of the three factors—state, market and civil society. Of course, it could also be a combination of the three, with any one of them initiating it and dominating it. The state (which incorporates institutions, elite and leadership) and its reform attempts will be taken up in the end and discussed in detail. Before that some brief comments about the other two are required. Taking the market first (Table 7.1), as already mentioned earlier, it is extremely small in Bihar and, that too, captive. What people forget is that, if any one of the three potential actors is practically absent, then the burden on the other two obviously increases. In the case of civil society, even a limited familiarity with Indian history of the last 200 years would indicate that emergence of a relatively strong civil society (wherever it has emerged in India) has been always preceded by decades of social movement—anti-Brahmin movement in south and western India, so called renaissance in Bengal and activities of the enlightened princely states. In the case of Bihar, with the failure of the Sepoy mutiny in 1857, in which its participation was substantial, the state was subjected to a series of repressions which crystalised into negative resistance to Westernisation and modernisation. Thus, the civil society in Bihar fostered on resistances did not have anything positive to build itself. Although the small size of the market and the absence of social movement characterise many parts of India, but in the case of Bihar the two phenomena have much deeper roots and have a relatively longer history. As such, for social and economic development, Bihar is left with no other actor than the state itself. As if these two factors were not enough, with one of the longest history of the politics of protest and assertion, starting from 1920's, the state in Bihar exists as a free standing social institution in India. It has no other institution to support and share its burden.

We can possibly discuss the state only during the 1990s. But one principal dimension of the state structure is its 'institutional structure' which is given to us as a historical outcome and what we have today is also what we had almost 100 years ago. The main foundations of this institutional structure are tenurial relations and land distribution within which the 'incentive structure' is indeed embedded. In the Bengal Presidency, of which Bihar was a part, the then Governor General Lord Cornwallis settled intermediaries permanently in 1793, known as *Zamindars,* between the state and the tenant. In the process, the incentive structure for 'production' for the tenant, the main generator of wealth, was aborted; on the contrary, an incentive structure for exploitation by the *Zamindars* got institutionalised which became part of the history of permanent settled area. Thus, the soil of Bengal Presidency with its best natural endowments (abundant ground and river water with alluvial soil) could not become the centre of green revolution. In contrast, in the *Rywotwari* and *Mahalwari* areas, with no intermediaries to poach the surplus, some accumulation was ensured in spite of relatively less fertile land. In the non-permanent settled districts, as comprehensively demonstrated by a study from MIT, Harvard, '25 per cent of area has higher proportion of irrigated area, 45 per cent higher level of fertilizer use and 25 per cent higher proportion of rice under high-yielding varieties. Overall agricultural yields are 16 per cent high, rice yields are 17 per cent higher and wheat yields are 23 per cent higher' (Banerjee and Iyer 2003: 7).The rise of a rich peasant class at least in *Ryotwari* areas has probably something to do with the lack of a stratum of pure rentiers lording over them. The tenants were further protected in large parts of the Rywotwari area with legislation against transfer of land to non-agriculturist that further limited the power of the pure moneylenders over cultivators. This resulted in some rich peasants gradually entering the industrial sector at a later stage. However, Bihar has not been a mute spectator to this social and economic change. There have been protests—freedom movement, peasant movement, socialist movement, communist movement including the still existing radical and extremist movement, euphemistically called Naxalite movement. But, it all converged on the protests that have been observed since the late 1980s. These protests had a strong caste basis since that time and it is basically because the deprived sections in general had a reasonably homogenous caste background.

In a sense, the present phase of the protests had actually started during the 1970s when Karpuri Thakur had become the Chief Minister of Bihar. He had emerged from the socialist movement, which definitely had a class foundation, and he was also from among the backward castes. Before him, there have been some Chief Ministers from among the backward castes, but they were not the true representatives. Their cooption by the traditional elites was more strategic than genuine.

After the assassination of Mrs Indira Gandhi, Congress politics weakened and consequently backward class consolidation resurfaced. Ultimately, in 1990 Laloo Prasad became the Chief Minister of Bihar. What was the condition of the state and the economy at that point requires to be recalled, otherwise the present strategy of the Nitish government will tend to get distorted: (a) Bihar was already a non-performing state with its economic ranking at the bottom. Its fiscal health was very poor. Several factors were responsible for this but the important one was that between 1972 and 1981 (a period of 9 years), the number of government employees increased by 2.73 lakhs (from 2.75 lakhs to 5.48 lakhs). This is in contrast with the increase in the previous decade, between 1961–1972 (a period of 11 years), when the number of employees had increased by 96,000 only (from 1.79 lakh to 2.75 lakh). Obviously, the pressure was too much to bear. Thus, in the next 16 years, increase in the number of employees was even smaller, bare 30.5 thousand. (b) Later, another fiscal blow was the division of the state. This weakened the finance of the State even further. (c) The process of liberalisation started around 1990. By that time the state as an institution had already become very weak. Thus, when liberalisation implied that now efforts of the state should be to facilitate the functioning of the market, the weakness of the state in itself became an impediment to growth. A weak state could not simply facilitate the functioning of the market. (d) Adding insult to injury, against the limited resources and the constraints imposed by liberalisation, the expectations of the people (obviously the socially backward and economically deprived) rose to a new height. Laloo Prasad had started functioning under these circumstances. Laloo Prasad had to politically respond to the above circumstances. Admittedly, he had a charismatic appeal. But many forget to note that much of his political strength arose from certain sections of the people. Initially, they were upper backward classes and Muslims. Later, some sections of the upper backward classes left him. But this loss in mass base was more than compensated by the joining in of large sections of lower backward classes and Dalits. Thus, Laloo Prasad developed a strong class and caste base. His charisma, thus, was an icing on the cake. But then the cake, i.e., his social constituency was more important. What was the profile of his social constituency until recently, before they abandoned him in the 2005 Assembly election? And what was the profile of the political elites before his emergence? These two crucial queries have to be addressed in a comparative framework. The dimensions of this are: (i) Asset/Land: In terms of land endowment, Laloo Prasad's supporters are either landless or marginal or small farmers. Here, we must note that by virtue of doing cultivation for mainly self-consumption, they are not bothered whether market exists or not. But they are bothered about how the village-level state functionaries are tormenting them. As Hobsbawm, the famous historian, currently in Delhi, has put it, peasants are interested in 'working the system... to their minimum disadvantage'. (ii) Caste: For historical reasons, as mentioned, the distribution of population by land and the distribution by caste are parallel to each other. (iii) Cognitive world: The cognitive world of Laloo Prasad's social base was very narrow. In a sense, this is as good as saying their education level was very low. But I prefer to use the concept 'cognitive world' because, for some people, they may be uneducated and yet their cognitive world may not be that narrow (e.g., migrant workers). This cognitive world is important because it is from this world that one derives his or her world vision. In the last 15 years, the democratisation of polity in Bihar has changed the cognitive world of this social segment. They are, unlike the general impression, open to get connected to the world. Nitish will find Bihar now more connected, with much of its insularity aborted. In tracing out the evolution of the political elites in Bihar, it is noticed that the traditional elites who were generally with the Congress were high on land, high on caste, high on education, but had a poor world vision because of the limited size of their cognitive world. Thus, in spite of holding power for long, they could not develop the productive forces in Bihar. The limitation of the traditional elites to develop productive forces was somewhat reversed by a new type of elites in the 1960s and 1970s who were responsible for whatever green revolution had taken place in Bihar. They were what I have referred to as 'vernacular elite'. They could not proceed much at first because of their limited land endowment and second, they did not receive as much support and subsidy from the state as was received by the farmers in Punjab. Alongwith these, there emerged yet another type of elite belonging to the deprived and the backward caste. They had realised by now that they already had the numbers to their advantage. To assert their right even more strongly, what they needed to do was to capture the state. For that, they needed to enter the electoral arena as competitors. And it was not a difficult job for them, since they had been working all these years in electoral politics as political operators of 'traditional' or 'vernacular elites.' So they not only entered the electoral process but also won.

I have preferred to name them as 'cockney elite' not in the pejorative sense, but to indicate their social stratum as one, which is 'subaltern within the subaltern.' Their cognitive world earlier was narrow, lingua franca were local dialects spoken with rustic defiance and they got cultural subsidy (cultural and folk traditions of the particular area were given more salience in political strategy) through folk.

Yet, in the last couple of years, there has been a new paradigm shift. Bihar is possibly one of the first states in the hindi heartland, which has given up its reservation about English language teaching in schools. This was possibly the most important reform that was initiated in Bihar. For the 'cockney elite', capturing of the state was not an end in itself. That it could be utilised for development of productive forces, which could also benefit them, was now within their agenda. The strong political base of Laloo Prasad thus initiated an agenda of reform, specially related to dismantling the state as an institution without encountering much opposition. Reforms agenda, though belated, had entered into the cognitive world of the 'cockney elite' in Bihar. The state was not capable of even performing some of its minimal functions earlier, because of extremely fragile financial position. But at the same time, one could note that it did function when it was serious about its agenda, set either voluntarily or under compulsion. For the former, the example is how the state functioned to prevent any communal unrest. For the latter, as already mentioned earlier, the example is the implementation of Bihar's Medium Term Fiscal Reforms (MTFR) Programme which was aimed at improving the fiscal situation of the state.

The size of the market in Bihar being small in proportion to its population and whatever industrial base it had going, to its truncated portion, the political economy of non-development in Bihar since the 1990s, therefore, actually indicated two things. First, how social issues combined with electoral empowerment can create an unprecedented power structure. Nowhere in the country, other than Bihar, a new social segment in the state could be imagined to rise to the helm of political power through the existing democratic institutions. Second, the threat of a crisis or the problem of governance here seemed to be that this new political mobilisation had not taken up multi-class/caste sub-national agenda of economic development. These developments have helped in a significant manner in freeing the poor from mental enslavement. This feat in itself is a tremendous achievement. 'Cockney' brand of 'assertive' populism, entails abstract values of 'right' and 'dignity' rather than mere material gains (Scott 1985:xv). That is why, he could succeed in dismantling the state as an institution. For the 'vernacular elite' from the propertied strata, however, 'empowerment' was to have a component of material gains, an euphemism for subsidy, which demanded, among other things, good governance. In the absence of an understanding regarding these subtle differences, one often has an erroneous understanding of the phenomenon of development in Bihar. To quote Scott again, 'for Gramsci, the proletariat is more enslaved at the level of ideas.... The historic task of "the party" is, therefore less to lead a revolution than to break the symbolic miasma that blocks revolutionary thought' (Banerjee 2004: 295). Given the class base of supporters of Laloo Prasad and their bare minimum expectations, his reign remained unchallenged until recently, inspite of the failure of the refrigerated wagon to make forays into Delhi. Where Laloo failed, will Nitish succeed? Will the process of reform in Bihar get reversed or accelerated? Who will choreograph the reform—the resurrected traditional elite or the buoyant vernacular elite?

Notes

1. The role of the states was to implement Central government policies without many variations. The Indian Constitution, following the Government of India Act (1935), is famous for dividing the responsibilities between the centre and the states; and there was hardly any occasion when a province took a tangential stand even in the matter of state list.
2. Generally, the sales figure of the CST indicates trade figures of traders or small industrialists, who do not operate through their formal sales network. But, bigger industrial houses or manufacturing concerns, trade their inventory through 'transfer of stock', for saving to pay CST. So these transactions do not get reflected in the market size of the state of the respective industrial location or in the figure of CST.
3. a) Extensive vacancies and an imbalance in the staffing mix in several departments creates capacity constraints for the processing and implementation of projects. Around one-third of Bihar's 533 blocks lack Block Development Officers, generally an important post for project preparation and implementation. Shortages of engineers and DDCs at the Zilla Parishad level is also serious, particularly for Rural Development schemes, for which engineer staff fail to reach even one-third of the staffing norm. Senior staff shortages also result from delays in promotions in several departments, apparently arising from court cases (because of prolonged litigation in the court, many promotions are due). b) 'In the Cabinet meeting of Government of Bihar on August, 25, 2004 it was decided to handover the renovation and strengthening work of the state highways to the central agencies. The state cabinet while approving the proposal also cleared the decks for MOU that will be signed between the state government, center and the central agencies.' (*The Economic Times*, Calcutta, 27 August 2004).
4. Now it is endearing itself to the corporate world bringing the sobriety of 'Country's best Chief Minister, that has inspired business confidence across corporate India' (*The Economic Times*, 20 November 2004) from Azim Premji, Chairman of Wipro and one of Forbes' ten most powerful billionaires in the world. Apart from Premji, even Mukesh Ambani, the powerful CEO of Reliance Industry is going to make his presence felt in the city with massive investment. Calcutta's municipal corporation, run by Trinamool Congress, an NDA outfit, is not playing a less decisive role in creating investment ambiance. It has not only innovated strategies for raising resources, for investment in the water supply system, but also resurrected a heritage cinema hall which got burnt down in a fire accident. It almost competes with the left wing state government in entering the intellectual space of the city, which in turn makes it an attractive destination.
5. In Andhra Pradesh and Madhya Pradesh the duality of the economy was more pronounced than expansion of the market. Over and above, possibly the reform attempts were disproportionate to its market size. However, both the states have created some industrial and trading base, which get reflected through their CST collection.
6. Jagannath Mishra was Chief Minister of Bihar thrice.
7. Memorandum to the Twelfth Finance Commission, Government of Bihar, 2004.
8. To achieve the national SDP growth of 8 per cent per annum, Bihar has to grow at the rate of 15 per cent for the next 15 years. This growth would entail investment of Rs 38,500 crores annually. This was mentioned in the Joint Memorandum to The Twelfth Finance Commission for Bihar by several political parties, business and industrial organisations, and research organisations.

References

Banerjee, Abhijit and Lakshmi Iyer (2003). 'History, Institutions and Economic Performances: The Legacy of Colonial Land Tenure System in India', BREAD Working Paper No. 003, MIT, Depertment of Economics, Cambridge, MA 02142, January.

Banerjee, Mukulika (2004). 'Leadership in West Bengal and Tamil Nadu: Mamta & Jayalalithaa compared', in Rob Jenkins (ed.), *Regional Reflections: Comprising Politics Across India's States*. New Delhi: Oxford University Press.

Byres, Terence J. (1988). 'Charan Singh 1902-87: An Assessment', Reprint, People's Book House, Patna.

Common Minimum Programme of the United Progressive Alliance (2004). Available at www.pmindia.nic.in/cmp.pdf.

Dreze, Jean (2004). 'Employment as a Social Responsibility', *The Hindu*, (Delhi edition), 22 November.

Gupta, Shaibal (1995). 'Nitish Returns to Sicily', *The Hindustan Times*, (Patna edition), 8 February.

Howes, Stephen, Ashok K. Lahiri, and Nicholas Stern (2003). 'Introduction', in Stephen Howes, Ashok K. Lahiri and Nicholas Stern (eds) *State Level Reforms in India—Toward More Effective Government*. Delhi: Macmillan India Ltd.

Hindustan (2004a). 'Mol Ke Mol Biki Bihari Tarkari', (Patna edition), 23 June.

Hindustan (2004b). 'Thanedaron Ko Sabzi Ki Kharidari Ka Jimma', (Patna edition), 24 June.

The Hindustan Times (*HT*) (2004). 'Laloo's Green Flag to "Green van"', 21 June.

Kohli, Atul, Chung Moon and Georg Sorensan (eds) (2004). 'Introduction', in *States, Markets & Just Growth: Development in the Twenty-first-century*. New York and New Delhi: United Nation University Press and Rawat Publications, Jaipur.

Memorandum of Understanding (MOU) of Bihar with Government of India on Medium-Term Fiscal Reform Programme (MTFRD) (2004). Unpublished government document.

North, Douglass C. (1990). *Institutions, Institutional Change & Economic Performance*. London: Cambridge University Press.

Saxena, N.C. (2005). 'Central Financial Transfers to Bihar', World Bank Monograph (unpublished).

Scott, James C. (1985). *Weapons of the Weak: Everyday Forms of Peasant Resistance*. New Haven and London: Yale University Press.

Sundaram, Panchampet (2003). 'Issues in Governance Reform in Bihar', World Bank Monograph (unpublished).

World Bank (2004). 'Bihar: Towards a development strategy', Washington DC: World Bank.

Section III
Social Dimensions

8

Caste, Class and Globalisation: Continuity and Change

K.L. Sharma

INTRODUCTION

Though caste has been questioned from time to time as a holistic system of stratification, however, it has functioned more or less as an encompassing arrangement of social groups (castes and sub-castes). Dynamics and ramifications of caste as a system indicate that it has neither been uniformly rigid and elaborate in different parts of India, nor it has been so with regard to specific caste groups. A scale of 'elaboration' or 'rigidity-fluidity' dimension of caste suggests possibility of change in the system and that too not of the same magnitude. As we know that economic and political considerations have penetrated into the caste system from time immemorial, and therefore, at times this has made the ideology of 'pure' and 'impure' with regard to caste 'weak' and 'upside down' in certain respects. Even though 'individual' is not quite significant and visible in the caste system, but due to onslaught of certain economic and political factors, 'group' as the basis of caste ranking has received a setback, and 'individual' has shown his presence. Such a situation explains the incorporation of class and power into the core of caste system. One can also say that *ritual status* implies power, i.e., higher the rank of a caste, higher would be its corresponding power and vice-versa. Crystallisation of social (caste), economic and political domains calls for a study of change and mobility in the caste system. Our concern is to understand the extent and magnitude (both internal and external factors) of social mobility in the Indian society. We have noticed an increased presence of 'individual' in the patterns of migration, mobility, decision-making, etc.

While analysing the dynamics of social stratification, we would like to locate middle castes and middle classes in contemporary India to see how colonialism, education, social reforms, land reforms, green revolution, adult franchise, etc., have brought about social mobility. Some questions may be posed here: Is there a middle class? Is there a new middle class? What is the nature of clash of interests among different castes and classes? What is the nature of migration from rural to urban? Which are the areas of new spaces for the traditionally deprived people? Is a new social formation in the offing? In the light of these questions we intend to understand the role of 'globalisation' in the transformation of India's social stratification. What is 'globalisation'? How does it affect different social groups (castes and classes)?

Social Stratification

'Social stratification means the differentiation of a given population into hierarchically superposed classes. It is manifested in the existence of upper and lower layers. Its basis and very existence consist in an unequal distribution of rights and privileges, duties and responsibilities, social values and privations, social power and influences among the members of a society. Concrete forms of social stratification are different and numerous' (Sorokin 1959: 11). This conceptualisation by Sorokin applies to the caste system to a great extent. While analysing members of a society economically, politically and occupationally stratified, Sorokin observes, 'A real picture of social stratification in any society is very complex. In order to make its analysis easier, only the most fundamental traits must be taken. Many details must be omitted, and the situation simplified, without, however, disfiguring it' (ibid.: 12). One more statement from Sorokin's classical work, *Social and Cultural Mobility*, is quite relevant here. He writes, 'Any organised social group is always a stratified social body. There has not been and does not exist any permanent social group which is "flat" and in which all members are equal. Unstratified society, with a real equality of its members, is a myth which has never been realised in the history of mankind' (ibid.: 12–13).

How does a society get stratified? What is the main unit/basis of social stratification—individual or group? Take the example of Karl Marx (1888: 12) who pronounces class (group) as the basis of high and low positions. Marx observes, 'The history of all hitherto existing society is the history of class struggles. Freeman and slave, patrician and plebeian, lord and serf, guildmaster and journeyman, in a word, oppressor and oppressed, stood in constant opposition to one another, carried on an uninterrupted, now hidden, now open fight, a fight that each time ended, either in a revolutionary reconstitution of society at large, or in the common ruin of the contending classes.' Thus, the group is the basis of formation of society and it has never been stable. Industrialisation, for example, has transformed the earlier structure into two classes, namely, bourgeoisie and proletariat. No fixed and frozen relation exists between the two because the bourgeoisie constantly revolutionise the instruments of production, and consequently, their relation with society. Though the proletariats are an instrument of production, yet they alone are a revolutionary agent of social change. No significant middle class exists. The lower of the middle class—the small tradespeople, shopkeepers, and retired tradesmen generally the handicrafts men and peasants—all these sink gradually into the proletariat ... (Marx 1988: 12–32). The proletariat is special and essential product of the capitalist society, because it stands face-to-face with the bourgeoisie, and the lower-middle classes do not survive in the fight against the bourgeoisie, and therefore, manufacturer, shopkeeper, artisan, peasant, etc., are not revolutionary but conservative.

A different view is proposed by Max Weber. He observes: 'A class is any group of persons occupying the same "class status"' (1948: 429). A class could be (a) a 'property class', (b) an 'acquisition class', and (c) the 'social class'. Individual is the axis of class. An aggregation of individuals based on common traits may constitute a particular class. Like Marx, Weber also recognises a 'positively privileged property class' and a 'negatively privileged class' ('outcastes/ proletarians'). However, Weber recognises the 'middle classes' more significantly than Marx. Between the two—the upper and the lower classes stand the 'middle' classes. They have all sorts of property or marketable abilities through training. Some of them may be 'acquisition' classes. Entrepreneurs fall in this category. Merchants, shop-owners, industrial and agricultural entrepreneurs, bankers and financiers, members of the 'liberal' professions, and workers with special skills commanding a monopolistic position may constitute the middle classes (ibid.: 424–29).

Caste and Class

We may discuss briefly also about the caste system, and particularly, about the empowered castes with a view to know the role of the Indian state, education and exogenous forces. For a long time, caste has been perceived as an overarching ideological system of status-determination. Two logical queries would be: In what way caste is a normative system? And how is it a system of social relations? Louis Dumont (1970) considers caste more specifically as a special type of inequality as ideas and values are basic to know actual and observable behavior of the people. As such, caste is certainly a means of identity. But then, the question is, can caste not be an interest group? We have discussed earlier (Sharma 1994: 50–78; 1996: 130–46; 2001: 45–74) that caste and class are not polar opposites and antithetical to each other. Caste and class are nearly inseparable as one can be transposed into other by way of appropriating caste-status for class-gains and the latter for social superiority and cultural enhancement. P. Bourdieu's concept of 'capital' (1991: 14–15) is in tune with our understanding of the caste-class nexus. The two refer to intertwined processes along with their internal differentiations. 'The caste-class divide was never as rigid as reported in various writings, and hence Indian society was also not as rigidly structured as depicted in several accounts of the caste system' (Sharma 1998: 1). The 'ideal' and the 'actual' statuses were never the same. The intercaste marriages produced 'mixed castes'. Thus, there were status incongruities in ancient India. 'Production' rather than kinship was given premium in shaping the social formation in olden times. As such neither homo hierarchicus in India nor homo equalis in Europe were the absolute systems of hierarchy and equality.

Contradictions within the caste system and influence of external forces of social change on it rule out the possibility of it being homo hierarchicus. A long history of discontinuities, breakdowns, contradictions and changes in the caste system negate its absolutist, unchanging and holistic nature as perceived by some scholars (Dumont 1970; Srinivas 1998). Both inequality and equality are built into the ideology and practice of the caste system, and both have changed from time to time, providing scope for continuity, change and nexus of the two aspects, namely, 'social' and 'economic' in India's social formation. It is the caste system, which provides priest and contra-priest, inequality and equality, and as such a semblance of the 'unity of opposites'. Because of this confluence, caste has always acquired a new form and functioning in Indian history. It has not been a static (closed) system of social relations. Changes in the caste system have resulted into changes in class structure and power relations. 'The emergence of a new middle class disproportionate to the forces of production and the size of the upper and the lower classes has forged a new nexus between caste, class and power' (Sharma 1998: 2). The principal agricultural castes have given a new direction to the nexus between caste, class and politics. Economic and political power has become a focal theme today of the study of the caste system. Incongruities between caste, class and power clearly hint at the diminution of caste as an all encompassing system and the emergence of a new nexus of caste with economy, polity, migration and religion as interlocking sub-systems. Agrarian relations, economic transactions and service relations have set in a process of role-reversal in the caste system. Several studies have emphasised on the role of migration, education, occupation, political power, style of life, ownership, control and use of land, intercaste feuds, competition and bargaining for higher wages as the new criteria of status-determination and the caste-class nexus. Agrarian relations and green revolution have affected caste, class and land relations by creating divides of gainers and losers.

Today, processes of pauperisation, proletarianisation and downward social mobility on the one hand, and upward mobility and embourgeoisiement on the other, are found simultaneously among different castes and sub-castes. In such a situation, caste cannot be a precise equivalent or opposite of class and vice-versa. Castes are 'discrete' (Gupta 1992: 110), and therefore, they are flexible and segmentary.

The changing nature of nexus between caste and class not only refers to the multifaceted form and substance of social stratification, it also implies that there is considerable departure from the hierarchical model of consensus, resilience, and summation of roles and statuses in the context of caste. Various social segments and families have witnessed visible change in their social standing. Beteille (1966a; 1966b) has observed 'caste free areas' of social activities. We have observed (Sharma 1973: 59–77) 'downward social mobility' and incompatibility of the pollution-purity principle as a result of the entrenchment of the middle and the lower castes in politics and modern jobs. The problems such as exploitation, domination, poverty, alienation, distributive injustice, suppression of human rights, etc., call upon a reconceptualisation of the caste stratification (Sharma 2001). We can say that caste is transforming itself rapidly, finding a place for itself in new and secular domains of social, political and economic life. It gives coherence and meaning to actual social relations and, as such, it is both an actual structure of social relationships and an ideology (Harriss 1982: 42–56). It is realised that today a dominant caste is also a dominant class. However, there is no uniform pattern of caste-class congruence. Assam and Kerala, for example, show correspondence between caste stratification and corresponding class positions. Bihar has a different pattern as it is characterised by the Forwards (the twice-born), the Upper Backwards, the Lower Backwards, the Minorities, the Scheduled Castes and the Scheduled Tribes. West Bengal has considerable radical mobilisation due to an overwhelming presence of the lower castes who are extremely poor. We may like to infer here that the emergence of a well-off peasantry belonging to the intermediate castes, white-collar groups from among the upper castes and enhanced migration and mobility of these groups (country-town nexus), politicisation of caste identity, differentiation among the SCs and the STs, considerable presence of the class of capitalists, entrepreneurs, professionals, white-collar workers, a select group of elites from among the SCs and the STs, etc., are some of the recent actual developments. A continuous change in the caste-class nexus and levels of occupational and social mobility have contributed to the survival of caste as a means of mobilisation for economic and political goals.

In a very forthright manner, Nicholas B. Dirks (2001: 3–18) starts with a statement—'When thinking of India it is hard not to think of caste.' But there is a paradox. Dirks observes: 'Caste defines the core of Indian tradition, and it is seen today as the major threat to Indian modernity' (ibid.: 3). However, according to Dirks, caste is not in fact some unchanged survival of ancient India, not some single system that reflects a core civilisational value, not a basic expression of Indian tradition (ibid.: 5). A more important point in his analysis is that caste is a modern phenomenon, the product of historical encounter between India and Western colonial rule. The British (Risley 1969; Hutton 1946) made 'caste capable of expressing, organising and above all "systematizing" India's diverse forms of social identity, community, and organisation' (Dirks 2001: 5). Thus, colonialism made caste what it is today. Castes were transformed into middle classes as B.B. Misra observes in *The Indian Middle Classes* (1961). Dirks writes, 'Caste itself was seen as a form of colonial civil society in India, which provided an ironic and inferior, anthropological analogue for the colonised world' (2001: 12). Caste served the interests of a private domain at the instance of the British. As such, caste was opposed to the basic premises of individualism, voluntarism and reinforcement of the modern state. Its functioning remained restricted to social and ritual spheres, rather than political domain and individual and social mobilisation. Thus, during colonialism, caste was more pervasive, totalising and uniform than it had ever been before (Dirks 2001: 13). There were multiple identities (other than caste) during the British period. However, caste was always a political phenomenon and a way of classification of people in terms of high and low, superior and inferior, and pure and impure ranks.

Caste has not disappeared despite the claim of having enhanced urbanisation and industrialisation. The Constitutional stroke regarding its annihilation has also been falsified. Challenges to dominant caste(s) have been frustrated. Caste violence occurs frequently. Reservations have generated a lot of violence and animosities. Despite all this, 'caste did not die, it did not fade away, and it could no longer be diagnosed as benign' (Dirks 2001: 16). 'At the same time, caste remains the single most powerful category for reminding the nation of the resilience of poverty, oppression, domination, exclusion, and the social life of privilege' (ibid.). Caste provides the basis for new forms of social mobilisation and progressive politics. At the same time 'it has become the subject of national shame' (ibid.: 17). Today, as in the past, caste is imagined and then appropriated for social and political mobilisation; hence it becomes 'Castes of Mind' as Dirks rightly names his book to explain caste as a political creation. At the empirical level, castes are segments and not organically interlinked units of a holistic system. Dipankar Gupta (2004: 77–8) observes, 'The distinguishing characteristic of the caste order is the discrete character of its constituent units that resist being forced into a single hierarchical frame. As these castes are discrete and semaphore their separation on multiple fronts, caste competition is built in at various levels. It is only by accepting the reality of multiple hierarchies that we can conceptually make room for the existence of caste politics. If one were to go by the traditional understanding of a single hierarchy of purity/pollution, with brahmins at the top, then any evidence of caste conflict should have meant the dissolution of the caste order'. A similar view was articulated by Leach (1960: 1–10) that as soon as castes began to compete with each other, they ceased to be castes. However, castes have not only been competing with each other, they have had intense fights and violence, and never ceased to be castes or transform themselves into antagonistic classes in the Marxian sense.

A caste is in mind, it is a means of identity of the people, and so is class based on certain criteria/indices (Sharma 2001: 45–74). Landowners, landless labourers, traders and moneylenders are not abstractions or conceptual constructions; they are existential structural entities of India's class structure. Both conflict and cooperation refer to life-situations of different classes. One can see interconnectedness of the mode of production and production relations in caste, kinship, family and marriage (Gough 1980: 337–64). Class relations have been seen as the 'domain assumption' in the treatment of caste and kinship in India (Namboodiripad 1979: 329–36; Ranadive 1979: 337–48). Thus, to a large extent, caste and class represent the same structural reality. 'Classes operate within the framework of castes' (Singh 1968: 31) Since the hiatus between the upper and the lower castes is the same as it is between the upper and the lower classes, caste conflicts tantamount to class conflicts. At times, castes function as classes with a view to realise their economic (class) interests. Caste associations serve economic interests of their members.

Middle Class

In French literature, the English middle class corresponds with the bourgeoisie, whereas Marx considers the middle class as petty bourgeoisie. However, Marx and Engels did not make a systematic distinction between the 'old middle class' (of small producers, artisans, independent professional people, farmers and peasants) and the 'new middle class' (of clerical, supervisory and technical workers, teachers, government officials, etc.) (Bottomore et al. 1983: 333). Two other considerations in the understanding of the middle classes are: (i) political orientation—conservative or radical, and (ii) size or growth in numbers. In the wake of the recent global developments and also in the context of Indian society in particular, these two points may be worth discussing.

The middle class is a heterogeneous social layer. Income, property, natural or physical, civil and political inequality are the main criteria for defining commonality of a group of people as a class (middle). Education, standard of living, nature of occupation and wealth determine varying qualities of social prestige and power. The growth of the middle class in England was initially characterised by differentiation of the industrial and commercial functions. Production and trade became distinct activities. Entrepreneurship and management were required vis-à-vis factory production. This heralded a new social order replacing the feudalism in England. Industrial workers emerged from the differentiation of industry and trade. Thus, a number of new groups and categories emerged from the expansion of trade and industry, education and professions (Misra 1961: 1–7). Further, capitalism made the middle classes an integral part of a unitary social order (ibid.: 7). The old trading middle class was called 'middle' because it was situated in between the baronage and the peasant or artisan class (ibid.). The new middle class was not simply the capitalist or the worker; it had a wide range of occupational interests and was bound together by a common style of living and behaviour pattern. The new middle classes stood for certain liberal, democratic values which they expressed in their social and political conduct (ibid.). There was respect for the individual, intellectual freedom and social mobility, liberal individualism and political democracy. Thus, the new middle classes reflected a new standard of values (ibid.).

Before the advent of the British in India, the immobility of caste organisation and the despotism of bureaucracy precluded development of a middle class bourgeois. Even Buddhism, Jainism and Bhakti movements could not reduce the rigidity of the caste system to a noticeable extent (Misra 1961: 9). The caste system remained static because it was related to the law of property, land, economy, inheritance, etc. These were fixed status groups and intermediate categories and there were no middle classes. Under the British rule there was a rise of a middle class in India. Administration, education, business and occupation played a significant role in the emergence of a new middle class. The British-born Indian middle class exhibited in great measure an element of behavioural uniformity and style of life, and similarity in their mode of thinking and social values. The middle classes comprised of the members of the educated professions, namely, government servants and lawyers, college teachers and doctors in general. The merchants and industrialists were a minority and limited to big cities (ibid.: 12–13). Excluding the top people like owners of industries and corporations and top political leaders, and the people at the bottom like small peasants, agricultural workers, all the people such as merchants, agents, proprietors, salaried executives, officers, civil servants, judges, professionals, peasant proprietors, rentiers, shopkeepers and hotel-keepers, rural entrepreneurs, full-time higher education students and senior level school teachers and officials of the local bodies were all included in the middle classes as a result of the British rule in India. A confluence of official hierarchies, professional hierarchies and caste hierarchy was quite evident at the end of the 19th century in most parts of British India. Despite reactionary revivalism, liberal reformism was quite visible in the Indian society. What happened to such a formation after India's Independence?

The middle classes are not necessarily the middle castes. On the contrary, they may be from among the upper castes to a great extent, and only a minority of them may belong to the middle and the lower castes, minorities and the scheduled tribes. As such correspondence between caste and class remains quite unrealistic as well. Broadly speaking, there are three main classes—the bourgeoisie/capitalist class; the middle classes; and the working class. No doubt, all the three are internally differentiated and they cannot also be seen independent of each other. In the first category, we may include the property-owning, entrepreneurial, capitalist-employer. In recent times, capital and industry are controlled by professional salaried management. In developing countries like India, due to the new state formation, middle classes have grown enormously. The material standards of workers have also improved.

After Independence, the middle classes have changed in terms of their size, role and functions mainly due to the nature and character of the Indian State. Ghanshyam Shah (1986: 149–83) reports that the middle class has grown in size disproportionately with economic growth in Gujarat. In the new middle classes, the members are from among the upper and the middle castes on the one hand, and the lower castes on the other. Since the middle classes are a product of both the capitalist development and the state, there would be a conflict situation between the entrenched middle classes and the lower classes aspiring for the status of the middle classes by having access to lucrative white-collar jobs.

Satish Deshpande (1997: 294–318) observes that in the post-independence years, the ideology of development helped to create and sustain a strongly synergistic relationship between the developmental state, a relatively small but significant middle class and the nation. However, in due course of time due to decline in the development ideology, a new middle class emerged with different interests and desires. The new middle class can be characterised by transnationally dominant ideologies of globalisation and structural adjustment. This has resulted into the growth and differentiation of the Indian middle class. The developmental state of the Nehruvian era resulted in swelling the ranks of the middle classes. The era of 'globalisation' has marked a new phase in the growth and differentiation of the middle classes, and this calls for an examination of continuity and change in development, the state and middle classes in India.

However, it is not an easy task to ascertain the exact nature and contents of 'middle class'. In everyday life, the term middle class is referred in a very vague sense. Deshpande (2003: 125–50) observes that it is more of a symbolic term than a factual description. Now the question is: Can we conceptualise 'middle class' based on per capita consumption? What about the assets possessed by people? According to Deshpande, consumer as the basis of the middle class is too narrow to capture the critical multidimensional role of the middle class in post-colonial societies. A couple of observations by him may be useful in the conceptualisation of the middle class. (i) The middle class is the class of the people that articulates the hegemony of the ruling bloc by way of the language of legitimation and mediation between the ruling bloc and other classes. (ii) The middle is most dependent on 'cultural capital' and on the mechanisms for its reproduction. (iii) The middle class specialises in the production and dissemination of ideologies.

Despsite the ideological base and moorings as the strongest point of the Indian middle class, the consumerist thirst of the present middle class cannot be overlooked, and it is a clear indicator of the Indian market. Pavan Kumar Varma (1998: 170–214) talks of three middle classes based on a survey by the National Council of Applied Economic Research (NCAER) in 1994. These are: (i) the Consuming class (150 million people); (ii) the Climbers (275 million); and (iii) the Aspirants (275 million). Besides these middle classes, at the top are the very rich (6 million people). However, Varma does not endorse the consumerist view of the new middle class in India. The middle class in India has a 'history' and its specific characteristic features and relations with the higher and the lower classes. Hence, it is a socio-economic and political phenomenon because mere economic standing does not make a class a middle class. It is a systemic construction and an action entity.

A study of elite formation in India (Navlakha 1989) shows that select positions are usually taken by persons from select social strata. Such a group controls the positions of prestige, power and responsibility. Higher education is under the grip of upper castes, hence it is 'status stabilizer' (Jayaram 1977) or it results in social/cultural reproduction (Bourdieu 1996: 50–1) rather than in an increase in status-rigidities. A couple of studies on lawyers, university teachers, technocrats, scientists and managers have brought about social-structural and organisational aspects of the upper middle class professionals (Sharma 1997: 124–29; Lal 1988). The members of the middle classes have their origins in agriculture and industry (Rudra 1989: 142–50). Besides these, there is the class of intellegentsia, which has co-opted a number of members and both the classes have their social origins in agriculture and industry (ibid.). The intelligentsia include all white-collar workers, all office workers, teachers, writers, journalists, artists and skilled workers, professionals, journalists, politicians, trade union leaders, etc. They do not themselves produce any values in the material product sense of the value. Members of this middle class (intelligentsia) depend for their economic gains on the largesse of the other two ruling classes as well as the state. Middle classes are not direct rulers nor are they economic producers like the industrialists, workers and peasants. At the same time, there is a marked lack of homogeneity among different middle classes (Sharma 1997: 129).

The foregoing account of the middle classes shows that the upper castes constitute the middle classes in Indian society. Widespread political consciousness and democratisation of politics and land reforms and massive irrigation schemes, education and migration have resulted in the attack on the age-old hold of the upper castes on high-status positions. India's Independence has created various contradictions and conflicts of interests between the better off and the deprived sections of Indian society (Kamat 1980: 1673; Das 1984: 1616–19; Prasad 1979: 1955–58; and 1980: 215–19). The entire gamut of social change and mobility centres around caste, class and state (power). Social change could be gauged in terms of gain and loss between groups of people, and by both persistence and emergence of tensions, contradictions and conflicts (Sharma 1998: 159). For example, in Bihar, the middle castes have registered a stiff opposition to the upper castes and have further legitimised their meteoric rise in the class and power hierarchies leading to rapid decline of the persisting 'semi-feudalism'. Caste-based mobilisation by the middle castes in favour of the policy of reservation of jobs has further sharpened and intensified the class contradictions. Capitalist transformation in agriculture in Tamil Nadu, for example, has created a middle class, though caste and kinship have blocked the process of change to reach at the top level. To some extent the process of modernisation needs to be viewed in relation to caste, family and village community.

No doubt, 'new status groups' or 'new castes' (Beteille 1969) have emerged due to role-differentiation and occupational diversification which can be characterised by both upward and downward social mobility (Sharma 1973). Such a situation of differentiation and diversification has arisen due to interpenetration of caste into class and vice-versa and also due to change in the perception of caste which can be characterised by 'micro-ideology and micro-utopia' (Kolenda 1989: 1831–38) and functioning of varna-ideology merely as a social practice rather than an effectual praxis (Franco, Chand and Sarvar 1989: 2601–12). K.L. Sharma (1997: 161) observes: 'Social mobility in the caste system is evident in the ever increasing violations of the traditional criteria of status, namely, hereditary occupations, *Jajmani* obligations, observance of certain rituals, and in the acceptance of modern secular occupations, education, migration and positions of power in formal political bodies. At times, competition between different castes accentuates into conflicts and violence.' I.P. Desai (1984: 1106–16), in the wake of the problems arising out of the Mandal Commission (1978–80), recognises type of society, role of political power and social mobility movements as significant factors to understand social and educational backwardness and does not consider these as an offshoot of the ascribed status of a community/collectivity. Desai observes that today contractual relationships and performance matter a lot in the occupational field. Caste plays a minor role in it. However, this view is contradicted by G. Shah (1985: 132–36) by way of persistence of caste consciousness and ineffectiveness of the state in the annihilation of caste system. Immobility generates contradictions and tensions; and such a situation brings about mobility, hence dilution in the rigidities of the caste system. Today, we are talking of the scheduled caste and the tribal elites and the *Kulaks* among the upper backward castes.

The state in India has consciously encouraged participation of the backward sections of the society in the body polity and economy. Equality and participation are positively correlated. From social participation of a cross-section of society comes out equality and genuine citizenship. 'Equality of outcome' is very difficult to achieve and to sustain over any length of time. Bryan S. Turner (1986: 120) observers, 'The historical origins of equality are bound up with the preconditions for the development of rational capitalism—the occidental city, Roman law, the system of monetary exchange, administration by officials and a this-worldly religious ethic. Equality requires equity in terms of the delivery of a service and the achievement of desirable standards of efficiency and reliability requires bureaucracy' (ibid.: 121). Turner follows strictly the Weberian approach on rational development of capitalism as a sure means of equality. Without reaching a certain level of capitalist development, equality cannot be achieved in Indian society. However, Turner is right in his observation that 'equality emerges out of the active and conscious struggle of social groups to achieve social participation through citizenship rights' (ibid.: 123).

Earlier, I have observed (Sharma 2001: 61) that intercaste and intracaste relations are no more the basis of caste hierarchy, division of labour, and asymmetrical power relations. Today, people identify themselves as very rich, rich, well-off, not-so-poor and poor. In a different sense, they perceive themselves as 'powerful' and 'weak' families or as 'superior' and 'inferior' people. And yet in another sense, people identify themselves as engaged in lucrative and prestigious jobs, and in middle and lower level occupations. Thus, economic status, esteem and power are clearly the underlying criteria in the current evaluative expressions. Today, people prefer to have equal etiquette and equal rights. Intercaste relations based on the traditional *jajmani* system have become rarest of the rare. Intercaste marriages are no longer a taboo. Such a trend signifies violation of the rules of marriage based on caste endogamy and clan exogamy. Caste is increasingly becoming a matter of interpretation rather than a pre-given substantialisation. It refers to purposive rationality, and therefore, provides a description, and an explanation of the pathologies of modern polity and economy. Occasional caste outbursts and ostracisations on the basis of the so-called violations of caste ethics may not be taken as an actual pattern of intercaste and intracaste relations. Intercaste relations are no more the bedrock of the caste system. Family and individual have largely replaced caste in everyday life. Caste is becoming a desideratum, a state of mind, a plastic and malleable institution. There is no more caste hypersymbolisation to express caste differences and typifications.

Despite the process of delegitimisation of the 'essential' of caste, the sporadic appearance of caste-based decisions, articulation of religion and metaphysical interpretations of caste and its divinity (preordained and creation of God) pose a serious challenge to the secularised understanding of social reality. Historically speaking, politico-economic interpretations of caste indicate its significance as the system of class exploitation, social distance and rivalry, an instrument of power and social injustice. Clustering of castes in the form of categories for political mobilisation, employment and resources have also been there with a view to question the supremacy of the superior castes. In everyday life, caste has become quite feeble. Summation of statuses at the levels of individual and family implies weakening of the caste system and strengtheing of the extra-caste considerations in Indian society.

Because of the incorporation of the economic and political considerations into the caste system, social mobility has become somewhat easy. Development in the post-independence era has brought about a substantial middle class in India which dominates the power structure of the society. Yogendra Singh (1993: 11–21) states that the Indian middle classes are a very articulate, active and powerful segment of our society. Expansion of market and trade, information networking and media exposure of the people, expansion of services and strengthening of the integrative impulses selectively are some of the economic, cultural and political consequences of the strong new middle class in India. At least four points may be noted as reported by Singh with regard to the role of the new middle classes: (i) structural cleavages in its composition; (ii) a lack of harmony with the national ideology/social change; (iii) dominance of the upper and middle castes among the middle classes; and (iv) creation of cleavages between the upper middle and the lower caste groups within the reserved categories.

Further, Singh states that the middle classes tend to have a mind-set, which decries values of liberalism, social justice, and principles of sharing or sacrifice. The middle class is rapidly taking to consumerism and short-run utilisation values. Such a situation creates conflict of values and expectations and misdirected radicalism alongwith ethical and social opportunism. In Singh's view, Indian society is faced with a situation of double crisis—one of success and the other of failure. No doubt, there is an ascendancy of a new middle class, and it implies both social and economic change and resilience. The middle class strengthens market, trade and media and provides a huge base of skilled manpower. But this is negated by their self-centered ideological moorings and narrow social base. This leads to a situation of double crisis—crisis of success and crisis of failures.

Globalisation and the Indian Society

Let us now see how 'globalisation' is impinging upon the Indian society in general, and with regard to specific segments and sections, in particular. However, before we map out the impact of globalisation, it is necessary to define this concept, which is still somewhat hazy and ad hoc. In the Indian context, the concepts of Westernisation, modernisation, development, etc., are being sidelined by the concept of 'globalisation' since the 1990s. In fact, with the increasing internationalisation of trade and investment in the developing countries, the developed and the developing countries have come to be regarded as superior and inferior entities in today's situation. The process of globalisation goes beyond transnationalisation or internationalisation of capital. It is a profound reorganisation of manufacturing, trade and services within a globally encompassing system. Globalisation, thus, refers to mega corporations and transnational corporations (TNCs) which operate worldwide (Martinussen 1997: 119–22). Besides accomplishment of an economy globally, globalisation refers to globalising knowledge and global consciousness based on its historical and social context. To restrict the concept to rapid harmonisation of the world in terms of the power and influence of the transnational corporations is only one side of this reality. The other side refers to destruction of diversity and marginalisation of democratic rights, culture, environment, etc., by way of external implosion. Thus, according to Robbie Robertson (2003: 3–13) 'globalisation is more than just McWorld or Westernisation'. He observes, 'It is about human intercommunications that have assumed global proportions and transformed themselves' (ibid.: 3). No doubt, globalisation is a modern strategy of power; it is to be seen also in terms of its historical and social depths. Robertson talks of 'three waves of globalisation', namely, the globalisation of regional trade, industrialisation, and the new world order after 1945. The three waves cover a span of nearly five hundred years. In a way, this applies to the Indian situation as well. The first wave was the pre-British period, dominated by the East India Company, the second may refer to the British rule, and the third naturally would be the post-independence period. All the three periods imply epochal structural changes characterised by internal dynamics and external influences. Trading groups and white-collar workers were the creation of the first two waves. The third wave partly transformed the earlier groups and partly created new groups in terms of India as a newly independent nation. Robertson puts more emphasis on 'human interconnectiveness' in the discussion about the three waves of globalisation and its historical and social dimensions. Another way to look at the concept of globalisation is freedom of investment, production, supply and sale without any constraints whatsoever. Such a conception, if actualised, may lead to a ruthless dominance of the strong MNCs over the people of the developing countries.

Globalisation is a process that changes sites and levels of economic decision-making. Christian Comeliau (2002: 96–108), while analysing 'the contradictions of globalisation' observes that it (globalisation) brings new players onto the scene, and transofrms the relationship of forces among those present in it. Three points are important today in the globalisation of economy: concentration of power in a small number of 'multinational' and 'transnational' corporations and their national branches; emergence of a small number of international public organisations at global and regional levels; and a significant change in the place and role of national public authorities. The new power relations with unequal power of decision-making are an obvious result of globalisation.

Pulapre Balakrishnan (2003: 3166–72) considers globalisaton as a policy, process and as justice in an interconnected manner. In the context of India, keeping in view these general features of globalisation, Balakrishnan observes that the economic constraints that bind its economy are very likely internal ones rather than anything external. 'The current bout of globalisation is unlikely to affect her fortunes dramatically either way' (ibid.: 3171). Poverty, health and education have continued to improve in the 1990s a period that has not witnessed either 'unprecedented improvement' or 'widespread impoverishment'. Some segments of economy have integrated with the rest of the world and some cannot be affected adversely because most Indians have either very low incomes or very low skills to be affected by globalisation either way (ibid.). Since integration of the possession of low incomes and low skills with the world economy is not possible, adverse effects are simply not there. The Report of the World Commission on the Social Dimension of Globalisation insists on conducting social dialogues within a democratic framework, at the local, national and international levels, to create a 'fair globalisation' that is inclusive (Kannan 2004). The Commission calls for 'fair globalisation' that will 'create opportunities for all'. Emphasis is on ethical, economic and social dimensions of globalisation, hence a strong plea for human development.

A Marxist critique of globalisation can be found in Samir Amin's recent work (Harshe 2002: 1407–12). Rajen Harshe, in his review of Amin's seminal work, looks at globalisation as an off-shoot of capitalism and modernity. Marxism, capitalism and globalisation have been seen as inextricably interrelated developments. While tracing the history of the world capitalist system (1945–90), according to Harsh, Amin looks at globalisation as a fresh crisis and a challenge in the management of the world capitalist system. Three limitations may be noted in this process: (i) a lack of evolution of compatible institutions beyond nation states to effect global transactions;(ii) a failure to take the newly industrialising countries of Asia and Latin America (including India) along with the developed ('global') countries; and (iii) absence of the process of competitive industrialisation. Further, with continuing strong 'ethnic complexities' and 'ontology of nation state' and hegemonic capitalism of USA, Western Europe and Japan, globalisation remains a new form of monopoly and dominance in the hands of the countries of the first world.

Recently D.L. Sheth (2004: 45–58) and others (Banerjee 2004: 89–93; Dubey 2004: 59–73; Kumar 2004: 114–16; Mayaram 2004: 80–88; Menon 2004: 100–04; Mukherji 2004: 109–13; Nandy 2004: 94–99; Nigam 2004: 72–79; Roy Chowdhury 2004: 105–08; Sundaram 2004: 64–71) in a series of 11 articles have discussed different aspects of globalisation. In a nutshell, globalisation has created 'new politics with old dilemmas'. Opposition to globalisation has resulted in micro-movements with a view to check the onslaught on the interests of farmers, women, artisans and poor sections of Indian society. This has raised a new discourse on democracy, beyond the conventional institutions of elections and political parties. Participatory democracy is being reinvented through such a discourse of politics and micro-movements, challenging globalisation as a new hegemonic development. Transnational activities are touching almost all aspects of India's social fabric, including religion, media, migration, economy, polity, women, labour, family, community, etc. India is confronted with the dilemma of joining the global race on the one hand, and to retain its national distinctive character on the other. Besides this, the differential nature of gains and loses of the globalisation process for the nation as a whole and for specific socio-economic entities in particular cannot be overlooked. But 'localisation' or insulation of a nation from the global order is no way as it would obstruct modernisation of economy and migration and mobility of the people. How does localism benefit the poor? Or how does globalisation harm the people at the bottom? It depends upon the strength of the indigenous economy in providing employment and security to the members of a given country, and the nature of globalisation may also affect the poor, but not necessarily, and may affect the middle classes alone.

To understand globalisation in the Indian context, we may have to know clearly the concepts such as 'individual', 'development', 'freedom', 'opportunities', 'market', 'state', etc., as formulated by Amartya Sen (2000). Sen looks for the 'social' behind all human endeavours. The concept of 'social opportunity' proposed by him becomes relevant for us as it covers a wide range of societal dimension having implications for Indian polity, economy and culture. Development is freedom, and freedom is social opportunity, and it is constrained by social arrangements. Thus, freedom is 'social' and 'unfreedom' is inequality. The removal of unfreedom is constitutive of development. Effective social arrangements alone can ensure freedom leading to development. Sen talks of 'substantive freedoms'. Is globalisation weakening the social arrangements? What happens to the marginalised groups due to globalisation? Does globalisation result in reproduction of the old middle classes and continuation of the dominance of the upper and the upper middle castes?

Bihar, Uttar Pradesh, Gujarat, Maharashtra, etc., have witnessed 'caste wars' which tantamount to 'class wars' between the landless and the landed people. 'Attacks' and 'counterattacks' have become quite frequent in Bihar in particular. Susan Bayly (1999: 355–59) observes that 'caste war'/violence has tended to become a conflict between urban centres and the rural hinterlands as many students and factory workers are drawn into such a situation. She observes, 'Such outbreaks are not then to be seen as a reversion to the "feudal" or "traditional" past. "Modern" institutions, especially the courts, the universities and the mass media, have figured prominently in the so-called caste feud phenomena' (ibid.: 355). The anti-Mandal agitation in the wake of 27 per cent reservation in jobs for the OBCs was geared by the urban middle class youth and students who normally looked for government jobs, which even today provide security and social status to the incumbents. Caste divides among students and staff have become a common feature in colleges and universities in India. Even hostels are dominated by students of specific castes/sub-castes.

Since the 1970s, the English-speaking intelligentsia have watched the growth and diversification of the Indian middle classes with considerable alarm (Bayly 1999: 360). This particular class of people was engaged in government jobs, professions and middle-level entrepreneurship. However, with the expansion of trade and industry and the commercialisation of agriculture, new aspirants for the jobs, cornered by the old middle class, have come up to claim their shares in professions and other white-collar jobs. Reservations have also added to the aspirations and claims of the formerly deprived groups. However, the gap remains unbridged between the upper and the middle castes or between the traditional middle classes and the newly aspiring groups of people for white-collar jobs, because the old middle classes have been looking for new pastures and possibilities in the wake of globalisation. The newly aspiring groups at this juncture are not in a position to compete with the traditionally privileged groups. More or less this was the case a few decades ago when the lower castes tried to move up by way of sanskritisation and the upper castes opted to desanskritise their cultural pantheon and decided to take up new and secular jobs and practices. A similar situation prevails today. Globalisation calls for new adjustments and alterations in our society and culture. The intensity of the hiatus between the upper and the lower social segments would remain despite very basic changes in economy and social milieu. This is how resilience of Indian society becomes a perpetual focal point.

Concluding Remarks

Indian society is characterised by a semblance of tradition and modernity, continuity and change, having differentiated effects on individual, family and group. Hence, no uniform pattern of change and its impact on different social units is noticed. The pre-British period had witnessed large-scale transformation as a result of the agrarian policy and administrative structuring. The British created a new class structure to serve its colonial interests and along with it a reconceptualisation of caste and intercaste relations. Constitutional provisions, five year plans, adult franchise, reservation policy, social movements have brought about a new consciousness and transformation of the pre-independence society and culture.

At any given epochal phase, no complete overhauling of the structure of Indian society has occurred. Part-continuity and part-change have characterised the Indian society. Such resilience is peculiar to it. The upper castes might have partly lost their traditional high status after independence, but at the same time, they remained as the main middle classes for quite sometime. Since, for some time, new middle classes from among the middle and lower castes have been showing their presence challenging the continuing middle classes in their new reincarnation, the latter are busy in search of greener pastures in India and abroad. Initially, when a challenge was thrown up to the upper castes living in the villages by the politically upcoming middle and lower castes, the former moved out of their villages in significant numbers to settle down in towns and cities. Today, they are either looking for those avenues in India which are not accessible to the upcoming mobile groups and individuals, or they are moving out of India. Rajesh Kochhar (2004: 20) rightly observes, 'Globalisation has prevented Indian upper castes from accepting a diminished role and status consistent with their actual numbers. Aspirations of an Indian middle class that revels in emulating the west are costing India dear and glorifying trivia in an unprecedented fashion.'

A sort of 'cultural lag' persists between the formerly privileged middle class and the new class of people aspiring for middle class status. Globalisation has created a new 'space', which is taken by the entrenched middle class, which is in an advantageous position. The 'space' vacated by this class is occupied by the aspiring class. The trajectory of the class structure demonstrates such dynamics all over the world. However, one has to see the class of people who get adversely affected or who remain stagnant due to global/local factors of social change. The question is: What is 'just globalisation'? How does it help or does not help the poor, the peasants, the artisans, the labourers, the petty shopkeepers and women? Primordial structures in India have not obstructed the processes of social change and globalisation. Adaptive capability of Indian society is evident in its continuity and change even in face of both external and internal threats.

References

Balakrishnan, Pulapre (2003). 'Globalisation, Growth and Justice', *Economic and Political Weekly*, 38(30).

Bayly, Susan (1999). *Caste, Society and Politics in India from the Eighteenth Century to the Modern Age*. Cambridge: Cambridge University Press.

Beteille, Andre (1966a). *Caste, Class and Power*. Bombay: Oxford University Press.

——— (1966b). 'Class and Open Social Stratification in India', *European Journal of Sociology*, Vol. 7.

——— (1969). *Castes: Old and New*. Bombay: Asia Publishing House.

Bottomore, Tom, Lawrence Harris, V.G. Kiernan and Ralph Miliband (eds) (1983). *A Dictionary of Marxist Thought*. Oxford: Basil Blackwell Ltd.

Bourdieu, Pierre (1991). *Language and Symbolic Power*. Cambridge: Polity Press.

——— (1996). *The State Nobility*. Cambridge: Polity Press.

Comeliav, Christian (2002). *The Impasse of Modernity*. London: Zed Books.

Das, A.N. (1984). 'Caste in Itself, Caste for Itself: Social Articulation in Bihar', *Economic and Political Weekly*, 19(37): 1616–19, 15 September.

Desai, I.P. (1984). 'Western Educated Elites and Social Change in India', *Economic and Political Weekly*, (19)15: 1106–16, 14 July.

Deshpande, Satish (1997). 'From Development to Adjustment: Economic Ideologies, the Middle Class and 50 Years of Independence', *Review of Development and Change*, 2(2): 294–318, July–December.

——— (2003). *Contemporary India: A Sociological View*. New Delhi: Penguin Books.

Dirks, Nicholas B. (2001). *Castes of Mind*. Princeton: Princeton University Press.

Dumont, Louis (1970). *Homo Hierarchicus—The Caste System and Its Implications*. London: Weidenfeld and Nicholson.

Franco F., Sherry Chand and V. Sarvar. (1989). 'Ideology as Social Practice: The Functioning of Varna', *Economic and Political Weekly*, 24(47): 2601–12, 25 November.

Gough, E. Kathleen (1980). 'Modes of Production in Southern India', *Economic and Political Weekly*, 15(5–7), Annual Number, 337–64, February.

Gupta, Dipankar (1992). 'Continuous Hierarchies and Discrete Castes', in Dipankar Gupta (ed.), *Social Stratification*. Delhi: Oxford University Press.

——— (2004). 'Caste Is Not Race: But, Let's Go to the UN Forum Anyway', and 'Caste, Race, Politics', in Sukhadeo Thorat and Umakant (eds), *Caste, Race and Discrimination*. Jaipur and New Delhi: Rawat Publications.

Harshe, Rajen (2002). 'Marxism, Capitalism, Globalisation', *Economic and Political Weekly*, 37(15). (This is a review article on Samir Amin's book—*Capitalism in the Age of Globalisation: The Management of Contemporary Society*. London: Zed Books).

Harriss, John (1982). *Capitalism and Peasant Farming*. Delhi: Oxford University Press.

Hutton, J.H. (1946). *Caste in India*. Oxford: Oxford University Press.

Jayaram, N. (1977). 'Higher Education as a Status-Stabliser: Students in Bangalore', *Contributions to Indian Sociology* (New Series), 2(1): 169–91.

Kamat, A.R. (1980). 'Politico-economic Development in Maharashtra: A Review of the Post-Independence Period', *Economic And Political Weekly*, 15(39 & 40): 1669–75, 4 October.

Kannan, K.P. (2004). 'For a Fair Globalisation', *Economic and Political Weekly*, 39(38). (A brief account of the *Report of the World Commission on Social Dimension of Globalisation* is given in this note by Kannan).

Kochhar, Rajesh (2004). 'Denationalised Middle Class: Global Escape from Mandal', *Economic and Political Weekly*, 39(1): 20, 3 January.

Kolenda, P. (1989). 'Micro-ideology and Micro-utopia in Khalapur: Changes in the Discourse on Caste Over Thirty Years', *Economic and Political Weekly*, 24(32): 1831–38, 12 August.

Lal, S.K. (ed.) (1988). *Readings in the Sociology of Professions*. Delhi: Gian Publishing House.

Leach, Edmund R. (1960). 'Introduction: What Should We Mean By Caste', in Edmund R. Leach (ed.), *Aspects of Caste in South India, Ceylon and North-West Pakistan*. Cambridge: Cambridge University Press.

Marx, Karl (1888). *Manifesto of the Communist Party*. Chicago: Charles H. Kess.

Martinussen, John (1997). *Society, State and Market—A Guide to Competing Theories of Development*. London: Zed Books Ltd.

Misra, B.B. (1961). *The Indian Middle Classes—Their Growth in Modern Times*. Delhi: Oxford University Press.

Namboodiripad, E.M.S. (1979). 'Caste Conflicts versus Growing Unity of Popular Democratic Forces', *Economic and Political Weekly*, 14(7, 8), Annual Number, 329–36, February.

Navlakha, Suren (1989). *Elite and Social Change: A Study of Elite Formation in India*. New Delhi: Sage Publications.

Prasad, Pradhan H. (1979). 'Caste and Class in Bihar', *Economic and Political Weekly*, 14(7 & 8): 481–84, February.

——— (1980). 'Rising Middle Peasantry in North India', *Economic and Political Weekly*, 15(4).

Ranadive, B.T. (1979). 'Caste, Class and Property Relations', *Economic and Political Weekly*, 14(7 & 8), Annual Number, 337–48, February.

Risley, H.H. (1969). *The Peoples of India*. Delhi: Orient Books (2nd edn).

Robertson, Robbie (2003). *The Three Waves of Globalization: a History of a Developing Global Consciousness*. London: Zed Books Ltd.

Rudra, Ashok (1989). 'Emergence of the Intelligentsia as a Ruling Class in India', *Economic and Political Weekly*, 24(3): 142–50, 21 January.

Shah, Ghanshyam (1986). 'Social Stratification among the Scheduled Tribes in the Bharuch and Panch Mahals Districts of Gujarat', in S.C. Malik (ed.), *Determinants of Social Status in India*. Shimla: Indian Institute of Advanced Study and Delhi: Motilal Banarasidas.

——— (1985). 'Caste, Class and Reservation', *Economic and Political Weekly*, 20(3): 132–36, 19 January.

Sen, Amartya (2000). *Development as Freedom*. New Delhi: Oxford University Press.

Sharma, K.L. (1973). 'Downward Social Mobility: Some Observations', *Sociological Bulletin*, 22(1): 59–73.

——— (1994). *Social Stratification and Mobility*. Jaipur and New Delhi: Rawat Publications.

——— (1996). 'Conceptualisation of Caste-Class Nexus as an Alternative to Caste-Class Dichotomy', in A.R. Momin (ed.), *The legacy of G.S. Ghurye—A Centennial Festschrift*. Bombay: Popular Prakashan.

——— (1997). *Social Stratification in India: Issues and Themes*. New Delhi: Sage Publications.

——— (1998). *Caste, Feudalism and Peasantry: The Social Formation of Shekhawati*. New Delhi: Manohar.

——— (2001). *Reconceptualising Caste, Class and Tribe*. Jaipur and Delhi: Rawat Publications.

Sheth, D.L. (2004). 'Globalisation and New Politics of Micro-Movements', *Economic and Political Weekly*, 39(1): 45–58, 3 January. (Other special articles in this number are by Abhay Kumar Dubey, Ravi Sundram, Aditya Nigam, Shail Mayaram, Madhulika Banerjee, Ashis Nandy, Nivedita Menon, Supriya RoyChowdhury, Rahul Mukherji and Vivek Kumar).

Singh, Yogendra (1968). 'Caste and Class: Some Aspects of Continuity and Change', *Sociological Bulletin*, 17(2): 165–86.

Singh, Yogendra (1993). *Social Change in India: Crisis and Resilience*. New Delhi: Har Anand Publications.
Sorokin, Pitirim A. (1959). *Social and Cultural Mobility*. New York: The Free Press.
Srinivas, M.N. (1998). *Village, Caste, Gender and Method—Essays in Indian Social Anthropology*. New Delhi: Oxford University Press.
Turner, Bryan S. (1986). *Equality*. New York: Tavistock Publications.
Varma, Pavan, K. (1998). *The Great Indian Middle Class*. New Delhi: Penguin Books Pvt. Ltd.
Weber, Max (1948). *From Max Weber: Essays in Sociology*. (trans., edited and with an Introduction by H.H. Gerth and C. Wright Mills). London: Routledge and Kegan Paul Ltd.

9

Globalisation and Agriculture: 'Crises' of Farming in Contemporary Punjab

Surinder S. Jodhka

Introduction

The sudden spurt in cases of suicides by small and marginal farmers in different parts of India over the last couple of years has created a sense of unprecedented crisis in Indian agriculture. The fact that this has happened simultaneously in different regions of India—from Karnataka and Andhra Pradesh to Maharashtra and Punjab—has understandably made social scientists, activists, and policy makers wonder about the causes and connection that such a phenomenon may have with the wider processes of change operating at the national/global levels. At another level, this sense of crisis has brought agriculture back to the centrestage of Indian social science discourse once again. Though they differ in their emphasis, a large majority of scholars have tended to attribute this crisis directly to the policies of economic reforms that foregrounded the urban middle classes and industry at the cost of rural poor and agricultural sector of the economy. Even the state agencies have responded to the crisis with a similar understanding.

While it might at times serve some useful political or even academic purpose to talk about the existing state of affairs in terms of crisis, such a language could also foil any recognition of the processes of social and economic change being experienced on ground, desirable or undesirable. It is precisely this that I wish to attempt in this chapter, viz. looking at the socio-economic changes that have come about in rural Punjab and how we could best conceptualise the existing state of affairs of agriculture in Punjab.

The Background

Located on the northwest border of India, Punjab is a rather small state occupying less than two per cent of the total geographical area inhabiting a little more than two per cent of the total population of the country. Bengal and Punjab were the only two provinces that were partitioned when the formation of independent nation states of India and Pakistan was announced by the colonial rulers in 1947. Punjab thus, became a border-state, located in the 'periphery' of India, not only geographically, but also socially and culturally. Ever since its reorganisation in 1966, Punjab has been one of the few regions of the country where Hindus, who constitute more than 80 per cent of India's population, have been a minority.

Notwithstanding its peripheral location, Punjab has always been an important region in the political and cultural imagination of the nation. As mentioned above, until recently the state was viewed as the most dynamic and progressive in the country, particularly for its successes in the agrarian sector. The green revolution was successful in other parts of India as well, but it was Punjab that it primarily came to be identified with.

The available statistics on various indicators of agricultural growth speak for themselves. Of all the states of India, Punjab's growth rate was the highest during 1960s to the middle of 1980s in agriculture. Annual rate of increase in production of food grains during the period 1961–62 to 1985–86 for the state was more than double than that for the country as a whole. The percentage of high yielding variety (HYV) of seeds in the total area under food grains in Punjab was as high as 73 per cent in 1974–75 (all India 31 per cent) and 95 per cent in 1983–85 (all India 54 per cent). According to one estimate, of all the tractors in India, one-third are owned by farmers in Punjab (Singh 2005: 31). While Punjab had 17,459 tractors per hundred thousand holdings, the all India figure was only 714. The same holds true for most other indicators (Kohli and Singh 1997). These achievements have also been very widely recognised. The opening lines of the recent World Bank report on the state, for example, summarises Punjab's achievements quite well:

> Punjab is India's most prosperous and developed state with the lowest poverty rate. At the end of the 1990s, more than 94 per cent of Punjab's citizens were above the poverty line, 70 per cent were literate, 94 per cent of the six year olds were enrolled in primary schools, 72 per cent of children under twelve months were immunised, 99 per cent of households had access to safe drinking water, and the average life expectancy of its citizen was 68 years. The remarkable development record of Punjab can also be inferred from the fact that it has already achieved, or is well on track to achieve, most of the Millennium Development Goals (MDGs). According to India's National Human Development Report (2001), Punjab was ranked second only to Kerala in terms of the overall level of human development among the major Indian states. Most citizens of Punjab have thus already achieved a level of socio-economic status that the majority of Indian citizens are unlikely to experience in their lifetime (World Bank 2004: 3).

Apart from the prosperity that the success of green revolution in the 1960s and 1970s brought to the people of Punjab, it also played a very important role in solving the immense problem of food scarcity in the country. The state rightly came to be known as the food basket of India. The official website of the state government proudly claims that 'Punjab produces 22 per cent of the country's wheat (12.7 million tons), 9 per cent of rice (6.8 million tons) and 24 per cent of cotton (0.3 million tons). It contributes 60 to 70 per cent of wheat and 40 to 50 per cent of rice to the central pool'.[1]

The discourse of green revolution also changed the politico-cultural dynamics of the state. It was not only to the new agrarian technologies and the high yielding varieties of seeds that the success of green revolution was attributed. Credit was also given to the enterprising rugged farmers of the region and their hard work. Their love for land and the high values they attached to the practice of self-cultivation (*khudkasht*) played an important role in making the green revolution a success story in the region, much before it took roots in other parts of India.

The local dominant agrarian caste, the *Jats*, have particularly been known for the pride they take in their rural identity. A sociologist working in a village of the Doaba region during the early 1980s had reported, 'the Jat might be employed as a school teacher, or serve in military but he saw his primary role as that of an agriculturalist; his connection with land was what he held most dear and what identified him' (Kaur 1986: 233). Another anthropologist similarly writes about the contempt that the *Jats* had for city life. They despised 'the townsman as lacking in physical bravery' and were viewed them as 'gasping, greedy and lacking in dignity' (Pettigrew 1992: 169).

As it happened in other parts of the country, the success of green revolution and the introduction of universal adult franchise brought the locally dominant castes to the centre stage of regional/state politics. This process was perhaps more intense in states like Punjab and Haryana where the agrarian life style came to be the norm. The triumph of agrarianism not only gave the agrarian elite political power at the local and state level, but also had important implications for the existing social identities. For example, though the land owning *Jats* had always been an important element of the Sikh community, it was after the green revolution that the Sikh image came to be identified with the Jats (Gupta 1996; Pettigrew 1995). And, perhaps more importantly, despite its urbanisation and industrialisation being above the national average, Punjab came to be popularly known as a land of prosperous agriculturists.

The decade of 1980s was a critical period in contemporary Indian history. Punjab witnessed a powerful ethnic movement during this period. The movement for Khalistan, a separate Sikh nation, generated a sense of 'crisis', which was felt much beyond Punjab (Saberwal 1987). Though Sikh militancy declined during the early 1990s, it had far reaching consequences for the society and economy of Punjab.

Further, effects of the so-called 'Punjab crisis' were not confined to the region alone. The 'new social movements' that came up around the same time in different parts of the subcontinent, though very different in their contents, also had several things in common with the crisis in Punjab. The 'new' mobilisations by women, farmers, Dalits, tribals and ethnicities all questioned the wisdom of state-directed development, the 'Nehruvian agenda' of social transformation and modernisation. Coupled with other changes at the global and national level, the decade of the 1980s saw an overall erosion of the developmental state. As Das puts it:

> The goals of rational organization of life, the scientific management of society, modernization and development, to which great energies had been devoted in the sixties and early seventies, now seem like signposts to cities that are abandoned and empty (Das 1990: 1).

While the 1980s was, in a sense, a creative period for Indian society, when many fundamental assumptions around which the post-colonial Indian nation was being built were questioned (Jodhka 2001b), for Punjab and for the Sikhs it was a traumatic phase. Fifteen long years of militancy and the manner in which the Indian State handled the 'Punjab crisis' not only caused bloodshed and suffering, it also quite fundamentally altered the popular image of the region. From a region (Jodhka 2001a) known for its economic vibrancy and progress, Punjab began to be seen as a 'crisis ridden state', a region with serious problems of law and order and political unrest, and therefore, not suitable for safe investments.

Interestingly, despite all problems, even during the 1980s the agrarian economy of Punjab continued to progress. The income of the primary sector of the state economy grew at an average of 5 per cent per annum while the corresponding figure for India as a whole was around 3 per cent.[2] The real implications of the crisis were to be felt in the following decade, during the 1990s, when the economic priorities at the national level witnessed a major shift.

Globalisation and Indian Agriculture

As discussed above, 1980s and 1990s were important turning points in the history of contemporary India. It was perhaps for the first time in the post-independence period that there was a general feeling of unease and doubt about the paradigm of development planning that the Indian state had embarked upon after its independence from colonial rule. There had been criticisms of the policies and programmes that the first democratic government of independent India had initiated under the leadership of Jawaharlal Nehru earlier also, but they emanated mostly from conflicting ideological positions of different leaders or political formations. The strikingly new feature in the 1980s was that, unlike before, the challenge this time came from 'below', from those who were supposed to benefit from development, or whom the independent Indian state had promised a better life.

In the following decade, the 1990s, the Indian state embarked upon a new framework of economic development. Pressed hard by the compulsion of a changing global economy and rising import bills following the 'first' Gulf War, the Government of India initiated a process of economic reforms. Though initially intended to deal with the immediate challenge of 'balance of payment', the reforms turned out to be the beginning of a new phase in the economic history of India. The collapse of the Soviet Union and end of the Cold War around the same time revived the confidence of advocates of free market economy. Breakthroughs in telecommunication technology and the increasing reach of capital to virtually every nook and corner of the world ushered in a totally different phase in globalisation.

These changes also initiated certain new trends in social sciences. The 'old' modernist theoretical perspectives gave way to a variety of 'post-modernist' ways of imagining the world. Not that everyone in social sciences quickly converted to these 'new ways of looking at things', yet their presence was felt everywhere. The language of development discourses and politics of social change witnessed many shifts. From class analyses, the focus moved to questions of culture, from revolution to empowerment, from politics to governance, from production to consumption.

Though it may indeed appear paradoxical, but historically speaking, the rise of 'new social movements' in India and the trends that appeared in the following decade, liberalisation/globalisation, followed by the ascendance of a variety of post-modernist perspectives in the social science academy, all seemed to converge at some level with the idea of development that the new economic policies advocated. The connection between the rise of new paradigms in social sciences and the emergence of 'new' social movements was not entirely accidental. They did seem to support each other. They also seemed to agree in their criticisms of the modern state, and invariably projected it as a villain. They all seemed to also emphasise on a greater role for civil society institutions, which in effect meant opening up spaces in the sphere of development for non-governmental organisations (NGOs). This kind of ideological shift, of course, suited the post-liberalisation/globalisation state well.

These shifts have had diverse implications for different categories of Indian population. For sections of the urban middle classes and the rich, the new economic policies have proved very rewarding. The NGO movement has also acquired a certain degree of respectability and strength. Questions of human rights, caste, gender, and ecology/environment have come to occupy the centre stage of social agenda in India and the world over, and can no longer be ignored by the State. However, these shifts have also marginalised certain 'old questions', questions that continue to be of critical significance, and have consequences for large number of Indian people.

The most obvious issue in this category is the marginalisation of the rural people in general, and of those dependent on agriculture in particular.

It is not only ideologically that agriculture experienced marginalisation in the popular imaginations of the Indian people over the last two decades; its share in the national income has also declined considerably. Though a large majority of Indians continue to live in the countryside, the share of agriculture to the national income has come down to less than a quarter. The growth rates in the agricultural sector have also been much slower than other sectors of the economy.

Declining significance of agriculture, one would think, is quite 'natural', and perhaps a desirable process. With the development of industry and modern servicing sectors, it has happened everywhere in the world. However, there is something quite unique about the Indian experience. Unlike other regions of the world, marginalisation of agriculture in the Indian economy is not being accompanied by a similar degree of shift of population to non-agricultural employment. Given that India is a democratic country, such a reality becomes even more challenging.

Liberalisation and the Punjab Economy

Though liberalisation and globalisation were important turning points in the recent economic history of India, the 'crisis' of Punjab agriculture, as mentioned above, was already evident by early 1980s, and had become a political issue in the state. Acknowledging that all was not well with the state of affairs in Punjab agriculture, the state government in 1985 appointed a committee under the chairmanship of S.S. Johal, an agronomist, to look into the problems of the agrarian sector.

In the report submitted in 1986, the Johal Committee expressed concern about stagnating productivity levels and deteriorating environment due to the cropping pattern dominated by paddy-wheat rotation. The Committee recommended that if agriculture in Punjab was to be made sustainable, the farmers will have to be encouraged to diversify cropping pattern, switching over from high-volume and low-value crops to low-volume and high-value crops. However, given the overall political atmosphere in the state at that time, no concrete steps could be taken to implement the report.

Introduction of liberalisation and globalisation during the early 1990s further increased pressure on the agrarian economy. The 'new' economic policy advocated withdrawal of the state from economic sphere, leaving it to the logic of market forces. While it might be a good thing for the industry to be allowed to freely import the latest technology from abroad or have a competitive atmosphere, leaving the agricultural sector to the vagaries of free market could prove disastrous. Small landholders cultivate most of the land in India and they often have to borrow from various sources for investments in the cultivation of cash crops. The cycle of agricultural production is such that virtually the entire farm yield comes to the market simultaneously. In a completely free and open market, the indebted small cultivator would obviously find it hard to bargain with the mighty trader.[3] The support price regime for food grain crops had been a great help to the farmers.

Notwithstanding the shift in economic policies, the agrarian lobby was able to prevail and the support price regime was not withdrawn. However, procurement agencies became lackluster and began to show lethargy in procuring crops from farmers. With the extension of green revolution to other parts of India, the demand for food grains from Punjab also declined. Thus, even when the support price regime continued, the Central government no longer raised the support prices much in the subsequent years.

This was most visible during the paddy procurement season of the year 2000. There had been a bumper crop of paddy in the state with no natural calamities like untimely rains or floods. But when the crop was brought to the *mandi*s (marketing centres) the farmers were surprised to find that procurement agencies were not willing to buy their grains at the minimum support price declared by the Central government. The officials claimed that they could not buy the paddy because it was of inferior quality. The FCI (Food Corporation of India) Chief went to the extent of saying that as much as 80 per cent of the Punjab paddy was spoilt—a claim that had no scientific basis. Indeed, the FCI officials rarely conducted any tests while rejecting a particular lot of paddy even when they were provided with the kits to carry out such tests.[4]

Interestingly, private traders and rice millers were quite willing to buy the same paddy, but at a price much lower than the official support price, which would have hardly met the farmers' costs for production of the crop. In the given situation, many farmers eventually sold their paddy to traders. The traders paid them Rs 400 to Rs 450 per quintal for the 'super fine' variety of paddy against the official support price of Rs. 550. For the common variety of paddy, traders paid them Rs 350 to Rs 400 per quintal against the official support price of Rs 510.[5] Some traders reportedly sold the same paddy to official agencies at the minimum support price a few weeks later.

Many farmers, however, chose to wait with their grains in the *mandis* for the official agencies, in some cases, for over two weeks. Local newspapers during the month of October 2000 were splashed with pictures of paddy piled up in the *mandis* and farmers sleeping over them. 'The grain was everywhere' and *mandis* were overflowing with heaps of paddy. Paddy was being downloaded wherever the farmers could find room—on roads, in school grounds, in public parks[6]. The farmers were obviously depressed and angry, perhaps more depressed than angry! As a newspaper report states:

> Though the farmer's anger is coming to a boil, his attitude towards the government officials is, surprisingly, the very reverse. With folded hands, he pleads with them to lift his produce, at times virtually falling at their feet to grant him a 'remunerative' rate. A telling symbol of the vice-like grip that the market binds him in.[7]

Farmers were at the mercy of officials! 'It is blood and toil for six months and we cannot afford to annoy the officials. The money we earn during these days will provide for our family during the next six months as well as help us purchase fertilisers for the forthcoming wheat crop',[8] a farmer in the Khanna Mandi, Asia's biggest grain market, told Bajinder Pal Singh, a newspaper reporter. However, not all of them could wait or bear the humiliation. There were several reports in the front pages of local newspapers during the month of October 2000 of the small and marginal farmers taking the extreme step of committing suicide out of frustration and humiliation.

Indebtedness and Suicides

Marginalisation of agriculture has had many far reaching implications for the farming population of the region and elsewhere. There has been a general stagnation of agricultural sector over the last decade or so. The available analyses showed that by early 1990s, paddy and wheat had already reached peak level of productivity in Punjab (Government of Punjab 2004b: 39). According to the *Economic Survey of Punjab 2003–04*, the primary sector of Punjab economy registered a negative growth at the rate of minus 2.38 per cent over the preceding year (2002–03). This stagnation of agriculture has been evident all through the decade of 1990s. As is shown in Table 9.1, while agriculture grew at the rate of 4.87 per cent during the decade of 1980s and 3.18 per cent from 1966–67 to 1979–80, during the 1990s this declined to mere 0.37 per cent.

The share of agriculture sector to the gross state domestic product also declined significantly from 33.06 per cent in 1993–94 to 24.43 per cent in 2002–03 (Government of Punjab 2007b: 45). More focused studies carried out by economists also show that over the last decade or so, cash expenditure on crop production has been steadily rising for different crops. The compound growth rate of cash expenditure between 1974–75 and 1991–92 was nearly 9 per cent for wheat and more than 11 per cent for rice, two of the main crops grown by Punjab farmers (Shergill 1998: 3).

Table 9.1: Growth Rates in Different Sectors of Punjab Economy

Period	*Industry (in %)*	*Agriculture (in %)*	*Livestock (in %)*
1966–67 to 1979–80	8.22	3.18	6.10
1980–81 to 1990–91	9.12	4.87	5.70
1991–91 to 1998–99	8.49	0.37	5.10

Source: Government of Punjab Human Development Report 2004—Punjab, (2004b: 50).

Much of this growth in expenditure has been a direct result of the increasing use of commercial inputs by the farmers of Punjab, such as pesticides, fertilisers and seeds. Since all these inputs are purchased with cash, farmers of Punjab have to invariably invest a substantial amount of cash in every crop. Given that their own resources are limited, they invariably have to borrow, either directly from the market, or via the commission agents through whom they sell the yields of their farm. In some cases, the situation has become so desperate that local farmers have put boards outside their villages stating 'the village is on sale'[9].

Some recent studies carried out by economists in different parts of the state provide us with abundant evidence of growing economic hardships of the cultivators of Punjab. A study carried out by H.S. Shergill during the middle of 1990s found that as many as 86 per cent of the respondent farmers had to routinely borrow from various credit agencies for short-term investment on crops. Nearly 27 per cent of all farmers borrowed for capital investments in farm machinery.

In terms of dependence on borrowed money, the smaller landholders were clearly in a much weaker position than bigger landholders. Though the bigger farmers also frequently borrowed for short and long-term investments on land, many of them also had savings. The average per acre outstanding debt of the small farmers worked out to be Rs 3,396 as against Rs 1,398 and Rs 1,599 for the medium and big farmers, respectively. As discussed below, other studies, carried out more recently, have found the levels of indebtedness much higher.

It is rather interesting to note that despite official efforts towards making institutional credit available to the cultivators, a significant proportion of short term borrowings (61.31 per cent) by all categories of farmers were from the commission agents in grain markets, the *arhtias*. As many as 63.85 per cent farmers regularly borrowed from them. The primary co-operative credit societies came next from where 51.31 per cent of the farmers borrowed for their short-term credit needs. Only 8.85 per cent of the farmers borrowed from commercial banks for short-term investments in land (Shergill 1998).

Another study by a team led by Sucha Singh Gill found that the indebtedness of the surveyed farmers who had committed suicide in the Malwa sub-region of Punjab ranged between Rs 10,000 and Rs 6.5 lakh and the average outstanding debt was Rs 1.25 lakh per farmer household.[10]

More recently, Singh et al. (2005) in their study of six villages selected from different sub-regions of the state found that as many as 78.40 per cent of all the farm households in Punjab were under debt. Only those with large holdings were relatively free from debts. Average outstanding debt of their sample population worked out to be as high as Rs 92, 394 of which nearly

58 per cent had been borrowed from non-institutional sources. The extent and the nature of debt ofcourse varied across different categories of farmers. While the absolute amount of outstanding debt with the marginal and small farmers was lesser (Rs 17,465 and Rs 43,598 respectively), the share of non-institutional debt in their outstanding debt was much higher (74 and 70 per cent, respectively).

This study also confirmed the overall domination of *arhtias* in the local credit market. They accounted for as much as 50.51 per cent of all the outstanding debt with their respondent farmers. Some other studies, such as by Gill (2000) and Kaur (2002) also found *arhtias* being the major source of credit for farmers of Punjab. There are obvious reasons for *arhtias* being so dominant in the local credit markets. The available institutional credit was simply not enough. The *arhatias* fulfilled the gap in availability of credit from institutional sources and the total demand for credit in rural Punjab (Gill 2004). Their credit also involved lesser paper work and other bureaucratic hassles.

Singh et al. (2005) in their study also looked at the purpose of borrowing. Money was borrowed for both 'productive' (41 per cent) and 'unproductive' (59 per cent) purposes. Though all categories of farmers borrowed heavily for 'social' needs, the share of 'unproductive' borrowings was highest amongst marginal farmers (71 per cent) and comparatively lesser amongst large farmers (48 per cent). Nearly half of the money borrowed for 'unproductive' purposes was spent on marriages and other social functions.

The cost of informal credit is almost always higher than that of the institutional credit. The *arhtias* typically charge a monthly interest of 2 to 3 per cent. Further, as was underlined by the classical literature on agrarian social structure in India (Bhardwaj 1974; Bhaduri 1984; Bardhan and Rudra 1978), informal credit invariably comes with other demands and pressures, i.e., the interlocking of credit with the product market. Though the context of contemporary Punjab agriculture is no longer semi-feudal in any sense of the term, the informal credit market is invariably tied to the product market. An indebted farmer not only has to compulsively produce for the market but also has to sell his produce to/through the *arhatia* to whom he is indebted. Anita Gill's study found as many as 84 per cent of the sample households in Patiala district and 51 per cent in Amritsar district being interlinked borrowers (Gill 2004: 3746). It may be useful to quote from her study:

> On the whole... informal lenders have survived despite all proclaimed policy measures. Their guise has changed to a lender, whose principal activity is not money lending. Rather, credit contracts are now interlinked with contracts in other markets. In the study area, it is the sale of crop (i.e., output) which is interlinked with credit and the arhtiya has emerged as the main informal lender. By shifting to a better collateral (crop, instead of land), these lenders have not only strengthened their bargaining power in their principal activity, but are also able to exploit the borrowers to the hilt by charging exorbitant rates of interest. And yet, borrowers are forced to turn to them because formal credit is not only inadequate, availing it is also a cumbersome process, involves ownership of land explicitly or implicitly, and a sizeable class of cultivators cannot offer much land for loans. A lower rate of interest in formal market, then, is hardly any incentive (Gill, A 2004: 3748).

As has happened in some other parts of India, Punjab too experienced an increase in cases of suicides by farmers and landless labourers during the decade of 1990s. The available literature tends to point to a clear link between the increasing economic hardships of the rural people, particularly the smaller farmers and landless labourers, and the growing numbers of suicides.

According to an internal report prepared by the Department of Agriculture of the Punjab Government (Government of Punjab 2004a) in 2004, though the phenomenon of farmers' suicides started sometime during the 1980s, it witnessed a sudden increase during the 1990s. The situation became alarming when in one year, i.e., 1997, as many as 418 cases of suicides were reported from rural Punjab. The report identified a total of 2116 cases of reported suicides since mid-1980s, and recognised that 'these figures were only of reported acts and many must have gone unrecorded' (ibid.). Further, it underlines some interesting facts about these suicides. They were mostly concentrated in the Malwa districts of Sangrur, Bhatinda, Ferozepur, Mansa and Faridkot. More than 70 per cent of those who killed themselves were small/marginal farmers or landless labourers. In most cases, agriculture was their only source of livelihood. A large majority of them were engaged in cultivation of wheat and paddy crops (65 per cent) or in wheat and cotton (20 per cent). More than 70 per cent of them came from Jat caste, and with the exception of one, they were all males, of a relatively younger age group.

The report also recognised that because of the declining growth rates, agriculture was no longer profitable, and the cultivators had no alternative sources of employment available. This scenario led to rising debts. However, in some cases, conspicuous consumption and drug addiction were also important factors that led to chronic indebtedness of those who committed suicide.

Another study conducted by Institute of Development and Communication (IDC) also pointed to a sudden increase in cases of suicides in Punjab. The number of suicides committed in Punjab experienced a sharp rise from the year 1992–93. During this period, suicides in Punjab increased by a staggering 51.97 per cent, while the comparable figure for the country as a whole was only 5.11 per cent. In the years 1993–94, the increase was 14 per cent in Punjab as against 5.88 per cent for the country. While there was a decline in the reported cases of suicides at the all-India level, the state of Punjab once again reported an increase of 57 per cent in 1994–95. The IDC report also recognised the fact that there was always a possibility of underreporting of suicides (IDC 1998).

Further, this study also pointed to the suicides being concentrated in certain pockets of the state. The district most prone in Punjab has been Sangrur from where as many as 22.39 per cent of all the suicides were reported that occurred during 1988–97. Another study reported that within Sangrur also, it was from certain blocks that most of the cases were reported. There were 12 specific villages in Lehragaga, Andana and Barnala blocks of the Sangrur district where most of the suicides occurred (Iyer and Manick 2000).

Though the IDC study recognised the presence of a link between indebtedness and suicides, the explanations offered for the indebtedness of those who committed suicide is at variance from the official report and some other studies. According to the IDC study, the contemporary crisis of the Punjab agriculture emanated from: a) limitations of the green revolution and lack of inner dynamism to build up forward and backward inter-sectoral linkages; b) decline in the size of operational holdings and fragmentation of land as well as pauperisation of small and marginal farmers; c) decline in the growth rate of productivity; and d) increase in input costs and a corresponding fall in income of the small and marginal farmers.

Inferring from Shergill's work, IDC study also pointed to the fact that small and marginal farmers had a much higher share of debt. However, it did not give much weight to indebtedness *per se* as being the main factor that explained the increase in suicides. Of the causes identified by the IDC study, indebtedness came at number three. Only 41.50 per cent of those who committed suicide were indebted. The corresponding figure for the 'general sample' was 71.40 per cent. The fact that 'only 6 per cent of the suicide victims had to sell land under the burden of debt' (IDC 1998: 69) implies, according to the IDC study, that the debt burden was not particularly severe. It also suggested that 'social factors' were much more determining while explaining the rural suicides in contemporary Punjab. The most important factor was 'family discord' followed by 'alcohol and illicit drug use'. Even indebtedness in most cases was 'socially induced'. It may be worthwhile to quote from the study:

> ... greater proportion of the debt of the small and marginal farmers originated from loans taken for non-productive purposes.... a large amount of debt is socially induced among these sections. Sixty eight per cent of the suicide victims' families have a debt on them because of unproductive expenditure as compared to 20 per cent of general households.
> ... A number of suicides were noticed among those for whom the use of credit for conspicuous consumption had aggravated the stress situation (ibid.: 36–37).

In contrast to the IDC study, Iyer and Manick (2000) treat the crisis of the agrarian economy and the growing indebtedness of farmers as the foremost cause of increase in suicides in the rural Punjab. They make a crucial distinction between the 'causative' and 'precipitant' factors while explaining these suicides. While the latter could be social and psychological, the former, in most cases, were economic (primarily indebtedness). According to them, the latter are the ones that produce those social conditions under which an individual begins to feel insecure and helpless.

In their sample, nearly 79 per cent of those who committed suicides came from poor families—mostly marginalised farmers or landless labourers. Only around six per cent were free from debts and most of them had borrowed money from informal sources, generally from the *arhtias*. In some cases, drug addiction and marital disputes also became causative factors, but these were not as critical to them as they were for the IDC study. Similarly, though indebtedness was a crucial and determining factor, by itself it could not be a sufficient cause for committing suicide. In most cases, it was the loss of honour and constant experience of humiliation in the hands of lenders that seemed to have 'precipitated' them to take such an extreme step.

Explaining the Crisis of Agriculture

As mentioned above, one of the major implications of the shift in economic priorities during the early 1990s was a near complete marginalisation of the rural society and agrarian economy in the popular discourses in India. However, the sudden spurt in suicides by farmers in different parts of the country has brought agriculture back to the public arena. Academics, activists, and policy makers are all talking about agriculture once again. However, this time it is not being talked about in the manner in which it was during the early decades after Independence, when the farmer was presented as a food-giver, selfless and hard working, a symbol of national pride. Unfortunately, it is in the context of an unprecedented crisis of the agrarian sector, reflecting itself in seemingly unending reports of suicides by farmers, mostly from regions that had experienced agricultural development during the decades of 1960s and 1970s that agriculture is being talked about in India today.

Apart from public outcry on the subject, some scholars have also been looking into analysing this phenomenon. Though overlapping significantly in their orientation and arguments, we can identify broadly four different sets of perspectives in the current writings on the crisis of agriculture.

(*i*) First and foremost is, what could be described as, 'the thesis of neglect'. According to this line of argument, the crisis of agriculture is a direct offshoot of the shift in priorities during the early 1990s. Growing obsession with the so-called 'new economy', information technology, media and the urban consumers led to a complete marginalisation of the 'rural' and agrarian sector. The policies of economic liberalisation, according to this perspective, also required the state to open-up all sectors of the Indian economy to global market. Following this line of argument Chandrasekhar and Ghosh write:

> Public agricultural extension services have all but disappeared, leaving farmers to the mercy of private dealers of seed and other inputs such as fertiliser and pesticides who function without adequate regulation, creating problems of wrong crop choices, excessively high input prices, spurious inputs and extortion. Public crop marketing services have also declined in spread and scope, and marketing margins imposed by private traders have therefore increased. All this happened over a period when farmers were actively encouraged to shift to cash crops, away from subsistence crops which involved less monetised inputs and could ensure at least consumption survival of peasant households (Chandrasekhar and Ghosh 2004).

This neglect of agriculture and rural economy has affected not only the farming communities but also the landless labourers who, because of the crisis in agriculture, are finding it much more difficult to secure employment on viable wage. Commenting on this process, Jayati Ghosh writes:

> The complete collapse of rural incomes or job opportunities has created an almost unprecedented situation of desperation among the landless, who rely exclusively on wage labour to survive. Some of this problem originates further back, in the inadequate development of non-agricultural work opportunities in most of rural India. This was directly related to the decline in public expenditure on rural development, which had adverse multiplier effects on rural non-agricultural economic activity

in general. More recently, farm-related activities such as dairy have been hit by the decline of cooperatives (some of them killed by official design) and the pattern of trade liberalisation (Ghosh 2004).

The recent realisation by policy makers in the Government of India also seem to be working with a similar kind of understanding of the crisis of agriculture.

(*ii*) The second, and perhaps more popular, has been the thesis that links the rise in farmers' suicides to 'the crisis of ecology' and 'disintegration of community' caused by the new technology, and accentuated by globalisation. Commenting on the earlier crisis of militancy in Punjab, Vandana Shiva had, for example, argued that the green revolution was not merely a technological innovation meant for increasing productivity of land and bringing prosperity to farmers. Its negative social consequences far exceeded its benefits. Green revolution introduced a commercial culture in rural Punjab and destroyed the community. It changed social relations, from those based on mutual obligation to those based purely on the market principle. After the green revolution, 'Atomized and fragmented cultivators related directly to the state and the market. This generated on the one hand, an erosion of cultural norms and practices, and on the other hand, it sowed the seeds of violence and conflict' (Shiva 1991: 171). More recently, she along with some others attributed the suicides by cotton farmers directly to the ecological crisis generated by the introduction of new economic policies associated with the globalisation process.

> The tragedy of farmers committing suicides for a couple of years in some states, highlights some of these high social and ecological costs which are linked to globalisation of non-sustainable agriculture and which are not restricted to the cotton growing areas of various state but have been experienced in all commercially-grown and chemically-farmed crops in all regions. While the benefits of globalisation go to the seeds and chemical corporations through expanding markets, the cost and risks are exclusively born by the small farmers and landless peasants (Shiva et al.1999).

Elsewhere Shiva writes:

> ... as farming is delinked from the earth, the soil, the biodiversity, and the climate, and linked to global corporations and global markets, and the generosity of the earth is replaced by the greed of corporations, the viability of small farmers and small farms is destroyed. Farmers' suicides are the most tragic and dramatic symptom of the crisis of survival faced by Indian peasants (Shiva 2004).

Several other scholars have also tried to link the increase in farmers' suicides to a general breakdown of the ecological balance, disintegration of 'community' and kinship support system, and the rise of some kind of individualistic orientations brought in by the new technology and development philosophy to the Indian countryside (Ahalawat 2003; Vasavi 1999).

(*iii*) Some have also attributed the agrarian distress leading to suicides in Punjab to the generic 'irrationality of the peasant'. The fact that in most cases, the small and marginal farmers went into chronic indebtedness primarily because of 'unproductive' borrowings (as discussed above) implies that they had not acquired Weberian rationality characteristic of modern capitalism. Quoting Thomas and Znaniecki, B.P. Singh (2005) finds basic irrational traits among Punjab cultivators. Instead of investing their returns from agriculture in further expanding their capital base, he argues, the Punjab farmers tend to spend everything on 'consumer goods to seek physical and sensual gratification'. A similar kind of conclusion could also be inferred from the IDC study of farmers' suicides in Punjab discussed earlier.

(*iv*) There has also been another set of arguments that look at the current crisis of Indian agriculture as having been entirely a consequence of the new economic policy and globalisation, which, according this position is basically a 'return to the colonial logic' of the global economic integration. The most vocal advocate of this approach has been Utsa Patnaik. She draws a parallel between what happened during the colonial period when the Indian peasants were compelled to produce commercial crops like cotton, because the British needed it for the textile mills in England, and the current phase of globalisation. In an interview to a popular magazine she argued (Patnaik 2004):

> ... lakhs of small farmers, were switching from food crops to cotton as the world prices were rising. Many of them had not cultivated cotton before.... There was this sudden expansion of area under cotton—these farmers could not afford to do so except on the basis of credit. They took loans and the amount of loans they took to produce cotton was much higher than they had taken in the past, as they would have grown rain-fed food crops on the same land, which would not have cost much for production. *So the switch to an exportable commercial crop led to a scenario of rising indebtedness* (emphasis added).

She continues:

> ... there is an interesting parallel that one can find with what happened during the cotton boom. In 1861, when the American Civil War broke out and supplies of raw cotton from the United States to the manufacturing centres in Britain and Europe were cut off, they turned to alternative sources of cotton and India was a major source. Suddenly the prices of global cotton went up and the Indian farmer, being always very price responsive, switched over from food crops to cash crops. Immediately, there was a huge expansion of areas growing cotton and a switch from food crops like jowar and ragi to cotton. In order to do so, they borrowed from the *sahukars* [moneylenders].
>
> When the Civil War ended, the global prices crashed. The story repeats itself in 1996... But what happened was that when the people switched from food crops to cash crops,

the food prices went up. With the crash in cotton prices, the farmers found that they could not pay the *sahukars*. And the *sahukars* began to foreclose the debts. This led to the Deccan Riots. What happened then was that the Indian farmers actually took on the *sahukars* and unitedly fought against them, but this time they seem to be taking it out on themselves.

Beyond Crises

The above discussed explanations offered by different scholars are certainly quite persuasive and make several useful suggestions about the prevailing state of affairs in Indian agriculture. However, when one looks at these arguments a little dispassionately, with a specific regional context in mind, one also begins to realise that the story of agrarian distress is perhaps a little more complex and complicated than what is made out to be in most of these 'theses'.

The notion of agriculture and the rural social structure that they all seem to work with appears to be rather problematic. Even when vulnerability of small/marginal farmers is underlined in most of these analyses, they seem to treat agriculture in totality, as a sector of the wider Indian economy, which has been pushed into crisis by various policy changes. The social context of agriculture, i.e., the village, is also seen as a generalised category. Such populist frames tend to look at the village in communitarian terms, viz. peasant communities that were hitherto living undisturbed in peace and harmony, and have suddenly been pushed into crisis by commercial capital and global markets. Such analyses, thus, end up ignoring the internal differences of caste and class that are so obvious and important aspects of the Indian agrarian scene.

These analyses also tend to 'over-generalise' the nature of crisis and its causes, almost completely ignoring regional variations and diverse trajectories that mark the Indian agrarian scene today. Though globalisation has indeed had many negative implications for the agrarian economy in general, the crisis of agriculture today is not being experienced in a similar way everywhere. A close look at contemporary Punjab, for example, clearly shows that suicides were largely localised in certain pockets and only a few cases were reported from most other parts. The broader context of agrarian change also varies a great deal.

Emerging Scenario in Punjab Agriculture

As mentioned earlier, the most significant effect of the policies of liberalisation and globalisation on agriculture has been a shift in the discourses on agriculture. Notwithstanding India's continued need for food grains and the declining stocks, farmers are being told to diversify into the production non-food grain crops. While the immediate reason for this is the growing pressure on the state to withdraw the support price regime, which applies only to the food grain crops, it would also have its long-term implications in terms of integrating agriculture into the global market regime. Apart from the liberalisation lobby, diversification thesis also finds support from those concerned about the ecological balance of soil in Punjab. Production of paddy requires enormous amount of water, most of which is drawn from the ground. The growing number of tube wells in the fields of Punjab has meant receding water table, which has escalated the cost of production of paddy in the state. As per the official data, the area under cultivation of wheat and paddy went up from 47 per cent in 1970–71 to as much as 75 per cent in 2002–03 (Government of Punjab 2004c: 57).

Keeping all these considerations in mind, the Johal Committee had proposed an ambitious plan for crop diversification. With much fun and fare, the Congress Government in Punjab initiated an ambitious project in 2002 under which farmers were to be encouraged to shift from paddy to maize in the kharif season and from wheat to rapeseed and mustard in the rabi season. The state government also asked the Central government to fund its proposals.

The other major initiative to change Punjab agriculture was in the form of promoting corporatisation of agriculture and contract farming. Punjab was one of the first states in India where this was initiated when the multinational company, Pepsi Foods, set up its units in the state during the 1980s. Since then, contract farming has seen some growth in Punjab. Most of the multinational and local organisations involved with contract farming in the state have been focused around tomato, potato and chillies.

How have these twin processes altered the overall patterns of Punjab agriculture? The Congress Government in Punjab under the leadership of Capt. Amrinder Singh revived the Johal Committee proposals with much enthusiasm when it came to power in the state in 2002. It proposed to shift 38 per cent of land area from paddy and 29 per cent of land area from wheat to other crops. However, it soon developed cold feet. By 2005, no one was really talking about diversification with much interest and there had been no perceptible change in the cropping pattern. It was not only at the political level that the agenda of diversification lost appeal. To begin with, the proposals were perhaps too ambitious to be sustainable. Some local economists also pointed to their being economically unviable. According to one estimate, if implemented, the diversification as suggested by Johal Committee would have meant an annual loss of Rs 13,280 per hectare to the Punjab farmer (Shergill 2003: 7).

The situation is not very different withrespect to contract farming. As mentioned above, the corporations involved with contract farming in Punjab have been focusing around a few crops, such as potatoes, tomatoes, chillies and mustards. While individually, some of them might have been successful in procuring enough from the farmers of Punjab, the land under such farming still constitutes a miniscule proportion of the total agricultural activity in the state, and there is no visible sign of any significant growth in the land under contract farming in the state. It may be interesting to look at the operations of Pepsi Foods Limited that pioneered contract farming in Punjab and has been procuring potatoes through contract farming from the local farmers for production of chips and other potato based snacks. According to one study, it works only with 63 farmers and its factory located in a village in Sangrur district of Punjab employs only 75 persons (Singh, S. 2005: 75–82). Similarly, some other companies have their processing units located in Punjab but do not procure their crops only from Punjab farmers. They also have contract arrangements with farmers in the states of Haryana, Himachal Pradesh and Rajasthan (ibid.: 111). Thus, it may not be an exaggeration to say that at the macro level, contract farming is perhaps not yet a process worth taking note of.

The insignificance of processes like contract farming or corporatisation of Punjab agriculture, and at another level, the failure of crop diversification programme does not mean that the agrarian economy of Punjab, or its wider economy, is not experiencing any changes. On the contrary, I have tried to argue that in order to go beyond the discourse of crises, we need to look at the nature of changes taking place in Punjab economy and society and understand them in its own historical context.

From Crises to Change

It may be worthwhile to go back to the decades of 1970s and 1980s to make sense of what is happening to Punjab agriculture today. The green revolution technology indeed brought about significant change in the productivity of land and changed the cropping pattern of Punjab agriculture. However, the impact of green revolution was not confined to agriculture/economy alone. It transformed virtually everything—society, culture, politics. The economic development experienced during the green revolution period also brought the villages closer to the city life and its economy. S.S. Gill had reported this process some twenty years back:

> With the penetration of capitalist relations in agriculture, modern education has spread. Most of the Punjab villages have schools and some even have colleges functioning in them. Some of the capitalist farmers ...are actually sending them to urban centres to acquire better education. With this a large number of educated persons from rural areas have been coming forward to take up jobs in government and semi-government institutions and departments. This has produced a distinct category of middle class intellectuals of rural origin (Gill 1985).

This process has become further pronounced since Gill's observation some twenty years back. Most agricultural households in contemporary Punjab have become economically diversified. As Lindberg rightly points out, they are increasingly becoming pluri-active, 'standing between farming and other activities whether as seasonal labourers or small-scale entrepreneurs in the local economy.... Agriculture and farming is no more an all encompassing way of life and identity' (Lindberg 2005: 11).

The available official data on employment patterns in Punjab has also begun to reflect this process very clearly. As shown in Table 9.2, the proportion of cultivators of the total number of main workers in Punjab declined from 46.56 per cent in 1971 to 31.44 per cent in 1991, and further to 22.60 by 2001. While the share of cultivators has been consistently falling, that of the agricultural labourers had been rising until the 1991 Census. However, over the last decade, viz. from 1991 to 2001, even their proportion declined significantly, from 23.82 to 16.30 per cent. In other words, though nearly 70 per cent of Punjab's population still lives in rural areas, only around 39 per cent of the main workers in the state were directly employed in agriculture. The comparable figure for the country as a whole was still above 58 per cent.

Table 9.2: Proportion of Main Workers Engaged in Agriculture in Punjab

Category	*1971*	*1981*	*1991*	*2001*
Cultivators	42.56	35.86	31.44	22.6
Agricultural labourers	20.11	22.16	23.82	16.3
Total	62.67	58.02	55.26	38.90

Sources: Government of Punjab (2004b: 46); *Human Development Report 2004*. *Census of India* 2001(www.censusindia.net).

Table 9.3 further corroborates the point that agriculture in Punjab is undergoing some interesting shifts. As shown in the table, total number of landholding in the state declined from 13,75,392 in 1971 to 10,27,127 in 1981. This decline of more than 3 lakh holdings obviously suggests a sudden move away from agriculture. While this process experienced a reversal during the 1980s, perhaps because of the Khalistan movement, it again seems to have gained momentum during the post-1990 period.

Who is moving out of agriculture? If we look at Table 9.3 carefully, the decline is most clearly visible in the category of marginal land holdings (from 37.63 per cent in 1970–71 to mere 18.65 in 1995–96) followed by small land holdings. There is a correspondent rise in the medium and large land holding over this period of 25 years or so.

Table 9.3: Distribution of Operational Land Holdings

Size-class (in hectares)	*1970–71*	*1980–81*	*1990–91*	*1995–96*
Marginal (0–1)	5,17,568	1,97,323	2,96,131	2,03,876
	(37.63)	(19.21)	(26.50)	(18.65)
Small (1–2)	2,60,083	1,99,368	2,03,842	1,83,453
	(18.91)	(19.41)	(18.24)	(16.78)
Medium (2–4)	2,81,103	2,87,423	2,88,788	3,20,340
	(20.44)	(27.99)	(25.85)	(29.31)
Large (4–10)	2,47,755	2,69,072	2,61,481	3,05,792
	(18.02)	(26.20)	(23.40)	(27.98)
Extra-large (10 +)	68,883	73,941	67,172	79,612
	(5.00)	(7.19)	(6.01)	(7.28)
Total	13,75,392	10,27,127	11,17,414	10,93,073
	(100)	(100)	(100)	(100)

Source: Government of Punjab, (2004b: 41), *Human Development Report 2004*.

Though the average size of the holdings is growing in Punjab, the bigger farmer is not necessarily becoming more rural. While marginal and small cultivators seem to be moving out of agriculture, the bigger farmer is moving out of the village. The big farmers of Punjab invariably have a part of their families living in the town. Their children go to urban schools/ colleges, and they invest their surplus in non-agricultural activities.

Not only has there been a fragmentation of farming classes, the rural social structure has also undergone almost complete transformation over the last three or four decades. My recent study of changing caste relations in rural Punjab clearly reflects this process. As I have argued elsewhere (Jodhka 2002), commercialisation and mechanisation of agriculture on the one hand, and introduction of democratic political process on the other, have together transformed caste relations in rural Punjab quite fundamentally. Over the last twenty years or so, large proportions of Dalits in Punjab have consciously dissociated themselves from their traditional occupations and have also been trying to distance them from everyday engagement with the agrarian economy, which were the sources of power for the locally dominant castes over them. Their autonomisation from the 'traditional' rural economy and structures of patronage and loyalty has created a rather volatile situation. While the institutions supporting ideas and structures of hierarchy have nearly disintegrated, the upper castes have not yet shed their prejudice against the former 'untouchable' groups. Nor have they yet reconciled to the changed ground realities. In the emerging scenario, local Dalits have begun to assert for equal rights and a share from the resources that belong commonly to the village and had so far been in the exclusive control of the locally dominant caste groups or individual households (Jodhka and Louis 2003; Jodhka 2004).

These processes of change have had a direct implication for the political agency of the farming classes in Punjab. The earlier solidarity of farmers reflected in their powerful mobilisation during the 1980s is nowhere to be seen today. The Bhartiya Kisan Union (BKU), which had provided leadership to Punjab farmers during the 1980s, is split into four factions. Apart from the different factions of BKU, communist parties and other leftist groups also have their farmers' unions. Put together, there are a total of 10 different organisations claiming to represent farmers' interests in Punjab (Gill S.S. 2004). Though some of them occasionally come together on a common platform, most of the time, they remain divided. This fragmentation of farmers' movement during the last decade or so cannot be understood without referring to the growing internal differentiation within the landowning classes/castes and the changing political and class balance at the local and regional level.

Further, the process of globalisation/shift in economic priorities and consequent weakening of Indian state, have all played their role in making the farmers' politics less effective. As in other parts of Asia, green revolution was primarily a state-driven programme. Liberalisation and growing emphasis on withdrawal of state and growing involvement of corporate sector in agriculture has changed the opportunity structure of farmers' politics (Lindberg 2005). The moral high ground of Punjab's farmers as producers of food for the nation is lost when they are told to diversify into non-food grain corps that can find markets, locally and globally, without any help from the state.

Notwithstanding all these new trends, the change on ground is still limited. Farmers in Punjab, as elsewhere in India, continue to be an influential block. Populist politics often resorted to by the regional elite works to their advantage. This is quite evident from the available data on agricultural subsidies and the state policies during more than a decade of liberalisation/globalisation. In the case of Punjab, for example, after facing problems with procurement for some two years or so, crops were being procured again by the state agencies and the support prices have also been rising, albeit slowly. Instances of farmers committing suicides in rural Punjab have come down in the last couple of years, when compared to the decade of 1990s.

However, this is not to suggest that the crisis of Punjab agriculture is over. On the contrary, as is reflected in the literature on growing indebtedness, the challenges before the farmers of Punjab seem to be growing. The fact that smaller land holders are increasingly finding it hard to stay in agriculture, and are moving to other occupations clearly shows the nature of pressures the agriculturists in Punjab, as elsewhere in India, are confronted with. However, one ought to also see it in relation to the larger changes being experienced at the village and regional levels, economic, social and cultural. This perhaps, would enable us to raise more meaningful questions about what is happening to agriculture today.

The analysis and arguments presented above also suggest that what we need in Punjab, and what is likely to happen in the near future is a further diversification of the Punjab economy, and that is where the challenge of governance lies. The state and other agencies involved with the agenda of governance, thus, need to encourage and promote diversification of the economy that could enable the rural population to move out of agriculture into viable alternative occupations. Agriculture in Punjab can easily sustain itself and grow further with much smaller number of workers than is the case today.

Viewed in this historical perspective, the future of Punjab, and its present state of 'crises', would perhaps not seem to be very different from what has happened with the process of development elsewhere.

Notes

1. As in the official website of the Punjab Government 2004 (http://www.punjabgovt.nic.in).
2. Income of the secondary sector of Punjab economy during the 1980s grew at the rate of 7 per cent per annum as against the all India average of 6.1 per cent (Gill and Ghuman 2000: 450).
3. There have been several reports on the growing indebtedness of the Punjab farmers, particularly those of small and marginal farmers. Their sources for borrowings are invariable, and informal, generally the *arhtias* (the commission agent) in the grain market, which obviously makes their bargaining position weak. (see Shergill 1998; Bose 2000).
4. H. Jaisingh, 'Growing Frustration of Kisan: Agriculture Needs Fresh Strategy', *The Tribune*, (Chandigarh), 11 October 2000.
5. As reported by Lalit Mohan, *The Tribune*, 10 October 2000.
6. As reported by Bajinder Pal Singh, *The Indian Express*, 5 October 2000.
7. As reported by Bajinder Pal Singh, *The Indian Express*, 6 October 2000.
8. As reported by Bajinder Pal Singh, *The Indian Express*, 6 October 2000.
9. These villages are Harkishanpura in Bhatinda district and Shergarh in Mukatsar district. (As in S.S. Gill 2004).
10. *The Tribune*, 21 October 2000.

References

Ahlawat, S.R. (2003). 'Sociology of Agrarian Crises: Peasant Suicide and Emerging Challenges', *Man and Development*, 25(3): 97–110.

Banaji, Jairus (1996). 'The Farmers' Movement: A Critique of Conservative Rural Coalitions', *Journal of Peasant Studies*, 21(3 and 4): 228–45.

Bardhan P.K. and Ashok Rudra (1978). 'Interlinkage of Land, Labour and Credit Relations: An Analysis of Survey Data in East India', *Economic and Political Weekly*, 13(6 and 7): 367–84, Annual number.

Bhaduri, A. (1984). *The Economic Structure of Backward Agriculture*. Delhi: Macmillan.

Bharadwaj, K. (1974). *Production Conditions in Indian Agriculture*. Cambridge: Cambridge University Press.

Bose A. (2000). 'From Population to Pests in Punjab: American Boll Worm and Suicides in Cotton Belt', *Economic and Political Weekly*, 35(38): 3375–77.

Chandrasekhar, C. P. and Jayati Ghosh (2004). 'Agrarian Crisis in Andhra Pradesh', *Business Line*, 5 October.

Das, V. (ed.), (1990). 'Introduction', in V. Das (ed.) *Mirrors of Violence: Communities, Riots and Survivors in South Asia*. Delhi: Oxford University Press.

Ghosh, Jayati (2004). 'The Rural Gloom', *Frontline*, 21(24), 20 November–3 December.

Gill, Anita (2000). *Rural Credit Markets: Financial Sector Reforms and the Informal Lenders*. New Delhi: Deep and Deep Publications.

——— (2004). 'Interlinked Agrarian Credit Markets: Case Study of Punjab', *Economic and Political Weekly*, 39(33): 3741–51.

Gill, S.S. (1985). 'Genesis of Punjab Problem', in Abida Samiuddin (eds), *The Punjab Crisis: Challenge and Response*. Delhi: Mittal Publishers.

——— (2004). 'Punjab Farmers' Movement: Continuity and Change', *Economic and Political Weekly*, 39(27): 2964–66.

Gill S.S. and R.S. Ghuman (2000). 'Crisis of Punjab Economy: The Alternative Options and the Role of the Government', in R.S. Bawa and P.S. Raikhy (ed.), *Punjab Economy: Emerging Issues*, pp. 437–58. Amritsar: Guru Nanak Dev University.

Government of Punjab (1999). *Statistical Abstract of Punjab 2000*. Chandigarh: Economic and Statistical Organisation.

——— (2004a). 'Suicides by Farmers in Punjab,' Chandigarh (Unpublished official note).

——— (2004b). *Human Development Report 2004: Punjab*. Chandigarh: Government of Punjab.

——— (2004c) *Economic Survey Punjab 2004*. Chandigarh: Economic and Statistical Organisation.

Gupta, D. (1996). *The Context of Ethnicity: Sikh Identity in a Comparative Perspective*. Delhi: Oxford University Press.

Institute for Development and Communication (IDC) (1998). *Suicides in Rural Punajb*. Chandigarh IDC.

Iyer, K.G. and M.S. Manick (2000). *Indebtedness, Impoverishment and Suicides in Rural Punjab*. Delhi: Indian Publishers Distributors.

Jodhka S.S. (1997). 'Crisis of the 1980s and Changing Agenda of "Punjab Studies": A Survey of Some Recent Research', (Review article), *Economic and Political Weekly*, 32(6): 273–79.

——— (2001a). 'Looking Back at the Khalistan Movement: Some Recent Researches on its Rise and Decline', (Review article), *Economic and Political Weekly*, 36(16): 1311–18.

——— (ed.) (2001b). *Community and Identities: Contemporary Discourses on Culture and Politics in India*. New Delhi: Sage Publications.

——— (2002). 'Caste and Untouchability in Rural Punjab', *Economic and Political Weekly*, 37(19): 1813–23.

——— (2004). 'Sikhism and the Caste Question: Dalits and Their Politics in Contemporary Punjab', *Contributions to Indian Sociology* (n.s.), 23(1 and 2): 165–92.

Jodhka S.S. and P. Louis (2003). 'Caste Tensions in Punjab: Talhan and Beyond', *Economic and Political Weekly*, 38(28): 2923–26.

Kaur, Ravinder (1986). 'Jat Sikhs: A Question of Identity', *Contributions to Indian Sociology*, 20(2): 221–40.

Kaur, Gian (2002). 'Role of Informal Rural Financial Markets in Punjab—A Case Study', Working Paper-1, Mumbai: NABARD, Department of Economic Analysis and Research.
Kohli D.S. and N. Singh (1997). 'The Green Revolution in Punjab, India: The Economics of Technological Change', Conference paper. 'Agriculture of the Punab', The Southern Asian Institute, Columbia University, 1 April 1995.
Lindberg, Steffan (2005). 'Whom and What to fight?: Notes and Queries on Indian Farmers Collective Action under Liberalisation and Globalisation', Unpublished seminar paper, Patiala: Punjab University.
Patnaik, Utsa (2004). 'It is a Crisis Rooted in Economic Reforms', *Frontline* (net edition), 21(13), 19 June–2 July.
Pettigrew, J. (1992). 'The Jats of Punjab', in Dipankar Gupta (ed.), *Social Stratification*. Delhi: Oxford University Press.
——— (1995). *The Sikhs of the Punjab: Unheard Voices of State and Guerrilla Violence*. London: Zed Books.
Saberwal, S. (1987). *India: The Roots of Crisis*. Delhi: Oxford University Press.
Shergill, H.S. (1998). *Rural Credit and Indebtedness in Punjab*. Chandigarh: Institute for Development and Communication (monograph series IV).
——— (2003). 'Crop Adjustment Programme for Diversification of Punjab Agriculture: Can it Deliver the goods?', unpublished Working Paper.
Shiva, Vandana (1991). *The Violence of the Green Revolution: Ecological Degradation and Political Violence in Punjab*. London: Zed Books.
——— (2004). 'The Suicide Economy of Corporate Globalisation', *Znet*, www.zmag.org, accessed 5 April.
Shiva, Vandana, Ashok Emani and Afsar H. Jafri (1999). 'Globalisation and Threat to Seed Security: Case of Transgenic Cotton Trials in India', *Economic and Political Weekly*, 34(10): 601–13.
Singh, B.P. (2005). 'Punjab Peasantry in Turmoil', Unpublished seminar paper, Patiala: Punjab University.
Singh, Sukhpal (2005). *Political Economy of Contract Farming in India*. Delhi: Allied Publishers Pvt. Limited.
Singh, Sukhpal, M.S. Toor and V.K. Sharma (2005). 'Magnitude and Determinants of Indebtedness in Punjab Agriculture', Unpublished seminar paper, Patiala: Punjab University.
Vasavi, A.R. (1999). 'Agrarian Distress in Bidar: Market, State and Suicides', *Economic and Political Weekly*, 34(32): 2263–68.
World Bank (2004). *Resuming Punjab's Prosperity: Opportunities and Challenges Ahead*. New Delhi: Poverty Reduction and Economic Management Sector Unit, South Asia Region.

10

Globalisation, Governance and Labour

Sharit K. Bhowmik

This chapter attempts at an assessment of the impact of globalisation and economic liberalisation on labour. The focus is on the developments after the Industrial Policy Statement was laid before Parliament on 21 July 1991, by the then Finance Minister, Manmohan Singh. This statement, in fact was the basis of structural adjustment and liberalisation of the economy. We shall attempt to look at the main issues raised by the policy, namely, downsizing and outsourcing, growth of insecure employment, and gradual dismantling of the public sector. The chapter also analyses the responses of trade unions and the government to the changing situation.

INTRODUCTION

The process of structural adjustment as a result of globalisation has adversely affected the working class throughout the world. Labour in developing countries has suffered the most because restructuring of industry has invariably led to unemployment due to closure of 'unprofitable' industrial units. The World Bank has been pushing forth the idea that the only way countries of the South can promote growth is by encouraging private enterprises and reducing the protection for labour. The argument is that, too much protection to labour in the formal sector has resulted in a small section of the working class who are more privileged than the vast majority of ill-paid workers. Thus, the World Development Report of 1995 noted that, 'In many Latin American, South Asian and Middle Eastern countries, labour laws establish onerous job security regulations, rendering hiring decisions practically irreversible; and the system of worker representation and dispute resolution is often subject to unpredictable government decision-making, adding uncertainty to firms' estimate of future labour costs' (World Bank 1995: 34). In order to facilitate this process many countries (especially those in Central and South America) have relaxed or removed legal protection to workers in the formal sector. In India too, there have been persistent pressures to allow closure of industries and reduce the protection given to permanent workers.

Since independence, India decided to adopt the path of planned development as implemented in socialist countries such as the erstwhile Soviet Union. It was also decided that it would have a mixed economy with both the state sector (public sector) and private enterprise. However, private sector would exist under regulations and controls. This included issuing of licenses to start industry and these industries could be started only in areas that were not designated as core industrial areas. This system continued till the mid-1980s. In 1985, the then Prime Minister, late Rajiv Gandhi, called for a review of these policies. He wanted the economy to open up to foreign competition and a more proactive role for the private sector. He was unfortunately not able to see his reforms through because of his assassination in 1991, when he was campaigning for the oncoming general elections. However, the Congress Party that was elected continued the policies and on 21 July 1991, the Finance Minister (who is now the Prime Minister) laid before Parliament the Industrial Policy Statement that radically differed from the past policies. The policy, keeping in line with the post-1985 changes, envisioned a greater role of private enterprise in economic development. It was very critical of the public sector and recommended that its role should be restricted only to core or basic sectors. What was more important was that it scrapped the licensing system in almost all sectors and encouraged foreign investment.

The new industrial policies were in tune with the prevalent approach of structural adjustment and globalisation of finance and investment. Other developing countries and the former socialist countries (Soviet Union and the East European Countries) too changed their policies in a similar manner. Two glaring features of the policy are: undermining the public sector and, reduction of employment in the formal sector.

The policy statement contains a string of anti-public sector statements. It would seem that all the ills of this country was due to the existence of the public sector and its continuous expansion. These statements barely fall short of abuse. The policy then proceeds to stress on the need for reviving the economy through privatisation. The government then began to dismantle the public sector organisations through a number of strategies. An interesting feature is that the principle of privatisation has been accepted by the major political parties and the past governments. Hence, though there may be other political differences between the major political parties in the country, the policy of privatisation is common. For example, the NDA government was at one time interested in privatising the petroleum companies. This was deferred because of sharp resistance from some of the alliance partners. Soon after the decision to stop the sale of petroleum companies was announced, the Finance Minister of the UPA government, P. Chidambaran, wrote a hard-hitting article in a leading newspaper (*Sunday Express*) criticising the government's failure to privatise the petroleum companies. The NDA government had appointed Arun Shourie to speed up the process of privatisation who was honoured by associations of industry as 'man of the year'. He was able to off-load public sector enterprises at throw away prices. Most of them were sold at prices that were well below the value of the assets they possessed (Balco, Modern Bakery, VSNL, etc.). The Congress and NDA are not the only ones fascinated by privatisation. In fact, even the CPI(M) Chief Minister of West Bengal, Buddhadeb Bhattacharya, admitted in a long interview to a TV channel (which was reproduced in the *Indian Express*) that one of the major mistakes of the state government in the past was opposing privatisation.

The formal sector has been under threat as the policies of the government as well as the World Bank insist that labour laws have to be less protective to permanent employment. It would have liked to change labour laws, especially the Industrial Disputes Act (IDA), so as to make it easier to close factories. According to the IDA, any industrial enterprise employing 100 or more permanent workers cannot shut down its operations without the permission of the concerned departments of the state government. The government, instead, tried to promote an 'exit policy' that would ease the rules to shut down enterprises. This was opposed by the trade unions and the idea was shelved for sometime. There are other ways of promoting such a policy. The most important one is the Voluntary Retirement Scheme (VRS) through which companies can downsize their work force through 'voluntary' retirement of their workers. It is significant that one of the conditions for availing of income tax relief for compensation paid to the worker under this scheme is that the retired worker's post must not be filled up in future. In other words, every instance of voluntary retirement reduces a permanent job. The impact of this policy is shown in a later section.

Growth of Insecure Employment

The distinction between the formal and informal sectors is crucial for understanding employment relationship. Workers in the formal sector are engaged in factories, commercial and service establishments and their working conditions, wages and social security measures are legally protected. The bulk of the labour force, however, is engaged in the informal sector.

The 1991 Census noted that the total working population in the country was 317 million, of which 290.2 million (91.5 per cent) was in the informal sector while only 26.8 million (8.5 per cent) was in the organised sector. The earnings of the workers in the two sectors differed considerably. Though the organised sector employed only 8.5 per cent of the total labour force, the workers collectively earned around 33 per cent of the country's total wages and incomes (Davala 1995). Composition of workers in the informal sector showed that an overwhelming majority was in agricultural. There were 75 million agricultural workers and 110 million small and marginal cultivators who were also engaged as agricultural labour (Dutt 1997: 10). Therefore there were around 100 million workers in the non-farm rural sector and the urban unorganised sector.

The figures quoted above are mainly from the 1991 Census that was conducted before the new policies were introduced. The situation has changed since then. A report of the Ministry of Labour, Government of India (GOI 2004) has given the figures for the year 2000 based on the report of the National Sample Survey Organisation (NSSO). It carried out a sample survey (55th Round) in 1999–2000 and its results showed that out of total workforce of 397 million, only 28 million workers were employed in the organised sector and remaining in the unorganised sector. This means that a decade after reforms were introduced, employment in the formal sector has been almost stagnant or has slightly declined. The *Economic Survey* for 2004–05 (GOI 2005: 230) states that the total employment in the formal sector on 31 March 2003 was 27 million. In other words, employment declined by one million since 2000. Moreover, there seems to be no change in employment in terms of numbers since 1991. The informal sector, on the other hand has grown tremendously. One of the reasons for the decline of the formal sector is closures of the public sector enterprises.

In 1993, around 70 per cent of the workers in the formal sector were employed in government, quasi-government and public sector enterprises (Papola 1994: 34). This proportion fell by one per cent in 2003. The *Economic Survey* for 2004–05 notes that in March 2003, the public sector employed 69 per cent of workers in the formal sector. In fact, the formal sector employment fell by one per cent because of a decline in public sector employment of 0.8 per cent (GOI 2005: 230). The private sector provides employment to only 30 per cent of the labour in the formal sector. The wages of formal sector workers are substantially higher than those engaged in the urban informal sector. Moreover, a range of labour laws, guaranteeing permanent employment and provision for retirement benefits, protect their jobs.

Though in principle, labour laws in India are expected to apply to all sections of industrial labour, there are in-built provisions in these laws which exclude large sections of the labour force. The most important law regulating work in industries is the Factories Act. All other laws such as Employees State Insurance Act, Workmen's Compensation Act, Provident Fund and Family Pension Act, Payment of Gratuity Act, apply only to establishments covered by the Factories Act. This Act is applicable only to manufacturing units which employ a minimum of 10 workers and use power in manufacturing or alternately, a minimum of 20 workers if the unit does not use power. Hence, a large section of workers employed in small industries do not have legal protection in their workplace. We can thus see that the composition of the labour force in India shows wide contrasts.

While the formal sector shows a negative growth in employment, the small-scale manufacturing sector shows a lot of buoyancy. The annual pre-budget economic surveys show that small industries have been growing steadily. The 2004–05 survey shows that this sector employs around 28 million workers and its employment is growing by over 4 per cent per annum. The total number of workers in this sector alone is more than the employment provided by the entire formal sector. The remarkable growth of this sector is again a thrust area of the industrial policy of 1991, which stated that the small-scale sector would be encouraged to play a dynamic role in growth and employment. The *paid up capital* for small scale industry has been increased considerably. This means that it is possible to upgrade technology and include high technology industries in this sector. In this case too, we find that the NDA government operated in the same way as the Congress government had earlier. As a result, small scale industries contribute to 35 per cent of India's export earnings (GOI 2003). This is certainly a good sign, but it could have been appreciated even better if the condition of its labour had shown a similar improvement in terms of better wages and social security.

The rapid growth of the small scale industries is due to the above mentioned policy measures and restructuring of large industries, especially in the consumer goods and pharmaceutical sectors. These industries were originally based in urban centres like Mumbai, Ahmedabad, Kolkata, etc. They started closing down their operations by downsizing the labour force and shifting their production to smaller towns where labour is cheap and there are no unions and stringent labour laws as in the urban industrial sector. On the other hand, the government, in its bid to promote industrial development of these areas, demarcates special areas called 'industrial development zones'. These are operated through the state's industrial development corporation. The concerned state government usually grants an array of incentives to induce industrialists to set up their units in these areas. These include, availability of land on low rent and existence of industrial sheds and exemption of local taxes such as sales tax and excise, for a specific period of time (usually for the first five years).

Several large companies take advantage of such offers and move production from the larger cities to these smaller centres to avail of the benefits that lead to reduction in costs. This does not necessarily mean that the consumers will benefit by getting the goods at cheaper rates. This process is similar to the type of outsourcing in production witnessed between countries of the North and the South. Just as industrial production in the developed countries of Europe is outsourced to the less developed countries, similarly, the large-scale sector in India outsources its production to the small-scale sector in non-urban areas, as production costs are low.

Impact on Women: Feminisation of Labour

Let us now examine what effects the policies have had on women workers. Women have been losing their jobs in the formal sector for a very long time, much before the present policies were even conceived. We saw in the previous section that employment in the formal sector has been sluggish, resulting in loss of job for many. However, job losses among women workers in this sector took place at a time when this sector was, in fact, expanding. In the 1920s, employment of women in the three traditional industries, namely, jute, cotton textile and mines, was over 20 per cent which came down to less than 5 per cent in the 1970s. The only industry where women were employed in large numbers was the plantation industry where they constituted 50 per cent of the total permanent labour force and this number continued to be high. An analysis of this phenomenon is outside the scope of this chapter as it concentrates mainly on the post-liberalisation era. The main observation we can make in this regard is that women faced job losses after certain laws were passed. The Factories Act does not permit women to work in night shifts in factories. The Mines Act prevents women from working underground. These laws were ostensibly passed to protect women as it was believed that it would be unsafe for them to return home late in the night after the shift ended and, in the case of mines, working underground was detrimental to their health. Moreover, factory work was projected as activity for men and thus, unfit for women. The most significant in this whole process was that women were never asked whether they wanted to work at night, or underground. It was presumed in a patriarchal society that they needed protection.

The 1991 Census data shows that women workers formed one-seventh of the formal sector workforce and one-third in the informal sector (Davala 1994). In fact, female workforce in the formal sector increased its weightage mainly because of their large number in the plantation sector. This sector comprises tea, coffee and rubber. It employs around 1.6 million permanent workers, which includes about 8 lakh women. This large number of women in one sector can increase their weightage in the formal sector. It should be noted that the plantation sector offers the lowest wages in the formal sector. Women are mainly employed as nurses, airhostesses, primary school teachers, receptionists and secretarial staff. Salaries in each of these categories, with the possible exception of airhostess, are the lowest in the concerned industry/profession. We can thus see that women in the formal sector are assigned to jobs that are identified and categorised as 'feminine'.

We have mentioned earlier that the argument for preventing women from working at night was mainly their protection and safety. Even the International Labour Organisation has a convention to this effect besides another that states that women should not work underground. In fact, these are two of the very few conventions that have been accepted by most countries. At the same time, when it becomes necessary for women to participate in the labour force, these conventions are overlooked. This happened during the Second World War when men had to fight the war and women were recruited to work in factories and mines to keep production going. At that time, the safety norms were conveniently overlooked.

In the present phase, when there is a growth in call centres (discussed later) and production in small scale sector, the issue of women working in the night has once again surfaced. On 29 March 2005, the Union Cabinet took a decision to amend the Factories Act of 1948 so that women could work in night shifts. The main reason that guided the cabinet's decision was that, after January 2005, the quota system for garments and textiles was lifted by WTO. Hence, this made it possible for India to enter the international market in a big way, provided the goods were cost effective. What could be cheaper than employing women in these factories? Concerns on women's safety were conveniently sidelined.

Though women occupy a better position in the informal sector, in terms of numerical strength, their position in the work hierarchy and income are low. The better paid jobs are taken by men and the lower paying ones are reserved for women. In fact, the type of work performed by them are those that can be replaced by technology. For example, in the construction industry, women are assigned to carry building materials to the work site. They carry bricks or crushed stones in baskets on their heads to these places. This however, can be replaced by conveyer belts and consequently, women lose their jobs.[1]

The example of construction labour is one of the many activities that are performed by women as labourers. Bhagalpur in Bihar is regarded as the centre of the silk spinning industry. The entire task of spinning silk and twisting the yarn is done by women. This is low-paid but requires long hours of work. This industry is now facing a crisis because imports of silk from China and Korea is fast replacing the domestic product. The obvious losers are the impoverished women weavers of Bhagalpur.

Technical changes taking place at rapid rates presently, result in job losses if no new jobs are created. In agriculture, weeding is done by women. The use of pesticides has removed the need for manually removing weeds and hence this reduces the employment of women. Similar is the situation in cotton cultivation where women are employed to pick cotton buds. However, their work has been replaced by the use of combined harvesters.

In most of the cases mentioned above, women are paid wages that are lower than those of men. This is a violation of the law, but women are made to believe that the type of work they do is inferior hence, they are paid less. The Equal Remuneration Act was passed in 1976. This was meant primarily for workers in mines, plantations, construction industries, etc. Initially it was found that employers, especially in plantations, continued to pay less to women workers on the ground that the workload of men was higher than that of women and equal wages would discriminate against male workers. The government clarified in December 1976 that equal wage had to be given to male and female workers when the nature of work was similar and not the volume. In other words, the nature of work in construction or in plantations is similar even though women may be assigned less workload than men. Tea plantations in West Bengal started paying equal wages soon after this clarification. However, in Assam, which employs half the plantation workers in the country, equal wages were paid as late as in 1990. In other industries and in agriculture, women continue to get lower wages than men.

Besides those that are employed on wages, a major section of informal employment comprises self-employed workers.[2] Street vending is one of the activities of the self-employed. Studies show that there are around one crore street vendors in the country of which women constitute roughly 30 per cent. Their income was less than that of the male street vendors. On an average a male street vendor earned between Rs 50 to Rs 70 a day whereas, women earned between Rs 40 and Rs 50 a day. The reason is that women vendors are from poorer families and therefore cannot invest much resources in their enterprise. They are also expected to do household work such as cooking and cleaning. This means that they can spend less time on their profession. In cases where male members of the household helped the women, their income was higher as they could spend more time in selling their goods.

Along with the above mentioned problems, women vendors face harassment from male vendors as they are seen as competing with them. In Patna, it was found that women vendors prefer to sell from door to door rather than squat on the pavements with others, mostly men. Mobile vendors have to carry their goods in baskets on their heads which means that they sell only limited quantities of their wares. Women are forced to do this because they feel threatened when they try to occupy spots on the pavements. The male vendors harass them and therefore, they have to leave. Thus, we can see that in these professions too, women occupy the lower levels. Moreover, most women vendors in all cities are engaged in selling vegetables, which are the least profitable, if sold in small quantities. One rarely finds them as independent sellers of more profitable goods such as garments, fruits, prepared food, etc. In fact, food vendors have the highest earnings and they are mainly men. Ironically, many of them have the pre-cooked food prepared at home by their wives who are not involved in the selling.

Hence, we find that even in the informal sector, women are assigned the lowest paid jobs and even these are shrinking. At the same time, it would be incorrect to assume that after liberalisation and globalisation, jobs in the informal sector have decreased. In fact, in the construction industry, demand for women head loaders may have declined but there are higher demands for other services such as carpentry, plumbing, electrical etc. Women workers are unable to access these jobs because, first, these are categorised as jobs meant for men and second, they are not trained. The second point follows from the first. In most cases, plumbers, carpenters and electricians learn their skills from their fathers. Boys are taught these skills when they accompany their fathers to work. Girls are never imparted such skills as these jobs are not meant for them. Hence, if women are to access these jobs they need training. If the state or NGOs provide such training to women construction workers, they could be more flexible in their work. This would also help in eroding the gender based barriers in work.

Voluntary Retirement Scheme

Many of the large companies have resorted to downsizing in order to reduce labour costs. The concerned workers are forcibly made to 'voluntarily' retire. The methods were earlier subtle, but crude. The targeted group of workers could be frequently harassed by the management, they could be transferred to other plants or offices of the company in other areas etc. All these were done with a view that the workers would not be able to bear this harassment and would seek a compromise.

After the reforms of 1991, the employers' organisations demanded that government should frame an 'exit policy' that would enable any industry to close down. This was fiercely opposed by trade unions and the government then decided against such a policy. At the same time, it allowed companies to reduce their workforce through a process known as the Voluntary Retirement Scheme. Through this, the companies could offer voluntary retirement to their workers by giving them a better retirement package than what they would have got under law. This would lure workers to accept these terms and quit. In reality, it was noticed that companies did offer VRS but if the response was not as much as expected, they would use other tactics to 'convince' their workers. For example, one of the commonest methods employed was spreading the rumour that the concerned factory or office would close down within a short period and workers would be transferred to another plant far away. Hence, if workers did not accept the time-bound offer of VRS, they would have to either move to the other factory or if they wanted to resign then, they would get only the compensation provided by law and nothing more. Hence, it was found that the first offer of VRS had luke warm response, but for the second round (after these rumours were spread) the response was much better.

Myrtle Barse (2001) has studied the impact of this scheme in some large companies in Mumbai. She finds that it has had a marked impact on the nature of employment and in changing the quality of life of the workers. The paper has case studies of workers who have taken VRS and how their lives changed. Most could not find alternative work and their compensation evaporated within a few years. Their living standards reduced drastically and some managed to find low paid work in the informal sector. She suggests that the government or other organisations such as trade unions or NGOs should help workers who accept VRS in investing their money properly and also in providing health insurance.

Noronah (2001) studied the Bombay Dock Labour Board (BDLB) and how globalisation has changed its functioning. He notes that by setting up the BDLB, a modicum of social security was provided for sudden economic crisis and at times of recession when work was not readily available. However, the advent of globalisation and containerisation reduced the need for labour. The Board then had to resort to VRS for the workers which turned out to be disastrous for them and for the Board too, as it faced a funds crunch after paying large sums as compensation. This is one case of when both employer and employee suffered because of VRS.

Ratan Khasnobis and Sudipti Banerjea (1996) have come to similar conclusions while studying VRS in Durgapur in West Bengal. The study explores the mechanisms behind the workers' acceptance of VRS in the Durgapur Industrial Area of West Bengal. Though there was willingness on the part of workers to accept compensation in some cases, there were several instances of coercion from the management, forcing the workers to accept the deal. Moreover, the amount was used for unproductive purposes. The worker thus, had little left to start a self-employment venture.

OUTSOURCING

Unilever: A Case of Internal Outsourcing[3]

We will briefly discuss the case of outsourcing by Unilever, an MNC operating in India. Unilever is an Anglo-Dutch MNC and is known in India as Hindustan Lever Limited (HLL). It has been operating since the days of colonial rule and is the market leader in detergent and toilet soap industry with a market share of 60 per cent and 40 per cent respectively. HLL also dominates the shampoo market with a 64.5 per cent share and has a 54 per cent market share in skin creams.

At the same time, the huge increase in production is not matched by an increase in the workforce employed by HLL. In fact, there has been a sharp decline in the number of workers employed in the company's manufacturing units. We can take the case of the company's largest unit, namely, the factory at Sewri in Mumbai (Bombay). In 1985, this unit employed around 4,000 workers. By 1996, the workforce had shrunk to 1,800. Even this, the company felt, was too high. In every shift, a few workers were not given any work because the management stated that there was not enough to do. By 2003, the workforce was reduced to around 1,200 workers. In other words, the workforce in this factory had been downsized to a little over one-fourth of its size twenty years ago. Simultaneously, we find, the production of HLL products manufactured has increased substantially. This is mainly through outsourcing production through other units.

The author had conducted a study on outsourcing at HLL in 2001–02. We located several industrial units in the small-scale sector where outsourcing was carried out. There were some units that were promoted by HLL as its subsidiary, though, a majority of them were owned by private companies or individuals that manufactured goods for HLL. The units covered were located in the Industrial Development Zones that are set up by the state governments in non-conventional industrial areas (as discussed in the previous section).

The HLL sponsored units had large number of workers but we found that most of them were engaged through labour contractors and not by the company. The total number of permanent workers employed by HLL in each of its units did not exceed 100. This was done on purpose. The Industrial Disputes Act states that any manufacturing unit employing 100 or more permanent workers could not close down without the permission of the state government. Thus, by employing less than 100 workers, HLL could close down any of its units with ease. This happened quite often. In fact, HLL has built up a dubious reputation of closing down its unit when the period of subsidies expire. The company sets up its unit in the industrial development zone and avails all the facilities given to a new unit. As soon as the period of getting the facilities is over (usually it is for first five years), it closes the unit and moves to another industrial area where it can avail of the same facilities.

Wages paid to HLL workers at these industrial development zones are substantially lower than wages of workers in its factory at Mumbai. For example, the average wage of a work in Daman was Rs 4,500 per month and in Khamgaon this was Rs 6,500 per month. Wages of workers in HLL factories in Mumbai and Kolkata were between double and three times the wages of workers in these units. The outsourced industries paid wages that were even lower, ranging from Rs 1,500 to Rs 2,500 a month. Lower wages are mainly because workers in the industrial zones have low bargaining power. As these regions are less developed, there are few employment opportunities outside the industrial zones. Moreover workers in these units are not unionised, which further reduces their bargaining power.

This large-scale outsourcing had two advantages for reducing costs. First, the exemption from income tax and second, lower labour costs. Both factors should have helped in lowering prices of HLL products, but this does not happen. Consumers pay higher prices mainly because of the brand name. In fact, the author found that in 2001, prices of HLL brands in India (soaps, shampoos) were more than the prices of the same products in Germany! For example, a small container of shampoo cost Rs 65 in India and the larger one cost Rs 130 whereas in Germany, the same large container cost DM 2.50 (Rs 50). A cake of Dove soap cost Rs 45 in India while its price in Germany was DM 1.50 (Rs 30).

Internal Outsourcing in Other Industries

The kind of outsourcing discussed above is done not just by MNCs like Unilever, but by other large companies as well. For example, since 1980s the large-scale textile mills have closed, rendering hundreds of thousands of workers unemployed. The main textile centres were Mumbai and Ahmedabad (Bhowmik and More 2001 and Breman 2001). There were around 80 large-scale textile mills in these two cities. At present, both these metropolitans have not more than 10 textile mills functioning between them. Production of textiles, however, has not decreased due to these closures. Instead, it is now outsourced to the thriving power-loom sector. Power-looms are similar to hand-looms except that they are run by electricity and not by human energy. The technology used is backward, and much lower than that of large-scale textile factories. The power-loom sector becomes viable because the wages paid to workers are very low. They earn around Rs 50 to Rs 80 a day for working for at least 10 hours. In this sector too, low level of technology and low labour productivity is offset by low labour costs. The textile companies by and large get their products by outsourcing to the power-loom sector. The wages of a power-loom worker is between one-third to one-fourth of the wages in the large-scale textile mills.

Similarly, several other products are outsourced to the small-scale sector as protective legislation and regulations are lax or non-existent here. Peter Knorringa (1996), a Dutch sociologist studied the footwear industry in Agra. The shoe-makers belong to ex-untouchable communities and have low social status. He finds that the relation between the small self-employed shoemaker and the exporter's agent is based on the traditional relations in the caste hierarchy. The agent assumes the role of the upper caste patron of the lower caste shoe-maker.

In traditional caste relations, the lower caste or untouchable castes comprised those who performed manual work and were usually associated with the so-called 'unclean' activities like working with hides, cleaning the village, providing labour for the upper castes etc. Their lower social status ensured that the remuneration they got, in an economy based on exchange, was much lower compared to the physical labour they were expected to put in. This, in fact, formed the basis of the exploitation of the lower castes by the upper castes in the traditional system. Knorringa's findings show that by recreating traditional caste relations, the agents recreate the traditional forms of exploitation based on caste status and they are in a position to pay them less for their work.

Apart from Knorringa's study, there are other instances in different cities where low caste leather workers are the main suppliers of good quality, high priced leather products for the domestic and the export markets. These centres are in Kanpur, Kolkata and Mumbai. Most of the branded shoes available in the domestic market, are in fact, manufactured by such workers. As in the case of HLL, we can see that large manufacturers of leather products have down-sized their labour force drastically. The largest manufacturer in this field, Bata, had two large factories, one in Batanagar in Kolkata and the other in Faridabad near Delhi. At present, both factories have drastic cuts in their permanent labour and in production. Most of its products are now manufactured in the small-scale sector. In Dharavi, Mumbai, which is reputed to be Asia's largest slum, there are clusters of sweat shops that employ leather workers to produce goods for the international market. These units use assembly line methods to ensure standardisation of the goods produced. The employees are largely Hindus (belonging to the *charmakar* or *dhor* castes that were traditionally engaged in leather work and tanning) and Muslims.

Outsourcing can be possible only if labour costs are very low and so is the technology. Production is thus, labour intensive. Hence, low labour costs means lower costs of production. The combination of these factors, has in fact, promoted outsourcing. This is exactly what happens at the international level too. The less developed countries have an edge over the developed ones mainly because labour costs are low. This has to be coupled with technology that is labour intensive since only then can costs be reduced. Let us now look at outsourcing at the international level.

Outsourcing for the International Market

India is a land of contrasts. On the one side, there is high level of illiteracy (40 per cent) and on the other, there is a highly qualified work force that has spread all over the world due to its superior skills. Hence, it is not surprising that India should be sought after by international companies for outsourcing. These can be seen in diverse activities that are labour-intensive. Costs of labour, as mentioned earlier, are very low as compared to international standards.

Outsourcing in India is prevalent at two extreme levels. At the bottom end, there are poorly paid workers who work in 'sweat shops' and put together goods for the international market. On the other end, there is outsourcing at the micro-electronic sector, involving large contracts for developing software etc. The more current trend is that of Business Process Outsourcing (BPOs). This involves operation of call-centres on a very wide scale and other forms of outsourcing such as back office functioning. Legal companies, banks and other loan agencies outsource their office work to these Indian companies. Most of this is from the USA though the UK also has a fair share.

The extent of outsourcing can be seen from the large number of call-centres operating in various cities. Gurgaon, a city very close to Delhi, has a large concentration of call-centres. Similarly, on the outskirts of Hyderabad in South India, a township known as Cyberabad has sprung up to accommodate the call-centres. In Mumbai, the suburb of Andheri has a large number of call-centres and other BPOs. In Kolkata, the government has demarcated an area for software companies in its suburb, Salt Lake. Bangalore, in South India is known as the 'Silicone Valley' of India given the large concentration of software companies in the city.

Outsourcing in India began in the software industries over a decade ago. Bangalore was the city where this started. The Micro-Electronic Revolution of the 1980s brought about radical changes in production. The sudden improvement in communications led to rapid transfers of capital as well as production between countries. The change in technology made it possible for countries, like India, that had a pool of technical personnel to take advantage of the changed scenario. Several leading MNCs and other international companies took advantage of this revolution and decided to shift their main activities that involved communication and computer technology to countries like India. These countries had trained personnel who could be employed for low wages (compared to wages in developed countries). This led to the first form of outsourcing. Mark Holmstrom, a British anthropologist, has done an excellent study of Bangalore as a techno-city where flexible specialisation was introduced (Holmstrom 1997). A more recent study on Bangalore details the problems of the software industry (Heitzman 2004). It traces the relationship between information technology and social organisation in the city.

Outsourcing in the software industry is done by the larger companies in the developed countries. For example, the entire accounting work of the German MNC, Seimens, is done in Bangalore and so is the ticketing for international airline companies like Lufthansa and British Airways. Similarly, the software upgrading of cell phones for US companies are also done in outsourced units.

India has a comparative cost advantage as far as software is concerned. The cost of living here is lower and around Rs 25,000 a month would be a very decent salary for a qualified software programmer. Similarly, the call-centres have flourished because the operators know English and are available at much cheaper rates than their counterparts in the USA and UK. The operators are paid around Rs 8,000 to Rs 12,000 per month and supervisors/group leaders earn around Rs 18,000 to Rs 25,000 per month. These are several times lower than a person with a similar job profile in the USA or in Europe. This is why companies in USA, Australia and the English speaking parts of Europe have moved to India for outsourcing the call-centres. This boom has happened in the past five years with the sudden and rapid improvement in communication technology in India. It has provided employment to several thousands of youth in the different cities. A news report (*India Today* 2002: 36–49) noted that that in late 2002 there were 336 centres employing 110,000 people and estimated that the total number of jobs would increase to two million by 2008.

The other form of outsourcing is the back office activities. These offices provide back-up services to companies in the developed countries, especially in the USA. They provide information on various legal and other activities for the company that has hired them. The costs in this case, too, are very low compared to costs in developed countries for the same services. We have described the type of outsourcing that is done at the upper end of the market. Let us see what happens at the lower end.

Outsourcing in the developing countries is mainly prevalent in certain industries that involve low technology and labour costs. Thus, we can see that in industries such as textiles and garments, outsourcing is quite popular. In India, outsourcing in this sector is not very popular because there was a quota system for export of garments. However, this has ended in 2005. Bangladesh is at present, the main area for outsourcing in the garment industry. In India, the textile industry is involved in export of better quality fabrics. We have discussed in the section on outsourcing in the domestic market how the power-loom industry has replaced large textile mills. In cities such as Surat, in Gujarat, the power-loom industry is engaged in outsourcing for markets abroad. Other industries that engage in outsourcing are the leather and the handicrafts industry. In all these, the literacy rate of the workforce is low and there is impoverishment. Besides, the wages are low and working conditions are extremely poor. In most cases, workers are paid at piece rates (i.e., they are paid according to the number of products they produce). The rates paid are usually very low and the worker has to put in 10 to 12 hours of work a day in order to produce enough for getting a minimum wage.

Trade Union Response

Trade unions have by and large opposed the above policies. They have organised nation wide strikes, *bandhs* and rallies in different parts of the country. However, these have hardly had any effect in changing the policies. The only assurance given so far is that there will be no 'exit policy'. This is of little value as we have seen earlier that workers continue to lose their jobs through VRS and lay-offs caused by downsizing.

It is evident from this that all these forms of conventional protests have lost their teeth. There is a need for revaluating the situation and developing new forms of opposition as well as alternatives to the present policies. The trade union movement, on the other hand, has by and large remained conventional and still believes that traditional forms of protest are the only means of highlighting problems concerning labour. While it cannot be denied that traditional means of protest, which includes mass action, play an important role in mobilising of the working class and making them articulate their problems as a collective unit, under the present circumstances, these methods may not fully achieve the purpose in changing onslaughts on workers' rights.

Unfortunately, the trade union movement has by and large restricted itself to unionising labour in the formal sector. The last verification of union membership by the Labour Department showed that of the total membership of the seven recognised national federations, only one per cent of their membership lay in the informal sector (Davala 1995). Trade unions have ignored the vast sections of labour in the informal sector. In fact, even when the informal sector exists within the formal sector, trade unions ignore them. A study of contract and casual labour in eight industries (Davala 1994) showed that casual and contract labour formed between 30 per cent to 50 per cent of the labour force. Except in one industry, tea, these workers were not unionised. In some cases, unionised workers regarded them as rivals who would take away their jobs. Except for rare instances like the Self-Employed Women's Association (SEWA), there are hardly any instances of trade unions among the informal sector. We shall return to this issue of unionising the informal sector later.

Globalisation is something that cannot be wished away. It has undoubtedly led to pauperisation and insecurity of the working class all over the world. Labour in developed countries, too, has to face its consequences. But is this new for human society? Any sudden change results in situations that are not easily perceived. It is, therefore, labelled as anti-people and there are moves to oppose it. A similar, if not worse, situation occurred in the middle of the 18th Century at the time of Industrial Revolution. Hundreds of thousands of artisans and craftspeople lost their traditional jobs in the villages because factory produced goods replaced traditionally produced goods. These people, along with the other sections of the rural poor, were forced to migrate to the industrial centres in search of poorly paid factory jobs under inhuman working conditions. The working class responded to the situation by forming a distinct, and hitherto unknown, organisation—the trade union. It was through trade unions that the working class was able to fight for their rights. They did this first by, challenging the employers' total control over the labour process and, second, by challenging the state and pressurising it to pass protective legislation.

Globalisation has raised similar challenges to the working class movement. The question now is: can the labour movement adapt itself to face these challenges? Or rather, is the labour movement willing to adapt to the challenges thrown up by globalisation and develop new strategies to face these? Given the present orientation of the mainstream trade union movement in the country, this seems unlikely in the near future. Trade union strategies, as of now, revolve on two issues. First, use of traditional means of protest, such as strikes, rallies and *bandhs*, whenever the issue of closure or redundancy arises in the organised sector. Second, opposing globalisation itself. Both strategies have achieved very limited success in their objectives. The question is, therefore, of not opposing globalisation per se, but rather, how best can the interests of the working people be safeguarded?

The question then is, is mere opposition enough to combat the adverse effects of globalisation or should the labour movement promote some positive alternatives? A related, but more crucial question is, can trade unions function merely as opposition bodies? Or, should they offer alternatives?

In fact, searching for alternatives could be an effective way of counteracting the present ill-effects. Let us take the case of privatising the public sector. Though this move was started by the Congress government under Narasimha Rao, it in fact, reached its zenith at the time of the NDA government. Soon after the Industrial Policy Statement came into force, the government appointed the Privatisation Committee. This committee submitted its first report in 1995. It drew up the guidelines for privatisation and even made a list of those undertakings that should be privatised. There was no debate on this report. Both trade unions and the major opposition political parties, with whom the national federations were affiliated to, did not think that this deserved much discussion. Only a few statements were made condemning privatisation. The basic issues were never debated or even discussed.

One of the major suggestions made by the Committee was that the money realised through privatising public sector organisations should be kept aside to form a fund for promoting education and health. This would help in decreasing the government's expenditure on these two important items. However, when the organisations were privatised the amount recovered from the sale was, in most cases, used for covering the budgetary deficits. Even then, none of the trade unions enquired on how the money was spent. They were too busy opposing the sale. Had there been a concerted demand by trade unions on how the amount should be invested, it could have been an act of constructive opposition.

Workers' Takeovers

Another aspect of privatisation is the alternatives it can provide for employee takeovers. This has been tried with success in some other countries such as Canada, where trade unions have backed the employees in taking over the companies. They have encouraged the workers to form co-operatives to run the companies and have also helped in securing loans (Quarter 1993: 37–38).

The Industrial Policy Statement has indicated some encouragement in this direction, though not in a particularly positive manner. Paragraph 16 of the document reads: 'Labour will be made an equal partner in progress and prosperity. Workers' participation in management will be promoted. Workers' co-operatives will be encouraged to participate in packages designed to turn around sick companies.'

The attitude of the policy is quite clear: Workers will be encouraged to manage companies only after these become sick and are of no use to the owners. However, 13 years have passed since the policy was accepted by parliament, and till now there is not a single instance of workers' take-over of any company. In fact, there are successful cases of workers' take-over but these have nothing to do with the liberalisation policy. Let us discuss this issue.

Worker co-operatives are industrial or commercial organisations which are owned and controlled by employees of these organisations. They are fairly recent in India, as compared to their long history in the more developed countries, especially Britain and Europe. There are a number of instances of worker co-operatives in plantations, mines and in industrial units. The workers of Sonali Tea Estate, a tea plantation employing around 500 workers in the Jalpaiguri district in West Bengal, established the first worker co-operative in plantations in 1974. In Tripura, five tea plantations are being run successfully by their workers since the early 1980s (Bhowmik 1992). In Dalli Rajhara, near Bhilai Steel Plant in Madhya Pradesh, there are around half a dozen worker co-operatives operating in the open cast iron ore mines. In Kolkata, there are at least 20 industrial units that are managed by worker co-operatives since the early 1980s (Bhowmik and Sarker 2002). The fact that these have survived for more than two decades in itself speaks of its success.

Unfortunately, despite the impressive track record of the existing worker co-operatives, their significance is glossed over by those interested in alternative policies. Indeed, the current debates on industrial policy range around the pros and cons of the state sector versus private enterprise. Neither the national trade union federations nor those critical of privatisation have tried to seriously consider the possibility of developing a third sector, namely, a workers' sector in industry.

The relations between workers' self-management and trade unions in India are complex. The national trade union federations have remained indifferent to the idea of worker takeovers. At the same time, every successful case has had the backing of the respective trade union. The union has motivated the workers of the unit to form the co-operative and takeover the ownership. This type of trade union initiative remains only at the local level. The local union leaders take a pragmatic stand as they are faced with a concrete problem—if the industrial unit closes, workers will lose their jobs. Hence, when help does not come from any quarter for revival of the unit, the workers and their trade union have to devise means of helping themselves through their own resources. This pragmatic approach has guided the formation of the existing worker co-operatives.

The main drawback of this approach is that the co-operatives remain largely local endeavours. In most cases, they do not have links with other co-operatives, even though the trade union may be the same. This is especially true of those in Kolkata. The workers in almost all the co-operatives are members of the CITU and they were motivated to takeover their respective units by the local CITU leaders. These co-operatives, nonetheless, remain local initiatives. The CITU, at the state level, rarely recognises the contributions of these workers to the working class movement. There is also no attempt to establish a network of these co-operatives so that they can form a joint forum to deal with common problems.

The situation in Tripura is somewhat different as the CITU at the state level has initiated the move to form co-operatives in the tea plantations. In fact the General Secretary of the state CITU, and a former Speaker of the Legislative Assembly, late Bimal Sinha, had keenly propagated worker takeovers. However, even in this case we find that the CITU has not highlighted these achievements as a part of the working class struggle.

The same situation is found in the case of the worker co-operative in Sonali Tea Estate in Jalpaiguri district of West Bengal. Workers of this plantation took over the plantation after its management abandoned it in 1973. A year later, they formed a co-operative to manage the plantation. The union was affiliated to AITUC. Within a span of three years, the workers were able to increase production, expand the plantation and undertake several welfare measures. As a result, its former owners staged a comeback by filing several legal suits against the co-operative. At this stage, the AITUC promptly backed out leaving the workers to fight their battles on their own. The co-operative eventually won its legal battle but after fighting for 21 years.

In Golaghat district of Assam, the INTUC-affiliated union took over the Woka Tea Estate in 1975 through its co-operative. The plantation was about to close and the union decided on the takeover to save workers' jobs. The co-operative was able to revive the plantation within two years of its takeover and at minimum costs. However, the INTUC has till date not highlighted the achievements of these workers in reviving production.

Trade Unions and Worker Takeovers

The reluctance of trade unions to support worker takeovers arises from an ideological dilemma. One of the primary functions of trade unions is to defend workers against exploitation by capital. Hence, trade unions are expected to function mainly as opposition groups. Once workers themselves become owners of capital, the conventional role of trade unions has to change, as it can no longer function as an opposition. This in fact, creates the dilemma for most trade unions, especially the radical ones.

There is no disputing the fact that the focus of trade unions is the struggle between labour and capital. But, does conventional trade unionism provide a radical framework for challenging the existing relations? Conventionally, trade unions defend workers' rights in a number of ways. These include fighting for security of employment, improvement in living and working conditions, increase in wages, and so on. In addition, they act as pressure groups to change or modify existing policies of government that affect labour. However, in conducting these activities, the actual domination of capital over labour is never challenged. In fact, trade unions accept this domination, explicitly or implicitly, depending on the ideology of the union.

The right wing unions do not dispute this domination and they may advocate co-operation between the two in order to get benefits for labour. The radical unions, especially those that swear by the supremacy of the working class over capital, resign themselves to this domination till the time is ripe for a social revolution. Thus, when an industry becomes sick or it closes, the trade unions start looking out for another supplier of capital to revive it. In most cases, they press for takeover by the state. Ironically, even the radical unions clamour for nationalisation, even though, most of them regard the state as pro-capitalist and anti-labour. The fact that labour itself can be organised to save production and employment is rarely given a serious consideration.

Organising the Unorganised

We have till now discussed the alternative strategies that the labour movement could have adopted to protect the interests of the working class. There is, as pointed out earlier, a more serious divide in the movement, namely, that between the formal and the informal sectors. Trade unions do not seem to play any role in protecting the interests of these workers, who in fact are most needy of this protection.

It cannot be denied that the trade union movement has largely concentrated on problems of the organised/formal sector workers. These constitute around 8 per cent of the workforce.

The remaining sections of the working class have not had the benefit of organising themselves. The formal sector workers have been the main targets of liberalisation and the reasons are not difficult to find. This sector, through its past struggles, was able to consolidate its gains to improve its conditions of work and living. Unfortunately, it is due to these gains that this sector has become the victim of liberalisation. The informal sector is now being pitted against the formal sector. On the one hand, jobs in the formal sector are shrinking and on the other hand, there are a spate of new types of employment in the informal sector. The growth of labour in the small-scale industries is one such example.

As mentioned earlier, the total labour employed in the small-scale sector in 2003–04 was around 28 million. An overwhelming majority of these workers were not unionised and they were engaged in poorly paid jobs with little or no social security. They were also not covered by the existing labour laws. Unfortunately, the trade union movement ignored the problems of these workers. The main argument put forth by the unions is: as there were no laws or job security for these workers, unionisation is difficult, if not impossible. This argument is not very plausible. The trade union movement in the country started at a time when industrial labour was in similar conditions. In 1918, when B.P. Wadia started the Madras Labour Union, factory workers were perhaps in the same situation as the informal sector workers of today. There were no labour laws and no protection for workers or social security. In fact, Wadia started the union precisely after hearing about the woes of workers at Binnys mills. After forming his union he tried to press for improvement of the working conditions but without much success. When he organised a strike, the employers went to court and the Madras High Court ruled that he should pay Rs 50,000 as compensation for the losses he had caused. Wadia finally reached a compromise by promising to opt out of the trade union movement as he was unable to pay the fine.

Similarly, in the post-World War I period there were a spate of labour unrests in all industrial cities. In Ahmedabad, Mahatma Gandhi started the Majur Mahajan in August 1918 to fight for workers' right to bonus. In Mumbai, trade union leaders of the mill workers were leading them towards militant struggles. All these movements took place when there were no laws or any form of protection for workers. In fact, whatever laws had come up were due to the initiatives of the trade unions. On 31 October 1920, the All India Trade Union Congress (AITUC) was formed as the first federation of the trade unions. Soon after this, in 1921 the Factories Act was passed granting 8 hour working day to male workers (earlier only women were allowed to work for 8 hours and there was no regulation of working hours for males). In 1926, the Trade Union Act was passed that for the first time gave recognition to trade unions. In fact, most of the labour laws granting protection in employment and social security in the post-independence period were passed mainly due to the earlier struggles of the working class. Hence, it was trade unionism that brought about changes in laws. In the present context, it is unfortunate that the mainstream trade unionists should want the government to pass laws first, before they can unionise. In fact, unionising these workers would help in throwing up their problems and solutions could then be worked out.

While it is true that unionising workers in the unorganised sector is a difficult and painstaking task, it is also true that the conventional methods of unionising may not be very successful.

In these cases too, trade unions need to develop new tactics. The example of the Self-Employed Women's Association (SEWA) is worth emulating in such cases. SEWA's focus has been on unionising the poorer women. It has organised rag-pickers, street vendors and a host of other trades by unifying them through various strategies such as, co-operatives, credit societies, health and child care services etc. It has a membership of over 500,000 and is the largest trade union in Gujarat. To the cynic, much of this work would appear as NGO activities. However, SEWA has used these different strategies with the prime objective of unionising these women so that they can articulate their demands as a group and can influence the state in changing its laws in favour of the working class.

After SEWA started organising women workers of the most oppressed sections of the working class, the government was forced to look into their problems. First, the government appointed a committee to look into the problems of self-employed women workers. Their report, *Shramshakti* served as an important document for further action. The report of the Second National Labour Commission, too, had a focus on the informal sector (as compared to the First National Labour Commission that had devoted only 36 pages on informal sector workers). Hence the issues of informal sector workers have come to the fore mainly through the actions of trade unions like SEWA and other unions of these workers. The struggles of other sections of the informal workers have also helped in getting them some social security. Two major achievements in this regard are the Beedi and Cigar Workers' Welfare Act and Construction Labour Welfare Act (which has not been implemented). Both these came into force only after long drawn struggles of these workers and their unions. Similarly, in Kerala, where unionisation of informal sector workers is high, there are a number of Welfare Boards for different sections of the informal sector. In Tamil Nadu too, there are such Boards. In Mumbai and Pune also, the Boards of the head-load workers are fairly strong and they are able to get minimum wages for their members. In addition, they provide for insurance and unemployment benefits etc. The concerted efforts of these unions and other organisations of the informal workers have led the present government to agree to an 'Umbrella Legislation' for the informal sector. The attempt is to have a common set of laws granting social security to workers in this sector so that there are common benefits. The draft legislation has been framed and is being discussed by different organisations.

Concluding Remarks

In this chapter we have tried to bring out the major problems of the working class as a whole after the intensification of the process of globalisation, economic liberalisation and structural adjustment. We have tried to show how all sections of the working class, both formal and informal sectors, have had to face problems because of these processes. We have critically looked at the role of the trade union movement in the country in dealing with the new problems. The objective was not to show that the movement is incapable of responding to the new problems, but on the contrary, the need to stress that the problems of insecure jobs and lack of social security can be tackled only through trade unions. Whatever minor gains achieved by the workers of the informal sector are due to their ability to unionise. However, the more important issue is that the trade union movement, that has largely been confined to the formal sector, needs to think afresh about the ways and means of unionising this sector. The problem of unionising workers to fight for their rights becomes more significant in this period when their rights are being effaced and the government is gradually withdrawing its support to the working class.

Notes

1. The data presented in this section is based on the study by Renana Jhabvala and Shalini Sinha (2002). The paper is a summary of the report of the Study Group on Women and Child Labour for the second National Labour Commission.
2. This part is based on the study on street vendors in seven cities conducted by the author on behalf of National Alliance of Street Vendors of India (Bhowmik 2000). The findings of this study was presented to the Ministry of Urban Development in 2001 and subsequently the Ministry appointed a National Task Force on Street Vendors/Hawkers to frame a notional policy for street vendors.
3. The data presented in this section is based on a study conducted by the author titled 'Outsourcing at Hindustan Lever Limited'. The Federation of Trade Unions of Netherlands (FNV) had sponsored this project as Unilever is an Anglo-Dutch MNC. The study was undertaken in 2001–02 and we covered most of the outsourced units in two states in western India, namely, Maharashtra and Gujarat.

References

Barse, Myrtle (2001). 'Social Implications of Voluntary Retirement Scheme: A Study in Mumbai', *Economic and Political Weekly* (Review of Labour), 36(52): 4828–35.

Bhowmik, Sharit K. (1992). 'Worker Co-operatives in the Plantation System: A Study of Tribal Tea Plantation Workers in Eastern India', *Labour, Capital and Society*, 25(2): 180–97, November.

——— (2000). 'Hawkers in the Urban Informal Sector: A Study on Street Vending in Seven Indian Cities', National Alliance of Street Vendors of India. (http://www.nasvinet.org and http://www.streetnet.org).

Bhowmik, Sharit K. and Nitin More (2001). 'Coping with Urban Poverty: Ex-Textile Mill Workers in Mumbai', *Economic and Political Weekly*, Mumbai, 36(52): 4822–27.

Bhowmik, Sharit K. and Kanchan Sarker (2002). 'Worker Co-operatives as Alternative Production Systems: A Study in Kolkata, India', *Work and Occupations*, Nashville, 29(4): 460–82.

Breman, Jan (2001). 'An Informalised Labour System: End of Labour Market Dualism', *Economic and Political Weekly*, Mumbai, 36(52): 4804–21.

Davala, Sarath (eds) (1994). *Employment and Unionisation in Indian Industry*. New Delhi: Friedrich Ebert Stiftung.

——— (1995). 'Introduction', in *Unprotected Labour in India*. Delhi: Friedrich Ebert Stiftung.

Dutt, Rudder (ed.) (1997). 'Introduction', in *Organising the Unorganised Workers*. Delhi: Vikas Publishing House.

GOI (Government of India) (2003). 'Small-Scale Sector', in *Economic Survey 2002–03*. New Delhi: Ministry of Finance.

GOI (Government of India) (2004). 'Informal Sector in India', http://www.labour.nic.in/ss/INFORMALSECTORININDIA, accessed on 2 December 2004.

——— (2005). *Economic Survey 2004–05*, Ministry of Finance, www.nic.in, accessed on 21 November 2004.

Heitzman, James (2004). *Network City: Planning the Information Society in Bangalore*. New Delhi: Oxford University Press.

Holmstrom, Mark (1997). 'A Cure for Loneliness? Networks, Trust and Shared Services in Bangalore', *Economic and Political Weekly*, Mumbai, 32(35): L14–L28.

ILO (International Labour Organisation) (2001). *World Employment Report 2001: Working in Information and Communication Technology Sector*. Geneva.

India Today (2002). 'Housekeepers to the World', Delhi, 27(46), 18 November.

Jhabvala, Renana and Shalini Sinha (2002). 'Liberalisation and the Woman Worker', *Economic and Political Weekly*, Mumbai, 37(23): 2037–44.

Kabeer, Naila (2001). *Bangladesh Women Workers and Labour Market Decisions: The Right to Choose*. New Delhi: Vistaar Publications/Sage.

Khasnobis, Ratan and Sudipti Banerjea (1996). 'Political Economy of Voluntary Retirement: Study of "Rationalised" Workers in Durgapur', *Economic and Political Weekly*, Mumbai, 31(52): L64–L72.

Knorringa, Peter (1996). *Economics of Collaboration: Indian Shoemakers Between Market Hierarchy*. New Delhi: Sage Publications.

Noronah, Ernesto (2001). 'Dock Labour Board 1948–94: From Security to Insecurity?', *Economic and Political Weekly*, 36(52): 4851–57.

Papola, T.S. (1994). 'Employment, Growth and Social Protection of Labour in India', in P. Sinha, C.S. Venkat Ratnam and G. Botterweek (eds), *Labour and Unions in a Period of Transition*. Delhi: Friedrich Ebert Stiftung.

Quarter, Jack (1993). *Canada's Social Sector*. Toronto: Lorimer.

World Bank (1995). *World Development Report 1995: Workers in an Integrating World*. Washington DC: Oxford University Press.

11

Governance and Development in the Era of Globalisation: Understanding Exclusion and Assertion of Dalits in India

Vivek Kumar

INTRODUCTION

Here, an attempt is made to understand the process of exclusion of the Dalits from the institutions of governance and policies of development in the contemporary Indian society in a specific socio-political context of globalisation. The chapter highlights the point that any system of governance is shaped by the social structure of that particular society. In doing so, it deliberates upon one of the most important structure of the Indian society, i.e., caste. We have tried to see how caste played a dominant role in shaping Indian administrative structure in the past and how it continues to influence it even today. The terms Dalit and globalisation have been defined. The history of exclusion of the Dalits in the institutions of governance and its continuance in contemporary Indian society forms the main part of the chapter. Further, the chapter depicts the status of the Dalits during the process of globalisation along with liberalisation and privatisation. Following this the issue of reservation in the private sector, which has emerged specifically because of the compulsions of globalisation in the Indian society, has been discussed. An important issue of governance in this era of globalisation is the emergence of NGOs. This is critically analysed in relation to their specific role in ameliorating the condition of the Dalits. Finally, an analysis of the issue of Dalit diaspora as a part their assertion forms part of the chapter, as it is the most important positive impact of globalisation on the Dalits.

The traditional social structure influences the modern structure of society. It is true for a hierarchically arranged society like India. It can be said beyond doubt that the Indian social structure had a direct impact on the Indian administrative structure. The so-called upper castes, which dominated the Indian social hierarchy, also dominated the Indian secular hierarchy in the judiciary and bureaucracy. But the Untouchables, Tribals and even Shudras were left out of the institutions of governance in the Indian society. The direct impact of domination of the so-called upper castes has been total and that is why they have reaped the fruits of the policies of development. On the contrary, the lower strata, as it was left out of the structures of governance, has been denied the fruits of development which is proved by the poor social indicators of the Dalits related to poverty, illiteracy, atrocity, unemployment, etc. This low status is a testimony to the fact that the Indian governing elite has not functioned on the universalistic principles where everyone is treated as equal. They have suffered from structural tensions of familistic, caste, kin-oriented particularism, and personal loyalty clashing with legal anonymity. Because of the traditional social structure, the Dalits have been out of the market, and hence have no economic power to compete in the globalised economy wherein the so-called upper castes dominate and most of the big business houses belong to them. Further, as the Indian society has been hierarchical, Dalits were of course excluded from the civil society and the same trend still continues. No doubt the democratic structures of governance have loosened the shackles of caste rigidity, but yet the accessibility to the secular spaces has been denied to them. Now a moot question is whether the total dominance of so-called upper castes will continue in the institutions of government, market and civil society—the three key players in the realm of governance—in the era of globalisation? Or is there a hope for the Dalits in this era to get their fair share. The most worrisome aspect of the era of globalisation is that there are no institutions administering social justice to the weaker sections. Earlier, there was the Indian state to take care of their needs and if they were not fulfilled they could go to the court of law for remedy. But now when the state is withdrawing and civil society and market continue to play an increasingly dominant role, and there is virtual monopoly of the so-called upper castes in these realms, where will the Dalits go for remedy?

Concepts

The terms Dalit and globalisation have been used in the chapter with a specific meaning. At the outset, we define these terms used in the chapter for our convenience and for the general readers.

Term Dalit

The Dalits in the annals of Indian history were addressed with different nomenclatures like *Chandalas, Avarnas, Achhuts, Namashudra, Pariahs, Adi-Dravida, Adi-Dharmis,* Depressed Classes, Oppressed Hindus, *Harijan*s etc. at different points in time. But especially after the emergence of Dalit Panthers movement in 1970s in Maharashtra, they preferred to be called as Dalits. The definition of Dalits as propounded by Dalit Panthers included members of Scheduled Castes (SCs), Scheduled Tribes (STs), the landless and poor peasants, women and all those who were exploited politically, economically and in the name of religion (Murugkar 1991: 237). This was a class definition of the term Dalit. It can be argued in this context that political compulsion forced the Panthers to propound such a definition as they wanted to forge an alliance between these aforesaid groups so that they can get maximum support from them. But it is a fact that the movement first took roots among the ex-untouchables of the Hindu society and the usage of the term Dalit was also restricted to this section only.

The class based definition of Dalits given by Dalit Panthers does not represent any sociological category in existence because ex-untouchables, tribals, women and proletariat are not the same. The definition blurs the differences between economically poor persons and ex-untouchables, tribals and ex-untouchables, and also women and ex-untouchables. It does so because the poor may be deprived in economic and political realms, but they may not be necessarily deprived in the social realm, i.e., they may not face the same type of exclusion and seclusion in the social and cultural life as ex-untouchables face. For instance, penury stricken Brahmins, Kshatriyas, Vaisyas or Shudras are never forced to live outside the boundaries of the main village. Though there is a hierarchy of status but untouchablity is totally absent in their interaction. They interact within themselves at least in secular realms on more or less equal terms. Contrary to this the Dalits were/are excluded from the main residential area of the village and were also kept outside the interaction pattern of the social life. Hence, we see that an ex-untouchable is deprived in the three—social, economic and political—realms. Therefore, the construction of consciousness of the Dalits is shaped by these three types of deprivations. Oommen has rightly pointed out, 'Dalit consciousness is a complex and compound consciousness which encapsulates deprivations stemming from inhuman conditions of material existence, powerlessness and ideological hegemony' (Oommen 1990: 256).

The social exclusion of an ex-untouchable is so overpowering that even though he attains economic and political mobility through his hard labor, he is not accepted by those located higher up in the caste hierarchy. His identity remains stigmatised and his achievements are basically associated with that social identity only. An example in this regard will make the fact clearer. It is a fact that as soon as K.R. Narayanan became the President of India, everyone tried to evaluate his achievement only on the basis of his caste identity and argued that he was elevated to the post of President because he belonged to the Dalit community. Here Narayanan's personal achievements in the educational and political realms became peripheral and his social identity became the basis of evaluation of his achievements.

Another impact of social deprivation on Dalits is that the loss of 'social capital' that could give them the potential to develop consciousness and motivation for their amelioration. And because of the lack of this consciousness, they could not revolt against the Hindu social order for long. Their cultural co-option in the Hindu social order, even though they were not of the part of V*arna* hierarchy, was effected by the artificial consensus which was a part of Hindu hegemony legitimised by the *Karma* theory which believes in the deeds of previous births determining one's status in the present.

Further, who can deny the differences between the ex-untouchables and tribals? Tribals are not a part of Hindu social order and have their own independent social system with its own social hierarchy. They did not face the same type of social exclusion as the Dalits. Their exclusion was more because of their geographical location in the hilly or forested terrain. On the whole, the tribals differed from Dalits in political, religious, economic and psychological aspects. These aspects have kept them away from the Hindu hegemony in terms of their status in the caste hierarchy, occupation, commensality etc. Further, this differentiation from the Hindu social order has resulted in a different type of construction of consciousness among the tribals and therefore, unlike the Dalits, they revolted against their exploitation a number of times in the past. That is why we cannot include them along with the ex-untouchables in defining the term Dalits.

Women also cannot form a part of the category of Dalits as propounded by the Dalit Panthers. The reasons are very clear. One, women in Indian society, no doubt exploited on the gender basis, do not constitute a monolithic whole. There is differentiation among the Indian women on caste and class lines. For instance, the women belonging to the castes located in the upper echelons of the caste hierarchy have the same attitude toward the Dalits as their male counterparts. They practice untouchability in the same manner, as any Hindu male would do. In fact, general caste women have never revolted or organised any movement against the exploitation of the Dalit woman by their men. Not only that, their revolt against the Hindu religious sanctions for the Hindu women has also been very mild. Hence, how can we differentiate them from Hindu men and include them in the category of Dalits.

Based on these facts, the term Dalit is being regularly used for ex-untouchables in the contemporary sociological parlance. Now, here an enigmatic situation exists as the caste Hindus want to lay a claim on the Dalits as being part and parcel of the Hindu social order and on the other hand the Dalits claim an independent status of a separate community. Therefore, based on this claim for separate identity anchored in the three types of deprivation—social, economic and political, where social deprivation assumes more significance, we can carve out an analytical category namely Dalits. This categorisation is very necessary because only then we can pinpoint the exact contours of this collectivity which can be used for analytical purposes without confusing it with other collectivities. The term Dalit has been used in this sense in the present chapter.

Globalisation

Explaining the process of globalisation, Oommen (2003) has emphasised that increase in the impact of a common communication system in the current epoch, has converted the universe into a 'world society'. This can be said so because whatever happens in one part of the world can instantly be communicated to the rest. Therefore, we can broadly conceptualise the universe as a world society. However, he argues that a world culture is different from a world society. It is different because there are four interrelated processes involved in the creation of what is called the global culture. These are: i) homogenisation, ii) pluarlisation, iii) traditionalisation, and iv) hybridisation. Hence, to understand the impact of globalisation on the Indian society, it is very important to look at how these four processes are at work. In this context, Oommen emphasises that the vast network of communication system which produces a world society results in the process of homogenisation. That means the traits, culture or institutions (say jeans or democracy), have all become global.

However, underlining this is the process of pluralisation. This means that it is one thing to adopt an item from the package of global culture but it is another thing to use it on a regular basis. For instance, consider Indian democracy with its numerous parties anchored in the values of caste, religion or region etc. It is quite a different phenomenon compared to the democracy in USA with two party systems. Yet, they both are said to be democracies.

Oommen has called this process pluralisation, which refers to the necessity to adapt to the needs of local/national situation. The third interrelated process which Oommen mentions in the process of globalisation is that of traditionalisation which emerges out of the process of assimilation of minority and weaker groups into the mainstream dominant culture. According to him, the process of homogenisation leads to hegemonisation and hence the weaker and the smaller cultures have a tendency of search for their roots which forces them to go back to the roots of the little tradition.

Last but not the least is the process of hybridisation which also accompanies globalisation. Oommen explains lucidly that in the process of adaptation, we often try to mutate some aspect of the alien culture when it interacts with the indigenous culture and add to the alien culture some indigenous traits. In this process of mutation of the modern culture and merging it with the traditional culture elements, a hybrid product is produced resulting in the process of hybridisation. For instance, take the case of local adaptation of McDonald's burgers in which beef and pork has been replaced by potato cutlet. Similar is the case of the Hindi version of MTV programs. Therefore, we can see that the local adaptations of cultural traits differ from the original process ruling out any possibility of a world culture.

Further, Oommen suggests that by cultural globalisation, we mean spread of cultural elements which has been ongoing from the days of colonialism. The only difference is that because of superior technological advancement there has been greater compression of time and space. But we have to take into account the advantage and disadvantages of these technological advancements. One disadvantage of this process of globalisation can be withering away of primary groups because of high technology that might effect the whole civilisation. Second, there is also the element of availability and accessibility of modern technology, the great instrument of globalisation which increases disparities in society and diminishes the possibility of a common humanity.

Seen in the light of the above, the process of globalisation in India has proved more harmful than beneficial to Dalits, specifically the process like pluralisation, traditionalisation and hybridisation. These processes have made it further difficult for researchers and administrators to measure and observe the bases and levels of discrimination in the institutions of governance. Because we never exactly know on which basis of value, universalistic or particularistic, the incumbent of an office in the legislature, judiciary, and bureaucracy functions. It is easy to camouflage one for the other with the help of the processes of globalisation in India. And unless we really diagnose the real basis of discrimination, it will be impossible to formulate the principles of governance and development in the era of globalisation.

Governance and Dalits: Past and Present

Sociologically speaking, governance can be defined as the formulation and implementation of policies and programmes, management and distribution of economic and social resources among the masses on the basis of universalistic principles. Further, the institutions of governance like legislature, bureaucracy, and judiciary should have fair representation of the members of diverse social groups without any monopoly of one group or the other.

In a hierarchically arranged society like India which is divided on the basis of caste, religion, class etc., it is all the more important that the institutions of governance are organised on universalistic principles so that each strata gets its fair share in decision-making and policy formulation. But that has not been the case in Indian society. Since the inception of modern institutions of governance viz. legislature, bureaucracy, judiciary etc., the so-called upper castes have dominated them. For instance, Misra (1960: 322) writes that 'most of the Hindus in the service of the Government were upper caste men, especially Brahmins and Kayasthas, who dominated the field.' The Indian Public Service Commission reported in 1887 that of 1866 Hindu members of the judicial and executive services, as many as 904, i.e., nearly half were Brahmins, and 454, i.e., nearly a quarter were Kayasthas who were called Prabhus in Bombay. The number of Kshatriyas or Rajputs was 147; Vaishyas, 113; Shudras, 146; and others, 102. The Brahmins were especially dominant in Madras with 202 of the total 297, and in Bombay with 211 out of 328. Similarly, Seal (1968: 118) reveals that in the year 1886–87, the caste of persons employed in the executive and judicial branches of the uncovented service in the Bombay Presidency—the elite of the Indian administrative hierarchy—shows that of the 384 persons employed in this capacity, 328 were Hindus, of which 211 were Brahmins, 26 Kshtriyas, 37 Prabhus, 38 Vaishyas, 1 Shudra and 16 others. In this context, if we take note of the Miller Committee (named after its British Chairman, a judge), it showed that in Mysore 9712 of the 13946 jobs in the state service were occupied by Brahmins (Mendelshon and Vicziani 1998: 129). In the same vein Ambedkar also highlighted the dominance of the caste Hindus in the public services after the issue of Indianisation of services emerged in the public domain with the establishment of Islington Commission in 1915 and Lee Commission later on. He opined, 'It is notorious that the public services of the country in so far as they are open to Indians have become by reason of various circumstances a close preserve for the Brahmins and allied castes. The Non-Brahmins, the Depressed Classes and the Mohamdeans are virtually excluded from them' (Ambedkar 1982: 394).

From the above data it is evident that the traditional hierarchy of the Hindu social structure was replicated in the bureaucratic structures as well. This strengthened the position of the Brahmins, Kshtriyas, Vaishyas who clubbed their social privileges and positions with the secular one, which emanated from bureaucratic and legal structures and reinforced their dominance over Dalits and other marginalised sections. Hence, the growth of rational legal authority and bureaucratic social structure of universalistic principles was thwarted. Weber has remarked that traditional India did not have a developed socio-culture foundation for the growth of rational legal authority and bureaucratic social structures (Weber 1946: 416–17). Looking at the data of contemporary India the same can be said for today as well. The institutions of governance have been functioning more or less on particularistic values, and therefore, the lower strata like Dalits and tribals have been discriminated against. The administrative machinery dominated by the so-called upper castes does not sympathise with the Dalit cause and interests, is not charged with their pain, wants, desires and cravings and is inimical to their aspirations. That is why there has been a wide discrepancy and gap between the formulation and implementation of state policies as well. That is why cumulatively the resources could never reach the targeted groups, making Dalits and other marginalised groups suffer.

After independence and the commencement of the democratic Constitution with the principles of equality and equality of opportunity, it was envisaged that the administrative structure will get democratised with a fair representation from most of the sections of society. But the irony is that the composition of the institutions of governance hardly changed. In fact, the dominance of the so-called upper castes substantially increased soon after the partition of the country and further increased over the years. They monopolised the institutions of governance. Their representation in the institutions of governance has increased over the years, whereas the representation of Dalits, tribals and other marginalised sections has remained negligible. The community-wise population and their representation in various services have been given in Tables 11.1, 11.2 and 11.3 which are self explanatory.

Table 11.1: Percentage Population of Various Castes and Communities and their Representation in Class-I Government/Non-government Services

	% of population		*Representation in services (%)*	
Castes/communities	*1935*	*1989*	*1935*	*1989*
Brahmins	3.5	5.20	3.00	70.20
Rajputs	2.5	3.80	2.00	1.70
Kayasthas	0.85	1.03	40.00	7.00
Banyas	1.20	1.78	1.00	3.50
(Total so-called upper castes)	(6.15)	(11.81)	(46.00)	(82.40)
SC/ST/OBC	64.00	68.85	1.00	8.00
Muslims	21.00	10.13	35.00	3.20
Others	7.95	9.21	18.00	6.40

Source: National Commission for Scheduled Castes and Scheduled Tribes, Fourth report, 1996–97 and 1997–98, p. 22.

Table 11.2: Representation of Various Social Groups in Various High Courts as Judges and Additional Judges

Year	*Total no. of Judges*	*Scheduled castes*	*Scheduled tribes*	*Others*
March 1982	325	1.23%	–	98.77%
March 1993	547	2.38%	0.73%	96.89%

Source: National Commission for Scheduled Castes and Scheduled Tribes, Fourth report, 1996–97 and 1997–98, p. 20.

It is a fact that as the representation of Dalits and the other marginalised groups of the society has gone up in the institutions of governance, the same has acted as one of the most important bases of discrimination against them. The discrimination can be explained by the

Table 11.3: Representation of Scheduled Castes, Scheduled Tribes, Other Backward Classes and Upper Castes in the Indian High Commission Offices

Class	*Scheduled Caste*	*Scheduled Tribes*	*Other Backward Classes*	*Upper Castes*
Class A	8.00	1.00	0.00	91.00
Class B	4.20	0.60	5.00	94.00
Class C	4.30	1.20	1.50	93.00
Class D	7.00	1.00	0.20	91.33

Source: National Commission for Scheduled Castes and Scheduled Tribes, Fourth Report 1996–97 and 1997–98, p. 20.

continuing monopoly of the so-called upper castes. Instead of functioning on the universalistic principles and values where every individual should be treated equally, they function more on particularistic values related to caste, region, religion, language etc. There is a bias towards the Dalits and other marginalised groups in these institutions of governance and that is why either service is denied to them or there are delays in the delivery of services. It has been reported in many quarters that the members of administrative machinery treat them with contempt, and hence, there is undue harassment of these sections. It has also been reported that often the members of the administration in connivance with the local dominant castes transfer the facilities meant for the Dalit localities to those of the upper castes. There have been regular instances where the funds earmarked for the Dalits are transferred to other heads, sometimes funds meant for the programmes for the Dalits lapse and at other times the funds are siphoned off illegally (see the recommendations of various SC/ST Commission reports).

In this context, the Audit report of the Comptroller and Auditor General of India (C&AG), reviewing grant Number 85 of the Ministry of Social Justice and Empowerment revealed, 'Unspent Provision: The unspent provision during 2000–20001, was Rs 136.89 Crores, during the previous years 1999–2000 and 2000–2001, it was Rs 169.07 Crores and 242.98 Crores respectively' (GOI 2004a: 76). Further the report reveals, 'Unrealistic Budgeting: During the period 1999–2002, there were as many as 560 sub-heads where 47 to 100 per cent of the budget provisions were re-appropriated to other heads, defeating the original purpose for which it was authorised by Parliament. Above 60 cases included 32 cases where entire budget provisions remained unutilised' (ibid.). In evaluating a specific scheme viz. National Scheme of Liberation & Rehabilitation of Scavengers and their Development, the report has rebuked the ministry in the harshest words. It says, 'it [scheme] has failed to achieve its objective even after ten years of implementation involving investments of more than Rs 600 Crores' (ibid.). Underlining the main causes of failure of the said scheme, which can be equated with that of the failure of most of the programmes of the government, the report highlights, 'it failed working out a coherent strategy for policy initiatives.... Absence of base line survey, non-involvement of district development authorities,... lack of purpose in aligning the parameters of the scheme and lack of will in implementing it led to the scheme floundering on its own assumption' (ibid.). The strong rebuke by C&AG to one of the highest offices of governance concerned with the welfare of Dalits and other marginalised groups is self explanatory regarding how the rules are flouted by the functionaries. In this context, one can imagine the plight of the Dalits because they are the most dependent lot on the State. From the public distribution system where they get their subsidised food, to birth, death, income, caste, domicile certificates, the dependence of Dalits is total, that is from 'cradle to grave and beyond'.

Against this background of high dependence of Dalits on the State, their problem becomes complicated because it is difficult for them to garner courage to lodge a complaint against the erring officials who are generally from the so-called high castes. Second, even if a complaint is lodged, because of monopoly of the so-called upper castes in different echelons of governance, the guilty is seldom punished. Because of this it is difficult to have a democratic structure of governance in the Indian society where the Dalits and the other marginal groups are treated as equals.

The only way left to democratise the institutions of governance is to break the monopoly of the so-called upper castes and diversify the representation of the marginalised sections like Dalits, tribals, OBCs, minorities and women in the different echelons of governance. It is a fact that the phenomenon of diversification of representation in the institutions of governance had started with the educational development among the Dalits and other marginalised sections. The process would have got a fillip had the recommendations of the Mandal Commission got implemented a decade before they were finally implemented in 1994. But the irony is that as soon as this process started taking roots and more and more members of the deprived sections started entering the different arms of governance, the process of globalisation was unleashed. With the onslaught of the process of globalisation and its economic agenda of liberalisation and privatisation, the government has virtually stopped the recruitment in general. The recruitment in the government, public enterprise, banking, and insurance sectors has been frozen and there has also been retrenchment through voluntary retirement and compulsory retirement schemes. The jobs have been lost also because of the disinvestment policy of the public sector. On the other hand, there is no reservation in the private sector at all. Clubbed together, the Dalits have been the worst sufferers with the onset of the process of globalisation because earlier too they were not in the institutions of governance and as soon as they enabled themselves to be part of them, globalisation has ruined their chances. In this manner, the monopoly of the so-called upper castes in the institutions of governance has been kept intact and it will never be challenged in the future as well, because the members of other marginalised groups will never be inducted in large numbers.

Therefore, a moot question about the relationship between Dalits and the institutions of governance in this era of globalisation is whether these institutions will be democratised or not and whether they will continue functioning on the particularistic values related to caste, religion, region, language etc. The second question is whether in the process of democratisation, the Dalits and other marginalised sections will get a fair share so that the monopoly of the so-called upper caste is broken and they can also be part of the decision-making and policy formulation.

Dalits in the Era of Globalisation

Dalits, India's ex-untouchables constitutionally known as Scheduled Castes, account for 16.37 per cent of the total population of the country according to the 1991 Census. Historically Dalits have been among the most subordinated and poorest people in India who have been structurally subjected to various kinds of social discrimination and economic deprivation. It is also a fact that the cumulative deprivation suffered by the Dalits has a tacit support of the Hindu social order that took refuge in its sacred texts to justify the seclusion of one-fourth (SCs and STs together) of the Indian population.

Historicity apart, what is disturbing in this regard is that even after 57 years of independence, with the completion of nine Five Years Plans and when we have entered the 21st century in this era of globalisation, all the efforts to ameliorate the condition of Dalits have proved largely futile. The efforts of the state and the expenditure incurred on the programmes and policies for their upliftment have not produced commensurate results. There has not been any marked improvement in the socio-economic condition of the Dalits. Otherwise 50 per cent of Dalits would have not been below the poverty line, 68 per cent of them would have not been illiterate, 80 per cent would have not been dropouts after high-school, 63 per cent would have not been wage labourers in the rural areas, only one-fifth of them would not have been cultivating land as independent self-employed cultivators, two Dalit women would have not been raped and three Dalits would have not been murdered per day in the country. The plight of the Dalits is evident from Table 11.4 that depicts the prevalent poverty, illiteracy, and dropouts among them.

The socio-economic and cultural inertia and lack of what Pierre Bourdieu calls 'culture capital' are internal reasons for the arrested development of the Dalits in Indian society. Education is one of the most potent instrument of social mobility. But the lack of primary education centres and non-allocation of enough funds for it have retarded the growth of education among Dalits. Further, the educational curriculum, course content and the fee structure still favours the upper strata of the society. The Dalits have failed to identify themselves with the educational content in the books.

Their labour, history and cultural elements are mostly absent in the books taught in the schools, colleges and universities. And if at all they find a place, they are ridiculed or have a stigmatised identity. We can argue that the lack of identification with the course content by the Dalits is one of the most important bases for them to become dropouts. That is why we find the maximum number of dropouts among this section of society. Similarly, the vast army of 63 lakh educated SC/ST youths have demoralised parents to send their wards to educational centres as they have no hope for the future, and on the other hand, once educated, they also turn away from their hereditary occupation, making livelihood difficult. Today with the privatisation of education and demand of management graduates and computer engineers in the job market on the one hand, and introduction of courses of *Purohiti* targeting Dalit youths on the other, the chances of Dalit youths getting vocational education to earn their livelihood have further worsened. They have already lost their traditional occupations with the introduction of modernisation. Now, with the contract system in the era of globalisation

Table 11.4: The Socio-economic and Educational Profile of Dalits in Different Indian States

Sl. no.	*State*	*SC population (1991) %*	*SC literate population (1991) %*	*SC under poverty line (1993–94) %*	*Dropout rate SC at secondary stage (1990–91)*
1.	Andhra Pradesh	15.93	31.59	34.92	86.00
2.	Arunachal Pradesh	0.47	57.27	–	–
3.	Assam	7.40	53.94	29.86	62.42
4.	Bihar	14.56	19.49	62.91	89.39
5.	Goa	2.08	58.73	–	81.07
6.	Gujarat	7.41	61.07	38.62	71.29
7.	Haryana	19.75	39.22	35.07	78.12
8.	Himachal Pradesh	25.34	53.2	27.70	67.78
9.	Jammu & Kashmir	–	–	–	79.09
10.	Karnataka	16.38	38.06	54.00	75.03
11.	Kerala	9.92	79.66	34.01	51.05
12.	Madhya Pradesh	14.54	35.08	55.41	61.58
13.	Maharashtra	11.10	56.46	52.10	71.96
14.	Manipur	2.02	56.44	–	81.70
15.	Meghalaya	0.51	44.27	–	30.57
16.	Mizoram	0.10	77.92	–	–
17.	Nagaland	–	–	–	–
18.	Orissa	16.20	36.78	48.2	81.54
19.	Punjab	28.31	41.09	25.02	79.34
20.	Rajashan	17.29	26.29	43.50	82.07
21.	Sikkim	5.93	51.03	–	91.51
22.	Tamil Nadu	19.18	46.74	52.77	77.32
23.	Tripura	16.36	56.66	–	87.29
24.	Uttar Pradesh	21.04	26.85	58.50	72.20
25.	West Bengal	23.62	42.21	41.51	88.81
26.	Delhi	19.05	57.60	–	65.36

Source: Sixth Report of The National Commission for Scheduled Castes and Scheduled Tribes, 1999–2000 & 2000–01, New Delhi, pp. 40, 41, 172–74, 177.

and privatisation, their traditional/hereditary occupation like sweeping, washing (specially in the government hospital, railways, banks etc.), supply of leather and hide of the dead animals etc., are being taken away by the highest bidder, rendering the Dalits poorer.

Protective Discrimination

To ameliorate the Dalits from their wretched condition, the framers of the Constitution gave the slogan of establishing equality in the society. For the same reason they enshrined in the

Constitution the value of equality of opportunity under Article 16. But they knew that in this hierarchical Indian society as some individuals and groups have been privileged by mere chance of their birth, they will take all the advantages of this policy of equality of opportunity and hence they tried to create equality of condition with the policy of protective discrimination better known as the policy of reservation.

Accordingly, reservation has been provided for the Dalits systematically, since independence, in three areas: i) political reservation of seats in the Parliament (Lok Sabha) and the State Assemblies (State Legislatures), urban and rural local bodies; ii) reservation in government jobs—central and state services, public sector enterprises, banking sector and insurance sector, and iii) reservation of seats in admission and related facilities in educational institutions. It may be mentioned here that reservation has produced by now significant results, though the evaluation of its precise impact on the Dalits in the country is overdue. In the light of the above, it is interesting to note that till date except for political reservation under Articles 330 and 332, which were to lapse after ten years following the commencement of the Constitution but have been extended till 2010 (Article 243-d and 243-t), the central and state governments have never completely filled the allotted quotas of jobs for the Dalits under Article 335 of the Constitution (which has no time stipulation). The figures in Table 11.5 amply explain the gross violation of constitutional provision meant to uplift and bring a vast population into the mainstream of the society.

The situation in different educational institutions along with the four Indian Institutes of Technology and different management institutes is even worse (see Table 11.6). For example, it was reported that out of 422 faculty members in IIT Chennai, there were only two belonging to SC/ST communities, and even they had been selected on the basis of merit. It is evident from the figures that the policy which was envisaged to empower the Dalits to participate in governance and other aspects of social life was never implemented on one pretext or the other. At the inception of the policy, it was argued that enough candidates are not available for recruitment, and later on it was declared that the seats are vacant because of want of suitable SC candidates. With over four decades of negative history of poor implementation of reservation, since 1990, the policy started facing the onslaught of new economic policy which is rendering the whole policy of reservation ineffective.

Table 11.5: Representation of Scheduled Castes in Different Services with respect to 15 per cent Reservation in them

Class of service	*Central services*	*Public sector undertaking*	*Public sector banks and financial institutions*	*Insurance sector*
A	11.29	10.35	12.51	13.67
B	12.68	11.05	14.88	12.40
C	15.72	18.93	24.46	17.24

Source: Sixth Report of The National Commission for Scheduled Castes and Scheduled Tribes, 1999–2000 & 2000–01, New Delhi.

Table 11.6: Representation of Dalits in Various Central Universities

	Universities							
Type of service	*BHU*	*AMU*	*JNU*	*DU*	*JMI*	*Vishwa Bharti*	*Hydrabad C.U.*	*IIT Chennai*
Professor	1/360	0/233	2/183	3/332	0/80	1/148	1/72	Two SC
Reader	1/396	0/385	3/100	2/197	1/128	1/70	2/87	out of total
Lecturer/Asstt. Prof.	1/329	0/521	11/70	9/140	1/216	16/188	13/44	422 teachers

Source: Sixth Report of The National Commission for Scheduled Castes and Scheduled Tribes, 1999–2000 & 2000–01, New Delhi.

Globalisation and Reservation for SCs

It is abundantly clear that the with the onset of globalisation and its supplementary processes of liberalisation, privatisation and revolution in information and communication technology, the state is rolling back. This has resulted in substantial reduction of jobs not only in the different sectors of government, but in the private sector as well. The state has already opened up 10 out of 18 core public sectors for private bidders and soon the remaining eight will also be thrown open. By granting reservation of jobs in each public sector enterprise, Dalits were ensured their share in the sector prior to introduction of the policy of privatisation. However, Dalits are losing their share in the form of job reservations due to selling off and disinvestment of the public sector enterprises by the government. Moreover, though the government is generating revenue from the sale of public sector enterprises, it is not spending anything out of that on Dalits and thus denying their share in the resourse. Furthermore, many nationalised banks are being merged to compensate for their losses and private banks are coming up with no provisions for reservation. Even the insurance sector has been opened for the private sector. Further, the Fifth Pay Commission recommended a 30 per cent cut across the board in the jobs, over a 10-year frame at the rate of three per cent per annum. But in order to bring about fiscal prudence and austerity, the government imposed a 10 per cent cut across the board in the number of sanctioned posts as on January 1 1992. Instructions were issued in January 2000 directing a 10 per cent reduction in the number of posts created during January 1992 to December 1999. The Expenditure Reforms Commission recommended a further 10 per cent cut in the sanctioned strength of staff as on 1 January 2000, to be carried out by each ministry/department by 2004–05. The net result of the aforesaid process will be shrinking job opportunities, not only for the general masses but for Dalits as well. For the latter in comparison to general castes, it is more detrimental because reservation has played an important role in their empowerment and integration into the society. This is proved by the fact that they are found only in those realms where either reservation has been implemented or in the areas where their hereditary services such as sweeping and cleaning is required. Otherwise, there is complete black-out of their presence in other social and economic sectors where reservation does not exist, for instance, the Indian (private) market, in media, cinema, judiciary, army, different boards, Rajya Sabha, and PMO, to name a few.

Politics of Private Sector Reservation

Recently, the Congress (I)-led UPA Government has started a dialogue on affirmative action including reservation in the private sector for Dalits. In Maharashtra it introduced a bill in this regard before going into assembly polls. Further, in Madhya Pradesh it had implemented supplier and dealership diversity for Dalits in January 2002. A moot question is, why at all Congress-led governments are so eager to provide reservation to Dalits in the private sector? This question becomes more significant because there has not been any genuine demand by the Dalits for reservation in the private sector. There have been no movements worth mentioning for the same. Even the Backward and Minorities Communities Employees' Federation (BAMCEF), the biggest group of Dalit employees has not demanded this kind of reservation. Yet, the Congress (I) is thinking along these lines.

In the distant past too, it was Congress (the then Indian National Congress led by Mahatma Gandhi) which forced Babasaheb Ambedkar to accept reservations under the Poona Pact, though he had demanded separate electorates for the Dalits and achieved that as well. But he had to sacrifice them to save Mahatma Gandhi's life. Since then, it is an established fact that the Congress has benefited from political reservation by getting elected only those Dalits who speak their party language (Ambedkar 1991: 88–102, Ram: 1982). But since the inception of reservation the Congress lacked political will to implement the policy of reservation for the Dalits in the service sector. For instance, the first Prime Minster of India, Jawaharlal Nehru once wrote to his Chief Ministers in June 1961, 'It is true that we are tied up with certain rules and conventions about helping the Scheduled Castes and tribes. They deserve help but, even so, I dislike any kind of reservation, more particularly in service. I react strongly against anything which leads to inefficiency and second rate standard' (Nehru 1989: 456–57).

Therefore, notwithstanding the importance of dialogue on reservation in the private sector because of shrinking job opportunities in the Government/Public Sector and spread of private sector in wake of liberalisation, privatisation and globalisation, Dalits have their own doubts about the policy. They wonder whether it is only a political gimmick or is the government serious!

Need of a White Paper on the Status of Reservation

Dalit skepticism is easy to understand. Various Governments formed at the centre, in which the Congress party has been in power for longest duration, have not been able to completely fill in the vacancies under the allotted quota of reservation for Scheduled Castes (15%) (see Table 11.5) and Scheduled Tribes (7.5%) in the central services and public sector, as per Article 335 of the Constitution, even after about six decades of Independence. The record of various state governments in this regard has been even worse. Similarly, different governments took 44 years in identifying the OBCs and implementing reservation for them. So the logical question is that, if the governments have not been able to implement the reservation policy for so long, how long will they take to implement a policy which is not yet born? Can any one specify the exact time that the legislature, judiciary, and bureaucracy will take to dovetail the policy so that it can be implemented smoothly?

If the government is truly sincere about opening up employment opportunities to the socially oppressed, it must first review the existing policy of reservation and come out with a white paper on the present status of reservation. Such a document must detail how many jobs were identified for reservation in various sectors, how many have been filled, and how many vacancies remain vacant. It should look into the causes of omission and commission and help plug the gaps as well. If there are problems at the government end, it should specify them; and if at the Dalit community's end, then some immediate policy measures should be taken for their capacity building. Further, if the government is convinced that reservations can uplift Dalits, it should enumerate the timetable in the paper to fulfill the backlog of vacancies within the government and public sector. In the same vein, the government should extend reservations to Dalits and OBCs in the key offices of the country like the judiciary, army, Vidhan Parishads, Rajya Sabha and various regulatory bodies in different sectors which are still under its control. Instead of taking these aforesaid steps, the present government is having a dialogue with the private sector and that too, without any concrete preparation. It should ideally have done the groundwork on certain issues, which would aid in negotiating with the private sector.

How Private is the Private Sector?

The Government should reveal what is so private about the private sector. It has not analysed whether the private sector should be referred to as the private sector at all, especially in the light of the concessions given to it by the government—like land and its registration at concessional rates, tax holidays, bank loans, besides the indirect contribution made by government in their development in the form of maintaining law and order, supply of technology, research and development, trained human resources, road, rail, air, other communication facilities, etc. Has the government documented the total cost of these subsidies? Had they done so, it would have been easier for it to show the real worth of the private sector. There is also a need to inform the masses how the private sector was doled out with government money during its infancy. Today's Tatas and Birlas have thrived only on the public money in the past and enjoyed full government patronage. Under these circumstances can we say the private sector is really private?

Evaluating Merit and Efficiency

Similarly, the government should have prepared a concept paper on the issue of 'merit' in general and 'merit and efficiency' of the private sector in particular. It is necessary because whenever the issue of reservation comes up, it is certain that the whole Dalit community is portrayed as devoid of any merit. The rest of the society is depicted as meritorious. This view is one sided. Nobody even cares to note that there are millions of Dalits who survive without availing reservation. The merit of the other side is never assessed. It is pertinent now that the government critically evaluates the performance of the private sector in terms of its inefficiency, and uncompetitiveness. It is true that, 'The case for the efficiency of capitalism rests on the theory of "invisible hand", which Adam Smith first set forth two centuries ago...The producer has the incentive to make what consumers want and to make it in the least costly way. Nobody is asked to evaluate what is good for the system or for the society' (Okun 1975: 50). But even then the private sector asks for help from the state and society. The government may reveal the efficiency of the Indian private sector, for instance, revealing the amount of money lost by the public sector banks as 'Non-Performing Assets' because of the private sector companies, and also the total loss government suffers on account of tax evasion by them. The government should also reveal the number of private industries which die out every year or declare themselves bankrupt. It must declare the number of fraudulent non-banking financial companies, which have duped the public of their money. In this regard, the Ministry of Company Affairs (MCA) has released a concept paper on the Companies Act in which it has dealt with the concept of 'vanishing Companies', the concept paper has identified 122 such companies (which raised public money to the tune of Rs 838 crore) (Bhutani 2004).

The merit and efficiency of the private sector can be easily assessed by the contribution it makes to the world export market, which is a meager 0.7 per cent only. Similarly, the same private sector has been demanding level playing field for itself with the onset of the process of liberalisation. How can the private sector then boast of its efficiency and merit? If the Indian industry was so meritocratic, why is it that they have not produced a single brand or item, which can be internationally prescribed or has become an international commodity? Above all, what right do the industrialists of today have to call themselves meritorious, when most of the owners of the established business houses have inherited their business from their parents. None of the top industrialists is a first generation industrialist. They might have expanded the business but they could do so because they belong to certain pedigree only. That is why a number of social scientists have rejected the view of 'merit'. They have argued that the rewards in the educational and economic system are not based on merit. The educational and occupational attainments are related to family background rather than talent and ability. Thus, the children of the wealthy and powerful tend to obtain high qualification and highly rewarded jobs irrespective of their ability. It is this that the educational system disguises with myth of meritocracy (Bowles & Gintis 1976). In the same vein, social scientists have also rejected the narrow definition of merit in terms of intelligence which is a measure of just one portion of the total spectrum of human mental abilities associated with knowledge and memory rather than the ability to reason (Jensen 1973).

The government should, in fact, seek the assistance of the progressive intelligentsia—particularly the Dalit intelligentsia—to explode the myth of merit once and for all. Theories to defend the Dalits on the issue of merit are needed. Starting from the contribution made by Dalit labour in running the economy and polity of the nation to the midwifery role played by the Dalit women should be evaluated and highlighted. Who decides which occupation is of 'functional importance' and therefore to be accorded higher prestige (Tumin 1967)? And why should merit only be evaluated in terms of performance of these 'functionally important' occupations? Why can labour of the Dalits not be a commodity worthy enough to be regarded creative, artistic, and hence prestigious? Second, to detonate the myth of merit the government should use its own data to show that enough trained and qualified Dalit students are available for the jobs in the private sector (see Table 11.7). From the available data, one can negate the argument put forward by the private sector that the Dalit candidates are not available or suitable. Further, the government should also collect data on other streams of professional education gained by Dalits to prove the exact pool of talent among the Dalits. Till now the data published by the SC/ST Commission includes only the traditional educational degrees like BA, MA, BE, which does not suggest their real potential.

Table 11.7: Number of Dalit Students Available in Different Streams

Arts graduates (1)	*Science graduates (2)*	*Commerce graduate (3)*	*B.E. (4)*	*MBBS (5)*	*B. Ed. (6)*	*M.A. (7)*	*M. Sc. (8)*	*Profes-sionals (4+5+6)*	*Total (1-8)*
3,61,894	14,2,686	82,118	30,193	12,615	13,004	44,093	10,134	55,812	6,32,689

Source: National Commission for Scheduled Castes and Scheduled Tribes, Sixth Report, 1999–2000 & 2000–01.

Merit of the Other Side

Dalits wonder—are the communities that do not avail of constitutional reservation meritorious? They evaluate the Indian performance on the basis of traditional social structure to asses the 'merit' of the aforesaid groups. There were Varnas—Brahmin, Kshatriya, Vaishya—assigned with particular functions, which were initially open but became closed later. The Brahmin had the privilege of teaching, the Kshatriya of protecting all creatures, and Vaishya living by commerce (Dumont 1970: 69). Today Dalits ask, if the Brahmins were so meritorious, then why is it that still half of the country's population is illiterate? If the Kshatriyas were so meritorious, then why could they not defend our borders? The Tartars, Moughals, British etc., all defeated them and subjugated us. Similarly, if the Vaishyas were so meritorious, then why is the trade and commerce of India in shambles?

Presently India is placed as low as at 124th position in the Human Development Index (HDI), in the group of 174 countries. In the 'Corruption Perception Index' for the year 2004, India ranks 90th in the group of 146 countries as indicated in the Transparency International India report 2004 (*The Indian Express* 2004). Above all, the external debt of India is a whopping Rs 5,11,861 crores (GOI 2004b: 128). All the meritorious economists and administrators are managing the affairs of the country without availing of any reservation, even then why is the situation so bad? The situation in science and technology which is considered the realm of high specialty and hence kept out of bound of reservation is not encouraging. In this regard, Nian Chai Liu and his colleagues at the Shanghai Jio Tong University in China spent two years collating and analysing the output of 2000 universities world-wide and published their results by ranking five hundred universities. Only three universities/institutions from India figure in top 500: Indian Institute of Sciences at 260 and the Indian Institute of Technology at Kharagpur and Delhi at 459 and 460 respectively (Mohan: 2004). In this context, it will be worth mentioning to look at the merit of the doctors working in the most prestigious hospitals in the country. If the Indian doctors and medical specialist are so meritorious, then why is it that most of the VVIPs run away to foreign countries to treat the simplest of illness? Even the former Prime Minister Atal Bihari Vajpayee, an ardent supporter of *Swadeshi* had to call an NRI orthopedic surgeon for his knee operation. Last but not the least, is it really logical and possible to measure the merit of the professionals passing out from the various private engineering, medical, management colleges etc., where a seat can be bought for a few lakhs of rupees.

Discrimination in Recruitment Pattern in Private Sector

It is a fact that there exists systematic discrimination in recruitments in the private sector. Beteille (1990: 203) observes that, 'Although the new occupations in the office and factory are in principle caste free, the association between caste and occupation is carried over from the traditional to the modern occupational settings. The various castes are not represented in the occupations according to their proportions in the population. The inferior castes in general, and the Scheduled Castes in particular, are very thinly represented in the superior administrative and managerial occupations. In a society which has adopted the principle of equality of opportunity but whose members remain acutely conscious of caste distinctions, these disparities are now a source of anxiety and concern.' Further, he argues, 'There are several reasons why the untouchables and other inferior castes are so thinly represented in the higher occupations. While Article 15 prohibits discrimination on the grounds of caste and Article-16 guarantees equality of opportunity in public employment, there is, in fact, widespread prejudice against the inferior castes in general and the untouchables in particular. This prejudice is not easy to measure and by its nature it is difficult to establish in the individual case. It operates more actively at the lower levels of employment where recruitment, tenure and promotion are to large extent personalised than perhaps at the higher levels where these processes are organised in a more impersonal way. But there is reason to believe that some candidates are at every level rejected on account of prejudice even when they have the necessary qualification' (ibid.: 203–4).

Discrimination exists in the private sector on account of denial of equal employment opportunity especially because of the informal and opaque medium of recruitment. In the name of cost-effective choice of the most suitable person, private sector industries make appointments often based on personal choices without even advertising for the jobs. Vernacular newspapers and backward areas are deliberately blacked out to reduce the pool of talent; a foreign degree and high pedigree becomes the basis of evaluating merit. This recruitment pattern is increasing day by day. Human Resource Head of Adobe India says, 'Employee referrals are a major source of recruitment for us. Our employees understand our requirements very well and have friends with a similar academic background and skills'. In the same vein, director of MAQ Software argues that 'we reach candidates with better profiles who cannot be reached otherwise through other channels like online sites or placement agencies'. Apart from Abode and MAQ software, there are a few more in the same league like Infosys and Wipro who have an internal employee's referral scheme for employment. Not only that, they hire an employee on the basis of referrals; rather if the hired employee fits the bill then the employee who has referred is paid an increment as well (Singh 2004). This is a discriminatory practice, which has gone on since the inception of the private sector in India.

Though there is no research on the demerits of this system of recruitment in India, but studies abroad suggest that discrimination does exist. Commenting on the demerits of the informal system of recruitment in United Kingdom, the Commission for Racial Equality once observed, 'As far as informal recruitment methods in many industries are concerned, ethnic minorities never come to know of vacancies because they have never worked in those industries. They are unable to pass on to their friends and children the information on vacancies. Therefore, such establishment will always remain all white' (Anwar 1990: 58). Further, 'The commission's investigations have shown that the word of mouth recruitment is unlawful as it discriminates indirectly against particular racial groups. However, even when these methods of recruitment are corrected to remove their unlawful effect, it can take many years before an impact is made on the opportunities for ethnic minority people'. Though the aforesaid fact is concerned with an alien land and communities, but they can be easily equated with the situation of the Indian industrial system and the plight of the Dalits, who are underrepresented in the private sector industries.

Therefore, unless the government debates, highlights and discusses, the aforesaid issues, the general masses and Dalits will not be aware of the myths and reality of both private and public sector reservation. If they fail to do so, then the dialogue on reservation in private sector will be considered only a political gimmick on more than one account: One, it is a ploy to garner Dalit votes; two, it is for granting legitimacy to the whole private sector and that too via the most deprived section of the society; and last but not the least, it may thwart the emerging independent Dalit assertion and thereby, the independent Dalit movement.

Atrocities on the Dalits: The Test of Dalit Status

Atrocities on the Dalits are continuing unabated in the era of globalisation. Right to equality and right to be treated equally are different sets of prepositions. There are a number of laws and constitutional clauses which give the Dalits the right to be treated at par with others, yet the number of atrocities against them reveal that they do not receive equal treatment from other members of the society. The perpetuation of the 'upper caste' hegemony through purporting atrocities on the Dalits has proved detrimental for them. Atrocities on Dalits is not a new phenomenon, though there are no historical records on the same.

As far as the nature of atrocities on Dalits is concerned they can be divided into two broad categories. First the 'traditional' category where they were denied every right whatsoever in the Hindu society and suffered grave forms of exclusion. The second type of atrocity emanates from modern forms of resistance on part of Dalits or is a caste Hindu response to the changing situation of Dalits. It is a fact that though the first type of atrocities still persist, the second type is becoming more and more rampant. The barbaric killing of five Dalits, when they refused to bribe the police, in Dulena, Jhajjar in Haryana on 16 October 2002, falls under the first category of atrocity. The mob in Jhajjar had no sympathy with the Dalits because of a psyche that Dalits are to be treated shabbily and are worse than animals. This was evident when after lynching them, instead of ordering an inquiry, the authorities ordered the postmortem of the cow as if the life of a cow is more precious than five human beings (as five Dalits were killed). Not only that, though the sacred text of the Hindus have assigned this stigmatised job to the Dalits, yet the same Hindus treated them without any consideration of humanity and took refuge in the symbol of cow which has been declared as sacred by the Hindu Shastras. The second incident in the first category of atrocity on Dalits occurred at Chakwara in Jaipur. Here the caste Hindus denied Dalits access to the water tank and temple on 22 September 2002, lest they defile both. And when they asserted their right, they were beaten up. Again the caste Hindus took refuge in the scared symbol of the Hindus, that is, sanctity of the Hindu temple.

To mention a few glaring examples of the second category of atrocities on the Dalits, we can take the example of Tamil Nadu the land of Dravidian movement. On September 5, at Kaundampatti in Dindigul district, a Dalit agricultural worker was forced to drink urine—for having lodged a complaint with the police of trespass against a caste Hindu (Vishwanathan 2002). If this was not enough, at Thinniyam village in Trichi, two Dalits, Murugesan and Ramasami were forced 'to feed each other' human excreta. The crime they committed was that they stood by another Dalit, who was engaged in a prolonged struggle against a former Panchyat president (ibid.). Now the irony is that the number of atrocities of this kind are on the rise and the state is a mere spectator. The rising number of these types of atrocities on the Dalits is evident from Tables 11.8 and 11.9.

Table 11.8: Atrocities Committed on Dalits During 1997–2000

Year	*Murder*	*Grievous hurts*	*Rape*	*Arson*	*Others*	*Crime under POA*	*Total*
1981	493	1,492	604	1,295	10,343	14,318	28,636
1982	514	1,429	635	1,035	11,441	15,054	30,108
1983	525	1,351	640	993	11,440	14,949	29,898
1984	541	1,454	692	973	12,327	15,987	31,974
1985	502	1,367	700	980	11,824	15,373	30,746
1986	564	1,408	727	1,002	11,715	15,416	30,832
1995	571	4,544	837	500	11,056	13,925	31,433
1996	543	4,585	949	464	13,862	9,620	30,023
1997	504	3,462	1,002	384	12,149	7,831	25,338
1999	506	3,241	1,000	337	11,820	7,289	25,093

Source: Annual Reports of Commission for Scheduled Castes and Scheduled Tribes, New Delhi.

The true nature of governance comes to the fore once we look at the processes of delivering social justice to the marginalised sections of society. In this context, it is really astonishing

Table 11.9: Pending Cases under SC & ST (POA) Act 1989 in Some States

Sl. no.	*Sates*	*Pending cases*	*% of dalit population of state*
1.	Uttar Pradesh	74,303	21.04
2.	Maharashtra	8,218	11.10
3.	Rajasthan	5,836	17.29
4.	Orissa	5,669	16.20
5.	Andhra Pradesh	1,845	15.93
6.	Tamil Nadu	1,810	19.18
7.	Karnataka	1,794	16.38
8.	Kerala	1,768	9.92

Source: Sixth Report of National Commission for Scheduled Castes and Scheduled Tribes, 1999–2000 & 2000–01, New Delhi, p. 213.

that despite so many laws and legislation, not only the atrocities on the Dalits go unabated, but they also do not get justice in time. Article 17 of the Indian Constitution, Untouchability (offences) Act 1955, Protection of Civil Right Act 1976, The Scheduled Castes & Scheduled Tribes (prevention Of Atrocities) Act 1989, with their deterrent penal provisions and provision of Special Courts for the trial of such offences, have proved futile in preventing the Dalits from the physical and mental violence perpetrated by the 'Upper Castes'. The number of pending cases despite the provision of special courts and appointment of special public prosecutors under Sections 14 and 15 of the SC & ST (POA) Act 1989, prove the plight of the Dalits and thereby the prevailing unrest in society and the failure of governance.

Further, the existing paradoxical socio-political context in which these atrocities on Dalits are inflicted is further complicated by the onset of the process of globalisation in contemporary India. This along with its appendage processes of information revolution and privatisation has not had any impact on the stigmatised status of the Dalits. Regarding globalisation, it was argued that with the onset of these processes, the interaction pattern on the basis of primordial loyalties would be replaced by global identities. Needless to say that the national leadership also had more or less the same hopes with the processes of modernisation and industrialisation in Indian society after the commencement of the Constitution. But the irony is that it neither happened then, nor it is happening now. We can observe ourselves that still the caste Hindus are interacting with the Dalits on the same primordial identities as is evident from the aforesaid incidences. Further, there is an attempt by the political-Hindutava, led by Bharatiya Janata Party to co-opt the Dalits into their fold without actually empowering them. The legitimacy provided by the NDA government to the Anti-Conversion Act passed in the different states, formation of coalition government with Bahujan Samaj party in Uttar Pradesh, co-option of Dalit youths in various states as party cadres with their *Malin Basti* (slums), *Rakshabandhan* (thread of protection usually tied by a sister to her brother's wrist) and *Khichri* (a food item having mix of rice and pulses) distribution programmes are few significant steps, which Hindutava forces have taken in this direction.

Governance and NGOs

Another feature of governance in the era of globalisation is greater participation of civil society through non-governmental organisations (NGOs) or voluntary organisations (VOs) in India. Both national and international organisations are working with the masses with national and foreign aid. In this context, what we have to observe is which collectivity constitutes the civil society, or the individuals of which strata of society have control over the NGOs/VOs working for the Dalits and receiving government and foreign grants. It can be argued beyond doubt that the so-called upper castes dominate here as well like in the government services. As they have access to offices and information and also the capital to start NGOs, they were the first to capture the space. It is interesting to note here that the government grants aid to only those voluntary organisations which have successfully functioned for three years. Therefore, to run an organisation without any help from the state is a big challenge. As the Dalits are excluded from the society and have hardly any capital to pool or any access to state assistance, it is difficult for them to organise a Voluntary organisation. Hence, they are again left behind in the area of NGOs and VOs. A detailed study of NGOs—their composition, their structure of governance, and members of executive etc.—is long overdue. But even without such a study, we can argue that their functioning has been far from satisfactory.

For instance, in the year 2003–04, the Ministry of Social Justice and Empowerment allocated Rs 24 crore to 361 voluntary organisations working for the Dalits in different states (see Table 11.10). But what is astonishing about the functioning of these organisations is that the Ministry has no detailed report on their performance. There is no regulatory authority which has established any provision of punishment for the erring NGOs. At most, an NGO can be blacklisted and its grant be cut or stopped. But this does not act as a deterrent for the voluntary organisation as it can come back with any other name. Second, there is no rationale for allocation of funds to these organisations except a report from the state authorities where the organisation has been functioning for a minimum of three years. Also, there is no proper ratio between the percentage of Dalit population in the states and the number of government-funded NGOs/VOs working in a particular state. For example, Gujarat has only 7 per cent of Dalit population but there are as many as 28 voluntary organisations working for them, while West Bengal has 23 per cent of Dalit population but there are only 8 voluntary organisations working for them. Similarly, Punjab has the highest Scheduled Caste population (28 per cent) in the country but there is not even a single organisation working for the Dalits. Under these circumstances, can we really hope that even civil society through NGOs or Voluntary organisations can be of any real help for the amelioration of the wretched condition of the Dalits?

Globalisation and the Dalit Diaspora

An important development that has taken place in the Dalit society with the current process of globalisation is the increasing visibility of the Dalit diaspora and their pattern of mobility

Table 11.10: Number of Voluntary Organisations Working for Scheduled Castes Across States during 2002–04 with the Help of Grants-in Aid from Ministry of Social Justice & Empowerment, Government of India

Sl. no.	*State*	*% SC population (2001)*	*No. of voluntary organisation*
1.	Andhra Pradesh	16.23	37
2.	Assam	6.85	8
3.	Bihar	15.72	7
4.	Chhattisgarh	11.61	2
5.	Delhi	16.92	21
6.	Gujrat	7.09	28
7.	Haryana	19.35	4
8.	Jammu & Kashmir	7.59	1
9.	Jharkhand	11.84	1
10.	Karnataka	16.20	37
11.	Kerala	9.81	1
12.	Madhya Pradesh	15.17	40
13.	Maharashtra	10.20	38
14.	Manipur	2.02	9
15.	Orissa	16.53	35
16.	Punjab	28.31	Nil
17.	Rajasthan	17.16	40
18.	Tamil Nadu	19.00	5
19.	Tripura	17.37	1
20.	Uttar Pradesh	21.15	31
21.	West Bengal	23.02	8

Source: Annual Report 2003–04, Ministry of Social Justice & Empowerment, Government of India, New Delhi, pp. 90–101.

in the different countries of the world. An unique feature is that the Dalits in India have developed links with the Dalit diaspora which in turn has helped their community in India to use the most advanced technology—computers, internet, websites, etc., for the development of their community in this era of globalisation. Otherwise, there has been nothing for them to cheer. The process of globalisation has broken the national boundaries and taken the Dalit movement to international levels, making not only their diaspora more visible but has also exposed the hypocrisy of Indian society and Indian State regarding the human rights violations of Dalits in India. In this context the Dalit diaspora with the help of Dalits in the India have successfully pressurised the international funding and law-making agencies like International Monetary Fund, World Bank, United Nations Human Right Commission, United Nations Development Program, Asian Development Bank, etc., to ask Indian government to take up their issues in right earnest. Here, it can be said that this type of mobilisation at different levels would not have been possible before the advent of globalisation which, with its various processes like information and an increased role of civil society, has helped them. To have a better understanding of the whole process, we will have to look at the genesis, development and assertion of Dalit diaspora in more detail.

The Dalit diaspora can be divided in to two major streams—the 'old' and the 'new'. The 'old' comprises indentured and assisted labourers who were taken by the colonial powers and the contractors to different countries. This diaspora is confined to South Asian and African countries. The other stream of 'new' Dalit diapora includes semi-literate and professionally trained Dalits who have emigrated especially to London and the US as industrial labourers, technicians, other professionals and students.

Dalits as Indentured Labourers

Indian Dalits were not only taken to different countries as indentured labourers by colonial masters, but they also migrated themselves. According to Lal (1984: 126–30) out of 60,965 Indian indentured labourers who migrated to Fiji between 1879 and 1916, about 11,907 or 26.2 per cent belonged to low menial castes like *chamar*s, *kori*s, *pasi*s, etc. Similarly, Brereton (1974: 26) writes that between 1876 and 1885, those who arrived in Trinidad were *brahmin* and other high castes (18 per cent); artisan castes (8.5 per cent); agricultural castes (32 per cent); low castes (41.5 per cent). In this context (Jain 1984: 175) also accepts that many untouchable castes (adi-dravidas) migrated to Malaysia, but he says that it is difficult to substantiate it statistically. But Sandhu (1969) elaborates the presence of south Indian Dalits belonging to *cheruman*s, *parayan*s, *pallan*s and other depressed castes as indentured labourers in Malaysia. According to him, 'Of the people of the subcontinent the south Indian peasant, particularly the untouchables or low caste Madrasi, was considered the most satisfactory type of labourer' (Sandhu 1969: 56).

A click at www.ambedkar.org will reveal the presence of another stream of Dalit diaspora in UK, US and Canada. This 'new' Dalit diaspora migrated as free labourers and professionals. Dalit activists from Punjab put their migration to UK to pre-independence, but according to Muman (2000: 71) a Dalit from Punjab, 'I came to Britain in the late 1960s from a remote village in India. During this period mostly semi-literate Dalits migrated as industrial and domestic labourers. Indian Dalits started migrating to the US in the 1970s. They were first generation literates and professionals. This "new" stream is politically conscious and has in-fluenced politically subdued 'old' Dalit diaspora as well.'

Dalit Diaspora and Caste Discrimination

It is true 'that caste was increasingly an aspect of culture rather than of social stratification per se...'[Jain 2003]. But caste identities were (are) strong within the Indian diaspora, which restrict the interaction pattern of non-Dalit with the Dalit diaspora. For instance, 'there is evidence that some of the traditional methods of showing differences between status still exists. Thus in Trinidad the residence of lower castes is restricted. In South Africa there [persists] some idea about unclean occupations. There is also some restricted commensality, for example that of the

Trinidadian brahmin priests as rituals, or the Guyanese who told Singer that he would not eat in the home of a low-caste, and restricted feeding of valmikis in East Africa' (Jain 1993: 15–16). Similarly, '...in Wolverhampton the customer refused to take the change from the vendor lest he found their touch polluting and instead that the change be placed on the counter to avoid contact. On the factory floor, again in Wolverhampton, we know of women of so-called upper caste jats not taking water from the same tap from where the so-called lower caste person drink...(in another incident of practice of untouchability). The Sikh temples hold annual inter-temple sports tournaments. One such tournament was held in Birmingham where the "Langar" (sanctified food) will be served by one of the participating temples who happened to be belonging to the Ravidasia community. Whilst their teams participated in the tournament but the langar did not get eaten by the jats because it came from the chamars' (VODI Report 2000: 73). Ironically, this persistence of caste distinction has not been wiped out even with inter-caste marriages between Dalits and non-Dalits. Jain (2003: 74) saw this when he revisited Tamil plantation frontier in Malaysia in 1998–99. He argues, 'also the stigma of caste did not die out completely. Women of high caste married to low caste men when they reached the age of 34–35. (When the men were ageing, their wives still enjoyed health and youth superior to their husbands. They looked down upon their husbands. They looked upon the latter, and even told their children how their fathers were of a lower caste than them).'

Dalit Diaspora and Social Solidarity

In these circumstances, Dalits settled abroad did not remain aloof from each other though they migrated from different parts of India and belonged to different sub-castes. They created their own organisations to develop social solidarity with different Dalit communities. In this context, members of 'new' Dalit diaspora took the lead. For instance, Dalits in UK established Buddha Vihars (Buddhist praying centre) and gurudwaras (Sikh praying place) in the late 1960s. A Buddhist Council was established in the year 1985 here which is a federation of seven Ambedkarite organisations working for Dalit Indians. The Federation of Ambedkarite and Buddhist Organisation (FABO) and Voice of Dalit International (VODI) are also working in UK to uplift Dalits back in India. A more organised effort came in the US from literate NRI Dalits when they formed 'Volunteers in Service to India's Oppressed and Neglected' (VISION) in 1975. In fact, they aligned with the Black Panther movement in the US and highlighted their plight, which became the symbol of Dalit and black unity. According to a VODI report 2000, the Ambedkar centre for Justice and Peace was established in Canada, a decade before the issues of Dalits were highlighted at different International forums.

In 1999, Backward and Minorities Employees' Federation (BAMCEF) also launched its international networking with UK as its headquarters. The organisation has already organised conferences in the UK, US and Malaysia to sensitise people about the wretched conditions of the Dalits back home and about the role of Vishva Hindu Parishad (VHP) which collects funds from abroad in the name of Hindus. Dalits have also donated unknowingly but now they have stopped. Now, it is also making an effort to wean away Dalits from the VHP. The organisation is still at a nascent stage and has yet to formulate its concrete plans.

The UK and the US are becoming the hub of activities of the Dalit diaspora. Dalits here celebrate and commemorate Ambedkar's, Buddha's, and Ravidas's birth and death anniversaries with lots of fanfare. In UK, for the last three years, Dalits have taken the initiative to organise Ambedkar memorial lecture in Manchester Metropolitan University with a vision of spreading his thought throughout the world. Another unique effort of the Dalit diaspora in UK in the cultural realm is establishement of an Ambedkar Museum at Wolverhampton on 23 April 2003. This museum now houses over 40 items belonging to Babasaheb Ambedkar and is now the place of pilgrimage for Dalits visiting UK from different parts of the world and has become a new cultural symbol for the Dalit diaspora.

Assertion of Dalit Diaspora

The mobility which Dalits have attained in different countries has motivated them to assert that they are not inferior to anyone. They have argued, 'look we have demystified the ideal type image of Dalits as dirty, drunkard, devoid of any merit, beast of burden, etc., by developing ourselves without any governmental help.' In the same vein, 'by attaining the mobility in different realms of foreign society without the help of the protective discrimination we (Dalits) have made a point that nothing is inherently wrong with us. It is only because of lack of democratic social conditions in Indian society that we have lagged behind. If we are provided a democratic social order we can also perform like any other person and will not need any type of reservations'. In their effort to demystify their ideal type image and enhance their self-esteem the Dalits boast of their contributions to the country by pointing out that they also send in foreign remittances.

Dalit diaspora has used the internet to unite the Dalits world over. There are about 51 sites, which provide information about Dalits in India and abroad. Few important ones are www.ambedkar.org, www.dalitusa.org, www.dalitistan.org, www.dalitawaj.com, www.dalitindia.com, etc. Similarly Dalits also run their E-magazines like—Dalit-International@yahoogroup.com, dalits@ambedkar.org, Buddhistcircle@ yahoogroup.com, Sakyagroup@yahoogroupcom. Their numbers are increasing day by day. Through these site magazines, the Dalit fraternity world over keeps itself update about the latest happenings within their diaspora and community in India, which helps them to take prompt action based on these information. All this was not possible earlier because they had no links with each other. The whole process of sharing information about themselves has sensitised them and made them conscious that distance is no more a hurdle in the path of unity. And today, their efforts are bearing fruits as Dalits world over have approached the United Nation's Human Rights Commission and organised various conferences for ameliorating the situation of Dalits in India.

The Dalit International Organisation organised the first Dalit World Conference in Malaysia on, 'A Vision Towards a Caste-less Society' during October 10–11 1998. Till 1997, Dalits in Malaysia who are mostly from Tamil Nadu organised Tamil Conferences in league with their non-Dalit Tamil brethren showing their Tamil solidarity and identity. But when they realised that the latter are using them for their own gains and political mileage, the Dalits have begun to organise themselves independently. They formed parties with the Indian Progressive Front and organised many rallies under the slogan, 'Nidhiketu Nedudhurum Payanam' (Long March to Demand Justice). Today they revere and highlight Ambedkar and have developed a separate political and social identity, which has enhanced their political clout. Some Dalits have even been nominated to the Malaysian parliament.

The second international conference by the Dalit diaspora was organised by Dalits in UK on Dalit Human Rights in London on 16–17 September 2000. This was unique in the sense that representatives from all Dalit communities in UK belonging to Shri Guru Ravidas, Bhagwan Valmiki, Amedkarite and Buddhists and Christian organisations not only attended and participated in the conference, but also generously donated money and other resources for it. It chalked out a two-pronged approach attacking the problems of the Dalits at the national and international level. The problems to be tackled at the national level included the practice of untouchability, and lack of educational, health, food and other facilities. Further, it was suggested in the conference that a 'Dalit Research/Information Centre' be established in north. Similarly, the conference decided that all the northern governments, non-governmental aid agencies, multi and bi-lateral agencies, World Bank, UNICEF, UNDP, and other groups that give aid to India's poverty alleviation programme should review their policies and must see that at least 50 per cent of aid is allocated to programmes that focus on Dalits (VODI Report 2000).

In the follow up of September 2000 conference, VODI organised another international Dalit conference in India during 19–20 February 2003. This was specially organised on the issue of 'Dalit and International Developmental Aid'. Discussing the report of Charity Aid Foundation (CAF) and Voluntary Action Network India (VANI) the conference showed that there were 18,000 NGOs in India registered under the 1976 Foreign Contribution (Regulation) Act which receive a sum of Rs 26,000 million as foreign contribution. But Dalits who constitute 90 per cent of poor in India are deprived of their due as upper strata-dominated NGOs usurp this money. The World Conference against Racism, Racial Discrimination, Xenophobia and Related Intolerance (28 August–7 September 2001 in Durban) is a testimony to the fact that Dalit organisation in this era has reached a different level. The Dalit diaspora has played a dominant role in helping Indian Dalits in achieving their desired goal. In this conference, Dalits represented by National Campaign for Dalit Human Rights (NCDHR) participated in large numbers (Kumar 2001). They have shown that international institutions can be used for redressal of grievances if a national government is not taking care of a group of people. In the same conference, Dalit women led by National Federation of Dalit Women raised their voice separately, which was later on included in the NGO Declaration on Gender and Racism. Today NCDHR has a network of 26 international organisations. The Dalit diaspora in Vancouver, Canada under the banner of Association for International Dalit Conference organised a world conference during 16–18 May 2003. The theme of the conference was 'Charting Dalit Agenda for 21st Century'. The conference in the end adopted 11-point declaration. One of the important demands was, 'The United Nations and its affiliates and non-governmental agencies concerned with human rights, social and economic development, must recognise that the Dalits are a special group and create separate Dalit divisions managed by the Dalits themselves. The World Bank and other financial institutions should attach conditional special component clause and must ensure the rightful share of the Dalits in the funds they lend to India for socio-economic and sustainable development' (Declaration of Vancouver Conference 2003).

Conclusion

To conclude, it is abundantly clear that the structural location of Dalits in Indian society is different from most of the other collectivities. They suffer from the cumulative deprivation in the social, economic and political realms and hence, cannot be treated at par with any other economically poor groups. It is also evident from the above analysis that their exclusion from the institution of governance results from their unique location in the Hindu social structure. On the other hand, the dominance and virtual monopoly of the so-called upper castes emanates from their respective location in the social structure. Therefore, it can be held that the location of collectivities in a social structure in a hierarchically arranged society plays a dominant role in its inclusion and exclusion in the institutions of governance and policies of development.

As far as the issue of development of the Dalits is concerned, the available data reveals that in spite of constitutional safeguards, legislation, modernisation, industrialisation and now globalisation, Dalits have been excluded from having a fair share in the fruits of development. If at all there is any change in their socio-political situation in the country, which can be proved by the available data on poverty, literacy, atrocity, unemployment, reservation, etc. it has come because of protective discrimination policy and state intervention. They are virtually absent from other realms like market, media, voluntary organisations etc., to name a few, which are going to be the most important institutions of governance in this era of globalisation. The most worrying aspect about Dalits is their economic future and social safety, as economic liberalisation offers no prospect of early advantage to these people. One is forced to argue that these paradigms of development have become redundant for them. Do we have some alternative paradigm for the development of the Dalits who are structurally located at a lower pedestal in the Indian society?

Further, the wretched condition of some 160 million people in the Indian society, which signifies the failure of constitutional measures, legislations, socialist paradigm of planned economic development, and other international institutional help etc., has forced the Dalits to assert their rights. The increasing number of atrocities on them and other forms of discrimination are testimony of their assertion and their resolve that they are not willing be treated as a dumb vote bank. That is why they are charting out their own independent politics, literary movement, religious conversion, certain NGO-led movements including that of the Dalit diaspora, etc. Hence, the planners and the leaders should note the level and horizon of their aspiration which the programmes and policies of the state have created over the years. If the gap between their aspiration and policies is not reduced soon, it can take a destructive course.

References

Ambedkar, B.R. (1982). *Dr. Babasaheb Ambedkar: Writings and Speeches. Vol. 2*, Mumbai: Education Department, Government of Maharashtra.

——— (1991). 'What Congress and Gandhi have done to the Untouchables', *Dr. Babasaheb Ambedkar: Writings and Speeches. Vol. 9*, Mumbai: Education Department, Government of Maharashtra.

Anwar, Mohammad (1990). *Redressive Action Policies in the United Kingdom*. Bombay: Popular Prakashan.

Bhutani, Mukesh (2004). 'Keeping Company with Phantom', *The Indian Express*. New Delhi, 25 September.

Beteille, Andre (1997). *Society and Politics in India*. New Delhi: Oxford University Press.

Bowles, Samuel and Herbert Gintis (1976). *Schooling in Capitalist America*. London: Routledge and Kegan Paul.

Brereton, Bridget (1974). 'The Experience of Indentureship 1845–1917', in John LaGuerre (ed.), *Calcutta to Caroni*. Trinidad and Jamica: Longman Caribbean.

Declaration of Vancouver Conference 2003. The International Conference, Vancouver, Canada, 16–18 May.

Dumont, Louis (1970). *Homo Hierarchicus: The Caste System and its Implications*. New Delhi: Oxford University Press.

GOI (Government of India) (2004a). *Annual Report 2003–04*. New Delhi: Ministry of Social Justice and Empowerment.

——— (2004b). *Economic Survey 2003–04*. New Delhi: Ministry of Finance, Economic Division, Government of India Press.

Jain, Ravindra K. (1984). 'South Indian Labour in Malaya,1840–1920: Asylum Stability and Involution', in Kay Saunders (ed.), *Indentured Labour in British Empire 1834–1920*. London: Croom Helm.

——— (1993). *Indian Communities Abroad: Themes and Literature*, New Delhi, Manohar.

——— (2003). 'Culture and Economy: Tamils on the Plantation Frontier in Malaysia Revisited, 1998–99', in Bhiku Parekh (ed.). *Culture and Economy in the Indian Diaspora*, London: Routledge.

Jensen, A.R. (1973). *Educational Differences*. London: Methuen.

Kumar, Vivek (2001). 'A Blow for Dalit Dignity and Pride', *The Pioneer*. New Delhi, 25 September.

——— (2003). 'Dalit Movement and Dalit International Conferences', *Economic and Political Weekly*, Mumbai, 38(27): 2799, 5 July.

Lal, V. Brij (1984). 'Bouring Men and Nothing More: Some Problems of Indian Indenture in Fiji', in Kay Saunders (ed.). *Indentured Labour in British Empire 1834–1920*. London and Canberra: Croom Helm.

Mendelshon, Oliver and Marika Vicziani (1988). *The Untouchables Subordination, Poverty and the State in Modern India*. New Delhi: Cambridge University Press.

Misra, B.B. (1960). *The Indian Middle Classes*. Bombay: Oxford University Press.

Mohan, Dinesh (2004). 'The Science of Dumbing Down', *The Indian Express*. New Delhi, 16 July.

Muman, Sat Pal (2000). 'Caste in Britain', in Report of the Proceedings of International Conference on Dalits Human Rights, VOD International, London, 16–20 September.

Murugkar, Lata (1991). *Dalit Panthers Movement: A Sociological Appraisal*. Bombay: Popular Prakashan.

Nehru, Jawaharlal (1989). *Letters to Chief Ministers 1947–64*. New Delhi: Oxford University Press.

Okun, Arthur, M. (1975). *Equality and Efficiency: The Big Tradeoff*. New Delhi: Oxford & IBH Publishing Co.

Oommen, T.K. (1990). *Protest and Change: Studies in Social Movements*. New Delhi: Sage Publications.

——— (2003). 'Approaching cultural change in the globalisation', Interview with Anand Kumar and Frank Welz, *Social Identity*, Vol 9, London.

Ram, Kanshi (1982). *The Chamcha Age (An Era of the Stooges)*. Delhi: Vedic Mudranalaya.

Sandhu, Kernail Singh (1969) *Indians in Malaya: Some Aspects of Their Immigration and Settlement, 1786–1957*. London: Cambridge University Press.

Saunders, Kay (ed.) (1984). *Indentured Labour in British Empire 1834–1920*. London and Canberra: Croom Helm.

Seal, Anil (1968). *The Emergence of Indian Nationalism: Competition and Collaboration in the later Nineteenth Century*. New Delhi: Cambridge University Press.

Singh, Rupashree (2004). 'Refer to Win', *The Hindustan Times*. New Delhi, 20 September 20.

The Indian Express (2004). 'Corruption Perception Index: India ranked 90,' (Express News Service), New Delhi, 21 October.

Tumin, Melvin M. (1967). *Social Stratification: The Forms and Functions of Social Inequality*. Englewood Cliffs, USA, Prentice Hall.

Vishwanathan, S. (2002). 'Preying on Dalits', *Frontline*, 25 October, p. 39.

VODI Report (2000). Report of the Proceedings of International Conference on Dalits Human Rights, London: Voice of Dalit International.

Weber, Max (1946). *Essays in Sociology* (trans. H.H. Gerth and C. Wright Mills). New York: Oxford University Press.

12

Governance, Reforms and Development: Scheduled Tribes in India in the Era of Globalisation

Prakash Louis

INTRODUCTION

In the era of globalisation, there are many streams of discourses doing the rounds within the realm of political economy and political sociology at the national and international levels. Development, democracy and participatory governance is one such stream. Governance, reforms and development is another stream. Liberalisation, privatisation and globalisation is the third. So is the discourse on state, civil society and collective action. These discourses bring to the fore, the innumerable issues that are surfacing in the arena of political economy and political sociology. In a special way, these deliberations highlight the relationship that exists between development paradigms and actual development, government and governance, common people and the state etc.

Governance, reforms and development are terms extensively used in the current economic and political debates. But they mean different things to different people. Since governments continue to play a central role in the lives of its citizens, governance came to be equated with government. Development and reform also constituted the functions of governments. Hence, they too were far removed from the citizens of a country. Now, when one talks of governance, one refers to participatory governance which works towards development of individuals as well as the society/nation.

Globalisation is also one of the most extensively used terms but less defined and even less agreed upon in economic and political discourses currently. Hence, some would argue that instead of trying to define the term globalisation it may be expedient to locate its impact. Once again, in understanding the effect of globalisation, it has been argued that most of the concentration has been on the economic aspects, and other elements like social, political, cultural, environmental etc. have not received adequate emphasis. Further, some consider globalisation to be a threat to a nation or society in general and to the marginalised in particular. There are others who see it as providing an opportunity to all.

In India too, the understanding of the effect of globalisation for a long time was confined to the economic aspects only. From this perspective, globalisation was seen as a uni-linear and uni-dimensional process. But today, social scientists are trying to unravel the multi-dimensional and multi-layered process and outcome of globalisation. Moreover, social scientists and activists are focusing on the impact of globalisation on specific groups like the Dalits, tribals/indigenous peoples, women, peasants and unorganised sector workers.[1] This chapter makes some preliminary observations about the impact of globalisation on the lives of the Scheduled Tribes (STs) with reference to development, reform and governance.

Globalisation

During the last one-decade there has been a lot of debate about the emergence and impact of liberalisation, privatisation and globalisation. There are some who acclaim the outcome of these processes, while there are others who oppose both the process of globalisation and its impact. It is argued that modern technology and communication have revolutionised the world in such a manner that it has resulted in easy access to information and quick contact with people across the world and hence, the world has become a global village. But what most of these theoreticians and experts fail to state is whether this unification of villages into a global unit is a reality to all the members of the global family.

Looking at the positive side of globalisation it is clear that it has led to technological transformation which has resulted in international mobilisation. Exchange of information, technologies, methods etc. have led to a decline in diseases, facilitated communication, made life more comfortable. It has also made human rights violations an international issue and has effected international solidarity.

In the words of A.K. Bagchi, the term globalisation used in 1985 by Theodore Levitt has been interpreted in several ways by different people. Roland Robertson speaks of globalisation as a process by which the world is becoming more and more 'a single place'. The author goes on to argue that at the risk of adding to the fragmentation in its connotation we can distinguish between two different generic classes of meanings attributed to it. i) The spread of human civilisation, globalisation, institutions, patterns of living, information and knowledge to span the planet earth. ii) A policy deliberately aimed at spreading certain institutions, modes of doing business, producing and trading commodities, services and information across all the states of the world (Bagchi 1999: 3219).

According to Bagchi, from this type of analysis one can distinguish the following features: i) There is a spread of international trade in goods and commodities. ii) People migrate from one country or region to another temporarily or permanently. iii) Money or means of payment are exchanged on an increasing scale between different countries and regions. iv) Capital flows from one country to another to help produce goods and services. v) Finance without direct link with production of goods and services flows between countries. vi) Trans-National Corporations or TNCs have replaced MNCs which increasingly engage in the activities listed above.

vii) Increasingly, with the spread of the patent regimes governed by the Paris Convention as modified by the provisions of the WTO, frontier technologies take an increasingly proprietary form. viii) The spread of print and electronic media. ix) The growth of international trade and production of services of all kinds like shipping, insurance, banking, health care, and of course, finance (Bagchi 1999: 3219).

As has been stated above, may be due to the ideological dominance of neoliberal capitalism today, the economic dimension is seen to be the cutting edge of globalisation. But this may not be the appropriate way of locating the phenomenon of globalisation. If a broader and multi-dimensional approach is not adopted to comprehend its reality, there is every possibility of losing out the most critical contradictions and crucial challenges. In this regard, Giddens' viewpoints provide some pointers. He states, 'globalisation is not only, or even primarily, an economic phenomenon; and it should not be equated with the emergence of a world system. Globalisation is really about the transformation of space and time. I define it as action at distance, and relate its intensifying over recent years to the emergence of means of instantaneous global communication and mass transportation' (Giddens 1994).

V.S. Vyas is of the view that globalisation implies weakening of the restrictions imposed by or inherent in a nation state. These restrictions were more severe in the first half of the 20th century. The 19th century had seen the weakening of the national barriers as the movement of goods and services and of capital, even of labour, was not more easier. The 20th century saw progressive liquidation of colonialism. There was a corresponding rise in the powers of the nation state. But the pendulum started swinging in the opposite direction since World War II, and the move towards globalisation started gaining strength. In this period, the mainspring of globalisation was the development in information technology which contributed more than anything else to the emergence of the 'global village' (Vyas 2002: 1109). But progressively it became clear that the fact of global village was beneficial only to those corporations and countries who could travel around without boundaries, to those who could shift factories and finances and their profits without restrictions. But the borders seemed to be open only for a few individuals, goods and countries.

There is the ever widening gap between the haves and have-nots, the rich and the poor, and the developed and developing nations. The UN Conference on Trade and Development (UNCTAD) has examined the issues of the growing worldwide gap between the rich and poor countries as a result of globalisation.[2] Some of its revelations are:

- Since 1994, the 200 richest people in the world have more than doubled their net worth to one trillion dollars (i.e., one lakh crore dollar).
- Industrialised countries of Europe and US hold 97 per cent of all patents worldwide.
- The income gap between the richest fifth of the world and the poorest fifth increased from 30 to 1 in 1960 to 74 to 1 in 1997.
- Tanzania's debt payment is nine times what it spends on primary health care and four times what it spends on primary education.
- The value of illegal drug trade was estimated at 400 billion dollars, that is, 40,000 crore dollars in 1995, about 8 per cent of world trade.

- In US, in 1960 a Chief Executive Officer of a company earned on average an income that was 40 times the average income of a factory worker. In 1993, it was 149 times more. The top 1 per cent has more wealth than the bottom 80 per cent.
- Among more than 600 professionals in the World Bank, the ratio of Economists to Social Scientists is 28 to 1. These economists with no hold on ground and also with no loyalty to their own country or society except their own self-interest determine the destiny of more than 75 developing countries by using charts and graphs.

The facts and figures presented above unravel the hard reality that the process of globalisation has accelerated the ever widening gap between the rich and the poor, developed and under-developed countries. But there is some ambiguity in spite of 'a burgeoning academic debate as to whether globalisation, as an analytical construct, delivers any added value in the search of a coherent understanding of the historical forces, which at the dawn of a new millennium, are shaping the socio-political realities of everyday social life, from the cultural to the criminal, the financial to the spiritual' (Held 1999). Thus, it can be stated that though the term globalisation has become popular among the academics and the activists, it still evades a common agreement.

Jan Nederveen Pieterse is of the view that globalisation or the trend of growing worldwide interconnectedness is presently accompanied by several coinciding and clashing notions of cultural change. A growing sensitivity to cultural difference coincides with an awareness of the world 'becoming smaller' and the idea of cultural difference receding. The growing awareness of cultural difference forms part of a general 'cultural turn' which involves wider self-reflexivity of modernity. Modernisation has been advancing like a steamroller, denying and erasing cultural differences in its way and now not only the gains (rationalisation, standardisation, control) but also the losses (alienation, displacement and disenchantment) are becoming apparent. Stamping out cultural variety has been a form of 'disenchantment of the world' (Pieterse 1996: 1389).

> The prime virtue of an authentic global ethic are liberty, justice, and love for a human world—a world without gender inequality, racial discrimination, stark income discrepancies, illiteracy, ethnic conflict, and religious bigotry. But the increasing economic disparities created by globalisation generate fanaticism, terrorism, moral indignation, and aggressive suffering. The severity of the contrast between the elite and the rejects feeds a pervasive mood of uncertainty. It divides the world into hegemony and domination on the one hand, and exclusion and threat on the other (Dasgupta 2004: 30).

It needs to be stated at the outset that globalisation as a process and a product has unleashed a powerful impact on human life. It has accentuated the divide between the rich and the poor nations, and between the rich and the poor within a nation. In a special way, globalisation has impacted upon the livelihood of the Dalits, tribals/indigenous peoples, women and the unorganised sector workers etc. But it would be untenable to state that these marginalised communities were further pushed to the margins only after the introduction of globalisation.

Exclusion, isolation, deprivation and discrimination of these weaker sections have been going on for centuries.[3] Globalisation has accelerated this process further.

Good Governance

Governance and good governance have become the theme for discussions, deliberations and discourse at the local, national and international levels. Good governance, people centred governance, responsive governance, all call for a collective sense of destiny and direction for human beings. Crisis in governance witnessed all over the globe has called for the re-examination of the broader tenets of governance. Malgovernance does not only affect the day to day delivery of goods and services to the citizens of a country, it fundamentally alters the principles of politics for the good of all.

Good governance refers to the ability to deliver goods to the stakeholders, which also refers to the elimination of malgovernance and the establishment of good governance through democratic processes and rule of law so that citizens of a country and members of a society do not suffer. It also means to make the various agents of a political system work for the betterment of all the citizens, especially, of the marginalised and the vulnerable communities.

At one time, the notion of 'governability' was also used to discuss the facets of good governance. The concept of governability directs attention to a state's capacity to govern. In the Indian situation, the issues of its growing crisis of governability refers to three types of problems: i) the absence of an enduring coalition; ii) policy ineffectiveness, and iii) incapacity to accommodate political conflict without violence (Kohli 1990: 22–24). One way of measuring governability is to set up standards whereby some objective definition of a society's problems would be sought and against which the capacity of a government to solve problems would be assessed. Most governments would fall short of these goals. A political establishment that repeatedly fails to globalise their stated objective is deemed to be a government with a low capacity to govern. It is at this juncture that crisis engulfs the government, which in turn affects not only the state but also the society.

It is of seminal significance to note that governance is wider than government, though government being the most powerful and coercive institution continues to be the major element of any system of governance (Mander 2004). Government, according to political theories, refers to three sectors—executive, legislative and judiciary. But this seems to be only the operational principle of government. Because, if it is accepted that government is for the people, by the people and of the people, then it is the people or the citizens who become the central focus of governance. To talk about good governance means ensuring the responsibility and accountability of various stakeholders like the community, the government, the civil society and the corporate sector. But the million-dollar question is, is it possible?

There is another trend that needs to be taken note of in a discourse on governance. In the era of privatisation, globalisation, free market, outsourcing of labour and capital, structural adjustment, decentralisation, restructuring, deregulation, sustainable development, empowerment etc., formulation and implementation of public policy (policy that benefits the public) seem be to increasingly delegated to or undertaken by non-governmental institutions. State is abdicating its responsibility and the corporate sector in a special way is entering into the service sector areas. The former on the one hand is slowly taking up many of the tasks which were once carried on by the state. While doing this, it also forces the government not to continue with subsidies. This will be a blow to the already poverty stricken masses. On the other hand, corporate sector does not fulfil its social responsibility though it receives various benefits from the government and also uses public money to carry out its business.

It was also taken for granted that in most of the nations, bureaucracy stands committed to a set of values enshrined in the constitution. The administrative structure in many countries could be relied upon for ensuring good and people-oriented governance. But the whole set of values for which the bureaucracy stands committed is under the threat of displacement in the name of liberalisation. In other countries where other primordial identities are surfacing either in terms of racism, casteism, regionalism and regionalism, the bureaucracy itself is undergoing major change. In a modern state where traditional or communitarian forms of administrative structures are sacrificed for the sake of state administration, it becomes all the more essential to insist upon good governance.

The ever sharpening understanding of good governance not only recognises the plurality of actors involved in the process but they also address themselves to the substance of governance. This means that it is no longer simply equated with civil service reform, or with the application of management strategies devised in the private sector to public organisations. Instead, now there is a greater emphasis on participation, decentralisation, accountability, and governmental responsiveness, and even broader concerns such as those of social equality and justice.

In a developing country like India, governance concerns necessarily have a wider ambit. The recognition that it takes place in domains other than that of exclusively formal institutionalised political and administrative structures, means that governance concerns encompass a variety of spheres. These include the political (equal application of rule of law, accountability and transparency, the right to information, and corruption in public life); the economic (corporate governance, the regulation of private sector, and financial markets); the civil society (in its various manifestations, not excluding uncivil associations) (Jayal and Pai 2001). It is these aspects that would lead to long term sustainability of communities, societies, nations and the universe at large.

Reforms

Economic reform has become a favourite term of the ruling elite. In India, with the introduction of New Economic Policy (NEP) in 1991, a series of reforms were introduced. The NEP envisaged a stabilisation programme (SP) and structural adjustment programme (SAP). The latter aimed at restoring balance on the fiscal side as well as in external payments. The fiscal imbalance was expressing itself in the growing budgetary deficit of the Central government. The resultant deficit financing was the principal cause of the inflationary pressure in the economy. Rising prices not only seriously hit the fixed-income earners, they also made Indian products costlier and thereby non-competitive. An inflexible exchange rate further exacerbated the difficulties in securing export markets. There were periodic spurts in economic activities but the underlying trend of stagnation was easy to discern. This necessitated cuts in expenditure. Given the political set-up of the country the cut would not be in defence or civil services but it would be in social expenditure. These cuts could be avoided if income was raised through taxation. This was not done since the taxable section of the population has greater political clout (Vyas 1993: 405). Cut in social expenditure would hurt the poorer sections of society. Cut in agricultural subsidies which is another measure of reform, would affect the small and marginal farmers even is case of increase in the price of agricultural produce as they do not produce much surplus for sale and also agricultural labourers without much increase in wages. Large majority of STs belong to this category of the poor in the country.

There are several areas where concerted action is indicated if the poor have to participate in the growth which NEP promises: i) greater investment in infrastructure to facilitate the 'spread effect' of economic growth and to generate productive employment; ii) greater investment in human resource development to strengthen the recipient system and improve its social status; iii) greater emphasis on IRDP, TRYSEM etc.; iv) strengthening a well targeted PDS catering to the basic needs of the poor; v) devising adequate and timely social security measures for the 'new poor'; and vi) the state should not embark on programmes whether with its own resources or with borrowed funds which are likely to remain a liability in the future (Vyas 1993: 405).

Development

The term 'development' usually refers to growth, progress, modernisation etc. There are various approaches to development—modernist, Marxian, positivist, Western or third world. In India, development definitionally and conceptually, denotes progress—social, economic, educational, cultural, scientific and technological—brought about by planned/programmed efforts to inaugurate an era of orderly and peaceful transformation of a society in a constitutionally desired direction. The need of the hour is to dovetail economic growth with social growth and equality (Srivastava 1998).

The UNESCO's Position Paper for the World Summit on Social Development (UNESCO 1994: 9) raised the argument that development is first and foremost social. It says, 'social dimensions is to be the starting point of development and should determine to a large extent the priorities of development policies'. The central trends of social development are:

(*i*) Economic growth is an essential but not sufficient condition to ensure social development; and strategies of development, in order to be more relevant, should focus on societies and not on economics.

(*ii*) Development should be human-centred and broad-based, effecting equal opportunities for all to participate fully and freely in economic, social, cultural and political activities.

(*iii*) People are the ends and not the means of economic progress and development.

(*iv*) Economic growth should subserve the cause of social development and ensure that development has a human face.

(*v*) Social development and economic progress are mutually reinforcing—social development helps reduce economic inequalities and bolsters economic growth, and equitable growth creates jobs and reduces poverty.

Development was perceived as a 'good for all' phenomenon. But now when we talk of development, we have to raise certain basic questions: What is development? Development by whom, for whom, at what cost? Who determines the parameters of development? The debate also questions the known paradigms of development, raises doubts about the directions it has taken place, and decries some of the contradictions. Questions are also raised about development on two accounts. First, the current development paradigms are not working well and second, the universality of the Western paradigm has proved to be a nightmare. While the political establishments and experts on economics want to continue with the present paradigm, civil society is in search of alternative forms which keep people in focus.

Scheduled Tribes

Historical records amply demonstrate the social fact that for several centuries in India, the tribals (popularly known as Scheduled Tribes—STs), the indigenous people, the *adivasis* or the original inhabitants who inhabited the river valleys, forest regions and practiced hunting, food gathering and shifting cultivation have been steadily pushed further back into highland forests and hills. This process possibly began in the 5th century when the so called 'great kingdoms' and 'empires' began to expand their civilisation around the fertile river valleys to eventually settle into permanent agriculture over the next 600 years. The original inhabitants thus managed to work on the new habitat and got the place ready and once again pushed further from there (Louis 2000: 4087–91).

In course of time, the tribals had developed their own forms of political participation. This is usually known as *'Adivasi Swashashan'*, that is, tribal self-rule. This form of governance was based on the ideology, *'Hamare gaon mein hamara raj'* (our rule in our village), that is, 'We rule ourselves, our culture, our economy, our religion and our society, which is both local and regional'. But this well-knit and well-integrated tribal society was brought under alien rule by the outside forces who entered unscrupulously into tribal area.

It seems true that from the 11th to the 16th century, the indigenous people were left to themselves to a great extent. But with the aggression of each invading ruler they were further pushed from their original settlements and lost out in all the ways possible. With the arrival of the British, even the remaining isolation of the tribals was rudely shattered. Road and rail construction helped significantly in the penetration of the military and the markets into ever more remote areas. This was accompanied by the thrust for establishing permanent rights to the land. At the same time, the commercialisation and control of the forests became necessary in order to make timber and charcoal available for housing, transport and energy. These trends became sharper even after the British left, as mining and industrialisation, dams and settlements encroached on to the remaining territories where the original settlers lived. Their displacement was accompanied by drawing of their cheap labour into production, markets, and in a special way in the tea gardens, construction works, rickshaw pulling etc.

B.D. Sharma maintains that the subsistence economy of the tribals depends on the entire habitat—land, forest and water—and not any one of them. The habitat is accepted as a common heritage of the community; individual has the limited right of using the same. Individual ownership is an alien concept, which is insidiously introduced through superimposition of laws without their understanding. It is bitterly opposed wherever people have become conscious about its implications and traditional institutions are strong. Land alienation is a possible consequence only if ownership is individual (Sharma 1995: 17).

In terms of number, as per the 2001 census, groups and communities described as tribes were enumerated at 84.3 million representing 8.2 per cent of country's population. This is evident from the fact that as per the Constitution Order (Scheduled Tribes) 1950, as large as 212 tribal communities in as many as 14 states were declared to be scheduled tribes. As per the Scheduled Tribes Order (Amendment 1976), nearly 300 tribal communities were listed in the constitution. The Anthropological Survey of India under the People of India Project identified as many as 461 tribal communities in the country.[4]

Tribal population is found almost all over the country. Yet, it is in the central region that their concentration is found the most. Out of the total tribal population, over 54.70 per cent are concentrated in central India and about 12.51 per cent inhabit the north-eastern region (Table 12.1). Western and southern regions have about 10.80 per cent and 4.15 per cent respectively. There are also differences in terms of the size of population among the various groups of the tribals.

Moving from the analysis of number, if one focuses on the social milieu of the tribals one would understand that the tribal population has a strong culture and value with which they had organised their social, cultural, economic and political practices and structures. This is precisely the reason why they continue to remain a distinct people in spite of every attempt by the dominant caste and class to bring them under the 'mainstream'. The *adivasi* ethos recognises and respects the basic and fundamental truth that the harmonious relationship between the human community, animal kingdom and the environment should be maintained at any cost. In this process they also respected and valued human labour.

For them the forest was their abode. They were also well aware of the fact that they belonged to the forest but the forest did not belong to them. The forests were alive and active with their gods and spirits of the ancestors. It is wrong to call them dead, since the ancestors are never dead for the tribals. They are part of the entire *jal, jungle aur zamin* (water, forest and land) and their ancestors are also part of them.

Table 12.1: Tribal Population

States	*Total population*	*% with respect to total population in the state/UT*	*% with respect to total tribal population*
1. Central Region	3,92,47,365	12.7	46.6
Jharkhand	70,87,068	26.3	8.4
Chhattisgarh	66,16,597	31.8	7.8
Bihar	7,58,351	0.9	0.9
Madhya Pradesh	1,22,33,474	20.3	14.5
Orissa	81,45,081	22.1	9.6
West Bengal	44,06,794	5.5	5.2
2. Western Region	2,33,07,364	11.4	27.6
Maharashtra	85,77,276	8.9	10.2
Dadra & Nagar Haveli	1,37,225	62.2	0.2
Daman & Diu	13,997	8.8	—
Gujarat	74,81,160	14.8	8.9
Rajasthan	70,97,706	12.6	8.4
3. North-East	1,04,65,898	26.8	12.4
Arunachal Pradesh	7,05,158	54.2	0.8
Assam	33,08,570	12.4	3.9
Manipur	7,41,141	34.2	0.9
Meghalaya	19,92,862	85.9	2.4
Mizoram	8,39,310	94.5	1.0
Nagaland	17,74,026	89.1	2.1
Tripura	9,93,426	31.1	1.2
Sikkim	1,11,405	20.6	0.1
4. Southern Region	95,06,600	4.3	11.3
Andhra Pradesh	50,24,104	6.6	5.96
Tamil Nadu	6,51,321	1.0	0.8
Karnataka	34,63,986	6.6	4.1
Kerala	3,64,189	1.1	0.4
5. North-Western	17,14,658	0.9	2.0
Uttar Pradesh	1,07,963	0.1	0.1
Uttaranchal	2,56,129	3.0	3.0
Himachal Pradesh	2,44,587	4.0	2.9
Jammu & Kashmir	11,05,979	10.9	1.3
6. Island Region	86,790	20.8	0.1
Andaman & Nicobar	29,469	8.3	0.3
Lakshadweep	57,321	94.5	0.5
Total	8,43,28,675	8.2	100

Source: Census of India 2001. New Delhi: Government of India.

As illustrated in Figure 12.1, the entire life cycle of the indigenous people is in consonance with nature and culture. The resources and the produce from hunting, food gathering, shifting cultivation or settled agriculture was and to a great extent owned by the concerned village community and not by the individual who was always recognised to be a part of the community. Various mechanisms were evolved, functionally and culturally integrated with the community life system, to ensure that egalitarian values of equality and cooperation sustained. Equality among all the members as well as among men and women was the edifice of community existence. The governance of the community was vested with designated functional heads, hereditary or otherwise, without 'power' but with 'responsibility'. Power was ultimately vested with the community. Participatory democracy was the method evolved by the community to govern themselves as well as the ecosystem. Every resource was to be preserved not only for themselves but also for the future generation and for all human beings.

Figure 12.1: Adivasi Life Cycle

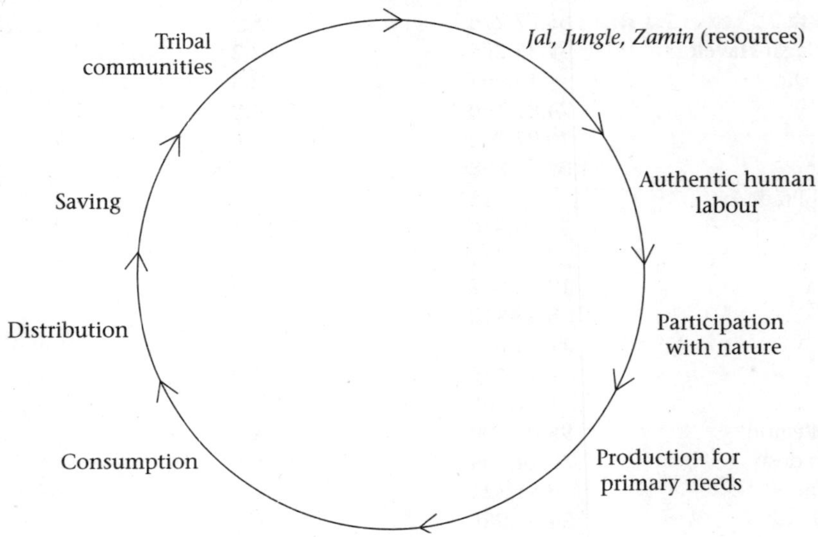

In the process of production, surplus generated was utilised to take care of the young and the old, sick and the needy. But it was not for boosting up a market economy. After taking care of themselves, needs of others, and the animals, the rest was used for leisure. The arts, crafts, science, technologies, dance, music etc. are created under the conditions that they are useful for the society. To present an instance, even the houses in the traditionally tribal areas are same in size, shape and colour.

Natural resources constitute the very lifeline of the tribal population. These resources make up the economic, social, cultural, political and religious universe of the tribal community. The tribal women in a special way had a say and control over these resources. With the introduction of development-induced displacement, vast segments of the tribal population have been displaced from their natural habitats and also are subjected to innumerable forms of exploitation. While land alienation and displacement have become an integral part of tribal history, their rehabilitation does not seem to be a part of the national agenda. A careful examination of displacement and rehabilitation of the tribals at the all-India level unravels this fact that among the 2 crore population who are displaced, more than 40 per cent are tribals (Table 12.2). Out of the 2 crore population who were displaced, only 54 lakh were resettled. Among the total resettled the tribals are only 21.2 lakhs, that is, only about 25 per cent of the tribals are resettled. Thus, from this data it becomes clear that though the tribals constitute only 8 per cent of the national population, more than 40 per cent among them are displaced. But when it comes to resettlement just about 25 per cent are resettled. This clearly indicates the bias against the tribal communities in India. Thus, the tribals who are used to living in symbiotic relationship with nature are reduced to becoming aliens in their own land. Women in a special way lose out control over resources and this increases their burden in terms of finding fuel, fodder and food (Louis 2003: 191–204).

Table 12.2: Total Number of Persons and Tribals Displaced and Resettled by Various Development Projects in India during 1951–1990

(in Lakhs)

Type of projects	*Total displaced (No.)*	*Tribals displaced (No.)*	*Tribals displaced %*	*Total resettled (No.)*	*Total resettled %*	*Tribal resettled (No.)*	*Tribal resettled %*
Dams	164.0	63.2	38.5	41.0	25.0	15.8	25.0
Mines	25.5	13.3	52.2	6.5	25.4	3.3	24.8
Industry	12.5	3.1	25.0	3.8	30.4	0.8	25.8
Wild-Life	6.0	4.5	75.0	1.3	21.6	1.0	22.2
Others	5.0	1.3	25.0	1.5	30.0	0.3	23.0
Total	213.0	85.4	40.1	54.0	25.4	21.2	24.8

Source: Annual Report (1991). Ministry of Rural Development, New Delhi: Government of India.

This continuing process of land alienation, eviction, marginalisation and exploitation of the indigenous people is what we call development in modern language. This begins to control the resources and labour of the majority (in this case the tribals) so that a minority may enjoy the benefits. Obviously, it is this minority which also defines 'development'. One hears now a new concept, 'development induced displacement'. There is also the other process of assimilating the tribals into the mainstream. The Draft National Policy on tribals[5] in a subtle way tried to stress point this, which the tribals rejected in toto.

Tribals, Governance, Reform and Development

The Constitution of India in clear and categorical terms has demanded that all the citizens of this country should be provided with the basic minimum facilities and their rights should be protected. Article 43 of the Constitution states, 'The State shall endeavour to secure, by suitable legislation or economic organisation or in any other way, to all workers agricultural, industrial or otherwise, work, a living wage, conditions of work ensuring a decent standard of life and full employment of leisure and social and cultural opportunities and, in particular, the State shall endeavour to promote cottage industries on an individual and co-operative basis in rural areas.' If this legal provision were to be implemented by the political establishment of the country, there would have been two interrelated consequences. On the one hand, productivity, safety and security as well as economic well being of the entire population would have been ensured over the last five decades. On the other, it would have also enabled in reducing the ever-widening gap between the resourceful and powerful minority and resourceless and powerless majority population.

This notwithstanding, the framers of the Constitution of India, legally guaranteed affirmative action or positive discrimination in favour of the weaker sections. 'The State shall promote with special care the educational and economic interests of the weaker sections of the people, and in particular, of the Scheduled Castes and the Scheduled Tribes, and shall protect them from social injustice and all forms of exploitation' (Article 46). From the perspectives of the framers of the Constitution, the Scheduled Castes and the Scheduled Tribes constitute specially marginalised and discriminated segments of the population. In the last five decades of development, outcome has driven home this message that the Scheduled Castes, the Scheduled Tribes, women, children and labourers in the organised sector constitute the weaker sections of Indian population.

Protecting the tribals is a far cry, but in the last five decades the tribals have been subjected to innumerable forms of oppression and exploitation. Sharma presents a vivid picture of the changes that are taking place among the tribals. 'An important change has occurred in the intervening period in the population matrix of the tribal areas. In many cases, they have been reduced to a minority. Moreover, a new generation of migrant population—children of officials, traders, contractors and such like have majored who forcefully claim equal status with the tribal people as 'sons of the soil'. Moreover, among the tribal people themselves, a small group comprising the educated has been formed having no interest in the habitat and anxious to join the 'other side'. Thus, the tribal people's undisputed command over their habitat is not only being questioned de jure by the state and other exotic interests but even by an influential section of the local population itself, making their position still more vulnerable (Sharma 1995: 24).

In the edited volume, *Globalisation and Indigenous Peoples in Asia*, Dev Nathan and Govind Kelkar argue that globalisation comes to the local communities largely through the market. New goods may be seen on the television or come to be known through other ways. But it is through the market that they become available to be consumed or can be used by people. It is also through the market that producers come to know what they can sell. Often they may not know the uses of to which their products are put to. For instance, only recently, after the logging ban imposed by the Indian Supreme Court, indigenous women in the North-Eastern state of Meghalaya, India, began selling the bark of some trees, but had no idea at all of the uses of that bark. The indigenous peoples of Andhra Pradesh, India, had for decades been collecting and selling gum called *karaya* without any idea of its use in making denture (Nathan, Kelkar and Walter eds. 2004: 293–94).

They go on to state that market, of course, is not new to indigenous people. But with globalisation there is a great increase in the scope of the market. Virtually any product can be traded. And, unlike with production for self-consumption, which is necessarily limited by the extent of local consumption, production for sale in the market is not similarly locally limited, of course, when the aim of trade is no longer to incorporate exotic products into a subsistence system, but becomes part of a process of accumulation.

The authors argue that the growth of the market has led to a process of privatisation of formerly communal land; of devolution of ownership, at least de facto if not also de jure, from supra-village and community or clan to the family. The market for timber and Non-Timber Forest Products (NTFPs) grew in the colonial or immediate post-colonial periods. To that extent they certainly pre-date the 1990s, which is generally regarded as the era of globalisation, with the growth of global financial markets. But the process of privatisation through market-induced transformation is a feature that has become even stronger in the current era. Consequently, an analysis of the privatisation process, even if it pre-dates the 1990s, can tell us a lot about the effects of the growth of global markets on what were formerly relatively self-contained, subsistence-based economies (Nathan 2004: 294).

Some economists argue that economic reforms initiated in 1991, which have included liberalisation and deregulation along with structural adjustment, were directed at industry, trade, banking, capital markets, exchange rates, taxation, public finance, and infrastructure. The impact on agriculture has been indirect. However, the reforms have had a considerable impact on the poor, whether in the cities or rural areas, employed in agriculture or industry or service. Economic growth and increases in standards of living are almost always associated with a rapid decline in the number of persons working in agriculture. Economic growth which can absorb labour into industry and the services sector is the process by which a substantial decrease in poverty can be attained. India has failed on this account (Parikh 1999: 50).

In a study undertaken by Astha Sansthan in Rajasthan on 'Impact of SAP and the New Economic Policy on the Poor in Rajasthan', it has been highlighted that inflation is one of the most important reasons for the misery of the poor (Table 12.3). In this study which was conducted between 1996 to 1998, the respondents rated inflation, lack of regular employments and loans and debts as the crucial facts which lead them to poverty. In five districts out of the nine taken up for study, there is a sizeable tribal population which is higher than the state average which is 12.4 per cent. The respondents rated in all three years price hike as one of the central aspect that affects them now.[6] Lack of inputs for agriculture, loans and debts for consumption purpose and denial of minimum wages constitute the second level factors which drive the people of this state and especially among them the tribals to poverty and misery.

There is no doubt that various development programmes initiated by the government has brought in some change in the lives of the tribal communities, especially in the areas of education, health and employment. During the Fifth Five Year Plan in 1974–75, the Tribal Sub-Plan was adopted to promote development among the tribals and also to protect their interests. From then on, specific programmes were worked out in addition to the general poverty eradication programmes. In the year 1999, an exclusive Ministry of Tribal Affairs was

Table 12.3: The Reasons for Deteriorating Economic Conditions

	Phase I		*Phase II*		*Phase III*	
Reasons	*Respondents (540)*	*%*	*Respondents (492)*	*%*	*Respondents (492)*	*%*
Inflation	129	24.0	153	31.0	143	32.4
Lack of regular employment	88	18.0	65	13.2	86	19.5
Lack of inputs for agriculture	39	7.2	61	12.4	71	14.4
Loans and debts	140	26.0	46	9.3	17	3.8
Denial of actual wages	60	11.0	42	8.5	73	16.5
Natural disaster	11	2.5	4	0.8	11	2.5
Increase in population	13	3.0	4	0.8	13	3.0
Sickness	5	1.1	22	4.5	5	1.1
Fragmentation of family	2	0.5	7	1.4	2	0.5
Exploitation	1	0.2	5	1.0	1	0.2

Source: *Impact of SAP and the New Economic Policy on the Poor in Rajasthan*. Rajasthan: Astha Sansthan, 2000.

constituted to deal with tribal welfare and development. But all these attempts seem to have not really benefited the tribals to the extent it should have.

Literacy is one of the indicators to measure the progress of a country and of a community within it. If one pays attention to the literacy of tribal communities and relate it with the general population of India, it becomes clear that they are a discriminated lot. Table 12.4 makes the point clear that there has been a substantial increase in literacy rate among the tribals in the last four decades. But if one examines the data given in the table, one becomes aware of the fact that the gap between literacy rate of STs and that of the general population is not only persisting, but widening. This goes to establish the fact that the general population due to their social location benefit from various programmes. The tribals on the other hand, do not benefit from these programmes. With land alienation as their lot, most of the tribals are forced to migrate and the steadily increasing literacy rate among them will witness decline in the future.

Table 12.4: Literacy Rate of ST and General Population

Category	*1971*	*1981*	*1991*	*2001*
General Population	29.45	36.23	52.21	65.38
Scheduled Tribes	11.30	16.35	29.60	43.10
Gap between the STs and general population	18.15	19.88	22.61	22.28

Source: *Report of Steering Committee on Empowering the Scheduled Tribes for the Tenth Five Year Plan 2002–2007* (2001). New Delhi: Government of India, p. 15.

Disinvestment of BALCO and Tribals: A Case Study

We present here a case study of disinvestment of a public sector undertaking and its impact on the citizens of the country, especially of the tribals.[7] Bharat Aluminium Company Limited (Balco) was set up at Korba (now in Chhattisgarh) as a Public Sector Unit (PSU) for the manufacture and sale of aluminium metal including wire rods and semi-fabricated products such as extrusions, sheets/coils and foils and in 1984 the company was asked to take over a sick unit in Bidhanbag, West Bengal which added to the downstream facilities in sheets, foils and alloy rods. The then Madhya Pradesh Government had allotted about 1650 acres of 'Tribal Land' to set up the unit.

Balco has its Research & Development (hereafter R&D) unit at Korba, which was set up in 1984 by Government of India (Department of Scientific Research) for developing special alloys for fuel tanks and casting for ballistic missiles like *Agni* and *Pritivi*. It is the only company in the country supplying special alloy metals developed on its own R&D to defence and space organisations for the production of ballistic missiles and space accessories. It is also the only aluminium industry in South Asia having its own hot rolling mill capable of fabricating defence products from special alloys.

The Korba facility includes a fully built township spread over 15,000 acres (about 6,000 hectares) in which over four thousand families live. At the time of disinvestment, with 15 per cent of the market share, Balco was the third largest player in India's aluminium industry having a relatively sound financial situation. Ministry of Disinvestment had indicated in the Parliament that Balco's financial health was slowly deteriorating by citing the current year's performance. This was a misleading statement by the Minister. The drop in the profit was mainly due to breakdown of one unit of Balco's captive power plant for a full year. This had resulted in purchase of power from Madhya Pradesh Electricity Board (MPEB) by paying very high tariff. Despite this, Balco was also a cash rich Public Sector Undertaking (PSU) which had reserve surplus worth Rs 460 crores at the time of disinvestment as it is evident from Table 12.5.

The Disinvestment Commission[8] outlined well thought out long-term objectives and strategy to address the disinvestment process (Table 12.6). Besides, the Commission also recommended comprehensive study of all loss making PSUs to classify them as:

(*a*) those which the government can sell as a growing concern;

(*b*) those which can be restructured, turned around and disinvested;

(*c*) those which may need closure.

The Commission repeatedly emphasised the need to conduct such a study especially since one of the main objectives of the disinvestment is to reduce budgetary support to the unprofitable PSUs. It should be noted here that 60 per cent of the budgetary support goes to unprofitable PSUs. However, there does not seem to have been any move on this front. The Commission strongly argued for setting up a disinvestment fund separate from other government receipts where the proceeds of disinvestment should be put and used for restructuring of loss making PSUs and workers benefits in case of closure.

Table 12.5: Financial Position of BALCO from the Financial Year (FY) 1992 to 1999

Financial heads	*FY 1999*	*FY 1998*	*FY 1997*	*FY 1996*	*FY 1995*	*FY 1994*	*FY 1993*	*FY 1992*
Operating income	756.56	738.71	665.09	601.4	598.9	506.5	389.6	394.3
Operating profit	134.77	134.79	127.17	197.6	162.3	65.3	51.8	46.5
Profit after tax	76.32	79.84	61.79	163.3	90.5	15.3	1.9	0.9
Equity capital	488.8	488.8	488.8	488.8	488.8	488.8	488.8	488.8
Tangible net worth	873.23	847.91	794.34	747.5	608.2	517.8	502.6	500.7
Gross margin (%)	25.03	24.86	26.82	32.9	27.1	12.9	13.3	11.8
Net margin (%)	10.08	10.80	9.29	27.2	15.1	3.0	0.5	0.2
RONW (%)	15.39	15.91	15.90	21.6	14.9	3.0	0.4	0.2
Earning per share (Rs)	1.56	1.63	1.26	3.34	1.85	0.311	0.04	0.02
Dividend (%)	4.7	4.1	2.9	2.9	—	—	—	—

Source: Disinvestment Commission Report 2 (1997). New Delhi: Government of India, http://www.divest.nic.in/comm-reports/reports-main.htm.
Note: RONW = Return on net worth.

Table 12.6: Objectives and Strategies of Disinvestment

Objectives	*Strategy*
Strengthen PSUs	• Strengthen profitable PSUs to promote greater competitiveness and profitability to enable payment of higher dividends to the Government and to enhance share values • Strengthen other marginally profitable PSUs and reduce their further dependence on the budget. • Financially restructure and revive loss making PSUs to invite private capital for long term turn around
Protect Employee interest	• Sustain long term employment by turning around of loss making PSUs • Providing fair and adequate VRS for surplus worker force • Provide for employee participation in management
Broad based ownership	• Enhance retail reach of PSU shares to small investors and offer at suitable price discount as compared to the institutional investor
Augment receipts for government receipts	• Enhance Government receipts by disinvestment in profitable PSUs • Eliminating the need for budgetary support for loss making PSUs

Source: Disinvestment Commission Report 1 (1997). New Delhi: Government of India, http://www.divest.nic.in/comm-reports/reports-main.htm.

In order to study the impact of various aspects of disinvestment or privatisation policy on the tribal industrial workers in Balco, a survey was conducted among 5 per cent of the total strength of 6,400 workers in Balco[9] which is about 320 as indicated in Table 12.7. Out of the total sample size, 45 per cent belong to the ST category, and rest belong to other social groups.

The relatively large percentage of workers belonging to the ST category of the total sample size has been taken for two reasons. First, the central objective of this study was aimed to solicit the opinion of tribal people on the issues relating to privatisation. A relatively larger percentage of tribal workers, therefore, would give us a cross-section of opinion from among the tribal workers on the issues relating to privatisation as well as in the context of the disinvestment of Balco. Second, other social groups of the sample size would be used for comparison to see the similarities and contrasts of views between the tribal and non-tribal workers on privatisation. Keeping this in mind, 16.9, 15.9 and 22.2 per cent of workers have been interviewed from among the scheduled castes, other backward castes and general category respectively.

Table 12.7: Classification of Workers According to their Social Groups in the Sample

Social Groups	*Number*	*%*
ST	144	45.0
SC	54	16.9
OBC	51	15.9
General	71	22.2
Total	320	100

Table 12.8 represents the opinion of the workers on the privatisation of PSUs. We can see that an overwhelming percentage of the respondents irrespective of their social category have declared that privatisation of PSUs is a 'Bad Policy'. The battle-lines against the struggle for privatisation are clearly drawn and there cannot be any middle ground in this struggle. The 67 day long labour strike, by almost the entire working force of Balco is a simple evidence, which speaks volumes about the unanimity of opinion among the workers against privatisation. It also received tremendous solidarity and support from other workers and unions.

Table 12.8: Opinion of Workers on the Privatisation of BALCO

Social groups	*Good policy*	*Bad policy*	*Both good and bad policy*	*Can't say*	*Total*
ST	1	111	27	5	144
	[16.7]	[48.7]	[35.5]	[50.0]	[45.0]
	(0.7)	(77.1)	(18.8)	(3.5)	(100.0)
SC	1	35	17	1	54
	[16.7]	[15.4]	[22.4]	[10.0]	[16.9]
	(1.9)	(64.8)	(31.5)	(1.9)	(100.0)
OBC	2	36	11	2	51
	[33.3]	[15.8]	[14.5]	[20.0]	[15.9]
	(3.9)	(70.6)	(21.6)	(3.9)	(100.0)
General	2	46	21	2	71
	[33.3]	[20.2]	[27.6]	[20.0]	[22.2]
	(2.8)	(64.8)	(29.6)	(2.8)	(100.0)
Total	6	228	76	10	320
	[100.0]	[100.0]	[100.0]	[100.0]	[100.0]
	(1.9)	(71.3)	(23.8)	(3.1)	(100.0)

Notes: [ ] represents column percentage.
( ) represents row percentage.

In April 2001, when the workers of Balco struck work, they were willing to enter into negotiations even though they were opposed to privatisation in any form. They had offered four options to the Union Minister of Mines. But the government instead of considering these options tried to lure the workers with service conditions. Even the *Swadeshi Jagran Manch* (SJM), a sister organisation of the ruling Bharatiya Janata Party vehemently criticised the privatisation process saying that politicians, bureaucrats and private vested interests were manipulating the privatisation of public sector companies. It alleged that these companies had been rendered sick for extraneous considerations (Sridhar 2001a).

In the month of May 2001, when the workers of Balco realised that their struggle has reached a dead end, they were willing for a negotiation with the new management. The union leaders repeatedly stated that the workers were only seeking a just and equitable solution. Instead of looking into this, the Sterlite Industries had only offered to pay the workers as an advance what was due to them. In their view, there was nothing magnanimous about Sterlite's offer. The union leaders also stated that the leadership of the unions was under pressure to reach an 'honourable solution' after a long battle involving thousands of people who had sacrificed a lot in the battle against privatisation. Keeping this fact in mind, the workers rejected Sterlite Industries' offer (Sridhar 2001b).

During the course of data collection, the workers of Balco termed the entire process as bad. As clearly indicated in Table 12.8, over 71.3 per cent of respondents out of the total sample of 320 have designated privatisation and disinvestment as a 'Bad Policy'. Respondents also gave very specific answers while declaring privatisation as a bad policy. Some of the reasons are ideological and conceptual while others are related to the immediate problems faced by the workers after privatisation. A number of respondents said that after privatisation their over time (OT) has been cut and they also fear job insecurity. A number of them also felt that the workload has increased since privatisation and workers are treated as machines. Some felt that workers are being exploited in the absence of inadequate government control of the management.

As noted earlier, much of the neoliberal doctrine has seen labour solely as input into production, just like any other input. But if improving living standards is the objective of economics then improving the welfare of workers becomes an end in itself; and if one believes that markets leads to efficient outcomes one can feel confident in not paying explicit attention to workers' welfare, trusting that the market will make the correct trade-offs, which has never happened. Nevertheless, a small section of workers, nearly 23.8 per cent have given mixed opinion on the privatisation of PSUs, whereas only 1.9 per cent of the respondents have found some merit in it to call it a 'Good policy'.

If development were merely a matter of capital accumulation, then successful development would entail primarily making a country more attractive for capital, enhancing the 'security of capital'. However, if development is to be broad based, then we must pay at least much attention to workers and their security. But if they are exposed to increased insecurity and higher unemployment it will not; and many of the reform policies have done exactly that. On a more positive note, successful democratic development entails questioning authority and participation in decision-making which involves more democratic structures at all levels.[10]

The state-industries relations have not been very encouraging in our country either in public sector or in the private sector. This often leads to conflict of interests between the workers and the management. Privatisation was expected to reduce the points of friction between the management and the workers. Our empirical finding as presented above, however, contradicts this understanding. In fact, in the post-privatisation situation, the relationship between the workers and the management has further deteriorated. The data presented in Table 12.9 demonstrates that privatisation as both government and its disinvestment minister are trumpeting, is not necessarily 'good policy'. It is obvious that only a miniscule 1.3 per cent of the workers found the new management of Balco conducive to better working conditions which is the most important factor in the enhancement of growth. By contrast, more than half of the respondents (51.3 per cent) do not find any virtue in the new management.

Table 12.9: Opinion of Workers on the Post-privatised Management of BALCO

Social groups	*Good*	*Not good*	*Not as good as the old one*	*Can't say*	*No response*	*Total*
ST	1	80	56	5	2	144
	[25.0]	[48.8]	[41.2]	[41.7]	[50.0]	[45.0]
	(0.7)	(55.6)	(38.9)	(3.5)	(1.4)	(100.0)
SC	2	27	22	2	1	54
	[50.0]	[16.5]	[16.2]	[16.7]	[25.0]	[16.9]
	(3.7)	(50.0)	(40.7)	(3.7)	(1.9)	(100.0)
OBC	1	25	20	4	1	51
	[25.0]	[15.2]	[14.7]	[33.3]	[25.0]	[15.9]
	(2.0)	(49.0)	(39.2)	(7.8)	(2.0)	(100.0)
General	—	32	38	1	—	71
		[19.5]	[29.7]	[8.3]		[22.2]
		(45.1)	(53.5)	(1.4)		(100.0)
Total	4	164	136	12	4	320
	[100.0]	[100.0]	[100.0]	[100.0]	[100.0]	[100.0]
	(1.3)	(51.3)	(51.3)	(3.8)	(1.3)	(100.0)

Notes: [ ] represents column percentage.
( ) represents row percentage.

In contemporary times, participation is the dominant slogan across the world and more so in the developing world. But it has been sent for toss by the state and its accomplices in India. After all, workers remain the most important 'partners-in-progress' of any nation. But here the government did not even consider seeking the opinion of the workers employed in Balco for more than 35 years. As Table 12.9 makes it clear that over 99 per cent of the workers who later tried to resist the privatisation of Balco were not even informed about the government's decision to privatise it.

Much more deplorable is the fact that even the agreement made between the *Balco Bachao Samyukta Abhiyan Samiti* (BBSAS), that is, Joint Committee for the Defence of Balco and the

Sterlite Industries, the new management of Balco was violated. On March 2 when the agreement was signed to sell off Balco's largest plant at Korba to Sterlite Industries, the workers under the leadership of BBSAS went on a strike. On May 8, after 67 days an agreement was reached between BBSAS and Sterlite Industries with the following conditions: a) workers would be paid two months wages; b) there would be no retrenchment or victimisation. But within 48 hours, Sterlite Industries laid off 2000 workers on the grounds that their contracts had expired. Moreover, the management reinterpreted the payment agreement, declaring the two months pay was an advance towards workers' future wages (Wickremasinghe 2001). Thus, both the government and the management did not bother to respect the rights of the workers and the management did not care to adhere to the agreement made with the workers' union.

Going further, it needs to be stated that Balco deal violates the fundamental rights of the tribals. The Constitution of India has clearly and categorically established the fact that the tribals have an inalienable right over their land. While this law was being violated, the Supreme Court of India in its historical judgment given in the landmark 'Samata Case', once again vested ownership of tribal lands in *'adivasi'* people and forbade its transfer to private companies or any other party. In the judgement delivered in July 1999, the Supreme Court of India declared that government land, forest land and tribal land can not be leased out to non-tribals or private industries (Samata 2000: iii). The judgement also directed the authorities to stop 'forthwith' all industrial and mining activities in tribal areas.

Balco's mining lease falls mainly in such areas of Chhattisgarh—Katghora, Bilaspur, Manpur, Monla and Rajnandgaon, which are predominatly tribal areas. A year after the Samata Judgement, the government went ahead and sold another PSU and thus, gave away the tribal land to a private company. Thus, Sterlite, the company that has bought 51 per cent of Balco's stakes cannot enjoy the mining rights in the area. Therefore, the Balco deal has created a contradiction of sorts between the disinvestment policies of the government, the constitutional protection for the tribals and the law of the land.

Praful Bidwai in his perceptive analysis argues that, the judgment interprets the Indian constitution's Fifth and Sixth Schedules, which apply to tribal lands as part of the statue's 'integrated scheme'. It declares that the custodianship of tribal lands must be vested with tribals alone. It therefore asks all states 'to ensure that all industrialists concerned be they natural persons or juristic persons, stop forthwith mining operations', etc. further, one-fifth or all their profits must be given to tribals. This includes all past profits. Praful Bidwai bemoans the fact that instead of implementing this order, or specific directions from the court to set up a special committee to legislate special protection for tribals, the centre has done its best to subvert it (Bidwai 2001). Thus, the fundamental right of the tribals to own land has been violated by the state and the corporate sector.

With the advent of globalisation, the tribals have been further marginalised. While outlining the impact of globalisation, especially of the market on the tribals, Dev Nathan amplifies the fact that the outcome of the growth of the market led to a process of privatisation of formerly communal land, and of devolution of ownership from supra-village and community or clan to the family. Dev Nathan also identifies the following impact due to this process: the rise of big men or big families and their links to the external world; the decline of earlier forms of reciprocity that inhibited accumulation; the separation of the objective conditions of labour (chiefly land) from labour itself, leading to the creation of what Marx termed 'not-land-ownership'; the growing domination of men in economic matters; the breakdown of norms of collecting forest products only for self-consumption and in regulating collection for sale; the gradual or rapid decline of NTFPs in the unregulated commons and domestication and shift of valuable NTFP species into the home gardens or privately owned fields (Nathan 2004: 294).

Questions are being raised about the very source of reform policies introduced and carried out by successive governments of India from 1990 onwards. C. Rammanohar Reddy states,

> A disappearing consensus on reforms is a complaint that Mr. Yeshwant Sinha, Union Finance Minister, has voiced on more than one occasion in recent weeks. The context has been the strong protests over the hike in ration shop prices of rice and wheat, the reduced subsidy for urea and the increases in price of petroleum products. A disappearing consensus assumes there was a consensus earlier. But if the truth be told, there never has been a consensus on economic liberalisation—if by consensus is meant a broad based democratic support for reform because after a decade of reform, there has been no widespread percolation of its benefits in terms of income and employment gains. The reforms were initially designed and administered by a small group of officials and economists. Liberalisation, in short, was not in any way rooted in the domestic policy (Reddy 2000).

If the benefit of reform has not percolated to the general citizens of this country, it reaching the tribals is far removed reality. Since the tribals are isolated, deprived and marginalised, they are all the more denied any benefit from the outcome of liberalisation, even if there is some benefit.

B.D. Sharma taking into account the present state of affairs of the tribals, presents the important features of the tribal scene at the beginning of the new era marked by globalistion and free market. i) Virtual rejection of the tribal sub-system: The constitutional scheme of an autonomous tribal sub-system within a nation committed to the establishment of an egalitarian society stands virtually rejected. ii) Habitat and community concepts are spurned: With the collapse of sub-system frame, there is no place for the habitat as the life-support system of the tribal people. Even before the community as the basic unit of tribal life could get formal recognition, the stage is set for its final burial under the cross of liberalism. iii) Shaky basis of individual and community rights and usage: The superimposition of the concept of individual rights in total disregard of the community and suppression of oral tradition has made the tribal people aware about their rights over land-water-forest resources most tenuous. iv) A new frontier spirit: In the earlier phase of the opening up of the tribal areas, there was fear of the unknown, risk of retaliation, constraints of state's moral responsibility. The constraints of state responsibility towards the tribal people have gradually vanished because of studied indifference and non-action. The new milieu is enterprises not being constrained by any guidelines which is an important feature of public sector enterprise. v) State committed to support the frontier spirit: As the state is now formally wedded to the so-called liberalisation, the message to the administration (to all the vested interests) is clear. This is leading to the loot, plunder and genocide of the tribals (Sharma 1995: 24–27).

Concluding Remarks

Before we conclude, let us raise some of the issues that need to be squarely addressed with regard to the state and the tribal communities in India. We will also present some of the alternatives that are carried out in some of the places. Moreover, we will spell out some pointers for responding to this deplorable condition of the tribals which was created by the globalising forces.

It is often argued by social scientists that the ruling establishment does not have the political will to implement its own policies. This on the face value seems to be true. But if one examines closely the performance of the ruling class, one becomes aware of the fact that there is a strong political will among the political regime not to do anything which will improve the lot of the tribals, whom the constitution refers to as the weaker section. It is evident that the ruling class has its own agenda and priorities based on these acts, in favour of some and against the interest of others. Consequently, it is the interests of the tribals which is not a priority of the ruling elite of India.

To a careful reader of the development initiatives taken by various state governments, the priorities of the ruling elite become clear. The Economic Survey 1994–95 (p. 105) of the Government of India presents the priorities of the ruling establishment as under:

- Haryana has set up high-powered committee to take on-the-spot-decision on foreign investments, NRI projects and 100 per cent export-oriented projects; it has also announced that all projects will be cleared through State Pollution Control Board within 15 days.
- Kerala has constituted a Green Channel Scheme to expedite clearances and all unnecessary licensing and clearance will be abolished;
- Punjab has constituted a committee to provide land 'off the shelf' and it is formulating a policy to ensure clearances within 24 hours of the submission of a proposal;
- Rajasthan has exempted 155 Small Scale Industries (SSI) from obtaining an NOC (No Objection Certificate) from the state control board and reduced the number of industries to be inspected under the Factories Act from 15 to 3;
- West Bengal has constituted an Empowered Committee at the State level, under the Chairmanship of the Chief Secretary to take quick decisions on investment proposals.[11] While these priorities clearly show the political will of the government to respond to the interests of the corporate sectors, it engages only in lip service with regard to the tribals.

Even the collective power of the labour class seems to have been weakened by the process and outcome of globalisation. Based on his examination of the review of case studies of trade unions in Asia, Latin America and Africa, Thomas Henk (1995) states that the trade unions are in precarious situations in the era of globalisation. The finding that stands out is the loss of power, in economic, social and political terms, of the trade union movement during the last decades. In particular, broad societal problems of access to, and quality of, employment pose challenges which the trade unions generally have not been able to address. Henk goes on to appeal that the challenges faced by the trade union movement in many parts of the world call for new approaches that may imply institutional renovations, new tasks, and even new ways of cooperation with other societal institutions. New roles for trade union movement are naturally related to the old traditions of protecting workers and better equipping people for work, and for struggling for wider emancipation and democratisation. However, given the fast and dramatic structural changes taking place in national and international labour markets, it appears that so far the trade union movement has been unable to assert itself with respect to both employment conditions and worsening power relations (Henk 1995: 236).

One of the international alternatives for the process of globalisation in the last few years has been the World Social Forum (WSF). The advocates of globalisation propagate that, 'Globalisation is a fact of life and it is a natural phenomenon'. They also go on to declare that, 'There Is No Alternative (TINA) to globalisation'. Against these pronouncements at the global level, there has been a trend to mobilise and organise those who want to counter the trends and effects of globalisation. This attempt has resulted in what has come to be known as 'World Social Forum' (WSF). Those who have been part of the WSF process have engaged themselves in search of alternatives for globalisation forces. In response to the slogan 'There Is No Alternative to globalisation', they have come out with the slogan 'Socialism Is the Alternative' (SITA). Some others would argue that 'There Are Many Alternatives' (TAMA). Thus, the debate continues unabated both in favour of and against globalisation.[12] Thousands of tribals who were present in the 4th World Social Forum at Mumbai in January 2004, reiterated this fact that they oppose neoliberal model of development which leads to land alienation and displacement and are searching for their own models of development.

A common view that is emerging among those who oppose globalisation is that serious and systematic attempts should be made to comprehend liberalisation, privatisation and globalisation processes and their effects. Further, there is also a need to redefine the foundational principles and practices that underline the alternatives. Those who outrightly decry the global model, need to search for local and sustainable model of sustenance and development. This would be possible and profitable if participation and good governance are introduced at all levels.

The tribals are becoming aware of the fact that though there is big talk about mainstreaming them, they are being denied opportunities in various fields. Hence, they are asking for the enactment of Equal Employment Opportunity Act. This would provide enormous scope for the tribals to be gainfully employed, which in turn would have an impact on the community. Along with this they are also demanding for an Equal Employment Opportunity Commission which would ensure time bound implementation of the provisions of this act.

According to Pieterse, growing cultural difference and globalisation are not simply contradictory but interdependent. Growing awareness of cultural difference is a function of globalisation. Increasing cross-cultural communication, mobility, migration, trade, investment, tourism, all generate awareness of cultural difference. The other side of the politics of difference is that the very striving for recognition implies a claim to equality, equal rights, same treatment: in other words, a common universe of difference. Accordingly, the clash between cultural diversity and globalisation may be considered a creative clash (Pieterse 1996: 1393). The crucial question at this juncture is, how should one carry forward this struggle for equality, equal rights, justice, participation etc., especially from the perspective of the tribal communities.

Ram Dayal Munda, the ideologue of the tribals taking into account the discrimination and exploitation suffered by the tribals, calls for a coordinated effort to bring together the awakened groups of people. These coordination efforts will have to be accomplished at all levels, that is, ethnic, social, linguistic, religious, political, economic and gender. Unless this is systematically undertaken, the tribal movement itself would whither away. Thus, with the arrival of tribal states if the tribal movement for self-determination, preservation of their *jal, jungle* and *zamin*, socio-cultural assertion and tribal self-rule withers away, then the tribals would be annihilated once and for all from the tribal region (Munda nd).

Finally, it needs to be stated that the ruling elite of this country advocates only economic reforms. Irrespective of party affiliation, all the political parties that came to power from 1990 onwards have shown their unambiguous commitment to economic reforms. But the common masses and the civil society members have been asking for reform in electoral system, in the judiciary, in the legislature, land reform, reform in educational system etc. The tribal community in a special way have been demanding a review of development paradigms and calling for ban on all those undertakings which violates their rights. But the ruling elite have not paid any attention to this demand. Yet, the tribals have continued their struggle for participatory governance. This resolve of the tribals can be clearly and categorically seen in their declaration as presented below:

The Final Declaration of the National Assembly of Tribal, Indigenous and Adivasi Peoples held in New Delhi on 21 September 2004 highlights some of the Non-Negotiable Principles for a National Policy for Tribal, Indigenous and Adivasi Peoples:[13]

(*i*) Principles of Fundamental Respect of Difference, by which is implied the acceptance and respect for different societies with our distinct identity, culture, ethos and ways of life.

(*ii*) Principles of Recognition of the Natural and Juridical Socio-Economic, Cultural and Political Rights of Tribal, Indigenous and Adivasi communities by which is implied the recognition of the Rights to

(*a*) Life and livelihood with dignity,
(*b*) Land, including our ancestral homelands and command over our natural resources, and protection and regeneration of natural resources in our lands,
(*c*) Express and uphold our distinct identities, cultures, ethos and ways of life.
(*d*) Protect and advance our traditional systems of governance, customary laws and jurisprudence,
(*e*) Protect and further our own cultures and civilisations, and
(*f*) Self-governance and determination of our development and our futures.

(iii) Principles of Participation and Primacy of the People in formulation of laws and policies that affect us.

(iv) Principles of Responsibility of the State to safeguard the rights and genuine aspirations of our peoples and ensure their fulfilment.

(v) Principles of Responsibility of the State to rectify historical injustices and restore our legitimate rights.

From the above presentation it can be stated that the tribals were and continue to be the isolated, deprived and marginalised segment of Indian population. Keeping this fact in mind, the framers of the Constitution made specific provisions for their upliftment. But, these have not really benefited the tribal communities at large. With the introduction of privatisation, liberalisation and globalisation, the rights of the tribals have been further violated. Yet, they continue to wage relentless war to safeguard their interests and rights. As stated above, it seems that the struggle will go on to establish the principles that uphold the rights of the tribals.

Notes

1. Many books and articles have been published on the process and outcome of globalisation in the last one decade. It is only recently, that some attempts have been made to understand the interface between globalisation and specific social groups. Dev Nathan et al. (eds), *Globalisation and Indigenous Peoples in Asia: Changing the Local- Global Interface*; P.G. Jogdand et al. (eds), *New Economic Policy and Dalits*; M. Bhattacharya (ed.), *Perspectives in Women's Studies: Globalisation*; Thomas Henk (ed.), *Globalisation and Third World Trade Unions: The Challenge of Rapid Economic Change*, and Akbar Ahamad's work, *Islam, Globalisation and Post-Modernity* are some of the works that are pioneering, but more research needs to be done to unravel the interface between these social groups and globalisation.
2. UNCTAD. *Fragile Recovery and Risks: Trade, Finance and Growth—Trade and Development Report 1999*. Bookwell: New Delhi, 2000. The data given by the UNTACD points out the growing gap between rich and poor countries and between rich and poor within countries.
3. For more discussion on exclusion, deprivation and discrimination suffered by the weaker sections of Indian society, especially by the Dalits of India refer to Prakash Louis (2003). *Political Sociology of Dalit Assertion*. New Delhi: Gyan Publishing House. In the past, social scientists discussed the issues from the perspective of poor but now the poor are further identified as excluded and marginalised.
4. Virginus Xaxa. *The Adivasis of India*. An Unpublished Document. There is no agreement on the exact number of tribal communities in India. This arises from the fact that there is no clarity or unanimity as to who constitutes a tribal. The ambiguity is also about the defining features of caste. For instance, there are communities who in their way of life, customs and practices are very much like the tribals but are enumerated as Scheduled Castes. As of now those who were included in the Constitution order (Scheduled Tribes) are considered to be tribals.
5. For the text of Draft National Policy on Tribals check the Ministry of Tribal Affairs' website. This draft policy was prepared by the National Democratic Alliance Government in the year 2004 and the present United Progressive Alliance Government has shelved this and is preparing a new draft policy.
6. Unpublished document 'Impact of SAP and the New Economic Policy on the Poor in Rajasthan'. Astha Sansthan: Rajasthan, 2000, p. 193. It needs to be stated here that now there are some field based studies being done to assess the impact of privatisation, liberalisation and globalisation. Some of the studies are general in nature but there are some studies which keep in focus specific social groups. The above mentioned study is one such example.
7. 'Disinvestment of BALCO: A Case Study of its Impact on the Tribal Workers'. This case study is taken from the unpublished document of the Research Study undertaken by the Indian Social Institute, New Delhi, 2002.

8. Ministry of Industry (Department of Public Enterprises) vide a resolution dated 23 August 1996, constituted a Public Sector Disinvestment Commission for a period of three years under G.V. Ramakrishna along with four other Members. The term was further extended till 30th November 1999. The Commission submitted reports on 58 PSEs. The Commission was reconstituted vide Ministry of Disinvestment resolution No.11012/1/2000-Adm dated 24 July 2001 for a period of two years under R.H. Patil as Chairman along with four other Members. The term of the Commission was subsequently extended till October 2004. Source: www. D:\backup\Economic Aspects\Disinvestment\Department of Disinvestment- Addresses.htm
9. Though there are varying estimates of the total strength of BALCO's work force but the figure of 6400 was mentioned by Sagir Ahmed, Vice President of the Union during the interview.
10. By contrast, the World Bank and IMF conditionality often serves to undermine democratic processes, especially when the conditionality extends beyond issues directly related to the crisis into core political issues. It is here, that the very sovereignty of a country is at stake and the power of these international financial institutions increase.
11. *Economic Survey 1994–95*. Ministry of Finance: Government of India, 1994, p. 105. Every year during the Budget presentation, the government brings out this document known as Economic Survey. This document presents an overall economic status of the country. In contrast to the government view points and data, the Alternative Survey Group brings out Alternative Economic Survey challenging many of the claims of the government.
12. Prakash Louis (compiled). World Social Forum 2004. Indian Social Institute: New Delhi, 2004, p. 1. World Social Forums are being held from 2001 when it was first held at Port Alegre in Brazil. Over thousands of people participate in this forum to raise their issues in view of globalisation and the alternatives they are pursuing. This forum has also raised questions about the very ideology of neo-liberalism and rules of governance and investment set by the World Economic Forum in Davos, Switzerland. The Fourth World Social Forum was held in Mumbai, India on 16–21 January 2004.
13. Final Declaration of the National Assembly of Tribal, Indigenous and Adivasi Peoples. This National Assembly was held in New Delhi from 21 to 23 September 2004 to review and respond to the National Draft Tribal Policy.

References

Bagchi, A.K. (1999). 'Globalisation, Liberalisation and Vulnerability: India and Third World', *Economic and Political Weekly*, 34(45): 3219.

Bidwai, Praful (2001). 'Balco Sell-Off', *Frontline*, 29 April–5 May: 3–6.

Chossudovsky, M. (1997). *The Globalisation of Poverty*. Pune: Madhyam Books.

Dasgupta, Samir (ed.) (2004). *The Changing Face of Globalisation*. New Delhi: Sage Publications.

Giddens, Anthony (1994). *Beyond Left and Right: The Future Radical Politics*. Cambridge, UK: Polity Press.

Held, David et al. (1999). *Global Transformations: Politics, Economics, Culture*. Cambridge: Polity Press.

Henk, Thomas (ed.) (1995). *Globalisation and Third World Trade Unions: The Challenge of Rapid Economic Change*. India: Madhyam Books.

Jayal, Niraja Gopal and Sudha Pai (eds) (2001). *Democratic Governance in India: Challenges of Poverty, Development and Identity*. New Delhi: Sage Publications.

Kohli, Atul (1990). *Democracy and Discontent: India's Growing Crisis of Governability*. Cambridge: Cambridge University Press.

Louis, Prakash (2000). 'Jharkhand: Marginalisation of Tribals', *Economic and Political Weekly*, 35(47): 4087–91.

Louis, Prakash (2003). 'Empowerment of Weaker Sections: The Myth and the Reality', *Jharkhand Journal of Development and Management Studies,* 1(2): 191–204.
Mander, Harsh (ed.) (2004). *Good Governance*. Bangalore: Books for Change.
Munda, Ram Dayal (nd.). 'Adivasi Identity: Crisis and Way out. Rising Fascism', *Update Collective*. New Delhi: Delhi Forum.
Nathan, Dev, Govind Kelkar and Pierre Walter (eds) (2004). *Globalisation and Indigenous Peoples in Asia: Changing the Local-Global Interface*. New Delhi: Sage Publications.
Parikh, Kirit (ed.) (1999). *India Development Report 1999–2000*. New Delhi: Oxford University Press.
Pieterse, Jan Nederveen (1996). 'Globalisation and Culture: Three Paradigms', *Economic and Political Weekly*, 31(23): 1389.
Reddy, C.R. (2000). *The Hindu*, 15 April.
Samata (2000). 'Surviving a Minefield: An Adivasi Triumph—A Landmark Supreme Court Judgement Restoring the Rights of the Tribals'. Hyderabad: Samata.
Sharma, B.D. (1995). *Globalization: The Tribal Encounter*. New Delhi: Har-Anand Publications.
Srivastava, S.P. (ed.) (1998). *The Development Debate: Critical Perspectives*. Jaipur: Rawat Publications.
Sridhar, V. (2001a). 'Blocking Privatisation', *Frontline*. 28 April.
——— (2001b). 'Fighting on: The Struggle Over Balco Continues', *Frontline*. 25 May.
UNESCO (1994). *World Summit for Social Development* (Position Paper). Paris: UNESCO.
Vyas, V.S. (1993). 'New Economic Policy and Vulnerable Sections: Rationale for Public Intervention', *Economic and Political Weekly,* 28(10): 405.
——— (2002). 'Globalisation: Hopes, Realities and Coping Strategy', *Economic and Political Weekly,* 37(12) 1109–14, 23 March.
Wickremasinghe, N. (2001). 'Collapse of Balco Strike Opens Way for Further Privatisation in India', www.wsws.org.

13

Retreat to Governance under Globalisation: Lessons from the Poverty Eradication Experience in Orissa

Manoranjan Mohanty

Retreat to Governance in Development Discourse

Like the term 'empowerment' in the 1990s, the term 'governance' seems to have already dominated the public discourse in the first years of the twenty first century. It is important to discuss the reasons underlying the shift from the usages of terms such as the 'state' and 'government' or even 'public administration' to the newly encoded term 'governance'. A vast amount of literature has already emerged in just a few years on this concept from a variety of sources including think-tanks and academic researchers. The term is not only used by policy makers of the international agencies such as the UN and the World Bank but also by political parties, non-governmental organisations (NGO) and the media.

What is clearly noticeable is the initiative taken by funding agencies and global networks to popularise the concept in the recent years. The World Bank sponsored numerous projects in the 1990s to promote research and discussion on governance (World Bank 1991). The UN followed suit and the Human Development Report focused on the crucial relationship between governance and human development. Ford Foundation adopted it as a priority area for funding. It financed for example, the setting up of the Centre for Law and Governance at the Jawaharlal Nehru University, New Delhi in 2001 among many such programmes worldwide. The Department for International Development (DFID), an agency of the British government sponsored setting up of Institutes of Good Governance in several States of India including Andhra Pradesh and Orissa in 2003–04.

Just as the notion of NGOs was promoted with great force in the 1980s by the global agencies, the concept of governance has been propounded with enormous emphasis in the recent years. And this new concept is no longer used in the sense of the business of the state at every level—central, provincial and local. It is presented as the business of all institutions and organisations. We now hear less of local government or local democracy and more of local governance, less of university's academic performance, more of university governance. This change in discourse is not innocuous, but is highly charged with political meaning.

Governance means governing or conducting the business of ruling according to rules and norms. The growing usage of the term governance signals a shift of focus away from policy to instruments of policy. It signifies that political issues have been settled and policies have been formulated. The task remains to implement the policies. It implies that issues of structural transformation are not to be dragged to the public realm. No doubt, the votaries of the term will say otherwise and assert that indeed governance included taking all kinds of decisions and acting upon them. Even though there are debates among governance theorists as to whether it replaces or complements government using new instruments of policy (Jordan et al. 2005) and merges private and the public (Stoker 1998) or extends state activity upward, downward and into multilevel processes (Kooiman 2003; Pierre 2000 and Kjaer 2004), the context of the emergence and currency of the term makes the actual meaning clear.

The context is the post-Cold War world in which the so-called consensus on market reforms has been presented as the global trend. Liberalisation of the economy by reducing state control, privatisation of public enterprises and globalisation of the movement of capital crossing state boundaries and consumerisation of people of the world to continuously expand market for goods constitute the new package which is cited as the inevitable path of human development in the present era. It is assumed that political decisions have been made on this issue and there are no choices to reject this path. The question according to this viewpoint is, how to implement this line of thinking and policy.

This is the context of contemporary corporate enterprises practicing governance or corporate governance, so that they can maximise profit while competing with each other. It focuses on continuous upgrading of technology of production and human organisation and steadily expanding their market. This perspective of governance is projected as the mode of rational action. It is said to possess rationality and effectiveness in terms of pursuing its goals of profit. In effect this notion of corporate governance has been generalised for all sectors of society.

There are however, alternative goals that people pursue. They seek a process of development that is not only materially productive, but also socially just, culturally compatible, environmentally sustainable, aesthetically pleasant and morally fulfilling. For the world of people's movements, globalisation as the current phase of world capitalist economy presents the opposite scenario. Therefore, issues of politics, policy and structure are very much on the agenda. Hence, there is a contestation over the discourse on governance.

The political history of human society records the emergence of the *laissez faire* state in Europe in late seventeenth century with the government mainly performing the law and order functions. Politics was limited to the entrepreneurial class exercising power to pursue its business activities. Welfare state followed as a result of rise of democratic consciousness of common people who demanded that state should ensure minimum welfare to the masses. By the middle of the twentieth century, we saw the operation of an activist state taking initiatives for collective welfare and social justice. Several developments took place leading to inefficiency and corruption in the body politic. That is when neoliberal assertion emerged in Western capitalist countries challenging the welfare state and propagating the rationality of market economy. The current turn towards governance is in a sense a retreat to the philosophy of the *laissez fair*e era which restricted the realm of politics.

In this chapter we discuss the limits of the governance approach by analysing how the NGO sector developed as an extension of state and capital facilitating globalisation rather than functioning as instruments for realisation of people's rights. To illustrate this argument we take the issue of poverty eradication experience in Orissa as a case study to argue that the governance approach to human development can hardly meet the aspirations of people. An alternative set of organisations which may be called PDOs (People's Democratic Organisations) have emerged in many parts of the country to advance the cause of people's rights. They symbolise a structural-political approach to poverty eradication and other aspects of human development as against the governance approach.

Disillusionment with NGOs in the New Environment

If we look closely at the field experiences in India it will be noticed that the NGO phase of developmental work has begun to wane. State agencies as well as non-governmental organisations have lost credibility with the common people at the grassroots level. Traditional political organisations namely, political parties and trade unions had long ceased to win the confidence of people as far as solving basic problems of livelihood of the rural poor was concerned. Community organisations hardly ever had poverty alleviation on their agenda.

This critical view is particularly targeted at the NGO sector, because they had attracted the maximum attention of policy makers, scholars and the media during the past two decades in the development process, especially in the international discourse related to poverty. Now we may be entering a new phase of seeking newer organisational initiatives in the context of the emerging environment of globalisation on the one hand and rising democratic aspirations on the other. This is the feeling one gets from the last ten years experience with anti-poverty programmes in the chronic drought prone Kalahandi region of Orissa. But it seems to be a wider trend in the country as a whole.

It is argued here that there are many reasons for the declining effectiveness of the NGOs and new ways have to be evolved for activating all the existing forms of the state and non-state organisations. It is stressed that efforts are needed for forging new organisations which attend to the structural roots of poverty and seek power for the struggling people to transform the existing structure. Thus, the search for organisation of the people is sought to be linked with the issue of political power. All forms of organisation have their own value, but they have to be tested on the structural-political scale so as to determine to what extent long term solutions to the problem of poverty in terms of land reforms, access to capital and human resources have been accomplished and how far the deprived sections have acquired rights to exercise control over their resources, plan their utilisation and monitor the development process.

The new focus on governance in the era of globalisation and liberalisation has been evident in the policy documents at every level—global to local. The state functionaries as well as those in NGOs are called upon to stress governance as the key to achieve their targets.

The Approach Paper to the Tenth Five Year Plan announces, 'Reform of governance perhaps has to be one of the centerpieces of the Tenth Plan' (GOI 2001: 47) and then goes on to spell out what it calls a programme for 'civil service renewal'. It is not only about making the state personnel and government institutions 'perform' and 'deliver' what is expected of them under the policy (GOI 2002b). In addition, the idea is to make governance the main preoccupation of everybody in all the institutions—public and private. In the context of poverty alleviation programmes, the emphasis is now squarely put on improving governance rather than on other explanations for persisting poverty such as faulty approaches. Orissa Government's Annual Plan for 2002–03, for example, states, 'State Government has taken several initiatives to improve governance and to monitor the implementation of RLTAP (Revised Long Term Action Plan) in the KBK (the undivided Kalahandi, Bolangir and Koraput) districts' (GOO 2002: Chapter 14, p. 25). One can cite many evidences to indicate the change in the mind set of the Indian ruling elite from examining roots of a problem and debating approaches to paying attention mainly to implementation.

The global emphasis on governance evolved together with liberalisation and globalisation. First of all, it was pointed out that the inefficient state apparatus in the post-colonial countries along with a corrupt bureaucracy created obstacles to economic development. Second, the elite, which defended the autonomy of the nation state, was discredited as preventing economic growth and grabbing the spoils of the welfare state. Thus, the post-colonial state was delegitimised by the tidal wave of globalisation. It was facilitated by the fact that indeed crises of state and development had intensified in most of the third world countries. There were numerous people's movements reflecting the expanded levels of democratic consciousness making new and legitimate demands on the state. The 1980s saw a variety of autonomy movements, agrarian struggles, tribal people's movements, anti-caste movements, environment movements and above all a fast growing women's movement. This is the time when the economies of UK and the US had been revived while those of the USSR and Eastern Europe had become more crises-ridden. After the collapse of the Soviet Union, the US emerged as the sole superpower. The Western capitalist countries now reinvigorated their policies to expand their market in the world. They used global economic institutions as well as the UN for this purpose. The national elites, which found it difficult to cope with the growing challenges to their power now leaned upon the forces of capitalist globalisation to maintain their power and the latter welcomed them if they adopted the terms of globalisation. Gradually it became clear that economic globalisation, military hegemony and communications monopoly were a unified package though with some internal contradictions.

When the post-colonial state was discredited, the West reached out to non-state actors in the developing countries. Thus emerged the NGO sector in the third world. The World Bank as well as the UN made it a part of their policy to directly involve them in all their programmes—directly in effect, even though clearances were required from the government. National and local plans and programmes now adopted the role of the NGOs as a component at every level.

The NGO phenomenon was now put in a theoretical framework of civil society as the sphere of non-state activities. It was argued that the more the activity of the civil society, the more a country is democratic. In other words, transfer of power from the state organs to civil society groups and organisations became the indicators of democratisation and development. Civil society in its current meaning is the sphere of articulate interest groups who are engaged in the pursuit of their interests. That civil society had in it powerful interests as well as less powerful or even powerless groups was not highlighted in this campaign to promote civil society in the third world and the former socialist countries. Even though the discourse on civil society has brought out these complications, it still remains as a powerful concept—a weapon in the hands of those who wish to attack the state (Mohanty 2000). There is much literature that highlights the class, caste, ethnic, gender and other contradictions in society and that the power structures in society are also closely connected with the operation of state power (Mohanty 1998). The civil society focus practically ignored these multiple contradictions.

The new ideology of globalisation had an attractive agenda called 'empowerment' of civil society, of women, of people and of disadvantaged groups. Attractive because that was the demand of the oppressed groups for long. They wished to achieve political power and were not satisfied with trickle down process of growth or relief programmes or even small grants in the name of integrated development. Now they were told, that was what was being given to them. Women's empowerment with Panchayati Raj was the most important accomplishment as a result of the 73rd amendment to the Indian Constitution, which reserved one-third seats for women. The same was provided for in urban councils under the 74th Amendment. The whole country now celebrated political empowerment of women (B. Mohanty 2001). This after all was the call in the world summits organised by the UN since the Copenhagen Summit on Social Development and the Beijing Summit on Women. But the concept of empowerment gave the illusion that only with statutory representation in the councils, women achieved power. It overemphasised procedures of electoral democracy than substantive power. It shifted the focus from land reforms, succession rights for women, access to productive assets, employment opportunities, education and such other rights of women to formal representation. Even this reservation was a welcome development and it could be used by people's organisations to pursue their struggle. But this in itself did not amount to 'power for women' (Mohanty 2000).

Rather than respond to the issues that can transform the power structure in the society, the new mantra that is being spread vigorously is that of governance. It is part of the global current pushed by the West. The *Human Development Report 2002,* which has an inspiring message as its theme—*Deepening Democracy in a Fragmented World*—leaves no doubt about the centrality of governance, 'Around the world, discussions on development are placing more emphasis on institutions and governance. These debates have focused on the effectiveness of the public institutions and the rules for making markets work and promoting economic growth—from professionalism and transparency of tax reforms to the capacity of judicial systems to enforce commercial contracts' (UNDP 2002: 2). Indeed it has affirmed some key components of democracy—to make it so both in form and substance, that it is inconsistent with rule by a small elite, that it has to be built from within, that only a sustained human development requires promoting democratic politics and so on. Then it goes ahead to present a scale to *gauge governance*—measures of democracy and political and civil rights. Conceding that there can be controversies, it spells out objective indicators as well as subjective indicators of governance (ibid.: 36–45). One can expect now that the whole world will internalise this ideology of democratic governance in the coming years like it did the concept of human development and gender empowerment measure. Already considerable academic and NGO writings have appeared promoting the centrality of the NGOs in the pursuit of Governance (Mohanty and Tandon 2002).

No one can minimise the significance of governance if it means effective implementation of policies or acting according to law and the rules to the last word. What is questioned here is the attempt to raise it to the level of an ideology that undermines the significance of politics. It is an apolitical ideology that assumes that questions involving structural change are already resolved and what remained was to implement the declared policies. In this case, they are the market-oriented policies of globalisation and liberalisation. On the other hand, struggles are continuing over basic rights to livelihood and dignity. In all societies there are movements going on for transformation of unequal status over caste, race and gender. In this context, the governance ideology seeks to impose its policies and allow only those changes that are compatible with the logic of the market economy. The struggles carried out by the people's movements are considered disruptive of the programme for the high growth economy. Therefore, the workers are asked to refrain from strikes; peace and stability in society are maintained if necessary by force and draconian laws. The welfare state may have retreated and public entreprises privatised. But the state is given actually more power—coercive power—to create conditions favorable to the market economy.

Social mobilisation in this context has acquired a new meaning. It is not for social transformation as was the original meaning. It is to enthuse people to participate in the newly accelerated institutions. The electronic media has developed as a major instrument of social mobilisation for the capitalist market. Development of communications has produced many new opportunities for all kinds of mobilisation, ranging from religious-communal objectives to electoral purposes. In the context of the anti-poverty programmes, it has come to mobilise target groups for the rural development schemes including the now popular self-help groups.

Participation was an essential value of democracy so that it could lead to self-governance. With the growth of the complex modern society, representative government became the practical mechanism for liberal democracy. It too has acquired a restricted meaning. People's participation in Gram Sabha is built into the Panchayat Raj system. The villagers as a whole are expected to decide on the appropriate beneficiaries for various schemes (B. Mohanty 2001). But it has degenerated into a formality of a meeting to put on record. Recent decades witnessed great interest in participatory development and even participatory action research. In some places, a new concept by the name of Participatory Adaptive Research (PAR) was launched to experiment new agricultural technology (Singh 2000). But participation has come to mean participation as per the norms of the new economy. Even the elected Panchayat functionaries are unable to participate in the making of policies. They participate in the implementation of projects that come down to them. Thus, the governance ideology has delimited the parameters of participation at the grassroots level.

In this environment all the organisations—state as well as non-state, have adjusted their role to meet the challenges of the market forces. The nature of the NGO activity came under sharp debates in the new context.

There are many ways to classify the NGOs. One study speaks of four categories: welfare NGOs, development NGOs, empowerment NGOs and social action groups (Murthy and Rao 1997: 74). According to this view, the first two categories work as extention or in collaboration with the government while the other two often confront the state. Actually, the classification has to centre on a criterion. If the criterion is attitude towards the state—not just government, then there may be three kinds: extension NGOs who help the government to implement some of its policies, perhaps more effectively, then there are those who are autonomous organisations and pick up those issues which may not currently attract the interest of the government and may have long term value. Then there are those groups who work for social transformation, and therefore, do confront the local power structure in course of their work (Mohanty 2000).

The reality is much more complex. The globalisation milieu has changed the classification and standardised the popular meaning of NGO—a funded organisation working professionally on a developmental issue. That separates the Sarvodaya groups and the religious charities from the modern NGOs. Action research has confused academic and service activities and many research institutes have appeared on the scene, which are actually modern NGOs. They have to be distinguished from numerous social action groups who would be offended if they are designated as NGOs. Today, it has acquired such a negative meaning that at the grassroots level they are included in the same list of exploiters of the poor as the moneylender, the contractor, the bureaucrat and the politician. Therefore, to take the NGO role as the central element in the process of democratisation and empowerment of civil society needs to be re-examined. Yet, as the Kalahandi experience tells us, every organised effort has to be utilised in the desperate human conditions, but only within a framework of people's democratic transformation. For the poor are now asserting their democratic right to shape their own destiny.

Anti-Poverty Programmes in the Kalahandi Region: Governance Approach in Action

The national and the global outlook on the centrality of governance in the changing development scenario has been so pervasive that programmes on poverty alleviation continue to be formulated at the higher levels and sought to be implemented at the grassroots level (Radhakrishna and Sharma 1998; Dev 2001). Local organisations including the Block, the Panchayats and the NGOs are given the role of the executing agency for the already formulated programmes. Since Central government together with the international agencies contribute the bulk of the funding for the anti-poverty programmes the Planning Commission and the concerned Ministries of the GOI formulate these programmes. When a think-tank of the government in power comes up with a new idea, the earlier framework changes. One such shift was made when the Integrated Rural Development Programme (IRDP) and many other programmes were replaced by a newly integrated programme called Swarnajayanti Gram Swarozgar Yojana (SGSY) in 1999 after the NDA Government came to power. It again is a top-down programme of the Indian state which directs the local organisations to carry out the schemes (DCRC 2004). No doubt people often make demands on the Central government to pay special attention to the poor people and allocate appropriate funds to them. But that does not mean that the local organisations will not have the proposals from below for their perspective. In a structural-political perspective, the process is reversed and the poverty eradication programmes are to be formulated by people's democratic organisations at the local level for which there would be statutory resource allocations. Let us examine this question in the context of the experience of the Kalahandi region.

Orissa has the largest proportion of the poor among the states of India with 47.15 per cent people below the poverty line in 1999–2000 according to the Planning Commission estimates. In the Human Poverty Index, Orissa has the second lowest rank of 31 among the States and the Union Territories of India, followed by Bihar. The order was the same both in 1981 and 1991 as is evident from the National Human Development Report (NHDR) (GOI 2002a: 142–43) though the value decreased from 59.34 to 49.85 indicating improvement in the aggregate profile of the state in terms of the deprivation in economic, educational and health related indicators which constitute human poverty according to the NHDR.

It should be noted firstly that while the rate of the decline in poverty at the all India level is substantial, in case of Orissa it is much less. Second, between 1993 and 2000 there was only a marginal decline in total proportion below the poverty line, whereas in case of urban poverty there is actually an increase (Table 13.1). Taking into account the methodological debates on the quantification of poverty, one would get an even more dismal picture. But if we go down to the districts of Orissa, the magnitude of poverty is much higher in some areas. Poverty is widespread both in the coastal as well as the inland districts of Orissa. While the inland region which includes Kalahandi had got wide publicity since the drought of 1985, the extent of poverty in the coastal region got exposed during the super cyclone of 1999 which claimed about 10,000 lives and destroyed 16 lakh houses, schools and other public facilities. However, we get a clear idea of the performance of the anti-poverty programmes from the way they have operated in the KBK districts.

Table 13.1: Percentage of Population below Poverty Line in Orissa and India

	Orissa			*India*		
Year	*Rural*	*Urban*	*Total*	*Rural*	*Urban*	*Total*
1973–74	67.28	55.62	66.18	56.44	49.01	54.88
1983–84	67.53	49.15	65.29	45.65	40.79	44.48
1993–94	49.72	41.64	48.56	37.27	32.36	35.97
1999–00	48.01	42.83	47.15	27.09	23.62	26.10

Source: Planning Commission (2001).

Table 13.2 shows the high incidence of poverty in the KBK region. In Nuapada district, which was carved out of the old Kalahandi district, the number of BPL families has actually grown by over two per cent during the five-year period 1992–97.

Table 13.2: Census of BPL Families in KBK Districts, 1992 and 1997

	1992			1997		
District	*Total No. of families (lakh)*	*No. of BPL families*	*% of BPL families*	*Total No. of families (lakh)*	*No. of BPL families*	*% of BPL families*
Kalahandi	2.42	2.07	85.77	3.08	1.93	62.71
Nuapada	0.94	0.79	83.64	1.27	1.09	85.70
Bolangir	2.39	1.81	75.82	3.30	2.01	61.06
Sonepur	0.92	0.57	62.29	1.10	0.80	73.02
Koraput	1.88	1.63	86.59	2.65	2.22	83.81
Malkangiri	0.80	0.68	84.81	1.09	0.89	81.88
Nawrangpur	1.52	1.38	90.56	2.15	1.59	73.66
Rayagada	1.42	1.22	86.04	1.88	1.36	72.03

Source: Panchayati Raj Department, Government of Orissa, 2001.

Since 1985, Kalahandi has been in the news for drought related distress including reports of starvation deaths, sale of children and distress migration (Mohanty 1999; Currie 2000). What is significant is that such conditions have recurred since 1966 again in 1977, 1985 and almost every five years with enormous severity. Every Prime Minister since Rajiv Gandhi has visited the place to affirm commitment to alleviate poverty. After widespread condemnation of the failure of the Indian state in mitigating the recurrent distress of the people of the region, the Central government decided to formulate a Long Term Action Plan (LTAP) for the KBK region as a whole (DCRC 1998). The common characteristics of this region acknowledged by the first LTAP document were: low per hectare yield of rice of 1,430 kgs, low irrigation (12 per cent), heavy soil erosion, poor water retention capacity of the soil, low employment in the agricultural activity, high rate of out-migration from the state, chronic malnutrition and nearly 90 per cent of the population living below the poverty line. After circulating several drafts, one version of the seven-year plan for 1995–96 to 2001–02 was announced in 1995. It had a budget of Rs 4,859 crores with two objectives: i) Drought and distress proofing, and ii) Poverty alleviation and Development Saturation (sic). As it turned out, the amount was only Rs 561 crore more than the cumulative amount of all the existing schemes for seven years. On the ground, the LTAP was a non-starter. During the first three years till 1998, only a meagre amount of Rs 20.49 crores was received as additional assistance. As the Annual Plan 2002–03 puts it, 'LTAP 1995–2002 did not take off for want of sufficient funds' (GOO 2003: Chapter 1, p. 3). Thereafter, a fresh initiative was taken and the Centre approved a nine year Revised LTAP for the period 1998–99 till 2006–2007 with an allocation of Rs 6,251 crores (Table 13.3). It was announced that the Centre will include the Revised LTAP as an integral part of the Tenth Five Year Plan and will provide about Rs 1000 crores per year as a Special Central Assistance for this project.

Table 13.3: Projected Outlay for LTAP, 1998–99 to 2006–07

(in crores)

Scheme	*Central share*	*State share*	*Total (Rs)*
Agriculture	74.93	10.1	84.94
Horticulture	72.52	1.62	74.14
Watershed development	696.86	81.42	878.28
Afforestation	361.94	14.11	376.05
Rural employment	2235.05	558.76	2,793.81
Irrigation	812.11	...	812.11
Health	150.95	...	150.95
Emergency feeding	88.50	...	88.50
Drinking water supply	67.74	67.74	135.48
Rural connectivity	534.70	65.00	599.70
Welfare of ST/SC	257.12	...	257.12
Total	5452.42	798.66	6,251.06

Source: Annual Plan, Orissa 2002–03 (GOO 2003: Chapter 14, p. 4).
Note: There is a slight difference in total because of rounding off.

There was some reformulation in the objectives and strategies, but only in breaking up some of them into more specific items. The Revised LTAP aims were listed as: i) drought proofing, ii) poverty alleviation, and iii) improved quality of life in the KBK districts—the third figuring specifically as if the former plan did not aim at that through the stated policies. Similarly strategies were rearranged:

(*a*) building rural productive infrastructure (roads, bridges etc.) and conserving natural resources (forest, soil and water);

(*b*) developing income generation programmes on a sustainable basis Swarnajayanti Gram Swarozgar Yojana) (SGSY), Employment Assurance Scheme (EAS), micro-credit support etc.;

(*c*) mobilising and energising the rural poor (e.g., self-help groups (SHG), Vana Samrakshana Samitis (VSS), Pani Panchayats, and Bhumi Panchayats);

(*d*) restructuring and energising social security system (e.g., emergency feeding, mobile health units, education among SC/ST girls).

Some of these did not figure as the main strategies in the earlier documents, especially the specific forms of mobilisation of the rural poor such as SHG, VSS, Pani Panchayat and Bhumi Panchayat. The question is whether they qualify to be called people's organisations. Since the framework imposed from above is one for efficient credit utilisation and management of reduced subsidies, they have hardly acquired the legitimacy of grassroots democratic organisations. The allocations of funds were on familiar lines.

Rural employment attracted the maximum funding because of the need to provide earnings through construction and similar work in times of distress. Irrigation and watershed development naturally deserved high priority in drought prone areas followed by rural connectivity mostly for road construction. Relatively low priority given to afforestation and horticulture in an area where the tribal population is high is noticeable, though the tribal people would benefit from the other items as well. But the high priority items are those, which involve contractors, political maneuvers at the Panchayat Samiti level, and various other means of patronising middle men. In other words, the reasons for which the IRDP and other rural development programmes over the decades failed to make a serious dent in the situation of poverty will continue to operate in this very special programme. This programme has now become a symbol of the welfare role of the Indian state even in the era of globalisation and liberalisation that seeks cutting of subsidies and fiscal deficits.

The programmes under the LTAP are distributed among different departments of the government thus depending heavily on the bureaucracy and the ministerial interest of the concerned department. However, a 'senior' level officer was appointed for the LTAP as a whole and has been posted in Koraput since 2001. The fact is that no senior level officer likes to be posted in the KBK region with its present living and working facilities especially because he/she is eligible to live in Bhubaneswar or New Delhi. The only exceptions are the Revenue Divisional Commissioners for the three divisions of the State who live in Cuttack, Sambalpur and Berhampur. Unless of course, some highly motivated senior officer offers his/her services to work for the upliftment of the poor in the KBK region. But that is only one aspect of 'governance' problem relating to the coordination between departments of the government, releasing funds on time and monitoring implementation. The perspective governing this plan is itself defective because it relies more on bureaucracy than on Panchayats and NGOs, let alone other people's organisations. In 2003, the Planning Commission and Government of Orissa decided to authorise the KBK Commissioner to directly draw its annual allocation of nearly Rs 1000 crores (but then reduced to Rs 250 crores), thus simplifying the procedures, which had created hurdles thus far. Further, the UPA Government at the centre merged the RLTAP with the Backward Regions Grant Fund (BRGF) under the eleventh plan maintaining the same allocation. In protest the Government of Orissa launced the KBK plan in April 2007 with an annual allocation of Rs 120 crores. But the perspective remained unchanged. (GOO 2003).

The intention of the plan makers is noble, though. A State Level Committee with the Chief Minister as its head and a Project Level Committee with the Chief Secretary as its head have been constituted to periodically review and monitor the LTAP. The Planning Commission has also been involved in monitoring it through the Institute of Applied Manpower Research, New Delhi. But whether the concerned people, the poor of KBK have any role in monitoring the plan through some mechanisms does not seem to be part of the thinking of the planners. As mentioned before, they have no role in the formulation of the plan (DCRC 2003).

Alternative to the Governance Approach: People's Democratic Organisations

Persistence of massive magnitude of poverty in Kalahandi demonstrates the failure of the governance approach. The KBK initiative was a centrally sponsored bureaucratic intervention by the state which involved NGOs in a big way. The anti-poverty programme mainly focused on food for work and road construction, besides some water works. It did not go into the issue of rights of tribals over land, forest and water. Land reforms was never considered a crucial component of the anti-poverty programme, though 'land distribution' nominally figured in the plan. The trend of deprivation of tribal people's rights over forest produce and forest resources does not seriously concern the policy makers. On the other hand, the government was determined to locate more and more mining projects in the tribal areas displacing tribal people and destroying the environment. In other words, the structural issues of development relating to rights over productive resources are constantly ignored in the governance approach. At the same time, people suffering from destitution and underdevelopment have no role in the formulation of policy. The role of the panchayat institutions is confined to helping in implementation—consistent with the governance approach. The Palli Sabha or the Village Assembly is a nominal provision to fulfil a formality. There is a disjunction between the panchayats and the NGOs and between panchayat and organisations such as Self-Help Groups (Antyodaya 2000). The state bureaucracy has promoted professional NGOs for organising Self-Help Groups. (Gram Vikash 2000; Parivartan 1999). Panchayats are seen by the bureaucracy as faction-ridden and inefficient institutions. It is also observed that when programmes do not emerge from people themselves they do not acquire legitimacy in their mind (Sainath 1996). They remain as government programmes, either operating directly through the *babus* or through NGOs. It had happened with IRDP, it is also happening with SGSY (Mohanty 2004). So the efforts of NGOs and other non-state organisations to help in 'empowering people' are seen as similar to government efforts. Therefore, the assumed uniqueness of a civil society initiative does not operate in practice.

This is why we have to search for an alternative approach that addresses structural issues of development such as those of land rights, and access to capital as well as health and education (Mohanty 2002). It has to emerge from people's own deliberations over the appropriate method of achieving it. In other words, people—especially the poor landless, small farmers, Dalits, adivasis, women and minorities have to design policies for their upliftment and monitor their implementation. The state has to enable them in carrying out that process. For that role, there is the need for new kinds of organisations—People's Democratic Organisations (PDO), who derive resources from among the local people and are accountable to them. The PDOs can make the working of panchayats and other political institutions more effective.

There are three main differences between PDOs and NGOs. First, a PDO is a political entity that emerges from a struggle, whereas an NGO is a legally incorporated entity formed by a group of people which may not necessarily have a background of struggle. Once the formation acquires an identity, it may go for legal registration under the Societies Registration Act in India. Even if it is denied registration by the government, the entity may continue as a substantive force. Chhattisgarh Mukti Morcha got registered much after it had emerged as a people's organisation through struggle. This background makes it a bulwark of strength to uphold people's rights and resist the governance agenda of the state and global capital. Second, the PDO derives its main resources—money and personnel from the local area where it is active. On the other hand, the

NGO generally is funded from outside the area, by external funding agencies and to some extent by the state. This critical difference has many implications. The international funding of NGOs has made them extensions of programmes of globalisation; sometimes the national government. It is true that many of the internationally funded NGOs take part in the World Social Forum criticising globalisation. But as was pointed out by the organisers of Mumbai Resistance in 2004, such NGOs did not constitute a fundamental challenge to globalisation. Sometimes the national government develops problems with international funding agencies and the latter turn out to be promoters of democracy and human rights. It may actually be the case that state violates people's rights while international voices uphold them. But as a general phenomenon the debate between NGOs and PDOs gets reflected locally, nationally and internationally. Since the funding agencies are responsible to Western governments or Western entrepreneurs who give donations, they are more likely to be part of the overall tendency of globalisation which their governments and corporations promote. This is why NGOs cannot become non-state people's organisations. They are 'funded professional organisations'. The Sarvodaya Mandal or the Ryot Coolie Sangham collect small donations from people and carry on their programmes in the area. People's assessment of their contribution to the upliftment of the people decides the extent of local help they get.

The third element is the differing nature of accountability. While the NGOs are accountable to their funding agencies, the PDOs are accountable to the local people. The funding agencies get their receivers or partner organisations evaluated and on that basis the funding gets renewed. The government only ensures fulfillment of accounting procedures through auditing. The situation presents a complex picture as the PDOs as struggle organisations may confront the state and the NGOs in such a way that the state may resort to repression. That has actually taken place in many places of India including the drought affected areas of Kalahandi and Rayagada in Orissa. The people's organisations campaigning against the establishment of Aluminium Industries in the decade since 1995 have clearly differentiated from the NGOs who have participated in the governance process of the state and capital who are determined to go ahead with export-oriented industries in Orissa. At the same time, the PDOs may not have clear institutional methods of maintaining their accountability. They have sometimes resorted to coercion and extraction to secure support of the local people.

In fact such organisations have begun to appear in many parts of India. The National Alliance of People's Movements and the All India People's Resistance Forum are some of the examples where some of these organisations are visible. They question the unfolding development process of the neoliberal political economy in India and the world. Unless the PDOs become widespread, the much talked about concepts such as 'civil society mobilisation', 'participative development', 'human development' and 'empowerment' will remain extremely restrictive concepts only legitimising the top-down process of development currently promoted by the governance framework of the Indian state and the forces of globalisation. Struggling people are likely to resist the retreat to governance and continue to work for the realisation of democratic rights.

References

Antyodaya (2000). *Annual Report* 1999. Bhubaneswar: Action-Aid.

Currie, Bob (2000). *The Politics of Hunger in India*. London: Macmillan.

Dev, S. Mahendra, Piyush Antony, V. Gayathri and R.P. Mangain (2001). *Social and Economic Security in India*. New Delhi: Institute of Human Development.

Developing Countries Research Centre (DCRC) (1998). *Poverty Eradication and Role of Local Institutions: A Study of the Kalahandi Region*, Report by M. Mohanty et al. submitted to the Ministry of Rural Areas and Employment, Government of India.

——— (2003). *Poverty Eradication and Role of Local Institutions in Comparative Perspective with Focus on Kalahandi, Bhojpur and Chittoor: A structural-political perspective*. Report by M. Mohanty et al. submitted to the Planning Commission, Government of India.

——— (2004). *SGRY in Orissa*. Report by M. Mohanty et al. on the evaluation of the working of SGRY in Sambalpur, Angul, Cuttack and Kendrapara districticts, submitted to the Planning Commission, Government of India.

Government of India (GOI) (2001). *Approach Paper to the Tenth Five Year Plan 2002–07*. New Delhi: Planning Commission.

——— (2002a). *National Human Development Report 2001*. New Delhi: Planning Commission.

——— (2002b). *Report of the Steering Committee on Voluntary Sector For the Tenth Five Year Plan (2002–07)*. New Delhi: Planning Commission, (January).

Government of Orissa (GOO) (2002). *Economic Survey 2001–02*. Bhubaneswar: Directorate of Economics and Statistics, Chapter 14, p. 25.

——— (2003). *Annual Plan 2002–03*. Volumes I & II, Bhubaneswar: Planning and Co-ordination Department.

Gram Vikas (2000). *Annual Activity Report* (1990–2000), Orissa: Berhampur, Ganjam.

Jordan, Andrew, Rudiger K. W. Wurzd and Anthony Zito (2005). "The Rise of 'New' Policy Instruments in Comparative Perspective': Has Governance Eclipsed Government?", *Political Studies*, 53(3): 477–96.

Kjaer, A.M. (2004). *Governance*. Oxford: Polity.

Kooiman, J. (2003). *Governing as Governance*. London: Sage Publications.

Mohanty, Bidyut (2001). *Panchayats—Women and Food Security: Challenges in the Era of Economic Reforms*. New Delhi: Institute of Social Sciences.

Mohanty, Manoranjan (1998). 'Social Movements in Creative Society', in M. Mohanty et al. (eds), *People's Rights*. New Delhi: Sage Publications.

———(1999). 'Kalahandi: Destitution and Under development', in Ambrose Pinto (ed.), *State, Development and Alternatives*. New Delhi: Indian Social Institute.

——— (2000). 'On the Concept of Empowerment', in *Contemporary Indian Political Theory*. New Delhi: Samskriti.

———(2002). 'Changing Definition of Rights in India', in Sujata Patel et al. (eds), *Thinking Social Sciences in India: Essays in Honour of Alice Thorner*. New Delhi: Sage Publications.

——— (ed.) (2004). *Class, Caste, Gender*. New Delhi: Sage Publications.

Mohanty, Ranjita and Rajesh Tandon (2002). *NGOs and Governance*. New Delhi: Sanskriti, National Institute of Agricultural Extension Management.

Murthy, Rajni K. and Nitya Rao (1997). *Addressing Poverty: Indian NGOs and Their Capacity Enhancement in the 1990s*. New Delhi: Friedrich Eberit Stiftung.

Parivartan (1999). *Annual Report 1999*. Orissa: Bhubaneswar, Kalahandi.

Pierre, J. (ed.) (2000). *Debating Governance*. Oxford: Oxford University Press.

Radhakrishna, R. and Alakh N. Sharma (ed.) (1998). *Empowering Rural Labour in India: Market, State and Mobilisation*. New Delhi: Institute for Human Development.

Sainath, P. (1996). *Everybody Loves a Good Drought*. New Delhi: Penguin Books India Ltd.

Singh, J.P. (2000). *Socio-Economic Dynamics and Development Strategy for Participatory Adaptive Research Project*. Hyderabad: Institute of Participatory Adaptive Research.

Stoker, G. (1998). 'Governance as Theory', *International Social Science Journal*, 50(155): 17–28.

United Nations Development Programme (UNDP) (2002). *Human Development Report 2002*. New Delhi: Oxford University Press.

World Bank (1991). *World Development Report* 1990. New Delhi: Oxford University Press.

14

Globalisation, the Indian Diaspora and its Governance: Issues, Expectations and Solutions

Ravindra K. Jain

INTRODUCTION

What are the salient characteristics of globalisation as it affects social processes in the present conjuncture of political economy in multicultural societies? I shall focus on India as the major example of such societies but extend my analysis with reference to what I have elsewhere called 'settlement societies' as contrasted with 'non-modern' civilisations like India (Jain 1998a). Settlement societies evolving into modern, technologically advanced, civilisations are the prime recipients of 'new' diasporas[1] from South Asia and my purpose in what follows is to examine the interface (linkages and role) between Indian diaspora and governance problematic concerning the overall developments—economic, political and socio-cultural—of the Indian nation.[2]

Globalisation, as the very term implies, covers societies at all phases of development, viz., in this case the nation state of India as well as the countries to which Indian diasporics have migrated. The process of globalisation is driven by three major imperatives—the market, the new technology and transnational networks—that are themselves interconnected. Market forces, are in theory, based on free and fair competition but protectionist policies in trade, volatility and negative effects of short-term capital flows and biases in international investment agreements, permeate and vitiate the field to widen the hiatus between developed and developing countries. While this is the macro-picture, closer to our concerns are the phenomena of speculators manipulating financial markets and cartels of nation states of the North making policy decisions in institutions like the World Bank, the International Monetary Fund (IMF) and the WTO to the disadvantage of countries of the South and corner outstanding advantages in what should otherwise—in theory—be a level playing field (Khor 2001). As to the local effects of these forces, there is conspicuous increment in what has been called 'the consumption of modernity' which in a poor country may be termed as 'unbridled consumerism' (Jain 1998). Although market forces are, theoretically, determined through the balancing of demand and supply, the propensity of heavy consumption as compared to production in the play of market mechanism in an underdeveloped country like India may be explained by what one of my informants (an Indian petroleum engineer settled in Houston, USA) put as the excess of down-streaming (distribution and consumption or, in other words, buying) as against upstreaming (production and selling) in the flows of world markets. The cultural upshot of these processes is the 'production' of identities but 'consumption' of goods and symbols. And these processes of participation in the market and marketplace characterise middle class behaviour in both urban India and in the new diaspora. With regard to its deep significance for cultural politics in the latter context, Sandhya Shukla's (2003: 84) empirical observations are germane:

> Southall and Jackson Heights also exist as places with goods to offer residents and visitors. These veritable market places, replete with Indian restaurants, food stores, sari stores, beauty salons, record stores, and the like evoke images of an exotic bazaar, or of a self-sufficient ethnic community, and perhaps both, through which India as fantasy is made real, Jackson Heights to a large extent and Southall only a bit less so are spaces of consumption. Indians meet there, and buy and sell there, and essentially perform an Indianness that functions to consolidate their migrant subjectivities. Through these multiple acts of consumption, migrants become citizens of the local space, of Southall and Jackson Heights (and London and New York), of England and the United States, of the diaspora, as their experiences have a life outside immediate boundaries and perhaps too of India, and as this sense of becoming culturally India is translated into maintaining Indian political activity. If in the postwar and perhaps post modern age consumption qualifies as participatory citizenship, than Southall and Jackson Heights become ideal sites in which to comprehend how nations function, and function differently, for distinctly diasporic actors. When these sites become spaces for ethnics' own tourism, the picture becomes even more complicated.

Taking off from the example cited above, one could go into the details and varieties of the typical Indian and diasporic markets in the era of globalisation but let me, for the sake of brevity and focus, look at the technological revolution which constitutes the second major dimension of the socio-cultural impact of globalisation in India and the diaspora. In both its real (locomotionary) and virtual (telecommunication) senses the diaspora is about travel (Clifford 1997). And it is travel in the various forms—the capacity to physically travel very fast and repeatedly and the capacity of travel virtually through 'works of the imagination' (Appadurai 1997)—which has brought diaspora as a compelling theme in our day and age. However, technology has played a catalytic role in all this. Especially, information technology (IT) is leading to a new form of capital accumulation as is clearly evident in the IT industry itself. Regardless of its origin and amount, capital can be circulated and accumulated on a global scale, at an unprecedented speed, and therefore, with extreme volatility. An urgent task of the study of globalisation and migration is to understand the international labour system of the 'new economy.' In this context, unlike in the colonial past, it is capital chasing labour rather than the other way around. The structure of this 'chase' is admirably delineated in a recent ethnographic study of the agents that have been the main means by which Indian IT professionals move globally (Xiang 2001: 23–90).[3] Xiang conducted this field-study initially among Indian IT professionals' migration to Australia through spells of fieldwork in Sydney and Hyderabad. He later theorised this transnational stratum of Indian migrants to Australia as an 'ethnic transnational middle class in formation' (Xiang 2002). This exercise shows not only the spatio-temporal discontinuity but also, most interestingly, certain ethno-practical continuities between the old and new diaspora of Indians.

Before coming to the details of Xiang's studies of Indian IT professionals in diaspora, let me introduce the third major imperative of globalisation, namely, transnational networks. According to Tambiah (2000: 140), two broad sets of networks may be differentiated for purposes of analysis. 'Vertical' networks are formed within 'host' societies when 'communities' are constituted, either voluntarily or forcefully in order to devise conscious strategies to fight discrimination as well as to succeed economically. The second set of networks, i.e., 'lateral' may be subdivided further: (a) between host society and society of origin/homeland, and (b) transnational global networks where diasporas across the world communicate with each other and maintain transnational links especially through media and travel. What is lacking in Tambiah's concept of networks, however, is the dimension of social stratification, which we may analyse in terms of class, culture and mobility in both the old and new diasporas (Jain 2004). To generalise then, from my perspective, vertical networks are those which ramify across classes—these are inter-class asymmetrical networks—while horizontal and symmetrical networks rest on the intra-class solidarity. As regards their embeddedness, diasporic networks cut across locations because these are configured in 'space' rather than fixed 'places' (de Certeau) though locations are created (cf. Bhabha on 'location of culture' and 'social space' in Henri Lefebvre's sense) in the process of social life. In concrete terms, then, diaspora constitutes a space *sui generis*. As we shall see, Xiang's empirical demonstration of the formation of an 'ethnic transnational middle class' supports my conceptualisation.[4] To cautiously generalise further, a network analysis of globalisation process enables one to look at it from 'below' and 'above'; the exhortation, therefore, to 'think global and act local' from the perspective of underdeveloped societies is not innocent of its cutting edge of class connotation.

Indian 'IT' Specialist Diaspora in Australia

Xiang's study provides an excellent example of the meshing in of markets, technology and networks, thus constituting a case study of globalisation in the context of Indian diaspora. Let me first summarise the conclusion of the ethnographic study by Xiang. In the study of globalisation and migration, a distinction between 'transnationalism from above' and 'transnationalism from below' has been made recently (Guarnizo 1997; Portes et al. 1999). While the former refers to transnational activities of powerful institutional actors, such as multinational corporations and states, the latter focuses on the activities of ordinary migrants. Both trends have been widely discussed, but thus far the links between the two remain unexplored. Xiang's paper shows how capital and labour, key concepts of a political economy framework, and ethnic networks, which are central for 'transnationalism from below', work together in the structuration process of a new international labour system.

Unlike what is usually assumed, ethnic networks play a critical role in the migration of highly skilled professionals in the Indian's migration to Australia. Besides their role in recruitment, ethnic networks are also important in managing workers within body shops (particularly retaining worker when they are on the bench). For example, workers see it as 'immoral' or as potentially damaging for their own 'reputation' if they raise complaints against their Indian sponsors ('body shops').

Ethnic networks are important in this case because they reconcile the state and the market. Corporations in a volatile economy call for a flexible labour market to minimise their costs. A liberal global market inevitably creates social costs, such as the lack of security of workers. The state of the receiving countries requires employers to take social responsibilities for the migrant workers. Employers 'outsource' these responsibilities to placement agents. Big agents, yet again, pass them on to 'body shops'. Finally, ethnic networks enable 'body shops' to keep workers silent when the workers are on the bench. Agent chains and ethnic networks transfer the costs of a volatile market to the workers. In the US, wives of H1B visa holders are granted H-4 visas with which they are not allowed to work and are completely dependent on their husbands. *Maitri*, a San Francisco-based South Asian Women Organisation, received more than 1,500 calls from H-4 women reporting domestic violence over the year 2000–2001 (Srivastava 2001). Thus, even in the case of highly desirable professionals, globalisation is accompanied with high human costs.

The ethnicity-based labour supply system also has its bright side. Migratory Indian IT workers have been able to make a quick transition to transnational entrepreneurs. In California in 2000, Indians generating an estimated US$ 60 billion in sales annually ran more than 7,000 high-tech companies. These businesses increasingly rely on their networks back in India for labour, outsourcing the offshore investment opportunities (Saxenian 2000, cited in Xiang 2001). Arising from this labour system, India's IT industry grew at a rate ten times higher than that of the GDP over the last decade and reached US$ 10 billion revenue in 2000–2001 (*The Times of India*, Hyderabad, 4 July 2001). The scenario seems to support the new notion of 'brain circulation', which replaces 'brain drain' in migration studies. However, what is not clear is to what extent the brain circulation can benefit local society in India. The labour migration system is more likely to contribute to a new 'dual structure': a global sector where resources are calculated and accumulated in US dollars and a local sector where surplus value is pumped out to serve economic globalisation. Due to the ever expanding and enhanced transnational connections, the vital issue for the current research of skilled immigration may not be measuring 'brain gain' versus 'brain drain' of a particular country, but may be examining the relations between the global and local sector across borders. The structuration process of Indian IT professionals' migration to Australia is only one case illustrating how skilled labour from a periphery society struggle to join the global system at their own cost and ultimately of the periphery society.

Ethnic Transnational Middle Class (ETMC) in Formation

The context of globalisation is vital to an understanding of the social stratification framework into which the professional Indian diaspora of the last forty years or so belongs. One has often heard the exhortation, particularly in the developing societies of 'think global and act local'. What is not often uncovered is that the body of professionals working either as immigrants, off shore workers or engaged in outsourcing is vital for global capital not only as cheap skilled labour, but also because they facilitate penetration of global capital to the developing world. Xiang calls them the Ethnic transnational middle class (ETMC) who are not only in the 'middle' between capital and labour, but also between global and local. The body of Indian global professionals is generally not a class, which 'owns' the means of production (TCC or ETCC; Transnational Capitalist Class or Ethnic Transnational Capitalist Class) but is at the same time client to body-shoppers, who are not merely recruiters but also 'trainers'. The ETMC comprises at one end the conventional professionals—engineers, doctors and IT professionals in particular and, at other end, the 'Salaried' administrative and managerial, supervisory, clerical, sales, service and account jobs which would be called semi-professional. With respect to the former category, there is usually a glass ceiling for mobility but also to a limited degree advances from even ETMC to Ethnic Transnational Capitalist Class (ETCC) or Transnational Capitalist Class (TCC). Thus, it comes about that in terms of GDP, 21 per cent is controlled by 0.02 per cent persons. There is a firm nexus between local society and established transnational corporations, viz, IBM, Microsoft, GE, Google etc., and it is the local society (and ultimately the workers), which invests in the recruitment and placement of ETMC. The local society provides the wherewithal for professional specialists in the diaspora. As sociologists, let us look at the connection between the Indian ETMC and the institution of dowry. To quote Xiang:

> There are various social mechanisms through which resources have been channeled to the IT training. The most novel one is the institution of dowry. Dowry is a completely new institution in AP (Andhra Pradesh) and is largely a product of the introduction of the 'organized sector' during British time. I came across a village, which had its first dowry marriage in 1996 (previously bride-price was the norm) because at that year the first highly educated man in the village married. 'Computer people' bring in a new dichotomy of 'global versus local' and gave dowry a new boost. Dowry is either seen as a direct reward to the groom's parents for their investments in costly private education, or is used as sponsorship for IT study and/or emigration.... More effectively than by any other means high dowry gives 'computer people' a high social status.... (D)owry is a direct means to transfer surplus value from the unorganized sector to the organized, from rural to the urban, and from the local to the global (2002: 8).

The dowry rate for the IT professional is also closely associated with the country where the groom is based. An USA-based groom receives a dowry typically double that of an Australia-based groom.

The overall nexus between the local and the global in the ETMC is well illustrated in Figure 14.1.

Labour Flows in the New Indian Diaspora

As seen above, we are fortunate to posses an ethnographic account of the IT specialists' Indian diaspora in Australia, since that was a desideratum (along with the continuing lack of information on Western Europe) in the study of the new Indian diaspora. For USA, Canada and UK we have the demographic and economic profiling done by Deepak Nayyar (1994). The same source also goes into the labour flows and remittances from the modern Indian diaspora to the Middle East.

Figure 14.1: The 'Indian System' in the Global IT Industry

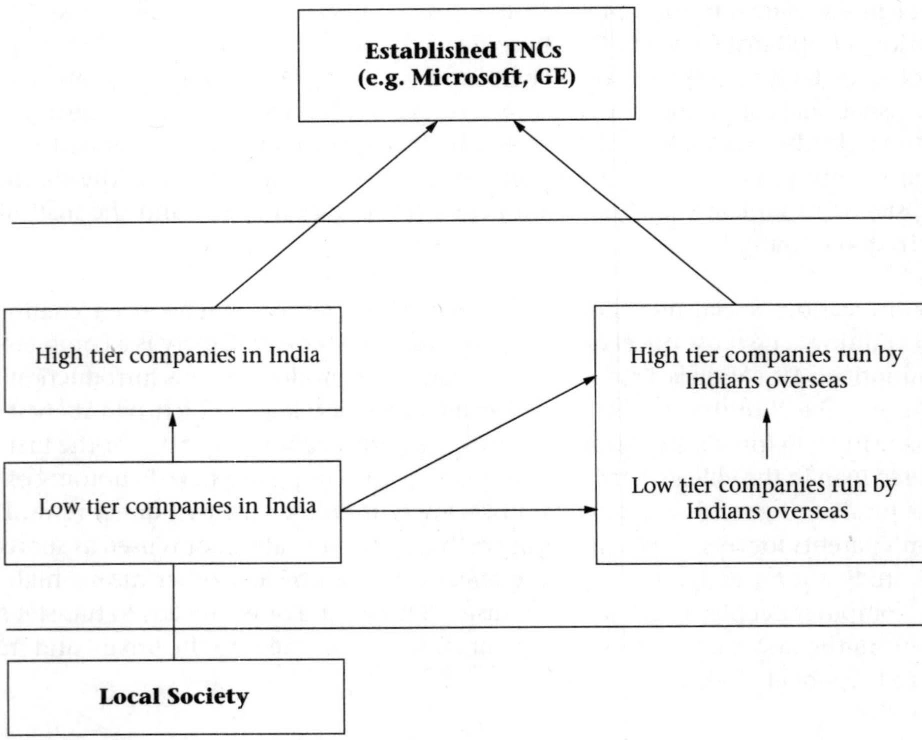

Source: Xiang (2002: 12).

Let me first summarise the findings about the dimensions and the composition of emigration to the industrialised countries. Nayyar points out that there are three basic characteristics of emigration from India to the industrialised world in the period since independence. First, such labour outflows made up almost entirely of permanent migration in so far as the population of emigrants who return to India after a finite period, is almost negligible.[5] Second, a good proportion of these migrants are persons with professional expertise, technical qualifications or other skills perceived to be scarce, or needed, in labour-importing countries, who would be at the upper end of the spectrum of incomes in India even before migration. Third, for an overwhelming proportion of these migrants, the destinations are the United States, Canada and the United Kingdom, possibly because of common ties with the English language.

Nayyar himself admits that the database for these generalisations is rather slender and also that, surprisingly, no governmental records are available within India to provide the database. We may add to this the fact that this profiling is a little out of date. In recent decades emigration from India—especially from the southern states of Andhra Pradesh, Karnataka and Tamil Nadu—to industrially advanced countries has multiplied many times over. Nayyar's discussion is based on immigration statistics of the countries of destination. Difference in his aggregate estimate of immigration from India to industrialised countries (USA, Canada and United Kingdom) from 1951 to 1990 and in the Report of the High Level Committee (2001), although not strictly comparable, may be seen from Table 14.1. It also gives a rough idea of the tremendous increase in the overall numbers. This can be attributed to the phenomenal increase in migration in the 1990s.

Table 14.1: Immigration from India to the Industrialised Countries

Immigration to	*1951–1990 (Nayyar)*	*2001 (High level committee)*
United States	467,255	1,678,765
Canada	180,731	851,000
United Kingdom	260,120	2,200,000

Note: The sources of the High Level Committee Report are not made public. Also, the figures of the Committee do not distinguish between immigrants and natural population growth. Further, the Committee's figures would also include Indian migrants of the colonial era (and other such twice-thrice migrants, viz., Indo-Fijians) who moved from countries such as Uganda and Kenya to the UK and other industrialised countries.

Immigration statistics in the selected industrialised countries provide information on the skills composition from India to North America but not to the United Kingdom. The available evidence on immigration from India to the United States (1971–2001) and Canada (1971–90), by major occupation group is set out in Tables 14.2a and 14.2b. The Tables show certain unmistakable trends. First, among diasporics in the affluent countries of North America migration has increasingly shown a trend of the proportion of non-working dependants to overtake that of workers. The figures for non-workers also include persons whose occupation is not recorded.

This omission too is significant. As recorded in a recent study of Asian Indian community in New York city (Khandelwal 2002), the occupational distribution in the borough of Queens is as follows: construction 1,042; manufacturing 3,342; retail 8,845; professional 1,553; health services 1,082 and *others* 12,605 (italics mine). As it is, the very small percentage of professional and health services employees shows the poorer status of the bulk of Indian residents in Queens; what is even more indicative of the poor status of Indian employees is the huge figure of 12,605 (44.3 per cent of all employees) in the category 'other'. This evidence supports the macro-figures provided by Nayyar: there has been progressive increase not only in the proportion of non-working immigrants (dependents) but also in the progressive employment of working diasporas in poorer occupations. It leads one to suspect a bracketing of the latter with persons whose occupations are not recorded. Further, rather inexplicably, in the occupational profile of Indian immigrants entering the United States in 1991–93 (Table 14.2a) there is a large quantum of those whose occupation is given as 'farming, forestry and fishing' (15.8 per cent of all immigrants). Even subsequently, a certain proportion of immigrants in this category is indicated, viz., 4.13 per cent in 1997–99 and 1.99 per cent in 2000–01 Who are these people? And, finally, while the proportion of immigrants in the category 'Professional and technical' registers an overall progressive increase, even in very recent years, the proportion of those with 'occupation not specified' registers high percentages of 68.73 and 63.68 in the years 1997–99 and 2000–01 respectively. Since this category includes persons with 'no occupation or occupation not reported' could it not cover a large number of persons in poorer occupations?

Table 14.2a: Immigration from India to North America by Major Occupation Group, 1971–2001, United States

number of persons (%)

Occupation group	*1971–75*	*1976–79*	*1982–85*	*1986–90*	*1991–93*	*1994–96*
Professional and Technical	31,623	20,586	15,461	19,160	20,395	19,603
	(43.4)	(26.9)	(15.7)	(13.5)	(16.7)	(17.1)
Executive, Administrative	1,503	3,574	5,059	8,292	6,174	6,246
and Managerial	(2.1)	(4.7)	(5.2)	(5.8)	(5.1)	(5.5)
Clerical and Administrative	1,620	2,491	2,326	3,982	2,719	2,390
Support	(2.2)	(3.3)	(2.4)	(2.8)	(2.0)	(2.1)
Sales	375	704	1,317	1,989	975	1,489
	(0.5)	(0.9)	(1.3)	(1.4)	(0.8)	(1.3)
Service	800	788	2,115	6,453	2,965	3,487
	(1.1)	(1.0)	(2.2)	(4.5)	(2.4)	(3.0)
Farming, Forestry	214	1,311	2,675	4,646	18,875	3,567
and Fishing	(0.3)	(1.7)	(2.7)	(3.3)	(15.8)	(3.1)
Skilled workers	1,637	2,512	2,823	3,583	1,263	1,613
	(2.2)	(3.3)	(2.9)	(2.5)	(1.0)	(1.4)
Total above with occupation	37,772	31,966	31,776	48,105	53,366	38,395
	(51.8)	(41.8)	(32.4)	(33.8)	(44.0)	(33.5)

(*Table 14.2a continued*)

(*Table 14.2a continued*)

Occupation group	*1971–75*	*1976–79*	*1982–85*	*1986–90*	*1991–93*	*1994–96*
No occupation or occupation not reported	35,140 (48.2)	44,595 (58.2)	66,403 (67.6)	94,035 (66.2)	68,574 (56.0)	76,133 (66.5)
Total immigration	72,912 (100.0)	76,561 (100.0)	98,179 (100.0)	142,140 (100.0)	121,940 (100.0)	114,528 (100.0)

Occupational profile	*1997*	*1998*	*1999*	*Total (1997–99)*	*%*
Professional & Technical	6776	5979	3492	16247	15.50
Executive, Admn. and Managerial	2065	1398	1112	4575	4.37
Clerical	819	520	576	1915	1.83
Sales	703	544	648	1895	1.81
Service	1224	573	559	2356	2.25
Farming etc.	1558	1447	1328	4333	4.13
Skilled workers	694	434	301	1429	1.36
Total with occupation	13859	10895	8016	32770	31.27
Occupation not specified	24212	25587	22221	72020	68.73
Total immigrants	38071	36482	30237	104790	100.00

Occupational profile	*2000*	*2001*	*Total (2000–01)*	*%*
Professional & Technical	8632	19935	28567	25.43
Executive, Admn. and Managerial	1644	3062	4706	4.19
Clerical	573	643	1216	1.08
Sales	689	842	1531	1.36
Service	798	1041	1839	1.64
Farming etc.	1080	1161	2241	1.99
Skilled workers	308	389	697	0.62
Total with occupation	13724	27073	40797	36.32
Occupation not specified	28322	43217	71539	63.68
Total immigrants	42046	70290	112336	100.00

Source: US Immigration and Naturalisation Service, *Statistical Yearbook*, Annual issues.
Note: Data are not available for fiscal years 1980 and 1981.

In a publication (Nayyar 2002), subsequent to the one used above, Nayyar has discussed the causes and consequences of the recent rise in demand of immigrant skilled labour from India. However, one should note three contrary trends in the 21st century that militate against permanent migration. First, the advent of outsourcing. Outsourcing is the process of turning over part or all of an organisation's service functions to external service providers. While it is technological progress that has replaced unskilled migration to skilled migration, it is the same imperative where it is the work rather than the persons that gets migrated. Second, there is an increasing trend of return migration. Few studies make the point that cultural factors and rising incomes for skilled professionals in developing countries like India are encouraging return migration. Places like Bangalore and Hyderabad are becoming hubs of returned *desis*

Third, World Trade Organization (WTO) plays a crucial role in today's globalised world with provisions that do not allow permanent migration. General Agreement on Trade in Services (GATS), which is an integral part of WTO, propounds temporary migration of people (through Mode 4 of the GATS Document). It basically facilitates intra-company transferees.

These trends provide a corrective to the rather rose-tinted and celebratory depiction of the affluent status of Asian Indian community in North America. As we shall see later, a realistic picture of the present status and future life-chances of Indian diasporics in these countries furnishes the background to the kind of expectations they have from their country of origin, more particularly from the Government of India.

No information is available on the occupational distribution or the skills composition of immigration from India to the United Kingdom. It is plausible to argue, though impossible to prove, that, until the early 1960s a large proportion of emigration from India to the United Kingdom was made up of unskilled, semi-skilled, or skilled workers. This was attributable in part to the post-war labour shortage and in part to the absence of immigration controls on Commonwealth citizens. Post-colonial ties and the associated bonds with the English language, perhaps reinforced the patterns of immigration, as also the underlying factors. It is possible that

Table 14.2b: Immigration from India to North America by Major Occupational Groups, 1971–1990, Canada

number of persons (%)

Occupation group	*1971–75*	*1976–80*	*1981–85*	*1986–90*
Professional and Technical	4,721	1,070	914	974
	(11.1)	(3.5)	(2.8)	(2.1)
Entrepreneurs, Managers and Administrators	567	210	221	687
	(1.3)	(0.7)	(0.7)	(1.5)
Clerical and Sales	2,337	800	484	774
	(5.5)	(2.6)	(1.5)	(1.7)
Services	549	179	236	432
	(1.3)	(0.6)	(0.7)	(0.9)
Farming, Horticulture and Animal Husbandry	2,063	454	1,225	2,208
	(4.8)	(1.5)	(3.7)	(4.7)
Skilled Workers	5,956	955	790	1,899
	(14.0)	(3.2)	(2.4)	(4.1)
Occupational not classified	1,814	3,694	6,139	9,430
	(4.2)	(12.2)	(18.8)	(20.2)
Total Workers	18,007	7,362	10,009	16,404
	(42.3)	(24.3)	(30.6)	(35.2)
Total non-workers not reported	24,625	22,909	22,648	30,243
	(57.8)	(75.7)	(69.4)	(64.8)
Total immigration	42,632	30,271	32,657	46,647
	(100.0)	(100.0)	(100.0)	(100.0)

Source: Canadian Employment and Immigration Centre, Ottawa.

the same pattern continued for some time in the 1960s, although the mix may have changed somewhat to encompass persons with professional experience or technical qualifications.

However, as immigration laws became progressively more restrictive, it is almost certain that during the 1970s and the 1980s the occupational distribution of immigrants from India was determined by skills or expertise perceived to be scarce in the United Kingdom. Thus it is reasonable to infer that after 1970 the skills composition of emigration from India to the United Kingdom was similar to the skills composition of emigration from India to North America, even if the occupational distribution was dissimilar in so far as the agricultural sector in the United Kingdom was probably not a destination for emigrants.

It is ironical indeed that the Indian labour migration to the Middle East can be characterised in terms that are almost the reverse of those for North America and UK. The expectations, which this diaspora has from the Government of India, are even more importunate and vociferous. First, the Indian diasporics to the Middle East are sojourners rather than permanent settlers. It follows that the number of dependents of these immigrants in the host countries is almost negligible. Second, it is unskilled and skilled workers who constitute the bulk of these migrants while the number of white-collar workers and high skill workers is very small (Table 14.3). Although our figures are a little out-of-date it would seem that the above characteristics of Indian migrants to the Middle East have endured.[6] It is also on record that the diasporic's adaptation in these countries is marked by relatively restrictive, stringent and even hostile policies on the part of host governments. The representations made by these migrants to the High Level Committee and their statements at the *Pravasi Bharatiya Divas* congregations in 2003 and 2004 bear this as a testimony to this fact. I now turn to that evidence.

Table 14.3: The Skills Composition of Labour Outflows from India to the Middle East, 1984–86

		1984		*1985*		*1986*	
Sl. no.	*Skills composition*	*Number*	*%*	*Number*	*%*	*Number*	*%*
1.	Unskilled workers	88,575	43.0	55,710	34.2	45,577	40.1
	– Constructions Labour	85,797	41.7	51,330	31.5	39,314	34.6
	– Farm labour and household workers	2,778	1.3	4,380	2.7	6,263	5.5
2.	Skilled workers	86,014	41.8	86,037	52.8	53,432	47.0
	– Construction sector	45,882	22.3	46,318	28.4	24,485	21.5
	– Other activities and services	40,132	19.5	39,719	24.4	28,947	25.5
3.	White-collar workers	7,477	3.6	5,753	3.5	7,351	6.5
4.	High-skill workers	6,495	3.2	7,378	4.5	5,958	5.2
	– Para-medical staff	2,630	1.3	1,205	0.7	1,175	1.0
	– Technical and supervisory personnel	3,865	1.9	6,173	3.8	4,783	4.2
5.	Others	17,361	8.4	8,157	5.0	1,331	1.2
	Total	2,05,922	100.0	1,63,035	100.0	1,13,649	100.0

Source: Ministry of Labour, Govt. of India, New Delhi.

Expectations

Based on the criterion of economic affluence and political leverage vis-à-vis the governments in the country of origin as well as host countries, Indian diasporics—both new and old—can be placed in a rough socio-economic hierarchy. Whenever Indian diasporic commonality is in question, a gradation appears along the history of colonialism and capitalism within which the different countries of immigration are located; the hierarchy from top to bottom runs somewhat like this: USA and Canada, Australia, United Kingdom, other European countries, South Africa, Trinidad & Tobago, Guyana, Mauritius, Malaysia, Nepal. At least this was my firm impression while listening to the deliberations under the aegis of umbrella organisations like the GOPIO (Global Organisation of the People of Indian Origin)[7] about common diasporic Indian matters, such as the issue and pricing of PIO (Persons of Indian Origin) cards by the Indian Government. This is further confirmed by an analysis of the Proceedings of Pravasi Bharatiya Divas (PBD) for 2003 and 2004. It is no coincidence that the countries to which Overseas Citizenship has been granted by the Government of India happen to be at the top of this hierarchy. (The statutory position of these countries having dual citizenship provision was, of course, the deciding factor). These sixteen countries, in alphabetical order include: (1) Australia (2) Canada (3) Finland (4) France (5) Greece (6) Ireland (7) Israel (8) Italy (9) Netherlands (10) New Zealand (11) Portugal (12) Republic of Cyprus (13) Sweden (14) Switzerland (15) United Kingdom (16) United States of America.

I report a sampling of the views expressed by the diasporics according to this hierarchy. I first outline some of the views presented by representatives from UK, USA, Canada and other European countries. According to Bhikhu Parekh from UK (PBD 2003: 30–32):

> Not cultural nationalism, but cultural universalism is really at the heart of our identity and I think what the diaspora does is constantly to remind India that a part of it lies outside. India will be untrue to its history, untrue to its destiny if it ever forgot that it was an inherently open and outgoing society.... It is very important that India should have a systematic policy on the diaspora. The Government of India alone cannot design this policy because policy relates to us in the diaspora. And therefore, there must be a systematic dialogue... we bring with us certain sensibilities. And if India is going to reassess its place in the world at large, it would need to know what the world at large thinks about itself, as well as about India. And we, whether we are in the United Kingdom or United States or wherever, can bring regularly to the Government of India our insight into how the world is changing and how India needs to change with it. We can be a remarkable pool of ideas, attitudes, information, knowledge and sensibilities. And the kind of forum that I am proposing would be a useful institutional space where this kind of dialogue can take place... I have seen in our deliberations today the second and third generations have been almost entirely ignored... The suggestion of 9th January cannot be entirely innocent. Is it your suggestion that we in the diaspora should emulate the example of the greatest Indian

of our generation, Mahatma Gandhi, and return to India for good? If that is your intention, then I don't think it will be in the interest of either of us.

The same message of the openness of India—not only as learnt from the earlier democratic transformation of Britain—but that was and has been part of our tradition since ancient times was the main theme of the speech by the distinguished NRI, the Nobel laureate, Amartya Sen (PBD 2003: 42–45). Academics from the USA have been more down-to-earth and outspoken. According to Devesh Kapoor of the Faculty of Arts and Sciences, Harvard University, five principles ought to be maintained in diaspora-related policies: 1) The overall policies regime should not create an incentive structure whereby it is easier to gain recognition in India by leaving India than by staying here. 2) On economic issues the diaspora should be treated at par with foreigners and only marginally different from residents. Else, it will simply create opportunities for arbitrage that will benefit the diaspora much more than it will benefit India. 3) In sharper contrast, in matters involving social, cultural and civil rights, the diaspora should be treated on par with residents here. This is specially the case in the right to work. The first barrier comes from professional associations here. The second is a problem with the shortsighted policies of the public sector. The third concerns higher education, which Indian liberalisation has bypassed. The diaspora can contribute the most by setting up institutions of higher education which are an asset not only to residents here, but also would provide a mechanism for second generation Indians to come and spend a semester or a year and that too, very cheaply. 4) On political rights, unless there is a tax obligation, dual citizenship should not carry with it the right to vote. 5) Finally, India's diaspora is usually a minority in the country of settlements. Both the Indian state and the diaspora must realise that claims of perfection of the diaspora in the countries of settlement are weakened if minorities here are not protected. One might also add that this has been the burden of 'deterritorialised Indianness' in the reflections of many of the representatives of the diaspora.

Coming to the mid-point in the diasporic hierarchy, Mewa Ramgobin, Member of Parliament in South Africa, noted that 'this conference has an obligation to engage its diaspora to find out whether we as a group, so-called, are indeed making South Africa livable for all who live in it. Are we helping to push back the frontiers of poverty, disease and homelessness? Are we an integral part of the African Renaissance? Whether special dispensations by India to the people of Indian origin in South Africa lead to political integration with cultural diversity?' (PBD 2003: 35). This attitude shows what I have earlier called 'multiple territorialisation', (Jain 1998) or better still, 'reterritorialisation' of the Indian diaspora. In a similar vein, Dato Seri S. Samy Vellu, Minister of Works, Malaysia spoke as a Malaysian with a stake in India, again not deterritorialised but multiple-and-reterritorialised agent: 'There is a large pool of talent to share with the world. Fostering partnership between India and the Indian diaspora is a two-way process. The key dimension is how can there be a win-win situation from multiple players.... Malaysians have been successful in investing and participating in infrastructure projects in India. We could further facilitate these through collaboration partnerships, which will be beneficial for both India and Malaysia' (PBD 2003: 33).

As we come down the hierarchical ladder, there are speeches from Mauritius, Fiji and Dubai. Dhundev Bauhadoor, Chairman of GOPIO International, Mauritius had this to say:

> We feel that the emphasis in this conference is more on NRIs than PIOs. NRIs are Indians, but residing in the UK, USA, and all these countries. PIOs are not Indians, but the people of Indian origin living in the South of the world. We have been observing the change in the attitude of the Indian government and the Indian officials. The emphasis is towards those who hold Dollars, Pounds, Rials and all these things. Those people who hold a Rupee are not considered to be real Indians. They have nothing to do with the people in Fiji. When Mahendra Chaudhary was held hostage for 20 days, India refused to comment. She opened her mouth only when a small country like Mauritius intervened with the United Nations. This cannot continue. If India is to play her role as a mother, she must protect her children wherever they are (PBD 2003: 55).

Bauhadoor went on to criticise the GOI for an exorbitant fee of US $ 1000 for the PIO and, its eligibility for only upto fifth generation, and the harassment faced by PIOs at the airports, in the shops and in the holy places.

Given the troubled background of Fijian Indian community, Mahendra Chaudhary, former Prime Minister of Fiji, made a special appeal to the Government of India to help this impoverished, footloose and embattled community. He too, like the representative from Mauritius, made a distinction between immigrants who went to affluent Western societies, 'who left India as emigrants to seek greener pastures and others who were taken often by force as indentured labour to the British colonies' (PBD 2003: 38). He went on to say, 'Given those two very different scenarios, focusing too much on how India and those in the affluent sectors of the diaspora can benefit from forging relationships with each other with little concerns for the needs of those members of the diaspora who are suffering and whose rights are under assault. That will indeed be a pity' (ibid.). He concluded by saying that India cannot abandon PIOs to fight their aim battles.

Similarly disgruntled was the representative from Dubai, Bharat Kumar J. Shah, and Chairman of Al Mustaneer Trading Co., who spoke mainly in Hindi. He said, 'Our resident brothers think we are the pampered children. Unfortunately, because of our bureaucratic hurdles these concessions, these facilities do not reach the medium and low-level bureaucracy. If it reaches, they do not read it. If they read, they don't understand it. If they understand, they don't digest it. If they digest, they don't implement it' (PBD 2003: 54).

Solutions

Responding to the problems and issues raised by the diaspora representative at the first Pravasi Bharatiya Divas, as well as to the problems presented before the High Level committee, the Government of India announced several measures for the amelioration of the *pravasis*. These constituted the main burden of the then Prime Minister, Atal Bihari Vajpayee's inaugural address at the second Pravasi Bharatiya Divas (9–11 January 2004). We may note the salient provisions announced by him. First, about overseas investments by Indian corporates. These will be freely permitted to make overseas investments upto 100 per cent of their net worth, whether through an overseas joint venture or a wholly owned subsidiary. The hitherto existing restrictions including a ceiling of US$ 200 million were being lifted. Second, Indian corporates were not only permitted, but also encouraged, to go global in the agricultural sector. This, said the Prime Minister, will enable Indian corporates to take advantage of global opportunities and also to acquire technological and other skills for adoption in India. Third, the enhancement of citizenships amendment bill was announced which provides overseas Indians in 16 countries (see above) the possibility of applying for dual citizenship. The Prime Minister clarified that these countries were chosen because their legal systems were compatible with the concept of dual citizenship and there was a strong representation of people of Indian origin in these nations. Fourth, as a sop for those Indian workers who travel to distant shores in search of higher remuneration, namely, migrants to the Gulf and Southeast Asia, a compulsory insurance scheme called Pravasi Bharatiya Bima Yojana was introduced since December 2003. Fifth, provision was being made for the same category of diasporics as above (migrants to the Gulf region and Southeast Asia) who have had to leave their children behind in India, the facility of one-third reservation out of the 15 supernumerary seats across different disciplines in educational institutions. Further, children of the NRIs in the Gulf would not be required to pay NRI fees. They would be treated at par with resident citizens. Sixth, the government decided to set up a Pravasi Bharatiya Kendra in New Delhi for which a suitable plot of land has been provided along with a seed grant of Rs 25 crore. The responsibility of running it will be entrusted to an autonomous body, which shall also raise additional resources from members of the diaspora. The Kendra will be a permanent center to deal with the multifarious needs of the diasporic community. Finally, expressing his faith in the abilities of the young people of Indian origin all over the world, the Prime Minister announced a scheme whereby each year a group of 50 second or third generation Indian youth from different countries will be invited to visit India for two weeks.[8]

Following the Indian General Elections in May 2004, the new UPA government took over and almost immediately announced the formation of a new Ministry of Overseas Indian Affairs with Jagdish Tytler as the Minister-in-Charge. The formation of this Ministry has followed the celebrations of the Second Pravasi Bharatiya Divas held at Vigyan Bhavan, New Delhi from 9–11 January 2004. The Proceedings of this celebration, again sponsored jointly by the Ministry of External Affairs (MEA) and the Federation of Indian Chambers of Commerce and Industry (FICCI) are not as voluminous as the first PBD, but they contain speeches by the ministers of the last NDA government which are no less celebratory and self-congratulatory as the previous ones. Yashwant Sinha, then Minister of External Affairs, spoke in a characteristically buoyant tone, hailing 'the feel good factor' and 'Brand India'. The rhetoric of his statement deserves to be quoted in his own words: 'It is true that we have a long way to go. Benefits of economic growth have to percolate down to the lowest rungs of our society. The "feel good" factor has to reach every corner of our country. But slowly and steadily, Brand India is making its presence felt. Instead of being associated with poverty, social turmoil and backwardness, India is today perceived as an emerging power, a highly successful democracy, an economy destined to become the third-largest in the world, a center of science and technology, and a land that can boast of people known for their talent, intelligence, hard work and extraordinary creativity. Yoga and the art of living, computer geeks and IITs, fashion and food, Bollywood and Bangalore – these are the symbols and images of the new India.' (BPD Proceedings 2004: 4).

The story comes full circle when the government of the day becomes a handmaiden of the consumerist culture of the middle classes.

Recent Trends

Among other signals that a dialogue between researchers and the controlling agencies may be in the offing is a small beginning that the Ministry of Overseas Indian Affairs made by organising a Roundtable Discussion on 20 December 2004 at the India International Centre, New Delhi. In a theme-note prepared for this meeting, I raised a sampling of issues that confront us:

The overall context of this brainstorming exercise is the expectations, which the Indian diasporics have of the Government of India and vice versa. Examples of the former orientation are vociferous demands by the NRIs in the Middle East to ameliorate problems in recruitment and conditions of work, and the educational rehabilitation of their wards during the guardians' absence overseas, and so on. Similarly, there is demand in the global Indian diaspora for dual citizenship and its pros and cons from the viewpoint of the GOI. There is the politically charged issue of loyalty to the host countries vis-à-vis attachment and patriotism towards the mother country. Sociologically, the cultural gap between the first generation and subsequent generations of the diasporics creates problems of adaptation. There is also the question of how successful the provision of PIO cards has been to rehabilitate and attract diasporic interests in India. Is the distinction between NRIs and PIOs relevant and useful now and in the future? Important too, are the economic questions arising out of remittances from overseas Indians on the one hand, and diasporic participation and leadership in FDI and portfolio investments in India. We may also examine the character and upshot of the sterling contributions of India to the diaspora in the field of ICT (Information and Communication Technology). How insightful in the economic and socio-cultural planning for the Indian diaspora can the experience of another Asian giant be, namely, the Peoples Republic of China?

Subsequent to the Roundtable, we had reports of the Third Pravasi Bharatiya Divas, held in Mumbai during 7 to 9 January 2005. In his inaugural speech, the Prime Minister, Manmohan Singh, concluded with the exhortation that we hold a vision of an 'open economy and inclusive society'. I take cue from this excellent summing up by noting the following.

(1) Let us analytically distinguish between the mapping and monitoring of issues and perspectives as was suggested at the Roundtable. In mapping the field, from a sociological point-of-view, it should be emphasised that the Indian communities overseas are not a monolith. According to their respective histories and economies, there is not only

a hierarchy and variation among the various communities in different countries, but also internal variation. The latter are often conflictual in the sense that, for example, in South Africa the older South Africa born Indians and their progeny in many instances regard themselves as 'Foreign Born Indians' (they use for themselves the acronym 'FBI') claiming socio-cultural and economic superiority over the newly-arrived, often poorer and disempowered, recent immigrants from India and Pakistan (Jain 2001). Similarly, there is an asymmetry between Indians (mainly Hindu) who have migrated to the Netherlands from Surinam and those Indians arriving recently direct from India. There is pervasive misunderstanding and antagonism between these groups. In Sri Lanka, although both the Jaffna Tamils and the plantation Tamils are ethnically homogeneous, there are acute differences of perception and life-chances in the circumstances of the two sub-communities. It has been noted in the literature on overseas Indians as well as in the High Level Report that there exists heterogeneity in the Indian communities based on region, language and religion not only among the PIOs but even in the NRI population of industrially advanced countries. Often enough, this lack of unity gives rise to parochial associations and cultural organisations. Usually, in government documents, including the High Level Report, this diversity is decried as making for disunity and discord. My point of view, which is in accord with the Human Development Report (2004), is that such cultural variety is inevitable among diasporics from such a vast and culturally diverse country as India. It may actually be judicially and tactically supported as positive cultural freedom. At the same time, however, steps should be taken to minimise this diversity's potential for conflict despite its somewhat inevitable expressions in day-to-day life. There can be no uniform formula for achieving mitigation of conflict, but its recognition and policies designed to handle it should be part of what we call 'monitoring' in addition to mapping.

(2) I think that the monitoring aspect comes into operation when we consider our policies towards the PIOs and NRIs in relation to issues such as dual citizenship. The Prime Minister's announcement that all overseas Indians who migrated after January 26 1950 will be eligible for dual citizenship is an important step in the direction of 'inclusion'. Of course, the application of this provision would be subject to the laws of the host societies and the fact that those migrating before the Republic of India came into being would be treated as per the law. A question was raised at the Roundtable whether there was a conceptual reason why the PIOs should be made eligible for dual citizenship. (Much would depend on what special benefits this status would bring as distinct from a PIO Card only). My submission is that in view of (a) the current spread of globalisation, and (b). the socio-economic mobility gained by PIOs *in situ* in the host societies, their potential for contributing to India socially and economically should not be underestimated. Thus eventually, as the Prime Minister stated, all overseas Indians should be welcome to enjoy a legal status in their country of origin. Whether the PIO cards should continue or not is in some ways an empirical question. My own impression is that there have not been as many takers of the card as originally stipulated and, also,

that if selected, PIO countries (those which have the provision for dual citizenship) too were offered dual citizenship by India, the prospect would be much more welcome.

In general, then, I do not subscribe to the view expressed in some quarters that the dual citizenship debate has been hijacked in favour of the PIOs. Of course, its application and extension to the recent NRIs (as has actually been done now) is a valid priority, but all in all, the drift of contemporary times does not much validate an enduring distinction from the viewpoint of the government between the NRIs and the PIOs.

(3) This brings me to another major point about the mapping and monitoring of the diaspora in so far as the academic perspective is concerned. The repeated incantation of the names of very big and successful Indian entrepreneurs abroad such as Swaraj Paul and Lakshmi Mittal in UK or the dot.com billionaires of USA is to my mind, succumbing to a media-hype. As far as I know, this is not the way China seduces its overseas benefactors to the mainland. There is, on the other hand, in the PRC, a largely decentralised, eco-geographically demarcated and localised approach to tap in the investment potential of countrymen settled abroad (Woon 1997). And, whereas, from a macro policy point of view, we do need the expertise, goodwill, lobbying (and even money!) of Swaraj Pauls and Mittals for investments in India, let us not forget—as the Secretary Shri Krishna Kumar pointed out at the Roundtable—small towns, medium-sized businesses and, if I may add, even retailers having direct trading links with manufacturers and buyers abroad. (for some suggestive leads, cf. Baru 2000). And in this activity networks would be crucial. I have already talked of vertical (inter-class) and lateral (intra-class) networks traversing India and its diaspora. These can be charted out and mobilised if regional businesses are informed and encouraged. On a slightly different track, our institutions of higher learning (like some universities and institutes in Gujarat) may become socio-economic centers of Diaspora Studies which can then be nodal points for passing on information and skills between diasporics and their Indian counterparts.

(4) The question of loyalty has been raised. Whenever there are migrants more or less permanently settled abroad, especially if they enjoy dual citizenship, the question of conflicting loyalties is bound to arise. The individuals concerned have both rights and duties in the two countries. The host society, in particular, is within its sovereign rights to expect the loyalty of all its citizens. At the same time, the very reason for retaining or obtaining citizenship of the country of origin by diasporics is to avail of the entailed opportunities. The Human Development Report 2004 discusses the subject of legal pluralism. It is argued that if the legal system of the larger society respects human rights norms, the problem of divided loyalties may be mitigated. However, there is another important issue at stake. The host society would, directly or indirectly, look to the society of origin whether or not it respects the cultural freedoms of its minorities (numerical or socio-political) and would reciprocally treat its own minorities (which the diasporics normally are). During the past regime in India, the kowtowing of the Hindu fundamentalist ideology raised serious questions about the ill-treatment of the Muslim minorities by the N.D.A. government, especially in relation to the diaspora-oriented state of Gujarat. When an Indian ambassador at large (Bhishma K. Agnihotri)

was—extra-legally—appointed to be the spokesperson for Indian minorities in the US and beyond, there was popular and academic questioning of his role bestowed upon by a government which itself failed to protect its Muslim minority in the homeland (van der Veer 2002). Therefore, one of the important policy imperatives for governance in India with respect to the welfare of its diaspora would be that its own policies and practices with regard to national minorities would be closely watched. This is a specific instance of what, among other items, the Prime Minister would possibly mean by an 'inclusive' society at home for a healthy diaspora.

Conclusion

It would have become clear by now that the post-independence governments of India have awakened to the needs, aspirations and contributions of the diaspora only recently. In its work of social engineering, the role of the academics may be defined as that of diagnosis and prediction, in a limited way, if those responsible for diaspora's governance wish to consult them. As part of a conclusion in the burgeoning field of diaspora studies and governance, the following observations arising from my recent comparative essay on Indian immigrants to Malaysia, Trinidad and Australia may have some relevance (Jain 2004: 1–26) First, ethnic networks and agent-chains have been in evidence for the whole gamut of Indian diasporics abroad. Second, there has been a pattern of 'circulation' (Markovits 2000) rather than a one-way passage between the region of origin in India and a number of diaspora nodes (Voigt-Graf 2004). Even in regard to labour diaspora, as distinct from traders such as Sindhis and Chettiars, Carter (1995) has shown the impact of returnees from amongst indentured recruits from India to Mauritius as far back as during 1834 to 1874. Similarly, even in old and distant locales such as Trinidad and Tobago the 'to-ing and fro-ing' of Indian cultural specialists like religious leaders and missionaries is very much in evidence. So also is the transmigration of Indian nationalism. Third, whether it is the high rate of suicides among plantation workers in Trinidad during the 19th century or the high incidence of domestic violence in the present-day professional Indian diaspora in the US, we learn that the human and social costs of overseas migration have been very high. Fourth, the internal socio-economic disparities and, externally, a hierarchical structure in the diaspora have been commonly found in the old and new diasporas. Khandelwal (2002: 104) has argued about the stratification existing between the well-to-do older immigrants from India in New York and the taxi driving, restaurant and other service-industry migrants. She writes: 'In 1987 the *Wall Street Journal* extolled the Indian "immigrant saga" with more success stories. But it also reported that "for every rising entrepreneur there are poor Indians scrubbing restaurant kitchens". According to the 1980 census, 9.9% Asian Indians were below the poverty line, a figure approaching the 12.4% poverty rate for all Americans'. Fifth, as I have argued in relation to Khandelwal's depiction of the internal disparities among Indians as coming close to 'blaming the victims' (Jain 2003a), the overall structure of 'receiving' societies, whether in Malaysia, Trinidad and Tobago or in developed countries like Australia and US has carried the stain of discrimination and disparity between the local and the global. In terms of external influences, what was caused by colonialism and imperialism in the old diaspora has been highlighted in the new diaspora through the consequences of globalisation.

Yet the situation of the Indian diaspora now and in the future is not a gloomy one. In the foregoing, it has been argued that the governance of this diaspora from the Indian end (as compared to the Chinese diaspora, for example) has been tardy and delayed. I have also argued that numerically perhaps the bulk of this diaspora does not merit being painted in very bright colours; in fact there have been problems and grievances that both the governmental and other public agencies controlling and regulating the Indian diaspora should be acutely aware of.[9]

Notes

1. The distinction between old and new diasporics may be made in terms of the 19th century predominantly labour migration from India in the former and the 20th century migration of educated and largely professional migrants in the latter although there are occupational overlaps in both the cases. The migration to the Middle East constitutes a sub-category by itself of 20th century diaspora.
2. Some observers of globalisation and diaspora have spoken of 'post-nation' as the category most relevant in the study of the 'flows' in the present conjuncture (Appadurai 1997). However, I am in complete agreement with Partha Chatterjee (1977: 30–34) that in the debate between 'beyond the nation' or within India, one veers towards a nationalist rather than 'beyond the nation' point-of view for the Indian socio-economic development.
3. It is heartening indeed that a young social anthropologist from Peoples Republic of China is employing exactly the same techniques of empirical field-study to investigate the recruitment process of Indian IT professionals what anthropologists and historians of the previous generation (e.g., Jain, Carter, Brijlal et al.) did for the study of recruitment of plantation labour overseas from India in the 19th and 20th centuries.
4. For a recent analysis of Indian IT workers' horizontal or intra-class networks (see, Upadhya 2004).
5. In the decade of the nineties this situation has changed drastically. There is an increasing tendency towards larger number of persons, especially IT professionals, who are migrating to the industrialised countries returning after a finite period. This could be mainly attributed to the high turnover rates prevelant in the IT industry and the altered demographics in the industrialised countries (ageing host population).
6. The 1990s witnessed a structural shift in the market for expatriate labour in majority of the Middle East economies. There is a marked change in demand for skills away from construction towards operations and maintenance, services and transport and communications. A recent field-survey conducted among Indian migrants in UAE shows that more than forty per cent who are migrating to the Middle East are those in skilled/professional categories (Zachariah et al. 2004).
7. The First Global Convention of People of Indian Origin was held in New York from August 27 to September 3 1989 at Sheraton Centre. Among American dignitaries present at the Convention as an active participant was the 2004 democratic arch contestant for Presidentship of USA, John Kerry, the then Senator. National Federation of Indian American Associations sponsored the Convention. Since its inception, GOPIO has grown steadily into a full global organisation. However, within a span of just three years a split occurred in GOPIO between what may be termed as GOPIO (M) with its headquarters in Mauritius and GOPIO (NY), being the original core. While the former represents PIOs and the old

diaspora, the latter broadly constitutes the new diaspora. Besides the pan-Indian global organization, there are the regional and linguistic global diasporic organisations, viz., the World Telugu Federation (WTF).

8. Besides these concrete steps, the Government of India has also instituted Pravasi Bharatiya Awards, 'search your roots' programme, and has proposed distance education capsules for the diaspora youth. If one may divide the ameliorative programmes into instrumental and expressive ones, those mentioned here are largely of the latter variety.
9. One reason why in this chapter I have focused equally on the poorer and not only on the rich diasporics from India is, perhaps, my own long-term research on the labour diaspora in Malaysia (viz., Jain 1970, 2003).

References

Appadurai, Arjun (1997). *Modernity At Large: Cultural Dimensions of Globalization.* Delhi: Oxford University Press.

Baru, Sanjay (2000). 'Economic Policy and the Development of Capitalism in India: The Role of Regional Capitalists and Political Parties', in Francine R. Frankel et al. (eds), *Transforming India: Social and Political Dynamics of a Democracy*, pp. 207–30. New Delhi: Oxford University Press.

Carter, Marina (1995). *Servants, Sirdars and Settlers: Indians in Mauritius, 1834–74.* Delhi: Oxford University Press.

Chatterjee, Partha (1997). 'Beyond the Nation? Or Within?' *Economic and Political Weekly,* 32 (1 and 2): 30–34.

Clifford, J. (1997). *Routes: Travel and Translation in the Late Twentieth Century.* London: Harvard University Press.

Guarnizo, L. E. (1997). 'The Emergence of a Transnational Social Formation and the Mirage of Return Migration among Dominican Transmigrants', *Identities,* 4: 281–322.

Human Development Report 2004: Cultural Liberty in Today's Diverse World (2004). Published for United Nations Development Programme (UNDP), Delhi: Oxford University Press.

Jain, R. K. (1970). *South Indians on the Plantation Frontier in Malaya.* New Haven & London: Yale University Press.

——— (1998). 'Reality and Representation: Aspects of the Electronic Media in Contemporary Indian Society and Diaspora', *Sociological Bulletin,* 47 (2): 167–84.

——— (1998a). 'Indian Diaspora, Globalization and Multiculturalism: A Cultural Analysis', *Contributions to Indian Sociology* (New series), 32 (2): 337–60.

——— (2001). 'Culture and Class in Indian Diaspora', *Economic and Political Weekly,* 36 (17): 1380–81.

——— (2003). 'Culture and Economy: Tamils on the Plantation Frontier in Malaysia Revisited, 1998-1999', in Bhikhu Parekh et al. (eds), *Culture and Economy in the Indian Diaspora,* pp. 51–80. London and New York: Routledge.

——— (2003a). Review of 'M.S. Khandelwal: Becoming American, Being Indian', *Indian Social Science Review,* 5(2), July–December 2003.

——— (2004). 'Indian Diaspora, Old and New: Culture, Class and Mobility', *Indian Anthropologist* (Journal of the Indian Anthropological Association), 34 (1): 1–26.

Khandelwal, M. S. (2002). *Becoming American, Being Indian: An Immigrant Community in New York City.* Ithaca and London: Cornell University Press.

Khor, Martin (2001). *Rethinking Globalization: Critical Issues and Policy Choices.* London and New York: Zed Books.

Markovits, C. (2000). *The Global World of Indian Merchants 1750–1947: Traders of Sind from Bukhara to Panama*. Cambridge: Cambridge University Press.

Nayyar, Deepak (1994). *Migration, Remittances and Capital Flows: The Indian Experience*. Delhi: Oxford University Press.

——— (2002). 'Cross Border Movements of People', in Deepak Nayyar (ed.), *Governing Globalization: Issues and Institutions*, pp. 144–173. Delhi: Oxford University Press.

Portes, A., L. E. Guarnizo and P. Landolt (1999). 'The Study of Transnationalism: Pitfalls and Promise of an Emergent Research', *Ethnic and Racial Studies*, 22 (2): 217–37.

Proceedings of the Pravasi Bharatiya Divas (PBD) (2003 and 2004). New Delhi Ministry of External Affairs and Federation of Indian Chambers of Commerce and Industries, Pravasi Bharatiya Secretariat.

Report of the High Level Committee on the Indian Diaspora (2001). New Delhi: Indian Council of World Affairs.

Shukla, Sandhya (2003). *India Abroad: Diasporic Cultures of Postwar America and England*. Princeton and Oxford: Princeton University Press.

Srivastava, R. (2001). 'H4 Visa Leaves Many Indian Women Dependent on Abusive Husbands', *The Times of India*, (Hyderabad edn), 22 July, p. 9.

Tambiah, S.J. (2000). 'Transnational Movements, Diasporas and Multiple Modernities', *Daedalus* (Winter): 163–94.

Upadhya, Carol (2004). 'A New Transnational Capitalist Class? Capital Flows, Business Networks and Entrepreneurs in the Indian Software Industry', *Economic and Political Weekly*, 39 (48): 5141–51.

Van der Veer, Peter (2002). 'Transnational Religion: Hindu and Muslim Movements', *Global Networks*, 2 (2): 95–111.

Voigt-Graf, C. (2004). 'Towards a Geography of Transnational Spaces: Indian Transnational Communities in Australia', *Global Networks*, 4 (1): 25–50.

Woon, Yuen-fong (1997). 'Qiaoxiang Mentality and Economic Development: A Comparative Study of Two Overseas Chinese Homelands in South China in the 1990s', *Journal of Canadian Anthropological Society* (JCAS), Symposium Series 4, pp. 45–65.

Xiang, Biao (2001). 'Structuration of Indian Information Technology Professionals' Migration to Australia', *International Migration*, 39 (5): 73–90.

——— (2002). 'Ethnic Transnational Middle Class in Formation: A Case Study of Indian Infor-mation Technology Professionals', Paper presented to the International Seminar on ICTs and Indian Development, Geneva: International Organization for Migration (IOM).

Zachariah, K.C., B.A. Prakash and S. Irudaya Rajan (2004). 'Indian Workers in UAE: Employment, Wages and Working Conditions', *Economic and Political Weekly*, 39 (22): 2227–34.

Section IV
Cultural Dimensions

15

Globalisation and Information Society: Cultural Dimensions and Governance Reforms with Reference to Print Media

J. S. Yadav

The world is fairly globalised today. Many say it has become a global village. In a village every resident knows each other personally and shares a common worldview. The world may not have integrated to that extent, but surely events in one part of the globe have reverberations and impact on other parts. Just as modernisation, globalisation has influenced various domains of the life of traditional societies, which tries to adhere and adapt itself in the field of economy, while still seeking to preserve its own identity and cultural values. Our everyday lives are becoming more global, more affected by events occurring far away.

Globalisation may be best defined as the integration of markets, finance, nation states and technologies to enable corporations, nation states and individuals to reach around the world—faster, deeper and cheaper than ever before. Globalisation's driving idea is free-market capitalism (Tremblay 2003). It has its own set of economic rules, which revolve around opening, deregulation and privatising economies worldwide. It has its own defining technologies: computers, satellite communications, fiber optics and the Internet. These technologies are the engines of globalisation. Its defining measurement is speed, and scale of communication and commerce. The symbol of the globalisation system is a World Wide Web that unites everyone (Bhagwati 2004).

As such, globalisation is a complex process affecting various facets of human life and is immensely facilitated by revolutionary developments in communication technologies. One can look at the human history and emergence of globalisation phenomenon from the communication perspective. As such, here in this chapter I will first discuss some significant features and trends in communication technologies, how these developments are forcing and facilitating liberalisation and globalisation. This will be followed by examination of its implications for reforms and governance and resulting cultural dimensions of globalisation and governance reforms with reference to the print media in India.

Revolution in Communications

The communication and information revolution is rapidly transforming economy, culture and politics the world over turning it virtually into a 'global village'. Events taking place in any corner of the planet become known the world over almost in no time. More and more economic decisions and operations have global ramifications. The increasingly greater integration and centrality of information and communication into the functioning of economy and society is taking place so rapidly and on such a vast scale that globalisation and emergence of information societies is becoming a reality. However, all nations, groups and individuals have not uniformly or equitably shared the benefits of globalisation and information technologies within a nation. Apprehensions about cultural imperialism are also there. Hence, the fierce debates all over about the hopes of utopian nature and despair of widening the digital divide; promising a prosperous peaceful world and fearing civilisation and cultural clashes (Huntington 1997). The reality, to my mind is likely to be somewhere in between.

No doubt information technology is a very powerful force but the human ingenuity, I am convinced, is even stronger and much will depend upon the way we put to use the information technologies to address our issues and concerns. Information is knowledge and knowledge is power. It has always been so, whether it is the case of how to make fire and stone tools in prehistoric times or nuclear or space science and related technologies in modern times. The significance of these examples, however, is neither the power nor knowledge, in fact that empowering was achieved because knowledge was held by a relatively small number of people. Man alone has the capacity to generate knowledge; conceptual abstract thinking and making tools and technologies. Through communication and information, knowledge is shared with others.

The power to communication and 'control' information and knowledge is one of the keys to power. As such, human beings have been devising more and more efficient methods, techniques and technologies of communications with a purpose of influencing others and increasing their areas of dominance and power. The central thread that seems to run through human history is the urge to reach out to more and more people; the largest number possible, fastest possible and most cost effectively possible. And to this end, human beings devise ever increasingly efficient methods and techniques of communications.

Throughout history, human beings have been utilising this capacity to generate knowledge and share it to their best advantage; to ward off enemy, search for food, acquire wealth, organise human relations, etc. Also, it is the history of struggle to control knowledge and even communication and technologies to share the knowledge by some for their own limited use and advantage as against others. Consequently, antagonistic socio-political groups, 'we' vs. 'they', are formed. People resist restrictions and recent developments in communication and information technologies which make control difficult, if not impossible. Emergence of Internet, Information super-highways and convergence of information/communication technologies is a revolutionary development. It makes control over knowledge difficult and sharing easy, promising almost near universal empowerment of people provided we make innovative use of these 'new' technologies.

Information Age

As a result, the winds of change now sweeping across much of the world is paving way for an open world. Today, the advances that man had made in the area of communication technologies is transforming the organised human life so fundamentally that many social scientists speak of the dawn of a new era—the Information Age.

Today, media has assumed significance which it had never seen before. Starting as an institutionalised approach to generate awareness and information to the masses, media has become an instrument governing our lives. Rather than a form of cultural expression, it has a culture of its own. It was supposed to report on the way of life of people. It has now become a way of life itself. Moreover, it is one of the most important industries of our time.

Many of the societies are already changing from being advanced industrial ones to 'information societies' in which computer technologies, their networks and other enhanced forms of interpersonal and institutional communication are a major force. Some of the Western countries have already entered into an information age. In the United States, the information activities engage more than 46 per cent of the workforce, which generates over 55 per cent of the labour income.

Multinational IT companies are in the process of building a vast web of electronic networks, 'information super highways', of fiber optics and computer. This network will deliver an abundance of goods and services at offices or homes—video images, phone calls, enormous amount of data on various required fields by a user or customer. They promise to change the way people work, live and leisure.

The vision of communication abundance has been possible because of the sharp decline in costs. According to an estimate, the cost of microprocessors has fallen by 22 per cent, computer memories cost is down by 40 per cent, and that of communication equipment by 11 per cent per annum. By the year 2010, may be even earlier, the cost of a computerised home system should be about the same as that of an automobile today, thus coming within the reach of the common man in developed countries. The protagonists of the new communication technologies have been promising a revolution of abundance and diversity of information for all.

Convergence

Let us briefly examine the characteristics of the new communication technologies that have been fast changing the information environment in the new millennium. As a matter of fact, most of the so-called new communication technologies have been with us for the last couple of decades. What is relatively new is this convergence and integration. Another feature of the present day situation in communications is the scale and affordability of operation enabled by the microprocessors and the 'chips'. The result of these two processes, convergence and scale, are revolutionary, making information technology user friendly and affordable.

The convergence of emerging telecommunication technologies and computers is transforming business operations, broadcasting, telephone systems and human interactions in general. We are on the threshold of having a high-resolution, two-way video and personal computers tied to networks, so that by sitting at home or office, one can receive and send information from and to anywhere in the world, and engage in a two-way video conversation across the world (Sambandan 2000).

As the world shifts to a service-oriented economy, vast amount of money, goods and services are being circulated as well. In the last few years, break-through in satellite and high-speed computing have given leading users an overwhelming economic advantage over those who have not kept pace. Thus, the stakes in new communication technologies are high and are of global dimension. Although for foreseeable future, the responsibility, if not power, to plan and decide about communication will continue to rest with the nation states, already many of the operations are beyond them. The result is enormous expansion and significance of multi-national corporations.

Through multinationals and other trade channels the advanced Western countries are pushing hard the new communication technologies in the Third World Countries to maintain their economic and political interest. The 'pull' force for the 'latest' and the 'best' on the part of the ruling elites in the Third World countries sustains the 'push'.

Thus, in brief, there have been revolutionary changes in information and communication technologies, which provide both challenge and opportunity. The new fervor for modernisation and progress through adoption of the latest information and communication technologies enhances the capabilities of communication at various levels, both within and outside the organisation. Technologies increase the efficiency in terms of speed and spread, and also in terms of looks and appearances. With latest communication technologies one is able to multiply messages fast enough and also make it reach the intended audiences quickly or even instantly. One may also produce attractive information/communication packages.

Amazing times are ahead. Goods and services can be acquired from anywhere anytime. Time and space have acquired new meanings. What used to be distance is no more that far. What used to be local has become global. Excitement abounds information technology. Telephone, television and computers are getting inter-twined with each other, holding out promises of a world in which innovation and human dynamism would be the driving force. In the seamless world of tomorrow, mind would matter. Some say, it will be a knowledge society. Innovations would lead to intelligent technologies and bits and bytes would dictate communication. In the world of convergence, a telephone would not be an end in itself, but a means to greater linkages with the PC, and through it, to the Internet. Similarly, a TV would not just be an entertainment medium but also a link to the worldwide Internet through cable TV. The emergence of the wireless web further facilitates connectivity (Singhal and Roger 2001).

The quality of images and the speed of downloads will improve significantly with the introduction of next or third generation techniques and technologies. The mobile phone will have computation and storage capabilities that will match the fixed devices. Multi-media mobile messages will be e-mails' next rival. But enhancement of capabilities is not necessarily an assurance for effective communication.

Digital Divide

The gap between the industrialised countries and the developing world is striking. About 80 per cent of the world's population lives in developing countries. Their share of income and consumption of world resources is less than 20 per cent. One fifth of the world population lives on just a dollar a day. The digital divide is even more striking. The developing countries' share of Internet access is merely 10 per cent (Bajaj 2001). In United States, 56 per cent of adults are online, while in most developing countries merely 2–3 per cent or even less have access to the Internet. All of Africa has just 14 million phone lines, lower than New York or Tokyo. A third of the world's people have never made even a phone call in their lifetime (Jishnu et al. 2001). In these circumstances, naturally, some strongly argue in favour of basic needs such as safe drinking water, adequate food, shelter, health facilities and education first and telephone and computers later. But as rightly emphasised by Vinod Thomas (2001), Vice President of the World Bank, it is not a question of choice between penicillin and pentiums. (On digital divide see Table 15.1).

Table 15.1: Ownership of Information Communication Technologies

Per 1000 people

Media	*India*	*World*	*USA*
Radio	121	418	2,090
TV	69	247	864
Telephone	34	146	666
Mobile	1	55	500
Internet	4.5	70.6	540

Source: Business World, 21 May 2001.

The power of information revolution is precisely that it can help deliver basic services in more efficient and innovative ways. Rather, not putting those technologies to work for the poorest people carries a huge and growing cost. It means missed economic opportunities and growing inequalities within less developing countries themselves as rural areas become more isolated and fall further behind.

As stated earlier, with 'push' from developed countries and 'pull' from within the developing countries, information technologies are spreading fast. While Internet users increase in number in Asia, Africa and other developing countries, most data flows out of the US, rather than flowing in. In 2000, some 60 per cent of the world's Internet hosts were based in the US, and visitors to the 100 most visited web sites were from the US. The US hegemony in this field is near complete.

The PC penetration and spending on IT in developing countries is low and is likely to continue to be so in the coming years compared to the developed countries, especially the US (Parikh 2000). Table clearly 15.2 shows this.

Table 15.2: Spending on IT and PC Penetration, 2000

Country	*IT spending as % of GDP*	*Per capita IT spend ($)*	*P C penetration per 1000 people*	*Per capita GDP ($)*
China	1.1	7.9	13.2	793
India	0.8	3.6	6.2	461
Indonesia	1.0	6.8	11.2	681
Malaysia	1.3	42.7	69.4	3,286
Philippines	0.6	5.9	19.1	981
Thailand	0.5	10.0	22.0	2,008
US	4.3	1,372.3	500.00	31,915

Source: Business World, 21 May 2001, p. 38.

Access, not Ownership

However, notwithstanding, the present limitation of IT penetration and PC penetration pattern in developing countries like India, access to and benefits of IT are possible to a much wider population through innovative use of limited facilities (Bajaj 2001). India has developed a niche for itself in the area of computer software development and providing services. In the free-trading globalised world, the gains would accrue to those who can use IT, besides improving efficiency, to generate new ideas, products and services.

While IT induced improvement cuts labour demand in traditional skills, it opens new possibilities as well. Indian computer programmers are in great demand the world over. Customer support services and medical transcriptions services have opened new opportunities for English educated young men and women in India. Thus, a secretary in Chennai works for a doctor in USA or Canada. It is true of customer support services. A customer in the US, Canada or UK or for that matter anywhere in the world dials a toll free 1-800 number and the call is attended at the customer support service centre based in Bangalore. But the gains of IT revolution should not remain confined to the developed Western countries or the urban educated elites of the developing countries. These should reach the poor as well. Some innovative strategy to IT access and use is to be thought of and put in place urgently. The hope of benefits trickling down to the poor in villages will take decades and it may never even happen.

Like other technologies, IT may remain the monopoly of few urban elites until it is actively developed to serve the needs of the wider population. Then, the economy of scale sets in. At one time radio, telephone, and television were status symbols even in urban India. However, things changed rapidly with the availability of transistor sets, public call offices (PCOs) and cable television in respective cases. Taking a cue from CNN broadcasting the Gulf War live on television in five star hotels in Delhi, entrepreneurs jumped at the technological possibility of satellite cable television in India. They wired their neighbourhood and started showing video films and some satellite TV channels through dish antennae to 200 to 300 households, setting in motion the entry of foreign and Indian private television in the country. It provided a spurt to private television production and a host of other related media activities. Today, about 30 thousand cable operators, each with 200 to 500 household clientele reach out to nearly 35 million people, though mostly in big cities and small towns (Yadav 2001).

Liberalisation and Reforms

After achieving Independence in 1947, India opted for planned development with mixed economy and strong reliance on socialist philosophy. It did make noticeable progress in many fields like food production, space research and infrastructure development through massive steel plants and other public sector undertakings. There was a strong license and control regime. Market was controlled and subsidies were provided in many areas for the benefit of the poor and the deprived sections of the society.

Restrictions on the operation of multinationals and tight regulation of the indigenous private sector were the order of the day. The public sector occupied the commanding heights of the economy. During Prime Minister Indira Gandhi's heyday in the 1960s and '70s, income taxes were very high on the extremely affluent, with the top marginal rate reaching as high as 97.5 per cent (though less than 2 per cent of the population actually pay the taxes). Politicians rhetorically attacked the dominant economic classes, such as the landlords and industrialists (while privately seeking access to their funds and influence). Tariffs on imported goods were among the highest in the world. Travel abroad was effectively curtailed due to severe restrictions on foreign exchange. Television in the country was restricted to a single state-run and a Central government monopoly.

When Rajiv Gandhi changed the course in mid-1980s, liberalised import of some of the consumable items and emphasised his vision of modern India with computers and other technologies, India did experience a foreign-exchange crisis. The country's foreign exchange reserves started depleting in the late '80s, mainly to hard currency payments for a flood of imports and an increasing amount of foreign debt. There was crisis in 1991, when the country only had enough foreign exchange left to pay for a few weeks of imports. The government sought the help of World Bank and International Monetary Fund.

Consequently, India opened up the economy and deregulated the private sector. Under Prime Minister P.V. Narasimha Rao and Finance Minister Manmohan Singh, who assumed office that year, restrictions on the multinationals and the private sector were greatly relaxed. The governing alliance, NDA, headed by the Bharatiya Janata Party's Atal Bihari Vajpayee, continued the same policies. The public sector was steadily, albeit slowly, dismantled. The current UPA alliance, headed by the Congress Party under Manmohan Singh, continues to follow the liberalisation and reforms policies.

Under liberalisation and globalisation, sectoral government reforms are being strongly advocated by the World Bank, IMF and other multilateral and bilateral development agencies for adoption by the third world countries. Privatisation and dismantling of the public sector, withdrawal or cutting down the subsidies, less and less of government control on production and services, and giving greater opportunity for operation of market forces are some of the key manifestations of the new paradigms of emerging globalisation (Jenkins 1999).

The agenda of 'Good/New Governance Reform' is being vigorously pursued by all the development aid agencies. A strong case is made out that governance reforms leads to national development and growth and greater satisfaction of common citizens. The guiding thoughts are that private corporate business management practices are more efficient and need to be introduced into public sectors to improve their performance. In place of traditional public administration approach based on hierarchy and controls, the more democratic management approach is recommended. In contrast, the new governance approach shifts the focus from administrative skills and controls of large bureaucratic organisations to empowerment and enabling of all the stakeholders in development processes (Bedi et al. 2001).

Consequent to adoption of liberalisation and reform policies, India witnessed a sea change in many areas of its economy, especially relating to consumer goods and services. Take the case of telephone. Before privatisation, one had to wait for years for a telephone connection and needed the recommendations from a MLA/MP. Now, telephone companies are running after the customers. Same is true of LPG gas connection, cars, credit cards, bank loans and many other sectors. The markets are full of foreign goods and almost all the best-known brands of consumer goods are available freely in Indian stores even in the remote countryside. Life style of the people has undergone major metamorphosis. India is shinning for at least the upper and middle class urban India.

In the field of mass communication, major changes have taken place since the adoption of the new liberalisation and reform policies. The founding fathers of the Indian constitution thought it fit to lay broad norms for mass media operations. Though freedom of expression was provided as a basic right to all citizens, it made broadcasting a Central government monopoly. Press was made free under Section 19a of the constitution with minimal restriction of liable etc. under Section 19b. Still there were restrictions on access to services of foreign news agencies, which are still in operation. Restrictions on foreign newspaper and magazine publications in India and FDIs in print media continue to be operative, not withstanding the persistent demand to abolish these from some quarters. There were restrictions on screening of foreign films as well that have gone now.

In the age of World Wide Web that has been made possible by technological developments over which no controls are possible, any restriction on news and media flows do not make much sense in any case today. As such, mass media, including newspapers have easy access to photographs, video clips and the text materials from anywhere in the world. Consequently, the print media has changed its character and now what has come to be known in popular parlance as the third page journalism has become an integral part of newspapers and magazines including language press which is read in small towns and villages of remote parts of India. As such, with increasing penetration of TV and language press with increased literacy, the images of the world reaches the huts of rustic poor farmers and labourers, ordinary people, just as to the sophisticated urban elites. All these developments have far reaching consequences for the lifestyle and culture of the people all over the country.

Press in India

The press in India came with the colonial rulers. Its history and growth coincided with early reformation and liberation struggles of modern times. The press was at once the product and a stimulant of processes of national regeneration, which led to freedom from colonial rule. Journalists functioned more as missionaries and social reformers than mere professionals.

In post-independence era, with the passage of time, the press increasingly became more professional along the lines of Western models of Free Press. A time came when a journalist would have felt insulted if he were asked whether he had an 'attitude' to news and had 'values' which guided him in his attitudes. In those simple days 'facts' were 'facts' and when reported became news if they were of sufficient interest to a sufficient number of people.

Along with the question of 'objectivity' in news reporting, Western doctrine of Free Press advocated free flow of information and right to information as fundamental human right. On a conceptual level, these tenets were very attractive. But in practice, it became increasingly clear that the freedom of press actually meant freedom of the powerful, those who control the press through advertisements or otherwise and free flow of information means one way flow from the Western developed world to the developing Third World.

As a consequence, the conflict between Western libertarian view of press and the social responsibility of press became sharper. Not only that, the demand for restructuring of the existing pattern of news flow and information order gained momentum under the influence of the non-aligned movement. The Western concepts and models need thorough scrutiny and if necessary adoption/modification to suit the demands of local conditions. News and communication are not culture free; they make sense only in a specific cultural context.

The press in developing countries like India in addition to all its problems of finance, equipment, paper, staff and the like faces a peculiar policy dilemma. On the one hand, the press is expected to serve as a watchdog of government and on the other, it is expected to carry, interpret, even propagate the government policies and development programmes to the people because the future of the nation rests on the success of these plans. The response to the policy dilemma varies from newspaper to newspaper but upon this response depends to a substantial degree, the nature and contents of coverage in the newspapers.

It is true that the press was at once the product and a stimulant of processes of national regeneration, which led to their freedom from colonial rule. With the advent of independence, the former leaders of freedom struggle became the new rulers of their countries. For the press, it marked a sea change in its role. The nationalist press during freedom movement had served more as 'views-papers' and looked at the leaders with some kind of adulation, fully supporting and propagating their views, programmes and actions.

The 'honeymoon' period between rulers and the press lasted for varying periods. In India, it was rather a long 'honeymoon'. This was natural in a way because the leaders, many of whom were journalists in their own right, and as journalists shared common values and experiences of working in close association as partners in freedom struggle. For newspapers the challenge was two fold: from adversary to the alien rulers to take on the role of constructive critic of the national government, and to remain vigilant against pressures to curb freedom of press. But sooner than later relations estranged between rulers and journalists, the latter taking the role of more of an adversary.

With the passage of time in post-independent era, especially since liberalisation and globalisation processes were set in motion through revolutionary developments in communication technologies and accompanying policy shifts in 1990s', the press instead of remaining stimulant of education and social awakening increasingly became merely a source of news about political events and politicians, a vehicle of consumerism and a guardian of commercial interests. No doubt however there, has been notable progress towards modernisation of printing technologies and professionalism of the press in terms of skills, techniques and production facilities (Jeffrey 2003).

As a result, the professional dilemma listed earlier in terms of the social responsibility seems to have been relegated to the background and now, mostly treated as irrelevant. The proprietors consider newspapers as nothing more than a commodity to be marked and sold just like any other product say soap cake (Yadav and Mathur 1998). The trend initiated by the Times of India has been followed by others as well in order to survive in the prevailing market competition. The importance of editors and editorial staff has been downsized while that of the advertising managers and the commercial staff upgraded. Consequently, what matters in newspapers is how much revenue you can raise and not how well you write news. Commercial interests seem to dominate the press most to the extent of relegating social and educational functions of the press in the background, if not totally ignoring them.

Three cardinal objèctives of newspapers as envisaged by Mahatma Gandhi do not seem to guide the functioning and operation of press in most Asian countries including India. It is time to reflect upon the press from the standpoint of these objectives if it is to serve as stimulant to social awakening in Third World societies. According to Gandhiji, the newspapers have three main objectives: (*a*) to understand the popular feelings and give them expression, (*b*) to arouse among the people certain desirable sentiments and (*c*) to fearlessly expose defects in public life. Gandhiji was a great journalist and his weeklies were probably the greatest the world has known. Let us critically examine the press today against these yardsticks and suggest ways and means for development of a more socially functional press in the context of the Third World societies (Yadav 1984).

Salience to Politics

Press in India has always been an important vehicle of political discourse. The political coverage has been the mainstay of news coverage and writings. But along with the coverage of political developments the press served as an instrument of social awakening as well. Before independence, the press was a weapon in the hands of freedom fighters like Mahatma Gandhi, Jawaharlal Nehru and many others to fight the colonial rulers and an instrument of social reforms and public mobilisation in the hands of social reformers like Raja Ram Mohan Roy, and others.

During the post-independent era, the press increasingly took upon itself the role of an adversary to the government, performing the function of a watchdog rather well and at times taking upon itself the role of opposition (political party). It gives salience to politics and is more concerned with political developments, events and personalities, than economic, social and cultural issues. Scanning of any daily would testify such an observation. Some systematic studies have also confirmed this notion. Coverage of socio-economic and development issues are not usually more than 5–10 per cent of the total news space. So much so that today, in India instead of the press following politics, politics follows the press. During the last couple of years in India, the proceedings in Parliament have been dominated by what was published in the press just before the beginning of the Parliament session.

Be that as it may, the coverage of political events and developments seem to have significantly contributed to the political education of newspaper readers and others too indirectly. Newspaper coverage in no small way influences the fortunes of the main actors in the political scene. It seems to facilitate voters to make 'informed choices' at the time of elections.

The press in India is basically and avowedly a political institution. It plays an active part in the political processes. As a consequence, all those associated with the newspapers, among other considerations like money, are often motivated by the influence they can command in the society. Many youngsters who join journalism as a profession make no bones about it and frankly admit that the main attraction to the profession is the power and influence it bestows on the practitioners of this profession and not necessarily money. Same may be the reasons for many businessmen, politicians and others venturing into starting their own newspapers or magazines.

Exposing the failures of the government and those in public life is age-old and a well recognised function of the press. It is true of the Indian press as well. However, the exposures of Bhagalpur blinding case by *Sunday,* an English weekly in 1979, brought in a new phase in Indian journalism. Some public-spirited lawyers took upon the case with Supreme Court giving a new turn to the watchdog function of the press. Since then, investigative journalism in India has covered many milestones and in the process many misdeeds of individuals and the governments have been brought to light.

Investigative journalism has been inspiring many journalists all over the world. But since there is a close association between the persons and the parties in office or those seeking power and the press, investigative journalism at times may lead to misdemeanor. The protection provided by the journalistic code not to reveal the source, is also at times misused by some journalists for fame or favour as it happened in the infamous case of 'Little Jim', the story of drugging of a small child by her baby sitter reported in Washington Post by a young lady reporter. At times, in the name of investigation, some journalists, tend to exaggerate facts and figures trying to authenticate their story and cross the limits of decency by poking their nose into other's personal lives. In many investigative stories, 'according to highly placed sources not to be identified' are found in galore in the news items.

Though most of it may be true, in some cases the reporters fall into the temptation of expressing their own opinion into quotes under the cover of 'unidentified sources' or 'according to highly placed sources'. Even few such cases might give the individual reporter instant fame but may ultimately damage the newspapers' credibility on which stands the effectiveness of the role newspaper performs in society.

But at times if the purpose of an investigative reporting is not to get to the truth but to get to a person, then it is bad journalism, a temptation to which some journalists seem to have fallen. Currently Lalu Prasad Yadav, RJD leader and Railway Minister, has been the favourite whipping boy of the media for the last 15 years and the media persons never stop to think and find out as to what clicks in favour of Lalu that he continues to win elections.

With the increasing fragmentation of Indian polity along religious, caste and regional lines, the press has not remained untouched. Some political parties and their leaders assiduously court and win over the journalists for favourable coverage in the media and in the process do not mind extending suitable favour to journalists which they readily accept. As a result, many journalists have become partisans covertly or not so covertly and their peer groups know about it, though not the common readers, thereby damaging the cause of true journalism. Such journalists become promoters and campaigners of cause or the political leader/party as such. The resultant biased coverage of news and news events become a major distortion in political discourse and hampers the common citizen from making 'informed decision'. The partisan reporting was more marked in the context of emotional issues like L. K. Advani's *Rath Yatra*, demolition of Babri masjid and Post Godhra communal riots in Gujarat.

This trend of campaign journalism for partisan and sectarian interests, and not for any higher national goal, purpose or values as was the case during national freedom days, is contributory to loss of credibility of the press and media to some extent. Concomitant to this is the general loss of interest in politics and public issues/concerns. Politics has become a dirty word.

Sensationalisation of political development has taken over. There is hardly any serious political discourse or debate. Instead, third page journalism has emerged in a big way and the reader's interest has shifted to light readings, reportage of parties, meetings of celebrities, write-ups about food, fashion, fun and travel or just turning of pages for glamorous pictures of foreign and Indian models and stars. The newspapers have taken over magazines' functions as well coloured and well illustrated by photographs and pictures. Special newspaper supplements daily, often more than one, are common these days.

It is the concern for the truth and the larger purposes of national development and moral well-being of the people that marks out a great newspaper from ordinary ones. Too much focus upon negative happenings in society creates despair among the readers. I for one, would like all events—good, bad and others—to be reported. The press instead of building hysteria for despair should aim at giving the readers a balanced picture of the environment in which they live. I would say that the 'journalism of despair' should be balanced with 'journalism of hope'.

Development Journalism

Along with the dominant stream of journalism obsessed with politics and concerned with urban issues and developments, there have been some other stains in Indian journalism as well. *The Hindustan Times* can claim some credit for starting developmental reporting. In 1950s, it undertook extensive reporting about the functioning and the problems of various public sector projects in India.

In the 1970s, village Chhatera became a familiar column in the *Hindustan Times*. For months the problems faced and perceived by the residents of this village were reported. In the process, a team of correspondents associated with this column articulated the popular feelings of rural India. The columns informed and motivated various functionaries to undertake development activities and solve the problems faced by the villagers. It was a unique experiment of a daily newspaper playing the role of catalyst in the process of rural development.

This inspired and prompted some others to take up development reporting seriously. Bharat Dogra has been doing this for years. There are others in the field. Many issues of development nature have been taken up. The campaign by newsmen against the Silent Valley project on the grounds of danger to the environment built up strong public opinion, of course, in close association with environment activists, so much so, that the project had to be abandoned.

The other function of the press of understanding problems of common concern and giving them expression is in some ways similar to development reporting. But it is a different cup of tea as well. It has two dimensions. One is to investigate and extensively report on a problem of a particular region or community. In other words, in-depth reporting on social problems. Some examples of such reporting are the disabilities caused by eating Kesari dal in Chhatisgarh area of Madhya Pradesh and drinking fluoride-rich water in certain districts of Rajasthan. The purpose is to arouse public conscience. In this area, weeklies have done better than dailies.

The second dimension of this strain of journalism is to understand popular feelings and give them expression. In addition to the usual journalistic techniques and methods, there has been a growing interest in using more systematic and scientific methods to gauge precisely public feelings on specific issues. *India Today* is the pioneer in using the services of public opinion experts and commissioning surveys to scientifically understand public feelings and opinion as a part of their reporting.

Press, Politics and Governance

Modern democratic politics requires endorsement and approval at regular intervals by people. To start with, it was in the form of open discussions; all concerned people coming to a convenient place, a kind of platform for political discourse, and airing their views. Today in the age of mass media, politics is largely mediated, experienced by most citizens through broadcast and print media of their choice. The media reports and interprets political events and issues, and in the process influences the political processes and shapes public opinion. As a result, it has become central to politics and public life in contemporary democratic India.

Over the years the regional and language press in India has grown many folds and its reach and impact in shaping public opinion is significant. For example, since 1990's the circulation of newspapers in Hindi has more than trebled from under eight million copies a day to more than 25 million. And Hindi language press is not the largest circulating daily newspaper; other regional language newspapers like that in Malayalam, Bengali, Telugu and Tamil have much wider circulation and readership even in rural hinterland.

In a highly hierarchical and unequal society in India, access to media, one of the key measures of power and equality, is not uniform. Its reach is limited in rural and remote areas and among poorer sections and among women. Even so, it plays an important role in shaping public opinion on various issues. Media can shape power and participation in society in negative ways, by obscuring the motives and interests behind political decisions, or in positive ways, by promoting the involvement of people in those decisions. In this respect, the media and governance equation becomes important.

In a vibrant democracy nurtured through freedom struggle and ensured through universal franchise, media occupies a space that is constantly contested by different political parties and interest groups. The changing contours of technology, commercial considerations, professional practices and reader's interest have affected patterns of agenda setting and political discourse in recent times. This in turn affects the public opinion on various issues of governance in the country.

In a democratic society, therefore, the role of the media assumes seminal importance. Democracy implies participative governance, and it is the media that informs people about various problems of society, which makes those wielding power on their behalf answerable to them. That the actions of the government and the state, and the efforts of competing parties and interests to exercise political power should be underpinned and legitimised by critical scrutiny and informed debate in press and other media.

Ascendancy of 'infotainment' over 'serious' reportage and analysis of politics is a matter of concern for some, while others see it as a welcome development in the profession. It is also often remarked that the quality of 'serious' political journalism is steadily declining, with a dilution in its substantive political content to the detriment of the democratic process. An opposite view asserts that there is not too little serious politics in the media, but too much. This is seen as a kind of information overload that bores audiences and diminishes public interest. The variety of content available today in print media is the result of available communication technologies and the prevailing dominant philosophy winds favouring liberalisation and globalisation. Quantitatively and qualitatively, the information being circulated has greatly increased manifold. You cannot dismiss some of these developments by simply stating them to be 'trash'. New content formats are becoming popular by the day. Popular does not imply irrational. Entertainment can be informative, just as serious news can also be of great human interest.

In brief, the relationship between media and governance is fraught with tensions and mean-ingful possibilities. Excessive assertions of both religious and other primordial identities and homogenising tendencies resulting from globalisation are a threat to the pluralistic and democratic fabric of Indian society. In this context, it is imperative that both polity and media become more sensitive on issues of democratic governance, people's struggles against social injustice and inequality, and rising aspirations of the common people for better life. Strong and steadfast commitment to democratic norms and values in governance is a must.

With the rapid inroads of globalisation processes, the role of multinationals and big corporate houses and bourgeois monopoly over print media has increased enormously and scope for a say/role of small players and the vast majority of the poor in media has been further marginalised.

In the circumstances, the role of people's organisations, social movements, and the civil society in monitoring the functioning of media and making it more people-centered becomes a critical issue. The role of civil society organisations becomes important since in the wake of globalisation media organisations of journalists and workers, have not only become weak but they also severely lack in their ability to raise critical issues pertaining to media governance and its functioning.

Notwithstanding increased commercialisation and decline in professional standards in terms of objectivity, fairness and balance, the media, particularly the print media, has managed to create conditions for a liberal democracy. Broadly, the history of press in India has been as a major liberating force.

CULTURAL DIMENSIONS

In a way globalisation is not new to India. People of many races, religion and culture have come to India for centuries as invaders or traders and settled here making their imprints and contributing to the rich tapestry of pluralistic Indian culture.

However, the pace of cultural flows has increased manifold with the advancement in communication technology and opening up of India with greater say to market forces, liberalisation and reforms. We have already discussed at some length as to how media in general and print media in particular have undergone transformation. These changes have significant bearings upon cultural patterns and the way of life of the common people.

McDonald, Pepsi and Coke, the symbols of globalisation, are now visible even in the remote villages in India. The values and worldview of people are undergoing transformation under the influence of globalisation forces and processes. Attitudes towards sex and sex partners are fast changing. Marital discord and divorce are increasing. Separated women or widows are no more looked down upon as they were in the past. Intra-village and intra-*Gotra* marriages unthinkable under the traditional cultural norms have been reported in recent months. People are fast adopting the latest trends in fashion and living styles. In brief, globalisation and modernisation have affected the way people live and think to which, the newspaper contents, especially of the third page and special supplements contribute in no small way.

For centuries, being round and chubby in India was a happy thing, a sign of affluence and health in an otherwise undernourished country. But today, the country's wealthiest and most prominent young people are trimming down, working out at health clubs and watching what they eat. 'Nothing is too skinny,' said Ranna Gill, a real-thin, 28-year-old fashion designer. 'We all have personal trainers. We all work out. My parents think it's mad.'

The shifting notion of beauty is just one of several cultural traits evolving in India today, a response, in part, to the arrival of satellite television, foreign magazines and Western-style advertisements. Jeans both for boys and girls in colleges and work places have become a common sight in urban India. There are increasing evidence of the imprints of Western influences in Indian society (Fuller 2004).

But it must be noted that the increasing cultural influences from the West as a part of globalisation processes have also given impetus to many for cultural revivalism as well. They are using the same communication technologies to promote traditional values and culture. Not only that many a times Western cultural traits are adapted, modified and then adopted. McDonald's burgers have been adapted to suite local taste and keep in line with religious sensitivities.

Page-3 Journalism

Having discussed the revolutionary developments in communication technologies leading to or more appropriately forcing globalisation and reforms in different aspects of economy and governance and tracking trends in press reporting, coverage of political developments and events, now we focus our attention on the emergence of what has come to be known as Page-3 Journalism, which is reflective of changing culture, world view and ideology. There is a notable shift in the way we look at the newspapers. Besides being a source of news of the day, newspaper is viewed, especially by its owners, as a commodity to be sold in the market place and as a vehicle of promoting consumerism. As such, the newspapers have become as a source of 'infotainment' to be packaged and marketed competitively. In this, developments in communication technologies, globalisation and liberalisation have come handy. As sex and violence sell well across all cultures, downloading and using liberally images from abroad became easy and routine practice to start with *The Times of India* followed by other English as well as regional language papers. Images of thinly clad foreign women, socialites, fashion shows, films, celebrities and social parties emphasising glamour and affluence giving boost to consumerism constitute the staple menu of the Page-3 Journalism and newspaper supplements having far reaching implication for indigenous culture and ideology. Access to such titillating and sensuous images in the context of traditional rural and tribal society and semi-literate population with possible multiple exposure are likely to have destabilising and disturbing influence, especially among the young/minor children.

As such, a fierce debate is on regarding the desirability of the emergence of page-3 journalism in India. There are many who strongly condemn this new trend in journalism. They see it as a threat to Indian values and culture. The proponent of this variety of journalism argue that any restriction on content is not only against the freedom of expression but not possible and desirable in the age of World Wide Web. A Public Interest Litigation (PIL) has been filed in the Supreme Court of India against the pages-3 journalism praying that the allegedly titillating material—obscene photographs, articles on pornography, SMS jokes and sex education are detrimental to the 'healthy' growth of the young/minors and should be marked as such to restrict their access to children (*The Hindu*, 19 August 2005). The Supreme Court has directed the Government of India, Press Council of India, Press trust of India, United News of India and some leading national newspapers to respond to the PIL. This is clearly reflective of the serious concern among many sections of the Indian society about the contents of the page-3 journalism.

One area where changes in cultural contours are most significantly manifested is the way media portrays women. The interface between women and media has long been a focus of public debate but a subject of only a small number of systematic research studies. The women and media interface can be viewed from three different perspectives. These are:

- Women as consumers of media
- Coverage and portrayal of women in media
- Representation of women in media.

Women as Consumers of Media

As discussed earlier, with the revolutionary developments in communication and information technologies combined with globalisation, liberalisation and privatisation, there has been rapid expansion of mass media in the recent years, especially the television, across the country.

There is a strong association between literacy, poverty and gender as far as the access and exposure to media are concerned. More women are comparatively illiterate or less educated and poor, hence less exposed to any media. But notwithstanding the rapid expansion of mass media, the actual reach and access to media are limited by six mutually reinforcing factors. These are:

- Low literacy
- Poor purchasing power
- Poor means of transportation and communication
- Irregular electricity supply
- Not very relevant contents from the perspective of rural and tribal population
- Cultural taboos and norms.

The women are particularly constrained in having access to television due to conservative fundamentalist religious considerations among certain communities. Even among others, strong patriarchal social system restricts access of television to women. It is the male world; they decide as to when and what television programmes are to be watched. Even if she has brought a television set in her dowry, the television is usually in the hands of the male members of the family. Otherwise also, she might be left with little leisure time to watch television amidst her busy working chores from early morning till late in the night.

Thus the picture of women as consumers of media vary from being extensive and equal if not better than men in urban upper and middle class families to almost negligible and access denial amongst rural poor and conservative families.

Coverage and Portrayal of Women

The media not only reflects upon the society but also moulds it. In a democratic society the media is a 'public sphere' for debate and discussions about various public issues. It would not be wrong to say that the media constitutes the eyes and ears of society. We see and perceive the world around us through the eyes of the media. We live in a mediated world. The pace and extent to which we live and perceive this mediated society is ever expanding. The choices are increasing and becoming global.

As such, expectation from media include, reporting development likely to impinge on the well-being of citizens, identifying key issues of the day and setting the political agenda, acting as spokesperson of various perspectives and interest groups, facilitating a dialogue between rulers and the public and across a diverse range of views. Further, the expectations from media include that it should not only be financially viable but also a profit-making proposition.

Common experience as well as well-documented researches indicate that sex and violence 'sell' better across all sections of societies and cultures. As such, the media including the newspapers are under enormous pressure, at times of conflicting pulls, and hence became even the butt of public criticism. In these circumstance how should the media handle women's issues? How should it portray women? Here again, opinions, often conflicting, abound, but these are only limited research findings and that too, are inconclusive. However, we can discuss these questions under three major headings:

- News and views
- Entertainment
- Advertising

News and Views

The news space or time to women and women's issues is generally negligible in the so-called mainstream news media. Our newspapers and magazines are full of politics. Some content analysis indicates that the development stories constitute just 2 per cent of the news space and women's issues less than 1 per cent. In an analysis of Doordarshan news bulletins, it was revealed that of 760 minutes news in 38 bulletins only 20 minutes were devoted to news about women.

In terms of display, women related items, if at all covered, are tucked in the pages inside or towards the end of the news bulletin and not given prominent display, are rarely put on front page or as a lead story.

If we take twelve major priority areas of concern identified in the Beijing Declaration and Platform for Action, whatever little attention is paid in news and views columns is mostly in relation to violence against women or women in armed conflict. Dowry deaths, harassment, rapes and victims of war find space in news media. But most often, the reportage leaves much to be desired from the perspective of women.

The rape stories are often made sensational, at times pointing the needle of suspicion to the victim herself as if she invited the trouble. So is the case of many dowry deaths, which are often made out to be caused by their own neglect and sloppiness in the kitchen. The women are shown as war victims, helpless refugees and queueing for relief, as was the case in Afghan war. Rarely the story of their valiant struggle is brought to light. Of all the stories portraying women in Afghan war, there was only one exception which was Ajay Shukhla's story on Star News, which showed how certain women, carried on with the school education of girls, defying the Taliban's ban.

Furthermore, women are rarely newsmakers in news media. This to some extent is reflective of the power structure of the society wherein relatively a miniscule number of women occupy positions of power and decision-making. But, more importantly, the stereotype image of women as soft and helpless deny the chances of being picked up as newsmakers even though they may be newsworthy in their own rights.

Finally, women's issues are rarely taken up as topics worthy of editorial comments and discussions.

Entertainment

Coming to the 'entertainment' space in the press and the electronic media, particularly the television, the women occupy a prominent place. The newspapers now-a-days, usually have special supplements, and even more than one supplement almost everyday. The women features abound; different women's issues do find sufficient coverage, though the issues are generally of concern or interest primarily to the elite and upper middle class women. The 'common' women rarely find a place in these supplements. It is true of television serials. Some old fashioned pressman may question the relevance and utility of these supplements, altogether but the new generation is quite hooked to this relatively new concept. They cannot think of newspapers these days without the supplements. According to them, these are an integral part of the daily newspapers. Some might even question the increasing trend of commodification of women in newspaper supplements just the way in many advertisements. But most young boys and girls in my Advertising and Public Relation class did not find these supplements and women's portrayal therein any particularly objectionable or negative. Rather, they find these interesting and informative readings.

As far as the current television serials are concerned, most of these revolve around women, their concerns, their struggle and turbulence in the family arena. Some find women portrayal somewhat unreal, submissive and irrational as compared to male characters as rational and positive, while many others are of the view that these reflect the reality in today's homes. The issues, which were swept under the carpet, are now being discussed through the media. In the process what was happening 'privately' becomes 'public' and hence, the limits of acceptable social norms get extended and expanded.

Advertising

Many prominent citizens and experts have expressed concern over excessive, unnecessary and undesirable portrayal of women in the media in general, and advertising in particular. Many voices have been raised against using women as a commodity to promote their product and business interest. The vulgar display of women is not only demeaning in itself but also contributory to the moral decay and degeneration with far reaching implications for the social and cultural fabric of our society.

Yet women form an integral part of the advertising world. They are extensively 'used' or 'portrayed' to advertise goods and services. In some cases, it may be excessive and unnecessary as well.

But the important question is, what image of women gets conveyed through their portrayal in advertising? The review of literature and research findings reveal predominantly traditional stereotype picture of women as a wife, homemaker, kitchen-fixer, and a caring mother. She is also often featured as a decorative sex object in selling various products and services, often submissive, emotional, and irrational, less intelligent and even dumb/stupid. But of late, thanks to protests by various activist groups and individuals, and debates in various academic and public forums, including the Parliament, there are perceptible changes for the better. The women in advertisements these days are more often shown as confident, intelligent, firm, decisive and a decision-maker.

Participation and Representation

Women's participation in the media has improved over the years and is not that bleak now in comparison to the 1960s and 70s. However, according to the Press Council report, it is still low, just about 8 per cent. This also is mainly in English media and in big metro cities. You hardly come across women reporters and sub-editors in Hindi and other language newspapers and media organisations. This is reflective of the continuing conservative outlook of the owners and proprietors of language press and atmosphere of smaller cities and towns. But the visibility of women journalists particularly in electronic media television news has increased manifold and some of them have acquired high profile as well. They are serving as a role model for many young aspirants. As such, there is a phenomenal spurt in journalism/mass communication training and education programmes in institutions and universities across the country. Girls are joining these courses in fairly large numbers. Many a times, the number of girl students is more than that of boys. This slowly but steadily is increasing the number of women entering media organisations at the professional level every year.

Although, women joining the media organisations at a professional level has increased they often continue to suffer old prejudices in a male dominated world. They are often assigned soft stories and desk jobs not withstanding the fact that some women journalists have done better than men in covering the so-called hard news stories. As such, the traditional way of viewing women in media organisations prevents the full potentials of the few working women from coming to the fore and making their due contribution to media and society.

As such, many factors impinge upon the issue of women and media. Of these, the traditional views and practices emanating from patriarchal ideology and system is most crucial. But with the coming of the liberal philosophy, democracy, free media, education and increased economic opportunities and independence, the age-old traditional views and practices are being threatened.

New equilibrium with constantly expanding limits of acceptable behaviour in favour of women is the emerging reality. It is a complex process. Mere economic well-being is not enough as was demonstrated by the decline in sex ratio, 'missing girls' in the latest census figures from Punjab and Haryana, the two most economically prosperous states in the country. Literacy and poverty are linked and in turn are associated with low status of women. Education and greater economic opportunities are necessary steps but not necessarily sufficient conditions to improve their status and participation similar to that of men in society. It is the worldview and perception that make a significant difference. And here, the media plays a vital role.

In a democracy, the media, particularly the electronic media, has occupied centre stage as a 'public sphere' for airing divergent and contesting views and perspectives. In this process media not merely reflects upon society but shapes and moulds it as well. Some media scholars have referred to the television as the 'third parent', perhaps because particularly the television, serves as a major influence upon our lives, especially that of children.

Consequent to portrayal, discussions and debates about women's issues in the media, women emerge more self-assured and confident than ever before. They also are better groomed today. They are acquiring new skills and capabilities to take up any challenge and tasks. They are visible and are heard. Their issues and problems are being addressed if not yet solved to the full satisfaction. Of course, the winds of change are more perceptible in metropolitan cities and towns, but the villages also no more remain untouched. The process of these changes is accelerating and the country is fast moving towards a stage when women instead of rocking the cradle would rock the system, and for the better. This will be feasible only when the public policy pronouncements about female literacy and empowerment are actualised in the context of rural India.

The single most effective way to address gender issue in India would be to enable girls and women to change from being passive recipients of social equity to becoming active agents of change. In this, media, especially the television has played and continues to play significant role. However, a more appropriate strategy is called for urgently to harness the full potentials of media, especially in the context of rural India. It should promote: a) girl literacy, b) create awareness among women and, c) impart skills to the elected women representatives of panchayats and local bodies about their roles and responsibilities so that women can be the agents of change. In this, local language newspapers and magazines can play an important role.

Socio-cultural Impact

The socio-cultural impact of ICT revolution, globalisation and liberalisation on Indian society is enormous. The developments in Information and Communication technologies made globalisation possible and liberalisation a necessity. Multinational companies (MNCs) pushed ICTs globally, including in the developing third world countries leading to the opening of their economy and reforming governance. The elites in the developing countries were equally eager to acquire the latest and the best of technologies to be at par with their counterparts in the developed countries. As such, both 'push' and 'pull' factors were responsible for the rapid spread of ICTs globally. Although profit motive was the driving force behind pushing of ICTs by the MNCs, they packaged these as the saviour and necessity of the developing countries in their search for development and growth. There is no doubt that many benefits and empowering effects have taken place as a result of ICTs, but not uniformly and equitably.

There is an enormous increase in connectivity for social, commercial and entertainment purposes. Today, thanks to telecommunication revolution in India, ordinary citizens have easy access to telephone services. The mobile phone has now become a common sight in towns, cities and even in villages, while earlier, a telephone used to be the status symbol of the rich and the powerful. We often come across a roadside shoe mender or a mechanic talking on mobile phone. A house wife or old parents from remote villages routinely talk with their husband or children working far away in cities/towns anywhere in the country or the world. What a change! Similarly, ordinary citizens routinely use landine phones or cell phones for their daily commercial activities, facilitating and giving boost to their profitability.

With the rapid spread and deeper penetration of other communication facilities like television, radio, magazines and daily newspapers, voices and images from across the nation and the globe are now routinely reaching the people not only in cities and towns but even in remote villages in their homes and huts. Now images of thinly clad 'foreign' women and Indian socialites on television and in print routinely reach to people living in rural and tribal areas disturbing their traditional sensibilities and values and giving boost to consumerism. This at times leads to generational and societal conflicts as is evident from the frequently reported incidents of rape, elopement and murder.

There is no doubt that with the onset of globalisation and liberalisation, trends towards homogenisation of Indian society and culture are evident. India was known for her ethnic and cultural diversity. It was said that at every 15 km, dialect and culture changes in India. Homogenisation is rapidly taking place in many spheres of life. For instance, broadly there is common dressing pattern across regions, especially among the young. The dressing styles are influenced by Bollywood films, which may in turn be influenced by the trends in Western countries. Same is true of eating habits. Pepsi, Coke and McDonalds have become the in thing with the younger generation, at least in major cities. Homogenisation ripples, both of indigenous and of global nature are making in-roads in the countryside as well. However, India is endowed with great heritage and traditions and Indians are endowed with enormous creativity. Taking advantage of the opportunities that have become available with the advent of globalisation and liberalisation, many 'influences', products, practices and processes have been not only adopted but also adapted to suit Indian conditions and tastes leading to 'hybridisation' and 'glocalisation' phenomena.

Not only this, the same communication technologies and facilities have been used to check Western influences and promote traditional Indian values, culture and practices. Take the case of Swami Ramdev and his Yoga lessons on television. He is using modern communication technologies to propagate traditional Ayurveda and yogic exercises to 'cure' common diseases and live a healthy life. The tremendous response his camps are getting across the country is clearly indicative of his success to revive interest in Indian traditions and practices and restrict the penetration of western influences and products.

Another response to the fast moving ripple effects of globalisation and modernisation has been towards revival of past traditions. For instance, recently the Muslim clerics issued a *Fatwa* quoting *Koran* to make it mandatory for Muslim women to cover their faces and banned their participation in elections in the context of the Panchayat elections in Uttar Pradesh (*The Indian Express*,17 August 2005). On the other hand, Indian-born Muslim novelist Salman Rushdie wants Islam to be reformed to bring it into modern era as reported in the *Times of India* (12 August 2005). As such, homogenisation, hybridisation, glocalisation as well as revivalism processes and phenomena are simultaneously going on, differently effecting different sections and different aspects of Indian society and culture (Singh 2002).

Be that as it may, globalisation and liberalisation have once again revived the fears of hegemonisation and neo-imperialism of the Western developed countries over the third world developing countries. The fears are not completely unfounded. As in the colonial period, the flow of ideas, technologies, products and processes are largely one way, that is from the West to the East. There is near monopoly in ICT processes and products as well as in the dissemination of media contents globally. They are able to push with near impunity, titillating and sensuous images in collaboration with the elite Indian counterparts through Indian media, including the language press. Griffin (2004: 262) argues that globalisation has strong homogenising influences that would weaken and destroy existing cultures, move towards a world culture under US hegemony. 'The American way of life, or more likely a pale imitation of it, will become the world's way of life'. However, creative responses in the form of hybridisation and glocalisation on the one hand, and reassertion of ethnic identities and revivalism phenomena and processes on the other hand, so forcefully witnessed in Indian society-will help in blunting the threats of imperialism/neo-imperialism.

CONCLUSION

To sum up, globalisation is a complex process affecting various facets of human life and is immensely facilitated by revolutionary developments in communication technologies. Developments in information and communication technologies open vast opportunities to Western developed countries and multinational corporations to expand their markets globally as well as to empower those who were bypassed by industrial revolution.

The press has not remained unaffected by the communication revolution and forces unleashed by liberalisation and globalisation. It has been modernised through adoption of latest printing colour technologies and faster dissemination of news globally. Page-3 journalism and special supplements have become common features of the newspapers today in India including the small regional language newspapers. Coverage of celebrities, fun, travel and food, that was earlier considered as soft stories is a regular feature of the print media today. Coloured photographs and features of film stars, models and glamorous people make newspapers lively.

The interest of readers, especially that of the younger generation, is shifting from politics to such light infotainment readings. This is giving fillip to consumerism and influencing the thinking and the way of life of the masses.

Even so, the politics continue to be the staple diet of the daily newspapers. The concept of freedom and objectivity are relative and derive meaning from the context in which these are practiced. The press in India faces a peculiar policy dilemma. The conflict between Western libertarian view of free and social responsibility of the press is becoming sharper. With this comes the question of whether we are to practice 'journalism of despair' exclusively or 'journalism of hope' as well, which covers both positive and negative events in our societies. In fact, press should cover all—good, bad and other—news worthy of coverage.

The press in ultimate analysis, along with exposing defects in public life should strive to understand the popular feelings and give them expression. More importantly as Gandhiji said, the press should strive to arouse among the people certain desirable sentiments. Thus, the press is evolving its own peculiar blend of Western model and Eastern concepts and requirements. The issue of 'development' and vision of future are important considerations, which provide peculiar flavor to the press in India.

Liberalisation in the 1990s paved the way for reforms in many sectors. It opened the path for ascendancy to market forces and liberal import of goods and services. McDonalds, Pepsi and coke have become symbols of the new era and are now available even in remote villages. Gone are the days when one had to wait for years for a telephone connection. Telephone and mobile phones companies are running after the customers. Same is true of cars and bank loans. Liberalisation and globalisation have brought in significant changes in the way we think and live today.

With enormous increase in penetration of television, computers, World Wide Web, newspapers and magazines, culturally alien and not so familiar images come in our homes affecting our thinking, attitudes and practices about a host of things and issues. Our lives are affected by the developments taking place in far off places. Our life style and worldview is undergoing transformation affecting our culture and traditions in numerous ways. Threats of cultural imperialism and homogenisation of culture are perceived and reassertion of national culture and local identities are also attempted using the same technologies and facilities thereby adapting and adopting globalisation to establish a new equilibrium.

While facing challenges of globalisation in a free market place through liberalisation and privatisation, the developing countries should not lose sight of their poor in urban and rural areas. It is possible now to reach the unreached and empower them with information and skills through innovative use of information technologies. This to happen, ownership is not the required precondition. Access to IT is the key. It can be done as demonstrated by cable operators, public call offices (PCOs) and now information centers. The innovative use of IT would help in meeting their basic needs of health, education, food and shelter, facilitating their economic and social well-being and in the process will enhance their productivity as such, contributing to the goal of national development and progress. This will also expand markets for all kinds of goods and services in the rural areas, thereby, further giving a boost to globalisation, free market and emergence of information society. This approach alone will lead to a win-win situation.

References

Bhagwati, Jagdish (2004). *In Defense of Globalisation.* New Delhi: Oxford University Press.

Bajaj, Sunil (2001). 'Rural India Abuzz with the Sounds of Mobile Phone', *The Economic Times,* 17 June.

Bedi, Kiran, Parminder Jeet Singh and Sandeep Srivastava (2001). *Government @ Net: New Governance Opportunities for India.* New Delhi: Sage Publications.

Fuller, Thomas (2004). 'Tuning Into Baywatch: Globalisation Brings New Cultural Traits to India In Sync With the West', *International Herald Tribune,* 16 July.

Griffin, Keith (2004). 'Globalisation and Culture', in S. Cullenberg and P.K. Pattanaik (eds), *Globalisation, Culture, and the Limits of Market.* New Delhi: Oxford University Press.

Huntington, S. P. (1997). *The Clash of Civilisations and Remaking of the World Order.* New Delhi: Penguin Books India (P) Ltd.

Jeffrey, Robin (2003). *India's Newspaper Revolution: Capitalism, Politics and the Indian Language Press.* New Delhi: Oxford University Press.

Jenkins, Robert (1999). *Democratic Politics and Economic Reform in India.* Cambridge: Cambridge University Press.

Jishnu, Latha, M. Anand and P. Hari (2001). 'India's Great Digital Hope—Cyber India', *Business World,* 21 May.

Parikh, Kirit S. (2000). 'IT, Globalisation and the Poor', *Business Standard,* 6 December.

Sambandan, V. S. (2000). 'Journeying towards convergence', *The Hindu,* 9 November.

Singh, Y. (2002). *Culture Change in India: Identity & Globalisation.* Jaipur: Rawat Publications.

Singhal, Arvind and Everett M. Roger (2001). *India's Communication Revolution: From Bullock Carts to Cyber Marts.* New Delhi: Sage Publications.

Thomas, Vinod (2001). 'Why the Digital Divide Muse be Reduced', *The Hindu,* 25 June.

Tremblay, Gaetan (2003). 'The Information Society: From Fordism to Gateism', *Canadian Journal of Communication,* vol. 5, pp. 20–36.

Yadav, J. S. (1984). *Politics of News: Third World Perspective.* New Delhi: Concept Publication.

Yadav, J. S. and P. Mathur (1998). *Issues in Mass Communication.* Vol. I & II, New Delhi: Kanishka Publication.

Yadav, J. S. (2001). 'Communication and Development: Indian Experience', in *Think India.* New Delhi, 4 (1): 58–70, April–June.

16

Communicating Culture and Culture of Communications: *A Study of Indian Television*

Biswajit Das

Introduction

With the onset of globalisation over the past two decades, new modes of viewing and thinking about culture and television have appeared. In this connection, there have not only been new questions but also new formulations of old ones. One witnesses an enormous variety of new forms of culture, and the changes in the technological forms of television which mediate such cultures. It is surprising that the term 'culture' did not receive significant attention in the initial years of Indian television. But in the recent years 'culture' has become the site of contest and suspect in Indian television. Further, it may be noted that the study of 'Culture' might have received significance in television studies elsewhere (Ang 1990), but it was viewed more or less as a static, objectified set of ideas, beliefs and behaviour in India, this thus foreclosed any attempt to view culture in a historical context and as a process. Few researchers (Blumler 1985; Rosengreen 1988) addressed the aforementioned issues, but confined their analysis within the conventional framework of communication and its supposed effects on national identity and culture. These studies did not shed much light on the cultural flows in the nation states in India and their experiences in adjusting to it, besides, they did not even take into account the importance televisual practices might have in its constitution of culture (Das 2003).

The recent developments in the field further aggravated the situation. The more the global-local encounter took place, the more the cultural issues received attention. For instance, questions like how can we understand culture in a renewed encounter of global-local interactions? And how did the changes in the Broadcast Policy affect our culture? And finally, how the local cultural productions competed in a global set up?

Culture remained almost a 'missing link' in the discourse of indian television prior to 1990s. Instead, television was always seen as a political project to cater to the requirements of nation state and nation building programme (Farmer 2000). Television, thus, grew within a territorialist construction of nation state in India, as a political rather than an economic enterprise, but the governments in the 1990s ended the state monopoly of television by privatisation. In order to present itself as an emerging market, the policies embraced the liberal vision of the role of the state. What made the policy in Indian television more contradictory were the explicit political ambitions of its policy makers to compete and promote a global communication in Indian society. The transition from a statist and regulatory approach to a market-driven deregulated one produced particularly turbulent manifestations in India (Das 2001).

Television in India was guided by Indian cultural policy developed with major initiatives in the domains of national heritage and the promotion of culture in the wider sense of shared values. Attempts were made to reconcile centralist conceptions often structured around state institutions. The state played a key role in the making of and sustaining of such a culture. For a long time there was nationalist resistance to foreign invasion of programmes. New legislations came almost every alternate year, attempting variously to engage with the debate on the relationship between television and state control (Ninan 1998). Cultural elites found themselves caught in the dialectics between cultural nationalism, with its hierarchies of distinction, and mounting evidence of a consumer culture, which resisted traditional cultivated practices. The relative failure of cultural programmes in the initial years of Doordarshan worried everyone in the 1970s, when it still seemed as if a desacralisation of culture and more thoughtful scheduling were all that was required to bring culture within the ambit of the initiated. Meanwhile, the proportion of programming that could be termed cultural in a broader sense was dwindling.

Among the dimensions of the crisis faced by public service in India, the dilemma was how to mediate traditional and high modernist culture in the midst of a communications boom in Indian society. Also, new questions surfaced: the autonomy of nation state communication systems and the idea of a public service closely linked to that of public monopoly. Furthermore, the emergence of new technologies projected the apparatus of television into much more complex communication networks, which no longer affected only entertainment and news reporting, but also the databanks of community television. In such a context, it was difficult to imagine how the notion of public service could remain untouched by any requisitioning. Thus, the 1990s saw the launch of a venture, which epitomised its contradictory policy in the domain of communication and culture. This contradiction further aggravated with the recent introduction of DTH system and the introduction of Convergence Bill in the Parliament. Technologically, this change amounts to a shift from analogue to digital television. This shift also builds interlinkage among the media and the demands for convergence of communications. Although the Convergence Bill is yet to be implemented, it will indicate a major shift, if implemented, in the years to come.

What is radically new today is that Indian Television is directly affected on the one hand by the structural transformation of international exchanges and on the other by the transformation of television systems. The restructuring of the world economy has necessitated the reshaping of the nation state. This in turn has granted a prime place to the cultural and television sector. The nation state is not supposed to dissolve itself in the current process of internationalisation (world without borders), but to manage its national economic and institutional life in the interest of the transnational corporations. In this reorganisation, television networks within national borders ceased to exist and lost its control over beaming the so-called modernist high culture in the country. In fact, culture has received a new meaning that could not be captured in territorially bound anthropological studies. Now culture is also routed through space bringing different cultures and practices into the country with the help of terrestrial television. In the earlier conception culture was territorially bounded and television was seen essentially as a technology that catered to national territory and boundary. As a result, Indian state had the monopoly to decide, what was to be telecast and what was not to be telecast on the air.

Political Economy of Culture

The recent rise and expansion of Indian television can be understood as an onward march of commodification of culture. This expansion provides new ways of perceiving and understanding culture. Today it is no longer confined to the domains of anthropology, but is also treated as a product or commodity in the market. These products can be consumed and appropriated in different forms—news, serials, quiz show and music. In the process we end up consuming intangibles expressed through image and words comprising of ideas and values (Thomas 2004). Almost every other day, one comes across news regarding synergy, merger, takeover, and new developments, especially in the field of television.

Although the Indian government allowed commercialisation of television way back in 1976 with the help of advertiser sponsored programme, television hardly took off, instead it remained guided and guarded by state control (Sinha 1998). Some of the foreign programmes were on the air, as the production process of programme was yet to catch the business imagination of industrial houses. Nor, did they think of television as a viable medium for investment in production. Some of the foreign programmes aired during this period caught popular imagination so much that *Lucy* became a pet name in an average Indian home after the teleserial, *Love Lucy*. Sensing the fear in the years to come, the Joshi Committee (as it is popularly known) highlighted the media policy for the creation of a national identity as evidenced in the title of the report: *An Indian Personality for Television* (Joshi 1985). The lamentation over Indian personality is not new. It also figured in the initial years of Radio Broadcasting in India (Das 2005), when Lionel Fielden, the first Director General of All India Radio visited post-independent India to see the functioning of radio, he commented that radio was yet to develop an Indian Personality after shockingly observing that the State and Status of Radio still continued the past colonial legacy. (Fielden 1960). Besides, in the name of protecting national identity, the Joshi committee (Joshi 1985) collapsed other allied categories such as cultural identity and collective identity with national identity (Das 2003). However, one of the major recommendations of this committee was very apt—to focus on the content of the programme to develop programmes based on the classics as well as the culture of Indian society and the need for such productions. But the emphasis on high modernist culture could not be sustained too long.

The entry of satellite and cable television in the 90s provided the opportunity for the global cultural industry to gauge potential revenues in the Indian cultural market. The Gulf War in 1991 provided an occasion for extensive live coverage by CNN to privileged Indian homes.

It also symbolised the nature of technologies used in the war field for physical intervention and broadcast technologies for cultural intervention in domestic spaces. After its success of staging 'live' combats and theatrics of war, the logical outcome was the penetration of electronic beams into the Indian territory from an alien destination with the help of satellite transmission technologies. Hong Kong based Star TV pioneered in introducing five channels into India with the help of ASIASAT SAT-I satellite. These channels immediately had a market and the viewership increased substantially within a short time span along with the sale of TV sets. As Sinha (1998: 28) comments, 'the advent of satellite-based television shook Doordarshan out of its complacency. It responded to the competition on two fronts: by increasing the number of channels and by changing the nature of its programming'. The mushrooming of channels and change in content of programme revealed the strategy to compete with foreign players in the field. As highlighted by one of the former ministers of Information and Broadcasting; this was a befitting reply to the cultural invasion with an indigenous programming strategy (Sinha 1998: 30). Besides opening various regional channels, Doordarshan also engaged itself in dealing with a cultural channel (DD3). Though this channel was short lived, it created many controversies in the political establishment. This channel was meant to be a 'janata channel' as reported by the officials, however it intended to cater to the English speaking high brow intellectuals (HT 1994). This was a reason why DD3 became orphaned on birth (Malik 1994) and was postponed indefinitly. The official claim for withdrawing the channel was based on the last minute discovery that the contents of this channel were extremely contentious and harmful for the moral fabric of the Indian Society.

Doordarshan's impressive plans for expansion were not only supported by the rising advertising revenues, but also by the growing diversity of genres in its programmes. As reported by a market survey undertaken by Lintas in 1996, the revenue in India has been on the upswing since the introduction of satellite television in the early 1990s. The report further noted that within one year (from 1994–95 to 1995–96), the Indian market grew from Rs 7,620 million ($223.5 m) to Rs 10,200 million ($ 299 m). For the year 1995–96, Lintas estimated, Doordarshan had the lion's share of the commercial revenue, by cornering a whopping $196.5 million (out of a total of $299 million). Zee TV was a distant second with an advertising revenue of $64.5 million and the Tamil language network, Sun TV, gathering a respectable $13 million during this period. From an all- time high commercial revenue of Rs 5,727 million in 1997, Doordarshan's share slipped to Rs 4,901 million in 1998 and Rs 3,999 million in 1999 as satellite and cable channels began competing with the state-sponsored network for viewer's attention.

According to Kumar (2005: 270), the Annual Report (1993–2000) of Doordarshan suggests that, from 1991–2001, the national network—the indispensable ideological cohort of the nation state—had grown phenomenally to counter the threat of its transnational and trans-local competition in India. In terms of its geographic reach, the network covered 14 per cent of the nation in 1982, 61 per cent in 1992 and 72.9 per cent in 1999. With the launch of DD-International channel on March 14 1995, the state-sponsored network extended beyond the political boundaries of the national community and reached viewers across Asia. From ten programme production centers in 1982 to 20 in 1992, Doordarshan's production facilities grew by over 100 per cent by 1999 to 46 centers. Similarly, the number of broadcasting transmitters in the national network increased from 19 in 1982 to 535 in 1992 and 1,041 in 1999. While Doordarshan reached a mere 26 per cent of the national population in 1982, it reached 81 per cent in 1992 and 87.6 per cent in 1999.

At present, Indian Television has expanded considerably. This is due to the phenomenal growth of satellite broadcasting and cable television in the last one decade. Indian telecommunication companies (both for basic and value added services), cable TV companies, internet service providers, advertising agencies, market research groups and TV production companies are now as free as the manufacturers of consumer products or consumer durables to tie up with multinationals, provided that majority equity control remains with an Indian registered company. With the offer of unlinking facilities to Indian satellite television companies, such as Asia net, Sun TV, Eenadu, and the likelihood of similar facilities to foreign companies such as Star TV, the path has been cleared for new competitiveness in Indian Broadcasting.

In spite of these developments, Doordarshan has not fully opened the floodgates for the market. For instance, most of the social issues based on drugs, environment and so on, still reflect Doordarshan's continued commitment to 'public service'. In this regard, it follows a strict advertising code. Some of the programmes based on classical dance, music, national integration, panel discussions and folk music have much less viewership in comparison to the prime time entertainment programmes, yet these continue to be transmitted (Das 2006)

It may seem to be the last remnants of public service culture. Day-by-day programmes on Doordarshan have become vulnerable to the pressures of audience ratings and advertising revenues. Since it already withdrew the license fee, coupled with the pressure of government to raise internal revenues, Doodarshan has no other way except to embrace the market. The relationship of Doordarshan with the market forces is not a cordial one. In fact, Star TV now challenges the political as well as the economic agenda. It threatens to subvert government's attempts at nation building which, according to Joshi (1989), is a primary objective of Indian television. Star TV also siphons off Doordarshan's advertising revenues, which were estimated at $115 million in 1992. Market analysts estimate that about 20 per cent of mass brands and 50 per cent of niche brands have moved their advertising from Doordarshan to Star TV. In 1993, the latter and Zee TV together had 20 per cent of the total advertising budget.

Besides Doordarshan, there was a phenomenal expansion of Indian broadcasting with the help of mega companies entering Indian market, such as, News Corporations, Star TV Network, Time Warner's CNN and Cartoon Network, Viacom's MTV, Sony Entertainment and Disney among others. In spite of their entry, the institution of monopoly has not been completely eroded, instead, it has changed hands, i.e., from the monopoly of the state to the global companies. New language of commerce such as merger, take over, acquisitions and synergy have been added to the meaning of culture. The recent discussions are no more on culture but on who merges with whom and who takes over what, for instance, the recent merger of Sony with BMG to capture music entertainment market. This merger would help Sony BMG to control a quarter of the total global market. The local monopolies also do not lag behind; most of the family-based business concerns such as Tatas, Ambanis, Modis, and media houses have benefited from such developments. Further, some of the monopolies at the regional level also quickly jumped in the fray to own and control the media sector. Some of the examples are—Eenadu in Andhra Pradesh and the Sun Group in Tamil Nadu and rest of South India. Besides, the larger media houses, including Living Media, Zee Telefilms, Eenadu, Bennet Coleman & Company have formed a lobby—the Indian Media Group, to compete with foreign players such as Murdoch's Star India. At the moment there are five major players in the cable industry—Siticable owned by the ZEE TV empire, IndusInd Media owned by the Hindujas, Hathway Cables owned by the property tycoons the Rahejas, Sumangali Cable Vision owned by Kalanidhi Maran of Sun TV and the cable TV network owned by Harsh Goenka of RPG (Thomas 2001).

In the name of culture there is a larger enterprise engaged in production, consumption, commoditisation and an army of viewers eagerly awaiting such products. As the FICCI-Arthur Anderson report suggests, there is a substantial increase and expansion of the Indian entertainment industry sector that expects a revenue of Rs 8,445 crore ($ 1.8 bn) in the year 2000 and Rs 33,984 crore ($ 7.5 bn) in the year 2005 (Dutta 2001). Further, Thomas (2005) points out that there are three potential growth areas in the entertainment sector in India, which include: 1) a) an overseas market for Indian film, b) music and c) entertainment software. The market for exports is located in the Middle East, Europe, North America and South East Asia. As Rao (2000) observes,

> ... the entertainment industry...is expected to see in five years, film exports grow from Rs 400 crore ($95 m) to Rs 1000 crore ($230 m), cable and satellite advertising from Rs 1,366 ($325 m) to Rs 2,050 crore ($480 m), music from Rs 1,700 crore ($400 m) to Rs 3,000 crore ($690 m). Entertainment software is expected to export $20 billion by the year 2008 and employ 15 million people.

2) Animation, specifically the outsourcing of products for global studios. Some of the leading companies are: Mumbai-based Unilazar Group and the Chennai-based Pentafour; 3) Investments in domestic broadbanding by multi-channel companies who are poised to take advantage of the demands for entertainment in the domestic market. As a result, some of the regional media moghuls like Subhash Chandra of Zee TV, Kalanithi Maran of SunTV and Ramoji Rao of Eenadu have taken advantage of satellite television and cable television. Some others like Adlabs-Mukta, Time Cinemas, Ultra Digital Cinema, Real Image and Broadband Pacenet have entered the business (Kohli et al. 2000). It shows that globalisation has provided tremendous opportunities at the national and regional levels to realign and adjust to compete with the global set up of media business.

However, these cultural goods and materials are not free from scrutiny, as the cultural flows are guided by general GATT measures and multilateral trade agreements. While cultural policy is by no means at the forefront of multilateral trade agreements; it is, as we have seen, implicated in various GATT regulation measures and connected to wider arguments about the direction and scope of free trade negotiations. The central instrument for drawing media and cultural flows directly into such regulations is certainly the GATS. With the launch of the new round of GATS negotiations in January 2000, it was expected that the audio-visual sector would be dealt with and the logjam from the Uruguay Round, finally confronted. One reason was that the Most Favoured Nation (MFN) exemptions (which allow members to opt-out of non-discrimination commitments) were taken out by a substantial number of WTO members over audio-visual issues. Critiques had given a number of additional reasons for the impending change to the status quo. For instance, Galperin (1999) argued that a more conciliatory climate between the US and the EU over audio-visual negotiations signal indications that the agreement to disagree in the Uruguay Round may not be a long lasting formula. Sauve and Steinfatt (2000) noted that general trade liberalisation had sharpened the tension between trade values and cultural values, between maximising export opportunities and protecting cultural sovereignty. There was therefore, the need for a new set of negotiations which would result in pressure for additional liberalising regulations that might require policymakers to strike a new balance between trade and cultural values. Finally, Murdock and Golding (2001) commented on the service sector companies (including media interests) and claimed that corporate awareness of the untapped potential for profits in these sectors had made the service industries a major target for further marketisation, spearheaded by the GATS. GATS negotiations on audio-visual were likely in the near future, therefore, because of: 1) a willingness to talk between previously hostile parties; 2) a pressing need to protect cultural industries in an era of liberalisation; and 3) pressure by media multinationals to extend their portfolios.

Although the process of 'GATTisation' of international communications is far from complete, the audio-visual industries, in particular, form a very fragile part of the WTO's domain. The Uruguay Round of GATT negotiations might have derailed due to French and Indian determinations to maintain its right to use audio-visual quotas and subsidies to protect its cultural identity, however, the cultural exemption, excluded in principle, was accepted *de facto* on a temporary basis, postponing the solution of the problem for the next round of negotiation (Lapadre 2000). As Hernan Galperin (1999) points out,

> ...no other industry [other than audio-visual] has been the subject of more exceptions and qualifications to free-trade principles, despite the present unchallenged reign of the neoliberal dogma among policymakers of most quarters. Annexes and side-agreements abound in references to communications industries, limiting trade liberalization and investment across borders.

The guidelines and assumptions on which audio-visual sector negotiations are based, further suggest that there is a need for (WTO 1998) the classification of the audio-visual sector and for regulating its industries. This document recognises audio-visual services as a sub-sector of communication services (along with postal, courier and telecommunication services) and divides it into six categories: motion picture and videotape production and distribution services; motion picture projection services; radio and television services; radio and television transmission services; sound recording; other audio-visual services. Further, the document acknowledges the complications between telecommunications and audio-visual classifications, particularly in the case of broadcasting transmission services due to technological convergence. In general, however, it resolves to classify issues concerning programming content under audio-visual while those involving the transmission of information are classified under telecommunications, a distinction that is far from helpful in the multimedia and online environments. This confusion between telecommunications and audio-visual reflects a larger problem within WTO rules as to the difference between goods and services, defined by one DTI negotiator as that of 'visible/invisible, physical/intangible' (DTI 2000). The problem is that all physical goods have to be distributed in a context where distribution has been defined by the WTO as a service (WDM 2000) while many intangible services assume physical form (videos, film prints, CDs). Such confusion is bound to produce serious controversies in future negotiations over both 'goods' and 'services'.

This document also acknowledges the need for cultural and political importance of the audio-visual industries and the consequential need for regulatory regimes and support mechanisms. However, it takes a prejudiced view and subscribes to the pro-liberalisation position proposed by the Organisation for Economic Co-Operation and Development (OECD) that takes regulatory reform for granted. The WTO concludes that to 'accommodate rapid technological change and the new multimedia services, governments will, according to the OECD, need to modify their regulatory structures, (WTO 1998). The OECD's arguments are themselves heavily swayed by technological determinism and a neoliberal commitment to free markets. For example, the OECD argues that 'rapid technical innovation and globalisation in the market' is undermining cross-media ownership restrictions and boldly states that 'the necessity for reviewing current regulations to determine whether they may continue as best practices to meet policy goals is arising from the viewpoint of stimulating further competition and developing new services and applications (OECD 1999). Ownership restrictions are seen here as impediments to business expansion and corporate profitability, no longer as necessary mechanisms to prevent concentration and conglomeration and extend cultural diversity. While the background paper does not take an explicit position on regulation, both the general obligation in the GATS to minimise regulation and the specific assumption that regulatory regimes in the audio-visual sector will impede technological development seem to reinforce the notion that audio-visual negotiations will focus on deregulation as much as liberalisation.

One major reason for the slow pace of the negotiations is that, apart from the USA, few countries are willing to seek commitments on audio-visual liberalisation if this requires them to open up their own markets and put further pressure on domestic regulatory regimes. Given the domination of US rights holders in the international audio-visual market, the likelihood is that there would only be one winner (in economic terms). This is what lies behind the WTO counsellor's statement that 'relatively few delegations speak on audio-visual as opposed to other sectors [because] the sector is not one where many delegations have offensive interests' (WTO 2001). The distinction between 'offensive' (i.e., liberalising) and 'defensive' (i.e., protectionist) interests is one that permeates discussion of trade negotiations in the audio-visual sector. Most developing countries have little to offer in terms of selling broadcasting and film products on the international market, however, the scenario has changed with the emergence of developing countries like Brazil, Mexico, Egypt and India as significant regional exporters of audio-visual materials to the developed countries.

Nevertheless, the change in policy in the global set up affects India's intellectual property regime (IPR). As Thomas (2005) points out that 'external pressure also includes the threats of sanctions inspired by the US Trade Representative's Section 301'. In fact, India features in the 'Special 301' Annual Review 2004 (Special 301: 2004). The review, after commending

India's progress in matters related to the harmonisation of its IPR law with global standards, nevertheless point to the gaps that remain.

> Piracy of copyrighted materials (particularly software, films, popular fiction and certain textbooks) remains a problem for US and Indian right-holders. India has not adopted an optical disc law to deal with optical media piracy. Cable television piracy continues to be a significant problem... (ibid.: 439).

Further, Thomas comments that

> 'while issues related to IPR can and do need to be seen in terms of a contestation over cultures, meanings, knowledge and representations—there is no getting away from the fact that the current global IPR regime is essentially about markets, monopolies, enclosures and the re-feudalisation of the economy' (ibid.: 437).

Thus, economic liberalisation in India, then, makes it an especially attractive market to target the upwardly mobile English-speaking population of multi-lingual, multi-ethnic India, and who are most likely to benefit from it. Contradictions abound in Star TV's Indian reception. The Information and Broadcasting ministry unleashes rhetoric decrying foreign cultural imperialism, yet does not attempt to regulate its competition out of existence. Is it because technological advance in the form of diminishing satellite dish size make attempts at regulation hopelessly unenforceable? Or is it because the business groups and the middle class, the same segment of population that favors economic liberalisation, are watching Star TV and liking it? In this context, Mattelart et al. (1984) discuss society as the 'site of confrontation and negotiation between social groups' that serves to mediate national communications policies. The 'organic alliances between national and transnational capital on the basis of common interests' that he points to help explain the existence of unlikely alliances among competitors. In India, for instance, while national and transnational capital both compete for the domestic market; fewer government restrictions have helped domestic as well as transnational companies.

Moral Economy of Television

The television scenario in India has undergone a sea change over the past two decades. This change can be summed up in the policy of liberalisation of the Indian economy initiated by the Congress regime in the early 1990s and later endorsed by the National front and the Bharatiya Janata Party (BJP)-led coalition regimes. The policy submitted uncritically to the conditionalities laid down by the World Bank and the International Monetary fund and the GATT agreement. Such an unexpected turnaround in public policy, which was discernible in the mid-1980s, is most convincingly reflected in the deregulation and privatisation of telecommunications and the commercialisation of television broadcasting in India (Sinha 1998).

Television broadcasting in India has been through several major reorganisations over the past decades in response to economic difficulties and changes in the political climate.

The advent of commercial television completely altered the circumstances for a debate on public service in India. A non-commercial monopoly existed until the late 1990s when satellite channels began beaming into the country. At that time, however, only a small portion of the population had access to cable systems and satellite dishes were quite rare. These channels had only a minor impact on viewing patterns except DD which had a major impact by opening the door for the idea of a terrestrial commercial channel. In part, the reasoning was that without a national commercial channel, a good deal of advertising revenue would, in the future, seep out of the country to such foreign commercial channels. More important, however, were the ideological arguments. Political parties of the centre and right as well as industrial and financial interests were not only clamouring for a commercial station, but also in many cases attacking the fundamental premises for public broadcasting. Market forces were evoked as the only justifiable and feasible way to finance broadcasting. Deregulation was in the air. At this time, the sterile debates on public policy and the lack of interest by successive governments and political will succumbed to the pressure of international institutions. There were many voices expressing concern and even distaste for the Doordarshan, and demanded for an 'autonomous Television'. It was not a question whether 'an autonomous television' would have provided an alternative to the state-run television system, in fact, one witnesses several autonomous organisations in Indian society and their extent of autonomy vis-à-vis the state. Besides, all the public service model of television in the world were in crisis, hence, it was difficult to assess to what extent this model would have been a suitable alternative to the existing system of television in India. Nonetheless, we have struggled enough to achieve a public service television! Today we have a peculiar system whereby the public-run channels compete with commercial channels for revenue. The obvious point of interest here is how the non-commercial channels have adjusted to commercial competition. Another interesting issue is how the commercial channels adjust to a socio-cultural climate which has been shaped for a public-service tradition.

With increasing competition from private channels, Doordarshan's public service role is under pressure, as, in order to remain competitive, it now has to provide entertainment as well as education. Because of the reach of the terrestrial broadcasting network (it now covers nearly 450 million people in 87 per cent of the country) (Doordarshan 1997: 2), the government has been supportive to Doordarshan by banning Direct to Home (DTH) reception, although it insists that the ban is temporary and once the rules have been laid down under the Broadcast Bill, DTH will be allowed through bidding. The Broadcast Bill, introduced in 1997, seeks to bring order to the broadcasting industry, currently regulated by the archaic Telegraph Act of 1885, and to create an independent Broadcasting Authority to regulate broadcasting services. It has been suggested that the bill be replaced by the 1990 *Prasar Bharati* (Broadcasting Corporation of India) Act, which came into force in September 1997 and led to the creation of Prasar Bharati Corporation, promising to give autonomy to Doordarshan and AIR. Surrindar Singh Gill, Chief Executive of this new body and a former Secretary of the Information and Broadcasting Ministry, is keen to realise the 'social obligations' of Doordarshan and reduce entertainment programming. A self-confessed leftist, Gill is against surrendering cultural sovereignty to transnational players such as Murdoch, whom he calls 'an international buccaneer' and has even commissioned and financed a critical documentary about the media mogul for Doordarshan (Bamzai 1998: 3).

However, Gill's fate and that of the Prasar Bharati hanged in the balance as the coalition government led by the right-wing Bharatiya Janata Party (BJP), which took office in early 1998, let the Prasar Bharati Bill lapse in Parliament. The BJP, keen to promote a Hinduised version of cultural nationalism, wanted what it calls 'calibrated' globalisation, allowing foreign involvement only in certain sectors of the economy and with adequate regulation. It proposed, for example, to limit foreign equity holding in broadcasting to 20 per cent of the total shareholding. The BJP reflected a widespread belief that the foreign broadcasters were only interested in maximising their profits at the expense of the social role of television, which was being constantly undermined, a sentiment which conformed to a survey of Indian journalists undertaken by the contributor of their chapter. Although Doordarshan's reach has been extended and new channels added (in 1998, it had 19 channels, and was planning to launch a 24-hour sports channel), the percentage of public-service programmes have declined to accommodate entertainment of a hybrid variety. A more fundamental issue is the ideological shift in television culture from public to private—from public service to profit-oriented programming. For the present, it seems, Doordarshan 'has accepted the new rules of the game as defined in terms of revenue maximisation and has shifted its agenda to providing entertainment rather than enlightenment' (Gupta 1998: 77).

Doordarshan became increasingly commercialised during the 1980s, a decade when the expansion of the satellite network in the country enabled the beaming of 'The National Programme', which many saw as 'part of the state's effort to build a consensual cultural narrative' (Gupta 1998: 89). However, it may have more to do with the growing commercialism of the national broadcaster, intensified by the increasingly neoliberal governments of the 1980s, which made television entertainment more oriented to meet the needs of the advertisers. As a result, Doordarshan began to draw large audiences and its commercial earnings rose nearly 20-fold between 1982 and 1992 (Doordarshan 1997)

Various committees ever since its inception contributed and pleaded for an autonomous organisation of Television. But the gap between the discourse and action reflected on the nature of body politik and their governance. Indeed, governance reflects anxiety, uncertainty and sense of fear to lose control over the populace. The more the control over broadcasting, the better was the governance in society. Broadcasting policy almost figured in election manifestoes and political agendas but no political parties had the political will to establish it as an autonomous organisation. While the Chanda Committee (1966) proposed and recommended the creation of an autonomous Television Corporation of India, the Verghese Committee (1977) recommended one step ahead by recognising the limitation for the creation of a unified national broadcasting corporation with a highly decentralised structure with the help of delegation of power to the regional and local level so that the organisation enjoys the advantages of quick decision-making, sensitivity to local problems, familiarity with local customs and taste, and close linkages with various governments and institutions. But the Joshi Committee (1985) sidelined the debates on autonomy, instead, it emphasised upon the need of television for social and economic development of the country and on its role as an effective medium for providing information, education and entertainment. Besides evolving a software planning, the government emphasised on hardware development to rapidly expand the geographic reach of the national network. By mid-1983, potential coverage for Doordarshan grew from 23 per cent to 70 per cent of the population as the number of television transmitters increased from 41 to 180 in less than one year.

Although Prasar Bharati Act came into existence in 1990, the ruling party could not remain in government longer to provide legal sanctity for an autonomous corporation for broadcasting in India. Lack of enthusiasm by Congress did not allow the act to be amended, On the contrary, the government started relaxing several government restrictions on private businesses to operate in the television industry to boost the sagging Indian economy. Some of the developments in 1990s forced the government to open its sky to the external agencies. Till 1990, broadcast legislations were confined to the national territory for national security reasons. But the event of Hero Cup International cricket tournament challenged the age old monopoly of sky of the Government. In its landmark judgment, the Supreme Court held that the airwaves are public property that must be used in ways that ensure the expression of a plurality of views and diversity of opinions in the national community (Bhargava 1991). The Court also ruled that the government of India had the responsibility to use the airwaves to advance the citizens' rights to free speech guaranteed by the Constitution.

In its ruling, the Court explained, 'The broadcasting media should be under the control of the public as distinct from Government. This is the command implicit in Article 19(1)(a). It should be operated by a public statutory corporation or corporations'. On the question of broadcasting by private individuals and commercial networks, the Court ruled:

> The question whether to permit private broadcasting or not is a matter of policy for the Parliament to decide. If it decides to permit it, its for the Parliament to decide, subject to what conditions and restrictions should it be permitted. Private broadcasting, even if allowed, should not be left to the market forces in the interest of ensuing that a wide variety of voices enjoy access to it.

In defining the airwaves as a public property that is free from both state-control and commercial forces, the judges pointed to the 'danger flowing from the concentration of the right to broadcast/telecast in the hands of (either) a central agency or of a few private affluent broadcasters' (Ninan 1998). The Supreme Court's historic judgement ordering the government of India to 'take immediate steps to establish an autonomous public authority... to control and regulate the use of the airwaves' intensified the demands for reform in Indian television (Varma 1995).

Shortly after the creation of the Prasar Bharati Corporation, the United Front—which had been most receptive to the ideals of broadcasting autonomy—lost power after a short stint of 12 months in government, when the Congress Party strategically withdrew its support and called for mid-term elections in 1998. The BJP came back to power, but once again, the government lasted for only 13 months, when one of the regional partner of the NDA, the AIADMK in Tamil Nadu, withdrew its support in the Parliament. The Elections were held in 1999, the NDA alliance gained a comfortable majority to form the government, and it appeared that the third time was a lucky charm for the BJP. However, the future of the Prasar Bharati Bill now appeared more uncertain.

In its election manifesto, the NDA had promised to conduct a thorough review of the Prasar Bharati Act after forming the government. What this 'review' would result in, was not clearly spelt out in the document, but some political analysts predicted that the BJP government was 'keen to do away with the half-baked autonomy Prasar Bharati had been provided with'. In the run up to the 1999 Elections, the then Minister of Information and Broadcasting, Pramod Mahajan, had categorically declared that he was not in favour of granting autonomy to Prasar Bharati as envisioned by the 1990 Act. 'I do not have faith in Prasar Bharati. I want Doordarshan under the control of the government. If we come back to power, we will dissolve Prasar Bharati', he proclaimed.

Explaining his aversion to the Prasar Bharati Act, Mahajan argued that the question of autonomy may have been relevant in 1990 when there was only one national network in Doordarshan. However, with the growing number of national, transnational and translocal satellite and cable channels competing with the state-sponsored network in the 1990s, Mahajan maintained that there was no longer any need for the government to provide 'autonomy' to Doordarshan. Instead he expressed interest in focusing his attention, and that of his Ministry, towards the development of a Conditional Access System (CAS) to enable the government to better regulate programming and distribution of satellite and cable television channels in India.

After the 1999 Elections, when the BJP-led NDA alliance returned to power, Mahajan was back at the helm of the Ministry of Information and Broadcasting, and he focused his attention on the development of a comprehensive Broadcasting Bill to regulate the activities of the private satellite channels such as STAR TV, ETV, Sun TV and Zee TV, and the commercially-owned cable companies. The goal of the Broadcasting Bill, introduced in 1997 was to create an independent authority known as the Broadcasting Authority of India to oversee a range of broadcasting services in India.

The Ministry of Information and Broadcasting set up a Committee headed by Nitish Sengupta, to suggest revisions to the Prasar Bharati Act which had been passed by the Indian Parliament in 1990, but was shelved by the Congress Party which came to power in 1991. In its report, published in 1996, the Sengupta Committee noted that the rapid proliferation of satellite channels had rapidly transformed the television landscape in India since 1991. Explaining the need for re-evaluating the Prasar Bharati Act which was passed by the Parliament in 1990, the Sengupta Committee wrote,

> A complete rethinking of the role, organisation and functions of Prasar Bharati became necessary in a multi-channel scenario, mostly driven by market forces, Prasar Bharati needs the requisite degree of flexibility and financial powers to hold on its own. There has been a constant debate concerning the quality and purpose of Indian Broadcasting for quite some time now. Some basic questions will have to be addressed to be able to evolve a vibrant and versatile model of a national broadcasting system, including a reinvigorated Prasar Bharati, in a vastly changed and fast-changing scenario.

Although the Sengupta Committee was created in December 1995 by the Congress government after the Supreme Court issued its order for the creation of a public broadcasting trust, the

General Elections of 1996 brought a new political formation led by the BJP, called the National Democratic Alliance (NDA). The government of India issued the necessary notification to turn the Prasar Bharati Act of 1990 into law. With the creation of the Prasar Bharati Board on 23 November 1997, the task of ensuring autonomy for television in India now rested with the 15 members of the newly constituted public broadcasting corporation. Now legally enshrined as an autonomous corporation, Prasar Bharati promoted the expansion of Doordarshan by adding more channels to the national network as a strategy to compete with foreign and domestic networks in the realms of entertainment, news and regional-language programming (Kumar 2005).

Thus, the rapidly changing mass media scenario in India is marked by contradictory trends: expansion and decline, deregulation and rigid control, liberalisation and censorship, globalisation and localisation. The boom in cross-border television channels and the growth of TV sets hooked to cable and satellite channels is offset by the decline in interest in radio and the press. The process of deregulation of state monopolies in broadcasting and telecommunications is going ahead, but the controls on cable and the cinema remain in place. Further, the globalisation of media industries, while giving free rein to the cultural invasion by the multinationals, is being challenged by the growth of, and audience preference for, local software. At the close of 1998, there were around 55 million TV households in India, out of which barely 15 million were in rural areas. Of the 40 million urban households with access to TV, around 18 million were connected to cable; only fifteen million of these were, however, hooked to trans-border satellite channels via cable networks. So, while an array of 70–75 TV channels could be assessed, a large majority of households has the potential to access only a dozen or so channels because the cost of set-top decoders and/or subscription to cable networks was beyond their means. Moreover, the cable operator in most cases decided the fate of the viewers in terms of the selection of satellite channels to be relayed.

The transition from a statist and regulatory approach to a market-driven deregulated one produced particularly turbulent manifestations in India. New legislations came almost every alternate year, attempting variously to disengage communications from state control. Today it has almost reached a stage wherein commercialisation of Indian communication radically questions the autonomy of the Nation State communication systems and the idea of a public service.

The lack of public debate on broadcast policy was not entirely a domestic responsibility. The international donors also kept the implications of their adjustments out of the public realm, and quite deliberately so. There was a fragile political contract between the governments and the majority. The slide to the neoliberal economic policies, imposed on a reluctant government, proved politically regressive and very nearly disastrous. More widely, the neoliberal ascendancy has not been associated with the growth or entrenchment of democratic accountability. Although its proponents were reluctant to acknowledge the fact, economic neo-liberalism was also a political project. Its political impact was to attack the existing political contracts, rather than building up alternatives. As such, it has not been beneficial for the overall broadcast policy in India.

Conclusion

The narrative of Indian Television during the last two decades has shown major shifts in the area of policy which has impinged on culture as well. The system of production and commercialisation played a complementary role within the transnational framework by promoting culture to compete in the global scenario. The main patterns to emerge from the installation of new technologies in the country showed that, far from homogenisation and standardisation, India found renewed spaces through geo-cultural and linguistic affinity in the global world to market its cultural products. In the process, the contestatory character of national culture witnessed the tensions and contradictions between national sites and transnational cultural processes. These tensions generated arenas where other registers of culture encountered, interrogated and contested one another in several new and unexpected ways. Thus, the so called 'national culture' sought to co-opt and redefine the more local, regional or folk cultural forms.

While analysing these developments and its implications on culture, we witness that there are widely divergent views on the cultural dimension of reforms in the context of globalisation (Choudhary 2004). Pieterse (1996) outlines three broad areas in which one can visualise the impact of globalisation on culture: i) Homogenisation paradigm leading towards standardisation and uniformisation. It refers to homogenisation of lifestyles as reflected in McDonalisation, CocaColisation, and Disneyfication of the world. ii) The second notion of change could be called the cultural clash/ identity paradigm. It implies that the market-centred globalisation is making deep inroads into local and regional cultures that is seen as a threat to their survival. The result is the increasing assertion of identities to defend against the onslaught of globalisation (Huntington 1997). iii) The third notion refers to the hybridisation process. It emphasises on the process of translocal cultural mixing manifested in cultural heterogeneity and hybridisation. Further, scholars (Panikkar 2002; Mohan 1999; Griffin 2004) also view globalisation's impact on culture in terms of commodification, decontexualisation and dehistoricisation, hegemony, and so on.

Most of these analyses are immediate reactions to the global consequences; however the development in Indian television can not be merely summed up within the categorisations developed by these scholars. The recent developments in the field are contrary to their experiences. Appadurai's (1997) insight may be useful partially in this context as he refers to the appropriation of global forms in the local context and to the diaspora which is a part of the cultural dynamic of urban life. Even, Singh's (2002: 64) analysis is useful in this context as he refers to 'enormous cultural autonomy which provides enormous cultural resilience to communities in India to filter the effects of globalisation through refractory and prismatic adaptations'. These writings contest universalist assumption of globalisation. Instead, the focus is shifted towards 'regionalisation' which provides a better insight to understand the recent developments. These developments may be termed as 'geocultural' or 'cultural-linguistic' markets as some of the scholars would like to name it (Wilkinson 1995; Straubhaar 2002; Thussu 1998, 2000; Thomas 2004) as it spreads across the globe. One of the important markers of this geo-cultural set up is the proximity across geographic or cultural-linguistic terms based on the history of immigration, colonisation and other cultural contacts.

This approach certainly provides an edge over the earlier 'totalising' or 'universalising' discourse on globalisation (Schiller 1969; Tomlinson 1997), and provides a different, decentred model for thinking about global information flows. This model of an unstable, decentered, world system has become increasingly popular in recent years (Giddens 1994; Garcia 1995; Castells 1996). In this context Simon During's (1997) analysis is insightful where he makes a distinction between the global populàr and the cultural globalisation. According to During (1997), the 'global popular' as a useful distinguishing concept refers to homogenisation of popular cultural production and its reception worldwide. It connotes western economic power and new technology and describes the increasing power and reach of US and western culture, leading to the undifferentiated adoption by indigenous entertainment industries of US media forms. Global blockbuster movies such as 'Titanic', 'Harry Potter', 'Arnold Schwarzenegger's Terminator' series can come under this category. However, global television has also created a new category of 'global events', such as the Olympic Games, the Word Cup, Tianmen square, both Gulf wars, princess Diana's death and funeral, and on. During (1997) cautions that the concept 'global popular' should not be applied universally to all types of media because it is not to be identified with cultural globalisation (or transnationalisation) tout court. During categorically observes

> Cultural globalisation takes many forms and has many different effects, some of which work in the opposite direction to the global popular. Globalised cultural technologies and networks of production have, paradoxically, generated more and more locally produced and consumed works from news shows to soaps (During 1997: 809).

Bicket (2005) also points out that the 'global popular' is movie-oriented and resides in the form of the big-budget Hollywood blockbuster, whereas the glocal is television-oriented and resides primarily in the soap opera and other relatively low-budget television content. This distinction helps to understand the cultural-linguistic information flows. Besides, global popular remains within the hold of US domination whereas the 'lower level' transnational cultural products are diverse and have no single monopoly, instead, there are monopolies within monopoly. It is within this context that the transnational cultural products can be located and understood. Further, the convergence between the transnationalisation of cultural products, and the transformation in the art of political governance contributes towards a renewed understanding of culture and cultural forms in India.

References

Ang, I. (1990). 'Culture and Communication: Towards an Ethnographic Critique of Media Consumption in the Transnational Media System', *European Journal of Communication*, 5(2–3): 239–60.

Appadurai, A. (1997). *Modernity At Large: Cultural Dimensions of Globalisation.* Minneapolis: University of Minnesota Press.

Bamzai, K. (1998). 'Gill Finds a Role in Swadeshi Starrer: Will take on Murdoch', *The Indian Express,* (New Delhi edn) 23 April.

Bhargava, G.S. (ed.) (1991). *The Prasar Bharati Bill: Government Media Autonomy and After.* New Delhi: Concept Publishing Company.

Bicket, Douglas (2005). 'Reconsidering Geocultural Contra flow: Intercultural Information Flows through Trends in Global Audiovisual Trade', *Global Media Journal*, 4(6), Spring. (Available at lass.calumnet. purdue.edn/cca/gmj/sp05/gmj-spos-bicket.htm–75k; accessed on 25 December 2005.)

Blumler, J., M. Gurevitch and E. Katz (1985). 'Reaching Out: A Future for Gratifications Research', in K.E. Rosengrens, L.A. Wenner and P. Palmgreen (eds), *Media Gratifications Research: Current Perspectives*. California: Sage Publications.

Castells, M. (1996). *The Information Age—Economy, Society and Culture*, vol. 1: *The Rise of the Network Society*. Oxford, UK: Basil Blackwell.

Chanda, Ashok Kumar (1966). *Radio and Television: Report of the Committee on Broadcasting and Information Media*. New Delhi: Ministry of Information and Broadcasting.

Choudhary, K. (2004). 'Globalisation, Governance Reforms and Development in India', Paper presented at Workshop on Globalisation, Governance Reforms and Development in India', Institute of Rural Management, Anand (Gujarat), 14–16 December.

Das, Biswajit (2001). 'Global Communication and Local Appropriation: Indian Experience', in Z. Zaidi and V. Ray (eds), *Mass Media in Third World*. New Delhi: Kanishka Publication.

——— (2003). 'Culture, Nation and Communication: Locating Indian Experience', Paper presented at Indo-French Seminar on Culture, Identity and Development, MSH, Paris, 21–23 May.

——— (2005) 'Mediating Modernity: Colonial Discourse and Radio Broadcasting in India: 1927–47, in Bernard Bel, Jan Brower, Biswajit Das, Vibodh Parthasarathy and Guy Poitevin (eds), *Media and Mediation*. New Delhi, Sage Publications.

——— (2006) 'Beyond Boundary? Globalisation of Communication of Indian Society', in B.N. Patnaik and S. Imtiaz Hasnain (eds), *Globalisation: Language, Culture and Media*. Shimla: Indian Institute of Advanced Study.

Doordarshan (1997). *Doordarshan 1997*. New Delhi: Audience Research Unit, Directorate General, Doordarshan.

DTI (2000). *A New Future for Communications*. DTI/DCMS Communications White Paper, available at http://www.communicationswhitepaper.gov.uk/, accessed on 15 December 2005.

During, S. (1997). 'Popular Culture on a Global Scale: A Challenge for Cultural Studies?', *Critical Inquiry*, 23: 808–21.

Dutta, S.N. (2001). 'Real Life, Reel Woes', *Business World*, 15 January, available at http://www.Businessworld India.com/archive.

Farmer, Victoria (2000). 'Depicting the Nation: Media Politics in Independent India', pp. 254–87, in Francin Frankel, Zoya Hasan, Rajeev Bhargava and Balveer Arora (eds), *Transforming India: Social and Political Dynamics of Democracy*. New Delhi: Oxford University Press.

Fielden, L. (1960). *The Natural Bent*. London: Andre Deutsch.

Galperin, H. (1999). 'Cultural Industries in the Age of Free-Trade Agreements', *Canadian Journal of Communications*, 24(1). Available http://www.cjc-online.calviewarticle; accessed on 25 December 2005.

Garcia, Canclini N. (1995). *Hybrid Cultures: Strategies for Entering and Leaving Modernity*. Minneapolis: University of Minnesota Press.

Giddens, A. (1994). *Beyond Left and Right: The Future of Radical Politics*. Stanford, Califfornia: Stanford University Press.

Griffin, Keith (2004). 'Globalisation and Culture', in S. Cullenberg and P.K. Pattanaik (eds), *Globalisation, Culture, And the Limits of the Market: Essays in Economics and Philosophy*. New Delhi: Oxford University Press.

Gupta, N. (1998) *Switching Channels—Ideologies of Television in India*. New Delhi: Oxford University Press.

Hindustan Times (HT) (1994). 'DD3 Planned as Elite Channel' (New Delhi edn), 7 May.

Huntington, S.P. (1997). *The Clash of Civilisations and the Remaking of World Order.* New Delhi: Penguin Books India (P) Ltd. (first pubn. in 1996 by Simon & Schuster).

Joshi, P.C. (1985). *An Indian Personality for Television: Report of the Working group on Software for Doordarshan.* New Delhi: Publications Division, Ministry of Information and Broadcasting.

——— (1989). *Culture, Communication and Social Change.* New Delhi: Vikas Publishing House.

Kohli, V. (2000). 'It's Show Time Folks', *Business World,* 10 January, pp. 1–7.

Kumar, S. (2005). 'In Search of Autonomy: The Nationalist Imagination of Public Broadcasting', pp. 255–81, in Bernard Bel, Jan Brower, Biswajit Das, Vibodh Parthasarathy and Guy Poitevin (eds), *Media and Mediation.* New Delhi: Sage Publications.

Lapadre, L. (2000). 'The Audio-Visual Sector in the GATS 2000 Negotiations', available at http://www.econ.union.it/sie/incontri/rsa41/paper/4/TXT-Iapadre.pdf, accessed on 22 December 2005.

Malik, Amita (1994). 'Dog Eats Dog on DD3: Death of Channel III', *Indian Express,* (New Delhi edn), 22 October.

Mattelart, Armand, Michele Mattelart and X. Delcourt (1984). *International Image Markets: In Search of an Alternative Perspective.* London: Comedia Publishing Group.

Mohan, Kamlesh (1999). 'Implications of Globalisation and Cultural Invasion for India', in Raj Mohini Sethi (ed.), *Globalization, Culture and Women's Development.* Jaipur and New Delhi: Rawat Publications.

Murdock, G. and P. Golding (2001). 'Digital Possibilities, Market Realities: The Contradictions of Communications Convergence', pp. 111–29, in L. Panitch and C. Leys (eds), *A World of Contradictions: Socialist Register 2002.* London: Merlin Press.

Ninan, S. (1998). 'History of Indian Broadcasting Reform', pp. 1–21, in Monroe E. Price and Stefaan G. Verhulst (eds), *Broadcasting and Reform in India: Media Law from a Global Perspective.* New Delhi: Oxford University Press.

OECD (Organisation for Economic Cooperation and Development) (1999). *Communications Outlook.* Brussels: OECD.

Panikkar, K.N. (2002). *An Agenda for Cultural Action and Other Essays.* New Delhi: Three Essays Press.

Pieterse, J.N. (1996). 'Globalisation and Culture: Three Paradigms', *Economic and Political Weekly,* 31(23), 8 June.

Rao, S.L. (2000). 'India's Rapidly Changing Consumer Markets', *Economic and Political Weekly,* 35(40), 30 September.

Rosengreen, K.E. (1988). 'The Study of Media Culture: Ideas, Actions and Artefact, Report no. 10, University of Lund.

Sauve, P. and K. Steinfatt (2000). 'Towards Multilateral Rules on Trade and Culture: Protective Regulation or Efficient Protection?', Paper presented at Achieving Better Regulation of Services conference, 26–27 June, Canberra, available at (http://www.pc.gov.au/research/confproc/abros/paper13.pdf, accessed on 22 December 2005).

Schiller, H. (1969). *Mass Media and the American Empire.* New York: A. M. Kelley.

Sinha, N. (1998). 'Doordarshan, Public Service Broadcasting and the Impact of Globalisation: A Short History', pp. 22–41, in Monroe E. Price and Stefaan G. Verhulst (eds), *Broadcasting and Reform in India: Media Law from a Global Perspective,* New Delhi: Oxford University Press.

Singh, Yogendra (2002). *Culture Change in India: Identity & Globalisation.* Jaipur and New Delhi: Rawat Publications.

Special 301, *Annual Review* (2004), available at http://www.ustr.gov/reports/2004/special301-pwl.htm#India, accessed on 22 December 2005.

Straubhaar, J.D. (2002). 'Beyond Media Imperialism: Asymmetrical Interdependence and Cultural Proximity', *Critical Studies in Mass Communication*, 8: 39–59.

Thomas, Amos Owen (2004). *Imagi-Nations and Borderless Television: Media, Culture and Politics Across Asia*. New Delhi: Sage Publications.

Thomas, P.N. (2001). 'The Political Economy of Communications in India', in *Critical Issues in Communication: Looking Inward for Answers—Essays in honour of K.E. Eapen*. New Delhi: Sage Publications.

——— (2004). 'Media Ownership and Communication Rights in India', in Pradip N. Thomas and Zaharom Nain (eds), *Who Owns the Media: Global Trends and the Local Resistances*. London: Zed Books.

——— (2005). 'That Persistent 'Other': The Political Economy of Copyright in India', pp. 436–65, in Bernard Bel, Jan Brower, Biswajit Das, Vibodh Parthasarathy and Guy Poitevin (eds), *Media and Mediation*. New Delhi. Sage Publications.

Thussu, D.K. (1998). 'Localising the Global—Zee TV in India', in D.K. Thussu (ed.) *Electronic Empires: Global Media and Local Resistance*. London: Arnold.

——— (2000) *International Communication: Continuity and Change*. London: Arnold.

Tomlinson, J. (1997). 'Internationalism, Globalization, and Cultural Imperialism', in K. Thompson (ed.), *Media and Cultural Regulation*, London: Open University.

Varma, S. (1995). 'Air Waves: Public Property', *The Lawyers*, 10(5): 4–11.

Verghese Committeee Report (1997). available at http://www.indian television.com/Indian broadcast/legalreso/legalresources.htm, accessed on 18 December 2005.

Wilkinson, K. (1995). *Where Culture, Language and Communication Converge: The Latin American Cultural-Linguistic Market*. Austin: University of Texas.

World Development Movement (WDM) (2000). 'General Agreement in Trade in Services: In Whose Service?' available at http://www.wdm.org.uk/cambriefs/WTO/Inwhoseservice.htm, accessed on 22 December 2005.

World Trade Organisation (WTO) (1998). 'Background Note by the Secretariat on Audiovisual Services', S/C/W/40, available at http"www.screenquota.org/menupage/ newsPage, accessed on 21 December 2005.

——— (2001). *GATS – Fact and Fiction*, available at http://www.wto.org/english/tratop_e/serv_e/gatsfacts 0109_e.pdf, accessed on 17 December 2005.

17

Globalisation, Culture and Information Communication Technology in India

Santosh Panda

INTRODUCTION

Globalisation has permeated almost all spheres of our lives, and information communication technology (ICT) is taking the globalisation agenda further with significant possibilities of broadband Internet access and promise of global information networks like Integrated Broadband Networks—a network which is global, robust, sophisticated and broadband. A global information society or a global village is proposed at the cost of cultural ethos of communities, societies and nation states. Reforms and concomitant developments are promised in all spheres of life, including governance and education. Information technology is being promised as a catalyst not only for the issue of access and equity, but more so as a new and modern way of life, lifestyle and worldview. This modern way of life also promises 'development'—a novel way of efficient and effective restructuring and deployment of all kinds of resources meant to enhance the quality of life. The 'developed' agendas and models are persuaded, and at times imposed through bi and multi-lateral agreements, to prevail upon the 'developing' and the 'underdeveloped' through joint ventures, aids and half-hearted experiments.

Of course, one would argue, not all of these spread the neocolonial hegemony. What is then the new agenda? Does globalisation contribute to our better understanding, widely acceptable reforms, life standards, and development which we can call ours, sustain it, consolidate it, and build on it? What is the agenda of the new technologies? Does it facilitate the way we learn, think, collaborate, contribute, and seek-grow-sustain our identity in the community and community of practice? Does ICT contribute to bridge the digital divide, to our development and development of our communities in the culture that we live and breathe in? What, then, is the new agenda for information technology towards reforms and development? This chapter shall subtly explore these, and critically document the developments, status and possibilities in this regard generally, and with a focus on India in particular.

Globalisation, Culture and Internet

Globalisation as a concept, as a process and as a product is an all pervasive monster which affects almost all spheres of our lives, cultures, societies and nation states. Choudhary in the introductory chapter conceptualises the multiple interpretations of globalisation—as a process of economic integration and interdependence (internationalisation of production and distribution/marketing of goods and services); as a multi-dimensional process affecting our social systems, environment, culture and ways of living; globalisation of values and rights; as a myth and ideology; as an abstract concept which requires clarifications regarding theoretical framework and empirical details; and so on. Five interpretations of globalisation given by Das (2006) are comprehensive as well as inter-related:

- *As internationalisation:* cross-border relations, international exchange and interdependence;
- *As liberalisation:* creation of an open borderless world economy, and international economic integration;
- *As universalisation:* cultural synthesis in a global humanism;
- *As westernisation/modernisation:* global spread of the social structures of modernity, defying existing cultural self determination of societies; and
- *As deterritorialisation:* reconfiguration of geography and social space, and supra-territorial relations between people.

Globalisation as a presupposed notion of mutual agreement, collaboration, promotion and exchange in reality becomes an unacceptable hegemony unless the intentions are clearly spelt out. However, the nation states across the globe have clear policies and agendas of societal production and consumption, and of development, which are shaped by cultural ethos and which determine media policies and developments. But subtly, media deployment and use also affect the worldview of communities and societies. With the upcoming global economy, nation states do make fundamental changes in the structures of production and distribution. With increasing replacement of the Fordist-Taylorist development model (based on factory system and mass production, scientific management, and assembly line production) by Innovation-Mediated production development model (based on increasing investment in R&D and increasing application of knowledge in the process of production), significant changes are taking place in the perception of the role of education and ICT in the process of globalisation and national development.

This chapter takes a transformationalist position in that globalisation has both positive and negative impacts, that collaboration and competition in the international spheres is essential, that structural reforms need to be culturally rooted, and that education and technology need to initiate and sustain collective social action and the capacity of community of people to reflect and critically appreciate needs to be enhanced within given situatedness of socio-cultural contexts. In the entire process, culture holds the key.

Culture

Culture in the context of globalisation assumes significant importance in that globalisation must ensure culturally-wrought change. Culture as an overarching concept broadly denotes a changing and dynamic process of diverse traditions, patterns of action, symbols and artefacts, values and behaviour which individuals assimilate, internalise, and contribute to (Branch 1997; Matsumoto 1996). The psychological constructs of the communities of people are grounded in the social construct; and for cognitive structure and its meaning repertoire of individuals, culture has significant effect on what and how one believes.

One is influenced by different cultures at the same point of time, and from this point of view, the community of practice may have its own culture (Rogers and Steinfatt 1999), and that a mediated communication for a learning community may still develop and be influenced by its own distinct culture. The above authors further point out that intercultural interpretation of messages is determined as much by variations within culture (i.e., Socio-economic Status [SES], circumstances, etc.) as by the cultures of individuals themselves. Therefore, this suggests that, in a mediated communication, especially in the context of Internet, these two dimensions play an equally important role in communication, interaction and meaning-making, and therefore location and transformation of individual and community identity. This is where globalisation and ICT need to converge. Since human understanding and assimilation is situated in culture, any external intervention for participation and development need to be grounded in the culture of the individual and community cognitive structure. Diffusion and adoption of Internet, whether through multipurpose community-based tele-centres or through a variety of other actions, must look through this reality. This is where social shaping of technology as a framework assumes greater importance within which analyses of globalisation, culture and information technology can be located.

Internet and Information Society

It is historically well established that culture and identity are inextricably related. Cultural changes in societies of nation states have led to structural and institutional reforms. Advancements in technologies have also had significant impact on cultures creating strong drive towards institutional changes. However, it is clearly not possible to establish a strong linkage between (economic) globalisation, cultural processes, technology adoption, and ideology and identity. At times the process of globalisation and technological changes (commensurate with individual freedom and global solidarity) go parallel with changes in culture and ideology (linked with justice, equity and welfare). It has been pleaded that all these happen and lead towards what is called an information society.

The post-industrial society, popularly termed as the information society, has necessitated the wider adoption and application of ICT, especially the Internet, to every sphere of human life. Economic, technological, sociological and historical explanations have been provided for its consolidation (Feather 2003). In so far as technology is concerned, it needs to be established whether technological revolution is due to the needs and demands of the society, or such developments force the users to behave in ways they are desired/instigated. After the availability of electronic computers in the 1950s, constant upgradations have hounded humanity—one is simply not able to do away with it. Computers have become a necessary evil—they have solved many human problems rather intelligently. It has often been argued that contemporary economic changes are driven by developments of global communication networks (Castells 1998). However, as Giddens (1999) puts it, socio-economic changes including adoption of ICTs are instrumentations of broader globalisation.

Feather (2003: 16) further remarked 'The information society is an essentially social phenomenon: it is about how people live and work both individually and with each other. Therein lies its importance and its unending fascination'. Presenting a secular view of information society—secular in the sense that it deals with temporal world affairs, and that it occurs over a long period of time—Black (2003) rejects blind faith on digitisation and the concomitant information society. Presenting a historical analysis of information, he criticises the reduction of information into bits of disaggregated data—an item rather a process, a thing rather than an action; and that it is a misnomer that the ancient societies were less information-based than the modern ones. Rather, 'the information society proposition is in reality a mirage: a vision built on the shifting sands of the disquietening social change that has characterised recent decades' (ibid.: 20). The information society could be seen in a continuum of industrialism-capitalism-modernity-surveillance. The information society as a modern society is also a surveillance society—there are public attempts for control and surveillance in the name of authentic information. This, therefore, raises the question if the technology-based modern information society is intended to really make information available equally and equitably, or that it is meant largely for information/data surveillance.

Though it is essential to have information—information as a process, and not as a thing—such information should not delimit one's own critical thinking and self-reflection. Bauman (1994: 24) notes that the modern life has become a 'life fragmented into a series of meaningless spectacles ... a world which looks suspiciously like a 20 channel satellite TV with a madman holding the remote control'. Rather, any information in a culture of community must empower the community to develop the capacity for imagination and 'resist submersion in a global information culture' (Beeson 2003).

Globalisation as a political and/or economic philosophy might bring in short-term gains, but for sustainability and sustainable development, technology needs to be geared towards culturally-induced reforms in all spheres of life which further sustain cultural and individual identity and develop critical reflection on what could be set right for progress and development. As shall be argued in a later section of the chapter, globalisation has brought in significant reforms in technology and technology deployment in India with significant individual and community development, though it has not as much affected the basics of culture and the process of identity in the community of practice. Significant changes are required in the way technology is designed and deployed so as to initiate and sustain culturally induced changes and reforms.

IT Policy and Developments

Telecom and IT Policies

Significant telecommunication and information technology policy and developments in India is a recent phenomenon, with initial leap frogging and subsequent booming. As a federation of states and union territories, its diversity includes culture, language, religion and climate. While the cultural diversity might be considered as a boon, the linguistic diversity might act as a hindrance to IT development and deployment in so far as communication is in English (though India is much ahead of others as a outsourcing destination mainly because of its advantage in English language capacity). The tremendous liberalisation of the economy vis-à-vis developments in ICT, dispassionately documented by Singhal and Rogers (2001) and Wolcott and Goodman (2002), are indicators of the emergence of an IT superpower, almost obsessively dominating the Silicon Valley and Texas-Dallas. However, the demographic, educational and allied realities back home may not match such astonishing achievements by Indians abroad, tremendous government and private liberalisation notwithstanding.

Since independence from the British Colonisers in 1947, India has pursued a policy of self-reliance in socio-economic development, including infrastructure, science and technology, and defence. However, the Indian economy was gradually opened up during the Prime ministership of Rajiv Gandhi; and in 1984 the IT industry was declared as one of the core sectors of the economy. In the same year, the establishment of C-DOT (Centre for Development of Telematics), an R&D centre funded by the Indian government to design indigenous telecommunications, changed the landscape and future of Indian telecommunications industry (Singhal and Rogers, 2001). This led to mushrooming of PCOs, and above 30 million telephones and 650,000 PCOs in 2000. Singhal and Rogers (2001) further note that the founding of WorldTel by Sam Pitroda in 1995 had led the expansion of telecommunications reforms in the developing countries, and in India in 1999 upgrading of the PCOs to ICCs (Internet community centres) in rural Andhra Pradesh, Tamil Nadu, Kerala, Karnataka, West Bengal and Gujarat with the help of the respective state governments for multimedia facilities including Internet in regional languages. The reorganisation of the Ministry of Post and Telegraph and creation of Department of Telecommunications (DoT) in 1985 under a new Ministry of Communications, and the formation of MTNL (Mahanagar Telephone Nigam Limited) for domestic services and VSNL (Videsh Sanchar Nigam Limited) in 1986 for long distance services further boosted telecommunications in the country. Pitroda's DoT and various Technology Missions had taken significant strides and turns in the subsequent regimes.

The New Economic Policy announced by the then Narasimha Rao government had incorporated drastic measures towards liberalisation and free-market economy. The DOT was taken over by N. Vittal, a visionary technocrat, and this was followed by the declaration of the National Telecommunications Policy in 1994 which promised telephone services on demand, and invited foreign direct investment (FDI) to the sector. A subsequent development had greater impact on the telecommunications scenario when in 1997 the WLL (Wireless in Local Loop) was deployed and MTNL started mobile telephone services (though much later such services were offered by private multi-national companies). WLL connected telephone to the local exchange through radio wave and thereby considerably reduced the cost and became extremely economical in rural areas. The establishment of TRAI (Telecommunications Regulatory Authority of India) in 1997 was to regulate telecommunications in the country (though the day-drawn battle between DoT and TRAI significantly marred the telecom policy and the expansion of telecommunications in the country). Subsequently, many private operators started offering fixed and cellular services in various states in the country.

Socio-economic reforms under the Vajpayee government had been phenomenal, and much more accelerated than before. The year 1999 was a turning point when the Prime Minister Atal Behari Vajpayee formed the Group on Telecommunications (GOT) of the National Task Force on Information Technology and Software, and the National Telecommunications Policy (which was an improvement of NTP of 1994) was drawn. Subsequently, both basic telephony and cellular services were opened up for further private competition and expansion. In 2000, the STD (domestic long distance calls) was opened to private competition, and the end of the monopoly of the VSNL on international long distance with FLAG (Fibre Link Around Globe) was declared so that private operators and ISPs have direct access to FLAG without going through VSNL gateways (Panda and Chaudhary 2001).

Wolcott and Goodman (2002: 4), in this context about India wrote, 'At the dawn of the new millennium, Vajpayee and a growing number of politicians, bureaucrats, industry leaders, foreign investors, and bright-eyed entrepreneurs are trying to teach this Asian elephant to dance'. In fact, both the IT Action Plan of 1978 as well as the National Telecom Policy of 1999 led India to dance. Since then, there has been no looking back. Further legal footing was provided to information technology with the Information Technology Act 2000.

Like many other nations, India's telecom and subsequent information technology developments are influenced and determined by government policies—national policies by the Union Government. In October 1998, the then Prime Minister announced that the government will permit licence to private ISPs, and in November the New Internet Policy came to effect and so the Union Government allowed private companies to provide Internet services, besides the VSNL. The New National Telecom Policy of 1999 (GOI 1999a) allowed private operators to offer services for national long distance from 2000; TRAI was strengthened further; and the service and regulator functions of DoT were separated. In the same year, the IT Action Plan III (GOI 1999b) was released which dealt with long-term IT policy of the government; facilitated domain name registration in India; created the much-hyped *Sankkya Vahini* project (to link IT, research centres and higher education institutions); provided up to 40-bit key length of use to private providers; and public ISPs were invited by DoT to provide for international gateways for Internet services.

The general objectives of the IT Action Plan of 1998 was to create globally competitive IT infrastructure, increase IT software and service experts, and ensure 'IT for All' by 2008 (which included telecommunications services, Internet services, and IT-enhanced public services either as government or private projects relating to rural development, e-commerce and e-marketing, e-governance, e-health, e-education, etc.). Other important recommendations included, provision by 2003 of Internet in all schools, creation of IT-enabled education centres like IIITs, increasing use of IT services by the defence services, and establishment of public information and access centres (internationally known as 'telecentres').

In 1999, there was bifurcation of DoT into two—policy making and licensing remained with the parent department, while the newly separated and created Department of Telecom Services (later in 2000 known as Bharat Sanchar Nigam Limited—BSNL) was to provide services. The year 2000 saw: i) the formulation of the Information Technology Act 2000 which dealt with all local and copyright aspects of IT—electronic documents and signatures and payments, encryption, e-commerce, security, privacy, hacking, etc., and ii) the approval of the Communication Convergence Bill 2000 in 2001 by the Group of Ministers and Union Cabinet, which stipulated mechanisms of convergence of broadcast, telecommunications and Internet. This is an important step towards all sorts of convergence of technologies and services, including the emerging concept of 'tele-learning' and community-based multi-purpose tele-centres for development, empowerment, education, information and other services; and availability of three-in-one services of telephone, television and Internet through one connection.

Development and Diffusion of Internet

It has been underlined that Indian internet development has gone through three phases: promising beginning in the mid-1980s, stagnation thereafter, and sudden growth in the 1990s (Hanson 2001). The VSNL which had monopoly over international services started offering internet to the general public for the first time in 1995. As of September 2002, 213 ISPs reported to provide for services at A, B and C categories, and as of November 2002, the Government of India permitted 93 ISPs to provide national, state and city level Internet services (GOI 2003). These included important service providers like Satyam Infoway, DishnetDSL, HCL Infonet, VSNL, BSNL, Wipronet, Bharti BT, Bharti Telesonic, Hughes Escorts, L&T Netcom, Godrej Infotech, etc. of which 55 had been cleared for provisional commissioning. This was an important development in the history of IT and Internet in India. Today, above 185 licencees (from a list of about 540 issued licenses) operate the services in the country.

A study of the history of IT networks in India suggests that till late 1990s, the union government had full control over all kinds of communication, including local and long distance calls, domestic and international transmission, and transmission of voice and data. As noted earlier, things have changed after the promulgation of the NTP 1994. The establishment of NIC (national informatic centre) in 1975 and the CMC (computer maintenance company) in 1976 boosted IT activities in the country, and especially in 1978 when CMC took over former IBM operations (Singhal and Rogers 2001). In 1986, Education and Research Network (ERNET) and a year later National Informatics Centre Network (NICNET) were established, and in 1991 VSNL started gateway e-mail service, followed by introduction of 64 kbps leased line in 1992 and offer of commercial Internet services in 1995. In this historical development, the initiation of the first nation-wide VSAT satellite network by NIC in 1987 was crucial for data communication in the government sectors by linking state capitals and district headquarters.

At present, NIC is working on extending the network to sub-divisional and block levels. The VSNL also operated international e-mail network through GEMS 400, and with the help of Global One provided in 1998, speedy connections to its 1400 worldwide points. In 1986, the Department of Education, Government of India took the lead (and also some other government organisations) in establishing the ERNET with support from UNDP. In the same year, there was nation-wide computerisation of the giant railway services, and in 1987 and 1989 respectively, the NCST (national centre for software technology) started inter-city and international e-mail.

Since 1995, NICNET has been offering Internet services through the gateways of VSNL in four metros in the country. In the same year, the VSNL offered dial-up Internet services in the four metros though Department of Telecommunications (DOT) or MTNL, and had the sole monopoly to provide services under the GIAS (gateway Internet access service). It was surprising that in the same year the Indian government also allowed private ISPs to provide such services, though through the VSNL gateway—and even this was deregulated at the end of the century. With the VSNL monopoly, from 2000 subscribers and 10,000 users in 1995, the numbers increased to 90,000 and 450,000 respectively in 1997, and to 1.8 million and 5.5 million respectively in 2001. However, the competition provided by VSNL especially by dropping rate by 50 per cent through its 'Monsoon' package in 2001 compelled the private providers to reconsider their charges, and increased its number of subscribers. The VSNL monopoly on all sectors including international voice telephony ended in 2002, leaving it as just one of the competitors. Today, less than 1 per cent of above 1 billion population are internet users, most of whom are concentrated in big cities, and adopting broadband services. The Information Technology for Masses Working Group has set a target of 100 million internet connections, IT kiosks and cyber cafes. Since international telephony has been liberalised, the competition is hotting up day-by-day. However, Internet telephony is yet to be made legal, especially when VSNL's significant income came from international telephony. One significant development that should bring tremendous revolution in the near future is the large scale conversion of the existing more than 700,000 existing PCOs into Internet kiosks, some of which may consider becoming paid multipurpose telecentres.

How has the development of Internet provision in India been diffused? This is an area of considerable interest since the growth in access must lead to ownership and effective deployment for benefit to the community and its members. Press et al. (2002) present a six-dimension framework for the analysis of diffusion of Internet in a nation, especially in their comparative study of India and China: i) pervasiveness, ii) geographic dispersion, iii) organisation infrastructure, iv) connectivity infrastructure, v) sectoral absorption, and vi) sophistication of use. These are briefly summarised for India as follows:

(*i*) Pervasiveness: While there were 0.2 million users in 1999, it was estimated to increase to above 10 million in 2002 (March 2005: 39.2 million users, with 3.6 per cent penetration). Also, there were 96 hosts with 68 'in' domain names. However, for overall percentage, it falls behind many developing nations. With a tele-density of 3.6 in 2002, India ranks in the 145th position globally. However, the cost of Internet connection has decreased—VSNL has reduced it by 80 per cent since 1998, and MTNL and Dishnet have tried to follow suit. Regardless of this, Internet use requires English literacy which only 5 per cent Indians have; and the DOE strategy of making available software programmes in regional languages through C-DAC shall go a long way in the spread of Internet use and bridging the digital divide.

(*ii*) Geographic distribution: In 1999, India had Post Office Protocols (POPs) in 17 of the 32 states and union territories, which increased to 600 POPs in 150 cities in 2002 (Wolcott and Goodman 2002). Obviously Internet has the highest penetration in urban cities and is virtually negligible in the rural areas. Conversion of PCOs to kiosks and establishment of rural tele-centres may change the situation dramatically.

(*iii*) Organisation infrastructure: With liberalisation, inter-connecting network competition is increasing; and of the 108 recommendations given in the IT Action Plan of 1998, only 56 have been implemented, and 22 are in the process, while 27 have not been implemented at all. However, India's telecommunication and IT action plans are publicly debated and are transparent. As of July 2002, of the 79 DOT-approved Class A licenses, only 44 have started providing services. Further, of the 357 limited region licences, about 90 ISPs are operating. Nearly 20 companies have been permitted to provide 45 international gateways in 16 cities (the largest being in Delhi, Hyderabad, Chennai, and Bangalore), though in the country one is free to install a VSAT connection to the Internet.

(*iv*) Connectivity infrastructure: Compared to other nations, India's aggregate international bandwidth is lower in Mbps—though it increased from 82 Mbps in 1999 to above 1510 Mbps in 2002—so also the broadband access.

(*v*) Sectoral absorption: With a 10 billion dollar software industry, the .com users in India are comparatively less in number. Indian education and research network ERNET does not have many users, and the number of PCs used for education was not more than 0.2 million compared to 1.6 million in China.

India though has an edge over others regarding government websites, and transparency and interactivity. Compared to China's 39 government agency websites in 2000, India had 110; and based on the indicators of transparency and interactivity developed by Cyber Policy Research Group (CyPRG), India had a score of 5.6 in transparency (compared to 2.4 of China) and a score of 1.7 in interactivity (compared to Chinese score of 1.0). Further, sectoral portals of some of the state governments like Andhra Pradesh, Karnataka, Maharashtra, Madhya Pradesh etc. have been amazing. Bangalore as the Silicon Valley of India was long pursued by the Government of Karnataka, and this has boosted India's dominance in the IT industry globally.

(*vi*) Sophistication of use: Though the use of e-mail service is increasing, there is no perceptible increase in domestic e-commerce, chat, games—only less than 10 per cent website owners do e-commerce. Further, there is enough room to improve the services of audio and video within multimedia transmission. A study conducted by the Confederation of India Industry (CII) in 2001 on the use of websites or home pages showed that while 83 per cent use was for product catalogue, selling products and services and advertising, only 3 per cent use was made for training. This is an area which needs urgent attention, and future e-learning and community-based tele-learning should address the issue of education and training, and its convergence with development. In a way, distance learning significantly qualifies to take the lead in this direction.

IT for Development and Digital Divide

Digital Divide

Information technology promises considerable development in social, economic and educational spheres. As we shall see below, developments in and deployment of information technology for rural development, agriculture and community development in the country, though not wide spread, have significantly contributed to socio-economic status of the communities. However, both at the macro and micro levels, the basic issue is that of digital access, or in other words, digital divide. The four types of digital divide acknowledged by Keniston (2004) are equally applicable to India.

(*i*) There is the classical divide between the rich, educated and powerful and those who are not. With above six million Personal Computers (PCs) and above one million Internet connections in 2002, there exists a clear discrimination in favour of the English speaking minority of the rich and the upper middle class. Only a few from the disadvantaged sections of the society have access to both public and private community kiosks and PC access centres/tele-centres. Even if community kiosks are available, data on their actual use are not readily available.

(*ii*) There is a cultural and linguistic divide. With about 5 per cent of the population being able to speak English, language obviously restricts access to education and Internet. Across the globe, above 80 per cent of the Websites are in English, followed by other dominant languages like German, French, Japanese, Spanish, Portuguese, Chinese/Cantonese and Hindi. In the United States, there is what is called Anglo-Saxon linguistic and cultural hegemony—the Asian Americans have the highest Internet and PC access, followed by White Americans, Hispanics and Blacks. In India, though word processing and related software are available in Hindi and other languages, their use is limited largely to official transaction in government offices. Further, unlike for instance, China, Japan, Korea, Taiwan, the number of Websites in Indian languages is very negligible.

(*iii*) The third divide is between the information-rich and the information-poor, internationally referred to as the North-South divide. While in the industrially advanced nations, access to PC and Internet is above 50 per cent, in India it is respectively less than one per cent and half a per cent, and this is restricted to metros and urban areas. Most of the 0.7 million villages are out of its reach (though the spread in south India is faster than the rest).

(*iv*) The above three have given rise to the fourth category, i.e., the divide between those who have significantly benefited from the growth of the IT industry and other knowledge-based sectors of the economy, and those who are not. The emerging elites are not the contribution of caste, economic status or family inheritance, but of education and entrepreneurial intelligence. These are the IT programmers, systems analysts, venture capitalists, biotechnologists, and the like, and their emergence in tech-cities of Bangalore, Hyderabad, Pune, Mumbai, Chennai and even Delhi is highly visible. Within the sector of IT, there is also another divide, i.e., those who own IT companies and dotcoms and those who make chips and work for them. The common citizen is completely excluded from this domain.

IT and Development

In spite of considerable digital divide, the adoption and deployment of IT especially by central and state governments in the country has led to considerable developments in various spheres of society and community. Globalisation has definitely brought in information technology deployment in many large sectors of public projects successfully: computerisation of railways, banking, air travel, public civic services like land records, water, electricity, telephone, fax, and others. A few developments are in order to exemplify the state of affairs in the country.

(*i*) *Rural networking*: The development of IT in the country has been the contribution of, as also has inspired many, public and private sector entrepreneurs and organisations to take up the cause of indegenising and taking technology to rural areas and communities. It has been realised that the government, private, autonomous and research institutions have to work hand in hand to make a significant difference in IT networking and applications. Net surfing, e-commerce, online shopping and even dotcoms are not exclusive urban phenomenon today. There is nothing like an exclusive digital divide between urban and rural sectors. The efforts of especially the central and state governments, and not-for-profit organisations have made some difference in the IT capacity between the two worlds. As noted earlier, the union ministry of information technology has gone ahead converting above 6,00,000 PCOs into tele-info-centres accessible to the public at large with facilities covering Internet, e-mail, DTP, fax, phone and browsing. While the Government of Maharashtra has planned to link 40,000 odd villages for the farmers through Agronet, the Government of Karnataka had to seek franchises to establish Internet *dhaba*s (kiosks) all over the state. Use of corDET technology which brings telephone and Internet together is a novel experimentation, and is being used by the Tamil Nadu government to network villages. An indigenously developed wireless technology, this network provides services starting from agriculture, health to videoconferencing and other customised services. Also, 70 villages had been networked through RASI (Rural Access to Services through Internet), and this was to cover 700 villages in 2004.

A rural networking portal *indev* has been set up by the British Council to empower the community by providing information on sustainable development efforts of various development issues, developmental and non-government organisations in the country. The *Vigyan Ashram*, an NGO, attempts to provide wireless Internet connectivity called WLL to villages near Pune. This is a fine example of financial viability and sustainability. The Kuppam region of Andhra Pradesh is to be the first e-enabled rural region in the state with collaborative support received from the state government and HP (Hewlett Packard). Today, there are plenty of such examples in rural India.

(ii) *Rural development*: Rural IT networking is the first step towards bridging the digital divide. Rural development covers a wide range of areas ranging from health, education and agriculture to marketing and governance, and empowerment of the disadvantaged. The state of Kerala is credited to have the first fully literate district in the country as also the first fully computerised *gram panchayat* in the country. Nearly 70 villages are part of the network of Warna Wired Village Project in Maharashtra. SARI (Sustainable Access in Rural India), a collaborative project of IIT-C, MIT Media Lab and Harvard's CID is a fine example of international collaborative project to network above 1,000 villages in each of the two districts of Tamil Nadu for fostering economic development and imparting health education. Nearly 700,000 PCO network of the Indian Telecom converted into community kiosks is the testimony to the recent IT proliferation in the country. As Noronha (2001) notes, with population over a billion, India needs above 200 million telephone and Internet connections—this is not an easy task either.

The most interesting case of rural development is the M.S. Swaminathan Research Foundation which provides networked Internet connectivity to a cluster of 11 villages in the region of Pondicherry started in 1998 by International Development Research Centre (IDRC) and Canadian International Development Agency (CIDA). An initial survey showed that the major sources of information were the villagers themselves, the shopkeepers, the market place and the agriculture suppliers. With support received from villagers, the Foundation networked villages for use of Tamil fonts, message communication, document composition, and hard disk maintenance by the village youth. The project retitled as 'knowledge system for sustainable food security', primarily focused on agriculture. Women are fully aware of everyday weather and market prices, and spread agricultural and health information. The success and international acclaim for the project has led to establishment of a virtual university for agriculture in the country. A significant development is the use of solar-mains hybrid power system by the village knowledge centers (VKCs), and this regular power supply has enabled creation of a system of on-demand and walk-in information access to the rural poor. The success of the project involved (and which has implications for our discussion) visionary leader, partnership with community, content generation and development based on client needs, and simplistic use of technology (Jhunjhunwala, Ramachandran and Ramachander 2006). Technology never intended to disturb the culture of the community. Other successful examples include Foundation of Occupational Development (FOOD) and *Drishtee*.

(iii) *E-marketing*: One of the facets of rural development is facilitating marketing of rural products at a competitive price, thus eliminating the middle person, and economically benefiting the rural citizens, especially the women, whose economic products do not pay them anything. Misra et al. (2001) underline a few challenges for rural *bazaar* faced by rural entrepreneurs: rural products being sold in the rural *haat* with limited demand thereby limiting the chances of competition and product improvement; with limited awareness of the global market, the products hardly create a market for themselves; with limited possibility of exhibitions, the products remain bleak to the promoters; and, in the absence of intelligent marketing analysis and poor marketing infrastructure, the market is neither created nor sustained. This, in a way, affects the rural inhabitants and entrepreneurs adversely, and does not provide a fair or equal chance to grow. In other words, this is sheer stagnancy and exploitation. In this context IT promises a lot.

Rural Bazar, an e-product of National Informatics Centre (NIC), Government of India (GOI) is a web store which allows consumers to search, view, buy and pay for any product they choose. The fishing boats of Kerala have installed systems to access the satellite database of the Global Positioning System (on information tracker) which can identify the fishing belt for the day as also connect to a host of sea food markets for sale at a good price while still boating and fishing in the sea. An important organised portal is *TARA haat*, an NGO promoted by Development Alternative and which had won the Stockholm Challenge Award. 'Turmeric online' is another example of such e-marketing which has enormously benefited the Kandha tribes of Orissa, organised by Kandhamal Apex Spices Association for Marketing (KASAM) for above 61 turmeric growing societies. With 10–25 per cent growth of demand for organic turmeric in the European countries above, KASAM visualises a growing market for its products, and more importantly for its tribal producers.

(*iv*) *E-governance*: With independence, India inherited a bureaucratic governance from the British, and the nation has come a long way often further bureaucratising the bureaucratic governance. The initiatives of both the central and state governments have shown significant results of transparency and people-friendly interactive governance. It has been observed that those state governments which have implemented IT in a speedy and sustained fashion have also been able to implement e-governance schemes. The NIC's Computer Retrieval of Information on Scientific Projects (CRISP) was meant to facilitate district rural development agencies to monitor poverty alleviation programmes. Subsequently, Rural Soft 2000 was developed as a robust and scalable solution for greater efficiency in online monitoring. The revised National E-Governance Initiative of the GOI in 2002 stipulated that there could be differing expectations between the government and the citizen on various issues relating to e-governance. The core policies are crucial for further establishment of core infrastructure and core projects viz. smart card, national ID card, computerisation of revenue departments, generic office management system, India portal, e-procurement, and human resource management system. *Gyandoot* of the Madhya Pradesh government, *Friends* of the Kerala government, and *Bhoomi* of the Karnataka government are important initiatives in this direction. *Lokvani*, a public-private partnership in e-governance also provides an interesting case to follow (Singh 2005).

However, as Vittal (2001) notes, the common citizens in this country are habituated to the government's style of governance—hierarchy, secrecy, corruption, half-hearted interest; this coupled with lack of a comprehensive package as well as fear of surveillance are believed to have resulted in minimal utilisation of e-governance provisions.

(v) *E-health/e-medicine:* The telemedicine consultation project of the AP government, sponsored by the Care Foundation-Hughes Escorts-Siemens-Karishma Software, at the district hospitals of Nellore and Mahabubnagar is serving the community effectively. This is reinforced by another project in which the Auxiliary Nurse Midwife (ANMs) are equipped with Personal Digital Assistants (PDAs) for collecting important information from village women on infants, children, diseases, preventive measures, etc., for further use by Primary Health Centres (PHCs), district hospitals and state level officials. In another project, ISRO has hooked up 10 rural hospitals covering eight states to its network (telemedicine network) for providing super speciality medical consultations in remote areas of Leh, Andaman and Nicobar Islands, Tripura and Assam. Telemedicine, of course, is one of the fastest growing areas of ICT for development in the country.

Comments

As would be seen above, the developments and networking of information technology in the country during the last five years is amazing, and this shows that there is much more to come in the near future. One of the crucial factors of success, though, would be the support of the Central government to the states. For the first time in the country, the Central government signed on 18 August 2002, a memorandum of understanding with the state government of Kerala to support e-governance, and address technology, financing, business models and organisational issues, decision-making, seed funding through National Institute of Smart Governance, and sharing of such national experiences including that of the NIC (*The Hindu*, 19 August 2002).

For quite sometime now, the Government of India (Ministry of Communications and Information Technology) has launched the *IT-for-the-masses* project. The project envisages setting up of 100 million Internet connections by 2008, and computerise and web-enable all government services and transactions. One of the very prestigious and ambitious projects, this also faces problems like many government projects. It has been commented that it has limitations of inappropriate revenue model and inadequate popular participation. Keniston (2004) comments on the inappropriateness of the model itself, with particular reference to e-governance, which is borrowed from other countries. There is the absence of a proper revenue model—who sets up the infrastructure, who pays for it, who is responsible for implementation—all these need to be economically worked out. *The Telegraph* (14 January 2003) quotes an officer from the Department of IT, GOI saying:

> While such initiatives are aimed at removing the existence of middlemen, a few instances in Madhya Pradesh and Andhra Pradesh have shown that there is strong resistance from the local politicians ... Bureaucrats derive their power by restricting the right to information and a thorough knowledge of the administrative system. They do not want the people to get direct access to information or the officials. Villagers have to depend on middle person to access local information from the computers that have been installed in the panchayats.

One of the NASSCOM (2003) studies shows that e-governance is the fastest growing segment of the IT market in India which grew above 18 per cent in 2001–02. However, there is much less investment by the governments for the development of e-governance in the country. Kiran Karnik, NASSCOM President underlined the fact that despite the government's policy commitment for 3 per cent budget expenditure on IT, they were not sufficiently parting funds for e-governance (*Business Standard*, 17 January 2003). Further, he mentions, out of the total government IT expenditure, only 15 per cent goes to software services, with 60 per cent and 25 per cent respectively going to hardware and software package development.

With fast growing rural connectivity, teething problems are but obvious to crop up. Even if the young kiosk manager under the *Gyandoot* project gets reasonably good money (for instance by charging Rs 5–15 for various services, Rs 10 for typing applications, Rs 50 for astrological charts and forecasts, Rs 250 for computer lessons to local kids, and so on), there are problems of power back up, slow download speed, slow response rate to complaints, etc. Shapoo (2003), quoting the NDTV, notes that Gyandoot which was started with much hype and expectations

> ... now has very few takers. The operator at the information centre in Nalcha Block in Dhar has no clients. He has no electricity for hours and his information kiosk is deserted ... Thirty nine information centres were set up to make people in 500 villages computer literate and serve as one-stop shops for information. Of these, seven centres have an average of 35 visitors a day and six centres are non-existent, as the phones do not work. The rest have very few visitors. 'Nobody has told us in the village that such a service is available' says Teji Singh Rajen, a villager in Dhar district.

This situation reflects the typical mindset of the prospective users of such innovative schemes—the users do not mind to know and the government providers do not mind to listen.

In so far as the national and state projects are concerned, piloting works fine; but its full scale implementation raises the question of sustainability, and largely fails. Though the Central government has ensured national policies along with implementation strategies and plays more of a catalytic role, most of 'IT for development' projects are run in the states by state governments, NGOs and private operators. There has not been any attempt to consolidate these fragmented efforts to provide direction to national development. On the other hand, as Dugger (2000) points out, these small projects attempt to link 'isolated rural pockets to the borderless world of knowledge'. A tall order indeed!

ICT AND CULTURE

The spread of IT culture is most visible through the proliferation of cyber cafes and cyber culture. With regard to communications technology, communication through mobile technology and its allied functionalities are the latest craze especially amongst the youngsters. Both IT and mobile technology are creating a new lifestyle and worldview. However, questions have been raised about the notion of cyber culture, the phenomena of surveillance, pornography and obscenity, and such other consequences.

Cyber Culture

As noted earlier, IT development in India is one of the fastest in the world. While internet service is available in more than 380 cities and towns (and also in many village clusters), above 12,300 cyber cafes/public access kiosks are reported to exist in the country (ISPAI 2004). Other sources (Glaser 2003) report a whopping 300,000 internet cafes all over the country. While they provide cheaper and instant access to the Net, they also provide opportunities for cyber crime including pornography and cyber crime, largely by terrorists.

Studies on cyber culture are rare, and the area is peaking up in many parts of the globe, including India. Scholarship in this area has developed across three stages: popular cyber culture (e.g., duality of life, internet-led development, etc.), cyber culture studies (e.g., virtual communicates, identity online, etc.), and critical cyber culture studies (e.g., interaction and discourse online, access and equity, cyberspace design, etc.) (Silver 2000). Cultural critics have suggested that internet reduces literacy, creates alienation from reality and social fragmentation (Birkerts 1994); on the other hand, other group, techno-futurists pleads that internet reduces economic and social inequities, fosters democratic participation, and exhales a new frontier of civilisation.

Scholars and journalists of cyber culture studies initially depicted a descriptive picture that the Web, while allowing full freedom and control to the user to manipulate the environment, facilitates the user to experience cyber rape, violence and other unwanted liaisons. Other cyber theorists present a very forthcoming picture of Net meeting face-to-face in a different world while still maintaining individual identities in a collective virtual community. Rheingold's (1993) articulation of virtual community while appreciates doing on the Net almost everything that we do in real world (except that things are done on screen while the body remains behind), also talks of potential perils like hyper-reality, online surveillance, commodified Internet, and the like. The Internet populace was more attracted to it in the late 1990s as a place for empowerment, creativity, community, and identity. In the later part of critical cyber culture studies, online interactions, influence of socio-cultural-political-economic variables on them, and design interface have assumed greater importance. Besides the possibility of creation of pseudo communities, there is criticality in the cultural construction of the cyberspace. Critical voices have been raised such that the Net, in the name of recreating such a society, may in fact undermine the notion of civil society and multiplicity in unity (Jones 1997). Qestions have also been raised about unacceptable language, ethical issues, wastage of time and resources, and additional technological skills to use the Net. Sometimes, due to lack of provision to mention gender/race/caste/religion in Net-based communication, there is in fact disrespect to these realities in interactions in the cyber society.

Pornography and Obscenity

The cyber society proposes to have an alternative or a parallel to the existing civil society. Has this alternative improved the existing civilised society, or has it provided a free and flexible space for increasing anarchy? The famous and widely circulated MMS at Delhi Public School, and those on many models and film stars—even if many of those are really false—are an uncontrollable hazard and beyond the clutches of cyber law. We must also not forget the case of cyber crime by a minor student of Bal Bharti School in Delhi under section 67. Of a total 130.8 million phone connections in India, above 63 per cent are mobile subscribers; and of the 32 million new subscribers in the last only one year, 31 million were mobile subscriptions (Mukherjee 2006). While this, along with its side effects, will increase in future, the most engendered phenomenon is pornography. It is not surprising, therefore, that mobile phones have been banned in public schools in Delhi. And, in Mumbai the cyber caféowners are directed to have valid government licenses, install software filters, and possess valid IDs for the sponsors.

It may be argued that though pornography itself is not bad, what is objectionable is showing this in a manner (i.e., through public outlets) which induces sexual excitement—obscenity—and which is against public policy. The crime or offence has been well defined in various Acts: Indecent Representation of Women (Prohibition) Act, Indian Panel Code of 1860, Information Technology Act of 2000. This last Act defines obscenity as 'any material which is lascivious or appeals to the prurient interest or if its effect is such as to tend to deprave and corrupt persons… who are likely to read, see or hear the matter contained or embodied in it' (Varadarajan 2001). While the spread of Internet and the mobile phones have increased their use for obscenity, what is required is not only legal provisions for this but more importantly developing a civil sense of social ethics.

Surveillance

As has been noted earlier in this chapter, there is a general feeling among the citizens that information technology, and more particularly, its various social uses, and the Net are really meant for general good or that it is used for not only data surveillance but also life surveillance. Like traditional landline telephone tapping, tapping of the Net communication, mobile phones and internet telephones have raised critical questions about IT itself. In the absence of clear-cut guidelines and laws, almost every user today has a lurking fear on its very use. Further, this also raises concerns about political control for monitoring its citizens (Lyon 2001). The author further writes, 'surveillance is not inherently sinister or malign. But the focused attention to persons and populations with a view to influencing, managing or controlling them—that we call "surveillance"—is never innocent either' (ibid.: 307). While surveillance is extremely necessary in so far as, for instance, terrorism is concerned, data and life surveillance through the schemes of 'IT for Development', it is argued, facilitates debilitating political action, suppresses social action, as also favours hegemony by the multinational companies. Modern life promises liberation, though the modern technological developments are creating more control, conflict and repression. Writes Black (2003: 32–33), 'Thus, whether prosecuted by the state or by private organisations (those of corporate capital included), the "information society" as "surveillance society" commands a long tradition'. As an extension of that tradition, preserved intellectual property has today become a property at the click of the mouse. Concerns about human rights issues in an information society have also been raised with regard to regulatory frameworks, ownership and right to privacy (see Jorgensen 2006).

Conclusion

As has been discussed, globalisation has brought in many structural changes in the Indian society, economy, culture and life style. The influence of IT and the Net has been pervasive, benefiting the civil society, communities and individuals in many ways. We seem to find it impossible today to function without the Net; and it has been argued that even the activists cannot afford to neglect it (Mehta 2001). However, at times one wonders: are these information and concomitant actions so essential for modern living? Diffusion of technology and more particularly the internet is not going to help as much as some cohesive policy on social shaping of technology may (Lievrouw 2002).

Technology is not ethically and socially neutral. Individual choice is important towards social shaping of technology. Therefore, it is unfair to talk about technological *impacts* on society; rather it is prudent to introspect the way individuals and communities make choices about technology and utilise it for social action. Development vis-à-vis technology needs to be seen in this perspective.

References

Bauman, Z. (1994). 'Deceiving the Twentieth Century,' *New Statesman and Society*, April: 24–25.

Beeson, I. (2003). 'Imaginative Communities: Turning Information Technology to Expressive Use in Community Groups', in S. Hornby and Z. Clarke (eds), *Challenges and Change in the Information Society*. London: Facet Publishing.

Birkerts, S. (1994). *The Gutenberg Elegies: The Fate of Reading in an Electronic Age*. Winchester, MA: Faber and Faber.

Black, A. (2003). 'The Information Society: A Secular View', in S. Hornby and Z. Clarke (eds), *Challenges and Change in the Information Society*. London: Facet Publishing.

Branch, R.M. (1997). 'Educational Technology Frameworks that Facilitate Culturally Pluralistic Instruction,' *Educational Technology*, March–April: 38–40.

Castells, M. (1998). *End of Millennium*. Oxford: Blackwell.

Das, B. (2006). 'Beyond the Boundary? Globalisation of Communication in Indian Society', in B. N. Patnaik and S. I. Hasnain (eds), *Globalisation: Language, Culture and Media*. Shimla: Institute of Advanced Study.

Dugger, C.W. (2000). 'Connecting Rural India to the World,' *New York Times*, 28 May.

Feather, J. (2003). 'Theoretical Perspectives on the Information Society', in S. Hornby and Z. Clarke (eds), *Challenge and Change in the Information Society*. London: Facet Publishing.

Giddens, A. (1999). *Runaway World: How Globalisation Is Reshaping Our Lives*. Cambridge: Profile Books.

Glaser, M. (2003). 'Indian cities on Verge of Restricting Access to Cyber Cafes', *Online Journalism Review*, 4 December, http://www.orj.org/ojr/glaser, accessed on 5 April 2005.

Government of India (1999a). *New Telecom Policy 1999*. New Delhi: Ministry of Communications and Information Technology.

——— (1999b). *IT Action Plan III: Long Term National IT Policy*. New Delhi: Ministry of Communications and Information Technology.

——— (2003). *Internet Service*. New Delhi: Ministry of Communications and Information Technology.

Hanson, E.C. (2001). 'Globalisation, Inequality and the Internet in India', Paper presented at Meeting of the International Studies Association, Chicago, Illinois.

ISPAI (2004). *Internet Services Industry—An Overview*. New Delhi: Internet Services Providers Association of India.

Jhunjhunwala, A., A. Ramachandran and S. Ramachander (2006). 'Connecting Rural India: Taking Step Back for Two Forward', *Information Technology in Developing Countries*, 16(1). (Available at http://www.iimahd.ernet.in/egov/ifip/feb2006/article1.htm, accessed on 1 June 2006).

Jones, S. (ed.) (1997). *Virtual Culture: Identity and Community in Cybersociety*. London: Sage Publications.

Jorgensen, R.K. (ed.) (2006). *Human Rights in the Global Information Society*. Massachussets: The MIT Press.

Keniston, K. (2004). 'Introduction', in K. Keniston and D. Kumar (eds), *Bridging the Digital Divide: Lessons from India*. New Delhi: Sage Publications.

Lievrouw, L.A. (2002). 'Determination and Contingency in New Media Development: Diffusion of Innovations and Social Shaping of Technology Perspectives', in L.A. Lievrouw and S. Livingstone (eds), *Handbook of New Media*. London: Sage Publications.

Lyon, D. (2001). 'Surveillance after 11 September 2001,' *Sociological Research Online*, 6(3). (Also *Sarai Reader*, 2002). Available at http://www.socresonline.org.uk/6/3/lyon.html, accessed 1 June 2006.

Matsumoto, D. (1996). *Culture and Psychology*. Pacific Grove: C.A. Brooks/Cole Publishing Company.

Mehta, A. (2001). 'Why Activists Cannot Afford to Neglect the Internet', *Sarai Reader 2001*, pp: 140–46.

Misra, D.C., Avijit Dutta, Omkar Rai, Rama Hariharan, Rajiv Goel and Manie Khaneja (2001). 'Rural Bazar—Ideas of Today for a Better Tomorrow', *People's Action*. (Available at http://ruralinformatics.nicin/files/4903/pdf, accessed on 1 June 2006).

Mukherjee, A. (2006). 'Going for Broke', *Outlook*, 27 February, pp. 42–43.

NASSCOM (2003). *IT Enabled Services*. New Delhi: National Association of Software and Service Companies.

Noronha, F. (2001). *Internet for All: Indian Village to get Access at Prices They Can Afford*. Chennai: TeNet.

Panda, S. and S. Chaudhary (2001). 'Tele-learning and Tele-learning Centres in India', in C. Latchem and D. Walker (eds), *Telecentres*. Vancouver: COL.

Press, L., W. Foster, P. Wolcott and W. McHenry (2002). 'The Internet in India and China,' *First Monday*, 7(10): 1–34.

Rheingold, H. (1993). *The Virtual Community: Homesteading on the Electronic Frontier*. Reading, MA: Addison-Wesley.

Rogers, E.M. and T.M. Steinfatt (1999). *Intercultural Communication*. Prospect Heights, IL: Waveland Press.

Shapoo, R.K. (2003). 'Gyandoot E-Governance Runs into Glitches', NDTV News, 27 January, available at http://www.ndtv.com/morenews/, Accessed on 5 April 2005.

Silver, D. (2000). 'Looking Backwards, Looking Forward: Cyber culture Studies 1990–2000', in D. Gauntlett (ed.), *Web Studies: Rewriting Media Studies for the Digital Age*. Oxford: Oxford University Press.

Singh, A.P. (2005). 'Lokvani: An E-Effort to Empower Citizens', *Information Technology in Developing Countries*, 15(2). Available at http://www.iimahad.ernet.in/egov/ifip/nov2005/article1.htm accessed 1 June 2006.

Singhal, A. and E.M. Rogers (2001). *India's Communication Revolution: From Bullock Carts to Cyber Marts*. New Delhi: Sage Publications.

Varadarajan, S. (2001). 'Policing the Net: The Dangers of India's New IT Act', *Sarai Reader 2001*, pp. 133–35.

Vittal, N. (2001). 'Resistance to E-Governance', *The Economic Times*, 10 June.

Wolcott, P. and S. Goodman (2002). 'Global Diffusion of the Internet I: India: Is the Elephant Learning to Dance?' *Communications of the Association for Information Systems*, 11: 560–646.

Section V
Political Dimensions

18

Globalisation and the State in India

Vidhu Verma

INTRODUCTION

If we read the Indian Constitution as a text about achieving social justice, then the idea of citizens prescribing equal laws for themselves take on a dimension that a society deliberately acts to transform social relations. However it is recognised today that this idea was realised only in the framework of the nation state; if this nation state is now being redefined by global society and global economy then is this connection between nation state and democracy weakened?

In addressing this question I will first examine how globalisation has changed the nation state by focusing on the concepts of sovereignty and democratic citizenship.[1] I shall then briefly describe four political responses to the processes of globalisation. Finally using this debate as a springboard, I shall map out some of the challenges to the Indian state and evaluate its responses to the context of globalisation with reference to the Information Technology industry and politics of decentralisation. This chapter ends with the proposal for a more profound global transformation that is responsive to distributional considerations.

A few preliminary points before I proceed further. Globalisation is difficult to define not only because there are multiple projects in progress but also because it has been explored from a multiplicity of intellectual angles, academic lenses and disciplinary epistemologies. It comes in many different versions.[2] This chapter only examines political aspects of globalisation that have caused major changes in the nation state system since 1980s.

Broadly, the term globalisation refers to the intensification of global interconnectedness particularly in trade, capital, technology and information within a single integrated global market. It also refers to innovations in technologies of communication and transportation, which are reconfiguring social relationships spatially, and temporally; and to international divisions of labour operated by multinational corporations that stretch the production and manufacture of commodities across regional and national boundaries.[3]

Although a great deal has been written on globalisation, an inquiry into its political aspects poses major challenges of both an analytical and normative kind. The analytical challenge centres on the range of misconceptions that have become associated with globalisation that it destroys sovereignty, or that it is a recent phenomenon and different from modernity.[4] The normative challenge is in considering the voices and interests that evaluate global processes. To respond to these challenges, I focus on two key notions in political theory that have been debated recently in the context of globalisation and which have a bearing on the state in India.

The first is the nation state and the nature and extent of its sovereignty. In modern Western political thought, the idea of the state is linked to the notion of an impersonal and legal or constitutional order with the capability of administering and controlling a given territory (Held 1995: 38–40). The classic concept of sovereignty entails that there is an authority in a political community that has undisputed right to determine the framework of rules and regulations in a given territory and to govern accordingly. Over time, in modern democratic states sovereignty came to mean the supreme law making and decision-making power of a community whose ultimate source of sovereignty lies with the people. The second aspect of sovereignty in the international context means states should be regarded as independent in all matters of internal politics and should in principle be free to determine their own fate within this framework. It implies the assertion of the states of sole rights to jurisdiction over a particular people and territory (ibid.).

Many issues raised by globalisation have significant implications for traditional concepts of state sovereignty at three levels; (a) traditional domains of state activity and responsibility (defence, communications, legal systems) can rarely be fulfilled without collaboration with other states (see Held 1995: 91); (b) states have to operate within a post cold war situation where the US has emerged as the sole military superpower in the Western world; (c) states face pressure from global civil society organisations on an increasing number of issues. The question is: whether sovereignty still remains intact while political autonomy of the state has diminished or whether state actually faces a loss of sovereignty; whether the nation state is being strengthened in certain respects in so far as it suits corporate interests or is weakened in both its economic and political sovereignty?

The second notion is democratic citizenship.[5] The main principle of democracy is that people should be self-determining. Scholars writing on globalisation in the 1990s assumed that the removal of commercial barriers by national governments, greater mobility of people and the cultural impact of global information flows would pave the way for democratic forms of government. These assumptions are rendered highly problematic by the growing gap between the democratic governments of nation states that have to be accountable for their performance (mostly through electoral politics) within their territorial boundaries, as opposed to the multinationals that are not accountable to the wider body of citizens of any nation. Indeed talk of a 'global democracy deficit' comes from many quarters most notably with regard to interstate agreements or interdependent financial markets that are not accountable to any democratic will formation (Bohman 1999; Anderson 2002); or whenever the set of those involved in making democratic decisions fails to coincide with the set of those affected by them. The case of the European Union is an example of democratic deficit caused by the shift away from national decision-making bodies to bureaucratic decision-making committees of experts.

Theoretically, both these concepts seem contradictory to each other since sovereignty of the state is incompatible with the needs of democratic citizenship that is more sensitive to governance. The shift from government to governance in some respects reorients the institutions of the state (party system, electoral participation) to a highly diverse range of actors who participate through networking and alliances between different groups in cooperative forms of action. Since sovereignty is unitary and indivisible, it has to stem from a single source. Promoting democratic citizenship in the world means that national sovereignty is inviolable except when tyrannical regimes do not provide democratic citizenship or if local groups, movements and nationalism question a nation state's representative and accountable nature. Following this principle, the US has rallied many states in the Western world while invading Kuwait in 1991, and later in Afghanistan and Iraq. In this context, the US has been following hegemonic social practices by promoting certain sets of values as well as norms of governance. As a corollary, promoting private initiative, minimising the role of the state to maintenance of law and order and building representative democracies have become part of its larger objective of constructing hegemony or what some call 'empire'.[6]

My argument is that while state sovereignty is highly conditional on global patterns of interdependence, the state as a political institution is far from being submerged, either by global capitalism or by transnational political organisations. The two factors that need to be kept in mind are first, global capital still requires state functions to be performed and second, the persistence of national identity and nation-focused sentiments in conjunction with ethnicity reaffirm the boundaries of the nation state.

This is not to deny that the processes of globalisation have introduced new players in the world economy or that in developing countries like India, governments have withdrawn from certain social sectors and instead imposed new set of obligations on their citizens. 'Global city regions' are fast emerging as spaces where proliferation of identities go on. Despite these changes, nation states remain the main political players but the political institutions and national markets are not the same. Governments now share aspects of governance with corporate entities and civil society organisations.

The only way of overcoming the contradictory aspects of state sovereignty and democratic citizenship is if on the one hand, the global rules of the game especially for multinational business become more sensitive to the democratic accountability of national governments, by playing a part in enhancing this accountability through a more transparent code of conduct that discourages corrupt and unfair trade and business practices. On the other hand, national governments need to recognise the gains that can be made from selective and yet greater international interdependence. The main challenge is to define an economic role for the state in countries like India within the global setting without rooting it in a narrow economic or cultural nationalism and a political role that is responsive to distributive justice for all citizens.[7]

THE NATION STATE AND GOVERNANCE: HISTORICAL DIMENSIONS

There is no single theory of the politics of nations and states but the nation state is indisputably associated with political integration in the modern age. The rise of the modern state can be seen as part of a set of parallel developments characterised by the rise of nationalism, mass parties, the transition towards new forms of legitimisation of power based on domination and the concentration of political power in the institutions of the state. Party organisations can be seen as closely tied to a concept of the political rooted in interest and power that in turn are intrinsically linked to a particular concept of the state.

According to David Held, 'the conditions involved in the creation of nationalism were also often the conditions which generated the democratic modern state' (see Held 1995: 58; 1991). In the second half of the 20th century, nationalism and democracy were generally taken as synonymous in the political thought of Western nations. At the heart of these arguments is the proposition that the rise of nationalism is normally associated with deep running social ferment and change which disrupt the old order of society and speed up the processes of social mobilisation. On this basis, nationalism is seen as one of the major manifestations of the fundamental democratisation of society, the stirring into action of those classes who formerly played a passive part in political life (Emerson 1960).

The nation state was regarded as the political expression of the democratic will of the people. It was spread throughout the world with an almost 'missionary zeal' to the newly colonised areas of Asia, Africa and Latin America as part of the ideological fight against colonialism. It became central to the twin projects of nation building and secular nationalism. Secular nationalist loyalties 'were based on the idea that the legitimacy of the state was rooted in the will of the people, divorced from any religious sanction' (Juergensmeyer 1993: 11).

In the post-World War II period, the role of the nation state was critical. The interventionist state took many forms around the globe: the Keynesian welfare state involved extensive state guidance of a predominantly private economy, the developmentalist state in third world structures focused on overcoming the underdevelopment caused by colonialism and the Soviet model of the state that ruled out private economy (Rapley 2003).

The concerns of the industrialised countries in the cold war period were strongly influenced by the misery caused by the depression that created the desire for full employment derived from the conception of a welfare state, and the legacy of the second world war which motivated the quest for peace and reconstruction. In the post-colonial states like India the state was committed to economic development through planning with the explicit purpose of raising productivity and output. There was a conscious attempt to limit the degree of openness and integration with the world economy in pursuit of a more autonomous, if not self reliant, development. The state was assigned a strategic role in development because the market by itself was not perceived as sufficient (Nayyar 2002a).

In the 1980s the debt crisis led to a devaluation of the dollar and gradually allowed for the introduction of a system of floating exchange rates in the world economy. The partial collapse of the world economic system coincided with a massive rise in the price of oil that led to profits for major oil producing countries. The international rules developed during the cold war were rendered largely irrelevant by the collapse of state bureaucracies and party dictatorships in the former Soviet Union, Eastern and Central Europe along with the growth of the international drug trade, new brands of terrorism, Islamic fundamentalism and the possibilities of cyber warfare.

Financial liberalisation and the emergence of a global capital market compelled virtually all governments to become far more responsive to the signals that emanate from that market. Given these changes, state firms almost everywhere were privatised, and policymakers shifted towards regulation as a means of using the state to influence economic policy. In the last decade, even countries like India adapted different strategies in order to integrate their domestic economic policies much more into the world economy and to enlarge the role of the market vis-a-vis the state.[8]

The widespread consensus in thinking about development came to be known as the Washington Consensus in the late 1980s. Despite many voices of dissent, international financial institutions imposed restrictions on debt-ridden third world countries which included trade liberalisation, clearing all hurdles to foreign investment, privatisation, deregulation, strengthening property rights and tax reforms. It implied that the state should be rolled back, particularly in third world countries from the social sector; the market should be central in the accumulation process and civil society organisations should claim some kind of autonomy from the state (Chandhoke 2002: 43; Harris 2001). It was during this period that NGOs in many third world countries including India proliferated in sectors like education, health, instituting income generating schemes, and rural areas.

However, the rhetoric of free and untrammelled markets faced a major setback in the mid-1990s with the financial crisis that hit many countries of East Asia, Japan, Brazil and Mexico. Many scholars and politicians blamed globalisation for the destabilisation of financial markets, political disorder and income disparities between nations (Rhodes and Higgot 2000; Mahathir 2000). It was argued that 'a global economic order had been forged through globalisation without any prospect for justice, or democracy, or redistribution' (Chandhoke 2002: 43). It was widely acknowledged that market liberalism if left to private corporations gave rise to its own problems and it was felt that if markets were to endure they had to be controlled (Krugman 1995).

In this way, the Washington Consensus lost some of its lustre in the 1990s and its prescriptions were subjected to question (Nayyar 1997). This led to a radical shift in the understanding of the role of globalisation; the replacement of the language of the market by that of governance, accountability, transparency and democracy. Even though the dominant concerns of neo-liberalism continued, it was now recognised that along with economic growth there was a need for governance (Jayal 1997).[9] It implied the need for regulation and moderation of the processes of globalisation. It had a lot to do with the growth of civil society organisations all over the globe that criticised the policies of international financial institutes for their policies on development.

In this way, where earlier the emphasis was on opening up of national borders to the free flow of global capital and free trade, the emphasis now is on governance of these very activities.

However despite these changes the significant elements of free market and a minimal state continue to be seen as important elements in a democratic society.

Does Globalisation Spell the End of the Nation State?

Kenichi Ohmae, author of *The End of the Nation State* argues that the advance of markets and economic interdependence will soon see nation states being replaced by city states. The claims for group-differentiated rights actually arise out of the space of the city. The concentration of immigrants, refugees, and their identities are intertwined with the articulation of various citizenship rights against the state. Further, he sees a future world of city states that define their identity primarily from involvement in a borderless world economy.

In a narrow sense, Ohmae's prognosis seems accurate since contemporary world challenges to state sovereignty come from the global economy (multinational companies, global capital markets), transnational bodies (World Bank, GATT, WTO, United Nations, European Union), International Law (legal conventions recognised by national courts), hegemonic power and power blocs (NATO). Powerful multinational enterprises are able to transfer investment across political boundaries, control the terms of technology transfer and negotiate favourable tax and subsidy deals with government. Global business strategies are themselves enhanced by radical changes in information technology and telecommunications. These flows of investment, technology, communications, and profit across national boundaries are often seen as the most striking symptom of a global challenge to the nation state.

However, scholars like Ohmae wrongly assume that due to these changes a political order is emerging that will produce worldwide homogenisation and a global civilisation. There are four common responses to globalisation in relation to the nation state that I will consider: (a) the functional interpretation of the nation state; (b) globalisation as an expression of the rise of the free market or of neo-liberalism all over the world; (c) globalisation undermines the scope for meaningful democratic citizenship and (d) nation state survives only in the form of cultural and religious nationalism.

The Functional Interpretation of the State

The functional interpretation of the state is based on three claims: that the state is no longer capable of performing the functions for the contemporary world; that all states are equally integrated in the world economy and that a decline in the freedom of action in the international arena implies erosion of sovereignty of the state. I will argue against these claims because by suggesting homogenisation, they ignore the complex ways in which though nation states persist, the way in which they operate has been greatly transformed (Rapley 2003).

Multinational corporations are involved increasingly in activities like licensing, outsourcing, and joint ventures including international marketing that are not captured in the measures of foreign direct investment (FDI) (Bhaduri 2002: 36). They become important in influencing the overall performance of the nation state through these channels. Domestic firms located in a developing country have greater access to commercial loans internationally through joint ventures, and can obtain a better credit rating if they are linked to a multinational. Through multinational investment developing countries hope to attract both modern technologies and other forms of international capital inflow, including portfolio investments (ibid.). The erosion of authority occurs because governments have far less control over domestic corporate tax rates, interest rates, or financial markets triggering off massive speculative capital flight.

In India, for example, flows of private capital through foreign institutional investors (henceforth FII) have displaced domestic mutual funds in importance in the equity market. Although FII investment of around $11 billion is a welcome sign for boosting the capital market for many, there is unease over the nature of these investments and their impact on the stock market (Mohan 2005).

Despite the onslaught of global corporations and new international actors, scholars like James Petras argue that the nation state plays a more decisive role or intervenes with more vigour in shaping economic exchanges and investment at the local, national or international levels (Petras 1999; Hirst and Thompson 1995). It is impossible to conceive of the expansion and deepening involvement of multinational banks and corporations without the prior political, military and economic intervention of the nation state. Nor is it possible to understand the expansion of the market in the former USSR, China, Eastern Europe and former radical third world countries without acknowledging the vital political role of the US in fuelling arms race and subsidizing cultural and religious propaganda.

Scholars like Panitch (1994) stress that the state is an agent actively promoting the political construction of globalisation through trade agreements and regionalism. The most elementary and important trade agreements (GATT, NAFTA, ASEAN) and trading blocs (EU) were formulated, codified and implemented by nation states. The major policies stimulating vast tax windfalls, massive subsidies, and lower domestic labour costs have all been formulated by the nation state (Holton 1998). The scale and scope of nation state activity has grown to such a point that one needs to refer to it as the New Statism rather than the free market.

As Michael Mann (1997) argues that one can only understand the changing role of the state during globalisation if one makes distinctions between powerful and weak states. Economic interdependence is asymmetrical since the reactions of a powerful state are going to be different from those of weak peripheral states in the post-colonial world like India. Economic globalisation is not an evenly spread process, when nation states themselves vary in size, wealth and power. To speak of the impact of the globalisation upon the nation state, as if this were a unitary process that took the same form in every sector of the economy and for every nation state is, therefore, highly misleading. Macroeconomic policies adopted in a national context, particularly by the major industrialised countries exercise an important influence on economies in the rest of the world through interest rates, exchange rates, or inflation rates.

Further, these emerging issues are difficult to control in countries like India because national laws are applicable to resident individuals or registered firms but their jurisdiction does not extend to individuals or firms across national boundaries. The reason is that 'individuals or firms are subject to national laws enacted by their parliaments. But countries are not subject to similar international laws for there is no world government or parliament that can enact laws binding on nations' (Nayyar 2002: 12).

A recent example is the debate on quotas in the textile industry. Trade associations from more than 50 countries including countries such as Bangladesh, Indonesia and Sri Lanka signed the Istanbul Declaration asking the WTO to keep the quotas for a further three years. The signatories feared that the end of quotas would mean the loss of important inflows of foreign exchange. Having no natural comparative advantage beyond abundant cheap labour they feared losing markets to China.[10]

Thus, variations in the capacities of nation states to regulate cross-border transactions are an important variable when we consider the impact of globalisation on sovereignty of individual nations. The position of powerful players such as the USA and other G7 nations such as Japan and Germany who exert considerable influence in World Bank or WTO, for instance, contrasts markedly with the bargaining power of developing countries such as India and more worse off states like Bangladesh and Mozambique.

Globalisation and the Neoliberal Paradigm

Globalisation has led to viewing the neoliberal paradigm as the only acceptable form for celebrating the market (Hirst and Thompson 1995).[11] Neoliberal theory has had a strong influence on the structural adjustment and stabilisation programmes introduced by many governments since the early 1980s (Rapley 2003; MacEwan 1999). It is characterised by an excessive optimism concerning the role of market forces in promoting development. It assumes that nation states can relatively easily break into export markets on the basis of their comparative advantage but the reality is somewhat different.

Since producers in the developed world monopolise the most advanced technology, research and development, and marketing practices in most situations, producers in the third world like India face non-tariff protectionist barriers in First World markets and are part of an unequal exchange. It is for these reasons that adjustment policies such as the blanket removal of import controls and state subsidies and tariff reduction can therefore be regarded as unjustified even from the narrow viewpoint of promoting economic growth.

Indeed, despite globalisation, many problems related to poverty, inequality and deprivation still exist (Falk 1999). One-eighth of the people in the industrialised world are affected by poverty. Almost one-third of the people in the developing world, an estimated 1.5 billion, live in poverty and experience absolute deprivation (Nayyar 2002: 5). Many scholars argue that globalisation may have created opportunities for a few countries in the developing world but a very large proportion of people are still marginalised by the same process.

This is because market forces not only may be inefficient, but also promote injustice. Markets are hierarchical institutions in which people are constrained by their initial position in the bargaining power even though the transaction is viewed as fair. The profits of a few, and growth for some, thrive in conditions of uncertainty, inequality and vulnerability of all those who sell their labour power and of most consumers. Although markets emphasise juridical equality between individuals they marginalise groups of people by emphasising on certain assets or skills that can be used to provide an income. In a national labour market, the state can step in to provide solutions for this exclusion because governments are accountable to the people. However in the changed context, the openness and interdependence between labour and capital has made it difficult for governments to preempt such exclusions.[12]

Further weaknesses in the neoliberal paradigm have been noted. First, the paradigm homogenises countries of both the West and third world. Moreover, by reducing development to good governance based on market forces, it overlooks alternatives that might be explored in different political and cultural contexts. The result is a technocratic approach that overlooks the deepening contradictions of the development paradigm that rests on a prevailing global power structure that is grossly inequitable and undemocratic. Indeed the commitment to electoral democracy ignores how inequalities at the global and local level restrict the institutions of good governance.

Indeed, these arguments have given rise to a critique of the international economic order in many third world countries like India. It is realised that third world is assigned a marginal place in the international economic order. Although economic growth has been made, the pressing issues of environmental degradation, exploitation, state oppression and impoverishment remain.

Democratic Citizenship Rights

It is widely acknowledged that national governments are no longer the site of democratic politics and democratic citizenship rights. Several scholars have argued that in an age of globalisation citizenship cannot be confined within the boundaries of nation states; it must become transnational. Proponents of cosmopolitan citizenship like David Held for instance, advocate the need for a cosmopolitan democratic law to which citizens whose rights have been violated by their own states could appeal (Held 1993). Whether the present institutional framework, the UN, UNICEF, UNESCO, UNDP, the Bretton Woods, WTO and IMF is adequate, appropriate, or sufficient to meet the governance needs of the contemporary world economy and polity is a major concern. Griffin calls for the scrapping of non-performing global institutions such as the World Bank, and the transformation of IMF into a world central bank, and the creation of new global institutions to enforce world civil and criminal laws (Griffin 2003).

However, focusing on institutions as David Held does, misses out certain issues that have gained significance in the contemporary world. Whether the present institutional framework is adequate or sufficient to meet the governance needs of the contemporary world economy and polity has a lot to do with the nature and scope of international economic transactions. Since there is considerable structural change in international trade flows and international capital movements, cross border transactions in technology and movements of a larger number of people, developing countries are spectators rather than participants. Thus, asymmetrical rules (a point made earlier) need to be reassessed. Moreover, there are almost no mechanisms, let alone institutions, which could coordinate macroeconomic policies and their management across the world. Institutional responses are obviously of great importance but global institutions are only effective when they promote and deepen democratisation and when they facilitate popular participation.

Another set of scholars view the growth of a global civil society consisting of transnational non-governmental organisations, political activists, social movements, religious denominations and trade unions to business and financial groupings as having a democratic basis. In many ways global civil society represents transnational associational life that challenges the state system in two ways (Lipschutz 1992). On the one hand, it has focused attention on issues such as human rights, the environment, development that are within the province of state sovereignty. On the other, it has challenged the contours of the world economic order as mandated by the World Trade Organization, the World Bank, and IMF. There have been major protests in Seattle, at Prague and then in Geneva. But, from these actions it is difficult to conclude that global civil society is autonomous of other institutions of international politics or can provide an alternative notion of governance (Chandhoke 2002). This gives rise to the question whether they can counteract deep-rooted structures of global capitalism and provide an alternative to the present system? While it is perfectly true that global civil society has critiqued the workings of the international economic order, it is found that most of these organisations rely upon states, their institutions and laws. While they might critique the practices of states, in the field of human rights, they also require states to create political and legal frameworks that facilitate setting up of the rule of the law, civil and political rights, or environmental protection. In effect as Chandhoke points out 'the very states that global civil society supposedly opposes enable the latter in the sense that only they can provide the conditions in which the civil society agenda is realised' (2002: 51)

Returning to my earlier argument it could be now safely asserted that the state cannot be ignored as a site of democratic politics. It is important in terms of democratisation because elected governments are susceptible to the influence of citizens using democratic political rights. There remains considerable scope for national policy making. Moreover countries continue to exercise their autonomy in very different ways, reflecting their different political cultures. Even if forces of globalisation put similar pressure on countries like India, China or Pakistan they do not respond in the same way. Furthermore, it is important to stress that citizens deeply care about maintaining their national differences in social policy and they provide considerable differences in political participation at the domestic level.

Nation State, Cultural and Religious Nationalism

Since 1980 new frames of reference related to cultural and religious identity have emerged along with local, regional and global interconnectedness.[13] These demands range from a greater share of political power and respect for cultural identity to a more balanced allocation of resources for development that would minimise the demands to which minorities are subjected to in multiethnic societies. These demands came along with radical changes in eastern European communist regimes that were overthrown in a dramatic manner in the 1980s and which then brought their economies into line with the requirements of a global market economy driven by competition (Haynes 1998).

Elsewhere in some third world countries, along with changes in approaches to the market, ethno-national entities, long considered extinct, and which had not been an integral part of the nationalist movements of the 19th century came forward with demands for independent sovereign statehood and many states were caught in a maelstrom of redefinitions of the nation state. The argument of nationalities asserting their political rights of autonomy have in recent years spread to countries like Indonesia, China and Africa. Some have noted a global religious revitalisation since the communications revolution has led to the development of transnational religious communities (Huntington 1996).

However, the matter is complex. Some scholars argue that nationality

> answers one of the most pressing needs of the modern world, namely, how to maintain solidarity among the populations of states that are large and anonymous, such that their citizens cannot possibly enjoy the kind of community that relies on kinship or face-to-face interaction (Miller 2000: 31–32).

This argument is pitched against those who see national sentiment as somehow an extension of the desire for a homogenous, local and immediate community. Summarising these contrasting trends, Robert Holton (1998: 156–59) proposes the idea of the complex interpenetration of global, national, regional and local elements. He is of the view that the nation state draws strength from its symbolic significance as a source of political and cultural identity and is in certain senses, a form of resistance to globalisation.

But the question is: can we formulate a normative and social theoretical account of a nation state that preserves a place for the distinctiveness of people without endorsing the exclusions typical of nationalism?

An answer to this question lies in viewing how early forms of anti-colonialism that drew heavily on classical European nationalism and were inspired by the idea of national self-determination assumed a different form from the European one because the assertion of national identity was a form of struggle against colonial rule and economic exploitation; it assumed to be a liberating force linked to other goals of liberty, justice and democracy. For African and Asian nations, the quest for political independence was inextricably linked to a desire for social and economic development and for an end to their subordination to the industrialised states of Europe. The goal of national liberation, therefore, had an economic, social as well as a political dimension.

Another feature of these nationalisms was that they were for most parts linked to state-building. Even when nationalism did not appear as a distinct ideology in as many Asian countries, it affected the path of nation-building they were to follow in the post-colonial period. Whereas some countries like India, Indonesia and Burma developed their nationalism in the face of imperialist threats, others began in earnest after independence. In contrast to the creation of European nations that sought statehood on the basis of a preexisting national identity many post-colonial societies tried to build nations on the foundations of the existing states. Yet all these countries were united in proposing visions of social and economic progress as part of a larger project for modernity; the emphasis was on the need to reform or reconstruct society and its traditions along modern lines. In this task, they produced a discourse that challenged the colonial claim to political domination while also accepting the premises of Western models of modernity (Chatterjee 1996).

In the 1960s, one of the main tenets of the then conventional wisdom regarding Third world development, modernisation theory, was that all societies would secularise as they modernised and industrialised. But the so-called primordial loyalties did not wither away in these societies over the following decades. There was no explanation except that processes of modernisation along with declining faith in both secularism and state-backed development, left many people with feelings of loss rather than empowerment. Additionally, modernisation not only undermined traditional hierarchical systems but also tried to allocate opportunities to people in highly unequal ways. It stimulated in many people the search for an identity to give them meaning and purpose during a period of historically unprecedented changes.

The Indian Situation

As argued above, anti-colonial consciousness in India revolved around conceiving the state as a democratic nation state. It was premised on the idea that the Indian state although a creature of constitutionalism must be based on an appropriate modern political idiom for articulating plural identities and loyalties. Such a state cannot discriminate against any religious group or impose a uniform pattern among its citizens. Consequently, there was on the one hand, a universal and abstract appeal to transcend primordial loyalties that stand in the way of full equality, while on the other, concrete interests and groups they represented appeared fragmented. In addition to making the new state reflect the diverse interests of society, they also assigned primacy to the state in the whole process of nation-building. The state intervention in the economy was not merely to invest, rapidly accumulate capital or protect domestic capital; its overall goal was to bring about far reaching transformations through a policy of affirmative action.

However in the process of nation-building many indigenous models of governing were marginalised. Many people suffered in the hands of nation-building efforts to suppress or assimilate culturally distinct peoples. In the last two decades, challenges to the state have come from at least three sources: first is the process of globalisation and economic reforms leading to liberalisation and withdrawal of the state from the economy; second, the emergence of multiple identities that question the idea of the nation. Along with this is the rise of a discourse of civil society defined substantially in terms of non-governmental organisations aspiring to take on the developmental functions that had so far been the concern of the Indian state (Jayal 1997).

In this section I shall limit myself to the following features characterising the nation state in India resulting from an engagement with the global economy mentioned above: a decline in state's capacities for control; a shift from government to governance (articulated in the movement away from the state as the major sponsor of economic development to the state as cooperating with other organisations to realise its objectives); problems in legitimation of decision-making processes (manifested in an increasing inability to perform certain kinds of state actions in response to citizens' demands); and finally that the state that continues to perform very poorly on the economic front may try to improve its accountability image by taking recourse to nationalism (like religious fundamentalism or increased military might). These challenges raise an intriguing set of questions discussed in the beginning of this chapter: what if any, is the relation between these developments, globalisation, state sovereignty and democratic citizenship? Furthermore, if there is a relationship what are the lines of causality? Are they necessary effects of globalisation?

Economic Reforms and the State in India

The Indian state is confronted since 1991 by economic globalisation that involves not only flows of finance, capital investment, technology and labour but also an expanding web of transnational regulatory institutions (Sachs et al. 1999). The introduction of economic reforms by the Congress government under Narasimha Rao in 1991 was due to the gross fiscal deficit of the Central government and the problem of external indebtedness. The reforms in India followed a gradual approach by focusing in the first phase macroeconomic stabilisation and in the second phase, simultaneous reforms of industrial policy, trade and exchange rate policies, along with tax reforms, financial sector reforms and public sector reforms. Most significantly, in addition to stabilisation measures, structural reforms were introduced that reduced the extent to which the public sector controlled and influenced the private sector.

While foreign-based Indian economists like Jagdish Bhagwati (1997) or Deepak Lal have been advocating neo-classical economics on which the globalised vision of the world of the 1980s was founded, India-based scholars see globalisation as a process that states must try to adjust but also critique (Kothari 1995; Patnaik 1995). Kothari claims that the legitimacy and authority of the nation state has been eroded by globalisation (1995: 1595). Some of the scholars view the emergence of a new form of international finance capital as serving the interests of neo-liberalism (Patnaik et al. 2004). Indeed the rhetoric of democracy now consists of a neoliberal globalising thrust and thrust towards localisation through self rule, diversity and decentralisation (Kothari 1995). They also argue that despite its macro integration design at the global level, globalisation would reinforce disintegrative tendencies within existing nation states. Patnaik claims that forcible integration of the third world societies into global financial and commodity market producers will produce disunity in these societies forcing their retrogression into a variety of separatist tendencies (Patnaik 1995: 2050).

With this debate as a backdrop, I will discuss the IT sector as an example of the unique opportunities offered by globalisation while reflecting the state's lack of control (sovereignty) over transnational capital. I also reflect briefly on some of the salient characteristics of class formation taking place in the Indian economy. I then examine the movement for decentralisation that has been encouraged by the state but which also tends to be guided by the concerns of a transnational cadre that insert their priorities into its agenda.

The IT Sector

India is one of the important players of the world in the information technology sector and it is one of the fastest growing foreign exchange earner for the country. The engine of growth of the booming Indian IT sector is the software industry, which has grown at an estimated average annual rate of 50 per cent between 1992 and 1999. India's software industry performed very well as compared to the other sectors of the Indian economy (Saxenian 2002: 194).

The IT industry underwent an unprecedented transformation in the 1990s as part of the liberalisation package set by the international institutions like IMF, WB and WTO. This implied removal of barriers on imports and pursuance of a free trade policy as specified by the WTO. Prior to 1991, FDI in India was limited to 40 per cent joint ventures and its approval was very time consuming. After 1991, the government introduced new guidelines for extending approval for ventures with upto 51 per cent foreign equity in 13 major industries. In January 1997, the government opened its securities market to FIIs taking the step towards selling of government debts to overseas markets.

As the extent of a company's research and development effort is driven more by technology and competition rather than firm size, the rapid growth of spending on technology requires internationalisation of companies if profitability is to be maintained. The last decade has seen a number of collaborative agreements and strategic alliances between leading multinationals. Strategic alliances typically in automobiles (as in Honda city, Fiat and Ford), pharmaceuticals (Ranbaxy), biotechnology, information technology, and textiles (Arvind Mills) substitute earlier international economic transactions.

Prior to 1984, the Indian software industry operated within the framework of a highly regulated model of import substitution-led industrialisation that guided the Indian economy. Rajiv Gandhi's administration emphasised new policies for electronics, software, and telecommunications and recognised software as an industry. They lowered import duties on software and PCs and permitted the import of computers in exchange for software exports at a special low duty. In 1986, the Computer Software Export, Development and Training Policy 'marked an explicit rejection of India ISI and the idea of self-reliance in software' (Saxenian 2002: 172). The import of software in any form was permitted and various procedures simplified.

The post 1984 policy changes were crucial to the growth of the Indian software industry because they allowed domestic producers to exploit domestic resources in global markets. But the shift to offshore production allowing the programmers to work at facilities in India was only possible following the reforms of the early 1990s, particularly the removal of licenses on imports of industrial equivalent and the establishment of the STPs (Software Technology Parks).[14]

Earlier, offshoring was mostly restricted to manufacturing. Technology was transferred to less developed countries when it entered into maturity and degradation phase. In the decades of 1960s and 1970s transfer of obsolete technology to developing countries was criticised and so was the manner in which multinationals relocated many polluting industries to underdeveloped countries to skip environmental regulations.

In recent years, taking advantage of the internet and corporate networks global corporations have found it easy to find their service providers in India (Mukherji 2004a). India's greatest asset is a skilled educated workforce that is willing to work for low wages. The difference in time zones facilitates efficient project execution and gives an opportunity to Indian firms to perform maintenance and engineering tasks for US customers by accessing their computers after regular users have finished their work for the day. Cheap satellite communications, internet and quality focus encourage corporations to increasingly outsource routine, labour intensive projects, such as coding and maintenance to Indian software houses.

Companies have located their operations in Bangalore, Chennai and Pune. These centres have emerged as branches of leading global players as well as fine academic institutions, IT-focused venture capitalists and innumerable small scale outfits. Such operations create job opportunities in Indian cities and help lower costs for foreign companies. Data transcription and transmission for hospitals in the US and telemarketing for US firms is also being undertaken by Indian companies based in various Indian metropolitan cities (Mukherji 2004a). The growth of offshore facilities also allows some established Indian companies like Wipro and Infosys to begin building a base of in-house knowledge and to develop internal training programmes, quality processes and productivity tools. This has transformed Wipro into a multinational that can compete with IBM, Accenture and other global companies.

It has led to a qualitative transformation of the economy in three ways. First, the emerging global economy is integrated through information systems and communication technologies rather than hierarchical organisation structures. Second, the dramatic increase in the scale of technology and intense competitive pressure in relation to prices and product development has led to the reorganisation of its operations both geographically and functionally. Finally, this sector has been able to secure the benefits of globalisation through strategic transnational alliances and forms of collaborative arrangements that provide a significant advantage to India as compared to other countries in Asia. Saxenian is of the view that these networks are increasingly structured among diverse actors, the IT start-ups, NRI community members, local universities and research institutions rather than through large multinationals (Saxenian 2002).

According to Carol Upadhya, this industry is distinguished by its close integration into the global economy and its relative autonomy from the old economy dominated by the public sector and national economic class. In the last decade, the emergence of new kinds of transnational linkages has been due to the operation of foreign venture capital (henceforth VC). This was possible when changes in financial regulations in 1995 permitted the entry of foreign VC funds and institutional investors. Much of the capital came from non-resident Indians especially wealthy entrepreneurs and financers but more significantly VCs provide important inputs such as advice on strategy, technology, management, or human resources (Upadhya 2004: 5141).

For these reasons, some scholars tend to view the flow of transnational capital into the Indian software industry as responsible for producing a new kind of a capitalist class in India even though most of the founders of software firms are drawn from the middle class, 'building on their cultural capital of higher education (engineering) and on the cultural and social capital (knowledge and networks) acquired through professional careers' (Upadhya 2004: 5148). This transnational business class or capitalist class comprises of NRI technological entrepreneurs, venture capitalists, the founders and top executives of large and medium size Indian IT companies and even top managers of MNC software centres in India (ibid.: 5146).

There is no doubt that the IT industry has developed a distinctive corporate culture that is more global and multicultural than other sectors of the Indian economy. However, I would argue that the identity of this emerging class and their politics is too early to assess even though they form transnational business networks. Moreover, to view them as part of a transnational ethnic middle class or capitalist class is difficult because their salaries and economic status varies in different countries.

What is important for the argument of this chapter is that this class has a 'disproportionate impact on public policy both directly by forging links with the state, and indirectly as icons of a resurgent India' (Upadhya 2004: 5148). This has occurred not because of their ownership of the means of production but because of their access to knowledge systems, technology and information flows.

The main charge against the IT sector is that the software boom has exacerbated the brain drain. Programmers in India are increasingly aware of the global demand for their skills and the substantially higher compensation available in more developed economies. Many thus aspire to work for foreign companies not only for high wages but to be transferred overseas.

The concentration of the software industry in a small number of cities in the south has the potential to exacerbate the already desperate rates of growth across states and regions in India (Ahluwalia 2002). These technological innovations, largely related to the processing of information, will lead to the growth of a relatively small elite of well-paid software engineers and executives and a mass of poorly paid information processors.

Offshore facilities for outsourcing commercial activities has expanded service trade significantly but it poses challenges for tax authorities in a poor country like India. It has been argued that globalisation can hurt the revenue collecting power of the state in India, more so as capital abundance and capital scarcity within different countries is bound to effect the rules of value creation. A capital-scarce producer country like India has an interest because it needs to invest the revenues it gets out of trade and commerce in physical and human capital. However, given that foreign direct investment can exit to low tax locations (with little economic infrastructure) there is an emerging consensus that globalisation constrains redistributive aspect of government. Recent studies show that social spending in developing countries was negatively affected by globalisation to a much greater extent than in developed countries (see Mukherji 2004b: 91).

Thus, it is important for IT to become more than an enclave in an otherwise backward economy. There is a need to develop a wider range of industries and institutions to support the economic and spatial diffusion of IT. Indeed, India should not seek to replicate other technologies or countries beyond a point. There are compelling reasons that India will need to define its own pathway in the IT era. The US economy has the advantage of a large domestic market, a widely educated population, and well functioning infrastructure and regulatory institutions. In India, by contrast, a vast rural, as well as urban population lives in poverty, lacking even minimal levels of education. The nation's transportation and communications infrastructure remain woefully inadequate. Furthermore substantial bureaucratic regulations continue to hinder the modernisation of the private sector.

Indian states like Andhra Pradesh, Karnataka, Tamil Nadu and Kerala have pioneered far reaching innovations in the IT sector and raised two concerns crucial for governance in India: a) the inadequacy of the infrastructure: telecommunications, roads, airports and power supply; b) the cumbersome bureaucratic hurdles and red tapism. India's telecommunications, roads and air transport infrastructures rank extremely poorly in the bottom 10 per cent of ranked countries on a global scale (Saxenian 2002: 182). Economic activity requires infrastructure because poor infrastructure adds to costs and creates uncertainty in delivery times, then buyers are likely to seek alternative sources in this competitive global environment (ibid.).

Given the implications of federalism and state level politics in India, these changes are crucial for improving governance. With the decline of the Congress Party regional forces and leaders have become powerful. Many policies that have a critical bearing on the progress of economic reforms are on the state list in India's Constitution. For these reasons, the increasing role of private investment has afforded greater autonomy to the states to take the initiative to grow. The abolition of industrial licensing ensures that private investment would be attracted to the states where productivity gains would be the greatest. This makes it more urgent that infrastructure in the form of power, telecommunications, roads be rapidly improved. However, fiscal deficits are very high in many states and a cause for concern. In the future it is likely that private sector, rather than government would meet most of the enormous infrastructure needs of a growing economy. For good governance, states need to deliver essential services in areas such as health, education, civic amenities, infrastructure and a reliable legal system. This requires a more accountable bureaucracy that is responsive to public grievances (Mukherji 2004b: 111–12).

But scholars have cautioned that the Central government needs to continue to play a role in order to check disparities between regions. The inequality within the states grew during the reform period. Some scholars argue that relying only on the markets that is part of the neo-liberal agenda will worsen regional disparities and create grave consequences for the political economy (Ahluwalia 2002; Bhattacharya and Sakthivel 2004).

From the discussion above we find in the political economy a growing hold of corporate capitalism that is likely to increase with the growth in the high-tech variety of industries. These changes will widen the class, caste and regional divisions and increase unemployment following retrenchment and exclusion of people (mostly women, child labour and migrants) belonging to the unorganised sector (Kothari 1995). Will these changes in the political economy have an impact on democratic and decentralised politics in India? I attempt to address this question in the next section.

Decentralisation and Governance

After independence, the government of India embarked upon a path of major social and economic transformation in which the state played a major role. A structure of centralised administration in which ministries of agriculture, health and rural development which is primarily state government responsibilities received funds from the central exchequer on the basis of five year plans prepared by the Planning Commission. This arrangement was carried successfully through the National Development Council, chaired by the Prime Minister through schemes designed by the ministries and often implemented by them through agencies set up by them in a uniform manner across the states. Through central planning, an increasing number of economic activities were placed in the public sector—steel, fertilisers, heavy chemicals, machine tools, hotels along with infrastructure activities.

Meanwhile, a massive bureaucracy emerged over the years to implement the many schemes of the government in the social sphere. The civil servants while subject to a code of conduct and to disciplinary action enjoy protection through articles 310 and 311 of the Constitution. Although the impact of these schemes was well below expectations, the civil servants were not accountable to citizens but their seniors in their services. What resulted in the field was inefficiency and corruption on a massive scale. The result was a people unfriendly local bureaucracy that politicians took advantage of for rent seeking activities followed by corruption and inefficiency (Vyasulu 2004).

Despite these problems, the sheer conception of a decentralised development particularly of the Panchayati Raj type has always a great appeal since it represented the spirit of Article 40 in the Directive Principles of State Policy. The constitution had envisaged that the state shall take steps to organise village panchayats and endow them with such powers and authority as may be necessary to enable them to function as units of self government.

The Balwant Rai Mehta Committee (1957) was the first of its kind that looked into the bureaucratic framework of these local institutions. Despite its claim that community development could endure when the community was involved, not much was gained. There are various reasons for this, such as, the political and bureaucratic resistance at the state level to a sharing of power and resources with local level institutions and a takeover of these institutions by the rural elite. The lack of progress in the social sector, in areas like health and education, began to be taken seriously when Ashok Mehta Committee (1978) spoke strongly of the need for locally elected governments. Some of its recommendations were carried out in Karnataka, Andhra Pradesh and West Bengal.

Although the state was engaged with the issue of decentralised democracy, the debate on panchayati raj focused narrowly on how people could be made to participate in the implementation and development schemes of the Union Government. Instead of correcting imbalances in the local power structures that get reflected in the panchayati raj institutions, the latter are viewed as a vehicle for progressive social transformation. Critics of decentralisation point to the lack of control by local authorities over the allocation of funds, their planning capabilities and the design of macro-economic policy, and to the undemocratic nature of the selection of local officials.

A new phase of decentralised democracy to overcome these problems began with the 73rd and 74th amendments to the Constitution which devolved power to institutions of local self government. It made it mandatory for 'a uniform two to three-tier panchayat system to be constituted in every state, with direct elections to each of the three levels, viz, the village, block/taluka and the district' (Jayal 2001: 148). Apart from reserved seats for the scheduled castes and tribes provision was also made for one third of the seats to be reserved for women representatives. The amendments enabled the state legislatures to endow the panchayats with such powers and authority as may be necessary to enable them to function as institutions of self-government (Jayal 2001).

The idea of giving constitutional status to the panchayati raj institutions is sometimes viewed as a state response to the increasing recognition that the institutional initiatives of the preceeding decades had not delivered the goods. However the decentralisation of government for the most part can be traced back to initiatives from below.

The demand for greater representation of women in political institutions in India was taken up in a systematic way by the Committee on the Status of Women in India (CSWI) which published its report in 1976. The CSWI report suggested that women's representation in political institutions, especially at the grassroots level needed to be increased through a policy of reservation of seats for women. In 1988, the National Perspective Plan for Women suggested that a 30 per cent quota for women be introduced at all levels of elective bodies.

Apart from the womens' movement, for several decades social movements had protested and interrogated the basis of development as economic growth. This process had created some of the mechanisms and conditions for popular participation in public decision-making. Along with this, the governance agenda favoured by multilateral agencies, like the World Bank, promoted and funded participation through a network of non-governmental organisations. They focused on women empowerment, environmental conservation and compensation to people displaced by large projects. They funded NGOs to reach relatively inaccessible areas and for their capacity for innovation and experimentation. Eventually, the two-pronged strategy of the state making way, simultaneously for NGOs and market forces, made a strong plea for a greater role for the voluntary sector through strategies of decentralisation and people's participation (Jayal and Pai 2001).

The trend towards decentralisation due to pressure from grassroots is evident in the way laws like the Official Secrets Act that governed civil servants have been critically assessed. It has led to serious introspection about the lack of information with citizens about the development establishment and its administration. The Right to Information (henceforth RTI) demand formulated initially by members of the Mazdoor Kisan Sangathan (MKSS) is indeed a story of the extraordinary efforts of ordinary people in Rajasthan. The right to access government records was an assertion of many democratic principles and a claim on a share of governance. The right to information campaign includes public hearings, institutionalisation of RTI through social audit forces and equal standards of transparency and accountability on the users of information that include NGOs and citizen groups (see Roy and Dey 2002). Legislation on right to information has been passed in several states in India. And even though the resulting laws have been far from perfect, they may still recognise these as solid achievements by the people at the local level.

In the face of globalisation, decentralisation seems to offer the most feasible way to create a just political process in India. So those who worry about the demise of the nation state in India have turned to the emancipatory potential of local-level institutions (Kothari 1995). A consensus seems to be emerging among critics of the nation state, multilateral agencies and NGOs that the idea of participation—whether it is equity-based or agency-based—privileges the idea of the community and the local. The debate about the status of the 'local' has come to centre on 'how the institutions in which people are enmeshed structure, and are themselves structured by, the experience of locality…and how these institutions are implicated in wider networks of relationships' (Day and Murdoch 1993: 93). In this manner the discourse of participation found among basic needs theorists, environmentalists, sustainability groups, feminists and human rights activists, presents a valorisation of the local, as well as a critique of nationalist agendas of political elites that focused on projects of nation building and heavy industrialisation. What is surprising is that the privileging of the local space is linked to the decline in the capacity of the nation state.

Now, while it might be correct to argue that most sources of community problems lie beyond their spatial boundaries, organising around communities may reinforce the very patronage caste and religion driven political mobilisation in the first place. The context of decentralisation has also changed making these dilemmas appear greater than ever. On the one hand, the electoral triumphs of lower caste groups and women promise greater representation and accountability and on the other, economic restructuring, income inequality and continuing poverty undermine and wipe out the gains of local actions.

I would argue that this terrain of the local is fairly problematic. In its basic form many proponents forget that the local is a space of internal differentiation and power contestation. If by civil society we mean voluntary associations of citizens, then this interpretation will find it difficult to accommodate the existence of a variety of global NGOs that are not created through a democratic process or lack representation from local people. Many of them have their own agendas and adopt a very professional approach towards local problems. In this way, citizens are unlikely to engage with them or influence their agendas. Although many NGOs have demanded transparency and accountability from public agencies, they have for the most part, been fairly vulnerable to similar charges. Finally, the question of consultation and accountability central to the idea of democratic citizenship is not possible if most agendas affecting the local originate elsewhere.

State and Cultural Nationalism

The movement to centre stage by BJP in contemporary Indian politics raises theoretical and political issues of great complexity. Although the dramatic rise of cultural nationalism in India has been possible due to the resources found in our own anti-colonial heritage there have been other explanations as well. It is evident that the evolution of democratic institutions in India has led to ideological and structural transformations. In the years after independence, political mobilisation based on language, religion or region were unleashed. The political assertions of the historically disadvantaged lower castes, primarily the Dalits and the castes designated as the Other Backward Classes undermined the rigidity of the caste system. But the militant Hindu right wing—the Sangh Parivar—has asserted what they consider the claims of a culturally majoritarian community.

Another explanation is that since the 1980s, there has been intensification of ethnic, religious and nationalist movements in various parts of the world as a result of the processes of globalisation and its link with the economic immiserisation and marginalisation of populations. If national identity may be formulated on the basis of the differentiation of a nation from others and/or the affirmation of a specific vision of the historical continuity of a nation, resurgent cultural nationalism by the BJP has promoted the sense of the specificity of a Hindu identity among the people mainly through the process of symbolic boundary marking of culture. The principal ground for their ascendance has been a critique of the premises of the secular nationalist project.

BJP's membership and its public profile arose dramatically after it gained political power in 1996. Initially, apart from the BJP the Shiv Sena, VHP and Bajrang Dal were engaged in religious fervour, thus isolating the minorities and members of lower castes. The appeal to a Hindu identity with its emphasis on culture and Hinduism became a rallying point in moments of perceived Muslim threat in a multicultural society. In this situation, BJP offered a distinctive identity for the fears and anxieties of the Hindu community and later the political cooptation of the scheduled castes and tribes were attempts to strengthen the legitimacy of the BJP amongst its political constituency. But the political rhetoric in the last decade is quite different from its earlier statements and understanding this difference is essential in coming to terms with the new political terrain. The mechanisms through which this change has occurred include a combination of electoral politics, resurgence of religious identity and their popular mobilisation.

In May 2004, they were further changes related to the politics of cultural nationalism that arose with the BJP. The first is the change in political thinking that reduced the Atal Bihari Vajpayee-led National Democratic Alliance government to a minority in the 14th parliamentary elections. The voters also rejected important coalition partners at the state level, Chandrababu Naidu in Andhra Pradesh, S. M. Krishna in Karnataka and J. Jayalalitha in Tamil Nadu. One obvious reason for this defeat is inner party disputes and differences among the coalition partners within the BJP. The other factor relevant for the argument of this chapter is that government claims about the economic growth and development the country achieved were inaccurate. Middle class consumerist dreams without being matched by distributive justice that were sold to rural folk living in abject poverty were completely rejected. Within the RSS, there is a perception that the BJP lost the election because it did not follow the Hindu line rigorously enough while others claim that the communal riots in Gujarat, among the worst in the nation's history led by Narendra Modi, caused the debacle. The party's loss could also be related simply to anti-incumbency against state governments across the country.

Today we still are confronted on the one hand with a militant Hindu revivalism trying to define India in terms of an upper caste Sanskritic Hindu identity (an ethno-cultural conception of the nation) and on the other hand, with voices from below from tribals, Dalits, religious, linguistic and ethnic groups which are demanding acceptance of their cultural identity along with distributive justice.

Conclusion

In this chapter, I argued that the world inhabited by nation states is rapidly changing. The forces of globalisation represented by transnational corporations and international bureaucrats are a significant source of the change that has set limits both to state sovereignty and democratic citizenship. Globalisation is characterised by a basic asymmetry of scope between political and economic organisations or between nation states and national markets. Thus, while the mode of organising politics remains grounded within the state's territorial boundaries, the economy is increasingly organised in terms of wider transnational networks (Held 1993). These networks transfer wealth and capital across national boundaries and deepen and extend the nature of the international division of labour triggering changes in class formation.

This perspective is important in the light of the growing awareness that state capacity and authority are essential for protecting rights of citizens. Having said that I argued that the state is being displaced as the centre of economic activity and its sovereignty is being undermined in areas of foreign trade, taxation and contract laws. This erosion of economic sovereignty can be explained by the location of the Indian economy, its place in the international financial system and its relations with other international organisations. Meanwhile, the state in India has notably withdrawn from public expenditure in the social sector but it is misleading to assume the demise of the nation state because this fails to see the relationship between nation, state and democracy. If the market economy marginalises sections of society and denies public goods to a majority of the people then the government as an accountable institution has to intervene otherwise its political authority will be called into question through electoral politics and civil society organisations. Indeed the same government may rely upon the politics of cultural majoritarianism to assert its authority. These actions have seriously challenged the nation state framework for resolving minority rights.

My argument is, whatever the character of globalisation, it has led to growing social inequalities, greater social polarisation and increasing transfer of state resources to transnational capital. The distributive consequences of globalisation cannot be separated from the analyses of ownership and control of institutions, the class structure and the state. Thus, there is a need to make globalisation more democratic, not just through decentralisation, and such other institutional changes at the global level, both of the United Nations and intergovernmental type, but through a process of looking for new alternatives for dispersal of power among citizens.

Notes

1. An introductory point is necessary to distinguish between two aspects of what is bundled together in the concept of the nation state. Broadly, the idea of nation has been understood in two ways in modern times—nations as cultural communities and nations as political communities. The former views community as based on objective characteristics such as common heritage, language, a distinct territory, shared religion, customs and history. In its more recent versions, cultural nationalism is characterised by a commitment to one particular ethnic, religious or linguistic group over others. Political nationalism highlights political values, citizenship and loyalty for the nation. This describes the way a political community that occupies a defined territory is organised under the political authority of the state. Throughout this chapter, I use the term nation state and state as having overlapping concerns although I am aware that the latter is commonly used as a legal concept. The characterisation of the modern state as a nation state and being composed of culturally homogenous people is also inaccurate although it is very much alive. It gives rise to a range of complex issues that are outside the scope of this chapter. I am using the Nation State in a very general way even if the political and ethnic/cultural boundaries are not congruent.

2. There are three schools of thought on globalisation, the hyperglobalisers, skeptics and the transformationalists. For more see introduction to Held et al. (eds) (1999: 3–7).
3. There are many definitions of globalisation. Harold Levitt (1983) and Kenichi Ohmae (1990) promised boundless prosperity in their earlier writings whereas Paul Kennedy (1993) and Dani Rodrik (1997) warned about our lack of structures to deal with a global world. Some scholars see it as set of processes inscribed within the structures of the capitalist mode of production. They see it as something inevitable to which necessary alterations can be made. From this perspective, the challenge for a particular country is to adjust to changes in the world economy under the most favourable terms. Others view it as the outcome of a consciously pursued strategy or the political project of a transnational capitalist class. (See Petras and Veltmeyer 2001).
4. The origins of globalisation are a contested issue (see Held et al. 1999; Petras and Veltmeyer 2001). World system theorists view the expansion of European capitalism in the 16th century as the beginning of this process. Some see globalisation as arriving only after Second World War. I believe that although the end of the cold war signified the opening of a new chapter in the history of the globalisation of capital, it is useful to remember that capitalism is by its nature global in character. During the 19th century globalisation, rate of export of capital, international trade, migration was much more, but in the matter of communications the volume, range, density and speed of global communications today are far superior to those in the 19th century.
5. Due to the limited nature of this chapter I do not explore the two strands in the concept of citizenship, the strand with its origins in Greek polity, civic republicanism (participatory model), and the modern liberal strand (focus on citizen as bearer of rights against the state). In India most debates rage around the range of social citizenship.

   Theorists particularly those who are committed to a civic republican conception of citizenship are deeply suspicious of cosmopolitan citizenship which they view as endangering democratic forms of government (Mouffe 1992). David Held tries to develop a sociological understanding of cosmopolitan democratic governance. He argues that the autonomy of the nation state is severely limited by global processes as sovereignty is divided between national, regional and international agencies. He is principally concerned with democratising formal political institutions at the international and transnational levels.
6. There is a narrative of globalisation that links it with the unraveling of pax Americana in the early 1970s. Due to lack of space I shall not focus on these aspects in this chapter. (See Chatterjee 2004).
7. The 1980s and 1990s witnessed a dramatic upsurge in the popularity of the BJP and its ideologically disparate partners. Although, they did not speak in a single voice, proponents of hindutva identified nationalism with a rediscovery, redefinition and reaffirmation of Hindu uniqueness. The use of political power for promotion of cultural nationalism further led to inter-community polarisation and set aside the discourse on distributive justice. See section on 'State and Cultural Nationalism' in this chapters for more details.
8. These economic reforms are seen as a consequence of internal crisis situations in economy, polity and society, influenced by the collapse of India's planned economy and excessive state intervention in market economies. I will not go into the debate regarding whether these economic reforms could have been averted or not. (See Sachs, Varshney and Bajpai, eds 1999).
9. Again there is an extensive literature on governance that follows different theoretical approaches. According to Martin Doornbos, it was vague enough to include both donor and academic definitions. He writes 'the notion of good governance was broad enough to comprise public management as well as political dimensions, while at the same time vague enough to allow a fair measure of discretion and flexibility in interpretation of as to what good governance would or would not condone' (Doornbos 2003: 7).

10. The row over quotas is an illustration of my view that I develop in the end of this chapter. The row became more intense as manufacturers in USA argued that China would destroy the American textile industry. China's sales in America and Europe will surely grow once quotas are lifted. They wanted their government to maintain 15 of the 91 quotas that was to expire at the end of 2004. This whole debate shows how globalisation can affect different classes and nations differently. See Special Report on The Textile industry, in *Economist,* 13 November 2004.
11. Since the 1990s neoliberalism has been used for global market liberalism and for free trade policies.
12. Many scholars are of the view that the brunt of the capitalist globalisation process has been borne by labour, the restructuring of which in effect has been the major mechanism of structural adjustment. (For more, see Petras and Veltmeyer 2001).
13. Due to the scope of this chapter I do not examine definitions of nationalism; nationalism as modernisation; nationalism as a religion; nationalism as construction of language and literature; nationalism as a discourse of gender, sexuality and ethnicity.
14. Software Technology Parks is like an export processing zone for software. It gives guaranteed access to high speed satellite links and reliable electricity.

References

Anderson, James (2002). *Transnational Democracy: Political Spaces and Border Crossings.* London and New York: Routledge.

Ahluwalia, Montek S. (2002). 'State-Level Performance under Economic Reforms in India', pp. 91–124, in Anne O. Krueger (eds), *Economic Policy Reforms and the Indian Economy.* New Delhi: Oxford University Press.

Bhattacharya, B. B. and S. Sakthivel (2004). 'Regional Growth and Disparity in India. Comparsion of Pre and Post-reform Decades', *Economic and Political Weekly,* 34(10): 1071–77, 6 March.

Bhaduri, Amit (2002). 'Nationalism and Economic Policy in the Era of Globalization', pp. 19–48, in Deepak Nayyar (ed.), *Governing Globalization: Issues and Institutions.* New Delhi: Oxford University Press.

Bhagwati, Jagdish (1997). 'Globalization, Sovereignty and Democracy', pp. 263–81, in Axel Hadenius (ed.), *Democracy's Victory and Crisis.* Cambridge: Cambridge University Press.

Bohman, James F. (1999). 'International Regimes and Democratic Governance: Political Equality and Influence in Global Institutions', *International Affairs,* 75(3): 499–544.

Chandhoke, N. (2002). 'The Limits of Global Civil Society', in H. Anheir, M. Glasius, and M. Kaldor (eds) *Global Civil Society: A Reader.* Oxford: Oxford University Press.

Chatterjee, P. (1996). *Nationalist Thought and the Colonial World: A Derivative Discourse.* New Delhi: Oxford University Press.

——— (2004). 'Empire after Globalization', *Economic and Political Weekly,* 34(37): 4155–65, 11 September.

Day, G. and J. Murdoch (1993). 'Locality and Community Coming to Terms with Place', *The Sociological Review,* vol. 7: 82–111.

Doornbos, Martin (2003). "'Good Governance': The Metamorphosis of a Policy Metaphor", *Journal of International Affairs,* 57(1): 3–17.

Emerson, Rupert (1960). *From Empire to Nation: The Rise to Self Assertion of Asian and African Peoples.* Boston: Beacon Press.

Falk, R. (1999). *Predatory Globalization: A Critique.* Oxford: Polity.

Griffin, Keith (2003). 'Economic Globalization and Institutions of Global Governance', *Development and Change,* 34(5): 789–807.

Hadenius, Axel (ed.) (1997). *Democracy's Victory and Crisis*. Cambridge: Cambridge University Press.
Haynes, Jeff (1998). *Religion in Global Politics*. Harlow: Longman.
Harris, John (2001). *Depoliticising Development: The World Bank and Social Capital*. New Delhi: Leftword.
Held, David (1991). 'Democracy, the Nation State and the Global System', *Economy and Society*, 20(2): 138–68.
——— (1993). *Prospects for Democracy*. London: Polity.
——— (1995). *Democracy and the Global Order*. London: Polity.
Held, David, Anthony McGrew, David Goldblatt and Jonathan Perraton (eds) (1999). *Global Transformations: Politics, Economics and Culture*. Stanford: Stanford University Press.
Hirst, Paul and G. Thompson (1995). 'Globalization and the Future of the Nation State', *Economy and Society*, vol. 24: 408–42, August.
Holden, Barry (eds) (1996). *The Ethical Dimensions of Global Change*. London and New York: Macmillan and St Martins Press.
Holton, Robert J. (1998). *Globalization and the Nation State*. UK: St Martins Press and Macmillan.
Huntington, Samuel (1996). *Clash of Civilizations and the Remaking of World Order*. New York: Simon and Schuster.
Hutchings, Kimberly (ed.) (1996). 'The Idea of International Citizenship', pp. 113–34, in Holden (ed.), *The Ethical Dimensions of Global Change*. London and New York: Macmillan and St. Martin's Press.
Jayal, N. G. (1997). 'The Governance Agenda: Making Democratic Development Dispensible', *Economic and Political Weekly*, 32(8): 407–12, 22 February.
——— (2001). 'Reinventing the State: The Emergence of Alternative Models of Governance in India in the 1990s', pp. 132–50, in Jayal and Pai (eds), *Democratic Governance in India*. New Delhi: Sage Publications.
Jayal, N. G. and S. Pai (2001). *Democratic Governance in India*. New Delhi: Sage Publications.
Juergensmeyer, Mark (1993). *Religious Nationalism Confronts the Secular State*. Berkeley and Los Angeles: University of California Press.
Krueger, Anne O. (ed.) (2002). *Economic Policy Reforms and the Indian Economy*. New Delhi: Oxford University Press.
Krugman, Paul (1995). 'Dutch Tulips and Emerging Markets', *Foreign Affairs*, 74(4): 28–44.
Kennedy, Paul (1993). *Preparing for the Twentieth-century*. New York: Random.
Kothari, Rajni (2004). 'Issues before Indian Democracy', pp. 45–54, in Rajendra Vora and Suhas Palshikar (eds), *Indian Democracy: Meanings and Practices*. New Delhi: Sage Publications.
——— (1995). 'Under Globalisation: Will Nation State Hold?', in *Economic and Political Weekly*, 30(26): 1593–603, 1 July.
Lipschutz, Ronnie (1992). 'Reconstructing World Politics: The Emergence of Global Civil Society', in *Millennium: A Journal of International Studies*, vol. 21: 389–420.
Levitt, Harold (1983). 'The Globalization of Markets', *Harvard Business Review*, 61(3): 92–102.
MacEwan, Arthur (1999). *Neoliberalism or Democracy*. Canada: Fernwood.
Mahathir, bin Mohammad. 2000. *The South Summit*. Speech on 12 April, Havana, Cuba.
Mann, Michael (1997). 'Has Globalization Ended the Rise and Rise of the Nation State?', *Review of International Political Economy*, 4(3): 472–96.
Miller, David (2000). *Citizenship and National Identity*. Cambridge: Polity.
Mohanty, Manoranjan (2004). *Class, Caste and Gender*. New Delhi: Sage Publications.
Mohan, T.T. Ram (2005). 'Taking Stock of Foreign Institutional Investors', *Economic and Political Weekly*, 40(24): 2395–399, 11 June.

Mukherji, Rahul (2004a). 'Privatisation, Federalism and Governance', *Economic and Political Weekly*, 34(1): 109–13, 3 January.

——— (2004b). 'Globalisation and the Politics of International Corporate Taxation: A View from India', *India Review*, 3(2): 89–113, April.

Mouffe, C. (1992). *Dimensions of Radical Democracy: Pluralism, Citizenship, Community*. London: Verso.

Nayyar, Deepak (ed.) (1997). *Trade and Industrialization*. New Delhi: Oxford University Press.

——— (ed.) (2002). *Governing Globalization: Issues and Institutions*. New Delhi: Oxford University Press.

——— (2002a). 'The Existing System and the Missing Institutions', pp. 356–84, in Nayyar (ed.), Governing Globalization: Issues and Institutions. New Delhi: Oxford University Press.

Ohmae, Kenichi (1990). *The Borderless World*. New York: Harper Collins.

——— 1996. *The End of the Nation State*. London: Harper Collins.

Panitch, L. (1994). 'Globalisation and the State', in R. Miliband, L. Panitch and J. Saville. (eds), *Socialist Register*. London: Merlin Press.

Patnaik, Prabhat (1995). 'Nation State in the Era of Globalization', *Economic and Political Weekly*, 30(33): 2049–53, 19 August.

Patnaik, P, C.P. Chandrashekhar and Jayati Ghosh (2004). 'The Political Economy of the Economic Reform Strategy: The Role of the Indian Capitalist Class', in M. Mohanty (ed.), *Class, Caste and Gender*. New Delhi: Sage Publications.

Petras, J. (1999). 'Globalisation: A Critical Analysis', *Journal of Contemporary Asia*, 29(1): 3–30.

Petras, James and Henry Veltmeyer (2001). *Globalization Unmasked: Imperialism in the 21st century*. London: Zed Books.

Rapley, John (2003). *Globalization and Inequality*. Colorado: Lynne Rienner.

Roy, Aruna and Nikhil Dey (2002). 'Fighting for the Right to Know in India', *Development Dialogue*, 1: 75–90.

Rhodes, Martin and Richard Higgot (2000). 'Asian Crisis and the Myth of Capitalist Convergence', *Pacific Review*, 13(1): 1–19.

Rodrik, Dani (1997). *'Has Globalization Gone Too Far?'*, Washington DC: Institute for International Economics.

Sachs, Jeffrey. D., Ashutosh Varshney and Nirupam Bajpai (1999). *India in the Era of Economic Reforms*. New Delhi: Oxford University Press.

Saxenian, Anne OLee (2002). 'Bangalore: The Silicon Valley of Asia?', pp. 169–209, in Anna Krueger (ed.), *Economic Policy Reforms and the Indian Economy*. New Delhi: Oxford University Press.

Upadhya, C. (2004). 'A New Transnational Capitalist Class?', *Economic and Political Weekly*, 39(48): 5141–151, 27 November.

Vyasulu, Vinod (2004). 'Transformation in Governance Since 1990s: Some Reflections', *Economic and Political Weekly*, 34(3): 2377–385, 5 June.

19

Health in India in the Age of Globalised Governance: Some Issues

Mohan Rao

Introduction

The 1990s in India saw the initiation of policy measures that are frequently described as liberalisation, privatisation and globalisation; indeed an acronym created for this triumvirate of policy measures is LPG. As with many other mantras, there are serious problems with this policy prescription. One is, of course, that liberalisation and privatisation were some of the policy options of the project of neo-imperialism, which involved a whole range of other policy measures, fiscal and otherwise, to change the nature of economy and society. Along with this mantra, was another one, that of governance, which too adumbrates, emanating from the same set of actors driving reforms across the world, and within India.

India, of course, was never a welfare state in the European tradition. Nevertheless, there was a policy commitment to provide universal, comprehensive and free health care, going back to the Bhore Committee report of 1946 which affirmed the principle of access to health care 'irrespective of the ability to pay for it'. This was seen both as a citizen's right in itself and in the interests of the welfare of the nation. Since the onset of liberalisation, however, this policy commitment has disappeared from the public agenda as under the aegis of institutions like the World Bank, a range of measures, brought together under the rubric of health sector reforms have been initiated.

Health care reforms in India have to be located within the context of the 'transnational health care reform movement' (Twaddle 2002: 341) commencing in the 1980s and enveloping the entire world in the 1990s under the aegis of international financial institutions. The impetus supposedly came from rising health care costs in the developed and developing world. More significantly, the impetus arose from the rise of a global neoliberal agenda, with the collapse of the Berlin wall as much as with the overthrow of the Keynesian ideas on the role of the state—in demand management, the creation of effective demand on a mass scale that was to see the world through its Post-War golden age of capitalism. The profound new ordering of the world also saw a new direction to health policy: reducing the role of the state and increasing that of the private sector. Central to this was the ideology of introducing market principles into hitherto sacrosanct areas of public good, converting health care into a market-driven, profit-driven enterprise.

In its influential 1987 document, *Financing Health Services in Developing Countries: An Agenda for Reform*, the World Bank stated, 'the approach to health care in developing countries has been to treat it a right of citizenry and to attempt to provide free services for everyone. This approach does not work' (cited in Gershman and Irwin 2000: 30). The role of the state, then, was to be confined to regulation—and hence the salience of the phrase governance—while the private sector was to be encouraged, often through state subsidy, to take on the role of provisioning of health services, with the exception of a minimum clinical package, that ironically included family planning. Over this period, of course, the role of the World Bank in health sector development had increased enormously, while that of the WHO had shrivelled; indeed World Bank loans for one programme, malaria, exceeds the entire budget of the WHO (Rao and Lowenson 2000). The Bank is today 'the largest single source of health care finance in developing countries with an unparalleled degree of policy-making authority' (Kim et al. 2000: 143). At the same time, the health sector itself emerged as a leading source of multi-national profits as the health sector in developing countries was prised open for investment in a range of areas from high-level technologies to insurance.

The social base for these changes within India was provided by a large middle class, who, having benefited in the post-Independence period from state-led import substituting growth, were now anxious to secede from the country, gather the fruits of international integration, even on neo-colonial terms. Equally, they were anxious, in post-Mandal times, to do away with state intervention itself, not least for those who had not benefited from it in the past.

This paper does not discuss what the factors were that shaped this transformation of polity and society. These same factors also however governed the reforms of the health sector that were undertaken during the same period. What this paper does do is to look at some indicators of health in India, briefly survey the reforms that enveloped the health sector and make some concluding observations.

The Current Health Scenario

Commencing with Independence in 1947, India has made some substantial gains in health. The Infant Mortality Rate (IMR) was 134 per thousand live births at the time of Independence (GOI 2002a) and has declined to around 70 in 1999. The Crude Birth Rate (CBR), reflecting the huge mortality load, stood at 39.9 per cent in 1941–51, declining to 26.1 per cent in 1999. The Crude Death Rate (CDR) declined from 27.4 per cent in 1941–51 to 8.7 per cent in 1999. As a consequence, expectation of life at birth is now in the early 60s, from a figure in the early 30s at the time of Independence.[1]

Despite this, as data we survey reveals, India has worse health indices than a number of comparable countries in the world. It has the world's highest proportion of malnourished children and women. It also has the highest load of preventable and communicable diseases. Yet, the very first health policy adopted by the Government of India in 1983 set out to provide 'universal, comprehensive primary health care services, relevant to the actual needs and priorities of the community' (GOI 1983: 3). India is also a signatory to the Alma Ata Declaration which resolutely states: 'The Conference strongly affirms that health, which is a state of complete physical, mental and social well-being, and not merely the absence of disease or infirmity, is a fundamental human right and that the attainment of the highest possible level of health is a most important world-wide social goal whose realisation requires the action of many other social and economic sectors in addition to the health sector' (WHO 1978: 2).

Clearly then, there has been a wide chasm between policy commitment and its transformation into reality. What are the reasons for this chasm? Could it be that lack of governance is one fundamental reason? Or could this be due to other more fundamental factors? The following section provides an overview of the current health scenario, surveying some indices of health such as the IMR, the Child Mortality Rate (CMR), the Sex Ratio, Maternal Mortality Rate (MMR), the nutritional situation and so on. It also provides data on one of the important determinants of the current scenario, namely the financing of health care in the country. In particular, it surveys private health care in the country, with whatever data is available. The final section briefly surveys the efforts underway towards health sector reforms and raises some questions.

Infant and Child Survival

Table 19.1 and Figure 19.1 provide data on a key indicator of the health of the country, namely the IMR.

The data in the table and in the figure reveal that the IMR has indeed shown a secular, if relatively unspectacular, decline. But what the data also makes evident is that the rate of decline of the IMR has significantly slackened in the last decade since reforms were initiated: in the decades 1971–81 and 1981–91, the percentage decline in IMR was more marked than in the period 1991–999. The percentage decline in IMR between 1971 and 1981 was 14.7; between 1981 and 91 it was even more marked at 27.3 per cent. However in the period 1991–99, there has been a marked stagnation with the rate of decline in the IMR at 10 per cent. Further, as the data in the table reveals, despite policy commitments to the contrary, marked rural-urban differences persist unchanged.

There are also remarkable differentials between the states. Kerala of course had the lowest IMR at 14, while Maharashtra, Tamil Nadu, Punjab, Karnataka and Himachal Pradesh had met the national goal of reducing the IMR to 60 or less by 2000. Major states such as Madhya Pradesh (91), Orissa (97), Uttar Pradesh (84), and Rajasthan (81) were lagging far behind. These are combined figures for rural and urban areas; the rural areas of these states have figures of 96, 100, 87 and 85 respectively. It is not surprising that these states are often collectively referred to by the telling acronym BIMARU (sick) states.[2] It is possible to argue that these are precisely the states which have poor governance, as indeed they do.

But the National Health Policy 2000 (NHP 2000) draws attention to further differentials when it notes that the IMR is 83 among the Scheduled Castes, 84.2 among the Scheduled Tribes, 76 among other disadvantaged groups, and 61.8 among Others (GOI 2001: 12). Data from the National Family Health Survey indicate that the IMR among households with a low standard of living was 76.1 compared to 33 among households with a high standard of living.

Table 19.1: All India Infant Mortality Rates

Year	*Total*	*Rural*	*Urban*
1971	129	138	82
1976	129	139	80
1981	110	119	62
1984	104	113	66
1985	97	107	59
1986	97	105	62
1987	95	104	61
1988	95	102	62
1989	91	98	58
1990	80	86	50
1991*	80	87	53
1992*	79	85	53
1993*	74	82	45
1994*	74	80	52
1995*	74	80	48
1996*	72	77	46
1997*	71	77	45
1998[i]	72	77	45
1999[ii]	70	75	44

Source: Office of the Registrar General of India (1999), *Compendium of India's Fertility and Mortality Indicators*, Sample Registration System (SRS), New Delhi.

Note: * Excludes Jammu and Kashmir.

i) Office of the Registrar General of India (2000), *Selected Socio-Economic Statistics: India 1999*, New Delhi.

ii) ORGI, Sample Registration System (2001), *SRS Bulletin*, Vol. 35, No. 1.

Figure 19.1: Infant Mortality Rates in India

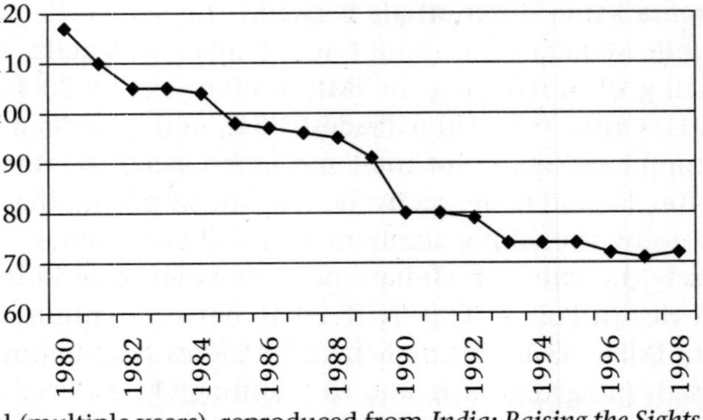

Source: Registrar General (multiple years), reproduced from *India: Raising the Sights – Better Health Systems for India's Poor*, World Bank, 2001.

The post-neonatal mortality rate is almost three times as high in households with a low standard of living as in households with a high standard of living (IIPS 2002). These differentials extend across states—the so-called well governed ones, and those not well governed.

In sum, not only is the IMR still unconscionably high, with marked rural-urban differences and differences among states and regions, there are even more marked social differences between groups within the population, which do not receive the attention they deserve. Thus, the SCs, STs and OBCs bear a disproportionate burden of infant deaths as indeed do the poor in general. What should be more worrying is the slackening in the rate of decline over the last decade, which has extended across the so-called governance divide in the country.

As in the case of the IMR, there has been a secular decline of the Under 5 Mortality Rate (U5MR), as revealed in Figure 19.2. Closely parallel to the levels of the IMR, there are marked differences in the U5MR among the states. While Kerala has a U5MR of 18.8, the figure is 137.6 in Madhya Pradesh, 122.5 in Uttar Pradesh, 114.9 in Rajasthan, 105.1 in Bihar and 104.4 in Orissa. These are composite figures, but obviously the rural areas would have markedly worse figures.

Figure 19.2: IMR and U5MR in India

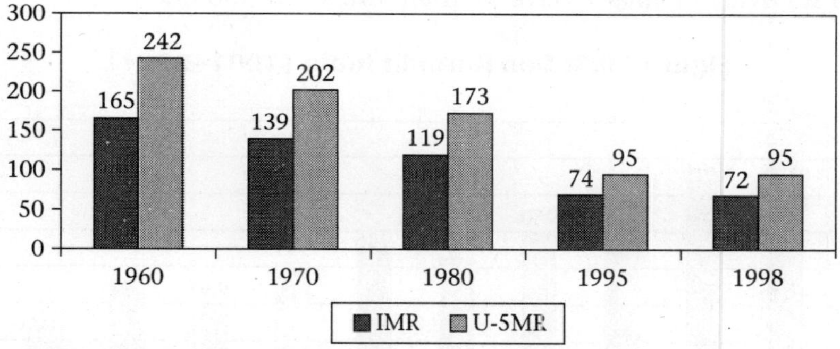

Source: UNICEF (2001), *State of the World's Children.*

In rural areas, the U5MR was 103.7, while in urban areas, it stood at 63.1 (IIPS 2002). While in urban areas it was 39.4 among households with a high standard of living, it stood at 112.2 in households with a low standard of living. In rural areas, the U5MR was an astonishing 127.3 among SC (Dalit) households, 131.4 among ST (*adivasi*) households and 112.2 among the OBCs (other backward castes), compared to 93.1 among others. Again, in rural areas, households with a low standard of living had levels of 131.8, more than three times higher than in better-off households in urban areas.

While there has been a decline in the U5MR, the pace of decline has come down and is currently hovering around 95. During 1971–81, the percentage decline was 20.6. The decline was much sharper during the 1980s, with a percentage decline of 35.7. However during the 1990s, with the onset of policies of liberalisation, the rate of decline has reduced to 15.1 (Misra et al. 2003).

Sex Ratio

The female male ratio (FMR) in the world—that is the number of females per thousand males—is 990. Western Europe has a figure of 1,064 females per thousand males and Africa, 1,015. Asia as a whole has FMRs of 953, but India shares extremely negative sex ratios with a number of her neighbours in Asia. Values of less than 950 females per thousand males are found in countries of West Asia (940), Pakistan (929), India (933), Bangladesh (939), and China (41), an arc of anti-female countries, cutting across religions.

In India, there has been a steady decline of the sex ratio over the 20th century (see Figure 19.3). The 1901 census showed 972 females per thousand males. It declined steadily to 946 in 1951, 941 in 1961, and 930 in 1971. The 1981 Census threw up a happy figure of 934 females per thousand males. The optimistic thought this indicated a halt in the decline in the sex ratio. The 1991 figure however put paid to this optimism: it revealed a further decline to 927. The 1981 figure, it is now accepted by demographers, was caused by a significant under-counting of females due to a decline in the quality of the 1971 census. Demographers have agreed that the 1991 and 2001 Censuses are free from this infirmity. This is to say that the 2001 census figures, of 933 females per thousand males, are real and indicative of an improvement in the overall survival of females. Have we then turned the corner?

Figure 19.3: Sex Ratio in India (1901–2001)

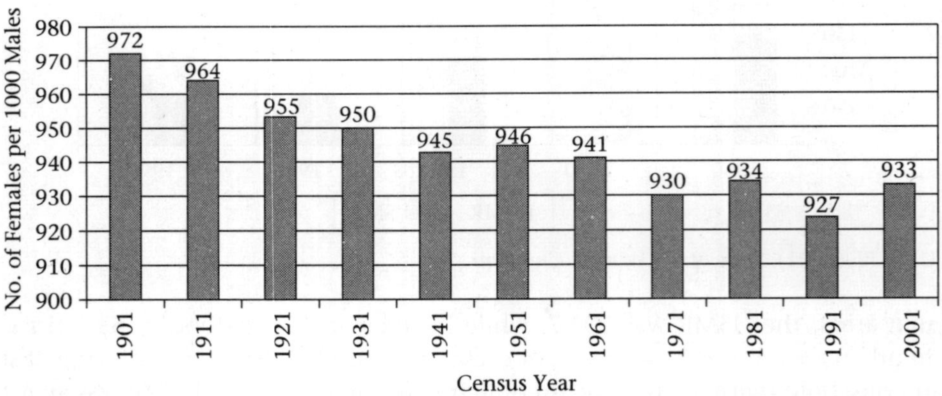

Sources: Census of India 2001, *Provisional Population Totals*, Registrar General and Census Commissioner, India.

The Sex Ratio could turn feminine simply because more men than women have migrated. But the Juvenile or Child Sex Ratio (CSR) is not subjected to this limitation. And it is this that is deeply worrying. Despite the slight overall improvement in the SR, the CSR in India as a whole has declined significantly—from 945 in 1991 to 927 in 2001. It is estimated that there are 35 million missing females in India as per the 2001 census (Patel 2004).

This decline in the CSR has been particularly notable in Himachal Pradesh (897), Punjab (793), Chandigarh (845), Haryana (820) and Delhi (865). In all these states, referred to as the Bermuda triangle for missing females, the number of female children per thousand male children in the 0–6 years age group declined by more than 50 between 1991 and 2001. Gujarat and Maharashtra, better governed states, have also unfortunately joined this group of states.

A part of the declining CSR is due to continuing anti-female rates of infant and child mortality. But more significantly, there has also been a marked masculinisation of the Sex Ratio at Birth (SRB) In India a figure of 105 male births for 100 female births is considered the norm. However, estimates of the SRB for 1998 reveals an all-India figure of 111 males per 100 females (Premi 2001). This is indicative of sex-selective abortion (SSA) of females, or the Pre-Birth Elimination of Females (PBEF). Figures above this national average of the SRB are seen in Gujarat (113.9), Haryana (123.3), Punjab (122.8), Rajasthan (114.8) and Uttar Pradesh (118).

A 2003 report simply titled, *Missing,* prepared by the United Nations Population Fund (UNFPA), Ministry of Health and Family Welfare and the Census Commissioner, which mapped the adverse CSRs in India captures the decline in the number of girls (UNFPA 2003). It reveals that 70 districts in 16 States and Union Territories have recorded a more than 50-point decline in the CSR between 1991 and 2001. The decline in CSR has spread to regions and populations hitherto considered immune, namely the states of the south and west of India and populations of Dalits and adivasis. What is also interesting is that the decline is more marked in the more developed and better-off regions and in more literate and better-off social groups. What is significant of course is that the worsening of the sex ratio is most marked in those states which can claim to be better governed, and have a higher density of private medical care services, and lower birth rates.

Maternal Health

Though reliable national estimates of maternal mortality are not available for many countries, South Asia is believed to have among the highest maternal mortality rates in the world. As Table 19.2 indicates India's MMR is still extremely high especially compared to China, not

Table 19.2: MMR by Select Country

Country	*MMR*
Korea	30
Sri Lanka	30
Malaysia	34
China	95
Pakistan	340
Indonesia	390
India	440
Bangladesh	850
Nepal	1500

Source: UNICEF (2001), *The State of the World's Children.*

to mention Sri Lanka. India and Pakistan have extremely high MMR, India's being markedly higher than poorly governed Pakistan. The latest National Family Health Survey (NFHS) estimate is 540 deaths per 100,000 live births, compared to 350 among low and middle-income countries. Indeed the NFHS II reveals that the MMR has actually increased in the seven years since NFHS I which recorded a MMR of 424 deaths per 100,000 live births. In both NFHS I and II, the rural MMR was much higher than the urban (434 and 385 in NFHS I and 619 and 267 in NFHS II).

The 1998 Sample Registration Survey places MMR at 407 per 100,000 live births, apparently an underestimate given the variations in state estimates (GOI 2000). Even at this rate, more than 100,000 Indian women die of pregnancy related causes every year, which is about 18 per cent of total global maternal deaths.

While it is indeed the case that the MMR is extremely high in India, it is also the case that this is primarily due to the poor health status of women in general. In all age groups, causes related to pregnancy account for 12 per cent of all deaths. In other words, causes other than pregnancy and childbirth account for much the larger proportion of deaths, so that solutions to the problem focusing on maternal deaths alone would be to miss the woods for the trees.

The trend of major causes of maternal death in rural India over a period of time shows no significant improvement. Haemorrhage and sepsis top the direct cause list, and anaemia the indirect. Abortion-related deaths show a downward trend, while toxaemia and malposition of the child remain almost at the same level. In short, they attest not only to the poor health status of women in general, but to the lack of adequate health facilities during pregnancy and childbirth, in particular the lack of emergency obstetric care.

Communicable Diseases

Figures 19.4 and 19.5 reveal the relative weight of communicable and non-communicable diseases in India and in China and in high-income, low and middle-income countries. The data on Burden of Diseases (BOD) reveals that India is yet to go a long way in her epidemiological transition due to the failure to control the quintessential diseases of poverty and deprivation, namely communicable diseases. These diseases together account for 50.3 per cent of the burden of diseases in India compared to 18.1 per cent in China, and 43.8 per cent in low and middle-income countries. Another study not surprisingly indicates for example that UP has the same BOD as Sub Saharan Africa: communicable diseases account for 62 per cent of the burden in UP, compared to 65.9 per cent for Sub-Saharan Africa (Ad Hoc Committee on Health Research, WHO 1996, cited in Mishra et al. 2003).

While there has been a decline in the prevalence and incidence of communicable diseases, they nevertheless account for a substantial proportion of deaths in the country, accounting for an estimated 2.5 million children below the age of five years and an equal proportion of young adults. As we also saw, communicable diseases also account for the largest proportion of deaths among women.

Figure 19.4: Burden of Disease by Cause, India and China, 1998

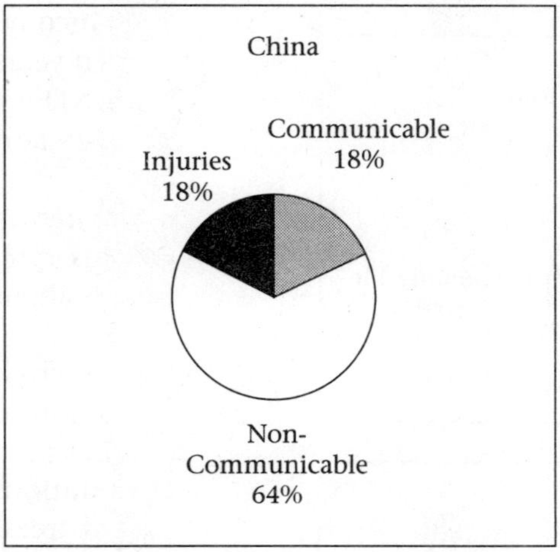

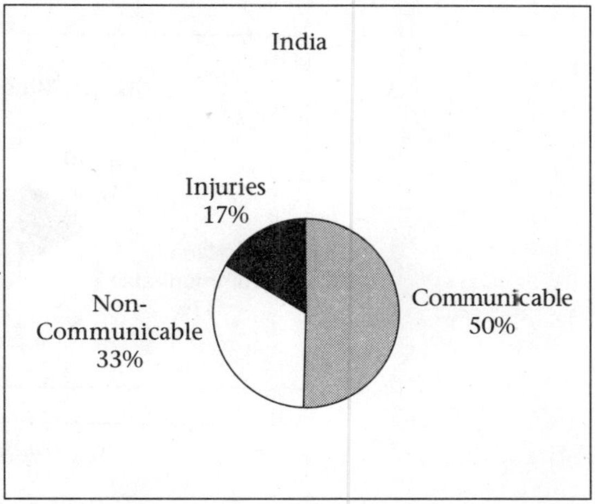

Source: World Bank (2001), *India: Raising the Sights—Better Health Systems for India's Poor.*

Reproductive Health

India commenced Mother and Child Health (MCH) and family planning services in the very first Five Year Plan; indeed India was one of the first countries in the world to initiate an official policy and programme for family planning. During the initial years, the focus was on antenatal care and the training of traditional birth attendants to provide safe deliveries, along of course with family planning which has always stood at the heart of the programme, its *raison d'etre*. Subsequently, under the CSSM (Child Survival and Safe Motherhood) programme launched in 1992, the focus was on encouraging institutional deliveries, along with the Universal Immunisation Programme (UIP). These programmes have been integrated into the Reproductive and Child Health Programme launched in 1996.

Despite these initiatives, however, as the data we surveyed earlier revealed, they have failed to have the expected impact in reducing the MMR or indeed the IMR and CMR. The NFHS II provides data indicating that MCH performance and coverage has been extremely unsatisfactory. Only 65 per cent of mothers received antenatal check-ups, 67 per cent received 2 or more doses of tetanus toxoid, 58 per cent received Iron and Folic Acid supplements, 34 per cent of deliveries were institutional, and 42 per cent of deliveries were assisted by a health professional.

There are also significant disparities between states: Goa, Kerala and Tamil Nadu consistently rank in the top five, while UP, Bihar and Rajasthan show a consistently poor performance. Women not receiving antenatal check ups are disproportionately from among the Dalits, adivasis and OBCs. Among women with a low standard of living, the proportion receiving

Figure 19.5: Burden of Disease in the World, High, Low and Middle Income Economies

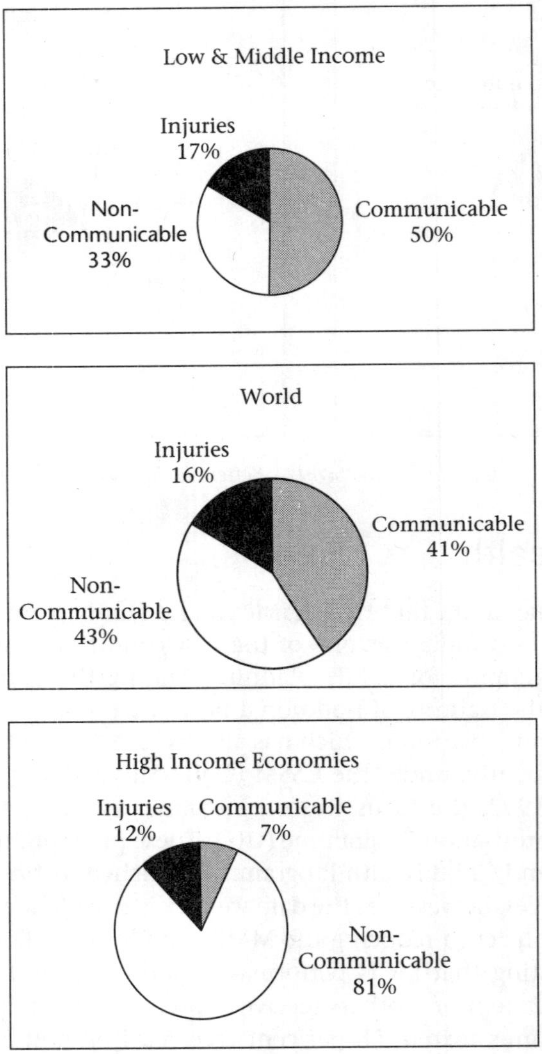

Source: WHO (1999), *World Health Report.*

no antenatal care was 45.1 per cent, compared to 12.4 per cent among women with a high standard of living. With reference to place of deliveries, 60 per cent of deliveries among the Dalits and 70 per cent among the adivasis took place at home, while the figure for 'Others' was 47 per cent. 66 per cent of women with a low standard of living delivered at home, compared to 27.6 per cent among women with a high standard of living.

Similarly, according to the NFHS II, vaccination coverage under the UIP left a lot to be desired. In urban areas, 52 per cent of children had received all immunisations by 12 months of age, while in rural areas only 29.3 per cent had. Boys (43 per cent) were more likely to have received immunisation than girls (41 per cent). Only 28 per cent of children of illiterate mothers were fully immunised, as compared to 73 per cent of children of mothers who had completed high school. Dalit children (40 per cent), adivasi children (26 per cent), OBC children (43 per cent) are less likely to be immunised than others (47 per cent). Only 30 per cent of children from households with a low standard of living were fully immunised as compared to 65 per cent of children from households with a high standard of living. Immunisation coverage ranges from 11 per cent in Bihar to 89 per cent in Tamil Nadu. Among the major states, Bihar (11 per cent), Rajasthan (17 per cent), U.P. (21 per cent) and M.P (22 per cent) had figures much below the national average of 42 per cent (IIPS 2000). In urban areas, 72 per cent of children were immunised by the public health services, 24 per cent by the private sector, and one per cent by NGOs or charitable institutions, while in rural areas the public health system was responsible for 85 per cent of immunisations, the private sector for nine per cent, and the NGO sector for less than one per cent.

Critics have argued that one reason for the failure of MCH programmes, indeed for a host of other programmes, has been the focus on vertical programmes in general and the family planning programmes in particular (Qadeer 1998). But as we see in Figure 19.6 the Total Fertility Rate (TFR) has declined over the years, along with a decrease in mortality, from 6.6 in 1960 to 3.2 in 1998. Here again, inter-state differentials are striking: the southern states, Maharashtra, Gujarat and West Bengal show a fairly rapid decline in both fertility and infant mortality; while the BIMARU states, accounting for over 40 per cent of the country's population, have the highest maternal and child mortality as well as fertility. Thus, while the TFR was 1.8 in Goa,

Figure 19.6: Total Fertility Rate (TFR), IMR & U5MR by Time Periods

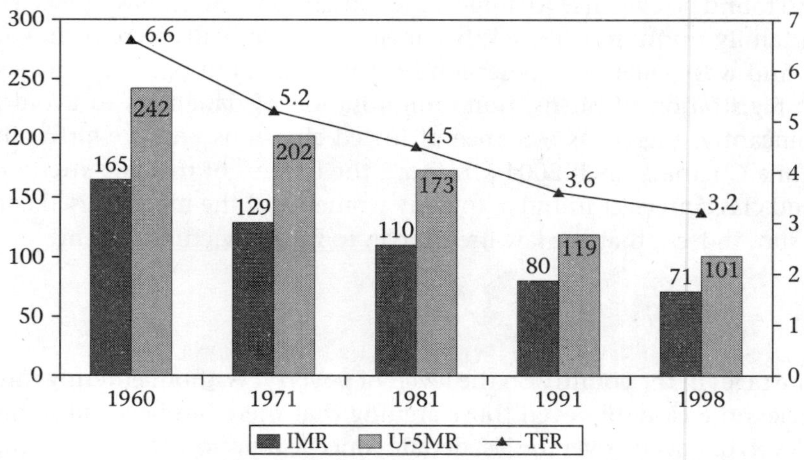

Source: SRS of various years, Census, NFHS (Under-5 mortality for 1991 covers 1988–93).

1.51 in Kerala, 2.07 in AP, 1.89 in Karnataka and 2.11 in T.N., it stood at 4.31 in UP, 4.06 in Rajasthan, 3.59 in Bihar and 3.3 in Madhya Pradesh. In other words, as could be expected, states which are lagging behind in epidemiological transition, and have a weak health care delivery system, are also the states lagging behind significantly in demographic transition. It is nevertheless significant that the fertility for the whole country has declined, between NFHS I and II, by about half a child per women. Thus, current policy initiatives, especially those initiated by several states, focusing on a Two Child Norm to be encouraged through punitive disincentives and targets and are not only in contravention of the National Population Policy (NPP) but also seriously misplaced (Rao 2002). Interestingly, the NFHS II also reveals that the fertility rate that is currently sought, 2.13, is lower by 0.72 child (that is by 25 per cent) than the current TFR of 2.85. This is to say, if unwanted births could be reduced, the TFR would drop to the replacement level of fertility. Indeed this is acknowledged in the NPP, which therefore marks as its priority, meeting the unmet need for health and family planning services. To propose punitive measures, in this context, is thus clearly absurd.

What is also important to acknowledge is that given the age structure of the population, population growth will continue despite fall in the birth rate due to what demographers call momentum, i.e., the effect of a young age structure caused by high population growth rates in the recent past. With a large proportion of the population—almost 60 per cent—below the age of 30 years, further growth of population is inevitable, unless of course mortality increases, which cannot be the aim of policy. Population momentum contributes to as much as 69.7 per cent of current population growth (Sen and Iyer 2002).

A study carried out recently in five states (A.P., Haryana, Orissa, Rajasthan and M.P.) indicated that the fallout of the imposition of the two-child norm on Panchayati Raj Institutions (PRIs) had been exactly as anticipated. The largest number of cases of disqualification from contesting elections was with reference to this law. Women formed 41 per cent of those disqualified; the Dalits, adivasis and the OBCs formed an overwhelming 80 per cent of those disqualified. The study also found no evidence to support the contention that the law induced the adoption of the small family norm; nor indeed that members of the PRIs were seen as role models. What it did find was evidence of desertion of wives, denial of paternity, neglect of female infants, non-registration of births, non-immunisation of daughters to avoid registration. Equally significantly, there was evidence of forced abortions and pre-birth elimination of females (Mahila Chetna Manch 2004). In short, the framers of this law utterly ignored how patriarchy and class intersect in India, to deny women and the marginalised communities a place in the sun. Indeed, that the law itself serves to further victimise them.

Nutrition

A fierce debate rages in the country on the levels of poverty. Without entering into the debate, it is nevertheless the case that even those arguing that there has been substantial improvement in the levels of poverty over the last decade concede that close to a third of the population still lives under the poverty line and thus unable to meet their calorie requirements. Data from the National Nutrition Monitoring Bureau (NNMB) indicate that there has been an improvement in the prevalence of severe under-nutrition in children between 1 and 5 years the level declining from 11.1 per cent in 1992 to 6.9 per cent in 1995. However, this compares to a prevalence rate of 6.2 per cent in 1982. While this relatively modest improvement is heartening, the levels of moderate under-nutrition remains substantially unchanged at 43.5 per cent while mild under-nutrition has increased from 36.6 per cent in 1992 to 40.6 per cent in 1995. Overall, the proportion of children nutritionally normal has increased from 7.2 per cent in 1992 to 8.5 per cent in 1995. Again, this should be tempered with caution since the figure stood at 15.6 per cent in 1982 (NNMB 1997). This data needs to be placed in the context of a dramatic decline in per capita availability of cereals commencing in 1991. Data indicate that the per capita daily availability of cereals declined from 468.5 grams in 1991 to 428.8 grams in 1999; that of pulses declined from 41.1 grams to 38.6 grams (GOI 1999). Indeed the NNMB notes that the average calorie consumption in the population in 1995 was below the Recommended Daily Allowance (RDA) (NNMB 1997).[3]

Data from the NFHS II however indicate higher levels of hunger than the NNMB data; they also pertain to the whole of India rather than just seven states as is the case with the NNMB data. NFHS II reveals that almost half the children under three years of age (47 per cent) are underweight, and a similar proportion (46 per cent) is stunted. 18 per cent of children below three years of age are severely undernourished, down from 20 per cent in NFHS I. The proportion of children stunted stood at 23 per cent.[4] Wasting or acute under-nutrition affects 16 per cent of children under three years of age. Under-nutrition is substantially higher in rural areas than in urban areas, but even in the latter, more than a third of children are either underweight or stunted. Levels of under-nutrition are also substantially higher among Dalits (underweight 53.5 per cent, severely underweight 21.2 per cent; stunting 51.7 per cent; wasting 16 per cent) and adivasis (underweight 55.9 per cent, severely underweight 26 per cent; stunting 52.8 per cent; wasting 21.8 per cent). Anaemia affects nearly three quarters of children (74 per cent), with 46 per cent having moderate and 5 per cent having severe anaemia. Anaemia affects 78.3 per cent of children among the Dalits, 6.6 per cent severely, and 79.8 per cent among the adivasis, 6.9 per cent severely. The highest prevalence rates are found in Bihar, Rajasthan, and surprisingly, the agriculturally advanced states of Haryana and Punjab. The proportion of children weighing less than 2.5 kilograms at birth stood at 24 per cent in rural areas and 21 per cent in urban areas.

The NFHS II data also reveal a far from satisfactory nutritional status of women in the country. Data reveals that more than a third (36 per cent) of women in the country had a Body Man Index (BMI) of less than 18.5 indicative of chronic hunger or chronic energy deficiency.[5] The proportion of women who are poor, and thus more likely to be illiterate, with BMI less than 18.5 is 42.6 per cent. Among Dalits the proportion is 42.1 per cent and among adivasis 46.3 per cent. Women in households with a low standard of living index have chronic hunger levels of 48.1 per cent, compared to 17.3 among households with a high standard of living. Prevalence rates of chronic hunger in rural areas (40.6 per cent) are almost double those in urban areas (22.6 per cent). The prevalence of chronic energy deficiency among women is also the highest in Rajasthan (39.3 per cent), Orissa (48.0 per cent), West Bengal (43.7 per cent), Uttar Pradesh (35.8 per cent), Maharashtra (39.7 per cent) and Karnataka (38.8 per cent), again cutting across the so-called governance divide.

The prevalence of anaemia is, not surprisingly, equally widespread; the overall prevalence rate was 52 per cent with 35 per cent mildly anaemic, 15 per cent moderately anaemic and 2 per cent severely anaemic.[6] Prevalence rates of anaemia are considerably higher for rural women (54 per cent) than among urban women (46 per cent). The prevalence rates are 60.2 per cent among women in households with a low standard of living, and as high as 41.9 per cent in those with a high standard of living. Among the Dalits the prevalence rates are 56 per cent and among adivasis, 64.9 per cent.

While there has been attention drawn to the poor health and nutritional status of women, not enough attention has been paid to that of men. Indeed the National Family Health Survey (NFHS) has no data on the prevalence of hunger among men. The NNMB however notes that 49 per cent of adult males also suffered from chronic energy deficiency in 1990 (NNMB 1997).

In short, the nutritional data unambiguously reveals the continuing high prevalence of hunger in the population. The issue is however complex, and goes beyond merely the availability of food: India now sits on a huge stock of food and indeed has, particularly since the onset of reforms, commenced export of food grains. The high prevalence of chronic hunger, in addition to acute hunger, is undoubtedly the cause of the continuing high mortality and morbidity load in the country. This is doubly tragic since it not only imposes suffering and diseases, it also represents a waste of the non-realised potential among these population of the country. Yet although food is so central to the health of the population, levels of hunger do not find mention in the NHP. If they do find mention in health discourses, it is frequently only anaemia as a cause of high maternal morbidity and mortality, and of high infant and child mortality.

Given this epidemiological blindness, as it were, it is not entirely surprising that policy initiatives are to place emphasis on the problems of obesity, and micro-nutrient deficiencies; 'a paradigm shift from food security to nutrition security' (GOI 2002b: 346). In another sleight of hand, there are moves to bring down the Recommended Daily Allowance (RDAs), and thus achieve a remarkable decline in levels of poverty. Thus, as India shines for those with problems of obesity, poverty gets eliminated by governance and the poor through family planning!

Health Finances

One extremely important cause for the high morbidity and mortality rates in the country, along of course with widespread hunger and poverty, is the remarkably low public investment in health. As the NHP itself acknowledges, 'public health investment over the years has been comparatively low, and as a percentage of GDP, has declined from 1.3 per cent in 1990 to 0.9 per cent in 1999' (GOI 2002: 7). As Table 19.3 reveals, health expenditure has declined as a proportion of GDP from 3.3 per cent in the Ist Plan, when issues of governance did not figure centrally, to 0.6 per cent in the IXth Plan, when they did.[7] Compared to health expenditures, family planning expenditures have shown a relative increase. What is also striking is the decline in the allocation to control of communicable diseases. In other words, the more the discourse of governance, the more policy has tended to discriminate against the people at large.

Table 19.3: Expenditure on Health and Family Welfare (in Rupees Crores)

				Health (Centre and States)		*Family welfare*		*Control of communicable diseases*	
Plan	*Period*	*Amount*	*Total plan investment (All development heads)*	*Outlay/ Exp.*	*% of Total Plan*	*Outlay/ Exp.*	*% of Total Plan*	*Outlay/ Exp.*	*% of Total Health*
First	51–56	Actuals	1960	65.2	3.33	0.1	0.01	23.1	16.5
Second	56–61	Actuals	4672	140.8	3.01	5	0.11	64	28.4
Third	61–66	Actuals	8576.5	225.9	2.63	24.9	0.29	69	27.7
Annual	66–69	Actuals	6625.4	140.2	2.12	70.4	1.06	23.1	10.2
Fourth	69–74	Actuals	15778.8	335.5	2.13	278	1.76	127	11.1
Fifth	74–79	Actuals	39426.2	760.8	1.93	491.8	1.25	268.12	11.5
	79–80	Actuals	12176.5	223.1	1.83	118.5	0.97		
Sixth	80–85	Outlay	97500	1821	1.87	1010	1.04	524	27
Sixth	80–85	Actuals	109291.7	2025.2	1.85	1387	1.27		
Seventh	85–90	Outlay	180000	3392.9	1.88	3256.3	1.81	1012.7	7.7
Seventh	85–90		218729	3688.6	1.69	3120.8	1.43		
	1990–91	Actuals	61518	960.9	1.56	784.9	1.28		
	1991–92	Actuals	65855	1042.2	1.58	856.6	1.3		
Eighth	92–97	Outlay	434100	7582.2	1.75	6500	1.5	1045	4.2
Ninth	97–02	Outlay	859200	5118.1	0.6	15120			

Source: Government of India, *Ninth Five Year Plan, 1997–2002, Vol. II,* Planning Commission, New Delhi.

This proportion of health expenditure is below the average of low-income countries and even Sub-Saharan Africa. The average health expenditure, as a proportion of GDP for low-income countries is 1 per cent, while the average in countries of Sub-Saharan Africa is 1.7 per cent (World Bank 2000). More significantly perhaps, India has one of the highest levels of private financing of health care expenses, with out-of-pocket expenditure estimated to account for 87 per cent of total expenditures. Indeed only Cambodia, the Democratic Republic of Congo, Georgia, Myanmar and Sierra Leone show a higher proportion of private funding (WHO 2000).

The high proportion of regressive funding for health care implies that the poor, who often have greatest need for health services, and the least ability to pay for them, bear the highest proportion of health care costs. Thus, a recent World Bank study concludes that 'the hospitalised Indian spends more than half his total annual expenditure on buying health care; more than 40 per cent of hospitalised people borrow money or sell assets to cover expenses and 35 per cent fall below the poverty line' (World Bank 2001, cited in Misra et al. 2003: 143). Out-of-pocket expenses alone are estimated to push 2.2 per cent of the population below the poverty line annually.

One extremely interesting finding is that the burden of out-of-pocket expenditure is highest in those states where public health infrastructure is least developed. This applies equally to government and to private facilities, to in-patient care as well as out-patient care. Thus, the treatment costs are least in Kerala, Tamil Nadu and West Bengal, and highest in Bihar, Assam, Punjab, Rajasthan, Haryana and Uttar Pradesh. Further, in all states, except Kerala, rural patients pay more for medical care and bear a higher burden of treatment (Krishnan 1999).

Total health expenditure by the public sector in 1998–99 was Rs 161 billion, or a per capita expenditure of Rs 165 at 1993–94 prices (Misra et al. 2003). In India, the states typically account for about 75 per cent of total public spending on health, with the rest being borne by the Centre. The proportion of health expenditure in the major states, which was in the range of 6–7 per cent during the 1980s, came down to about 5 per cent during the 1990s, the decade of reforms, the decade of governance.

Table 19.4 provides data on real per capita spending on health among the major states. As is evident, Uttar Pradesh has the least spending followed by Madhya Pradesh and Orissa. A substantial proportion, close to 80 per cent of these state expenditures are, however, geared towards payment of salaries alone, especially in the BIMARU states. This is indicative of course of not high salaries to personnel, but the remarkably low spending on health.

Table 19.4: Real Per Capita Spending on Health (Rs)

Sr. No.	*States*	*1985–86*	*1991–92*	*1995–96*	*1998–99*
1.	Andhra Pradesh	20.44	21.03	21.92	31.88
2.	Gujarat	24.32	30.51	28.77	45.44
3.	Haryana	26.79	26.65	24.39	33.78
4.	Kerala	25.97	32.15	30.98	35.05
5.	Maharashtra	27.46	30.87	30.73	33.67
6.	Madhya Pradesh	16.19	19.17	17.89	25.49
7.	Orissa	16.95	23.26	19.54	28.28
8.	Rajasthan	21.85	29.07	31.02	37.70
9.	Tamil Nadu	15.38	21.61	32.09	42.42
10.	Uttar Pradesh	16.12	20.38	19.01	18.10
11.	West Bengal	22.65	28.49	25.96	41.24
	Average Spending	21.28	25.74	25.66	33.91

Source: Misra et al. (2003), *India Health Report.*
Note: The figures are in constant prices 1980–81 = 100.

Here then, it seems, lies the singular explanation for poor performance in the health sector: poor public sector spending. What is more worrying, as the Figure 19.7 indicates, is that over the 1990s there has been a redistribution of shares within the primary, secondary and tertiary sectors, as compared to the period of the 1980s. While spending has increased by about 50 per cent at the primary and secondary levels, the increase at the tertiary level has been more than 100 per cent. In other words, although proportionately less funds were available for health, and a larger proportion went towards salaries, a larger proportion was also allocated towards tertiary level care. These are, of course, a result of political decisions made over this period, which was accompanied by a squeeze on finances. This is a consequence of reforms of the health sector, when issues of governance came to the fore. As in many other countries, then, reforms were slated to increase health inequalities, and were not fortuitous outcomes of the policy process. Again, these decisions were in line with policy prescriptions emerging out of the World Bank and institutions owing allegiance to it. The squeeze on resources for primary health care is the single most important factor for the dismal state of primary health care services in the country. This is not to deny that tertiary health care needed substantial strengthening. However, this is to draw attention to the fact that this has occurred at the cost of lower levels of health care.

Figure 19.7: Per Capita Real Expenditure by Levels of Care

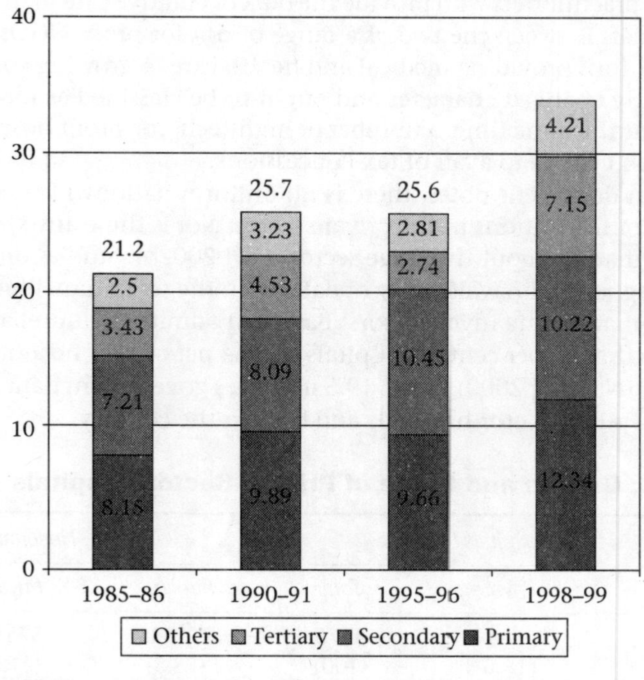

Source: Selvaraju et al. (2001). Background Paper, cited in Misra et al. (2003). *India Health Report.*

It is often argued that one reason why the government has introduced expenditure cuts is that there is a squeeze on government finances. What is not highlighted is that, over the 1990s, the government is either less willing or unwilling to collect taxes even at levels that existed before the onset of reforms. Thus, the tax GDP ratio has declined from more than 13 per cent in 1990–91 to 9 per cent in 2000–01. This of course implies that regressive indirect taxes as a proportion of revenue has increased, taxes paid for largely by the poor. But just the reduction in direct taxes represents uncollected revenues of 4 per cent of GDP, which is almost three times the entire expenditure on public health, medicine and family welfare by the central and state governments combined. At the same time, India substantially subsidises health care in the First World through transfer of skilled human power, trained at public expense, at an estimated cost of 160 million US dollars every year (VHAI 1997).

Private Sector in Health Care

Any generalisation about the private sector in the country would be hazardous, if not foolish, since it comprises a large and heterogeneous group of actors and institutions, and indeed among (in that phrase now so popular among governance-*wallahs*) stake holders.[8] On the one hand, are state-of-the-art super-speciality corporate hospitals in urban areas that even the middle classes find difficult to access, and which are to form the hub of the health tourism industry that the Government now plans to promote. On the other hand, are the vast numbers of ill-qualified individual practitioners who provide the bulk of curative care in the country, primary level care in particular. Between the two, is a range of not-for profit NGOs, trusts, charitable and religious institutions providing medical and health care. A growing concern is that some of these have recently changed character and ought to be classified as for-profit institutions (Misra et al. 2003). At the same time, a number of high-tech, for-profit hospitals are registered as trusts and research centres to avail of tax concessions.

As the Tenth Plan document notes, there is no uniform nationwide system of registering either practitioners or institutions in the private sector. Nor is there any system for obtaining and analysing information about this large sector (GOI 2002b). Studies on the private sector in India are thus plagued by unavailability of data, with the sector unwilling, by and large, to share data with even academic investigators. Based on admittedly unreliable available data, one study estimates that 93 per cent of hospitals and 64 per cent of hospital beds in India are in the private sector (Nandraj 2000). Table 19.5 indicates government data on the growth and share of private and public sector hospitals and beds in the country.

Table 19.5: Growth and Share of Private Sector Hospitals and Beds

	Hospitals			*Hospital beds*		
Year	*Public*	*Private*	*Total*	*Public*	*Private*	*Total*
1974	2832	644	3476	211335	57550	268885
	(81.4)	(18.6)	(100)	(78.5)	(21.5)	(100)
1979	3735	2031	5766	331233	115372	446605
	(64.7)	(35.3)	(100)	(74.2)	(25.8)	(100)
1984	3925	3256	7181	362966	137662	500628
	(54.6)	(45.4)	(100)	(72.5)	(27.5)	(100)
1988	4334	5497	9831	410772	175117	585889
	(44.1)	(55.9)	(100)	(70.1)	(29.9)	(100)
1996	4808	10289	15097	395664	228155	623819
	(31.9)	(68.1)	(100)	(63.4)	(36.6)	(100)

Source: (GOI) Health Information of India, CBHI, various years, (GOI) Directory of Hospitals in India, CBHI, various years.

Note: Figures in brackets denote percentage share.

The data clearly reveals that the share of private hospitals has increased remarkably between 1974 and 1996, while that of beds has shown an increase although not as significant as in the number of institutions. While there are exceptions, the majority of these are small institutions, with 85 per cent of them with less than 25 beds. Most such institutions offer maternity and general services and are managed by doctor entrepreneurs. Tertiary speciality and super-speciality private institutions comprise only 1–2 per cent of the private sector institutions (GOI 2002b).

The distribution of private sector facilities and doctors between states and regions is even more inequitable than the public health facilities, reflecting the tendency to concentrate in better-off states and in better-off regions. As in the case of public services, rural-urban differences are acute with a clear urban bias as shown in Figure 19.8. Indeed private hospitals are less urban-based than public ones at the all India level. However, what is to be remembered is that the bulk of medical care in rural areas, and a not-insignificant amount in urban areas, is provided by unqualified medical practitioners, estimated to be about one million. While the quality of medical care is said to be dubious, this is not a characterisation that sticks to the unqualified medical practitioners alone.

Figure 19.8: Rural-urban Distribution of Hospitals/Hospital Beds: Public and Private Sectors

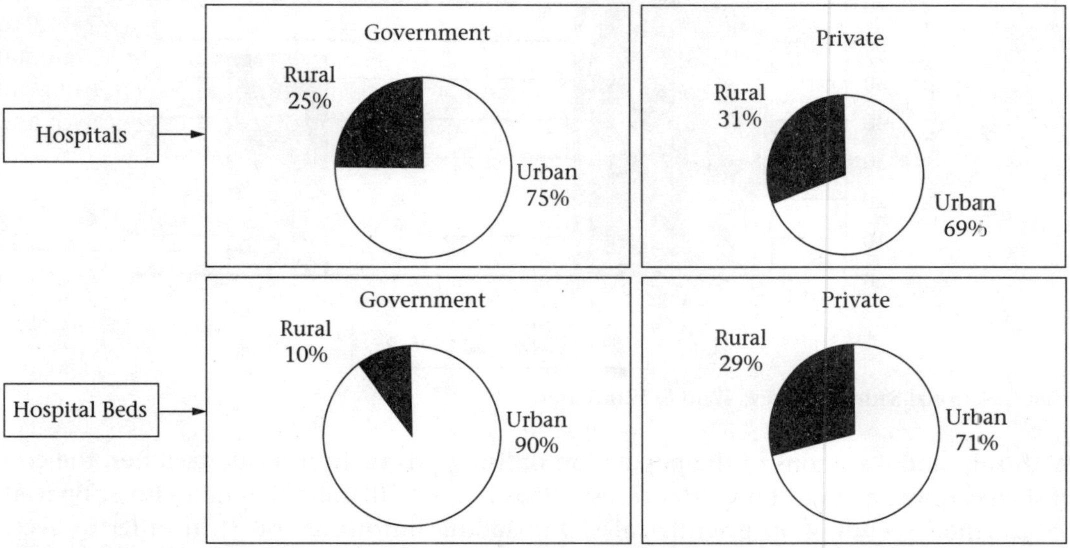

Source: GOI (1998) *Directory of Hospitals in India*; Nandraj (2000), *The Private Health Sector.*

The private sector today dominates the public in both in-patient care and in out-patient care. The reasons for this are many, and include the fact that medicines are not available in the public sector and indeed there are significant shortfalls of human power; it is also due to the preoccupation of public health services with the vertical programmes in general and the family planning programme in particular. Data from the National Sample Survey's 52nd Round reveal that 44 per cent of respondents preferred the private sector because the doctor was available, 36 per cent because they were dissatisfied with the quality of care in public facilities and seven per cent because medicines were not available in the public sector.

The private sector accounts for 82 per cent of all OP care at the all-India level and 56 per cent of all IP care (Figure 19.9). However, immunisations and antenatal care are overwhelmingly provided by public sector facilities. There are also significant inter-state variations. The better-off states, with a well-developed private sector such as Maharashtra, Kerala, Haryana, and Punjab show more utilisation of private facilities. On the other hand, poorer states with poorly spread private facilities continue to show the predominance of the public sector. Across the country, an interesting finding which perhaps explains the increasing neglect of public health is that the middle-classes have now forsaken the public sector (Baru 1998). It is this class, which is increasingly 'seceding' from the nation that provides the social base for the health sector reforms of increasing privatisation now under way.

Figure 19.9: Share of Private Sector in Out-patient & In-patient Care

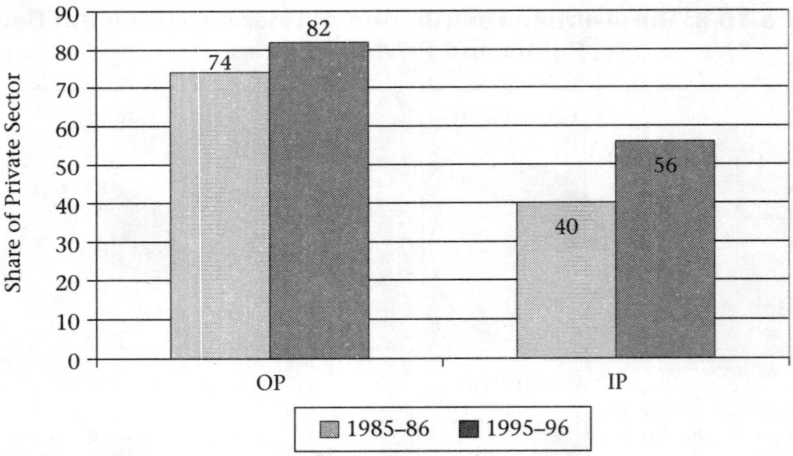

Source: National Sample Survey, 42nd & 52nd Rounds.

With substantial sections of the population utilising private health care facilities, the costs of such care assumes great importance, especially as the NHP notes that households typically reduce their spending on essential needs, including nutritional ones, in order to access medical care. Indeed as we already noted, medical care costs have emerged as a leading cause of indebtedness in the population. The NSS 52nd round reveals that per capita out-of-pocket expenditure per year to private facilities ranges from over Rs 500 among the richest, to Rs 75 among the poorest. In terms of percentage share of per capita expenditure by quintile to the private sector, the poorest quintile contributes 88 per cent, compared to 84 per cent by the richest quintile. The difference in costs between the private and public sector varies significantly across states as revealed in Figure 19.10.

Figure 19.10: Average Hospital Charge Per In-patient Day by Public and Private, by Select States

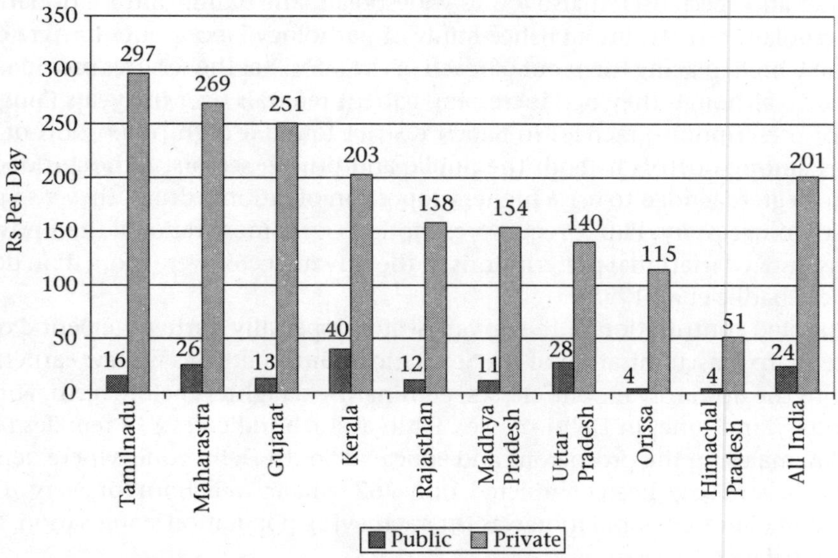

Source: Mahal et al. (2000), *Who Benefits from Public Health Spending in India*, NCAER.

Costs are ironically higher in the more advanced, and better governed, states such as Tamil Nadu, Maharashtra, Gujarat and Kerala than in the more backward BIMARU states. Here, again, is the evidence that market forces in the health sector do not necessarily supply cheaper care, and that competition in the medical care sector does not result in lower costs.

There is a general assumption that private medical care is of a vastly superior quality than that provided in the public. There is however little empirical data to substantiate this claim. A study of private hospitals in Chennai revealed that this sector has grown without any state policy to regulate its growth and development. As a result, the sector had grown without any regard to norms for infrastructure. There has also developed a complex network of private hospitals and physicians with diagnostic centres involved in policies of 'scalping'; it also shows a strong tendency to over-provide care, depending on the patient's ability to pay (Muraleedharan 1999). Another study of the private sector in rural Maharashtra revealed that only 55 per cent of private hospitals had registration, only 38 per cent maintained records of any kind, and that a remarkably high proportion lacked basic facilities. It also showed that close to 30 per cent were being run by doctors not trained in the allopathic system of medicine. They were being run without adequate facilities and human power, with only two per cent employing trained nurses. Of the hospitals, 39 per cent operated without a full-time doctor.

Only 10 per cent of hospitals had an ECG monitor, 65 per cent a steriliser and 56 per cent an oxygen cylinder (Nandraj and Duggal 1997). Yet another study found that Caesarean sections were performed three times more in private hospitals than public ones (Homan and Thankappan 1999). A study in Mumbai reported prevalence of widespread malpractices, with cutbacks for referrals—the scalping referred to—of the order of 40 per cent of the fees charged by laboratories and specialists. It also found widespread false billing and irrational treatment practices (Yesudian: nd). An unpublished study of pathology laboratories in Agra city found costs extremely high, placing them out of reach of the poor. Yet the services provided were not up to standards, although they had increasing patient referrals over the years (Singh 1993).

A study of prescription practices in Satara district found a high proportion of irrational prescriptions among doctors in both the public and private sectors. Although doctors with postgraduate degrees tended to use a higher proportion of rational drugs, they also prescribed more drugs than necessary. Public sector prescriptions were more rational than private sector prescriptions. Indeed irrational prescriptions in the private sector were more than double that in the public (Phadke et al. 1995).

One undoubted contribution of the private sector, especially during the period of reforms, has been the sharp masculinisation of the Sex Ratio at Birth (SRB), as we saw earlier. This is of course a gift to the upwardly mobile classes, eliminating daughters before birth. For example, between January and June, in Delhi the Sex Ratio at Birth indicates 819 females being born for every 1000 males; in the prosperous and educated South Delhi zone, where demographic transition has by and large been completed, only 762 females were born for every 1000 males. This well off and educated population was thus achieving population stabilisation, at the cost of population balance.

Perhaps the most telling comment on the private sector was during the plague epidemic in Surat of 1994. The epidemic itself is partly attributed to the decay of the public health system, including the slashing of budgets for the control of communicable diseases (Qadeer et al. 1994). But once the epidemic commenced, it was observed that the majority of private practitioners fled the city, while the government doctors tried, with hands tied, lack of medicines and funds, to fight the epidemic (Shah 1997).

Thus issues of quality of care that plague the public sector are not unique to it. Indeed, the private sector provides the lead and sets norms for a culture of medicalisation that the public sector is often forced to emulate. Yet, without taking many of the systemic factors that ail the public sector into account, efforts at reforms in the health sector all too often are facile and simplistic and involve increasing public subsidies to the private sector. While the private sector has thus grown, its quality, outcomes and cost have not been issues coming under a strong regulatory mechanism.

Health Sector Reforms

Citing inefficiencies of the public system, and financial stringency, India commenced health sector reforms. What was not clearly articulated was that these moves were initiated at the behest of international financial institutions to which we were indebted. The mantra was of course efficiency and governance. This section briefly surveys, on the basis of not very substantial evidence, what our experience has been.

The data reviewed on the health scenario and of the health system in India unfortunately project a none-too happy picture. A small recent study, widely quoted, for example, reveals the dismal state of public health services, even as it indicates that people spend substantially on health care largely provided by unqualified persons in the private sector where services were even worse (Banerjee et al. 2004). Yet, in the 1990s as India embarked upon the structural adjustment programme, as we saw earlier, state spending on health declined. The decline in public investments was matched with growing subsidies to the private sector in health care in a variety of ways (Baru 1998). What is interesting is that while wide-ranging reforms in the health sector were initiated, the NHP itself makes no reference to this important policy change.

In essence, the reforms intend to reduce the role of the state in financing and provision, while confining its role to that of regulation. The efforts underway in India could thus be seen as part of much larger processes shaping the health sector globally; in developing countries at the instance of international financial institutions. Given the fact, however, of the desperate poverty of large sections of the population, of the widespread prevalence of hunger, of the huge morbidity and mortality loads, and the abysmal role of the state in health sector provision in the country, the direction of such reforms as carried out in other countries, further curtail health care access to the poor.[9]

Health sector reforms in India have taken a variety of forms aimed at improving efficiency and effectiveness, and the quality of care provided by public health services. Some of these include contracting, public-private partnerships, user fees, and privatisation of public facilities.

Contracting has emerged as an important new mechanism for improving the efficiency of services in the public health sector. Some or all aspects of health facilities and functions could be contracted out to private parties, including clinical, para-clinical and non-clinical functions. The rationale for contracting was that it reduced costs, introduced greater flexibility in the use of labour, or could be utilised to provide services in areas that were under-served. In India contracting has been initiated under the blindness programme, the AIDS control programme, and franchising arrangements have been set up with private providers under the Revised National Tuberculosis Control Programme (RNTCP) (Nandraj et al. 2001). Many non-clinical support services in public hospitals have also been contracted out. It has been suggested that NGOs be contracted to provide primary health services in rural areas (World Bank 1995).

The experience of contracting services in other countries has been mixed. In India itself, given the systemic and wide-ranging nature of problems facing the health sector, it is not likely to prove a solution to these myriad problems. It is also necessary to systematically review the experience so far before extending it to other areas.

There is not enough documentation on the transfer of public health facilities to private providers on a contract basis. One recent case involves the transfer of ownership of a public tertiary care hospital in Mumbai as part of a state health system project funded by the World Bank (Nandraj et al. 2001). The municipal corporation of Mumbai has taken a policy decision to hand over many of its peripheral hospitals to the private sector. In a controversial move, a peripheral hospital was also handed over to a private medical college that did not have the necessary clinical facilities; the Medical Council of India had not recognised the concerned medical college. Other cities, such as Ahmedabad, have handed over facilities to NGOs. While it is indeed the case that some NGOs have provided excellent services and have served as models of Primary Health Care, this cannot be generalised. There are a number of other concerns that equally need to be addressed.

NGOs comprise a broad and heterogeneous category in terms of ideology, activities, funding, outreach and effectiveness. Generalisations about their effectiveness, efficacy and efficiency are made out of ideological concerns, not necessarily out of concerns for public health. Further, there is little empirical data to substantiate claims to justify greater public support to NGOs on various grounds. They are not necessarily demonstrably either more effective or efficient than any public funded institution and cannot be used as a substitute for a variety of reasons. First, NGOs, by definition, are discretionary and not mandatory. Thus, they can be socially exclusive, and indeed the fear that NGO-isation may be against the interests of Dalits has been frequently voiced by Dalit activists and scholars (Thorat 2001). Second, they are not necessarily accountable, certainly not to the people they work with. Third, the issue of monitoring and regulation of the private and NGO sectors is an urgent and vexed question, but we have only to remember that the scandal of quinacrine sterilisations in the country was largely carried out by NGOs (Rao 2001). Fourth, it is a well-worked out myth that NGOs are somehow more 'representative' than political bodies. Thus, the whole 'space' for 'Civil Society Organisations' in policy-making bodies that rigorously include NGOs but exclude other civil society organisations like trade unions is problematic. Finally, it is also not true that NGOs are internally more democratic: we have only to remember that the RSS and the VHP, the largest network of foreign funded Civil Society Organisations (CSOs) in the country are deeply hierarchical, non-representative, anti-democratic and indeed fascistic. It is to be borne in mind that typically NGOs are small and often scattered; they are neither universally available nor accessible. Baru has shown on the basis of available data that NGOs providing health services are typically located in the better-off states and in better-off areas among them (Baru 1999). Similarly, Visaria has noted that in both Rajasthan and Madhya Pradesh, NGOs involved in health and development activities are located in only a few developed districts (Visaria 2002). The same point has also been noted for the state of Maharashtra (Duggal et al. 1986).

It is still too early to assess the benefits and pitfalls of these experiments but they need to be examined for the benefits, if any, they bring to the poor. It could be argued that this transfer of public resources to private sources represents further strengthening of a private health care system that has shown itself to be exploitative and not sensitive to wider social concerns. This does not then represent moves to improve the administrative and managerial efficiency of the public health system as a whole, but instead a simplistic response to a complex problem.

Yet another scheme has been the provision of a range of incentives to the private health sector through provision of land at throw-away prices, grant of customs duty exemptions for import of sophisticated medical technology, and loans from financial institutions at low interest rates. These incentives have been provided for both private for profit and not-for-profit institutions. A study indicated that these had been utilised primarily by urban-based institutions that had not always provided free services to the poor as they were expected to as per the terms of the contractural agreement (Bhat 1998). Further, there were no mechanisms to monitor the project, with the government's limited institutional ability to do so. A Committee has been set up by the Government of India to examine the violations by private hospitals of the terms of their agreements.

Such arrangements have also led to the burgeoning of high-technology diagnostic centres in urban areas, with excess capacities. Between 1984 and 1986 over 60 diagnostic centres entered the market with an investment of Rs 20000 million (Nandraj et al. 2001). Thus, Mumbai has 13 body scanners, Delhi 11, Chennai eight, Kolkata three, Pune three and Hyderabad two (Jesani and Anantharam 1993). In such a situation, not warranted by public health considerations, there has occurred the irrational use and overuse of such technologies. The oversupply of doctors in the private sector has also led to unnecessary or over-medication of healthy people (Nandraj 1994).

Yet another reform measure has been the levying of user charges as an alternative source of health financing. Although the experience of other countries from Latin America and Africa indicated that user charges had neither generated adequate resources as to justify it, nor led to an increase in efficiency and effectiveness, and indeed had proved to exclude the poor and most needy, several states in the country have attempted, with varying success, to implement the scheme. These moves have met with varying degrees of opposition in the country, but nevertheless have been implemented over the 1990s in states such as Andhra Pradesh, Maharashtra, West Bengal, Madhya Pradesh, Orissa and Uttar Pradesh. Given the weak infrastructure in most public institutions and their poor outreach, user fees tend also to push more people to the private health sector. In India, the average across states for cost recovery through user fees was as low as 3.8 per cent.

The Tenth Plan document notes that an appropriate institutional framework for reviewing user charges has not yet been established and that the level of cost recovery has been minimal (GOI 2002b). Further, it also notes that mechanisms for identifying and exempting the poor were ill-defined.

Reviewing the cluster of projects that could be termed public-private partnership in health care, the Tenth Plan notes that many of the efforts have not been successful. Thus contractural appointment of health care staff and hiring of private practitioners has not been able to fill the gaps in infrastructure, nor has it been able to fill posts in under-served areas (GOI 2002b). It also notes that many of the project initiatives have not been evaluated and institutional mechanisms to monitor and implement these projects have yet to be evolved.

Further, over the 1990s, studies have documented a sharp increase in medical care costs. There have been far reaching changes in drug policies. Thus India—earlier characterised by relatively low costs of drugs and pharmaceuticals, along with a significant indigenous production of drugs—has witnessed a greater concentration of drug production, a larger role for multinationals, a higher proportion of imported drugs and unbelievably steep rises in the costs of drugs (Sengupta 1996). Concurrently, marked shifts have occurred in health care utilisation. Among people who sought out-patient services in 1995–96, more than 80 per cent did so in the private sector, a sharp increase in even the poorer states of the country (Sen et al. 2002).

In 1995–96, 55 per cent and 57 per cent in rural and urban areas were hospitalised in the private sector compared to 40 per cent in 1986–87. National Sample Survey (NSS) data indicates greater inequality in use of health facilities by economic class gradients. In rural areas the class gradient in in-patient use of public hospitals—which was insignificant in the mid-1980s—turned statistically significant in the mid-1990s. In urban areas, inequality in use of public facilities did not worsen significantly, but inequality in use of private facilities did. The steep fall in rural hospitalisation rates, along with increasing use by the better-off indicates that the poor are being squeezed out. Fee-for-services is undoubtedly one important mechanism that has succeeded in doing this.

Costs of both out-patient and in-patient care increased sharply in both rural and urban areas, compared to the mid-1980s. Private out-patient costs increased by 142 per cent as against 77 per cent in the public sector in the rural areas. In urban areas, private out-patient costs increased by 150 per cent compared to 124 per cent in the public sector. The increase in costs in in-patient care is even more striking: average costs rose by 436 per cent in rural and 320 per cent in urban areas (Sen et al. 2002). Thus, as Figure 19.11a reveals, a substantial proportion of patients borrowed money in order to meet their health care costs. Figure 19.11b provides data on in-patients below the poverty line who borrowed money or sold assets for hospitalisation in both the public and private health care systems.

Ironically, the better-off states, such as Andhra Pradesh, Tamil Nadu, Karnataka—states with a thick spread of private facilities—revealed more poor people borrowing money to pay for in-patient care. As is evident, the share borrowing money is greater in the private sector than the public. In states such as Rajasthan, Madhya Pradesh and Uttar Pradesh—given the thin spread of private care, the poor are borrowing money even to access the public health system for in-patient care. Clearly, this cannot be allowed to continue on grounds of equity, if not for epidemiological considerations.

Any effort to improve public health in the country must not only emphasise the important determinants of health but also the salient role of public spending. The reforms, however, singularly lack a health system perspective and instead comprise an agglomeration of projects with an implicit belief that the market will cure the problems that ail the health system.

Concluding Observations

There is a widespread assumption that India is characterised by widespread state presence in all sectors of the economy and polity. In the case of the health sector, this, as we have seen, is simply not the case. Along with a weak state sector, an unregulated and powerful private health care sector raises several issues of universal care, of comprehensive care and above all, of equity. Failing this, efforts at tinkering through projects, as we have seen, carry the risk of consolidating the dual health care system that the country now possesses: one weak and under-funded for the vast majority of the population with no access to primary health care,

Figure 19.11a: Proportion of Patients Who Borrowed for Hospitalisation Across States

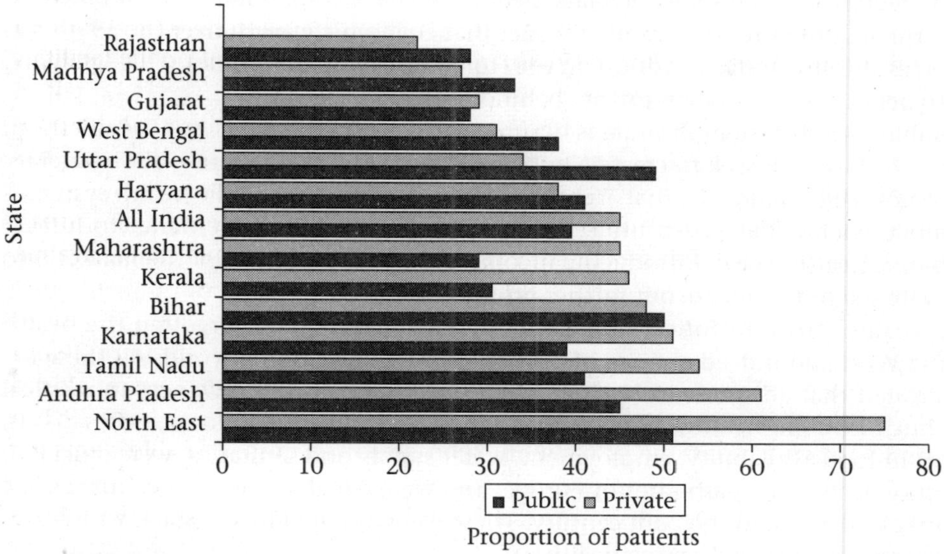

Source: NSSO 1995–96.

Figure 19.11b: Proportion of In-patients below the Poverty Line that Borrowed or Sold Assets for Public and Private Hospitalisations, by State 1995–96

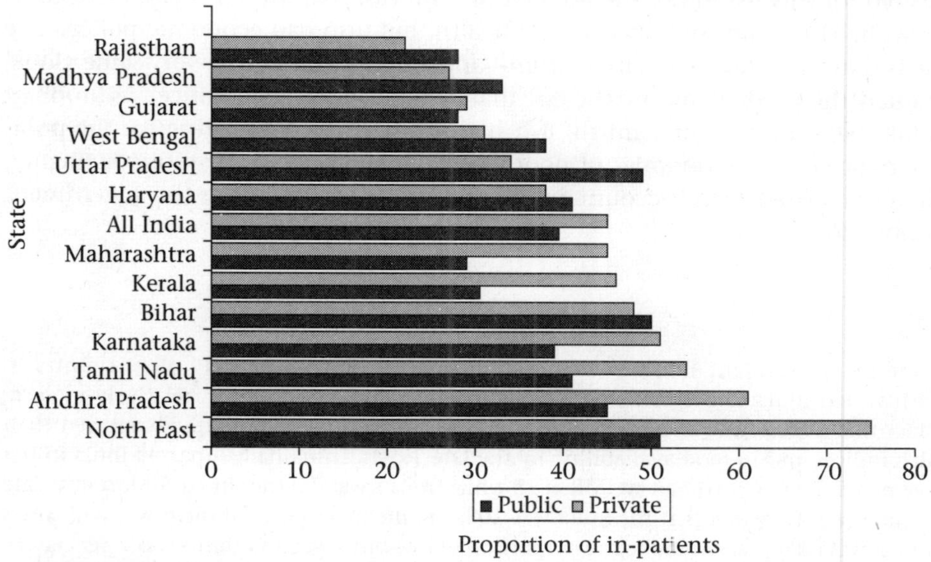

Source: NSSO 1995–96.

and the other largely urban-based curative high technology health care for a minority of the population whose public health needs are taken care of. Larger macroeconomic changes that have increased regional, rural-urban and class inequalities have compounded the problem. It is thus, not surprising to note that despite the fact that economic growth over the 1990s has been described as shining, India's position on the Human Development Index (HDI) globally, already low to begin with, has fallen further behind, from 127 to 132.

That the public health system in India is dysfunctional, or inefficient is not the question; the question is, did we ever seek to create a public system that was different—our budgetary allocations do not seem to indicate that. Yet these very features of the public health system—created by public policy—have been utilised in the age of globalised governance to further weaken the public health sector, introducing incommensurable principles of the market into it, for the private sector to squeeze out further profits.

We live in shamelessly a-historical times, when policy makers have forgotten the health histories of the West and indeed a range of countries in the developing world. All these experiences indicated that advances in health were a feature not just of advances in medical technology, but in public health, along with a range of socio-economic measures. Thus, improvements in food availability, employment, water supply and sanitation were crucial in the 19th century decline of death rates in Europe, and were equally crucial in countries like China, Sri Lanka and Korea in the 20th century. These were initiated by the state, which also provided universal and comprehensive health care.

What we have in India is a case of state-led collapse of the public health system, even as public funds are utilised to strengthen the private sector that provides medical care to a small section of the population. While medical care on par with the developed countries is thus supposedly created for this section of the population, the vast majority of the population is thrown to the wolf. This is not only bad public health, but also bad economic policy. The irony of course is that these moves emanate from—and are funded by—the very same global institutions, namely the World Bank and the IMF that demand 'good governance'. As Monbiot notes, 'this would be cause for bitter mirth, if it had not been so devastating for the poor; their own governance of the economies of poor nations could scarcely be more damaging, while in terms of transparency and accountability, they are as democratic as the government of Burma' (Monbiot 2003: 152).

Notes

1. While these are indeed substantial achievements, compared to China—the only other country in the world with which India can legitimately be compared—these are, however, relatively modest. Despite the fact that at the time of her revolution, China was relatively more disadvantaged than India in health indices and in food availability, by the late 1990s China had surpassed India in her health achievements. Thus, China had an IMR of 38 while India's was 71; the Under-5-Mortality Rate (U5MR) for China was 47, while that for India was 108; the life expectancy at birth was 69.8 years in China, while it was 62.6 years in India; the proportion of low-birth weight infants was 9 per cent in China while it was 33 per cent in India; the TB prevalence rate per 100,000 was 38.1 in China, while it was 136.9 in India (Acharya et al. 2000). One fundamental reason is of course the huge prevalence

of hunger and poverty in the country; indeed as the National Health Policy (NHP) notes, 44.2 per cent of the population of India survive on less than a dollar a day.

2. BIMARU stands for Bihar, Madhya Pradesh, Rajasthan, Uttar Pradesh and Orissa. Together they account for more than 40 per cent of India's population.
3. The average calorie consumption was 2172 Kcal as against the RDA of 2425 Kcal (NNMP).
4. A comparison cannot be made with NFHS I on stunting since height was not measured in five states during NFHS I.
5. The Body Mass Index (BMI) is defined as the weight in kilograms divided by the height in metres.
6. Mild anaemia is defined as haemoglobin levels between 10–10.9 grams/dl for pregnant and 10.–11.9 grams/dl for non-pregnant women; moderate anaemia as 7–9.9gms/dl and severe anaemia as less than 7.0 gms/dl. Anaemia is one of the leading underlying causes of death in the country among women, not just among the pregnant.
7. There are discrepancies in the Government documents, as is evident. The World Bank's *World Development Report, 1999–2000*, provides a figure of 0.7 per cent.
8. It needs hardly be added that this phrase more than metaphorically resonates with shareholders. This metonymic use of language is not accidental, but stems from the utilisation of market principles in health sector planning in the age of reforms.
9. While the consequences of reforms in Latin America and Africa are well known, that of China is equally apposite. Reforms in China, for example, have meant an annual real increase in GNP by 9 per cent, quadrupling the size of the economy in merely 20 years. Yet, this has been accompanied by increasing income inequalities between regions and in sharpening health inequalities. In 1994, the prosperous coastal province of Zhejiang had a Maternal Mortality Rate of 23.74 per 100,000 live births, while the poorer inland province of Quinhai had a figure of 215.37. Further, within provinces, rural-urban differences in wealth and well-being have sharpened: the IMR is higher in rural areas than in the urban, with a widening of the gap. A recent study of 30 of China's poorest counties found that the IMR actually increased from 50 per thousand live births in the late 1970s to 72 per thousand in the late 1980s, despite the relatively egalitarian base at which the reforms commenced. Surveys in 1987 and 1992 revealed that the proportion of stunted children in rural areas had increased. Data on growth of Chinese children also indicate increasing disparities in height between rural and urban areas. Despite the Chinese Government's commitment to gender equity, the reforms have led to an increase in gender differentials in child survival along with increased morbidity rates among females. The economic changes, along with the 'one child per family' norm, since officially abandoned, has accentuated the problem of 'missing girls'. Poignantly, as in countries like India, medical expenditure is emerging as a leading cause of the impoverishment of families as the health system collapsed. Efforts at decentralisation have merely sharpened the differentials (Liu et al. 2001).

References

Acharya, Alka, Rama V. Baru and Geetha B. Nambissan (2000). 'The State and Human Development: Health and Education', in G.P. Deshpande and Alka Acharya (eds), *Fifty Years of Crossing a Bridge of Dreams: India and China*. New Delhi: Tulika.

Baru, R.V. (1998). *Private Health Care in India: Social Characteristics and Trends*. New Delhi: Sage Publications.

——— (1999). 'The Structure and Utilisation of Health Services: An Inter-State Analysis', in Mohan Rao (ed.), *Disinvesting in Health: The World Bank's Prescriptions for Health*. New Delhi: Sage Publications.

Bhat, R. (1998). 'Private Health Care Sector in India: Issues Arising out of its Growth and the Role of the State in Strengthening Public-Private Interaction', Unpublished, IIM, Ahmedabad.

Banerjee, A., A. Deaton and E. Duflo (2004). 'Health Care Delivery in Rural Rajasthan', *Economic and Political Weekly*, 39(9): 944–49.

Duggal, Ravi, Manisha Gupta and Amar Jesani (1986). *NGOs in Rural Health Care*. Mumbai: Cehat.

Gershman, John and Alec Irwin (2000). 'Getting a Grip on the Global Economy', in Jim Yong Kim, Joyce V. Millen, Alec Irwin and John Gershman (eds), *Dying for Growth: Global Inequality and the Health of the Poor*. Maine: Common Courage Press.

GOI (Government of India) (1983). *National Health Policy*. New Delhi: Ministry of Health and Family Welfare.

——— (1999). *Health Information of India 1999*. New Delhi: Ministry of Health and Family Welfare.

——— (2000). *SRS Bulletin*, (vol. 34, no. 1), New Delhi: Office of the Registrar General.

——— (2001). *Draft National Health Policy 2001*. New Delhi: Ministry of Health and Family Welfare.

——— (2002a). *Health Information of India 1999*. New Delhi: Ministry of Health and Family Welfare.

——— (2002b). *Tenth Five Year Plan*, New Delhi: Planning Commission.

Homan, R.K. and K.R. Thankappan (1999). 'An Examination of Public and Private Sector Sources of In-patient Care in Trivandrm District, Kerala', Thiruvananthapuram: Achuta Menon Centre for Health Services.

IIPS (International Institute of Population Sciences) (2002). *National Family Health Survey (NFHS II) 1998–99*. Mumbai.

Jesani, A. and S. Anantharam (1993). *Private Sector and Privatisation in Health Care Services*. Mumbai: FRCH.

Kim, Jim Yong, Aaron Shakow, Jaime Bayona, Rhatigan Joe and Emma L. Rubin de Celis (2000), 'Sickness Amidst Recovery: Public Debt and Private Suffering in Peru' in Jim Yong Kim, Joyce V. Millen, Alec Irwin and John Gershman (eds), *Dying for Growth: Global Inequality and the Health of the Poor*. Common Courage Press, Muaroe.

Krishnan, T.N. (1999). 'Access to Health Care and Burden of Treatment in India', in Mohan Rao (ed.), *Disinvesting in Health: The World Bank's Prescriptions for Health*. New Delhi Sage Publication.

Liu, Yuanli, Keguin Rao, Timothy Evans, Yude Chen and William C. Hsiao (2001). 'China: Increasing Health Gaps in a Transitional Economy', in Timothy Evans et al. (eds), *Challenging Inequalities in Health: From Ethics to Action*. New York: Oxford University Press.

Mahila Chetna Manch (2004). 'Two Child Policy and Its Implications for Women', unpublished report for the Ministry of Health and Family Welfare, Bhopal.

Misra, Rajiv, Rachel Chatterjee and Sujatha Rao (2003). *India Health Report*. New Delhi: Oxford University Press.

Monbiot, George (2003). *The Age of Consent: A Manifesto for a New World Order*. London: Harper Perennial.

Muraleedharan, V.R. (1999). 'Characteristics and Structure of Private Hospital Structure in Urban India: A Study of Madras City', Small Applied Area Research Paper 5, Bethesda, Washington D.C.

Nandraj, S. (1994). 'Beyond the Law and the Lord: Quality of Private Health Care', *Economic and Political Weekly*, 29(27): 1680–85.

——— (2000). *The Private Health Sector: Concerns, Challenges and Options*. Mumbai: Cehat.

Nandraj, S. and R. Duggal (1997). *Physical Standards in the Private Health Sector—A Case Study of Rural Maharashtra*. Mumbai: Cehat.

Nandraj, S., V.R. Muraleedharan, R.V. Baru, I. Qadeer and R. Priya (2001). *Private Health Sector in India: Review and Annotated Bibliography*. Mumbai: Cehat.

National Nutrition Monitoring Bureau (NNMB) (1997). *Twenty Five Years of NNMB 1972–1995*. Hyderabad.

Patel, Tulsi (2004). 'Missing Girls in India', *Economic and Political Weekly*, 39(9): 887–89.

Phadke, Anant, Andrey Fernandez, L. Sharda, Pratibha Mane and Amar Jesani (1995). *A Study of Supply and Use of Pharmaceuticals in Satara District*, Pune : FRCH.

Premi, M.K. (2001). 'The Missing Girl Child', *Economic and Political Weekly*, 36(21): 1875–80, May.

Qadeer, Imrana (1998), 'Reproductive Health: A Public Health Perspective', *Economic and Political Weekly*, 33(44): 267–84

Qadeer, Imrana, K.R. Nayar and R.V. Banan (1994). 'Contextualising Plague: A Reconstruction and an Analysis', *Economic and Political Weekly*, 29(47).

Rao, Mohan (2001). 'The Rhetoric of Reproductive Rights: Quinacrine Sterilisation in India', in Imrana Qadeer, Kasturi Sen and K.R. Nayar (eds), *Public Health and the Poverty of Reforms*. New Delhi: Sage Publications.

——— (2002), 'Population Policies: From Bad to Worse', *Economic and Political Weekly*, 37(22): 2120–21.

Rao, Mohan and Rene Lowenson (2000). 'The Political Economy of the Assault on Health', *People's Health Assembly Discussion Papers*, Dhaka.

Sen, Gita and Aditi Iyer (2002). 'Incentives and Disncentives: Necessary, Effective, Just?', *Seminar*, 511: 46–51.

Sen, Gita, Aditi Iyer and Asha George (2002). 'Class, Gender and Health Equity: Lessons from Liberalising India', in Gita Sen, Asha George and Piroska Ostlin (eds), *Engendering International Health*. Massachusetts: MIT Press.

Sengupta, Amit (1996). 'Economic Reforms, Health and Pharmaceuticals', *Economic and Political Weekly*, 31(48): 3155–59.

Shah, Ghanshyam (1997). *Public Health and Urban Development: The Plague in Surat*. New Delhi: Sage Publications.

Singh, T.V. (1993). 'A Study of the State of Medicare Facilities in Agra City With Special Reference to Pathology Labs', Unpublished MSW Report, Agra: Agra University.

Thorat, Sukhadeo (2001). 'Strategy of Disincentives and Targeting for Population Control: Implications for Dalits and Tribals', Paper presented at the National Colloquium on Population Policies, New Delhi: Center of Social Medicine and Community Health and the Singamma Sreenivasan Foundation.

Twaddle, Andrew C. (2002). 'Health Care Reform and Global Hegemony', in Andrew C.Twaddle (ed.). *Health Care Reform Around the World*. London: Auburn House.

UNFPA (2003). *Missing: Mapping the Adverse Child Sex Ratio in India*. New Delhi.

Visaria, Pravin (2002). 'Population Policy in India: Evolution, Performance and Challenges', *The National Medical Journal of India*,15(Supplement 1): 6–18.

VHAI (Voluntary Health Association of India) (1997). *Report of the Independent Commission on Health in India*. New Delhi.

World Bank (1995). 'India: Policy and Finance Strategies for Strengthening Primary Health Care Services', Report No.13042-IN, Washington DC: Population and Human Resource Division.

——— (2000). *World Development Report 1999–2000: Entering the 21st Century*. New Delhi: Oxford University Press.

WHO (World Health Organization) (1978). *Primary Health Care: Report of the International Conference on Primary Health Care*. Geneva.

——— (2000). *World Health Report 2000*. Geneva.

Yesudian, C.A.K. (nd). 'Behaviour of the Private Sector in the Health Services Market of Mumbai', Mumbai: Tata Institute of Social Sciences.

20

Modernity, Nation-building and Globalisation: An Indian Anxiety

Anand Kumar

Introduction

The project of modernity and nation-building was first actualised in Europe. But later it travelled to the Asian countries, including India initially through European colonial interventions and later after Independence by the modernising elites' endeavour to develop their respective countries. In the recent decades, the project of globalisation has increasingly enveloped the third world countries including India and has elicited varied responses. In this light, the chapter delves upon the issue of modernity, nation-building and globalisation with a focus on the responses to globalisation in India.

Asian Engagements with Modernity

Let us first look at Asia and Asian modernity. The gradual establishment of authority of Europe over Asia began with arrival of Vasco da Gama and ended with the departure of the Western fleets from their bases on the Asian continent. Thus, the countries of Asia had been in contact with Europe for a period of five centuries and were subjected to Western domination for over a century. The period of European control of the states of Asia is a dividing line in their history. It is associated with resistance to colonisation and adaptation to modernisation. Both were crucial to generate new vitality and to enable them to consciously adapt themselves to new ideas by which alone they were able to gradually recover their independence and strength (Panikkar 1969: 313).

The most significant factor, which changed the intellectual relationship of Europe and Asia was the French Revolution. The doctrines of the French Revolution around the values of liberty, equality, fraternity, and revolution were the common characteristics of modernity (Habermas 1987). They became the corner stone of the first wave of modern political ideologies of the Asian people. The European contribution in the reform movements in the first half of the 19th century cannot be ignored. On the other hand, this was also the century which witnessed the all round progress of capitalism in Europe on the basis of exploitation of Asian colonial resources. J. A. Hobson (2006/1902), an economist and historian of imperialism and European expansion has noted that the exploitation of other portion of the world through military plunder, unequal trade and forced labour has been the one great indispensable condition in the growth of European capitalism. The period of imperialism which began in the middle of 19th century also intensified the contact of the people of Asia with a variety of Europeans. It was followed by the retreat of Europe between 1918 and 1945, which was dominated by two factors—the October Revolution in Russia and the rise of nationalism in Asian Countries. The development of nationalism is a major feature of Asian modernity and it grew directly through resistance to imperialism and indirectly by the recovery of historical sense and pride in cultural achievements as a result of Western contact. In other words, the sense of Asianism is exclusively the counterpart of the solidarity of European feeling around modernity. Before the end of the 19th century, there was no such feeling as Asianism in spite of the fact that from Japan to India, the civilisations of Asian countries have lived by certain common features in cultural, social, religious and philosophical spheres. They did not have economic and political unity but there has been a community of thought and feeling between the common people.

Apart from nationalism, the European impact on Asian societies has been most well entrenched in the sphere of law and legal system. Building of legal structure and transformation of legal systems have provided a modern framework for state system all over Asia. There was widespread introduction of the modern principles of government by the West throughout Asia in the last phase of its imperial command. Similarly, the growth of large cities as centers of political and economic dynamics is a result of European contacts and colonisation. These cities have become the base of middle classes in India, China and other Asian countries. They are also the receivers of the Western pattern of modernity and modernisation. The most critical consequence of Europe's long domination over Asia has been the integration of vast territories into great nation states of a kind unknown in the previous history of Asia, according to scholars. This process of territorial integration and construction of nation states has been furthered in the post-colonial phases in the Asian modernity (Eisenstadt 1987; Kaiwar and Mazumdar 2003).

But Asia has followed a different trajectory of modernity where it necessarily harmonises with history and cultural tradition. For example there are three different settings for modernisation in Japan, China and India. Then, there is a separate pattern in the Muslim majority nation states of Asia also. China and Japan had a predominance of familism, low status for the mercantile classes, tradition of xenophobia and a centralised political structure. Both engaged in modernisation after the break down of the traditional political structure. But in China, the political structure was fully dependent upon the cultural structure and social stratification was in congruence with the political system. This structural congruence between culture, polity and system of stratification was not conducive for the growth of modernisation which promotes differentiating structures and structural autonomy. In case of Japan, the cultural and political structures were highly symbiotic and not so congruent. There were many autonomous substructures, which gave sustenance to the processes of modernisation. In the Chinese case, modernisation was achieved in the second stage through communist revolution where it had to fabricate an alternate system of stratification and polity.

The arrival of modernisation in India was through the colonial passage. The colonial encounter was basically different from the engagement of China and Japan with modernity. At the same time the basic structural forms in the traditional Indian society were quite conducive to modernisation. This specialty of traditional India has led a number of scholars to argue in favour of rejecting the European experience about radical contradiction between modernity and tradition. According to Rudolph and Rudolph (1967: 3–15), there is need to accord tradition a higher priority in exploring the nature and processes of modernity and modernisation. They have underlined Gandhi's leadership, the transformation of caste system, and the continuity and changes in the Indian legal system as three instances of modernity of tradition as well as modernity incorporating traditional aspects.

There is also need to recognise the presence of another Asia dominated by the believers of Islam. Islam is a religion, which has experienced tension between reason and tradition during the period of Arab Islam World. The genesis of conflict between modernism and traditionalism in Islam today can be better understood by Islamic heritage. It is a fact that the rise and decline of rationalism in Arabic civilisation and Islamic societies has coincided with the florescence and fall of that civilisation. During its glorious period free thinking held its way. Philosophy had an upper hand over theology. Even skeptics were not excommunicated; although persecuted on political grounds. Therefore, any discussion about Asian modernity has to give separate attention to the Islamic countries of Asia today (Haq 1992).

In short, there is as much space for the concept of Asian modernity as there has been for European modernity. But the urge for modernity in Asia is co-mingled with the urge for identity, which was not so pronounced in the context of modernisation in Europe, which engaged in modernity with reference to itself. But the Asian modernity has been forced to deal with the hegemonic presence of the European modernity. For example, there is evolution of an eclectic ideology of modernisation in India and other post-colonial countries to accommodate the contradictions in the system from a short-term perspective. In the long run, however, the systemic restructure of this ideology cannot be postponed. It was argued in the 1970s that there has been a sharpening of choices between Marxism and Gandhism as the ideology for modernisation in India. At the same time, there was also thrust for a pragmatic synthesis, which could, promote a doctrinaire discourse (Singh 1978: 17). But today, it is being argued that India is experiencing cultural narcissism, assertion by the Dalit (depressed) castes, and mobilisation for gender justice. It is making a common path towards modernity very difficult. There is also disenchantment with modernity in certain sections. It has promoted social conflicts and lack of mutuality along the lines of caste, gender, and religion. What is the answer? It is suggested that 'spiritualising of modernity' is very important for the progress of modernisation (Pathak 2001). From another perspective, the sociologists have found the middle classes totally uncommitted to modernity and misfit to lead the process of modernisation as they are Westoxicated and self-possessed, without any respect for the rule of law, their role as citizens, and the rights of the others. So who can be the flag bearers of modernity in India? They suggest that the lower middle classes and the poorer sections of the nation are the genuine carriers of modernity (Gupta 2000).

Discourse on Globalisation and Dynamics of Nation-building

We may now look at the discourse on globalisation and its meaning for the dynamics of nation-building in the post-colonial societies, including India.

Globalisation has been the thrust of modern world system since the collapse of Berlin Wall and implosion of the Soviet Union. It has resulted in a contradictory situation—decline in the force of state and rediscovery of value of the process of nation-building around the world. The process of globalisation hinges upon inter-state treaties and international bodies. Thus, we are in stressful times, being caught between the dynamics of global integration and imperatives of identity (Roberts and Hite 2000).

How to make sense of the patterns of relationship between nation-building, globalisation, nation state, and people's communities in such a setting? There are a number of relevant questions, which are becoming more significant in the context of policy making, social mobilisation and political initiatives about these two aspects of contemporary human societies. For example, it is being asked that how can we ensure security as well as identity in the era of globalisation? What is the role and significance of nation-building in filling the gaps caused by the processes of regionalism, globalisation and consequential ethnification?

Are we witnessing the replacement of four centuries long process of European expansion by four decades old process of compression of space and time? Will there be an end of the era of nationalism due to the world wide waves of globalisation? Are we condemned to live with the fear of globalisation of most of the local and regional conflicts as they have been acquiring the potential of global inflation through terrorism leading to the declining significance of nation states as containers of conflict and promoters of equilibrium.

In my view, there are three important questions, which should be asked for understanding the present scenario: i) What is the political sociology of nation-building? ii) What are the major features of globalisation in the present times and what is its pathology? iii) Can they both exist together in the coming times?

Nation-building is contingent upon 'we' feeling around cultural and territorial identity. It has four major components which define the dimensions of belongingness and are present in most of the instances of nation-building, though in uneven patterns. They are political, economic, cultural and spatial (territorial). It should be also noted that the human family has experienced four phases of nation-building so far. The capitalist phase was prominent in the West European experiences. There was presence of anti-imperialist mobilisation in the experiences of the Asian and African people. This was followed by the phase of post-colonial nation-building, which directed the politics, and cultural policies of the countries of Latin America, Asia, and Africa soon after the end of the Second World War. Now we are in the era of post-cold War nation building, which is taking place in the countries of Eastern Europe and Central Asia after the end of Soviet Union.

In all these phases, the journey of nation-building has been undertaken through two major paths—liberal democratic regimes, and authoritarian governments in most of the cases. There has been conjunction of the processes of institutionalisation of freedom, citizenship, and modernity. There is also presence of linguistic, religious and territorial specificities in different degrees. As a consequence, we have a large number of nation states but no two nation states are identical in their nation-ness. In other words, the political sociology of nation-building suggests that it is a complex process, which creates a variety of interfaces between internal and external, local and global, ethnic and universal factors of interests and identity. It is a rational construction of the socio-political space through citizenship around the centrality of state. It is a dialogue between the past and the future in the context of the present and it is realised within a dynamic triangle of culture, power and society with due attention to the given global environment at a given point in time.

On the other hand, the present wave of globalisation appears to be contingent to the expansion of economic space beyond the nation state through global market mechanisms. It is located within a different dynamic triangle created by the interaction between

- national economies,
- international economic forces, and
- the political hegemony of modern world system.

From this perspective, nation-building and globalisation are neither complementary nor contradictory. They are converging in the core regions of the world economy. For example, the G-8 nations represent such a relation pattern. They have a harmonious co-existence in the semi-peripheral regions like China, India, Brazil, and South Africa. Then, there is contradiction between them in the peripheral regions of the World economy as in several of the post-colonial countries of Asia and Africa. A closer look at the German unification, decay of Soviet Union, and ethnic and religious violence in Yugoslavia, Southern Africa and South Asia may be useful to illustrate this perspective.

Globalisation has been defined as the process of social change which refers both to the compression of the world and the intensification of consciousness of the world as a whole. The processes and characteristics to which the concept of globalisation now refers to have been proceeding with some interruptions or many centers. But globalisation is not equated with or seen as a direct consequence of an amorphously conceived modernity. It is also associated with the discourse of globality and global sociology. Nineteenth century social theorists and sociologists had made modernity and globalisation two central features of their work. But in the late period of classical sociology, the situation became more complex because of the expansion of the apparatus of nation states and the strengthening of nationalism (Robertson 1992; Scholte 2000).

Currently, social scientists have challenges to deal with in four features of contemporary life settings simultaneously— i) individuality, ii) community, iii) nationality, and iv) globality. In an increasingly globalised world, there is a hyphening of civilisational, societal, ethnic, regional, national and individual self-consciousness. There are tensions between the local and the global. There is relativisation of local, national, regional and global. There is simultaneousness of homogenisation, heterogenisation and hybridisation. The increasing intensity of globalisation, which is compression of time and space beyond the nation states has several political and cultural implications for the latecomers in the discourse of modernisations like the Asians. The local-global interplay is not as smooth and functional in this region as it has been in Western Europe and North America. There are three prominent *antinomies* of modernity in full play in the post-colonial parts of Asia which centres around orientalism, racism and nationalism. The tension has been addressed in the discourse of Asian modernity by separating culture and economy and industrialisation and Westernisation. There is also revival of cultural xenophobia and religious intolerance in the name of resisting the cultural invasion by the West through globalisation (Le Rider 1993).

There is a need to look at the dimensions of globalisation and mediators of globality in India for taking a holistic view of the crisis of Asian modernity in facing the challenges of globalisation which necessarily demands continuous lowering of national barriers and dissolution of nationalism. There are five aspects of globalisation: i) capital, ii) labour, iii) technology, iv) commodity, and v) information. There is a rapid growth of globalisation of capital and commodity. There is selective expansion of technology and information network. But there is very low rate of globalisation of labour. This uneveness has been deepening disparities and promoting chronic poverty. It is by-passing a large section of rural Asia, particularly low skill workers, small land holding farmers and traditional craftsman. It is also rolling the state back, which increases the vulnerability of marginal groups and weaker sections including women, depressed castes and minorities. This has created a challenge for the sustenance of capitalist and consumerist globalisation in most of Asia excluding Japan, China and Vietnam.

The collapse of the East Asian economy causing the greatest economic crisis, which is the great depression, has sent shock waves and has alerted Malaysia, Korea, the Philippines, Indonesia and Thailand about the limits of the present pattern of globalisation in the Asian context. But it is equally important to note that Asian modernity is engaged in globalisation on the basis of a strong combination of internal and international factors. There are eight such factors, which are together mediating globalisation in Asia for last two decades. They are: i) market, ii) money, iii) middle classes, iv) modernity, v) multinational corporations (MNCs), vi) migration, vii) media, and viii) multiculturalism. Each one of these mediators encourage individuals and communities to get into the web of income and consumption beyond their localities. They together create networks and structures, desires and opportunities, campaigns and legitimacy for compressing time and space in search of prosperity and security.

Globalisation is associated with fears of homogenisation, leading to the loss of identity, which has been recently constructed in the course of anti-imperialist resistance, and the discourse of nation-building. It has also been promoting marginalisation of economically weaker sections, demographically smaller groups and culturally resourceless communities. There is always a fear of hegemonisation, which makes the post-colonial societies worried about their projects of decolonisation through development. There is growing de-sensitisation of the stake holders of globalisation towards the imperatives of social justice which has been a cause for concern in the context of promoting citizenship and humane social order beyond the agonies of want and fear of violence (MacGillivray 2006; Rosenberg 2000).

The Ideological Roots of Anti-Globalisation Responses

It is surprising that except the supporters of liberalism, there were no sympathisers of globalisation in India since 1991, when the country found itself succumbing to the pressures of international financial bodies in order to survive the economic crisis related to the depletion of foreign currency reserves. The Gandhians, the Marxists, the Nationalists, the Ambedkarites and the Maoists were all together in their pessimism about the wisdom of Indian government in the context of taking steps towards liberalisation and privatisation under the leadership of Narasimha Rao and Manmohan Singh. A large number of writings are available from these ideological quarters with grave warnings about 'the arrival of new imperialist', the threat to Indian freedom, and the danger for democracy. It is another matter that these moves created new hopes among the entrepreneurs, big farmers, neo-rich classes and certain other sections of the society.

In ideological terms, there are two most quoted authors in the anti-globalisation literature in India—Booker prize winner, author Arundhati Roy and Nobel Prize winner, economist Joseph Stiglitz. Let us have two examples of their analysis of the reforms introduced in the context of globalisation in India, Africa and elsewhere since 1991. According to Arundhati Roy (2002),

> The crisis in modern democracy is a profound one. Free elections, a free press, and independent judiciary mean little when the free market has reduced them to commodities available on sale to the highest bidder. On the global stage, beyond the jurisdiction of sovereign governments, international instruments of trade and finance oversee a complex wave of multilateral laws and agreements that have entrenched a system of appropriation that puts colonialism to shame... The World Trade Organization, the World Bank, the International Monetary Fund and other financial institutions like the Asian Development Bank, virtually write economic policy and parliamentary legislation. With a deadly combination of arrogance and ruthlessness, they take their sledge—hammers to fragile, interdependent, historically complex societies, and devastate them. All this goes under the fluttering banner of 'reform'. As a consequence of this reform, in Africa, Asia and Latin America, thousands of small enterprisers and industries have closed down, millions of workers and farmers have lost their jobs and land. Anyone who criticizes this process is mocked for being 'anti-reform', anti-progress, anti-development.

Arundhati Roy draws the attention towards two sets of global figures; about the rich getting richer and the poor getting poorer with deepening of disparities within and between various countries of the world. According to her, 'Countries that have been plundered by colonizing regimes are steeped in debt to these same powers, and have to repay them at the rate of about $ 382 billion a year. Ergo, the rich get richer and the poor get poorer—not accidentally but by design, by intention'. She further writes, 'according to Forbes Magazine, in the year 2004 there are 587 billionaires (individual and family units in the World), whose combined wealth is $ 1.9 trillion. This is more than the gross domestic product of the World's 135 poorest countries combined'.

Now let us look at the perception of the reforms from the economists' quarters. Joseph Stiglitz, Nobel Laureate in economics (2002) has argued that globalisation has been practiced in unfair ways and its benefits have disproportionately gone to rich people. Stiglitz (2000) says

> the policy issue is not "to globalize or not to globalize" or "to grow or not to grow". In some cases it is not even "to liberalize or not to liberalize". Instead the issues are; to liberalize short-term capital accounts—and if so how? At what pace to liberalize trades, and what policies should accompany? And are there growth strategies that increase poverty as they promote growth—strategies that should be shunned?'

In the perception of Stiglitz, the opening of markets to short term capital flows often increases economic instability and contributes to insecurity and poverty. To quote him,

> After the last round of trade negotiations—the Uruguay Round, a World Bank study showed that Sub-Saharan Africa was actually worse off. Asymmetric liberalisation had global terms of trade effects. The globalization studies suggest that Africa has suffered because it has not globalised. That may be partly true. But it is also true Africa has suffered from the way that globalization has been managed ... The anti globalization movement has often been charged with being unthinking in simply asking whether globalization is good or bad. But the econometrics studies, for all the seeming sophistication of their statistics, are equally guilty.

There are a number of objections to globalisation-related reforms among a large number of political formations and civil society organisations on the basis of such perceptions articulated by a wide spectrum of eminent global citizens from different walks of life. They create an ideological framework, which has provided the intellectual legitimacy to a number of anti-reform initiatives in India, Africa, and Latin America. They have promoted a consensus, which suggests the following as the basic features of globalisation-related reforms in India.

- There is an attack on the economic and political sovereignty of the Indian nation state.
- Multinational corporations are taking control of the infrastructure and natural resources of the country.
- This system allows unrestricted entry and exit of massive amounts of speculative capital and creates the threat of capital flight as a lever for international financial institutions.
- It has caused damage to the farmers and agricultural labourers causing further pauperisation.
- It is destroying the industrial base of Indian economy particularly medium and small-scale sectors by eliminating various protections causing closing down of close to 50 per cent of the industrial units.
- There is loss of jobs and growth of unemployment due to liberalisation, globalisation and privatisation (LPG).
- Allowing MNCs in fishing has grievously hit approximately two crore fishermen.

- The traditional life setting and livelihood of the *adivasis* is endangered due to mining projects, deforestation and other steps related with LPG.
- There is threat to access to clean water and food and other basic needs of ordinary people due to hazardous industrialisation by MNCs.
- Globalisation-related reforms are also causing threat to indigenous knowledge and risk of paralysing research in India.

Such a set of conclusions about the consequences of reforms around globalisation in India has promoted widespread pessimism among the community of socially concerned NGOs and other political forums. But, there is a growing group of advocates of 'globalisation with humane face' and reforms for promoting employment and eliminating poverty. It is a trend, which is visible among the major political parties who are engaged in governance in various provinces and the center.

Position of Major Political Parties

It is true that most of the political parties in India have moved from various ideological frameworks to the ultimate zone of convergence known as pragmatism. This has created problems of identifying these parties with specific positions about reforms in the context of globalisation. But, broadly speaking, there are two large alliances with most of the political parties belonging to one of the two—National Democratic Alliance led by Bharatiya Janata Party and United Progressive Alliance led by the Indian National Congress. The National Democratic Alliance has presented itself as being committed to make India an economic superpower by bridging the gap between the global and the national, between the urban and the rural, and between various regions of the country through a second green revolution and cautious dismantling of the *quota permit raj* (i.e., by adopting liberalisation-privatisation-globalisation) governed the country at the center from 1999–2004 in an uninterrupted manner. But it remained internally divided about its approach towards globalisation-related reforms. A number of its supporters were found to be working overnight to promote 'reforms' through channels like Ministry of Disinvestment. On the other hand, a good number of the sympathisers of the Bharatiya Janata Party were actively resisting it under the banner of Swadeshi Jagaran Manch. In the final countdown during the national elections of 2004, the NDA found itself deserted by farmers, artisans, salaried employees, and job seeking youths who perceived the NDA government pro-globalisation not favourable to their interests.

The Indian National Congress on the other hand, has been the prime mover of the project of 'reforms' since 1991. It argued in favour of taking hard decisions for the long-term interest of Indian economy and society by taking it beyond the shadows of subsidy and inefficiency. They disowned the philosophy of Nehru and Indira Gandhi regarding priority to national economic self-reliance and eradication of poverty and backwardness through five-year plans with a commanding role for the state. But after loosing power to an anti-Congress alliance, it was forced to review it position regarding reforms. They were also compelled to adopt a

Common Minimum Programme as a precondition to get support from the left parties where the limits of reformist agenda were recognised in clear terms. At present the Congress-led UPA is explicitly committed to ease the burden of debt, unemployment and poverty through a series of people friendly projects and policies. It remains committed to reform along with security of the interest of the weaker sections and backward regions.

A similar paradox is present in the political line of the left alliance parties who have been contributing towards anti-globalisation campaigns through their front organisations among farmers, workers, students and youths. But they do not have an anti-LPG stance in West Bengal, which is under their command for more than two decades. The party supports the ban on sale of agricultural land to foreign companies for agro-business. They promise guarantee of minimum wages to agricultural labourers. It supports food for work programmes to generate employment with campaigns for right to work as a fundamental right. It may be underlined that the left alliance parties have been consistently cautious about the problems of promoting Foreign Direct Investment in critical sectors of Indian economy.

There are a number of states, which are in command of a particular regional political formation like Uttar Pradesh (Samajwadi Party), Bihar (Rastriya Janata Dal), Orissa (Biju Janata Dal), Karnataka (Janata Dal Secular) and Maharastra (Nationalist Congress Party). These parties do have twin imperatives in the context of their orientation towards reforms. First, they have the pressure to appear as pro-people and not pro-MNCs. Second, they have to provide conducive environment for the entrepreneurs for investment and employment generation. Nearly all of them are found to be engaged in encouraging foreign investment and rolling back the state from industrial activities. But none of them are engaged in such reforms, which may antagonise the masses, particularly the farmers.

The issue of reducing agricultural subsidies, privatisation of social sector activities like health and education, encouragement of Foreign Direct Investment and increasing the cost of urban services are some of the zones of confusion within and between the political parties of India today. Each political party claims to have two commitments—creation of jobs and promotion of self-reliance with selective use of reforms and foreign investments. It is a win-win formula. But in practice, there are limits to such a strategy.

Profile of an Anti-Globalisation Campaign

After a brief overview of the orientation about globalisation and reforms among the political parties, it may be relevant to have an understanding of the characteristics of anti-globalisation initiatives for last fifteen years in India. There are a number of such coalitions and networks. National Alliance of Peoples Movement, Bharat Jana Andolan, Sarva Sewa Sangh, Swadeshi Jagaran Manch, Asian Social Forum, and Azadi Bachao Andolan are some of the better-known examples. We will present a short profile of one of the oldest and most active forums—Azadi Bachao Andolan.

In 1989, there was a proposal for General Agreement on Trade and Tariff (GATT). This was the beginning of the birth of World Trade Organization. A group of countries from the first World were found to propose a new set of norms for creating a new international economic order, which would promote interdependence instead of domination and dependence. However, a number of individuals and groups considered this initiative as the birth of corporate colonialism. They opposed GATT and WTO. Their opposition was ignored by the Central government, major political parties, Kisan Unions, Trade Unions and student and youth organisations. But they remained persistent by rallying together under the banner of—Azadi Bachao Andolan. For the past 15 years, the Azadi Bachao Andolan is engaged in (a) information, (b) dissemination, (c) mobilisation, (d) protest and resistance activities, (e) networking within India, and (f) cooperation with international initiatives and coalitions.

What are the objectives of Azadi Bachao Andolan? It claims that it is committed towards 'incessantly fighting for liberating India from corporate colonialism and to build a society based on Swadeshi, simplicity and self-reliance'. In ideological terms, it remains rooted in economic nationalism, social justice and political freedom as the three components of a vision termed *Swaraj* with a Gandhian flavour. But there is openness in terms of sharing concepts, analysis and solutions. Therefore, it finds every protest against foreign companies relevant and interesting. In terms of its social base, it has been engaged in cultivating support from artisans, small-scale businessmen, farmers, and students and youths from colleges and universities.

It has developed a group of activists from students and youths as well as intellectuals and social workers. The leadership is provided by a group of university scholars and freedom fighters. What is the pattern of mobilisation of Azadi Bacho Andolan? This campaign has been drawing people together against multinational corporations like Pepsi and Coca Cola as the biggest enemies of the nation. It approaches gram sabhas, schools and colleges for social resistance against bottling plants and wholesale dealers of soft drinks. Bringing together students and citizens through non-aggressive activities like human chain, personal abstention and collective resolutions are its basic techniques for mobilisation. It has also been engaged in brining together all those artisans, producers and entrepreneurs who had been adversely affected by the uninhibited entry of foreign goods in recent years.

The import of milk products has negatively affected the dairy industry and animal husbandry related households. The import of foreign edible oil hurts the interest of the farmers engaged in oil seed cultivation and the oil mill industry. Similarly, Pepsi , Coca Cola, Cadburies etc. have caused loss of market for the Indian Industries. Azadi Bachao Andolan has also taken the cause of farmers losing land to corporate companies.

The cultural pollution through entertainment industry, cable TV and internet is also underlined by the Andolan which bring them closer to the concerned parents and schools teachers.

What is the structure of their networking? Azadi Bachao Andolan has a three level mobilisational framework: i) study circles, ii) activist groups, and iii) sympathisers circle. It complements its network by associating with specific campaigns and resistance groups like boycotting Pepsi. It also seeks support from groups of experts and resource persons. These activities and activists are integrated in an information circuit through monthly magazines in Hindi and English. But everything is not good with this 15 years old network. For example, according to its Annual Report of 2003, the national office was burdened with a debt of Rs 1.5 lakh during the year 2002–03. Similarly it was still looking for a group of one thousand active persons to form Mukti Sahastra Nam (A network of one thousand activists covering different parts of India and to be available to respond to the calls of the Azadi Bachao Andolan in their area of influence) and establishing. Swaraj Vidyapeeth which would function as an open university to train such students who will be committed to create alternatives to corporate colonialism and corporate education.

What is the role of state in the affairs of Azadi Bachao Andolan ? There has been no direct interference by the provincial or the Central government in terms of preventing the campaigners of this organisation except occasional detentions during their *Satyagraha* at Pepsi and Coke plant. They have also not responded to their innumerable resolutions and campaigns against various products of MNCs. In short, Azadi Bachao Andolan represents the most characteristic example of anti-globalisation response in the civil society. It locates the genesis of globalisation in the foreign rule in India and aims at *Purna Swaraj* (total freedom), which will be based upon freedom from hunger and poverty as well as *Swadeshi* and self-reliance.

Towards Conclusion

What are the conclusions? According to empirical evidences, the present wave of market mediated globalisation has influenced nearly every aspect of Indian society, economy, and culture. The project of nation-building is getting affected by the LPG syndrome and related reforms.

At the same time, globalisation is not a new experience for Indian society. Therefore, it has found advocates as well as adversaries, because there are gainers as well as losers. Somehow, in recent years the gainers have been losing out to the losers in the context of the civil society responses to the 'reforms'. As a consequence, the marginalised and the bypassed have become more visible through a variety of anti-globalisation (corporate colonisation) mobilisations. Paradoxically, this process of disenchantment with the dynamics of globalisation is insufficiently articulated in the political discourses and inaccurately reflected in the media constructions. Therefore, it is important to have a systematic understanding of the power and paradoxes of globalisation in India today.

It may be obvious that modernisation and globalisation have different consequences in Europe and Asia. Europe is getting together by lowering the national frontiers as well as accelerating regionalisation as a response to the imperatives of globalisation. In case of Asia, there is rise of xenophobia as well as economic instability. There is simultaneous growth of economic integration and cultural fragmentation. There are limits to linking the local to the global, despite the phenomenal growth of the reach of finance capital, commodity networks, media accessibility, and information technology in Asia.

The process of globalisation has very limited impact in the context of the challenge of good governance and effective citizenship. There is continuous decline in the capacity of the state and the legitimacy of the government due to increasing role of transnational institutions and processes in the political economy of most of the Asian nation states.

Modernisation through globalisation has acquired a reputation of being friendly to the rich and indifferent to the poorer sections of the society due to its consumerist orientation. It has adversely affected the local artisans and the small and medium scale entrepreneurs. Informalisation of economy under the new international division of labour has created regression in the context of institution building in labour markets and in corporate-union relations.

There is also growth of anti-globalisation pressure in polity and culture through the coming together of a wide variety of groups and communities which suffer the consequents of increasing pressure of the global corporate forces upon the local resource base like forest, land and water.

Finally, the intensification of global integration is promoting politics of identity instead of citizenship-based politics of nation-building. The globalisation-related information technology revolution is developing highway of the global economy which connects the rising technopolies around the world. But they are bypassing the traditional localities, which have been the age-old habitat of millions of men, and women who can never be the beneficiaries of the present pattern of globalisation. Thus, it calls for exploring the meaning of modernisation and globalisation in different local settings to make sense of their responses to the imperatives of being in the era of modernity, nationality, and ethnicity with globality.

Notes

1. I am thankful to Dr. Kameshwar Choudhary for some very useful suggestions about the first draft of this paper which have contributed towards improvement in several ways.
2. All the information about Azadi Bachao Andolan is collected from *Nai Azadi*, a monthly periodical of the movement published from the central office of Azadi Bachao Andolan at Allahabad (Uttar Pradesh).

References

Eisenstadt, S.N. (1987). *Patterns of Modernity*. London: Frances Printer.
Gupta, D. (2000). *Mistaken Modernity*. New Delhi: Harper Collins.
Habermas, J. (1987). *The Philosophical Discourses of Modernity*. London: Polity Press.
Haq, M. (1992). *Reason and Tradition in Islamic Thought*. Aligarh: Aligarh Muslim University Press.
Hobson, J.A. (2006). *Imperialism: A Study*. New Delhi: Gaur Publishers & Distributors, (first foreign edition 1902).
Kaiwar, V. and S. Mazumdar (eds) (2003). *Antinomies of Modernity*. New Delhi: Tulika Books.
Le Rider, J. (1993). *Modernity and Crises of Identity*. London: Polity Press.
MacGillivray, Alex (2006). *A Brief History of Globalization*. London: Robinson.
Panikkar, K.M. (1969). *Asia and Western Dominance*. Bombay: Asia Publishing house.
Pathak, A. (1998). *Indian Modernity*. New Delhi: Gyan Publishing House.
Roberts, J. T. and Amy Hite (2000). *From Modernisation to Globalisation*. London: Blackwell.
Robertson, R. (1992). *Globalisation: Social Theory and Global Culture*. New Delhi: Sage Publications.

Rosenberg, J. (2000). *The Follies of Globalisation Theory*. London: Vasco.
Roy, Arundhati (2002). 'Globalization is Ripping Through People's Lives', in *Socialist Worker Online*, 27 September, pp. 6–7, www.socialistworker.org.
Rudolph, S.H.and L. I. Rudolph (1967). *The Modernity of Tradition*. Chicago: University of Chicago Press.
Scholte, Jan Aart (2000). *Globalization: A Critical Introduction*. London: Macmillan Press.
Singh, Y. (1978). *Essays on Modernisation in India*. New Delhi: Manohar.
Stiglitz, J. (2000). *Globalisation and its Discontents*. London: Penguin Paperback.

About the Editor and Contributors

Editor

Kameshwar Choudhary completed M.A. M.Phil. and Ph.D. in sociology at the Jawaharlal Nehru University, New Delhi. Currently he is Professor of Sociology at KSRM, KIIT Deemed University, Bhubaneswar. Prior to this he was Professor in the Department of Sociology, Banaras Hindu University, Varanasi. He has also taught at the Institute of Rural Management, Anand, and the Institute of Social Sciences, Agra. He has contributed book chapters and also many papers to a number of reputed journals on socio-political, educational and development issues. He is a member of several national and international social science and development bodies. He has held associateship of the Indian Institute of Advanced Study, Shimla. Recently, he was visiting fellow at the Jawaharlal Nehru University, New Delhi. He has published his book *Intellectuals And Society: A Study of Teachers in India* (Popular Prakashan, Mumbai, 2004). His current areas of interest include globalisation, development theory, governance reforms, and education in India.

Contributors

Dolly Arora is Professor of Political Science at the Indian Institute of Public Administration, New Delhi. Prior to this, she was with the University of Delhi. She has been working on governance and public policy related issues and processes. She has published research papers in national and international journals on governance, social policy, gender issues and participatory processes. Her recent work is focused on globalisation and reforms processes, local democracy, poverty and rural development. Her publications include *Political Economy of WTO Regime: Some Aspects of Globalisation and Governance* (co-edited) Rainbow, New Delhi, 2002, *Democracy and Competing Claims: Should Privileges be Privileged over Rights* (IIPA, New Delhi, 2004) and *Social Sector Development: From Outlays to Outcomes* (IIPA, New Delhi, 2005).

Sharit K. Bhowmik is currently Professor at the centre for Labour Studies, Tata Institute of Social Sciences, Mumbai. Prior to this he was Professor of Sociology at the University of Mumbai. He has done research on labour, urban informal sector and women and work. He has taught at

University of North Bengal, Indian Institute of Management Calcutta and Delhi School of Economics before joining University of Mumbai. His publications include over 50 research papers in peer reviewed journals or as chapters in edited books and three monographs: i) *Class Formation in the Plantation System*, ii) *Worker Cooperatives—Alternative form of Economic Growth*, and iii) *Tea Plantation Labour in India*. He is member of the Managing Committee of Indian Sociological Society and council member of the Indian Council of Social Science Research.

Biswajit Das is Professor at the Department of Sociology and Director of Centre for Culture, Media and Governance, Jamia Millia Islamia, New Delhi. Over his 20 years of teaching and specialized research in Communication Studies he has received many awards, including the Shastri Indo-Canadian Fellowship, Indo-French Scholarship and the Fellowship by Indian Institute of Advanced Studies. He has been Visiting Faculty at the Department of Communication at the University of Windsor, has lectured at the Department of Cinema and Audio-Visual, Sorbonne, University of Paris and Department of Communication at the University of Hawaii. He has contributed articles in selected volumes, and in international as well as national journals. He has jointly edited three volumes viz. *Communication Processes: Media and Mediation* (2005), *Domination and Appropriation* (to be published in 2006) and *Culture and Confrontation* (to be published in 2006) from Sage Publications, New Delhi. Currently he is completing a project of UGC on ICT and Governance in India.

Shaibal Gupta is an economist. He is presently the Member-Secretary of the Asian Development Research Institute (ADRI), Patna. Earlier, he was a faculty member at the ANS Institute of Social Studies, Patna. His main research interest is political economy of peripheral regions, particularly the studies on the relationship among sub-nationalism, regional markets and the nature of capitalist transformation in such regional economies. Within this framework, he has recently completed a comparative study of political economy of development in Madhya Pradesh and Bihar. He has prepared six research reports including memoranda consecutively for the Tenth, Eleventh and Twelfth Finance Commissions constituted by the Government of India. He held many important assignments including with the ILO Geneva, Research Consultant in BBC, Visiting Fellow, Institute of Development Studies, Sussex, Consultant of the World Bank to prepare report on Bihar Development, etc.

Ravindra K. Jain is a senior anthropologist and a leading international authority on the Indian Diaspora. He held the Chair of Social Anthropology at Jawaharlal Nehru University, New Delhi. He has taught in many parts of the world, including the Wolfson College at Oxford University, UK and the Australian National University, Canberra. After retirement in 2002 he was designated as Distinguished Scholar and is currently a UGC Emeritus Fellow in Sociology at the JNU. He is the author of several reputed publications including, *South Indians on the Plantation Frontier in Malaya* (New Haven and London: Yale University Press); (editor) *Text and Context: The Social Anthropology of Tradition* (Philadelphia: Institute for the Study of Human Issues), *Indian Communities Abroad: Themes and Literature* (Delhi, Manohar), *The Universe as Audience: Metaphor and Community among the Jains of North India* (Shimla, Indian Institute of Advanced Study), *Between History and Legend: Status and Power in Bundelkhand* (Delhi and Hyderabad, Orient Longman). His students are now occupying prominent positions in Anthropology and Sociology all over the world and a festschrift in his honour is in press.

Niraja Gopal Jayal is Professor at the Centre for the Study of Law and Governance, Jawaharlal Nehru University, and the Director of the Jawaharlal Nehru Institute of Advanced Study at the University. She is the author of *Democracy and the State: Welfare, Secularism and Development in Contemporary India* (Oxford University Press, 1999); co-author of *Drought, Policy and Politics in India* (Sage Publications, 1993); and editor of *Democracy in India* (Oxford University Press, 2001). She is co-editing two forthcoming volumes, both under publication by the Oxford University Press: *The Oxford Companion to Politics in India,* and *Local Governance in India—Decentralisation and Beyond.* Her current research interests include gender and governance; ethnic inequality and the governance of public institutions; and the Indian idea of citizenship in the twentieth century. She is also Director of a research project, funded by the Ford Foundation, *Dialogue on Democracy and Pluralism in South Asia.*

Surinder S. Jodhka is Professor at the Centre for the Study of Social Systems, Jawaharlal Nehru University, New Delhi (India). He has earlier taught at the University of Hyderabad, Hyderabad and Panjab University, Chandigarh. He has been working in the fields of agrarian change, social stratification and social identiities. He has published more than forty research papers in national and international journals and two books, including *Community and Identities: Contemporary Discourses on Culture and Politics in India* (edited volume, Sage Publications, New Delhi, 2001).

Anand Kumar is Professor of Sociology and Coordinator of Global Studies Programme at Centre for Study of Social Systems, School of Social Sciences, Jawaharlal Nehru University, New Delhi. He is currently engaged in studying the cultural limits of globalisation through a comparative study of India, France and Germany. He has been educated at Banaras Hindu University (M.A.), Jawaharlal Nehru University (M.Phil.), University of Chicago (Ph.D.) and State University of New York, Binghamton. He was invited as Visiting Professor at Institute for Sociology, Albert Ludwig University, Freiburg, and M.S.H., Paris. His published works include *State and Society in India* (1989), *Tibet Resourcebook* (1996), *Nationbuilding in India* (2000), *Parivartan Ki Rajniti aur Rajniti Ka Parivartan* (2000), and *Political Sociology of Poverty* (2004).

Vivek Kumar is Assistant Professor at the Centre for the Study of Social Systems, School of Social Sciences, Jawaharlal Nehru University, New Delhi. Prior to this he was Lecturer in the Unit for Sociology of Education, Tata Institute of Social Sciences, Mumbai for a brief period. He has contributed a number of research papers in books and journals. His books namely include *Dalit Leadership In India, Dalit Assertion and Bahujan Samaj Party, India's Roaring Revolution: Dalit Assertion and New Horizons,* and *Bahujan Samaj Party avm Sanrachnatmak Parivartan* (Hindi). He participated at the International Conference against Racism held at Durban in South Africa in 2001. His major areas of specialisation are social stratification, dalit movement, and diaspora.

Prakash Louis is Director of Bihar Social Institute, Patna. Prior to this he was Executive Director of the Indian Social Institute, New Delhi. He had done his doctoral studies on the Radical Agrarian Movements in Central Bihar from A.N. Sinha Institute of Social Studies, Patna. Two of his major publications are *People Power: The Naxalite Movement in Central Bihar*, and *Political Sociology of Dalit Assertion*. He contributes regularly to journals like *Economic and Political Weekly, Mainstream, Social Change,* Vikalp and Seminar. He also contributes regularly to national dailies *Hindustan, Jansatta, Prabhat Khabar* and *Rashtriya Sahara*. He has conducted research on 'People's Perception of Land Reform Policies and Practices: A Comparative Study of Eastern, Western and Central Regions of Uttar Pradesh', sponsored by the Ministry of Rural Development, Government of India, 2001.

Manoranjan Mohanty was Professor of Political Science and Director, Developing Countries Research Centre at the University of Delhi from where he retired in 2004. He is Co-chairperson, Institute of Chinese Studies and Visiting Professor at Institute of Human Development, New Delhi and President of Orissa Gaveshana Chakra. He has conducted studies on rural development process in India and China. His publications include *People's Rights* (1998), *Contemporary Indian Political Theory* (2000), *Class, Caste, Gender* (2004).

K. Ramchandran Nair retired as Professor and Head of Department of Economics, University of Kerala and is currently Chairman of Institute for Monitoring Economic Growth, Trivandrum. He held important positions as Member and Chairman of several state government committees/ task force/advisory board in Kerala. He has actively participated in the public discussions particularly on economic issues, and has also been associated with trade unions and social movements in Kerala. His publications include *Industrial Relations in Kerala* and *The History of Trade Union Movement in Kerala* (forthcoming), besides several co-authored ones in Malayalam, such as—*Dhanasasthra Tatvangal,* and *Agolavalkkaranam, Artham, Vyapthy, Sidhamtham.*

Santosh Panda, M.Phil & Ph.D. (Education), Cert. in ETV (BBC, UK), is Professor of Distance Education, Director of Staff Training & Research Institute of Distance Education, and Head, Inter-University Consortium for Technology-Enabled Flexible Education and Development, Indira Gandhi National Open University (IGNOU), New Delhi. A past Fulbright Scholar at the University of New Mexico, Albuquerque, Dr Panda has been Director of Policy and Research, Association of Indian Universities; and a Visiting Professor at the Manchester Metropolitan University and the University of London, UK. He has published widely in international journals. His latest works include *Planning and Management in Distance Education* (Routledge, London, 2003), and *Economics of Distance and Online Learning* (Lawrence Erlbaum, New Jersey, in press). Currently, his research areas include virtual research, benchmarking for online services, instructional design, mobile learning, online professional development, media and technology for education and development, etc.

Mohan Rao is Professor at the Centre of Social Medicine and Community Health, School of Social Sciences, Jawaharlal Nehru University, New Delhi. A medical doctor, specialised in public health, he has written extensively on health and population policy and on the history and politics of health and family planning. He has edited *Disinvesting in Health: The World Bank's Health Prescriptions* (Sage, New Delhi, 1999) and *The Unheard Scream: Reproductive Health and Women's Lives in India* (Zubaan/Kali for Women, New Delhi, 2004). He is the author of *From Population Control to Reproductive Health: Malthusian Arithmetic* (Sage Publications, New Delhi, 2004).

G. Krishna Reddy is Associate Professor in the Department of Political Science, Osmania University, Hyderabad. He has done his post-graduation and M. Phil. from Jawaharlal Nehru University, New Delhi and his Ph.D. from Osmania University. He has worked on media politics, and rural governance and decentralisation in Andhra Pradesh. His articles appeared in journals like *Economic and Political Weekly, Journal of Federal Studies*. His study on media interventions in politics of Andhra Pradesh will be appearing in a forthcoming volume on media anthology being published by the Sage Publications. He has done several projects including one on Rural Governance and citizen participation in Andhra Pradesh for the IDS, Sussex University as part of the Logo Link Programme. Presently he is engaged in the work on media and social movements in Andhra Pradesh.

K.L. Sharma till recently was Vice-Chancellor of the University of Rajasthan, Jaipur. He was Professor of Sociology at the Jawaharlal Nehru University, New Delhi where he also held various administrative positions including Rector, Chief Proctor, and Dean of Students. He was Visiting Professor at College de France in Paris. He has lectured in several countries like Holland, England and the Netherlands. He was member of UGC's Committee on the Teaching of Sociology and Social Anthropology and also of the OBC Commission of the Government of the NCT, Delhi. He has published several articles and papers in noted academic journals and has eighteen books to his credit which include: i) *The Changing Rural Stratification System,* (Orient Longman, New Delhi,1974), *Caste, Class and Social Movements* (Rawat Publications, Jaipur, 1986), *Social Stratification in India: Issues and Themes* (Sage Publications, New Delhi, 1997), *Caste, Feudalism and Peasantry* (New Delhi, Manohar Publications, 1998), and *Reconceptualising Caste, Class and Tribe* (Rawat Publications, Jaipur, 2001).

Vidhu Verma is Professor at the Centre for Political Studies, School of Social Sciences, Jawaharlal Nehru University, New Delhi, India. She was Visiting Fellow at Maison Des Science de L'Homme, Paris (1994), and Fellow at Developing Countries Reseach Centre (DCRC), Delhi University,(1998–1999), and Indian Council of Social Science Research, New Delhi (2000–02). Her areas of research include western political philosophy, feminist theory, politics of Southeast Asia and caste politics in India. She is author of two books *Justice, Equality and Community* (Sage, New Delhi,1999) and *Malaysia: State and Civil Society in Transition* (Lynne Rienner, Colorado, USA, 2002), besides articles in several national and international journals.

J.S. Yadav has Ph.D. in Social Anthropology (Delhi University) and Advanced Diploma in Communication Policy Planning and Development (UNESCO-AIBD, Pennang, Malaysia). His specialization is in development communication and preparing IEC strategy for effective communication and behaviour change. He was Professor at the Indian Institute of Mass Communication (IIMC), New Delhi and also Director of IIMC from 1987 to 1999. Currently, he is Founder Chairman of International Media Institute, Gurgaon, National Capital Region. He planned and coordinated a number of national and international media research projects and prepared several research reports and over 150 scholarly papers and a large number of journalistic articles. He has been member of many academic committees, and member/ chairman of Governing boards. His major books include *Politics of News: Third World Perspective,* and *Issues in Mass Communication* (2 vols).

Index